CW01209115

# CICERO AND ROMAN EDUCATION

*The Reception of the Speeches and Ancient Scholarship*

Cicero saw publication as a means of perpetuating a distinctive image of himself as statesman and orator. He memorialized his spiritual and oratorical self by means of a very solid body of texts. Educationalists and schoolteachers in antiquity relied on Cicero's oratory to supervise the growth of the young into intellectual maturity. By reconstructing the main phases of textual transmission, from the first authorial dissemination of the speeches to the medieval manuscripts, and by re-examining the abundant evidence on Ciceronian scholarship from the first to the sixth century CE, *Cicero and Roman Education* traces the history of the exegetical tradition on Cicero's oratory and reassesses the didactic function of the speeches, whose preservation was largely determined by pedagogical factors.

GIUSEPPE LA BUA is Associate Professor of Latin Literature at the Sapienza University of Rome. His research interests focus mainly on the relationship between religion and literature in the Roman world. His previous publications include *L'inno nella letteratura poetica latina* (1999) and numerous articles on pagan centos, Persius, archaic tragedy, Ciceronian rhetoric and oratory, Horace, Ovid, Apuleius, Roman declamations and the Latin prose panegyrics.

# CICERO AND ROMAN EDUCATION
## The Reception of the Speeches and Ancient Scholarship

GIUSEPPE LA BUA

*Sapienza University of Rome*

CAMBRIDGE
UNIVERSITY PRESS

# CAMBRIDGE
## UNIVERSITY PRESS

University Printing House, Cambridge CB2 8BS, United Kingdom

One Liberty Plaza, 20th Floor, New York, NY 10006, USA

477 Williamstown Road, Port Melbourne, VIC 3207, Australia

314-321, 3rd Floor, Plot 3, Splendor Forum, Jasola District Centre, New Delhi - 110025, India

79 Anson Road, #06-04/06, Singapore 079906

Cambridge University Press is part of the University of Cambridge.

It furthers the University's mission by disseminating knowledge in the pursuit of education, learning and research at the highest international levels of excellence.

www.cambridge.org
Information on this title: www.cambridge.org/9781107068582
DOI: 10.1017/9781107705999

© Giuseppe La Bua 2019

This publication is in copyright. Subject to statutory exception and to the provisions of relevant collective licensing agreements, no reproduction of any part may take place without the written permission of Cambridge University Press.

First published 2019

*A catalogue record for this publication is available from the British Library*

*Library of Congress Cataloging in Publication data*
NAMES: La Bua, Giuseppe, author.
TITLE: Cicero and Roman education : the reception of the speeches and ancient scholarship / Giuseppe La Bua.
DESCRIPTION: Cambridge, United Kingdom ; New York, NY : Cambridge University Press, 2019.
IDENTIFIERS: LCCN 2018042060 | ISBN 9781107068582 (hardback)
SUBJECTS: LCSH: Cicero, Marcus Tullius. Speeches. | Cicero, Marcus Tullius – Influence. | Learning and scholarship – Rome. | Education – Rome. | BISAC: HISTORY / Ancient / General.
CLASSIFICATION: LCC PA6285 .L3 2018 | DDC 875/.01–dc23
LC record available at https://lccn.loc.gov/2018042060

ISBN 978-1-107-06858-2 Hardback

Cambridge University Press has no responsibility for the persistence or accuracy of URLs for external or third-party internet websites referred to in this publication, and does not guarantee that any content on such websites is, or will remain, accurate or appropriate.

To Eloisa

# Contents

| | |
|---|---|
| *Acknowledgments* | *page* ix |
| *List of Abbreviations* | xi |
| Introduction | 1 |
| **1 Cicero Presents Himself: Writing, Revision and Publication of the Speeches** | 16 |
|    Written Oratory and Textual Longevity | 17 |
|    Self-Memorialization and Publication Theory | 22 |
|    Cicero the Editor at Work: The Policy of Self-*Emendatio* | 33 |
|    *Retractatio* and *Emendatio*: Cicero's Practice of Self-Correction | 42 |
|    Fashioning Himself: Revision and Edition of Undelivered Speeches | 47 |
| **2 Beyond the Author: Cicero's Speeches from Publication to the Medieval Manuscripts** | 55 |
|    *A Tirone Emendata:* Copying and Editing the Speeches | 59 |
|    A True Ciceronian Scholar: Statilius Maximus and His *Subscriptio* | 66 |
|    Late Collections of Ciceronian Orations | 70 |
|    Asconius Pedianus and the *Scholia Bobiensia* | 77 |
|    From Publication to the Medieval Manuscripts: Cicero's Speeches in the School | 85 |
| **3 Between Praise and Blame: Ciceronian Scholarship from the Early Empire to Late Antiquity** | 100 |
|    Ethics and Politics: Debating About Cicero | 106 |
|    Morality and Language: Cicero in the Early Empire Debate on Style | 112 |
|    *Latinitas* and *Eruditio*: Cicero, Icon of the Latin Language | 125 |
|    From Quintilian to the Scholiasts: Cicero's Authority on Latin | 130 |
|    *Alii . . . Dicunt, Alii . . . Legunt*: Late Ciceronian Scholarship | 162 |
| **4 Teaching Cicero** | 183 |
|    How to Read a Speech: Quintilian's *Praelectio* | 184 |
|    Introducing Cicero's Oratory to Beginners | 190 |

| | |
|---|---|
| Oratory, *Dissimulatio* and Irony: Cicero Teaches the "Art of Illusion" | 219 |
| *Eleganter Dixit Cicero* | 266 |
| Manipulating the Past | 298 |

## Conclusion 318

*Bibliography* 338
*General index* 384
*Index locorum* 388

# Acknowledgments

I started thinking about a book on the reception of Cicero's speeches in the Roman educational system after the completion of my doctoral studies when I had the chance to read Zielinski's seminal and inspirational study (*Cicero im Wandel der Jahrhunderte*). But I owe my passion for Cicero to Leopoldo Gamberale, who initiated me to the secrets of the art of oratory when I was a graduate student and a budding scholar. As a learned, generous and empathic mentor, he has assisted and supported me over the years, from youth to maturity, with benevolence and constructive advice. To him goes my first and greatest gratitude.

My research on Cicero has benefited from criticism and priceless comments of many friends and colleagues. I am deeply grateful to Bob Kaster for his never-ending generosity and advice always based on sound reasoning. He has not only helped me to improve my English prose but also prompted me to rethink many arguments. His wisdom has made *Cicero and Roman Education* a better book. In Cincinnati I had the good fortune to meet Harold Gotoff, one of the most distinguished Ciceronian scholars. Thanks to his helpful criticism and invaluable suggestions I have reworked many ideas on Cicero. I wholeheartedly thank him.

I am grateful to the former Department of Latin and Greek Philology (now Department of Ancient World Studies) at Sapienza University of Rome for a research fellowship in 2001–02, which allowed me to take a first look at many aspects of Cicero's oratory and its reception in antiquity. I am also very grateful to the Department of Classics of the University of Cincinnati for providing me with a stimulating research environment during my residence there as a Tytus Margo Fellow in 2005. The friendliness, commitment and professionalism of the staff of the Blegen Library have given me the opportunity to work on my project in a serene, welcoming atmosphere.

The bulk of this book was done during a year's leave from teaching in 2010–11, supported by a research fellowship from the Loeb Classical

Library Foundation. The Department of the Classics at Harvard University offered me the chance to carry out my research at the Widener Library. I am most grateful to all of the individuals who stimulated my thinking by generous conversations. I heartily thank Richard Thomas for his priceless support.

Over the years I have lectured on Cicero's oratory and its reception in many places and academic institutions – at Sapienza University of Rome, University of L'Aquila, Viterbo, University of Salamanca, University of Colorado at Boulder, University of Cincinnati, the meetings of the American Philological Association and the International Society for the History of Rhetoric, Princeton University, Columbia University and Harvard University. I warmly thank all the audiences attending my talks for their precious suggestions. I would like to thank the anonymous readers at Cambridge University Press for their criticism and helpful remarks. For discussion on specific aspects of my work I am grateful to Kathleen Coleman, Cynthia Damon, Jackie Elliott, Joe Farrell, Denis Feeney, Sean Gurd, John Miller, Carole Newlands, Michael Putnam, Wilfried Stroh, Richard Tarrant, Katharina Volk and Gareth Williams.

This book is dedicated to my little daughter Eloisa, the light of my life.

# *Abbreviations*

Unless otherwise indicated, abbreviations of ancient Latin authors and works are mainly from the *Oxford Latin Dictionary* or the *Oxford Classical Dictionary*. Greek authors and works are cited from Liddel and Scott's *A Greek-English Lexicon*. Abbreviations of periodicals in the bibliography follow the conventions of *L'Année Philologique*. English translations of the scholia are my own except in the case of Asconius where we possess the modern translation by Lewis. For other Latin texts I provide indication of text and translation at the first citation in the footnotes.

| | |
|---|---|
| B | C. Barwick (ed.), *Flavii Sosipatri Charisii Artis Grammaticae Libri V*, Leipzig 1925. |
| C | A. C. Clark (ed.), *Q. Asconii Pediani Orationum Ciceronis Quinque Enarratio*, Oxford 1907. |
| Cardauns | B. Cardauns (ed), *M. Terenti Varronis Antiquitates Rerum Divinarum*, Wiesbaden 1976. |
| Crawford | Jane W. Crawford, *M. Tullius Cicero. The Fragmentary Speeches*, Atlanta 1994. |
| FLP | E. Courtney (ed.), *The Fragmentary Latin Poets*, Oxford 1993. |
| FPL | W. Morel (ed.), *Fragmenta Poetarum Latinorum*, revised by J. Blänsdorf, Leipzig 1995. |
| Georgii | H. Georgii (ed.), *Tiberi Claudii Donati Ad Tiberium Claudium Maximum Donatianum filium suum Interpretationes Vergilianae*, Leipzig 1905. |
| GG | *Grammatici Graeci*, Leipzig 1867. |
| GL | H. Keil (ed.), *Grammatici Latini*, 8 vols., Leipzig 1855–1880. |
| GRF | G. Funaioli (ed.), *Grammaticae Romanae Fragmenta*, Leipzig 1907. |
| Hout | Michael P. J. Van den Hout (ed.), *M. Cornelii Frontonis Epistulae*, Leipzig 1988. |

| | |
|---|---|
| Iord. | H. Iordan (ed.), *M. Catonis Praeter librum De re rustica quae extant*, Stuttgart 1967 (orig. ed. 1860). |
| Jakobi | R. Jakobi (ed.) *Grillius Commentum in Ciceronis Rhetorica*, Munich, Leipzig 2002. |
| Jones | C. W. Jones (ed.) *Beda. De Ortographia*, CCSL 123, Turnhout 1975. |
| L | Wallace M. Lindsay (ed.), *Nonius Marcellus De compendiosa doctrina libros XX*, 3 vols., Leipzig 1903. |
| Lind. | Wallace M. Lindsay (ed.), *Sexti Pompei Festi de verborum significatu quae supersunt cum Pauli epitome*, Leipzig 1913. |
| LSJ | *A Greek-English Lexicon*, ed. H. G. Liddel, R. Scott, 9th ed., rev. H. S. Jones, Oxford 1940. |
| Marshall | P. K. Marshall (ed.), *Cornelius Nepos*, Leipzig 1977. |
| Marx | F. Marx (ed.) *C. Lucilii Carminum Reliquiae*, Leipzig 1904. |
| OCD | *Oxford Classical Dictionary*, ed. S. Hornblower, A. Spawforth, 3rd ed., Oxford 1996. |
| OLD | *Oxford Latin Dictionary*, ed. P. G. W. Glare, Oxford 1980. |
| ORF | E. Malcovati (ed.), *Oratorum Romanorum Fragmenta*, 4th ed., Turin 1976. |
| Ribbeck | O. Ribbeck (ed.), *Scaenicae Romanorum poesis fragmenta*, 2 vols., 2nd ed., Leipzig 1897–8. |
| Riese | A. Riese (ed.), *Anthologia Latina*, 2nd ed., Leipzig 1869–70. |
| Riesenweber | T. Riesenweber (ed.), *C. Marius Victorinus Commenta in Ciceronis Rhetorica*, Berlin, Boston 2013. |
| RLM | C. Halm (ed.), *Rhetores Latini Minores*, Leipzig 1863. |
| Reiff. | A. Reifferscheid (ed.), *C. Suetoni Tranquilli praeter "Caesarum" libros reliquiae*, Leipzig 1860. |
| Roth | C. L. Roth (ed.), *C. Suetoni Tranquilli quae supersunt omnia*, Leipzig 1858. |
| SB | D. R. Shackleton Bailey (ed.), *Cicero Letters to Quintus and Brutus. Letter Fragments. Letter to Octavian. Invectives. Handbook of Electioneering*, Cambridge, MA, London 2002. |
| SBAtt. | D. R. Shackleton Bailey (ed.), *Cicero Letters to Atticus*, 4 vols., Cambridge, MA, London 1999. |
| SBFam. | D. R. Shackleton Bailey (ed.), *Cicero Letters to Friends*, 3 vols., Cambridge, MA, London 2001. |

| | |
|---|---|
| Sbl. | M. T. Sblendorio Cugusi (ed.), *M. Porci Catonis Orationum Reliquiae*, Turin 1982. |
| SHR | B. Maurenbrecher (ed.), *C. Sallusti Crispi Historiarum Reliquiae*, Leipzig 1891. |
| St | Th. Stangl (ed.), *Ciceronis Orationum Scholiastae. Asconius. Scholia Bobiensia. Scholia Pseudasconii Sangallensia. Scholia Cluniacensia et Recentiora Ambrosiana ac Vaticana. Scholia Lugdunensia sive Gronoviana et eorum Excerpta Lugdunensia*, Vienna 1912. |
| Wessner | P. Wessner (ed.), *Aeli Donati Commentum Terenti. Accedunt Eugraphi Commentum et Scholia Bembina*, 2 vols., Stuttgart 1902. |
| Willis | J. Willis (ed.) *Martianus Capella*, Leipzig 1983. |

# *Introduction*

Rapuisti tum Ciceroni lucem sollicitam et aetatem senilem et vitam seriorem, te principe, quam sub te triumviro mortem, famam vero gloriamque factorum atque dictorum adeo non abstulisti, ut auxeris. Vivit vivetque per omnem saeculorum memoriam, dumque hoc vel forte vel providentia vel utcumque constitutum rerum naturae corpus, quod ille paene solus Romanorum animo vidit, ingenio complexus est, eloquentia illuminavit, manebit incolume, comitem aevi sui laudem Ciceronis trahet omnisque posteritas illius in te scripta mirabitur, tuum in eum factum execrabitur citiusque e mundo genus hominum quam huius nomen cedet.

(Vell. 2.66.4–5)[1]

"You took from Marcus Cicero a few anxious days, a few senile years, a life which would have been more wretched under your domination than was his death in your triumvirate; but you did not rob him of his fame, the glory of his deeds and words, nay you but enhanced them. He lives and will continue to live in the memory of the ages, and so long as this universe shall endure – this universe which, whether created by chance, or by divine providence, or by whatever cause, he, almost alone of all the Romans, saw with the eye of his mind, grasped with his intellect, illumined with his eloquence – so long shall it be accompanied throughout the ages by the fame of Cicero. All posterity will admire the speeches that he wrote against you, while your action against him will call forth their execrations, and the race of man shall sooner pass from the world than the name of Cicero be forgotten."[1]

Cicero never died. His assassins mutilated his *corpus*. They cut off his head and hands to eradicate his memory and spiritual legacy.[2] Yet Cicero's genius survived the accidents of time and stamped its mark on every age. As predicted by the Roman historian Velleius Paterculus, Cicero's intellect

---

[1] Text and translation (with minor modification): Shipley 1924.    [2] Plut. *Cic.* 48.6; *Ant.* 20.3.

I

and eloquence transcended the fragility and perishability of the human being.[3] Murdered by the sword of Antony's hitmen, Cicero survived the fragility of life through his writings.[4] The poignant scene of Cicero's violent death, recreated in dramatic forms by historians, poets and talented declaimers,[5] pays tribute to the statesman's and orator's accomplishments and immortalizes the last fighter for the liberty of the Roman republic as the "embodiment of verbal *ingenium*."[6]

From the last decades of the Roman republic and early empire to modern times, Cicero has wielded tremendous power over the minds of literate individuals and permeated every aspect of cultural life. His influence went well beyond prose writing. Modern scholarship has long dwelled upon the consolidation of Cicero's reception as orator and philosopher in the Fathers of the Church and Christian literature.[7] Scholarly attention has also been paid to the revitalization of the Ciceronian model in the Renaissance,[8] the centrality of Cicero's thought to the Enlightenment movement[9] and Cicero's pervasive presence in literature and popular culture over the course of the last two centuries.[10] As a philosopher, orator and statesman, Cicero has exerted a long-lasting impact on the history of ideas and the formation of a class of educated readers, destined for respectable careers as men of culture and politics.

Naturally, changing historical and cultural factors have impacted on Cicero's *Nachleben* over the times. Zielinski's influential study, *Cicero im Wandel der Jahrhunderte*,[11] claims that each epoch responded to Cicero with its own sensibility, its *Eigenart*, recreating a "single," one-sided Cicero, appreciated or imitated by virtue of a process of self-evaluation. As Altman makes clear, "Cicero in his integrity was the whole: it was we, his epigones, who repeatedly proved ourselves onesided in our appreciation."[12] Whatever the evaluation or reconstruction of Cicero over the centuries, a fact remains undeniable: Cicero's powerful and magnificent personality has stamped its mark indelibly on each age and continues to hold an endless fascination for readers and men of culture.

---

[3] Woodman 1983: 144–155; Schmitzer 2000: 184–9.  [4] Sen. *Suas.* 6.4; 5; 19; 7.2; 7–8.
[5] Sen. *Con.* 7.2; *Suas.* 6 and 7.  [6] Kaster 1998: 261.
[7] MacCormack 2013: 256–81; Kendeffy 2015. On the influence of Cicero's philosophy in Augustine, see O'Donnell 2015.
[8] Marsh 2013.
[9] Fox 2013. On Cicero's place in modern European (and American) culture and the role played by Cicero's rhetoric in Luther's Reformation, see Springer 2017. See also Manuwald 2016, for artistic and literary responses to Cicero in European and American culture from the thirteenth to the nineteenth century. For Cicero in the age of the Counter-Reformation, see Gatti 2017.
[10] Cole 2013; Fotheringham 2013b.  [11] Zielinski 1929 (first edition 1897).  [12] Altman 2015: 4.

The solemn celebration of Cicero's undying memory by Roman historians and declaimers started what has been defined as the "reduction" and simplification of the consummate statesman and orator to a cultural icon.[13] This was an untroubled process only in appearance. One might be reminded of Cicero's place in the so-called "quarrel of the ancients and the moderns," that is, the debate over imitation of the past and modernity of style that pervaded first-century literary criticism, discussed at length in Tacitus's *Dialogus*.[14] Recent analysis by Gowing has also called attention to the variable treatment of Cicero in the early empire, pointing to Quintilian's recuperation of Cicero as a good man and an ideal writer, in contrast with Seneca's moralistic vilification of the orator as an individual.[15] It is beyond question that Cicero's reputation had long suffered from this tension between opposing evaluations, condemnation and blame for his disputable political conduct, on the one side, and universal recognition of his excellence in the art of speaking, on the other. This is not to say that Cicero's personal achievements faded into insignificance. They continued to be a source of interest for late pagan and Christian writers.[16] In spite of his controversial life, Cicero's mastery of dialectical arguments and his moralistic approach to Greco-Roman philosophical and rhetorical doctrine exerted a considerable influence on literature and culture in late antiquity. Macrobius approached him as an encyclopaedic author, the source of all human knowledge.[17] To many Christians, he represented a paradigm of ethics and morality.[18] Lactantius, the *Cicero Christianus*, "shared Cicero's purpose to put eloquence in the service of a moral doctrine."[19] Yet Cicero played an influential role more as orator and prose writer than as man. Read and revisited in classrooms as the incarnation of the power of speech, Cicero "the icon of eloquence" and master of the Latin language gradually replaced Cicero the man.[20] In schools a new Cicero came into existence – Cicero the writer and man of letters whose memory had been preserved and carried forward by many generations of intellectuals over the times.

## Icon of Eloquence

Identified with his writings and words, Cicero soon established himself as the name and symbol of eloquence.[21] As we have said, at the end of

---

[13] Kaster 1998.  [14] Dressler 2015.  [15] Gowing 2013. See also Winterbottom 1982a: 254.
[16] MacCormack 2013: 252–5.  [17] MacCormack 2013: 282–9.  [18] Gasti 2016: 41–4.
[19] Kendeffy 2015: 91.  [20] Kaster 1998: 262.  [21] Quint. *Inst.* 10.1.112.

a process of historical erasure Cicero as a man, long censured as a prototype of political inconsistency and targeted as an example of an unphilosophical life, faded into the past. Cicero the statesman and politician was replaced by Cicero intellect and "pure form,"[22] abstracted from the social, political and historical preconceptions that had negatively affected his fame. One might say that this is the first, great legacy we have inherited from the school: the disentanglement of Cicero as a prose model from the historical and political Cicero and his consecration as the ideal orator, an image – passed down from generation to generation – that had dominated the history of education throughout the centuries and still remains at the heart of modern pedagogy.

The transformation into an icon of language and a model of Latin prose was a decisive moment in the history of the reception of Cicero in antiquity. If, as a historical figure, Cicero continued to encounter criticism and thereby elicit reflections on questions of Roman identity, offering space for debate about the survival of republican values in imperial times,[23] no one disputed his supremacy as a man of letters and an exemplary prose writer. Cicero met the high standards of ideal oratory. He was set as the example of the perfect orator, the *vir bonus dicendi peritus*, who combined moral virtues with the power of words and embodied therefore the ideals of Roman aristocratic culture. The truly Ciceronian Quintilian, as a schoolteacher and practicing advocate, held out Cicero's speeches as the models of the art of speaking. In the vast corpus of forensic, deliberative and civil law orations of Cicero, he found material for apprehending good Latin and the precepts for real-life oratory.

Reconfigured as an exemplary orator and prose writer, Cicero had a significant impact on the history of Roman education from the end of the republic onwards. We have rapidly noted that the early imperial debate about education and the persistence of established values pivoted on Cicero as the exemplar of eloquence and a model worthy of being imitated, emulated and reproduced by aspiring orators. Cicero did not only shape the form and practice of Roman rhetoric. He also shaped the ways in which the Romans reflected on education and its social and political function. By identifying Cicero with the art of eloquence Roman male elite students looked at the orator as the embodiment of successful oratory, the *vir bonus* who owed his pre-eminent social and cultural status to the rhetorical and oratorical skills that he had acquired and displayed over the years. Through Cicero they learned the ways by

[22] Dressler 2015: 147.   [23] Dench 2013.

which they could empower themselves and attain fame and prestige in Roman elite society. Rhetorical education, the result of an "amalgamation of practical training with broad cultural expertise,"[24] was an aristocratic cultural process strictly embedded in the social and political landscape of Rome. Cicero's oratory represented the cornerstone of this process. It provided the tools by which young elite men were turned into true orators, well-educated speakers with the knowledge and practical experience necessary to establish themselves as leading figures in the intense competition of Roman political life.

## Cicero and Roman Education

Abundant scholarship exists about the Roman educational system,[25] its three-stage arrangement[26] and the place of rhetoric in the formation of an educated Roman elite.[27] Analogously, the part played by Cicero as a master of Latin prose in literary instruction and rhetorical training has been well stressed.[28] As soon as one starts to examine the presence of Cicero in Roman education, it appears that there were two dominant scholarly approaches to his figure, closely related to each other. On the one hand, Cicero was reverently adopted as an unquestioned model of good and "pure" Latin, an invaluable source of linguistic and aesthetic devices to be successfully applied to real trials.[29] On the other, he was read, studied and imitated as the master of oratory as the "art of illusion,"[30] the model of ideal oratory devising and adapting persuasive arguments to the specificities of the trial at hand, manipulating the truth by means of pseudo-historical narratives, deploying verbal tricks and irony to destroy his opponent's credibility, delivering passionate and emotional performances and exploiting past events (as well as law decrees or statutes) to lend force and authority to his case. The speeches functioned naturally as the foundational texts of this didactic treatment of Cicero. Though delivered under different historical and legal circumstances, all speeches by Cicero

---

[24] Steel 2006: 65.
[25] Gwynn 1926; Marrou 1965; Bonner 1977; Harris 1989: 233–48; Morgan 1998a; Too 2001; Bloomer 2011b (for literate education in fourth- and fifth-century Gaul, see Haarhoff 1920). For Roman education in the republic, see Corbeill 2001. On rhetorical education and declamation, see Bonner 1949; Kaster 2001; Bloomer 2007.
[26] Kaster 1983.   [27] Clarke 1953; Corbeill 2007 (with further bibliography).
[28] On Cicero's ideal of oratorical education, see Bonner 1977: 76–89 (on standard rhetorical theory and Cicero: 287–308).
[29] Gasti 2016: 38–40 (on the *Tulliana dignitas* and Cicero as teacher of "good Latin").
[30] Gotoff 1993b.

displayed the potentialities of Roman language and oratorical art. Under the guidance of trained schoolteachers the young apprehended how to extract from a speech of Cicero all the linguistic and rhetorical material needed to display their oratorical talent and intellectual skills and perform thereby as accomplished speakers.

Any scholar trying to trace out a history of Cicero's place in Roman education should thus look at the reception process from two interconnected perspectives. From the standpoint of rhetorical education, our understanding of the reception of Cicero entails by necessity a study of the process of reinterpretation and re-evaluation of his rhetorical theory and practice in the light of the speeches, the texts most embedded in the political, social and cultural environment of the Roman republic. From a linguistic perspective, it involves an examination of the ways by which ancient scholars and schoolteachers approached Ciceronian language and style as a step towards defining the rules of correct Latin.

With respect to the linguistic side, it is well known that liberal education in Roman schools largely relied on Cicero's *auctoritas* in establishing the principles of good Latin. The *Attic Nights* of Gellius, the encyclopaedic dictionary of Nonius Marcellus, the collection of *singularia* of Statilius Maximus and late educational grammatical handbooks testify to the relevance of Cicero to the study of Latin language and style (*ars grammatica*). Proper pronunciation, vocabulary, word order and appropriateness of morphology and syntax were thought to be essential to the acquisition of *Latinitas,* the ideal of pure and correct Latin style and idiom, a notion firmly embedded in Roman elite culture. What seems much more significant is that, by learning Ciceronian language, the young members of the dominating classes expanded their opportunities to acquire a respectable place in Roman society. Since incorrect Latin diction was associated with immorality and the transgression of established social values, appropriation and mastery of Cicero's language promoted an elite ideal of Romanness and enabled the youths to play a part in the Roman community. As has been said, "in Roman society preference is given not to personal development and individual improvement, but to training youth for the community of the elite through replication by example."[31] By acquiring and replicating Cicero's *Latinitas* the elite male students learned how to become true Romans and establish themselves as educated promoters of Roman cultural tradition.

---

[31] Corbeill 2001: 282.

It goes without saying that Cicero as both a master of oratorical theory and practice and as an *exemplum* of successful eloquence had a dominant place in rhetorical training. Quintilian's construction of the ideal orator in his *Institutio* can serve as a case study for the deployment of Cicero's oratory in liberal education. At the heart of Quintilian's assessment of Cicero as a paramount model of oratorical prose is naturally the notion of imitation, which was integral to the development of the "good man" and "good orator." As an accomplished schoolteacher, Quintilian drew on Cicero's orations to clarify the correct exordial topic, illustrate different ways of dissimulating the truth and manipulating historical events and legal issues, underline wit and humor as productive rhetorical devices and offer examples of emotional delivery. Such an explanation of Cicero's technique of persuasion was preliminary to imitation and emulation of the great orator's rhetorical accomplishments. By propounding Cicero's speeches as models of oratorical excellence and elucidating relevant aspects of the manipulative strategy of persuasion Quintilian provided his pupils with all the most potent weapons in the armory of the orator and urged them to follow in the great orator's footsteps. To Quintilian, imitation of Cicero proved to be a powerful "tool of war" in the competitive arena.

Yet it is worth remembering that Quintilian's endorsement of Ciceronian oratory was also, and above all, a cultural and pedagogical project, based on imitation of the exemplary past as a means of inculcating elite young students with a set of values anchored in elite culture and society. In Quintilian's view, Cicero not only supplied students at the school of rhetoric with an impressive array of linguistic and rhetorical devices. He also helped to shape the youths' minds and make them mature individuals. Imitation of Cicero turned out to be an ethical concept, a notion embedded in the idealistic vision of education as an intellectual development from childhood to maturity, from young would-be Romans to "true" Roman citizens.

Quintilian was obviously not a voice in the wilderness. Cicero's place in the school curriculum and his importance as source of good Latin and a model of persuasion are amply demonstrated by the mass of exegetical material on the speeches, in the form of both independent commentaries and sets of marginal or interlinear notes, that goes under the name of *scholia Ciceronis* and ranges in date from the Neronian age, the time of composition of the commentary of Asconius Pedianus, to the late fifth or early sixth century.[32] A hitherto neglected chapter of the history of Cicero's

---

[32] Collected and edited by Stangl 1912 (= St). Edition of Asconius: Clark 1907 (= C); Lewis 2006 (with English translation); edition of the *Scholia Bobiensia*: Hildebrandt 1907.

reception, the scholia on Cicero's orations originated in the school environment, were the final product of the interpretative efforts of learned scholars and schoolteachers, reflected the multiple ways by which a speech of Cicero was approached, scrutinized and dissected, and ultimately presented to students a model for imitation. Just as Quintilian supplies us with insightful and precious comments on Cicero's oratorical art and its didactic use, Asconius enables us to establish the relevance of Cicero's speeches to the students' understanding of Roman republican history. Similarly, the *Scholia Bobiensia*, a linguistic-rhetorical commentary on a number of orations, is clearly rooted in a didactic context, connected as it is to basic training in linguistics and rhetoric. The commentary on the *Divinatio* and parts of the *Verrines*, which is commonly known under the name of Pseudo-Asconius, and the so-called *scholia Gronoviana* contain notes of some significance on Cicero's stylistic and linguistic features and his rhetorical practice. Taken all together, these scholiographic *corpora* join Quintilian in illuminating the multiplicity of roles played by Cicero in the school system, as a source of historical knowledge, a rhetorical theorist, a model of prose writing, a linguistic authority and a master of the art of speaking. To put it in different terms, Quintilian and the ancient scholiasts are essential to our reconstruction of Cicero's oratory as a foundational element in Roman education.

## Key Questions

Modern scholars dealing with Cicero's relevance to the Roman educational system unavoidably face two key issues: What was the role played by the school in the survival of Cicero's speeches? And how and to what extent has ancient exegesis influenced our understanding of Ciceronian oratory? The assumption is that *what* we read of Cicero is largely the result of a process of selection that began in the school environment in the late republic. Many speeches survived the accidents of textual transmission by dint of their didactic function. Not all of them, however. A good number of orations had been lost, in spite of their stylistic quality and their recognized impact on educational training. The case of the two speeches *pro Cornelio* is illuminating. Yet, if we are allowed to appreciate Cicero's style and oratorical art, we owe it to the school and its codified system that helped to preserve literary texts from their publication to the oldest medieval witnesses.[33] In our frustration at the lack of surviving original

---

[33] Pasquali 1952: IX; De Nonno 2010: 32.

autographs, the presence (or absence) of some texts in the school curriculum is crucial to our comprehension of significant stages of textual transmission. And it is not by chance that the majority of the speeches commented on in the scholia (presumably arranged in chronological corpora) reappear in the oldest papyri scraps or parchments. From the first authorial dissemination to the medieval manuscripts passing through the school, the story of the transmission of Cicero's orations (a story similar to that of the greatest number of Latin literary texts) had profoundly been affected by their didactic relevance and influence on the educational system.

To the schoolteachers' concern about the textual quality of the scrutinized orations we also owe *how* we read Cicero and *which text* of Cicero we read. Ancient scholarship on Cicero offers abundant comments on textual issues. As expected, variant readings, alterations, omissions, interpolations and erroneous conjectures by earlier critics constituted the subject of heated debates among scholiasts and commentators engaged in establishing textual correctness and accuracy. As has been stated, "the history of ancient textual criticism is a poor substitute for the history of the texts themselves, but in the absence of manuscripts it is the only one we have."[34] Applied to the reception of the speeches in the Roman school, this view makes sense of a large part of ancient scholarship on Cicero as a useful supplement to the history of textual transmission. In particular, the scholiasts' discussions of specific textual points, in line with or in opposition to earlier interpretations, illustrate the enormous interpretative work done on Cicero's speeches over the times. As "variorum works," the scholia or commentaries on the orations collect, assemble and discuss earlier opinions, often in polemical terms. They detail variant readings or comment on apparently unused linguistic forms in order to provide a text matching the standard criteria of philological accuracy. Along with the late grammarians and rhetoricians, the scholiographic *corpora* offer us the chance of investigating and identifying otherwise inaccessible strata of transmission.

Reflecting on oratory and its didactic use, schoolteachers in antiquity responded to precise educational demands. Rhetorical training included not only instruction on language. Roman elite students had to be prepared for real-life oratory by acquiring rhetorical devices and stratagems. Within this context, the surviving scholia on Cicero are of the greatest significance for understanding *the ways by which* students read and interpreted the speeches. Preoccupied with the intellectual development of their pupils,

[34] Zetzel 1981: 1–2.

the scholiasts guided them through the complexities and intricacies of Cicero's text, acting as learned and expert advocates acquainted with the manipulative art of persuasion. Through a close integration of text and commentary, they illustrated and elucidated Cicero's strategy of persuasion, his use of rhetorical tricks, artful argumentations and aesthetic/emotional devices, spurring knowledge of traditional rhetorical patterns and stimulating adoption and imitation of Cicero's oratorical tactics. What has been said about Quintilian is equally valid for late scholiasts and commentators. The principle behind explanation of Cicero was that of appropriation/imitation, that is, the acquisition of the rules of the art of speaking and the related practical replication of the precepts regulating the art of persuasion.

It has been noted that "a rhetorical theory can claim authority if it is understandable, usable and efficient – or, at least, perceived as such."[35] Quintilian and late scholiasts explained, commented on and used Cicero's rhetorical treatises and speeches to provide students with the main basis of rhetorical theory and offer guidelines on how to handle real trials and produce effective oratorical performances. If the youthful treatise *De inventione*, expounded at length by late rhetoricians such as Victorinus and Grillius, along with Cicero's other theoretical writings (*De oratore, Brutus* and *Orator*), offered the basic precepts of rhetorical theory, the speeches supplied students with the practical means of persuasion. In the speeches Cicero grounded the theory in his own experience as an advocate. He showed how to organize and arrange the arguments, provided examples of persuasive strategies and the proper use of aesthetic and emotional devices and taught students to make their texts authoritative through the application of traditional rhetorical tools. Cicero influenced Roman education as a rhetorical theorist and an authority on prose writing and the Latin language. But perhaps the most powerful impact he made on the ancient pedagogical system was through his speeches, the texts that, more than others, testified to the force of oratory as the art of illusion and manipulation of minds. Roman students transformed themselves into accomplished orators and respectable citizens by looking at Cicero's authoritative model. It might be tempting to say that they engaged in public speaking and entered the public arena holding a volume of Cicero's speeches in their hands.

---

[35] Guérin 2006: 62.

*Cicero and Roman Education* is a book about the reception of Cicero's speeches in the Roman educational system. It focuses on the role played by the speeches as practical supports for liberal education and rhetorical training in antiquity. Just as Virgil took a prominent place as a master of Latin poetry, Cicero dominated the world of Roman education as the exemplary model of prose writing and the ideal orator. And just as Virgil's epic poem illustrated the power of Roman poetical language, Cicero's orations served the needs of Roman elite male students, who looked at them as source of good Latin and instances of triumphant oratory. As its subtitle, *The Reception of the Speeches and Ancient Scholarship*, indicates, this book is also about the part played by the schools in the survival and propagation of the speeches. From the initial stages of textual transmission (publication and handwritten copies) to the earliest medieval testimonies, the educational use of the speeches acted as a sort of "guarantee" against the loss of a significant part of Cicero's oratorical output. In addition, since ancient scholarship on the speeches was beyond doubt connected to the school environment and didactic contexts, this study concentrates on the scholarly interpretation of Cicero's oratorical texts as a response to specific educational demands. Scholarly interest in chronology, the arrangement of the speeches, style and language, rhetorical patterns and linguistic/emotional devices originated in the schools: Cicero was the subject of scientific research as a scholastic *auctor* more than a source of human knowledge.

The evidence on which this book is based has been drawn not only from traditional sources, such as grammatical and rhetorical handbooks or the most representative work of Ciceronianism in antiquity, Quintilian's educational treatise known as *Institutio Oratoria*. The main evidence derives above all from the scholia on the speeches, the body of exegetical material of varying age and origin that has come down to us in the form of both marginal notes and continuous commentaries. As I said above, the *scholia Ciceronis* represent a valuable witness to Cicero's place in Roman education. More than for their relevance to Latin textual criticism in antiquity, this book constantly uses the scholia to illustrate relevant aspects of the reception of Cicero *orator* in the ancient schools.

Writing marks the beginning of any textual history. In the case of primarily "oral" texts such as the orations, the passage from orality to writing is the main determinant of the subsequent phases of textual transmission. In Chapter 1 I sketch out the figure of Cicero as "editor" and publisher of his own oratorical corpus. Relying basically on Cicero's continual reassessments of the power of writing as a means of promoting the self, I examine the social, political and cultural connotations behind the theory of publication through its three basic steps, that is, writing and composition, private circulation and revision, final publication. Writing was thought of as a vehicle for self-memorialization. By writing, revising and propagating his textual body, Cicero complied with a code of social obligations and helped to advance a larger educational and political project shared by the members of the dominating elite. Through publication he cultivated the oratorical and political self. Most importantly, by selecting his speeches for publication the orator showed his concern with self-aggrandizement. He perpetuated his message by means of self-referential pieces of writing.

The speeches put into circulation soon became models of style and political thought. Cicero's dream to educate young generations through his textual *corpus* came true. Yet he was not the sole guardian of his own literary and political fate. A good number of speeches, credited with literary dignity by the author himself, got lost in the first centuries of our era. As has been observed, material and/or cultural factors and changes in taste had considerable impacts on the preservation of Cicero's orations. Chapter 2 offers a survey of the transmission of Cicero's speeches, from the first handwritten copies to the earliest medieval manuscripts. Firstly, it focuses on the early imperial dissemination of editions of Cicero's speeches. The well-known passage of Fronto about surviving copies of Ciceronian orations (*Ad M. Caes.* 1.7.4: 15.11–16.1Hout) illuminates the established practice of copying out, emending and producing readable texts, certified by a final sign of authentication (*subscriptio*). The revision of a manuscript book of *De lege agraria* I by the second-century scholar Statilius Maximus provides a reliable proof of the routine process of editing that contemplated a careful reproduction of the exemplar by drawing on a number of earlier manuscripts. Then, it deals with the arrangement of collections and *corpora* of orations, a formative stage of textual tradition that started in late antiquity and had sensible effects on the current status of medieval manuscripts. Finally, it discusses the process of propagation of Cicero's speeches in the schools. A close comparison between indirect external evidence and the oldest extant papyri scraps and manuscripts points to the didactic use of the orations as the main determinant of their preservation over time.

The early history of Cicero's reception in antiquity is that of an ideological and literary conflict between enthusiastic admirers of Cicero and his detractors. In Chapter 3 I single out the basic moments of this prolonged debate about the republican orator and statesman, which aimed at the revitalization of the Ciceronian ideal and, amidst setbacks, ended in Quintilian's consecration of Cicero as the exemplary model of *Latinitas* and oratorical prose. This establishment of Cicero as an authority in Latin accounts for the early empire's interest in language and style. Relying on Gellius, Nonius Marcellus, grammatical handbooks and the scholia, I also offer a comprehensive overview of Cicero's place as icon of the Latin language in Roman education. As demonstrated by Statilius's compilation of obsolete or difficult words from Cicero's orations (*singularia*), the fondness for linguistic oddities or rarities appears to have been a regular feature of the reception of Cicero as *optimus auctor* in the school. But what most fascinated ancient grammarians and scholars was Cicero's creativity in Latin vocabulary, his linguistic acuteness and sensibility and propriety of language. Cicero taught the correct way of speaking and writing. And his speeches functioned as a sort of "Bible" of the ideal, perfect Latin. As the incarnation of the notion of *Latinitas,* Cicero instructed Roman students in acquiring a good, elegant Latin, reputed to be crucial to public reputation and social advancement.

Yet Cicero's genius and *elegantia,* his artistry and skill in the use of language, elicited divergent reactions throughout the centuries. Strictly connected to the establishment of Cicero as a linguistic *auctoritas,* textual correctness was one of the main areas of contention among literary critics and scholars. In the last section of Chapter 3 I call attention to relevant figures of ancient Ciceronian scholarship, pointing also to the nature and form of ancient commentaries and their function as auxiliary texts in reading and interpretation. I also re-examine a group of variants of collation and textual annotations in the scholia, reasserting the marginal role played by textual criticism in late Ciceronian scholarship. My focus will be on the academic contest over Cicero's language and style that pervaded early and late literary criticism. The commentaries on the speeches report and discuss a number of earlier opinions, often in polemical and censorious terms: they reveal that debating over aesthetics and rhetoric was intrinsic to the reception of Cicero in antiquity.

A discussion of the ways in which Cicero was read, interpreted and taught in the classrooms makes up the bulk of Chapter 4. Taking as my starting point the celebrated passage of Quintilian (*Inst.* 2.5.5–11) about the usual procedure followed in teaching rhetoric, I look into the scholastic interpretation of Cicero's orations as manipulative texts, deploying aesthetic and rhetorical artifices to persuade the audience and win approval. Oratory as the "art of illusion" was the principle that guided Quintilian and schoolteachers in explaining Cicero's mastery of persuasive and emotional strategies and encouraging students in the imitation/replication of the rhetorical subtleties used by the orator in his successful cases. Rhetoric was basically a weapon of deceit. By focusing on Cicero's strategic deployment of rhetorical and linguistic devices and his manipulation of truth in historical narratives (and legal issues) ancient educationists offered the speeches as models of virtuous oratory and artful deception of the minds of listeners/readers.

Cicero dedicated his entire life to constructing a reliable image of himself as ideal orator and consummate statesman achieving unrivalled and eternal fame by his personal qualities. He presented his speeches as a collection of prose models and *exempla* of political sagacity, emphasizing thereby the strict connection between oratory and politics, the act of public speaking and the supreme ideal of conservation of the *res publica*. By portraying himself as the epitome of Roman eloquence and a representative figure of Roman political culture, he stressed the importance of forensic and deliberative oratory to public life. Most importantly, he launched an educational and political plan aimed at forming a class of orators and politicians relying on a set of values traditionally associated with elite power and masculinity. This was Cicero's ambitious project: instructing Roman male students in the art of speaking and, at the same time, inviting them into a process of constant reaffirmation and reproduction of the rhetorical, linguistic and political elements that formed the backdrop for his literary works. Contemporary and later readers played a key role in Cicero's self-fashioning strategy. They shared – and replicated – the principles relevant for the "canonization" of Cicero as the perfect example of *vir bonus dicendi peritus*.

In assembling and disseminating a textual *corpus* of oratorical pieces Cicero "presented an edited account of himself" to his aristocratic reading audience.[36] Entering into an endless virtual dialogue with his young readers he required their support and involvement in the propagation of a distinctive image of *optimus vir* and first-class speaker. His memory relied on the readers' participation in his project of self-promotion. By providing Roman male students with a set of rhetorical models, a repertoire of stratagems intrinsic to the art of persuasion, and, at the same time, showing them how an effective speech could be delivered and reworked in writing, Cicero expected his readers to associate the very notion of oratory with the example set by his own work.

Readership in antiquity responded positively to Cicero's expectations. Commentators and schoolteachers identified Cicero with ordered style, *Latinitas* and masculine oratory. They explained Cicero's use of rhetorical and linguistic devices, repeatedly calling attention to the notion of

---

[36] Steel 2012: 254.

"illusion" as the key to success in Roman trials. In doing so, they excited passion for the model and stimulated imitation. One might say that, in approaching Cicero's oratory and his speeches as *exempla* of perfection of style, ancient readers and students played a sophisticated game of *imitatio/aemulatio*. They satisfied Cicero's desire for immortality by a never-ending sentiment of love and admiration, which resulted in the emotional and practical need to imitate and reproduce his acting, his gestures and behaviors, his rhetorical schemes and persuasive ornaments and, especially, his refined style.

Cicero was the incarnation of artistic language and the *exemplum* of oratory as the art of illusion. Roman students viewed Cicero as the only authoritative voice upon which they could rely to become accomplished orators and politicians. They loved and imitated him, trying to gain advantage from each of his teachings. By means of imitation they developed their intellectual abilities and transformed themselves into true Romans, "new Ciceros," holding respectable positions in Roman elite society. In some sense, it is this process of imitation and emulation/competition in the school environment that is at the very heart of the reception of Cicero in antiquity. Cicero's strong desire to monumentalize his oratorical power and eternalize his textual body passed through the renegotiation of his position in the school canon. But there is more. Roman students inherited a splendid legacy from Cicero, that is, the inseparability of powerful eloquence and personal glory in social and political life. What Cicero's speeches recorded for posterity is that power and authority depend on true eloquence. And maybe this is the reason why Cicero's reputation as orator had remained unaltered throughout the centuries.

CHAPTER I

# *Cicero Presents Himself*
## *Writing, Revision and Publication of the Speeches*

Thomas Habinek's sociological-materialist interpretation of Latin literature reminds us that writing was crucial to the preservation of Roman aristocratic identity.[1] As the response to the growth of Roman empire, Latin literature was an aristocratic enterprise, a means of unifying the sectors of elite society through a shared, identifiable language and propagating elite values through the circulation of a corpus of authoritative texts. As has been said, "many of the characteristics of Latin literature can be attributed to its production by and for an elite that sought to maintain and expand its dominance over other sectors of the population through reference to an authorizing past."[2] In creating, developing and transmitting a literature founded on the preservation of aristocratic ideals and authority, the Roman elite enhanced its political and social status and negotiated conflicts over values and power relationships. In other words, Roman aristocracy reinforced its dominance by means of writing.[3]

Applied to Roman oratory, a literary genre *per se* instrumental in maintaining political power, the aristocratic connotation of Latin literature is of much value. Oral performance, as an instrument for displaying intellectual and linguistic abilities, contributed powerfully to the construction of the self. By means of writing the intellectual elite crossed the boundary between orality and text and memorialized forms of social authority. As much as aristocratic power depended on the circulation of written texts, which perpetuated elite values and functioned as a replication of Roman tradition, rhetorical power maintained its elite nature by writing, seen as a form of reinforcement and transmission of social and political status achieved by fluency in speaking. A written speech inculcated aristocratic values, in the terms of preservation of the social order and promotion of elite ideals, for it "memorialized a performance carried out within a socio-culturally authoritative space by a socio-culturally authoritative

---

[1] Habinek 1998.  [2] Habinek 1998: 3.  [3] Moatti 2015: 98.

performer."[4] In the case of Cicero, a stunning example of political and oratorical success founded on the power of words,[5] writing gave the republican orator victory over past and contemporary writers and propagated his elite vision of Roman culture and politics. In Cicero's judgment, writing was the most powerful medium for preservation of political and literary memory. In addition to consolidating and transmitting Roman elite morality, the written word eternized Cicero as the icon of Roman eloquence and the ideal statesman.

## Written Oratory and Textual Longevity

To consider the role played by writing in Cicero's strategy of self-presentation, it seems useful to succinctly re-examine the beginnings of Roman oratory, as recounted by Cicero in the *Brutus*. As Narducci points out, "by the mid-point of the second century BCE, the orators who had the ability of putting their own speeches into writing were not very many; in certain cases, these speeches remained only sketches (*commentarii*), which in part were preserved in the archives of aristocratic families, or were put at the disposal of young orators for their education."[6] A first, notable change of course occurred with Cato the Elder, who was said to have left over one hundred and fifty written orations.[7] Modern scholars have long debated whether the Catonian speeches were assembled into a *corpus* or circulated separately.[8] Similarly, it is uncertain whether the delivered speeches were reworked before publication.[9] In any case, Cato's speeches were just flashes of Latin eloquence,[10] lacking stylistic refinement.[11] In Cato's view, writing was not a literary act. It was perceived as a professional elite tool, basically as a means of registering and memorializing a relevant political and social action.[12]

---

[4] Sciarrino 2007: 66.   [5] Habinek 1998: 10–1.
[6] Narducci 2002a: 403. For a survey of Roman oratory before Cicero, see Sciarrino 2007.
[7] Cic. *Brut.* 65.
[8] For a collection of Cato's speeches, see Calboli 1978: 6–10 (on the question, see also Sblendorio Cugusi 1982: 28–30).
[9] In a fragment of the oration *De sumptu suo*, transmitted by Fronto 90.15-9Hout as an example of *elegans praeteritio* (37Iord.; *ORF* 173; 169Sbl.), Cato depicts himself as re-enacting a prepared text, kept and filed away in a *caudex*. On Cato's passage and prose text composition, see Pecere 2010: 80; see also Kennedy 1972: 57–8; Dorandi 2007: 47–64. For Cato's speeches as "very close to the actual speeches which were delivered rather than semi-literary productions or revisions considerably removed from the originals," see Astin 1978: 134–6.
[10] Gel. 13.25.12.
[11] Cic. *Brut.* 294. For Cato's stylistic imperfection as a model of "republicanism," a paradigm of republican oratory alternative to "the exemplary perfection of Caesar's *commentarii*," see Gurd 2012: 61–2.
[12] On the connection between the act of writing and performing scripts in Cato the Elder and the creation of a "social identity," see Sciarrino 2004.

As a mnemonic device, writing does not preserve only the memory of an event. It also perpetuates the memory of one's self.[13] It is only through writing that the orator can preserve (and transmit) the memory of his own talents. In the *Brutus*,[14] "a teleological account of the development of Roman oratory and other Roman literary forms that valorizes a contrast between primitive, rough-and-ready early Romans and the sophisticated, philhellenic figures of the later Republic,"[15] Cicero frowns upon the laziness of past orators who spurned writing as an instrument of stylistic improvement and a memorial to their *ingenium* for posterity.[16] In meditating upon the eternizing power of writing and its lasting impact on the transformation of oratory into a literary genre,[17] Cicero canonizes himself as a national *exemplum* of orator-writer. The case of Servius Sulpicius Galba is illustrative of how important writing is to the definition of good oratory. One of the leading orators of the mid-second century BCE, Galba spoke differently from what he wrote. He was a man of great talent (*peringeniosus*), naturally gifted, but unlearned (*Brut.* 91–3).[18] As a result, he was unable to captivate the readers' attention by a passionate and vehement *oratio*.[19] Certainly, Galba was "an important oratorical ancestor whose stylistic innovations anticipate distinctive elements of Cicero's own style."[20] In contrast to Cicero, however, he failed in displaying his talent by writing.

Writing was vital to the evolution of Roman oratory towards literary forms. As has been remarked, from Cato onwards Roman oratory gradually progressed from unpolished texts to the refinement of the periodic style, associated with both Greek practices and the use of writing.[21] And it was Cicero's *corpus* of oratorical works that marked a turning point in the conversion of oratory into a canonical literary genre in Latin. As a harmonious combination of *ars* and *ingenium*, education and natural talent,[22] Cicero's work inaugurated a new, reinvigorated and stylistically balanced form of oratory, equally distant from rigid Atticism or

---

[13] Gowing 2000: 43 (with further bibliography).
[14] For an excellent discussion of the composition of the *Brutus*, see Narducci 1997a: 97–156; Narducci 2002a. On the rhetorical-political background of the treatise, see Steel 2003; Stroup 2003; Dugan 2005: 175–250; Stroup 2010: 237–68.
[15] Habinek 1998: 64.
[16] Narducci 1997a: 111ff., especially on publication in the pre-Ciceronian age as a "not regular practice."
[17] On the *Brutus* as a dialogue about writing and Cicero's representation of oratorical fame as "inescapably contingent upon the ability and willingness to write," see Stroup 2010: 267.
[18] On this passage, see Douglas 1966: 78. On Servius Galba "as a test case for how texts of speeches can be inadequate representations of an orator's *ingenium*," see Dugan 2005: 292. See also Webb 1997a: 113.
[19] Douglas 1966: 79.   [20] Dugan 2005: 296.   [21] Dugan 2005: 300.
[22] Cic. *de Orat.* 1.150; 257; 2.96–97; 3.190.

Hortensius's mannerism.[23] In committing his rhetorical and political project to writing Cicero invested a form of expression originally fitting an oral generic environment with literary dignity.[24] He bestowed on his written speeches "the powerful breath of *action*,"[25] recalling the centrality of good writing, an ideal reproduction of good speaking, to perfect eloquence and reasserting the effect of writing on the perpetuation of the image of the writer among future generations.

By converting himself into a writer, Cicero realized his ambitious project "of impressing upon his fellow-citizens the undeniable worth of culture."[26] An eloquent passage from the *Brutus* (122–3) emphatically proclaims that Cicero composed and disseminated an impressive number of volumes, benefiting thereby the rising generation through a more elevated and elaborated style. Even Scribonius Curio's masterpiece, the speech *pro Servio Fulvio de incestu*, had almost vanished from view, canceled by the advent of a new, sophisticated form of language.[27] Overwhelmed by the unprecedented literary output of Cicero, past oratory had ceased to be read.[28] By means of writing, then, Cicero transformed oratory from its original form as "display of oral skills" into "true literature." In other words, writing memorialized the modernity of Cicero's style and language.

Cicero's comments on writing are reiterated in the *Orator*.[29] As has been noted, in Cicero's last major rhetorical treatise "the performative aspect of oratory is overshadowed by the textual."[30] Great emphasis is placed on the vital function of writing to the literary evolution of Roman oratory.[31] Notably, Cicero consolidates his own reputation as an artist of speech and fashions himself as a Roman written authority by re-formulating the doctrine of the three styles of speaking (*Orat.* 100–112),[32] an inquiry upon ideal oratorical style and "the individual self of the ideal orator,"[33] which focuses primarily on the ability of the

---

[23] Narducci 2002a: 422–23.
[24] On the intimate relationship between speaking and writing in Cicero, see Bell 2013: 172–4.
[25] Narducci 2002b: 440.   [26] Narducci 2002b: 440.
[27] On Curio's lack of education cf. Cic. *de Orat.* 1.45–73; 147–59; 166–203. On Curio's oratory, see Rosillo López 2013.
[28] Bell 2013: 172–3.
[29] A good survey of the issues dealt with in the *Orator* is in Narducci 2002b. On Cicero's rhetorical project, largely indebted to the Aristotelian system, see Wisse 2002a; 2002b; May 2007a. For a brief account of Cicero's style theory in the *Orator*, see Albrecht 2003: 21–5.
[30] May 2007a: 259.   [31] Narducci 2002b: 440–1.
[32] Cf. also Cic. *Orat.* 20–1. A sound analysis of the passage of the *Orator* is provided by Dugan 2005: 303–6.
[33] Dugan 2005: 267.

truly eloquent speaker to master every one of the types of diction.[34] Most importantly, Cicero prides himself on attaining a varied and multifaceted eloquence and providing elite male students with a selection of speeches, which both recreated the vehemence and passion of the spoken orations and exemplified the varied aspects of his art.[35] In explicitly referring to his orations as readily available,[36] Cicero appears as a "confidently canonical author," well conscious of the achieved level of canonicity of his speeches.[37]

By merging Platonic aesthetics with the ideal of *prépon/decorum*, Cicero fashioned himself as the "Latin Demosthenes."[38] The first, among the orators of the past and the present, who may well be called the "good orator," Cicero portrayed himself as the only one capable of combining exuberant and mature style[39] and adapting his speech to fit all conceivable circumstances.[40] More significantly, by committing his idealized persona to the diffusion of his oratorical masterpieces, Cicero, an "engaged public figure,"[41] consecrated himself as an undisputed model of style and diction and presented "his textual corpus as the best Latin representation" of the ideal oratory.[42]

---

[34] On the threefold division of the types of diction into the plain, middle and grand styles, see Gotzes 1914; Douglas 1957; 1973; Kirchner 2007: 192–4 (on the middle style, see Winterbottom 1989).

[35] Cic. *Orat.* 102–3 (cf. also Quint. *Inst.* 12.10.58–76, on the *recta dicendi genera*). The low-key, plain style is represented by the civil law speech on behalf of Aulus Caecina, prosecuted in an inheritance case in 69 BCE (on the long-debated date of delivery of the speech, see Stroh 1975: 80–103; Frier 1983: 222–27). The middle style is used in the speech *de imperio Cn. Pompei*, delivered in 66 in support of Manilius's proposal to extend Pompey's military powers in the war against Mithradates (Rees 2007: 140). The grand, magniloquent style is exemplified by the speech in defense of Gaius Rabirius on a charge of high treason (*perduellio*), delivered in 63. The seven speeches against Verres, the *pro Cluentio Habito*, and the two speeches in defense of C. Cornelius charged under the *lex Cornelia de maiestate*, delivered in 65, finally, demonstrate Cicero's excellence in combining various oratorical styles.

[36] Cic. *Orat.* 103.    [37] Dugan 2005: 306.

[38] On Cicero's self-fashioning as a Roman Demosthenes in the *Brutus* and *Orator*, see Bishop 2015–16.

[39] At *Orat.* 107–8, the well-known passage of the *pro Sexto Roscio Amerino* about the punishment for the parricides (§ 72) is presented as an instance of youthful exuberance and abundance in opposition to the more mature style displayed in the *pro Cluentio* and the *pro Cornelio*. On the extraordinary fortune of this passage in the declamation schools cf. Sen. *Con.* 3.2; 7.1.1–2; 7.2.3; Quint. *Inst.* 12.6.4: Dyck 2010a: 137. According to the Gronovian scholiast **D** (310.18-20St), Cicero's description of the penalty for parricide in the *Rosciana* attracted some criticism because of the use of an elevated and magniloquent style: *Hic locus a criticis reprehensus est: hunc autem locum alibi laudat Cicero. Sciendum tamen est quia in hoc capite genus dicendi altum est, tractat enim de supplicio parricidarum* ("This passage has been censured: Cicero commends it in another place. However, it should be considered that in this chapter style is elevated; in fact it deals with the penalty for parricide"); cf. also 301. 30–302.1-2St.

[40] Cic. *Orat.* 123.

[41] I borrow this definition, applied to Pliny the Younger, from Riggsby 1995a: 123.

[42] Dugan 2005: 306.

But we might take one step further. In a sense, Cicero's choice of supplying readers and young orators with selective examples of style register represents a concrete attempt to exercise control on textual reception. In advertising some of his speeches as rhetorical models Cicero intended to create a small *corpus* arranged by stylistic criteria. The speeches on behalf of Caecina, in support of the Manilian law, and in defense of Rabirius formed, in fact, a restricted group of orations exemplifying specific stylistic peculiarities. Albeit there is no allusion to publication in the passage of the *Orator*, these orations already circulated and were, among others, available to a large readership. By enlarging this first group to include four more speeches, *Verrines, pro Cluentio, pro Cornelio* (both cited twice)[43] and *pro Sexto Roscio Amerino*,[44] Cicero equipped promising orators with a small collection of style models.

Obviously, the concept of selection contemplates the author's intervention in the process of arrangement and diffusion of his writings. In this case, Cicero grouped his speeches together in a *corpus* that, if not arranged with publication in view, at least was intended to perform as a style and diction collection.[45] Perfectly conscious of the social and cultural value of writing as the only instrument of a potential development of oratory from oral performance to "great literature,"[46] Cicero invented a stylistic canon and reflected upon the nature of his writings, selected by stylistic criteria and handed down to future generations as models of perfect eloquence. As Dugan observes, in the *Orator* "Cicero seeks to control and guide his reception not as a political agent or speaker in performance, but as a textual entity" and in order to do so he "turns his attention to solidifying an oratorical legacy that will of necessity be in writing."[47]

By drawing attention to the variety and extent of his written production Cicero explicitly "dismisses the rest of the Roman oratorical literature as unsuited to the exemplary function that his inquiry into rhetorical style requires"[48] and restates the key role played by writing in the process of canonization of oratory. Thus, Cicero's presentation of his stylistic achievements in the *Orator*, in combination with the above mentioned

---

[43] Cic. *Orat.* 103; 108.
[44] On Cicero's pride in taking on the defense of the young Sex. Roscius of Ameria in the year 80 BCE (an act of political courage), cf. Cic. *Off.* 2.51. Dyck 1996: 436 correctly argues that "the reference to the fact that the speech is extant (*quae, ut scis, extat oratio*) is an obvious invitation to read it."
[45] On the exploitation of body metaphors to explicate style notions in the *Orator* and the creation of a *corpus* as a textual physical unity, see Dugan 2005: 270.
[46] On the role played by writing in the consecration of oratory as a "literary product," see Narducci 1997a: 157–173.
[47] Dugan 2005: 250.  [48] Dugan 2005: 304.

passages from the *Brutus,* is an eloquent testimony to the importance of written oratory as a vehicle of self-presentation and reflects the orator's concern about writing as a form of "textual longevity." As Habinek puts it, "writing amplifies the persona of the writer" and the "circulation of a text extends the efficacy of the authorizing performance, thereby anchoring literary production even more securely in the elite cultural contexts from which it emerges."[49]

Cicero dissociated himself from lazy orators, admitted his strong desire for eternity, and played up the diffusion of his oratorical works.[50] In so doing, he re-evaluated the primary function of writing as "amplification and extension of persona." When dealing with Cicero's construction of his posthumous reputation in the *Philippics*, Steel points out that "writing matters in Cicero's case because it offers a simulacrum of oral performance. His actions continued to resonate with his imperial readers because his writings allowed them to play out, over and over again, the orator standing up and speaking in defense of the Republic."[51] By means of writing Cicero asserted his status of canonical author and acquired an authoritative space within the Roman elite.[52] In valorizing his corpus of texts, treated as "an inviolate body whose perfection any change would destroy,"[53] he provided a good example of how mastery of style, canonized in a large, unprecedented, literary production, contributed to secure his reputation and *fama* in the eyes of posterity.[54]

## Self-Memorialization and Publication Theory

Cicero's self-portrait as an orator-writer makes a good jumping-off point for a brief re-examination of the much-debated issue of the publication of the speeches. It is clear that self-promotion, consolidation of political status and search for fame dictated Cicero's selection and propagation of his judicial speeches. Publication was central to Cicero's self-fashioning

---

[49] Habinek 2009: 121 (who reformulates Habinek 1998: 103–21).
[50] Cf. also Cic. *Att.* 13.12.2 (320 SB*Att*); *Q. fr.* 3.1.11 (21 SB).   [51] Steel 2006: 61.
[52] On oratory, rhetoric and Roman politics in the late republic, see Alexander 2007.
[53] Dugan 2005: 305.
[54] An interesting parallel may be established with the publication of Cicero's letters. As Nicholson (1994: 60) notes, in spite of the confidentiality of the personal correspondence, Cicero was "always keenly sensitive regarding his *existimatio* in the eyes of his contemporaries" and saw publication of his letters as a means of self-advertisement. Revision and careful selection of the letters was then essential to promoting Cicero's social and political image. See also Hutchinson 1998: 4; on the order and disposition of Cicero's correspondence, see Beard 2002: 116ff. For a survey of scholarly arguments on the publication of Cicero's letters, see White (F.) 2010: 174–5; for a good discussion of the editing of the collection, arranged posthumously by an editor who selected and organized the series of letters with an eye to Cicero's self-portrait, see 31–61.

strategy. Opting for publishing and disseminating a text – as well as opting for *not* publishing – relied on a careful evaluation of the political, social and promotional advantages and outcomes resulting from the circulation of a "presentational" piece of writing. Crawford has opportunely insisted on Cicero's social status and the role played by oratory in enhancing and furthering the political career of a *homo novus*, pointing out that "by publishing his speeches, the orator could ensure the dissemination of his views and, if possible, his successes in court or government to a much larger audience than the one he originally addressed."[55] As Steel notes, "the written Cicero is a figure engaged in a successful and inexorable ascent of the *cursus honorum*."[56]

Cicero is abundant in comments on his status as "new man."[57] The first *homo novus* to be raised to the rank of consul at such a young age within living memory, as emphasized in a flattering message to the people in the proem to the second speech on the Agrarian Law (*Agr.* 2.3–4), Cicero parallels himself to those men who have been capable of achieving notability through manly talent and success in public office.[58] Sulpicius's attack on Murena's *nobilitas* prompts the orator to claim for himself a nobility achieved through his political merits (*Mur.* 15–7):[59] *virtus*, *ingenium* and *humanitas* are praised as the only virtues that enable the new man, *ex infimo genere et fortunae gradu*, to ascend to the highest offices (*Balb.* 18–9).[60]

Other passages might be usefully cited.[61] The importance of oratory in advancing the political status of a *homo novus* is well recognized in the late republican *Commentariolum Petitionis*.[62] Equally the opening sections of the *Pro Sexto Roscio Amerino* (1–5) highlight Cicero's rhetoric of "newness."[63] Fox rightly notes that the "rhetorical confidence of the speech

---

[55] Crawford 1984: 4f.  [56] Steel 2012: 254.
[57] On the ideology of *novitas* in Roman republic, see Wiseman 1971: 101ff.; 107–16; Shackleton Bailey 1986: 258–60. See Blom 2010: 35–59 for a survey of modern scholarship on the term *homo novus*; important also is Burckhardt 1990. On the "constructed nature of the political identity" of the new man, see Dugan 2005: 4f.
[58] Cf. also Cic. *Sest.* 136–47. Kaster 2006: 379 ("for a new man like C., it was an article of faith that his upward mobility was proof of personal manliness and a capacity for 'vigorous activity' (*industria*) that benefited the community").
[59] Cicero positively remarks on not-noble-born individuals attaining consulship in *Mur.* 24. See Bürge 1974: 101; Nótári 2008: 33.
[60] On Cicero's tactics in presenting Balbus's qualities and the ethical argumentation of the speech, see Kimberly 2004: 24–5.
[61] Cic. *Ver.* 2.4.81; *Sul.* 24; *Pis.* 2; *Planc.* 17–8.
[62] *Comm.* 2; 55. On the *Commentariolum* as a late first-century CE forgery, see Alexander 2009a. A commentary (with discussion about the authenticity of the treatise) is now Prost 2017.
[63] On this passage, see Dyck 2010a: 58 (cf. also Cerutti 1996: 49–82). For Cicero's emphasis on his own "newness," see Dench 2013: 130–4.

is effectively a manifesto for a more egalitarian form of political activity, one which relies upon education, and thus rhetorical skills, rather than contacts or hereditary access to office."[64] By naturalizing "newness" as a political and social category Cicero constructed his own *persona* and acquired a reputation as a brilliant speaker reliant on his own personal qualities.

It has aptly been noted that "the question of the reasons for publication has sometimes been looked in narrow or misleading terms."[65] Modern scholarship has often read Cicero's policy of publication in political terms. Approaching the issue from a didactic perspective, Stroh has stimulated scholarly interest in the pedagogical aims behind Cicero's theory of publication.[66] Stroh's argument, based on the *Brutus* and Cicero's correspondence with Atticus, focuses on Cicero's self-promotion as a rhetorical model as the primary motive for publication. In his view, the speeches were designed to develop and implement rhetorical training. As a paradigm of persuasion, Cicero's *oratio scripta* provided Roman elite students with a rhetorical pattern. Revision, rearrangement and publication of delivered speeches served Cicero's desire for a constructive dialogue with the youth. He invited his young readers and participants in training to rely on his authoritative texts in order to acquire facility in language and rhetoric.[67]

Stroh's arguments, shared by a good number of scholars,[68] bring attention to one of the main tenets of Cicero's cultural and rhetorical programme, his ambition to become an authority on oratorical matters and contribute to the formation of a class of educated speakers through models of persuasion.[69] The Roman youth was no doubt granted a privileged position in Cicero's search for *aeternitas*. Yet different reasons may have encouraged Cicero to publish and circulate his speeches. It seems useful, then, to take a fresh look at some relevant passages from Cicero's letters in order to clarify some basic points of the question. Let us start with Cicero's words about the publication of the *In Pisonem*. In a letter to Quintus, written in September 54 BCE (3.1; 21 SB), Cicero justifies his no-reply to

---

[64] Fox 2007: 120–1.  [65] Powell-Paterson 2004: 52.  [66] Stroh 1975: 21, 52–54.
[67] Stroh 1975: 53.
[68] Leeman 1982: 198–9; Classen 1982: 185–6; Vasaly 1993: 9–10. For a didactic approach to the issue of publication before Stroh, see Petersson 1920: 87; Plasberg 1926: 4; Laurand 1936–38: 1.2; Mack 1937: 11–2; Neumeister 1964: 106 and n117. The question must have been controversial already in antiquity, as may be argued from a passage from the late rhetorician Iulius Severianus (358.23–4 *RLM*): *edebat enim ille non solum patrocinia causarum, sed et exempla dicendi* ("he [sc. Cicero] published not only his performances as a *patronus* but also style and diction samples"); Stroh 1975: 52 and n93.
[69] On Cicero's speeches as models of *inventio, dispositio* and *elocutio* for the young, see Achard 2000.

Piso's rejoinder with a self-adulatory reference to his established role as a school author. He proudly proclaims that, in contrast to Piso's speech, destined to sink into oblivion if not dignified with the orator's response, his *in Pisonem* has already achieved the canonical status of textbook (3.1.11):

> Rescripsi epistulae maximae, audi nunc de minuscula. in qua primum est de Clodi ad Caesarem litteris; in quo Caesaris consilium probo, quod tibi amantissime petenti veniam non dedit uti ullum ad illam furiam verbum rescriberet. alterum est de Calventi Mari oratione; quod scribis tibi placere me ad eam rescribere, miror, prasertim cum illam nemo lecturus sit si ergo nihil rescripsero, meam in illum pueri omnes tamquam dictata perdiscant. libros meos [omnis] quos exspectas incohavi, sed conficere non possum his diebus. orationes efflagitatas pro Scauro et pro Plancio absolvi. poema ad Caesarem quod institueram incidi. tibi quod rogas, quoniam ipsi fontes iam sitiunt, si quid habebo spati, scribam.

> "I have answered the big letter, now for the little one. First you tell me about Clodius' letter to Caesar. I think Caesar was right to say no to the request you so affectionately made of him and not to write a single word to that embodiment of mischief. Next, as to Calventius Marius' speech[70], I am surprised that you think I should write a rejoinder to that, especially as nobody will read it if I don't reply, whereas all the schoolchildren learn mine against him by heart as though it were part of their lessons. I have begun the work which you are waiting for, but I can't finish it this trip. I have completed the speeches for Scaurus and for Plancius according to demand. I have broken off the poem addressed to Caesar which I had begun, but for you I shall write what you ask (since the very springs are now athirst), if I get any time."[71]

As usual in the private correspondence, the letter illuminates Cicero's massive literary activity. In addition to the *In Pisonem*, delivered in 55 BCE[72] and presumably revised and published in late 55 or early 54 BCE,[73] Cicero mentions his political treatise on the ideal state – yet at an initial stage, the revised speeches on behalf of M. Aemilius Scaurus

---

[70] L. Calpurnius Piso Caesoninus, consul in 57; his maternal grandfather was an Insubrian Gaul, named Calventius (cf. Cic. *Pis.* 14; *Red. Sen.* 13; *Prov.* 7); see Tyrrell-Purser 1901–33: 2.171; Shackleton Bailey 1965–1970: 1.208.

[71] Text and translation of Cicero's *Letters to Quintus*: Shackleton Bailey 2002 (SB).

[72] Cic. *Pis.* 65; Asc. 1.1-5C. On the recital of the speech between July and September 55 BCE, see Nisbet 1961: 199–202 and Marshall 1975, 1985: 81–82 (speech delivery in early August). See also Griffin 2001: 85; Lewis 2006: 193, without further discussion (*contra* Cavarzere 1994: 157).

[73] For a "quick" publication of the speech after its delivery, see Crawford 1984: 6; *contra* Nisbet 1961: 202 (publication at the end of 55 or beginning of 54 BCE); see also Gozzoli 1990, 451 n2 (publication not after February of 54 BCE). According to a tradition recalled by Asconius Pedianus (1.7-8C), the speech was erroneously believed to be the last delivered in 54 (on various attempts to identify the source of Asconius, see Marshall 1985, 81–3: Lewis 2006: 193–4).

and Cn. Plancius, and, finally, a cut-short poem to Caesar.[74] But the invective against Piso stands out for its exemplarity. In a deliberate strategy of self-fashioning, Cicero consecrates his *in Pisonem* as an example of rhetorical invective[75] and standard textbook, idealizing his persona of writer and canonical school author in overt competition with his enemy Piso.[76]

There is no reason to dismiss Cicero's self-advertising note as unreliable. It seems reasonable to suppose that the *in Pisonem* entered the school canon as an invective model immediately after its publication. If that were the case, the explicit allusion to the "schoolchildren" (*pueri*) would support Stroh's theory of the "didaktischer Zweck der Redenpublikation."[77] Yet one might also assume that Cicero opted not to counterattack Piso's provocations for political convenience.[78] From Quintus's words we may surmise that Piso's rejoinder damaged Cicero's reputation. In Cicero's view, an instant, angry reply would only have aroused curiosity about Piso's irritating words.[79] In the post-exile situation the republican orator, committed to re-establishing his public status and regaining his central position in Roman political elite, carefully balanced benefits of reply against its risks. With admirable diplomacy, Cicero expected silence to be a more productive alternative.[80]

Another passage, briefly touched upon by Stroh,[81] deserves attention. In a letter to Atticus written in early October 57 BCE (4.2.2; 74 SB*Att*), Cicero commends his speech *De domo sua* for its powerful style. Pressed by the youth's curiosity, the orator declares his intention to speed up the publication of the speech, delivered before the College of Pontiffs some days earlier (on 29 September):[82]

---

[74] Presumably the poem *De expeditione Britannica*, later restarted by Cicero and defined as a *suave epos*: cf. Cic. *Q. fr.* 3.6 (8).3 (26 SB); 3.7 (9).6 (27 SB). See Marciniak 2008: 214.
[75] On the invective material in the speech, see Nisbet 1961: 192–7; Koster 1980: 210–81; Corbeill 1996: 169–73. For a good presentation of invective oratory, see Corbeill 2002; Craig 2004; Arena 2007. Cf. chapter 4, pp. 193–4; 254.
[76] On the invective as a model of "calculated elegance," see Kubiak 1989.
[77] Stroh 1975: 52 and n95.
[78] Piso's reply was wrongly identified with Pseudo-Sallust's *Invectiva in Ciceronem*; on the question, see Nisbet 1961: 197–8; Marshall 1985: 83f. On "the Piso hypothesis," see Novokhatko 2009: 124.
[79] Crawford 1984: 8. As Nisbet (1961: 202) puts it, "when Piso criticized Cicero in the senate Cicero was no doubt prepared, and would not have refrained from replying. But he might have expanded his reply out of all recognition; a speech that was intended to cause pain and not to influence policy was particularly liable to such treatment." See also Gozzoli 1990: 452.
[80] On Cicero's attitude towards political friendships and enmities after his recall, as it is described in the *post reditum* speeches, see Riggsby 2002: 172–9. See also Raccanelli 2012.
[81] Stroh 1975: 52 and n95.
[82] On the immediate publication of the speech, lacking final revision, see Shackleton Bailey 1991: 38.

Post illas datas litteras secuta est summa contentio de domo. diximus apud pontifices prid. Kal. Oct. acta res est accurate a nobis, et si umquam in dicendo fuimus aliquid, aut etiam si numquam alias fuimus, tum profecto dolor et <rei> magnitudo vim quandam nobis dicendi dedit. itaque oratio iuventuti nostrae deberi non potest; quam tibi, etiam si non desideras, tamen mittam cito.

"After I sent that letter there followed a tremendous struggle over my house. I addressed the Pontiffs on 29 September. I dealt faithfully with my theme, and if I ever amounted to anything as a speaker, or even if I never did at any other time, I think I can say that on that occasion intensity of feeling and the importance of the issue lent me a certain force of eloquence. So our younger generation cannot be kept waiting for the speech. I shall send it to you shortly, even if you are not anxious to have it."[83]

Cicero had certainly to profit from an immediate publication of what may well be considered as his most significant political manifesto after exile.[84] It is well-known that the legal issue about Cicero's house was highly contested. Presumably, a rapid circulation of the speech was regarded by the orator as an appropriate demonstration of gratitude to the pontiffs. As a model of passionate plea fueled by the relevance of the conflict (over the confiscation of Cicero's house on the Palatine and the illegality of the consecration of the site),[85] the *De domo sua* reflects the orator's concern about possible deviances of the young members of the Roman elite, corrupted by Clodius's madness. Yet I find it hard to detect a pedagogical message behind Cicero's self-gratifying comment on the young's eagerness to read his speech. The publication of the post-exile speech might conceivably have been hastened by the grinding pressure of the current political circumstances that encouraged the immediate diffusion of pamphlets countering Clodius's allegations and helping the recalled orator to regain favor with the members of the dominating elite.

That political factors, combined with educational purposes, affected Cicero's policy of publication is fully demonstrated by the exemplary case of the consular speeches. In a letter to Atticus written on June of 60 BCE, Cicero promises to send out a textual *corpus* collecting orations delivered three years before, during his term as consul. He candidly

---

[83] Text and translation of Cicero's *Letters to Atticus*: Shackleton Bailey 1999 (SB*Att*).
[84] Narducci 1998: 12.
[85] On the legal issue and structure of the speech, see Classen 1985: 218–67; Stroh 2004. For Cicero's tactic of eroding the legitimacy of the act of *consecratio* by emphasizing Clodius's personal impiety and impurity, see Lennon 2010.

acknowledges that the zeal of his young readers has acted as a stimulus to rework and propagandize his consular performances (2.1.3; 21SB*Att*):

> Oratiunculas autem et quas postulas et plures etiam mittam, quoniam quidem ea quae nos scribimus adulescentulorum studiis excitati te etiam delectant. Fuit enim mihi commodum, quod in eis orationibus quae Philippicae nominantur enituerat tuus ille civis Demosthenes et quod se ab hoc refractariolo iudiciali dicendi genere abiunxerat ut σεμνότερός τις et πολιτικώτερος videretur, curare ut meae quoque essent orationes quae consulares nominarentur. Quarum una est in senatu Kalendis Ianuariis, altera ad populum de lege agraria, tertia de Othone, quarta pro Rabirio, quinta de proscriptorum filiis, sexta cum provinciam in contione deposui, septima qua Catilinam emisi, octava quam habui ad populum postridie quam Catilina profugit, nona in contione quo die Allobroges indicarunt, decima in senatu Nonis Decembribus. Sunt pratera duae breves, quasi ἀποσπασμάτια legis agrariae. Hoc totum σῶμα curabo ut habeas. Et quoniam te cum scripta tum res meae delectant, isdem ex libris perspicies et quae gesserim et quae dixerim; aut ne poposcisses. Ego enim tibi me non offerebam.

> "I'll send my little speeches, both those you ask for and some more besides, since it appears that you too find pleasure in these performances which the enthusiasm of my young admirers prompts me to put on paper. Remembering what a brilliant show your countryman Demosthenes made in his so-called *Philippics* and how he turned away from this argumentative, forensic type of oratory to appear in the more elevated role of statesman, I thought it would be a good thing for me too to have some speeches to my name which might be called 'Consular'. They are: (1) delivered in the Senate on the Kalends of January; (2) to the Assembly, on the agrarian law; (3) on Otho; (4) in defense of Rabirius; (5) on the children of persons proscribed; (6) delivered when I publicly resigned my province; (7) when I sent Catiline out of Rome; (8) to the Assembly the day following Catiline's flight; (9) at a public meeting the day the Allobroges turned informers; (10) in the Senate on the Nones of December. There are two further short pieces, chips, one might say, from the agrarian law. I shall see that you get the whole corpus, and since you like my writings as well as my doings, the same compositions will show you both what I did and what I said. Otherwise you shouldn't have asked – I was not forcing myself upon you."

Cicero himself details the origin of the *corpus*, set up in imitation of the analogous collection of Demosthenes's *Philippics*. Whether the cycle consisted of twelve speeches after the number of Demosthenes's speeches known from the ancient editions[86] or rather of eleven speeches[87] remains

---

[86] Manuwald 2007: 1.75ff.; Cape 2002: 118 n24 (with further bibliography).
[87] Canfora 1974: 49–51; Dugan 2005: 336 tends towards a corpus of ten speeches (*contra* Manuwald 2007: 1.75 n200).

in dispute. Whatever their number, the consular orations selected by Cicero and grouped together as a coherent unity convey the orator's wish "to cultivate, in rivalry/imitation of Demosthenes, a certain type of public image."[88] As Cape puts it, Cicero was "engaged in literary imitation."[89] Demosthenes shifted away from his past argumentative forensic oratory to take on the attitude of a consummate statesman.[90] Likewise, Cicero invested his *corpus* with an ideological and political goal. He embarked on the project of promoting his consular persona[91] and transmitting his idealized image of rescuer of the country to posterity.[92] By similarity with Demosthenes's *Philippics* that "portray a great statesman rallying his fellow citizens to action against as yet unperceived threats to their liberty,"[93] Cicero committed his figure of politician and high-minded consul to an organic textual unity in Demosthenic forms.[94]

The twelve-speech collection concretizes Cicero's ambition to convey his consular ethos through examples of "practical political negotiation."[95] What remains a vexed issue, however, is Cicero's postponed arrangement of the *corpus*,[96] an unparalleled case of publication three years after delivery.[97] Scholars have claimed that the delay was employed for an extensive reworking of what Cicero actually said.[98] In particular, some passages of the *Catilinarians* have been interpreted as later expansions or additions, or rather as "a retrospective justification added after the conspirators had been punished."[99] Certainly, later revisions are intrinsic to Cicero's "carefully orchestrated management of the recording of his

---

[88] Dyck 2008a: 10.   [89] Cape 2002: 118.
[90] On "Cicero's desire to be viewed as Demosthenes' Roman counterpart," see Ramsey 2003: 17. See also Weische 1972; Wooten 1983: 46–57; Dugan 2005: 303–14; Manuwald 2007: 1.129ff.; Bishop 2015–16: 174.
[91] Cf. Cic. *Pis.* 4–7: see Manuwald 2007: 1.76.
[92] On the similarity of the *corpora* of the two orators and the speeches' significance, which allows Cicero to compare himself with Demosthenes and to suggest the role of a senior statesman for himself, see Manuwald 2007: 1.76. For Cicero's aesthetic and didactic intent, see now Kenty 2017: 352.
[93] Cape 2002: 118.   [94] Cape 2002: 120.
[95] Cape 2002: 115. On Cicero's consular ethos, see Batstone 1994.
[96] For the uniqueness of the *corpus* (without parallels in antiquity), see McDermott 1972a; Cape 2002: 119.
[97] Settle 1962: 127–33; Helm 1979: 6–8; Kelly 2008.   [98] Dyck 2008a: 11.
[99] E.g. 2.28.9; 3.15.8–13; see Dyck 2008a: 11. Winterbottom 1982b: 61–2, argues that the Fourth Catilinarian was recast, especially at the beginning and end, to meet the young readership's expectations for exemplary forensic models: similarly, Lintott 2008: 30 reads the fourth speech as a "fiction" and a sort of cento, a combination of an introductory *relatio* with an *interrogatio* in the course of the debate (a different approach is in Martin 2011, who rejects the common-held view of a substantial revision of the speech). For a probable later addition to chapter 15 of the Third Catilinarian, see Barlow 1994. In general see Manuwald 2007: 1.77 n205 (with further bibliography). My friend Bob Kaster points out to me that the actions against the Catilinarians came under

consulship,"[100] but not to the exclusion of a swift publication of some orations after delivery, expected to make an immediate impact on Roman politics and Cicero's self-construction as the ideal Roman magistrate.[101] If it is true that the letter to Atticus suggests that the consular speeches were yet unpublished at the time,[102] nothing prevents us from supposing that the material selected and arranged in the consular *corpus* was already in circulation, at least partially. Compelled to justify his conduct (illegal?) during the Catilinarian conspiracy,[103] Cicero assembled a textual body that aspired to illuminate his consulship as a decisive moment for the restoration of the republican values and the safety of his fellow-citizens. Conscious of the impact of a calibrated political message on the Roman youth, Cicero conferred a pedagogical function upon his consular collection. Significantly, he set up a *corpus* after the model of Demosthenes's *Philippics*, an epic narration of the struggle for the freedom of Athens, in order to portray his consulship as a heroic act for the survival of the Roman republic.

Cicero built then up his textual persona on a selection of canonical texts designed to perpetuate his public image.[104] As Steel notes, "by creating a written narrative to sit beside his oral *persona*" Cicero increased his chances of electoral and other success.[105] By identifying himself with his text he publicized his values and *ethos*.[106] The invective against Piso, the post-exile speech on the restoration of the House and the consular speeches worked as texts by which the orator-statesman forged his identity and managed to re-establish and recuperate his social and political prestige.

---

attack immediately; this entails that Cicero would have had a motive to "improve" the speeches and make them documents of self-defense even if he had published them within days of their delivery.

[100] Steel 2005: 52.

[101] A passage from Sallust's historical monograph on the Catilinarian conspiracy (*Cat.* 31.6 *Tum M. Tullius consul, sive praesentiam eius timens, sive ira commotus, orationem habuit luculentam atque utilem rei publicae, quam postea scriptam edidit*, "Then M. Tullius as consul, whether intimidated by the man's presence or affected by anger, delivered a sparkling speech which benefited the commonwealth: he afterwards issued the written version of it." Text and translation: Rolfe-Ramsey 2013) is usually taken as referring to the publication of the First Catilinarian in 60 BCE. On the question, see Vretska 1976: 2.389; Ramsey 2007a: 147–8. It should, however, be observed that Sallust's words might also be alluding to a separate (after delivery?) publication of the First Catilinarian.

[102] Dyck 2008a: 10.

[103] For a good analysis of Cicero's defensive strategy in the years 60–58, see Steel 2005: 51ff. See also Nisbet 1965: 62–3.

[104] On the construction of the self in late republican Rome and in particular on the role played by oratory in the self-fashioning process, see Gleason 1995; Gunderson 2000; Dugan 2005. For Roman self-fashioning in the early empire, especially on the ground of Pliny the Younger's letters, see Leach 1990; Riggsby 1995a; 1998.

[105] Steel 2012: 253.

[106] On Cicero's manipulation of his persona and the "Ciceronian ethos," see May 1988.

The policy of publication integrated into Cicero's self-fashioning as a Roman cultural and political authority.[107] Engaged in conversation with the Roman youth Cicero configured the transmission of his writings as a crucial part of his educative program.[108] In his intention, publication provided young students with rhetorical models.[109] More, by means of publication Cicero invited the budding orator-politicians to read his speeches as exemplars of both the art of speaking and ruling the state.

It is time to go back to Stroh's arguments. Education of the young generations represents just an aspect of what Cicero planned to achieve through an accurate selection and dissemination of his speeches.[110] As we have seen, Cicero's no-reply to Piso's rejoinder and the immediate publication of the *De domo sua* were eminently political acts. Though appealing "to the rhetorically (and politically) minded youth,"[111] the Demosthenic assemblage of a group of consular orations may be interpreted as a gesture of literary and political imitation/emulation. Recording Cicero's consulship as the highest achievement in the life-long war waged in defense of liberty, the consular speeches aimed at directing posterity towards an eternal appreciation of the actions of the new *pater patriae*. Cicero's consular *corpus* conveyed a literary and political self-portrait. It served as the vehicle of a double authorial self-representation. It memorialized Cicero's consular actions and his live performances as exemplars of forensic oratory. That being so, in Cicero's theory of publication there is no clear split between pedagogy and politics.[112] Extension of his public figure, need for self-memorialization and consciousness of the potentialities of writing in advertising his political ideals determined Cicero's definition of his textual presence through publication.[113] In a word, Cicero's mind was dominated by the supreme

---

[107] Cicero's idea of publication as a self-fashioning medium is elucidated by the composition of his philosophical oeuvre. In the retrospective catalogue that opens the second book of the *De divinatione*, Cicero articulates his comments on his philosophical dialogues and creates a new canon of written works, selected and assembled later on (together with other philosophical texts) in a textual corpus to be survived, at least partially, in our medieval manuscripts (the so-called "Leiden corpus"). In so doing, he portrays himself as the "inventor" of Latin philosophy, elaborating on the sublime vision of writing as a means of achieving eternal fame. A commentary on the catalogue is now in Schofield 2013.

[108] In general on Cicero's educative and cultural project, see Narducci 1997a.

[109] Dyck 1996: 10, notes that the very fact that the conversation of the dialogue *de Oratore* includes the youthful Sulpicius and Cotta among its participants demonstrates that "discourse of this kind, too, was thought of as existing for the sake of its educative value for youth."

[110] For a good re-examination of Stroh's hypothesis, see Levene 2004.   [111] Cape 2002: 120.

[112] Dyck 1996: 10 ("In publishing and dedicating his works Cicero followed policies dictated by an amalgam of personal and political factors"). A good example of the polyvalent function, both political and didactic, attached to publication is offered by Cicero's *pro Sestio*: see Renda 2009.

[113] Steel 2005: 21ff; 49ff.

goal of transcending the limits of time and surviving eternal oblivion through his textual corpus.[114]

Cicero's option for *not publishing* was equally implicated in a self-fashioning strategy.[115] Cicero's no-reaction to Piso's verbal assault is particularly illuminating, since it supplies us with a good example of "political silence" reputed as rewarding in troubled times. Crawford rightly connects no-publication or suppression of a speech to Cicero's desire for good reputation and reinforcement of political alliances.[116] The speech *in Clodium et Curionem* highlights the political impact of uncontrolled publication, expected to hurt the author's credibility.[117] Cicero's fear and frustration over the circulation of an unauthorized, potentially harmful, version of his speech (*Att.* 3.12.2: 57 SB*Att*) stem from his perception of the potentially damaging effects of publication. Tagged as an *oratio perpetua plenissima gravitatis* by the orator himself in a letter sent to Atticus in the first days of July 61 BCE (1.16.8–10: 16 SB*Att*), the speech in its pirate version, "full of injudicious vitriol,"[118] contained unambiguous and inconvenient references to political figures involved in Cicero's recall. Similarly to what happens for the failed speech in behalf of Milo, reworked and partially rewritten to reassert its author's reputation for eloquence,[119] the invective *In Clodium et Curionem* was read as a political failure, dangerous for Cicero's interests. Once the speech was disseminated, the only way the orator had to regain credibility was to stigmatize the text as a forgery. However, the effort to pass off the speech as plagiarized was in vain.[120] Cicero's fierce

---

[114] Gildenhard 2011a: 1 (for Cicero's publication policy as animated not just by the "desire to imitate and emulate Greek and Roman predecessors" and the "didactic impulse to provide the next generation of Roman statesmen with exemplary instances of eloquence," but also by the "realization that published speeches constituted an ideal medium in which to fashion, promote, and justify his self and his actions, wish to maintain a permanent presence of sorts, perhaps even popularity, within upper-class discourse, opportunity to advertise further his convictions, policies, or, indeed, political program").

[115] Crawford 1984: 7. See also Steel 2013b: 162–3.

[116] Crawford 1984: 8. It should be observed that in some cases we are unable to determine whether the delivered speech was voluntarily suppressed by the author or published and then lost during the subsequent phases of textual transmission. This might be the case in at least four speeches, namely the *pro Titinia Cottae*, delivered in 79 BCE and regarded by Cicero as a *privata causa magna et gravis*, comparable to the Verrines and the Catilinarians for its "vigorous style" (cf. Cic. *Orat.* 129; see Crawford 1984: 35–6), *pro Tullio I* (Crawford 1984: 47–50), *pro Fonteio I* (Crawford 1984: 55–7), and *de C. Manilio*, delivered in 66 BCE (Crawford 1984: 64–9); although reasons for nonpublication exist, it might be supposed that these speeches were published and lost afterwards (they should thus be included among the *deperditae*).

[117] On the political background of the speech, see Crawford 1994: 227–33.  [118] Steel 2005: 120.

[119] See below pp. 51–4.  [120] McGill 2010: 113 n3; Higbie 2017: 159–60.

blame of Clodius and Curio kept circulating and damaging his political image.[121]

In conclusion, Cicero's involvement in the political and social life of the late republic was expected to play a decisive role in the policy of publication.[122] As Gildenhard puts it, Cicero's words "were his deeds as it were, his *res gestae,* monumental interventions in the history of the commonwealth that deserved to be put on record for posterity."[123] As a self-fashioning vehicle, intended to educate young generations and prolong political actions far beyond the temporal restraints, publication represented the response to Cicero's dream of portraying himself as both the ideal literate and the ideal politician through a textual body.[124] Steel comments that "Cicero's writing finally compels our attention because he made being an intellectual and a writer into part of what it meant to be a public figure."[125]

### Cicero the Editor at Work: The Policy of Self-*Emendatio*

Textual revision played a central role in the process of publication.[126] Given the effect, whether pedagogical or political, of a written text upon its intended readership, a piece of writing matching the rules of good Latin was reputed to be crucial to the public presentation of its author. It is well known that Cicero's engagement with revision implied submitting his orations to friends and advisers for comments. Textual production usually involved a phase of collective, or editorial, revision.[127] The final version of

---

[121] It is important to note that Cicero's letter does not contain any allusion to Atticus as responsible for the unauthorized publication of the invective. If that had been the case, Cicero would perhaps have made a direct statement about this. In another case, though in an apparently ironic tone, Cicero reproaches Atticus for the unauthorized propagation of the treatise *De finibus* (cf. *Att.* 13.21a: 327 SB*Att*). One might suggest, then, that, similarly to the first *pro Milone,* Cicero's pamphlet was "taken down" and circulated beyond the author's control.

[122] For an interpretation of Cicero's publication policy in social-political terms, see Powell-Paterson 2004: 52–7, who correctly point to the "advertisement" function lying behind publication and the positive impact on Cicero's public status following the divulgation of a successful speech among the elite circles.

[123] Gildenhard 2011a: 1. See also Steel 2012: 263 ("the oratorical texts which Cicero disseminated are not the unreflecting transcription of his public acts: they are elements in a planned narrative, which record his constant attempt to impose, on the sometimes recalcitrant raw material of Roman politics, order and success").

[124] For publication as a combination of political, didactic, self-promotional and artistic motives, see Butler 2002: 71ff.; Manuwald 2007: 1.58; see also Riggsby 1999: 178–84.

[125] Steel 2005: 146. On Cicero's written speeches as the "wherewithal to construct a narrative of Cicero's public career," see Gibson-Steel 2010: 121.

[126] On the process of publication in antiquity, see Starr 1987.

[127] For the distinction between "authorial revision" (reading and correction of the work drafts), "editorial revision" (submission of the text to the judgment of other readers) and "cultural revision"

a text resulted from a social debate. It has recently been argued that, in recognizing the force and authority of a community in a collectively revised text, Cicero associated revision with "republicanism" and the category of *res publica*. In particular, under Caesar's dictatorship Cicero saw his text as a "public thing," a charter of Roman community; by inviting his readers to debate on textual issues he valued stylistic imperfection as a feature of republican style, in contrast with Caesar's antisocial ideology of rational literary perfection.[128] To put it differently, a text revised and corrected by a literate community embodied a set of ethical (republican) values. By forging collective identity through collective revision Cicero responded to Caesar's tyranny by literary and textual means.[129] Incompletion and community-through-revision became, then, political notions, indirect instruments of opposition to an anti-republican regime. Cicero endorsed the culture of correction as a republican ideal.

Social-political connotations are certainly implicit in Cicero's concern with collective revision. Yet *emendatio* participates in the construction of the oratorical self. Questioning textual matters with a literate, culturally oriented community was intrinsic to Cicero's self-fashioning as a style model. Cicero's correspondence offers extensive evidence of authorial and editorial revision. Before proceeding further, a few words are in order on the usual practice of preparation and publication of a speech in late republic. From a long passage in Quintilian's *Institutio Oratoria* (10.7.30–2) we know that the orator customarily wrote out some parts of his speech, at least the opening lines (*necessaria et utique initia*), relying on mental preparation and improvisation for the rest and "making smooth transitions from the occasional written parts to extemporaneous speaking."[130] Cicero himself made use of written notes, or *commentarii*, composed at the occasion[131] and collected by the freedman Tiro afterwards.[132] Though the orator was allowed to glance at the prepared text while delivering, learning by heart and memorizing the sections of the speech written out beforehand seems to have been an established practice.[133]

---

(dissemination of the text, beyond the control of the author and its "appropriation" in terms of "adumbrations, imitations and re-inscriptions"), see Gurd 2007: 50 n5.

[128] Gurd 2012: 49–76.
[129] For Cicero's philosophical production as a response to the challenge posed by Caesar to republican values, see Gildenhard 2007.
[130] Ramsey 2007b: 130.
[131] Quint. *Inst.* 10.7.30–1: on the opposition between Cicero's *commentarii* and the notes of other orators, apparently composed for the benefit of posterity (*in memoriam posteritatis*), cf. 10.7.30. For *commentarius* as a rough draft of the speech, cf. Cic. *de Orat.* 1.5.
[132] Quint. *Inst.* 10.7.30.
[133] On Quintilian's discussion of improvisation in book ten, see Murphy 1990b; Celentano 2006; 2010; La Bua 2010a: 187–9.

## The Policy of Self-Emendatio

Further evidence confirms the diffusion of Cicero's *commentarii*.[134] Quintilian alludes to the presence of the speech on behalf of Scaurus in the *commentarii*.[135] Commenting upon a passage from the fragmentary speech *In toga candida* (87.9-12C),[136] Asconius Pedianus rejects Fenestella's assumption that Cicero acted in defense of Catiline on a charge of extortion in 65 BCE because of the absence of the preface to this case in the *Commentarii Ciceronis*.[137] A fragment of the speech *pro Gabinio*, furthermore, is known to have been discovered by Jerome in Cicero's *commentarii causarum*.[138] It is easy to assume that Cicero usually prepared the *exordium* or a simple outline of the speech ahead of time.[139] He then proceeded with delivery in accordance with the specific *quaestio* requirements,[140] relying essentially on memory and improvisation to handle his case successfully.[141] The only exception to this practice was the speech *post reditum in senatu*, which is known to have been delivered from a fully pre-prepared written text.[142]

After delivery the speech was commonly *retractatum*[143] and "written up" for publication.[144] Any Ciceronian scholar is familiar with the long-disputed question concerning the divergence or correspondence between the spoken and published versions of extant speeches, an issue opened up by the seminal volume of Jules Humbert in 1925, who claimed for a radical alteration and

---

[134] Bell 2013: 174. For the use of *commentarii* in declamations cf. Sen. *Con.* 1 *pr.* 17–8; 3 *pr.* 6.
[135] Quint. *Inst.* 4.1.69.
[136] *Verine ergo simile est haec eum Catilinae obicere, si illo defendente absolutus esset? Praeterea movet me quod, cum sint commentarii Ciceronis causarum, eius tamen defensionis nullum est commentarium aut principium* ("So is it probable that he would hurl these reproaches at Catilina, if he had been acquitted with Cicero defending him? Besides, I am also influenced by the fact that although there exist notes of Cicero's cases, even so there is no précis or preface extant for this one"). Text and translation of Asconius: Lewis 2006.
[137] For the question Crawford 1994: 197–8. On Fenestella as source of Asconius's commentary, see chapter 2, p. 58; 70.
[138] Hier. *Adv. Ruf.* 1.1.38–50 (Lardet 1993: 15); for the quotation from the *pro Gabinio*, see Hagendahl 1958: 174; Fantham 1975: 441 n37 (who associates Quintilian's mention of speeches in defense of Gabinius and Vatinius, at *Inst.* 11.1.73, with the passage quoted by Jerome). For denial of publication, see Settle 1962: 234; on Gabinius' trial, see Crawford 1984: 188–97.
[139] Marshall 1985: 298 argues that the *commentarii* could also contain the outline of a speech written up after delivery with a view to publication.
[140] Cf. Cic. *de Orat.* 2.101–4; 351–9.
[141] For the usual procedure of oral composition and the system of memorization from a written (at least partially) text, cf. also Plin. *Ep.* 9.36. See Small 2007: 204–5; Steel 2017a (for informal exchanges and improvisatory capacity in forensic oratory).
[142] Cic. *Planc.* 74; cf. also Cic. *Sest.* 129. On the sentence *dicta de scripto est* in *Planc.* 74 and the *post reditum ad senatum* as a notable exception to Cicero's usual practice of delivery, see Nicholson 1992: 15; Vössing 2008 (successfully opposing Bücher-Uwe 2006).
[143] For *retractare* as "to retouch, revise" a literary work, cf. Tac. *Dial.* 3.2; Plin. *Ep.* 9.15.2; 9.35.2.
[144] Cic. *Brut.* 91–2. Cf. also Cic. *Tusc.* 4.55; *Sen.* 38.

modification of the delivered text in its written form before publication. Since Roman legal procedure at Cicero's time did not allow continuous set speeches and a republican *quaestio* trial regularly went through a series of interruptions, altercations and adjournments, Humbert regarded Cicero's written speeches, as we have them, as artificial literary constructs, precisely as an assemblage of different "tours de parole" and a composite *post eventum* evocation of a real trial.[145] The reaction to Humbert's provocative theory has found its best interpreter in Wilfried Stroh.[146] As stressed in the previous section of this chapter, Stroh contended that Cicero's judicial speeches were designed to provide young students with models of persuasion. Whether or not we would expect that Cicero wanted his readers to have an enhanced and polished-up version of the actual performance, it appears that the didactic nature of publication prevented the orator from a radical modification of the delivered text. *Oratio* reproduced the key elements of the oral performance. Whether spoken or written, the orator's words had the potential to persuade.[147] What mattered more was the reading audience's reaction. And in readers' eyes the written text was nothing but a transcript of the spoken one.[148]

Learned and extensive discussion has been offered on this controversial, sometimes overestimated, topic.[149] With a few exceptions,[150] there is now general accord among the scholars as to the fact that Cicero's speeches have come down to us in a form that closely resembles that of the speech actually delivered by the orator in the court or in the Forum.[151] As Riggsby puts it, "a study of Cicero's implicit and explicit motivations for promulgating his speeches (advertising, information and education) shows that it would

---

[145] Humbert 1925.    [146] Stroh 1975: 7–25; 31–54. See also Laurand 1936–38: 1–23.
[147] On the so-called "persuasive-process criticism" in modern Ciceronian scholarship, see May 2007b: 75–7.
[148] Levene 2004: 118–9.
[149] Gildenhard 2011a: 14 reads the excessive importance commonly attributed to the question as "arising from commitment to the limited and limiting terms of a rather dated historicism and its peculiar priorities."
[150] Lintott 2008: 19–32, who warns against dismissing the interpretation of Cicero's speeches as "artificial compositions," encouraging the historian to be cautious about what the text of speeches actually represents.
[151] A detailed survey of the scholarly debate on this issue is in Craig 2002: 515–7; see also Ledentu 2000; Powell-Paterson 2004: 52–7; Manuwald 2007: 1.54 n148; Gildenhard 2011a: 14–5. For a valuable discussion of the arguments favoring the view that the published versions of the speeches represent a fair reproduction of the spoken ones, see Alexander 2002: 15–26; Morstein-Marx 2004: 25–30. For an extensive revision of the oral text in consideration of changing political circumstances (in the *pro Roscio Amerino*), see Berry 2004a (also Blänsdorf 2001). For the identification of oral devices in the written version, see Fuhrmann 1990: 55ff.; 59. On post-delivery revision of political speeches in Greek oratory, see Hubbard 2008 (with further bibliography).

have been to his advantage to reproduce fairly closely the texts of the speeches as he delivered them in court."[152] Recently, Powell[153] has attracted attention to the procedural framework of a republican *quaestio,* insisting on the potential correctness of Cicero's written speeches as an accurate record of what actually happened in a court trial.[154] Far from being literary fictions, amalgamated from bits and pieces delivered at different stages of the trial, the published speeches fit current legal procedures.[155] Cicero had no interest in falsifying "the very procedural conditions which made his success in advocacy such a striking achievement."[156] As Craig nicely summarizes, "we must admit that we can never know verbatim what Cicero actually said. Nonetheless, the proper way to appreciate one of his speeches as oratory is precisely to treat it as a transcript."[157]

It has opportunely been said that "a published speech, if it was to carry any plausibility at all, needed to conjure up the authentic phrases and rhythms of the forum or the senate, even if its precise text differed in some respects from what was said on the occasion."[158] Naturally, in transferring an oral performance to writing Cicero was authorized to display a more refined style or introduce minor linguistic changes (more appropriate to written communication). Scholarly research has paid attention to small-scale alterations, omissions and later adjustments in Cicero's extant speeches. Cicero presumably worked up the *Catilinarians,* mainly for apologetic reasons.[159] A post-Sullan revision has been argued for the *pro Roscio Amerino.*[160] Similarly, it has been supposed that modified political circumstances produced alterations in the published version of the *pro Murena*[161] and the *pro Sulla.*[162] Repetitions and doublets in the *pro Caelio*

---

[152] Riggsby 1999: 184. See also May 2007b: 74–5.
[153] Powell 2010a. For a brief outline of legal republican procedure, see Harries 2007: 12–20.
[154] Powell-Paterson 2004: 54 ("it is unlikely that Cicero would have inserted anything into a published version which would have been either impermissible or ineffective in a real speech").
[155] On the published speeches as rhetorical literature, aesthetically contrived pieces of discourse that transcended the immediate issues of litigation, see Enos 1988: 78–92. More reasonably, Dyck 2010b: 369–70 remarks that "the published speech did not need to be identical to the one actually delivered, but it needed to be true to the courtroom situation and the advocate's task."
[156] Powell 2010a: 36.     [157] Craig 1993a: 257–8.     [158] Powell 2013: 47.     [159] Dyck 2008a: 10–2.
[160] On some passages of the speech (§§ 3; 21–22; 130–1; 152–3) as ironic and hostile references to Sulla and their revision after delivery, see Berry 2004a (a different approach in Kinsey 1975); Dyck 2010a reads the swift publication of the speech in terms of self-advertisement strategy (esp. 19f; 62; 83).
[161] Boulanger 1940. On the discrepancies within the speech due to "Cicero's versatile persuasive technique," see Leeman 1982: 193–200. For the suppression of the defense of Clodius, involved in Murena's campaign for the consulate in 62 BCE, in the written version of the *pro Murena,* see Moreau 1980; Tatum 1999: 58–9.
[162] For explicit references to the suppression of the conspiracy as later additions, see Berry 1996a: 54–9 (on possible echoes of the *pro Murena* in Cicero's self-justification of his defense of Sulla, see 56 n264).

have been read as a sign of provisional status and posthumous publication.[163] The political segment of the *pro Sestio* (§§ 96–143), relating to the definition of the "Best Sort" (*Optimates*) and the ethical-political ideal of "tranquility joined with worthy standing" (*cum dignitate otium*), has commonly been considered as "a manifesto written and stitched into the speech after he had delivered it,"[164] though a more detailed analysis of Cicero's strategy may induce us to suppose that this "lesson for the young generation"[165] was a significant part of the delivered speech too.[166] Pliny the Younger's letter 1.20, finally, as we shall see, informs us of the suppression of irrelevant sections from the *pro Murena* and the lost *pro Vareno*,[167] indicated only by *tituli*, headings,[168] along with substantial abridgments in the written version of the *pro Cluentio* and *pro Cornelio*.[169]

It is not the purpose of this study to question the relevance of the scholarly dispute over the stylistic revision of the spoken speech to the history of Cicero's textual tradition. Our approach to the issue is here slightly different. Focusing on the orality-writing relationship in ancient rhetoric, we look at the written, published, speech *not as* witness of potential stylistic changes or modifications of the spoken version *but as* exemplification of what Cicero intended to achieve by disseminating a well-written speech. Let us first give a brief sketch of the debate over orality and writing in the late republic and the early empire. As we have seen, Cicero was conscious of the political and social impact of a written speech replicating the vehemence and passion of the spoken oration. Galba and even Cicero's rival, Hortensius, who had spoken much better than they had written,[170] failed in producing a written version of their speeches that could rouse in the reader "the emotions that they had known how to stir up in the listener."[171] In Cicero's view, the accord between orality and writing was vital to good oratory. The perfection of oratorical style could

---

[163] Austin 1960: 159–61; Loutsch 2007. On the doublets as features of oral discourse and the relative availability of arguments, reproduced at a distance "to get as much mileage out of them as possible," see Dyck 2013: 93 (on the process of publication of the speech: 26–7).
[164] Kaster 2006: 36.  [165] Kaster 2006: 33.
[166] A good discussion of the reasons against and pro the "stitching" hypothesis is in Kaster 2006: 35–7.
[167] On the lost speech *pro Vareno*, see Crawford 1994: 7–18.
[168] E.g. Cic. *Mur.* 57; *Cael.* 19; *Font.* 20. On the omission of framing material in the written text in accordance with the generic conventions of written speeches, see Gibson-Steel 2010: 121.
[169] For possible editorial interventions in the written version of speech and differences between what Cicero presented in his oratorical texts and what actually took place during the debate, see Steel 2017b: 18–23.
[170] Cic. *Orat.* 132. On the multifaceted relationship between Cicero and Hortensius, see Dyck 2008b.
[171] Narducci 2002b: 440.

be attained only through training in writing.[172] In a brilliant hymn to the *stilus* in the *De oratore* (1.150), Crassus emphasizes the positive effects of constant and diligent writing on oral performance, reasserting the value of the pen as "the most eminent teacher of speaking."[173] As stressed again in the *Orator* (200), the good speaker, even if he speaks extemporaneously, should be able to utter words and phrases perceived as they were written beforehand.[174]

The early imperial debate on eloquence centered around the relationship between "speaking well" and "writing well." In his *Institutio Oratoria* (12.10.49–56) Quintilian strikes out at the widely held view that the principles of speaking differ from those of writing. He fiercely claims that "speaking well and writing well are one and the same thing" and that "a written speech is nothing but the record of a spoken pleading" (12.10.51).[175] The good speaker should accommodate the subject and style of his speech to the audience's degree of education. He must speak as he writes, unless time and the jury's attitudes demand the omission of some arguments to be inserted into the published version afterwards (53–5).[176]

Pliny the Younger's approach is not dissimilar. In a letter addressed to the historian Tacitus (1.20),[177] he rejects his rival's arguments for brevity in forensic oratory, opposing any attempt to demonstrate that the orators of the past recasted substantially their oral presentations. On the contrary, as shown by Cicero's *pro Murena, pro Vareno* or the abridged *pro Cornelio*, orations were more long-winded in their oral version than in the published one.[178] The subsequent objection that there is substantial difference between *actio* and *oratio*, i.e. delivered and published speech, motivates Pliny to underscore the connection between oral performance and written text. It might happen that a well-delivered speech does not result in a good oration but it is not possible that a well-written oration fails when

---

[172] E.g. Cic. *de Orat.* 1.257; 2.96–7; 3.190.
[173] *Stilus optimus et praestantissimus dicendi effector ac magister*.
[174] On the "procedures of writing" and their influence on oral performance, see Narducci 2002b: 441.
[175] *Mihi unum atque idem videtur bene dicere ac bene scribere, neque aliud esse oratio scripta quam monumentum actionis habitae*. Text and translation of Quintilian: Russell 2001.
[176] On Quintilian's passage, see Austin 1948: XX–XXIII; 192f.
[177] On letter 1.20 and Pliny's literary ideas, Sherwin-White 1966: 132–5; Gamberini 1983: 27–32; Riggsby 1995a: 123–5; Cugusi 2003a; Zehnacker 2009: 126–30. For the relationship between Pliny's letter and Tacitus's *Dialogus*, in particular the figure of Maternus who advocates fullness and long speeches (cf. § 38.1), see Murgia 1985. On Tacitus as the privileged addressee of Pliny's collection, see Marchesi 2008: 97–143 (on the textual and chronological relationship between Pliny's letters and the *Dialogus*: 118–35).
[178] On Pliny's exaggeration of available evidence for Cicero's shortening of the published speeches, see Dyck 2010b. See also Riggsby 1995a on Pliny's claims for abridgment as based on a set of questionable inferences.

delivered, for the written speech is the *exemplar* and *archetypon* of the spoken version (1.20.9):

> "At aliud est actio bona, aliud oratio." Scio nonnullis ita videri; sed ego (forsitan fallar) persuasum habeo posse fieri, ut sit actio bona, quae non sit bona oratio, non posse non bonam actionem esse, quae sit bona oratio. Est enim oratio actionis exemplar et quasi ἀρχέτυπον.

> "Then it is argued that there is a great difference between a good speech as delivered and the written version. This is a popular view I know, but I feel convinced (if I am not mistaken) that, though some speeches may sound better than they read, if the written speech is good it must also be good when delivered, for it is the model and prototype for the spoken version."[179]

Pliny's case for lengthiness and his endorsement of the Ciceronian model[180] are clearly bound up with the debate over old and new style in the early imperial age. Riggsby has argued that Pliny's evaluation of *brevitas* reiterates Cicero's attack against the so-called Atticists and his predilection for *amplitudo* as a consequence of his engagement in politics.[181] However political Pliny's judgment may be, the letter restates the equivalence of the spoken speech to the written one. The procedures of oral performance are analogous to the literary ones. The good pleader can be defined as such only if he will be able to reproduce, within the written version, the stylistic qualities of a vehement and vibrant delivery. In Quintilian's words, the orator "writes to show how a speech should be spoken."[182]

Apparently, Pliny and Quintilian disagree on the formal edition of the delivered pleading (partial in Pliny's view, complete according to Quintilian).[183] Yet, both the discussions come to a similar conclusion. The oral version is a copy of the written one and the orator should speak as he writes. Both the authors share another argument, namely the prominent role assigned to writing in the sequence *actio-oratio*. Speaking well is dependent on writing well.[184] Pliny considers "the oration in paper" as the model of the spoken version:[185] Quintilian goes a step further and focuses on the didactic function of writing. He insists on the fact that the published version of a speech, directed to unlearned people, should not

---

[179] Text and translation of Pliny: Radice 1969.
[180] For Pliny's defense of Cicero's *amplitudo*, see Riggsby 1995a.
[181] Riggsby 1995a. See also Dyck 2010b: 373.
[182] Quint. *Inst.* 12.10.53 (*si modo eo scribimus ut doceamus quo modo dici oporteat*).
[183] For addition of some material to the delivered speech cf. Plin. *Ep.* 2.5; 9.13.24.
[184] Celentano 2010: 61.
[185] For Pliny's concern over the agreement between delivery and writing cf. also letters 1.16; 9.26. Riggsby 1995a: 125–8.

## The Policy of Self-Emendatio

admit any sort of suppression or cutting, as its main aim is to instruct the orator in the correct way of speaking. By endorsing the Ciceronian model of the ideal orator, Quintilian and Pliny see the agreement between spoken and written speech as crucial to oratorical success. Irrespective of the degree of revision of the pronounced text, the written version testifies to good delivery and those virtues that support the definition of the perfect orator as *vir bonus dicendi peritus*.

Cicero and his devout followers, Quintilian and Pliny,[186] invite their readers to consider the published version of a speech as a close reproduction of an oral presentation. The pen instructs in speaking and the ideal orator speaks as he writes. The written speech is an exact copy of the delivered text and a sort of exemplar of the spoken version. Even if stylization and refinement, mainly consisting in cutting off some technical and irrelevant parts of the spoken text, is encouraged, a well-written speech represents a photograph of a well-delivered speech. From this perspective, the long-debated reliability of Cicero's published speeches as accurate and credible reports of what was actually said in court turns out to be a pseudo-problem. By embellishing and polishing up the spoken version Cicero produced a style model, without departing from the substance of the delivered text. At the heart of Cicero's rhetorical program was his conviction that writing – and complete congruence between orality and writing – was crucial to good oratory. He constructed an ideology in which writing was central to the formation of the ideal pleader. No one doubts the fact that Cicero reworked his oral performances out of stylistic or even political considerations. Yet he was attentive to the criteria for excellence in oratory. As a result, he pursued the harmonious blend of *actio* and *oratio*, oral and written text, a cornerstone of his view of ideal oratory.

Cicero's choice to disseminate a good written text, retaining the force of a living performance, was deeply rooted in the Roman elite ideal of collective revision. We have already noted that, by submitting his writings to friends and advisers for review and comments, Cicero negotiated, established and maintained group coherence and identity[187] and enhanced his public reputation as an exemplary pleader and writer.[188] To Cicero, revision entailed self-integration in the community and production of a text acceptable to aristocracy. Addressed to a restricted group of the

---

[186] On Pliny the Younger and Cicero, see in general Weische 1989; Riggsby 1995a; Marchesi 2008: 207–40. On the parallelism between Cicero's and Pliny's literary careers, see Gibson-Steel 2010.
[187] Gurd 2007: 50.
[188] Gurd 2007; 2012: 49ff. On writing, publishing and social obligations in the Roman republic, see Stroup 2010.

republican elite, Cicero's textual corpus fashioned itself as the result of a collective reading. Socially marked, Cicero's written text derived its last and final *imprimatur* from a process of textual collectivization. "Writing well" was intended to be a cultural notion and a means of forging social and political ties. It follows that Cicero's concern with public approval and, accordingly, his constant search for perfection of writing was embedded in the cultivation of the self in relation to the community-oriented ethics. A well-written speech, an accurate copy of a well-delivered speech, was destined to bolster the orator's social and political visibility, achieved through public evaluation. It served as an insurance policy among the contemporaries and the generations to come.[189]

## *Retractatio* and *Emendatio*: Cicero's Practice of Self-Correction

If Cicero's editorial activity was part of a calculated self-fashioning manoeuvre, *retractatio* and *emendatio* of the spoken text created a culturally, politically and pedagogically effective speech in a context of text exchange and collective revision. The epistolary collection *ad Atticum* offers interesting examples of Cicero's practice of self-correction. In a letter sent to Atticus in late January 61 BCE (1.13: 13 SB*Att*), Cicero responds positively to his friend's suggestion to insert a topographical description of Misenum and Puteoli into one of the orations he was editing. Then, he confesses to having committed a date mistake, noted while checking over a rough draft of the text, and immediately emended it in the copy that had been sent to his friend (1.13.5):

> τοποθεσίαν quam postulas Miseni et Puteolorum includam orationi meae. "a.d. III Non. Dec." mendose fuisse animadverteram. Quae laudas ex orationibus, mihi crede, valde mihi placebant, sed non audebam antea dicere. Nunc vero, quod a te probata sunt, multo mi Ἀττικώτερα videntur, in illam orationem Metellinam addidi quaedam. Liber tibi mittetur, quoniam te amor nostri Φιλορήτορα reddidit.

> "I shall put in my speech the topographical description of Misenum and Puteoli which you ask for. I had noticed that '3 December' was an error. Of the things you praise in the speeches I had, let me tell you, a pretty good opinion, though I did not dare to say so before; now I assure you that they look to me far more Attic than ever in the light of your approbation. I have

---

[189] On Pliny the Younger's similar search for public approval through recitation and social reading, see Mayer 2003.

made some additions to the Metellus one, and shall send you the volume, since affection for me has made you an amateur of oratory."

It has been supposed that the description of Misenum and Puteoli (an epideictic excursus?) was added to the *Oratio Metellina,* namely the speech *contra contionem Q. Metelli,* delivered in response to a *contio* held by Q. Metellus Nepos at the beginning of 62 BCE.[190] Yet Cicero's words are vague about the exact placement of this *topothesia* (not preserved in any of the extant speeches). The scanty surviving fragments of the *Metellina* do not offer indications of any sort and the possibility of an addition to another speech cannot be ruled out.[191] Cicero's allusion to later additions to his sharp rejoinder, furthermore, raises the question of publication. If we accept the idea of a quick publication of the oration after delivery,[192] by virtue of its apologetic content,[193] it might be suggested that Atticus's request was probably for a more refined and polished version of the text.

The letter offers a fascinating picture of Cicero's ideal of revision. In addition to its primary meaning as "removal of *menda,* flaws in the text,"[194] the term *emendatio* includes style polishing and insertions of new parts into the reworked version. Embellishments or refinements to the delivered text originate from Atticus's informal, friendly encouragement to create a "more Attic" text, partaken of by both Cicero and Atticus,[195] a text matching the standards of perfect eloquence and meeting the expectations of an educated, aristocratic readership. The detection, and consequent *emendatio,* of an incidental chronological slip, moreover, testifies to the orator's effort at disseminating a reliable text. The use of a technical language, exemplified in the adverb *mendose* and the verbs *includo/addo* (both indicating textual addition), points to an "Alexandrian," rigorous, method of correction, very similar to the *labor limae* practiced on poetic texts.[196] The exquisiteness of the literary work is achieved only through *iudicium* and incessant correction of factual errors. The three-decades-long

---

[190] Shackleton Bailey 1965–1970: 1.305. On the speech, see Crawford 1994: 219–31.
[191] Gurd 2007: 52 n10.   [192] Settle 1962: 131–2; McDermott 1972a: 278 n4.
[193] Crawford 1994: 219 n5.
[194] Zetzel 1980: 42, who enlarges the semantic range of the word to include the correction of an author's rough draft, the proofreading of a copy against its exemplar, the addition of notes and the supplement of a variant reading (see also Zetzel 1973). On the basic meaning of the word as "revision" and removal of errors without any connotation of textual restoration, see Zetzel 1981: 7. For the semantic vagueness of the term, see Del Vigo 1990; 1995.
[195] Gurd 2012: 53 points out that the definition of both Atticus as a "lover of rhetoric" and Cicero's works as "more Attic" serves as a link between a stylistic virtue (Atticism) with a proper name (Atticus). The revised text becomes then a "shared property."
[196] For the poet as *emendator,* cf. Ov. *Pont.* 1.5.15; 3.9.17.

epistolary exchange with his friends conjures up an image of Cicero as an insightful *emendator*, dedicated to producing and releasing a high-grade literary product.[197]

Collective criticism was a significant part of the process of textual production, as said. Cicero's correspondence abounds in terms denoting textual actions.[198] Analogously, there is abundant evidence about the process of revision and textual collectivization. We know of comments from Atticus and other literary critics on two epistles to Caesar,[199] a letter to Brutus,[200] the *pro Ligario,* the lost *De gloria,*[201] the second *Philippic* and the *Academica*:[202] Cicero himself commented upon his friends' speeches and letters.[203] In this context of mutual correction, Atticus established himself as a symbol of philological rigor and proven literary quality. Assimilated to Aristarchus,[204] Homer's reader and exegete lauded for his carefulness in remarking errors and commenting upon relevant textual points,[205] Atticus cooperated with Cicero in producing a good literary product. His approval (*commendatio*) implemented the sense of collectivization connected to textual revision, setting the stage for the reception of Cicero's textual body.

Atticus is not the only textual authority to whom Cicero refers in his letters. Tiro, "the canon" of Cicero's writings,[206] Sallustius[207] and other distinguished personalities[208] are depicted as solicitous critics of the orator's style.[209] Nevertheless, Atticus seems to have played a key role in the circulation of Cicero's work.[210] Scholars have long debated on his

---

[197] For the practice of *emendatio* in early empire oratory cf. Quint. *Inst.* 1.4.2; 10.4.1–4; Plin. *Ep.* 1.2.1; 1.8.3; 7.17.7–13; 7.20.1; 9.35.2.

[198] For *desecare* as "to cut off a part from the text" cf. Cic. *Att.* 16.5.4 (414 SB*Att*); for *corrigere* cf. Cic. *Att.* 2.7.5 (27 SB*Att*); 13.48.2 (345 SB*Att*); 15.1a.2 (378 SB*Att*); 16.5.5 (410 SB*Att*); 16.11.2 (420 SB*Att*). On the *De gloria*, refashioned and sent to Atticus *crebris locis inculcatum et refectum,* "with numerous interlinings and alterations," cf. Cic. *Att.* 16.3.1 (413 SB*Att*).

[199] Cic. *Att.* 12.40.2 (281 SB*Att*); 12.51.2 (293 SB*Att*); 13.44.1 (336 SB*Att*).

[200] Cic. *Att.* 12.18.2 (254 SB*Att*).

[201] Cic. *Att.* 15.27.2 (406 SB*Att*); 16.2.6 (412 SB*Att*); 16.3.1 (413 SB*Att*); 16.6.4 (414 SB*Att*).

[202] On the revision history of the *Academica*, see Gurd 2012: 71ff. (141 n47).

[203] Cic. *Att.* 12.21.1 (260 SB*Att*); 15.1a.2 (378 SB*Att*); 16.4.1 (411 SB*Att*); *Fam.* 11.19 (399 SB*Fam*).

[204] Cic. *Att.* 1.14.3 (14 SB*Att*). For Atticus's comments marked with red wax (*cerulas miniatulas*) cf. Cic. *Att.* 16.11.1 (420 SB*Att*); cf. also 15.14.4 (402 SB*Att*).

[205] Del Vigo 1990. On Aristarchus and his textual and exegetical practice (on the praxis of *notam apponere*, "obelizing" a line regarded as spurious, cf. Cic. *Pis.* 73; *Fam.* 3.11.5: 74 SB*Fam* and 9.10.1: 217 SB*Fam*), see in general Pfeiffer 1968: 210–33; Porter 1992. For Aristarchus's use of technical terms and Stoicism, see Schenkeveld 1993: 273–8.

[206] Cic. *Fam.* 16.17.1 (186 SB*Fam*).

[207] On the role played by Sallustius and his "trial readings" in the genesis of the *De re publica*, see Gurd 2012: 53–8.

[208] Cic. *Att.* 13.48.2 (345 SB*Att*). [209] Gurd 2012: 53–4.

[210] Cf. Cic. *Att.* 2.1 (21 SB*Att*); *Fam.* 12.17 and 18 (204–205 SB*Fam*).

involvement in the bookselling business.[211] Phillips has aptly called attention to Atticus as a literary adviser more than a publisher of Cicero's works.[212] We will return to this issue, connected with the publication system in the late republic. Currently we emphasize Cicero's policy of self-*emendatio* as a search for textual correctness embedded in an aristocratic context of text exchange. Atticus, entrusted for his literary rigor, served as Cicero's "supervisor": his criticism – and commendation – was a decisive factor in disseminating a collectively approved text.

The revision of the speech *pro Ligario* provides us with a thought-provoking case of textual cooperation. In a letter sent to Atticus on 29 June 45 BCE (*Att.* 13.19.2: 326 SB*Att*), Cicero acknowledges that the *auctoritas* of his friend has been vital to the good reputation surrounding his oration on behalf of Ligarius:

> Ligarianam, ut video, praeclare auctoritas tua commendavit. Scripsit enim ad me Balbus et Oppius mirifice se probare ob eamque causam ad Caesarem eam se oratiunculam misisse. Hoc igitur idem tu mihi antea scripseras.
>
> "I can see that the weight of your approval has given my speech for Ligarius a splendid start. Balbus and Oppius have written to me that they like it wonderfully and for that reason have sent the little piece to Caesar. Well, you told me that earlier."

It is known that Cicero's defense of Quintus Ligarius, a former supporter of Pompey, was well received and admired in antiquity. According to Plutarch,[213] Caesar, dictator and sole judge in the trial, was amused and powerfully affected by Cicero's emotional delivery.[214] The speech stands out for its marked irony[215] and rhetorical excellence.[216] It had a special place in Cicero's *Fortleben*, as demonstrated by the impressive number of citations in Quintilian's *Institutio*.[217] The speech owed its popularity to public readings held at Atticus's home. A letter written on 23 June 45 BCE

---

[211] Carcopino 1947: 2.305–63. For Atticus as a private editor with any connection with the publishing industry, see Sommer 1926.
[212] Phillips 1986: 237; Murphy (T.) 1998: 495ff.   [213] Plut. *Caes.* 39.6–7.
[214] On Caesar's words and reactions as the result of a calculated search for political effect, see Gotoff 1993a: XXXIV–VI, who notes that the trial of Ligarius provided Caesar "with an opportunity to show himself engaged in dispensing justice, heavily laced with mercy, with an established crowd-pleaser leading for the defence" (XXXVI).
[215] Quint. *Inst.* 4.1.70.
[216] On the structure of the speech, see May 1988: 140–8; Gotoff 1993a: XXXII–XXXVII, and 2002: 241–51.
[217] For Quintilian's use of the speech as a rhetorical example of *deprecatio*, see Carilli 1984. McDermott 1970: 331–6 claims that the impressive fortune of the speech in Quintilian was due to its use as a classroom exercise.

highlights the role of Atticus as *praeconius* and *vendor* of Cicero's speech.[218] Commonly, the dinner-parties contemplated readings by a trained slave. As occasions of collective, aristocratic revision, they aroused interest in the text from a refined, literate audience,[219] as explicitly affirmed by Cicero himself in a letter written on 2 July 45 BCE.[220] The wide circulation of the Caesarian speech exceeded the author's power in controlling textual correctness, however. In a letter sent to Atticus on 14 July 45 BCE (*Att.* 13.44.3: 336 SB*Att*), Cicero pleads ignorance for a *lapsus memoriae* presumably committed at the time of delivery.[221] The error, namely the mention of a friend of Ligarius, L. Corfidius, who had died before the trial, was detected by Brutus. Cicero entreats Atticus to charge his slaves and freedmen with deleting the name of Corfidius from all the copies of the text:

> Cottam mi velim mittas; Libonem mecum habeo et habueram ante Cascam. Brutus mihi T. Ligari verbis nuntiavit, quod appelletur L. Corfidius in oratione Ligariana, erratum esse meum. Sed, ut aiunt, μνημονικόν ἁμάρτημα. Sciebam Corfidium pernecessarium Ligariorum; sed eum video ante esse mortuum. Da igitur, quaeso, negotium Pharnaci, Antaeo, Salvio ut id nomen ex omnibus libris tollatur.

> "Would you please send me Cotta? I have Libo by me, and I had Casca before. Brutus has sent me word from T. Ligarius that the mention of L. Corfidius in my defense of Ligarius is an error on my part. It was a mere lapsus memoriae, as they say. I knew that Corfidius was a close friend of the Ligarii, but I find that he died before the case. So pray commission Pharnaces, Antaeus, and Salvius to delete the name in all the copies."

Cicero's request had no effect in textual transmission. The name of Corfidius is preserved in all the extant manuscripts of the speech. Anyway, the letter shows Cicero's concern about textual correctness as a necessary requirement for social and collective approval. Though the error was a trivial one, if left (as it actually was), it would have testified to Cicero's *neglegentia*, "carelessness," and lack of historical accuracy,[222] a sign of

---

[218] Cic. *Att.* 13.12.2 (320 SB*Att*): *Ligarianam praeclare vendidisti. Posthac quicquid scripsero, tibi praeconium deferam* ("You have given my speech for Ligarius a splendid puff. Whatever I write in future, I'll leave the advertising to you"). On the meaning of *venditare* as *commendare* in connection with the sphere of the *munera amicitiae*, see Del Vigo 1990.

[219] For social readings and *convivia* at Atticus's home (cf. Nep. *Att.* 14.3), see Murphy (T.) 1998: 500; Parker 2009: 203; 208.

[220] Cic. *Att.* 13.20.2; 4 (328 SB*Att*).

[221] McDermott 1970:322 attributes the error to Cicero's lack of intimacy with Corfidius.

[222] On the use of the term *neglegentia* to indicate the confusion between the prefaces to the treatises *De Gloria* and *Academica* and their consequent displacement, cf. Cic. *Att.* 16.6.4 (414 SB*Att*). For the textual connotation of the term *diligentia*, see Perry 2000.

incompetence unacceptable in the social context in which the speech circulated. Cicero's attempt to justify his historical imprecision with a memory failure appears as an extreme (and vain) effort to cancel an unsatisfactory record of his virtues from collective memory. As we said, the error was spotted by Marcus Iunius Brutus, man of established literary reputation. In the case of the *pro Ligario,* authorial revision failed. Editorial revision replaced the author in certifying textual correctness. Atticus, along with others of Cicero's learned friends, supported – and implemented – authorial revision, shaping and improving the final form of the published text.

## Fashioning Himself: Revision and Edition of Undelivered Speeches

Behind publication was Cicero's desire to respond to particular political situations and promote his figure as ideal statesman and orator.[223] Though it is true that Cicero was generally disinclined to circulate speeches never delivered,[224] we know of at least two *scriptae orationes,* the *Second Philippic* and the *Actio Secunda in Verrem,* never delivered and put into circulation for self-promotion purposes. Analogously, a second "edition" (only in writing) of the *pro Milone* replaced a former, unsuccessful (and uncompleted) version of the speech. The *Second Philippic,* commonly held to have never been delivered,[225] was presumably published in reply to Antonius's attack delivered in the Senate on 19 September 44 BCE, in turn a response to Cicero's *First Philippic*.[226] As it happens for other pamphlets cast as orations, namely the Second *Actio* against Verres and the speech on behalf of Milo, Cicero strove to make his (fictional) invective as realistic as possible, composed as if it was actually spoken, by addressing his opponent in second person form and alluding to the physical setting as well as Antonius's demeanour on more than one occasion.[227] The speech documents Cicero's political action in the final struggle for the defense of the

[223] Crawford 1984: 10–1; Butler 2002: 72–3.
[224] Walters 2017: 81–5 (who also suggests that Cicero's *Post reditum ad populum* was written down first and disseminated before the occasion of delivery).
[225] Steel 2005: 141ff.; Manuwald 2007: 1. 59 n156 (with further bibliography). See also Lacey 1986: 16; Hall 2002: 275. For an attempt to demonstrate (without strong arguments) that the speech was delivered, see Cerutti 1994.
[226] Steel 2005: 142. For the content of Antonius's charges against Cicero, see Lintott 2008: 378–82. On the de-legitimization of Antonius in the *Second Philippic,* see Larsen 2008.
[227] E.g. *Phil.* 2.36; 76; 111. Steel 2005: 161 n55. Ramsey 2003: 157ff.; Shackleton Bailey 2009: 1.50. For the speech as a realistic representation of "an oral attempt to persuade a certain audience on a given date," see Craig 1993b: 149. On the speech as a pamphlet, see Ott 2013. See also Craig 2004: 191–2 (for a list of invective *loci* in the speech).

Roman republic.[228] Steel remarks that the *Philippics* "memorialize Cicero engaging in a particular set of public actions" and represent "the ultimate stage in Cicero's creation of himself as a public figure through writing himself as a public figure."[229] As powerful political weapons, the fourteen speeches were presumably disseminated individually soon after their delivery[230] (and later assembled into a corpus).[231] In the case of the *Second Philippic*, regardless of its date of publication,[232] it seems safe to assume that the propagation of what may be considered Cicero's final political manifesto was expected to make an immediate impact on the orator's public *persona*.[233]

The publication of the *Second Philippic* also relied heavily upon Atticus's *iudicium*. As may be argued from a letter written on late October 44 BCE (*Att*. 15.13.1: 416 SB*Att*), Atticus was charged with proposing the propitious time to release the speech:

> Orationem tibi misi. Eius custodiendae et proferendae arbitrium tuum. Sed quando illum diem cum tu edendam putes? Indutias quas scribis non intellego fieri posse.
>
> "I am sending you the speech to be kept back and put out at your discretion. But when shall we see the day when you will think proper to publish it? The truce you write of seems to me impracticable."

In a later letter (*Att*. 15.13a: 417 SB*Att*), Cicero's fear about a negative judgment (*existimatio*) from his erudite friend is joined with a lamentation over the current political situation. The restoration of a free republic appears to be the condition required for the publication of the invective against Antony (15.13a.3):

> Haec cum scriberem, tantum quod existimabam ad te orationem esse perlatam, hui, quam timeo quid existimes! Etsi quid ad me? Quae non sit foras proditura nisi re publica recuperata; de quo quid sperem non audeo scribere.

---

[228] Hall 2002: 275.    [229] Steel 2005: 146.
[230] Kelly 2008; see also Hall 2002: 281 n10; Ramsey 2003: 16; Steel 2005: 141 and 161 n54 (in reference to Cic. *ad Brut*. 2.3.4: 2 SB). Manuwald 2007: 1.60 notes that "it is a plausible assumption that the speeches including general statements on Cicero's political views and on his assessments of various protagonists were quickly made available, at least passed on to those people who might be influenced thereby." For copies of the *Fifth* and *Tenth Philippics* sent to Marcus Iunius Brutus, who approved of Cicero's choice of the "Demosthenic" title, cf. Cic. *ad Brut*. 2.3.4 (2 SB); cf. also Cic. *ad Brut*. 2.4.2 (4 SB); see Manuwald 2007: 1.50; 62.
[231] On the size and structure of the *corpus*, see Manuwald 2007: 1.65–90.
[232] For publication of the speech later than 5 Nov. (cf. Cic. *Att*. 16.11 [420 SB*Att*]), see Ramsey 2003: 158f. (late December: Shackleton Bailey 2009: 1.50).
[233] Walters 2017: 84.

"As I write this I think my speech must just about have reached you. Dear me, how nervous I am about what you will think of it! And yet what is that to me, since it won't see the light unless the free constitution is restored? What my hopes are on that point I dare not put on paper."

Atticus as a literary critic re-emerges in a letter written in early November 44 BCE (*Att.* 16.11: 420 SB*Att*). There Cicero reveals that his anxiety about his friend's potential censure has eventually been dispelled by an unexpected eulogy of speech arguments and style features (16.11.1):

> Nonis accepi a te duas epistulas quarum alteram Kal. Dederas, alteram pridie. Igitur prius ad superiorem. Nostrum opus tibi probari laetor; ex quo ἄνθη ipsa posuisti, quae mihi florentiora sunt visa tuo iudicio. Cerulas enim tuas miniatulas illas extimescebam.

> "On the Nones I received two letters from you, the first dispatched on the Kalends, the second on the day preceding. First then my answer to the earlier. I am glad you like my work. You have quoted my gems, and your good opinion makes them sparkle the brighter in my eyes. I was terrified of those little red wafers of yours!"

The relieved orator is now made ready to revise his text in line with his friend's suggestions (16.11.2):[234]

> Ita libenter ea corrigam quae a te animadversa sunt.

> "So I shall be glad to correct the points you notice."

The *Second Philippic* achieved thus its canonical status of literary work thanks to Atticus's criticism and well-advised political evaluations. Cicero's policy of self-*emendatio*, a combination of textual matters and social concerns, looked on a piece of fictional oratory – and its editorial revision accordingly – as a potential instrument of social and political self-promotion. In the end, tight cooperation between author and critic produced a text ready to start on its way to success.

If it is not clear whether Atticus, the "Latin Aristarchus," was involved in a professional activity of publisher, it is certain that Cicero's acquisition of a status of canonical author depended on the rigorous, Alexandrian criticism of his learned friend. As has correctly been remarked, "Atticus' standards of execution were of the highest and his name a guarantee of

---

[234] For later improvements in the text cf. §§ 3; 75; 103; 106 (all incorporated in the text transmitted to us). See Ramsey 2003: 158; 164–5; 267; 312–3; 317.

50                          Cicero Presents Himself

quality".[235] Cicero entered into a textual dialogue with his mentor, who acted as a literary adviser at multiple levels, by criticizing points of style and content, discussing the advisability of publication, holding private readings and sending out complimentary copies,[236] in a sort of modern advertising campaign. In connecting authorial-editorial revision to enactment of social and political visibility, Cicero and Atticus cooperated in creating a high-quality text, intended as a medium of propagation of literary and political values shared by the members of the upper class.

The self-advertising nature of Cicero's textual revision is stressed by the special connotation of the *Second Philippic* as a fiction. Disconnected from a concrete judicial occasion, the speech was primarily intended as propagandistic material. As has been noted, "there was no time at which the speech could have been delivered." This is not the case with the other known fictional speeches, the *Actio Secunda in Verrem* and the *pro Milone*, "all connected with a particular trial, even though the circumstances which would have allowed for their delivery did not arise."[237] To start with the former, the *Actio Secunda in Verrem*, "the largest single publication of Cicero's entire career, if not the biggest such undertaking in the first century BCE,"[238] was known to have never been delivered.[239] As far as we can assume, Cicero presumably composed the *actio secunda* speech for delivery in court. But the trial did not take place. Caught off guard by Cicero's successful handling of prosecution arguments in the first *Actio*,[240] Hortensius abandoned the defense[241] and Verres fled into voluntary exile (and was convicted *in absentia*).[242] Cicero decided to circulate a pre-written speech anyway,[243] maintaining the "similitude of a speech actually delivered."[244] By engaging his readers in a subtle dialogue, he employed the

---

[235] Reynolds-Wilson 1974: 23.    [236] Reynold-Wilson 1974: 22–34.    [237] Steel 2005: 141.
[238] Frazel 2004: 133.
[239] Plin. *Ep.* 1.20.10; Ps. Asconius 224–225.14St; Tac. *Dial.* 20 (Tacitus's passage does not contain any allusion to the supposed non-delivery of the five-book *Actio Secunda*).
[240] Frazel 2004: 131f.
[241] If Hortensius did not reply to Cicero in the *litis aestimatio*, following Verres's condemnation (Brunt 1980: 279 n44), it is likely that the speech by Cicero's rival, which Quintilian refers to in *Inst.* 10.1. 22–3, was given during the *Actio Prima*. On Hortensius's defensive strategy, see Alexander 1976.
[242] For an exhaustive discussion of the trial, see Frazel 2004.
[243] For *commentaria* of large sections of the *Verrines* written out before delivery, see Frazel 2004: 133.
[244] Greenwood 1978: XIX. For Cicero's allusions to the factuality of the trial, cf. Ps. Asconius 225.16-8St: *Neminem vestrum ignorare arbitror] Hoc totum figmentum est Ciceronis, ut sequentium librorum vera actio videatur: nam Verres iam sua sponte elegit exilium* ("You are probably none of you unaware] This passage has been invented by Cicero to give the impression that the trial, which is described in the subsequent books, actually took place: yet Verres had fled in voluntary exile"); cf. also 224.10-14St. For the repeated use of the verb *fingo* and its derivatives in the scholiast, see Gurd 2010: 81.

discussion of Verres's documents and consequent detection of damning erasures as "the template for projected responses to his own-writing."[245] As Butler puts it, "by publishing a record of the speech he had never delivered, Cicero did more than just redeem preparation that would otherwise have been wasted; he negotiated the part he had just played and was to play in Roman public life, transforming the success he had won as a clever detective into worthy monuments of a Roman senator's eloquence."[246] The publication (quickly after Verres's conviction)[247] of the *Actio Secunda* speech was then a major step towards Cicero's social and political promotion.[248] Similarly to what would happen for the *Second Philippic*, a fictional text memorialized and preserved Cicero's oratorical and political glory. At the beginning and end of his career, Cicero put into circulation two speeches that, albeit affected by their recognized unreality, were intended to exert a considerable impact on the formation – and consolidation – of his public figure.

Much more complicated is the case of Cicero's pleading on behalf of Milo. Ancient evidence supports the idea that the speech as transmitted to us is not the delivered one in the trial against Milo charged *de vi* in early April of 52 BCE.[249] According to the scholiast Asconius Pedianus (41.24–42.4C), Cicero, inhibited by the Clodians' shouts and jibes, lacked his usual "steadiness" (*constantia*) and was unable to keep on his delivery.[250] Yet the orator's words were taken down (*excepta oratio*).[251] An unauthorized transcript of the speech got into circulation and Cicero reworked the oral (failed) version of his *pro Milone*, providing his readers with one of his finest literary products. The account in the Scholia Bobiensia (112.7-13St) is not very different. Frustrated by a series of exceptional, out-of-hand events, Cicero interrupted his delivery.[252] Out of fear he uttered just rude words, preserved in the extant

---

[245] Gurd 2010: 82–3.   [246] Butler 2002: 84.
[247] For the publication and propagation of the *Actio Secunda*, see Frazel 2004: 136.
[248] Brunt 1980: 286–9.   [249] On the date of the trial, see Clark 1895: 127–9.
[250] For the circumstances of Cicero's debacle, cf. Plut. *Cic.* 35; Dio Cassius 40.54.1–4; schol. Bob. 111. 24–112.17St. On Asconius's passage, see Marshall 1985: 190–1; Lewis 2006: 247. See also Morstein-Marx 2004: 1–6.
[251] For the practice of "shorthand" in republican oratory, cf. Cic. *Att.* 2.20.4 (40 SB*Att*), in reference to Bibulus's edicts and *contiones*, see Marshall 1987. For skepticism on the diffusion of court stenography in the late republic, see Settle 1963, who erroneously claims that the first *pro Milone* was a forgery by Cicero's opponents or rather a later rhetorical exercise. On the surviving fragments of the first *pro Milone,* quoted by Quintilian *Inst.* 9.2.54 and the Bobbio scholiast (111.24–112.17St), see Dyck 2002 (also Crawford 1984: 210–8).
[252] The scholiast explains Cicero's unusual demeanor as a consequence of current unrest (*turbulenta res*), Milo's admitted guilt (*confessa caedes*), popular turmoil (*ad seditionem populus inflammatus*), placement of armed forces around the trial place (*circumpositi iudicio milites*) and Pompey's assessed opposition to Milo (*consul Pompeius obnixe studens in damnationem Milonis*).

transcript. Once free of anxiety, he revised and published a new, polished version of his *pro Milone*.[253] Quite similar are, finally, the reports of the trial in Plutarch's *Life of Cicero* (35) and Dio Cassius's *Roman History* (40.48–55). Both concur in describing Cicero's ineptitude as a demonstration of cowardliness in the face of Pompey's armed guards cordoning off the Forum.[254]

The ancient accounts of Milo's trial are likely to draw on an anti-Ciceronian tradition.[255] Whatever reason lies behind Cicero's powerlessness,[256] the *pro Milone* was a debacle.[257] Milo was convicted and, what is more, an unsatisfactory record of Cicero's skills, that is the first, taken-down speech began circulating and discrediting thereby the orator's credibility. As Steel notes, the "desire to supersede the pirated version" compelled Cicero to promote a new, more favorable, version of the facts,[258] passed off as if it was the speech actually delivered in the trial.[259] One might also suggest that the published speech faced competition from M. Brutus who, according to Asconius,[260] wrote and published (but never delivered) a *pro Milone*, presumably a rhetorical exercise,[261] "which took a different tack, not denying premeditated murder but claiming that the removal of a *malus civis* was justified."[262]

Modern scholarship has long debated on Cicero's revision of the first Milonian speech.[263] An extensive reworking of the oral version has recently been cast in doubt.[264] It has opportunely been suggested that Cicero's own version of Milo's case may have functioned as a corrective of the circulating unauthorized transcript of the speech.[265] Without diverging from the line of defense adopted at the trial, Cicero rewrote the speech (in good part, we presume) in order to delete the memory of his inglorious stylistic and

---

[253] For the publication of the revised speech in January 51 BCE, see Berry 1993.
[254] On the unreliability of Plutarch's and Dio's accounts and the picture of Cicero stumbling over his words through fear, suggesting an anti-Ciceronian climate, see Fotheringham 2015.
[255] Powell-Paterson 2004: 6–7; 55.
[256] In disagreement with Asconius and the Bobbio scholiast, Plutarch and Dio Cassius depict Cicero frightened by the view of the Forum encircled by Pompey's troops. For Cicero's later allusions to the placement of Pompey's army around the Forum as a protection measure, cf. Cic. *Fam.* 3.10.10 (73 SB*Fam*); *Att.* 9.7B.2 (174 SB*Att*).
[257] Lewis 2006: 247.
[258] Steel 2005: 118f. Crawford 1984: 212 argues that by writing up a separate speech for publication Cicero "wished to make clear his position and erase any doubts about his loyal support of Milo."
[259] Steel 2005: 120–1.
[260] Asc. 41.9-14C (= *ORF* 20); schol. Bob. 112.14-8St (Brutus made use of the *qualitas compensativa*).
[261] Quint. *Inst.* 3.6.93 (*exercitationis gratia*); 10.1.23.
[262] Dyck 1998: 221–2. On Brutus's *exercitatio* as a political pamphlet, see Balbo 2013b: 319–20.
[263] For a brief survey of scholarly arguments about the differences or similarities between the spoken and the published versions of the speech, see Crawford 1984: 211 n.6; see also Stone 1980; Clark-Ruebel 1985; Riggsby 1999: 110–2.
[264] Wisse 2007: 66–7; see also Fotheringham 2013a: 5–6.   [265] Powell-Paterson 2004: 55.

political failure. An extraordinary piece of rhetoric of advocacy,[266] the new *pro Milone* originated from Cicero's reaction to his past self-portrait, a "not well-written" speech, failing in meeting with standards of good oratory and transmitting a negative image of himself. If the late rhetorical treatise *De optimo genere oratorum* is authentic, as recent studies have convincingly proved,[267] still in 46 BCE, that is to say, six years after Milo's trial, Cicero exploited the trial's extraordinary setting, the Forum packed with Pompey's armed troops, as an implicit justification for his shameful withdrawal from the oratorical competition.[268] By linking his rehabilitation, as both an ideal orator and statesman, to the radical elimination of a wrong version and the subsequent dissemination of a revised, corrected, text, Cicero performed as an autonomous critic and editor of his own work. He neglected the consecrated practice of *emendatio* as an act of social obligation and mutual friendship. Pressed by the urgency to cancel an infamous past from collective memory, he emended himself by polishing and re-formulating his defense of Clodius's murderer.

The second, "right," *pro Milone* marks the highest point of Cicero's strategy of self-promotion. Revision, usually restricted to the correction of minor factual errors or style polishing, turns out to be a form of textual re-creation. Cicero had to re-establish his damaged reputation through a radical act of *emendatio*, that is to say, the replacement of a wrong text with a good one.[269] But Cicero's attempt failed, at least partially. An unauthorized transcript of the first *pro Milone* circulated still for a long time (at least to the first decades of the second century CE). As we have seen, through his policy of aristocratic and collective revision Cicero cultivated his political and oratorical self, trying to consolidate his leading role in a society dominated by learned upper-class figures. By means of his textual body the orator propagated a complex network of moral and stylistic values, shared by the members of the dominating elite. The casual and fluid nature of publication in the ancient world did not live up to the author's expectations, however. A good number of orations,

---

[266] On the magnificent narrative of the extant version that could have secured Milo's acquittal and Milo's famous comment (preserved in Dio Cassius 40.54.3–4) on the extraordinary effectiveness of Cicero's revised defense, see Steel 2005: 130; see also Crawford 1984: 211 n. 5. For the *pro Milone* as an accomplished piece of rhetoric, see May 1988: 129ff.; for its connotation as the "ideal" speech of an "ideal" orator, May 2001.
[267] Kennedy 1972: 258 n141; Berry 1996b; Ronconi (F.) 1998; see also Riggsby 1995a: 128 n8.
[268] Cic. *Opt. Gen.* 10. On the question, see now La Bua 2014a.
[269] On the revised *pro Milone* as an instrument of political propaganda and the twinned fortunes of patron and client (both exiles undeservedly), see Melchior 2008.

considered by Cicero as potential vehicles of self-promotion,[270] got lost. The text often took different ways, with no respect for the initial intentions of its author. But this is another matter. Once published, the speeches "became standard examples of oratory – as doubtless their author wished."[271] Amidst failures and setbacks, Cicero transcended the limitations of time through his textual corpus, entering the school canon as a style model.

---

[270] An example is the case of the lost speech *pro Cornelio,* regarded by Cicero as a style model and mentioned for its rhetorical relevance still in the second century CE (cf. Quint. *Inst.* 8.3.3; Tac. *Dial.* 39; Plin. *Ep.* 1.20). On the structure and fragments of the speech, see Crawford 1994: 65–144. See chapter 2, pp. 59; 86.

[271] Powell-Paterson 2004: 57.

CHAPTER 2

# *Beyond the Author*
## *Cicero's Speeches from Publication to the Medieval Manuscripts*

The authorial dissemination of handwritten copies of the speeches heralds the beginning of the reception of Cicero's oratory in the school. We have rapidly noted in the previous chapter that publication in ancient Rome was essentially a private process of textual production. In absence of a standard publication procedure, the usual form of book production was the making of private copies, circulating in selective literary circles for private use.[1] This operation required the service of professional trained scribes, known as *librarii*.[2] As has been observed, "writing *per se* was a non-elite activity":[3] accordingly, *describere*,[4] copying, was a lower-class practice.[5] On rare occasions we hear that a member of the upper class wrote his works *sua manu*, that is to say, without dictation to literary slaves or freedmen,[6] as suggested by the existence of Cicero's and Vergil's autographs.[7] Nevertheless, even when Cicero depicts himself as copying out a text of a friend[8] or the act is performed by highly educated people,[9] a commitment of this manual action to professional scribes should be assumed.[10]

---

[1] On publication at Cicero's time, see Philipps 1986; Starr 1987; Dortmund 2001: 45–186.
[2] Cic. *Att.* 4.13.2 (87 SB*Att*); 8.9.1 (188 SB*Att*); 12.14.3 (251 SB*Att*); 13.13–14.1 (321 SB*Att*); 13.21a.1–2 (327 SB*Att*); 16.5.4 (411 SB*Att*); *Fam.* 12.17.2 (204 SB*Fam*). For the transcription of speeches by professional scribes cf. Cic. *Agr.* 2.13; *Sul.* 42.
[3] Sciarrino 2007: 64.
[4] On the distinction between *scribo* and *describo* (more frequent than *transcribere*) and the use of verbs, such as *notare* (*adnotare*), *excerpere* ("take down short notes or excerpts") and *exscribere* to indicate copying of brief items as well as of longer documents, see McDonnell 1996: 482f. (for the occurrences of *describo* in Cicero: 483 n65). For the use of *describere* and *remittere* to signify the "gennanten Formen der Buchverbreitung, Buchhandel und private Abschrift," see Dortmund 2001: 285–9.
[5] Cf. *Rhet. Her.* 4.6. See Harris 1989: 249f.; McDonnell 1996.
[6] For the presence of full-time scribes in the households of literate Romans cf. Plin. *Ep.* 9.34. On dictation of a text worked out first in memory cf. Plin. *Ep.* 9.36 (Small 2007: 205).
[7] Quint. *Inst.* 1.7.20–2; Plin. *Nat.* 13.83. On the presence of Vergilian and Ciceronian autographs in public libraries in the first century CE and the archaistic renaissance, see Gamberale 1977: Pecere 2010: 83–4.
[8] E.g. Cic. *Att.* 2.20.5–6 (40 SB*Att*); *Fam.* 7.22 (331 SB*Fam*).
[9] Cf. Cic. *Att.* 4.13.2 (87 SB*Att*); 13.21a.1–2 (327 SB*Att*).
[10] For the causative sense of the verb *describere*, see McDonnell 1996. On the role played by the slaves in the formation of private book collections in the early empire, see Houston 2002.

Titus Pomponius Atticus played a key role in revising and propagating Cicero's works. As we have seen, by committing his writings to friends for review, Cicero publicized his textual body and stimulated collective debate on points of style and diction. Atticus "put his staff of trained *librarii* at the service of his friend":[11] copies and editions of Cicero's speeches proliferated, often with negative consequences on textual accuracy.[12] By holding private readings and passing out copies of Cicero's texts, in a relatively small number,[13] to literary personalities, Atticus cooperated with the author in the diffusion of exemplary speeches, enhancing then the social status of his influential friend and complying with the ritual and aristocratic gestures of mutual friendship.[14] A leading figure in late republic culture and politics,[15] Atticus took an active part in the preliminary dissemination of Cicero's works.[16] Rather than serving as a professional publisher,[17] he acted as Cicero's adviser and publicity agent.

It is not easy to determine whether other literary figures or scholars were engaged in what we may call the "editing phase" of Cicero's speeches. Collective dialogue about the process of textual composition is well-documented in the educated elite society at the end of the republic. As has been shown, Cicero participated in a textual world in which literary composition and dedication – and text exchanges accordingly – created a complex scenario of literary (not always hierarchical) relationships between individuals of equal social standing.[18] Good evidence exists about a textual interaction between Cicero and Cornelius Nepos,[19] who is generally held to have occupied a prominent position among his literary contemporaries.[20] A close friendship between the two men may be

---

[11] Reynolds-Wilson 1974: 23.
[12] For Cicero's vain attempts to exercise control on textual correctness, see Reynolds-Wilson 1974: 24.
[13] Sommer 1926: 414.
[14] For a good discussion of the Cicero-Atticus friendship, see Shackleton Bailey 1965: 3–59; see also Citroni Marchetti 2000: 3–99; 2009.
[15] For Atticus as historical and political figure, see Perlwitz 1992; see also Buckley 2002. On the portrait of Atticus in Nepos's biography, see Hägg 2012: 188–97; Stem 2012: 55–61.
[16] Dortmund 2001: 227–8.
[17] As Kenney 1982: 4 correctly assumes, "to style Atticus a 'publisher', as is still done in more than one current treatment, is to import into the reconstruction of his activities an entirely modern and obtrusive concept belonging in the world of the printed book." See also Zetzel 1981: 234; Horsfall 1989: 88–9.
[18] Stroup 2010: 1–20.
[19] For a correct re-evaluation of Nepos's literary qualities and a more appropriate analysis of the Cicero-Nepos relationship, see Geiger 1985b; Titchener 2003; a good survey of the issue is now in Stem 2012: 61–83. On Cornelius Nepos as Cicero's historical source and the use of the *Chronica* in the treatise *De re publica*, see Fleck 1993: 181–94.
[20] Stem 2012: 55–95. For Nepos's place within the cultural, intellectual and literary milieu of the late republic, see Geiger 1985a; see also Millar 1988.

*Beyond the Author: Cicero's Speeches* 57

deduced from the place of Nepos in Cicero's correspondence.[21] In a letter to Atticus written in early July 44 BCE (*Att.* 16.5.5: 410 SB*Att*) Nepos is featured as an assiduous reader of Cicero's writings, longing to see some of his friend's works, presumably his letters (not his philosophical treatises),[22] as may be argued by the subsequent mention of a group of seventy letters retained by Tiro, yet not collected and in need of scrutiny before publication. Nepos's interest in Cicero's letters as political documents receives confirmation from the biography of Atticus (16.4).[23] Nothing enables us, however, to argue for Nepos's involvement in the editorial plan of Cicero's correspondence.[24]

Nepos's positive depiction of Cicero comes to the fore in the biography of the orator, in at least two books.[25] Not surprisingly, excess of devotion to Cicero neutralized Nepos's celebrated historical preciseness. The misdating of Cicero's defense of Sextus Roscius attracted Gellius's attention for its "unusually troubling inaccuracy"[26] (15.28.1–2):

> Cornelius Nepos et rerum memoriae non indiligens et M. Ciceronis ut qui maxime amicus familiaris fuit. Atqui is tamen in primo librorum, quos de vita illius composuit, errasse videtur, cum eum scripsit tres et viginti annos natum primam causam iudicii publici egisse Sextumque Roscium parricidii reum defendisse.

> "Cornelius Nepos was a careful student of records and one of Marcus Cicero's most intimate friends. Yet in the first book of his *Life of Cicero* he seems to have erred in writing that Cicero made his first plea in a public trial at the age of twenty-three years, defending Sextus Roscius, who was charged with murder."[27]

Nepos's error was at odds with his historical *diligentia*. By counting the years from Cicero's birth to his delivery of the *pro Quinctio* we reach the

---

[21] Macrobius (2.1.14) refers to a second book of Cicero's letters to Nepos; see Geiger 1985b: 264–7.
[22] On Nepos's approach to theoretical philosophy, cf. Lact. *Inst.* 3.15.10 (frg39 Marshall): see Stem 2012: 64–5.
[23] White (P.) 2010: 32.
[24] Nepos's role in the process of publication of Cicero's letters is played up by Taylor (L.R.) 1964; for a survey of scholarly debate on the issue, see Setaioli 1976; Marchesi 2008: 208–9; Stem 2012: 77–83. White (P.) 2010: 33–4 focuses on the total absence of "any kind of editorial statement" in the published correspondence, observing that speculation over who was involved in carrying out the project of publication of Cicero's letters "has been pushed as far as it profitably can be without firmer anchor points."
[25] Gel. 15.28.1. On Nepos's praise of Cicero as a historian (in the *liber de historicis Latinis*: frg58 Marshall), preserved in a twelfth-century manuscript of the Herzog-August-Bibliothek at Wolfenbüttel, Guelf. Gud. Lat. 278, see Degl'Innocenti Pierini 2003:17–9; Stem 2012:73–5; on the circumstances surrounding the discovery of the text, see Marshall (P. K.) 1977: 8–9.
[26] Stem 2012: 73.    [27] Text and translation of Gellius: Rolfe 1927.

total of twenty-six, instead of twenty-three, as supposed by Nepos. As a result, the plea in defense of Roscius must have been delivered by Cicero at the age of twenty-seven. Gellius adds that a similar error (detected by Asconius Pedianus) was committed by the first-century CE antiquarian Fenestella, who assigned the speech on behalf of Roscius to the twenty-six-year-old Cicero.[28] But Nepos's misstating of Cicero's years appears more serious and unmotivated, though plausibly dictated by the scholar's admiration for the accomplishments of such a young orator (15.28.4–5):

> In qua re etiam Fenestellam errasse Pedianus Asconius animadvertit, quod eum scripserit sexto vicesimo aetatis anno pro Sex. Roscio dixisse. Longior autem Nepotis quam Fenestellae error est, nisi quis vult in animum inducere Nepotem studio amoris et amicitiae adductum amplificandae admirationis gratia quadriennium suppressisse, ut M. Cicero orationem florentem dixisse pro Roscio admodum adulescens videretur.

> "Asconius Pedianus has noted that Fenestella also made a mistake in regard to this matter, in writing that he pleaded for Sextus Roscius in the twenty-sixth year of his age. But the mistake of Nepos is greater than that of Fenestella, unless anyone is inclined to believe that Nepos, led by a feeling of friendship and regard, suppressed four years in order to increase our admiration of Cicero, by making it appear that he delivered his brilliant speech *In defence of Roscius* when he was a very young man."

As Holford-Strevens puts it, Gellius "suggests, without disapprobation, that Nepos was improving on the truth for his friend's sake."[29] In line with the canons of intellectual biography, Nepos idealized Cicero's extraordinary oratorical achievements and manipulated the chronology of the speeches for Cicero's benefits.[30] However it may be, the Gellian chapter tells us much about Nepos as a Ciceronian scholar. Within his eulogizing biography of Cicero, Nepos is likely to have commented upon the chronology of the speeches, presumably attempting to give indications about their order in parallel with the intellectual development of the biographic character. If this were the case, Nepos's biography would represent the first (as far as we know) scholarly effort at fixing the chronology of some orations. Regardless of the extent of Nepos's chronological interests, it appears that a scholarly debate over the chronology of Cicero's early speeches started already in the late republic and continued in the early empire, shaping the initial phases of Ciceronian scholarship in antiquity.

---

[28] On Asconius as Gellius's source, see Marshall 1985: 58.   [29] Holford-Strevens 2003: 162.
[30] Geiger 1985a: 67; 1985b: 262.

Whether Nepos's *Life of Cicero* contained a reference to a firsthand report of Cicero's speech on behalf of Cornelius remains an open issue. From a passage in Jerome's *Against John of Jerusalem* 12 (PL 23.381 Migne; frg38 Marshall) we are informed that Nepos attended *pro Cornelio*'s long performance, published with almost literal accuracy afterwards:

> Refert enim Cornelius Nepos se praesente iisdem paene verbis, quibus edita est, eam pro Cornelio, seditioso tribuno, defensionem peroratam.

> "Cornelius Nepos says that he personally attended the delivery of the defense of the tribune Cornelius and that the speech published afterwards matched up with the delivered one."[31]

It has been taken for granted that the anecdote on Nepos's presence at Cornelius's trial derives from the *Life of Cicero*.[32] The hypothesis of an edition of the *pro Cornelio* as Jerome's source finds no support in ancient evidence.[33] Interestingly enough, Jerome's report suggests that Nepos tried to clarify the relationship between the delivered version of the speech and the published one, a hotly debated topic of Ciceronian scholarship starting from the author's time. The trial against C. Cornelius, tribune of the plebs in 67 BCE, charged under the *lex Cornelia de maiestate*, lasted four days and Cicero delivered two speeches (*Pro Cornelio* I and II).[34] Highly regarded for its stylistic exemplarity[35] and the sublimity of Cicero's delivery,[36] the *pro Cornelio* fueled speculation in antiquity for its unusual length.[37] As we have seen, Pliny the Younger referred to the abridged published version of the speech in his discussion about orality and writing in forensic oratory.[38] Nepos weighed into the debate and testified to the agreement between the delivered speech and the published text based on his personal experience.

### *A Tirone Emendata*: Copying and Editing the Speeches

A much wider-ranging discussion can be opened about Cicero's freedman, Tiro, who is maintained to have composed a four-book *Life of Cicero*.[39] Credited with the invention of stenography or

---

[31] My translation.   [32] Geiger 1985b: 268.   [33] Geiger 1985b: 270.
[34] On the speech, of which a good number of fragments survives in Asconius's commentary, see Kumaniecki 1970; Marshall 1985: 214–80; Crawford 1994: 64–144. For the circumstances of the trial, the charge *de maiestate* and Cicero's defensive strategy, see Crawford 1994: 67–72; 97–101. Cf. below p. 86.
[35] Cic. *Brut.* 271; *Or.* 103; 108.   [36] Tac. *Dial.* 39; Quint. *Inst.* 8.3.3.   [37] Cf. Lact. *Inst.* 6.2.15.
[38] Plin. *Ep.* 1.20.8. Cf. chapter 1, pp. 38; 39–41.
[39] Ascon. 48.25-6C; Gel. 4.10.7; Plut. *Cic.* 41.7–8; Tac. *Dial.* 17.2. See Marshall 1985: 57–8; Lo Monaco 1990: 173 n11; 1995: 47.

shorthand,[40] Tiro acted as *litterarum adiutor* and *administer* of Cicero,[41] a learned friend trusted for his literary doctrine.[42] We do not know anything about Tiro as editor, with the only exception being what Quintilian affirms about an edition of Cicero's *Commentarii* (10.7.30–1)[43] and a three-book collection of Cicero's *ioca*, witticisms.[44] The issue is complicated by our extant evidence about the production and circulation of Ciceronian editions in the second century CE. The name of Tiro is associated with that of Nepos, Atticus and other copyists in a letter written by Fronto to the emperor Marcus Aurelius (*Aur.* 1.7: 13.17–16.3Hout). The emperor has copied out *sua manu* an oration of his eminent teacher, presumably the *De testamentis transmarinis*.[45] Fronto's smugness comes up with a flattering comparison between the high-rate copies of distinguished poets and orators, such as Cato, Ennius, Gracchus and Cicero, "certified" by the hand of well-known copyists, and the copy of his speech, whose survival relies on the emperor's subscription (1.7.4: 15.11–16.1Hout):

> Quid tale M. Porcio aut Quinto Ennio, C. Graccho aut Titio poetae, quid Scipioni aut Numidico, quid M. Tullio tale usuvenit? Quorum libri pretiosiores habentur et summam gloriam retinent, si sunt Lampadionis aut Staberii, Plautii aut D. Aurelii, Autriconis aut Aelii manu scripta e<xem>pla aut a Tirone emendata aut a Domitio Balbo descripta aut ab Attico aut Nepote. Mea oratio extabit M. Caesaris manu scripta. Qui orationem spreverit, litteras concupiscet; qui scripta contempserit, scriptorem reverebitur.

> "What fortune like this befell M. Porcius or Quintus Ennius, Gaius Gracchus or the poet Titius? What Scipio or Numidicus? What M. Tullius, like this? Their books are valued more highly and have the greatest credit, if they are from the hand of Lampadio or Staberius, of Plautius or D. Aurelius, Autrico or Aelius, or have been revised by Tiro or transcribed by Domitius Balbus, or Atticus or Nepos. My speech will be extant in the handwriting of M. Caesar. He that thinks little of the speech

---

[40] Cf. Cic. *Att.* 13.25.3 (333 SB*Att*). The invention of stenography is first attributed to Tiro in Jerome's *Chronicle*; for a history of Tironian notes, see Ganz 1990.
[41] On Cicero and Tiro, see McDermott 1972b.
[42] Gel. 6.3.8; 13.9.1. Cf. also Cic. *Fam.* 16.4.3 (123 SB*Fam*); 16.10.2 (43 SB*Fam*); 16.14.1 (41 SB*Fam*); 16.16.2 (44 SB*Fam*); 16.17.1 (186 SB*Fam*); 16.21.8 (337 SB*Fam*).
[43] On the diffusion of Cicero's *Commentarii* cf. Hier. *Adv. Ruf.* 1.16. Cf. chapter 1, pp. 34–5.
[44] Quint. *Inst.* 6.3.2; cf. also Macr. 2.1.12–4; schol. Bob. 140.16-7St. On a collection of Cicero's sayings in circulation by the end of 46 BCE, cf. Cic. *Fam.* 15.21.1–2 (207 SB*Fam*); see Geiger 1985b: 267.
[45] Astarita 1997: 56f.

will be in love with the very letters of it; he who disdains the thing written will reverence the writer."[46]

A curious assemblage of famous and less-known scholars,[47] the list of copyists mentioned by Fronto intends to "dare verosimiglianza al paragone tra i vecchi filologi e Marco Aurelio."[48] By connecting literary fame to high-grade *emendatio* Fronto links his own fortune to his pupil's scholarly merits and places himself (and his oration transcribed by the emperor)[49] at the peak of a list of authors (and their works) appreciated in virtue of their literary qualities.

Emphatically positioned at the end of the catalogue of past poets and orators,[50] Cicero was admired by Fronto amongst past prose-writers for the greatness of his oratorical performances,[51] less for his fondness for rare words.[52] Notably, Fronto was comfortable with revision and *emendatio* of Ciceronian texts. Evidence of that is provided by a letter addressed to Volumnius Quadratus (*Amic.* 2.2: 187.10Hout). There the rhetorician illustrates his usual practice of textual revision (in terms similar to those used by Suetonius to describe Probus's philology)[53] and promises to supply his friend with a number of Cicero's books "corrected, punctuated and annotated" (*emendatos, distinctos et adnotatos*).[54]

---

[46] Text and translation of Fronto: Haines 1920.    [47] Hout 1999: 40–2.
[48] Timpanaro 1986: 198. On the question, see also Timpanaro 2001: 161–3. On Fronto's "rhetorical manner of speaking," see Hout 1999: 40.
[49] On the relationship between Fronto and Marcus Aurelius, see Kasulke 2005. For Fronto's encouragement to Marcus Aurelius to read the old orators as a means of extending the emperor's awareness of his cultural inheritance and forging a sense of self-identification, see Stevenson 2004: 155.
[50] Hout 1999: 40.
[51] Cf. *Parth.* 10 (225.3Hout); *Amic.* 1.14 (180.10Hout). For Fronto's practice of making excerpts and copies from Cicero's correspondence, cf. *Ant.* III.8 (104.5-14Hout).
[52] Holford-Strevens 2003: 134–5.
[53] Suet. *Gram.* 24.2. On the Suetonian tricolon *emendare, distinguere, adnotare* and for a discussion of the common understanding of the three verbs as referring to the "correction of transcriptional errors, the placing of marks of punctuation and the addition of discursive notes" respectively, see Jocelyn 1984: 468–72; on the nature of Probus's commentaries (not line-by-line commentaries) and his marginal notes (not accompanied by explanations), see also Jocelyn 1985a and 1985b. Kaster 1995: 253 correctly observes that Suetonius's passage "implies nothing about any writings that Probus intended to produce for public circulation, and so provides no evidence that P. published 'editions' of the authors whose texts he gathered." Differently, Timpanaro 1986: 18–23 maintains (wrongly) that it might have been possible that Probus made "Alexandrian" editions (filled with critical signs and marginal symbols) of a good number of archaic and classical authors. On the *Anecdoton Parisinum* as a primary source on the use of Alexandrian diacritic symbols and annotations in the editions of Latin texts and the parallelism Probus-Aristarchus, see Del Vigo 1990: 80–4.
[54] *Pace* Champlin 1980: 40, *Ciceroniani* are not compositions by Volumnius in Ciceronian style but rather critical editions of Cicero's works: Hout 1999: 437. On the letter as testimony to Fronto's interest in Cicero's correspondence, see Piacente 2014: 45–8.

The mention of surviving copies of Ciceronian texts is not isolated in second-century scholarship. Elsewhere in his *Attic Nights* Gellius alludes to Ciceronian manuscripts, allegedly revised or overseen by Tiro and adduced in support of variant readings. At 1.7.1 the reading *futurum*, in the fifth oration of the *Actio Secunda in Verrem* (5.167), is said to have been found in "a copy of unimpeachable faithfulness, the result of Tiro's careful scholarship" (*liber spectatae fidei Tironiana atque cura factus*): the wrong reading *futuram*, replacing the old invariable future infinitive in *–urum*, may have originated from a textual violation of "good copies" (*boni libri*) from ignorant and impudent grammarians. Similarly, at 13.21.16, Gellius's approval of the Ciceronian forms of the ablative *perangusto fretu*, in place of the more archaic *perangusto freto*,[55] and *peccatu*, preferred to *peccato* for its rhythmic cadence,[56] rests upon "Tiro's copies, of very trustworthy antiquity" (*antiquissimae fidei libri Tironiani*). The old form *aedituumus*, instead of *aedituus*, used by Cicero in the fourth oration of the *Actio Secunda in Verrem* (4.96), is accepted on the ground of "Cicero's most authoritative copies" (*Tullii fidelissima exemplaria*), set apart from *vulgari libri*, less good manuscripts (12.10.6).[57] The scrutiny of several "old manuscripts" (*conquisitis veteribus libris*), finally, supports the genitive form *dies* (instead of *diei*) in the speech on behalf of Sestius (28).[58]

On the notion of *antiquitas* relies basically Gellius's assessment of the quality (and related trustworthiness) of the manuscripts.[59] Antiquity is a synonym for *auctoritas* and "*auctoritas* is the highest principle in Gellius' eye."[60] A good *recensio* was thus made on a closer inspection of the oldest handwritten testimonies, automatically classified as *optimi libri*.[61] As has been observed, the antiquarian Gellius "saw himself as living in an age of textual corruption, a time when ignorant grammarians changed perfectly correct forms in the works of Cicero and Vergil."[62] He devoted himself to

---

[55] Cic. *Ver.* 5.169.  [56] Cic. *Ver.* 2.191.
[57] On the form in *–tumus* and Gellius's passage, see Cavazza 1995; Santini 2006: 18–20.
[58] Cf. Gel. 9.14.6–7. Gellius's approval of the genitive *dies* (he explicitly mentions Caesellius Vindex as his source) is validated by the use of *dies* (for *diei*) in Verg. *Georg.* 1.208, reportedly inspected in an old Virgilian manuscript, allegedly an autograph. On the triplex genitive form *dies, die, dii* in archaic and republican Latin cf. Prob. *GL* 4.3.14; Charis. 69.8; 87.18B.; Priscian. *GL* 2.366.9; Diom. *GL* 1.305.5; *Fragm. Bob. nom. pron. GL* 5.555.8 (see Hofmann-Szantyr 1963: 357; 447). On the Gellian chapter, see also Astarita 1993: 53–4.
[59] E.g. Gel. 2.14.1; 4.16.2; 5.4.1. Gamberale 1977: 362(see also Gamberale 1969: 19 n26).
[60] Holford-Strevens 2003: 178.
[61] E.g. Gel. 5.4 (*bonae atque sincerae vetustatis libri*); 9.4; 9.14.6; 26 (*summae fidei et reverendae vetustatis libro*). On Gel. 18.5.11 and the manuscript of Ennius's *Annals* revised by Lampadio, see Gamberale 1989; Timpanaro 2001: 162–3.
[62] Grafton 2004: 334.

scrutinizing the earliest available manuscripts, even autographs or handwritten copies, in order to preserve the purity of textual tradition against scholarly incompetence.[63]

From Fronto's and Gellius's statements it is possible to suggest a wide circulation of old trustworthy Ciceronian manuscripts, marked by the name of Tiro and preserving good variant readings. Yet the presence of banal errors in the produced copies may "destroy the credit of their provenance."[64] As a result, substantial doubts have been cast about the authenticity and reliability of these "Tironian" manuscripts. Scholarly debate about this controversial issue has been sparked by a seminal study of Zeztel. Assuming a flourishing production and trade of fake copies of famous books in the second century,[65] he conjectured that the copies claimed to be descended from – or corrected against – manuscripts written by Tiro were not genuine: rather, they were "rare and expensive forgeries,"[66] created to meet the increasing demand for early books and editions in the second-century archaistic renaissance and misattributed thus to well-known copyists for financial profit.[67] A proof of the bad quality (and connected untrustworthiness) of these "plagiarized" manuscripts was implicitly provided by the inexactness of many variant readings allegedly found in these "Tironian" copies. As a logical conclusion, "the manuscript that Gellius considered Tironian was no such thing, but was either a deliberately eccentric text or merely a bad copy to which Tiro's name was falsely attached, in other words, a forgery."[68]

As expected, Zetzel's arguments have drawn reasoned criticism. Timpanaro has attentively re-considered Cicero's *usus scribendi*, demonstrating that the use of archaic or odd forms is consistent with the style of Cicero's early orations. To return to the cases discussed by Gellius, the future participle *futurum*, with no distinction of genre and number, is quite frequent in archaic Latin but it finds some, yet rare, attestations in classical language as well:[69] the variant readings *futuram/esse futuram* may be banal emendations by ignorant copyists.[70] Likewise, the archaic form of ablative in –*u*, defended by Gellius (*fretu/peccatu*), is well preserved in republican

---

[63] Grafton 2004: 334    [64] Holford-Strevens 1988: 139.
[65] Zetzel 1973: 233; 240–1; see also Zetzel 1981: 60–2. On book frauds, see White (P.) 2009; for a history of plagiarism in antiquity, see McGill 2012.
[66] Zetzel 1973: 242.    [67] Zetzel 1973: 239f. See also Holford-Strevens 1988: 139.
[68] Zetzel 1973: 232.    [69] E.g. Var. R. 1.68; Liv. 26.45.5. Timpanaro 1986: 203; 2001: 167.
[70] For a good discussion of Gellius's defense of the form *futurum*, see Santini 2006: 36–38.

Latin.[71] Charisius (164.7B) quotes the expression *a Gaditano fretu* from a lost work of Cicero.[72] The use of this type of fourth declension ablative is not isolated in the corpus of the orations against Verres, as the form *efflagitatu meo* in a passage from the fifth speech (*Ver.* 2.5.75) confirms.[73] According to Gellius, stylistic *ratio* prompted Cicero to opt for apparently disused forms,[74] as demonstrated by the use of *mille* with the singular number at *Mil.* 53 (*mille hominum versabatur*)[75] and the preference accorded to the accusative (instead of the ablative) in the expression *in praedonum fuisse potestatem sciatis* at *Man.* 33.[76]

If Cicero's archaisms emanated from authorial stylistic choices, it follows that the readings assessed as genuine by Gellius should not be interpreted as artificial or fictional products of late literate fakers. They are in their right place in Cicero's early orations, subordinated to specific style strategies. And their correctness can easily be proved by the fact that they come mostly from the *Verrines,* speeches composed in the 70s, in other words at an early stage of Cicero's career as orator.[77] An accurate investigation of Cicero's style validates, thus, Gellius's statements about the trustworthiness of old manuscripts transmitting good variant readings. Obviously, Gellius's affectation for rare forms and linguistic archaisms reflects a dominant literary tendency in the Antonine age. In spite of recent attempts to question the aptness of the term archaism to describe second-century Latin,[78] it may usefully be said that the second century of the empire saw a revival of Early and Republican Latinity, in terms of a return to a language pure and uncorrupted, the good Latin as opposed to the current linguistic degeneration. As has been observed, Gellius's concern for the *sermo purus et Latinus* was part of a larger politico-cultural programme, aimed at revitalizing the charismatic authority of the authors of the past as a pedagogical notion.[79] We will touch upon Gellius's classicism in the third chapter. That set apart, an incessant search for rare words and oddities marked out the archaizing movement of the early second

---

[71] The reading *fretu* at Cic. *Sest.* 18 (accepted by Klotz and Peterson) is attested in the oldest and most reliable manuscript of Cicero's post-exile speeches (Paris, Bibliothèque Nationale, Lat. 7794): Timpanaro 1986: 204.
[72] Timpanaro 1986: 204; 2001: 167.   [73] Timpanaro 1986: 205.
[74] Timpanaro 1986: 205. For Ennius's influence on Cicero's language, see Timpanaro 2001: 167.
[75] Gel.1.16.5 (the formation with the plural number is found in *libri minus accurate scripti*); for the Ciceronian expression, see Clark 1895: XLV. For Gellius's defense of *mille* as moderate archaism, see Santini 2006: 38–41.
[76] Gel.1.7.16.   [77] Timpanaro 1986: 208–9; 2001: 168.   [78] Holford-Strevens 2003: 354–63.
[79] Keulen 2009: 32–5.

century CE.⁸⁰ As Cameron states, "words, not ideas, were the business of the Antonine man of letters."⁸¹

As Zeztel puts it, "archaizing rhetoric demanded close study of the vocabulary of early writers, and therefore of manuscripts."⁸² High-quality manuscripts, claimed to be descended from older copies, circulated in good number among scholars. They preserved rare and exotic forms appealing to the archaistic taste of the age. Within this context, we may imagine that Gellius consulted some Tironian manuscripts, or rather copies of older manuscripts allegedly corrected by Tiro, in the public libraries.⁸³ In his copies he detected archaic or disused forms consistent with Cicero's early style. Yet the Tironian *emendatio* as a falsification remains a distinct possibility. The authority of a *codex optimus* does not authomatically imply genuineness of its *emendatio*. Cameron correctly observes that "the fact that a manuscript carried variants and marginal notes proved nothing about its credentials as a whole. What responsible prospective readers or purchasers wanted to know about a book they came across was whether it had been systematically corrected. That is what *legi/emendavi/recognovi* certified."⁸⁴ As a form of authentication (accompanied by the usual formula *emendavi*), the name of Tiro affixed to an allegedly old manuscript entailed that the copy had carefully been emended, and was therefore trustworthy. Since the routine procedure of emending a text consisted in "checking that copy conformed to exemplar, correcting scribal errors, and supplying missing words,"⁸⁵ Tiro became the symbol of textual accuracy. His name (no matter if falsely or not attached to the copy) guaranteed that the manuscript had attentively been revised and checked against its exemplar. To put it a bit more precisely, it is quite possible that the name of Cicero's freedman was later impressed on the manuscript to assess the authority of the text, in other words as a stamp of "textual authentication." If it is true that Gellius found old Ciceronian manuscripts that supported the rare and archaic forms he was fond of, there is no evidence of any kind that prevents us from supposing that the name of Cicero's freedman was later attached to the Ciceronian copy, checked against its exemplar, to certify the routine process of revision and credit the manuscript with the authority needed to guarantee its circulation.

---

⁸⁰ In general Marache 1952; 1957; Ronconi (A.) 1981: 273–91; Vessey 1994. On the cult of Early Latin in the second century CE and "the sentimental regard for antique virtue that attached itself to the cult of the past," see Holford-Strevens 2003: 356. See also Cameron 2011: 399–401.
⁸¹ Cameron 2011: 400.   ⁸² Zetzel 1981: 66.   ⁸³ Timpanaro 1986: 206.
⁸⁴ Cameron 2011: 464.   ⁸⁵ Cameron 2011: 443.

In the absence of certain evidence about Tiro as editor of Cicero's writings, what we can infer from Fronto and Gellius is that the Antonine age saw a good dissemination of ancient Ciceronian manuscripts, purportedly revised by Tiro – or Atticus and Nepos – or, better to say, bearing a formal indication of a Tironian, authoritative emendation. The name of the copyist or *emendator*, a sort of textual "signature," was presumably intercalated between the lines of the title and the *explicit* or, instead, in the margins of the manuscript. A copy signed by Nepos, Atticus or Tiro promptly transformed itself into a high-value textual product, the result of perceptive philological activity. The same can be said about Fronto's letter. While there is no explicit reference to the nature of Marcus Aurelius's transcription, presumptively divested of any intent of revision,[86] the formula *mea oratio extabit M. Caesaris manu scripta* makes it evident that the name of the illustrious copyist was placed after the title or at the bottom of the transcribed text in order to prove the manuscript's authenticity and ensure the fame and fortune of Fronto's speech.

## A True Ciceronian Scholar: Statilius Maximus and His *Subscriptio*

A copy preserving a Tironian *subscriptio* must have been in the hands of the second-century grammarian and scholar Statilius Maximus,[87] compiler of a collection of rare morphological items and words of obscure meaning (*singularia* or *semel posita*),[88] culled from the works of Cato and Cicero. The collection is preserved, in a fragmentary state, in the citations of the grammarian Charisius (who in turn reassembled fragments of Statilius's work, transmitted in Julius Romanus's chapters on adverbs and exclamations).[89] The name Statilius occurs in fact in the earliest subscription to have survived,[90] placed at the outset of Cicero's second speech against Rullus's agrarian law and preserved in some humanistic

---

[86] Timpanaro 2001: 161–2.
[87] Statilius is mentioned neither by Suetonius in the *De grammaticis* nor by Gellius. Zetzel 1974: 109 suggests that he was a contemporary of Fronto and Gellius; see also Zeztel 1973: 228; 1981: 64–5; Merello 1977: 116.
[88] Zetzel 1974: 109. On Statilius's collection, see chapter 3, pp. 139–44.
[89] We possess twenty citations from Statilius in Charisius (only in six cases is the grammarian named as Statilius Maximus, in the remaining fourteen as Maximus); on the technical use of the verb *notare*, see Zetzel 1974: 110; 117–8; Merello 1977: 113–4. On Iulius Romanus's *Ars*, source of Charisius, and Statilius Maximus, see Uría 2012.
[90] On late subscriptions in manuscripts of Latin texts, see Jahn 1851. For the cultural importance of the subscriptions and their impact on the history of textual transmission, see in general Pecere 1986 (on Statilius's *subscriptio*: 29–30). See also Zetzel 1980.

manuscripts descending from a copy made by Poggio Bracciolini.[91] Jahn printed the text of the *subscriptio* relying on a copy made by Mai.[92] The discovery of a manuscript of the Laurentian Library in Florence (*Conv. Suppr.* 13 = **M**), a fifteen-century copy of a copy of eight previously unknown Ciceronian speeches made by Poggio in Germany in the summer of 1417,[93] enabled Clark to print a better text of the subscription.[94] In 1948 Campana found Poggio's autograph in the Vatican Library (*Vat. Lat.* 11458 = **V**).[95] As it appears, Poggio transcribed, and added, the text of the *subscriptio* (two originally independent texts) in the top margin of fol. 56v after the end of the *De lege agraria* I at fol. 56 r and the *incipit* of the second speech.[96] The text of the *subscriptio*, improved after Campana's discovery, is as follows:

> In exemplari vetustissimo hoc erat in margine.
> emendavi ad tyrone(m) et laecanianu(m) / acta
> ipso cicerone et antonio coss. oratio XXIII.
> in exemplo sic fuit. Statili(us) / maximus rursus
> eme(nd)avi ad tyrone(m) et laecanianu(m)
> et dom & alios veteres. III. / oratio exi / mia.

Lines 1 and 4 are Poggio's comments. As has been shown, the distinction between *exemplar* and *exemplum*[97] implies that the *subscriptio* B (*in exemplo sic fuit . . . oratio eximia*) was written in the main body of the text, after the speech; the *subscriptio* A (*in exemplari vetustissimo . . . oratio XXIII*) was placed in the margin of Poggio's exemplar, evidently a note by the copyist who pointed to the presence of the subscription in the margin of the copy he was working on. The Italian humanist first transcribed the text of the *subscriptio* A, alluding to the manuscript (*exemplar*) from which his copy (*exemplum*) descended. Then, he copied the *subscriptio* B, preceded by the formula *sic fuit* as indication of the collocation of the second subscription in the *exemplum*.[98]

---

[91] For the textual tradition of Cicero's speeches *De lege agraria*, see Pecere 1982; Marek 1983: praef. V–XI.
[92] Zetzel 1973: 226.   [93] Marek 1983: praef. IX–X.   [94] Clark 1909: XI.
[95] The eight orations are the *pro Caecina* (found at Langres), *pro Roscio comoedo*, *De lege agraria I–III*, *pro Rabirio perduellionis reo*, *in Pisonem*, and *pro Rabirio Postumo* (all probably found in Cologne cathedral): Reeve-Rouse 1983: 91; Reynolds-Wilson 1991: 138. On Poggio's *antiquum volumen*, the archetype of the tradition of the *De lege agraria*, Pecere 1982: 84–9; see also Marek 1983: praef. VIII–IX. On the history of Poggio's discovery, see Sabbadini 1971: 35–8; see also Rouse-Reeve 1983: 83–4.
[96] Zetzel 1973: 226; Pecere 1982: 73.
[97] Zetzel 1973: 227 ("*Exemplar* refers to the physical form of a book, *exemplum* to the text written in it").
[98] Pecere 1982: 88–9.

As the *subscriptio* indicates, Statilius Maximus emended and revised Cicero's first speech on the agrarian law by relying on six manuscripts corrected (or claimed to have been corrected) by as many scholars, namely Tiro, Laecanianus,[99] Domitius,[100] and three other unmentioned copyists.[101] Presumably, the *emendatio* took place in two different phases. Statilius first revised the speech by making use of two exemplars claimed to be derived from copies corrected by Tiro and Laecanianus. The grammarian moved then to a new *emendatio* (*rursum*) and consulted four more manuscripts.[102] The number XXIIII in the closing phrase in the *subscriptio* A, *acta ipso Cicerone et Antonio consulibus oratio XXIIII*, placed after the title of the speech (f. 56 r), has been read as a reference to the place occupied by the *De lege agraria* I (not the second speech, as originally supposed by Zumpt)[103] in Statilius's collection, conceivably not a general edition of Cicero's complete orations but rather a collection assembled by the grammarian for private use.[104] As to the expression *oratio eximia* at the end of the *subscriptio* B, Zetzel's explanation of *eximia* as a "mistaken expansion of XXIIII, or whatever other number was originally written in the first part of the subscription"[105] has been rejected in light of similar encomiastic expressions in the exegetical tradition.[106]

It appears thus that Statilius Maximus revised and *emendavit* the twenty-fourth speech of his Ciceronian collection by drawing on a number of older, allegedly authoritative, manuscripts and adding a final comment on the speech's style. His revision was unique for its form and scope.[107] Far from being a dull calligrapher, Statilius acted as a professional philologist. In contrast to later subscriptions in Latin manuscripts "more concerned with stating the credentials of the subscriber than his text,"[108] he performed his correction of the *De lege agraria* I with the support of the six earliest copies of the speech, checking whether they witnessed the rare and archaic forms he was fascinated with. In other words, he "was a scholar who collected variants and had criteria for distinguishing between them."[109] Whatever his role

---

[99] On the correct form of the name, Laecanianus, Zetzel 1973: 228.
[100] Perhaps Domitius Balbus, the copyist mentioned by Fronto.
[101] The number III refers to *veteres*, not to *oratio eximia*: Pecere 1982: 193.
[102] Cameron 2011: 427–8.   [103] Zetzel 1973: 229.
[104] Pecere 1982: 112; 1986: 30; Cameron 2011: 452.   [105] Zetzel 1973: 230.
[106] E.g. Ps. Asconius 223. 4St; schol. Bob. 77. 9; 77.20; 103.18; 11C.29; 126.29St; Don. Ter. *Andr.* 295; *Eun.* 142. See Pecere 1982: 122.
[107] For the legal implications of the *subscriptio* practice in Statilius, see Martin 1984.
[108] Cameron 2011: 428.   [109] Cameron 2011: 429.

in Roman aristocracy,[110] Statilius distinguished himself from late subscribers for his scholarly qualities.

Statilius's activity has special significance for the history of Ciceronian scholarship in three aspects. First, it testifies to the practice of copying out and emending Ciceronian texts by collecting old manuscripts, trusted for their alleged antiquity and claimed to be derived from copies, even autographs, corrected by Cicero's intimate friends. These manuscripts, hunted out by enthusiastic scholars "in the hope of recovering an authentic reading,"[111] preserved a good, reliable text and contributed thus to a more appropriate evaluation of Cicero's linguistic oddities. Unlike the majority of the subscriptions that do not mention collation, Statilius revised his copy by relying on earlier manuscripts. As recently reasserted, in the manuscript culture the word *emendavi* usually referred to the process of checking copy against the exemplar from which it was copied, specifically an old, venerable manuscript claimed to be descended from a copy revised by earlier scholars.[112] Whether these copies were truly old as thought or rather falsifications, it is impossible to state. We have already called attention to the fact that the name of Tiro (or Nepos, Atticus and other emblematic figures) might have functioned as a symbol of textual correctness, a sort of insurance of the authenticity and reliability of the transcribed text, without ruling out the possibility of a false (later) attribution of a copy to earlier scholars. However it might be, the routine process of "editing," as shown by subscriptions in manuscripts, contemplated a careful, exact reproduction of the exemplar.[113] The newly made copy was invested with textual dignity, especially if its exemplar had been corrected by authoritative scholars. Statilius did more. His revision was embedded in his linguistic interests. He strove to improve the editorial quality of the text by consulting old manuscripts. More significantly, he displayed erudition and scholarly taste in detecting and discussing archaisms and variant readings.

Secondly, Statilius showed good interest in organizing and arranging collections of Ciceronian texts according to chronological criteria. The revision of the first speech on Rullus's agrarian law, not yet included

---

[110] On the identification of Statilius with the consul of the year 144 CE and the relationship between the "libro sottoscritto" and the literary interests of the ruling elite, see Pecere 1986: 30. For the connection between subscriptions in secular texts during the last years of the fourth century and the pagan opposition, see Reynolds-Wilson 1974: 41–3. A more appropriate analysis of Latin subscriptions is now to be found in Cameron 2011: 421–96, esp. 492–6, who opportunely revisits and corrects widely held views of the centrality of *emendatio* to the prestige of the pagan aristocracy.
[111] Reynolds-Wilson 1974: 31.   [112] Cameron 2011: 430–1.
[113] For a good discussion of the editing process in late antiquity, see Cameron 2011: 420ff.

in a separate, autonomous textual corpus and numbered as twenty-fourth in Statilius's collection, indicates that the subscriber and *emendator* possessed, or rather assembled for personal convenience, an edition of Cicero *orator* presumably starting from the earliest speeches. The chronology of the speeches was a hotly debated topic in antiquity, as we have noted in Nepos's miscount of Cicero's age at the time of the *pro Sexto Roscio Amerino*. Statilius involved himself in the dispute by providing some systematization to the impressive literary output of the *homo novus* from Arpinum.

Finally, by inserting a closing formulaic expression, such as *oratio eximia*, Statilius pointed to the stylistic excellence of the revised text and offered an illuminating example of how literary and textual criticism intermingled with one another in the exegesis of classical authors. The authority of Statilius's transcription was certainly enhanced by the exemplarity of Cicero's speech. This is of some significance, since the survival of a good number of Cicero's speeches largely depended on criteria of oratorical and stylistic exemplarity. In other words, Statilius's sophisticated *emendatio* reflects scholarly attention to style as a decisive factor in the process of textual selection.

## Late Collections of Ciceronian Orations

While it can be easily assumed that Statilius assembled a number of Cicero's orations for personal use, registered according to the usual system of consular chronology,[114] it is more problematic to conjecture an *ordo orationum* in the Antonine age. A second-hand reference to a speech numbered as thirteen in a collection of Ciceronian orations used by the late fourth-century grammarian Diomedes (*GL* 1.368.28)[115] has stimulated debate about a larger, more general, edition,[116] presumably arranged in the late second or third century, depending on Diomedes's source.[117] There is

---

[114] Lo Monaco 1995: 54.
[115] Hildebrandt 1894: 19 (for Diomedes's numeration as referring to the speech on behalf of Fonteius and a *corpus* including *pro Quinctio* I, *pro Sex. Roscio* II, *pro Vareno* III, *pro Roscio comoedo* IV, *pro Tullio* V, *in Verrem* VI–XII, *pro Fonteio* XIII). See also Lo Monaco 1990: 179 n36.
[116] According to Lo Monaco (1995: 56 n55), the order of the speeches might have been as follows: I *Pro Quinctio*; II *Pro Roscio Amerino*; III *Pro Vareno*; IV *Pro Roscio Comoedo*; V *Pro Tullio*; VI–XII *Verrines* (*divinatio, actio prima, actio secunda*); XIII *Pro Fonteio*; XIV *Pro Caecina*; XV *Pro Oppio* (I and II); XVI *De Lege Manilia*; XVII *Pro Cluentio*; XVIII *Pro Gallio*; XIX *Pro Manilio*; XX *Pro Fundanio*; XXI *Pro Cornelio* (I and II); XXII *De rege Alexandrino*; XXIII *In toga candida*; XXIV *De lege agraria in senatu Kal. Ian.*
[117] Kaster 1988: 270–2.

too little evidence to put forward theories about systematic collections of speeches in the early imperial age. Yet the question is of some relevance to the history of the reception of Cicero's orations in late antiquity and the early Middle Ages, by virtue of the visible effects of school collections on medieval manuscripts. It needs to be readdressed here by returning to the first stage of textual tradition, that is, Cicero himself.

It is common knowledge that Cicero published his speeches individually. The only notable exception to this practice, the group of consular speeches assembled in 60 BCE,[118] left its mark on the canon of orations incorporated into Pliny the Elder's resounding hymn to Cicero's *ingenium* (*Nat.* 7.116–7):

> Sed quo te, M. Tulli, piaculo taceam, quove maxime excellentem insigni praedicem? Quo potius quam universi populi illius gentis amplissimi testimonio, e tota vita tua consulatus tantum operibus electis? Te dicente legem agrariam, hoc est alimenta sua, abdicarunt tribus; te suadente Roscio theatralis auctori legis ignoverunt notatasque se discrimine sedis aequo animo tulerunt; te orante proscriptorum liberos honores petere puduit; tuum Catilina fugit ingenium; tu M. Antonium proscripsisti. Salve primus omnium parens patriae appellate, primum in toga triumphum linguaeque lauream merite et facundiae Latiarumque litterarum parens aeque.

> "But what excuse could I have for omitting mention of you, Marcus Tullius? Or by what distinctive mark can I advertise your superlative excellence? By what in preference to the most honorable testimony of that whole nation's decree, selecting out of your entire life only the achievements of your consulship? Your oratory induced the tribes to discard the Agrarian law, that is, their own livelihood; your advice led them to forgive Roscius, the proposer of the law as to the theatre, and to tolerate with equanimity the mark put upon them by a distinction of seating; your entreaty made the children of the men sent to proscription ashamed to stand for office; your genius drove Catiline to flight; you proscribed M. Antonius. Hail, first recipient of the title of Father of the Country, first winner of a civilian triumph and of a wreath of honor for oratory, and parent of eloquence and of Latium's letters!"[119]

Pliny celebrates Cicero's consular genius by commemorating the speeches on the agrarian law, Otho's unpopular measure for the reservation of the first fourteen rows in theatrical performances for the knights,[120] the

---

[118] Cf. chapter 1, pp. 27–31.   [119] Text and translation: Rackham 1938–43.
[120] A confusion between the actor Roscius, on whose behalf Cicero delivered a speech between 76 and 66, and Roscius Otho, tribune of 67, whose proposal was supported by Cicero during the consulship, occurs in the *Saturnalia* of Macrobius (3.14.11–2). Crawford 1994: 213 n1; Kaster 2011: 2.102 n121.

sons of the proscribed and the expulsion of Catiline from Rome, in partial accordance with Cicero's self-praise in *Att.* 2.1.3 (21 SB*Att*) and *Pis.* 3–4.[121] Probably relying on memory,[122] Pliny omits the orations *pro Rabirio perduellionis reo* and the speech on giving up the province of Gaul, sharing the omission of the *pro Murena* with the republican orator. The closing reference to the proscription of Mark Antony is hardly surprising in light of the good diffusion of the "Cicero-versus-Antony" theme in the rhetorical schools of the early empire.[123] As Winterbottom remarks, "*Catilinarians* and *Philippics* molded opinion after Cicero's death even more masterfully than when they were delivered."[124] Apparently unaware of chronological inconsistency,[125] Pliny breaks with the initial plan of limiting his celebration to the consulship and rounds off his list with the praise of Cicero's last political achievements, integrating Cicero's deadly fight against tyranny into a larger panegyric of his consular *ethos*.

"The first such attempt in the literature of the Silver Age,"[126] Pliny's listing and encomium, stylized in hymnic sentences and formulas through the use of anaphora, assonance, and final apostrophe (*salve*), consolidates the image of Cicero as both an ideal orator and virtuous statesman in early empire literature.[127] Notably, Pliny's register testifies to the survival, though partial, of the only corpus originally assembled by Cicero. The Roman encyclopedist creates a personal canon[128] and provides a new form of textual organization by combining a chronological-thematic scheme (the consular speeches) with criteria of exemplarity, as attested by the emphatic, closing memorialization of Cicero's last, ill-fated, fight in defense of the republican institutions.

The corpus of the consular speeches as a whole did not last through the accidents of textual transmission. Only eight speeches survived out of twelve (*de Othone, de proscriptorum filiis, cum in contione provinciam*

---

[121] In the passage of the *In Pisonem*, Cicero mentions the speeches on the agrarian law, *pro Rabirio perduellionis reo, de proscriptorum filiis*, his exchange of province with Antony (*cum in contione proviciam deposui*), and the *Catilinarians*, omitting from this consular list the speech *De Othone* (cited instead in the letter to Atticus), and once again the speech on behalf of Murena.

[122] Wolverton 1964: 160.

[123] Wolverton 1964: 161–2. On the treatment of the Cicero-versus-Antony theme in the schools of rhetoric, cf. chapter 3, pp. 107–8.

[124] Winterbottom 1982a: 238.   [125] Wolverton 1964: 161–2; Darab 1995: 38.

[126] Wolverton 1964: 161.

[127] For a good assessment of Cicero's influence on the literature of the first century CE, see Winterbottom 1982a. For further praise of Cicero in Pliny the Elder's encyclopedia, cf. *Nat. praef.* 7; 22; 13.83; 92; 33.34.

[128] On Pliny's canon as indication of a "polymath-possession of the complete works of Cicero," see McDermott 1972a: 284 n25.

*deposui*, and *De lege agraria* IV are lost).[129] The *Catilinarians*, frequently cited as *invectivae* in the grammarians and late rhetoricians,[130] often in a progressive numeration,[131] had an independent transmission.[132] The *pro Rabirio perduellionis reo* circulated separately as well. Parts of it survive in a palimpsest fragment in a seventh- or eighth-century manuscript in uncial from Lorsch, Vatican, Pal. lat. 24.[133] Badly preserved in the already cited manuscript Vatican lat. 11458, Poggio's autograph identified by Campana and containing Statilius's subscription (the final part is missing),[134] the speech seems to have been included in at least two alphabetical sequences, the first of which, *pro Rabirio perduellionis reo-pro Roscio Amerino*, is transmitted in the Vatican palimpsest,[135] the second one, *pro Rabirio Postumo, pro Rabirio perduellionis reo, pro Roscio comoedo*, in Poggio's manuscript (part I).[136] The speeches on Rullus's agrarian law also went their own way. Published individually, they were not grouped together in a homogenous corpus; the earliest attestation of a general title, *Kalendis Ianuariis de lege agraria*, in reference to the second speech, occurs in the late fourth-century grammarian Charisius (122.12B).[137] No matter whether the *codex* emended and revised by Statilius Maximus should be identified with the archetype from which all the medieval manuscripts descend, errors and lacunae shared by all the extant witnesses (the beginning of the first speech is missing) would lead us to suggest a derivation from a common ancestor.[138]

More fortunate were the seven-speech corpus of the *Verrines* and the fourteen-speech group designated as *Philippics* or *orationes in Antonium*, both of them surviving in the manuscript tradition in their integrity.

---

[129] The only extant fragment of *De Othone* (or *Cum a ludis contionem avocavit*) is preserved in Arusianus Messius's collection of *Exempla Elocutionum* (*GL* 7.490.23): Crawford 1994: 217–8. A fragment of the *De proscriptorum filiis* survives in Quint. *Inst.* 11.1.85 (Crawford 1994: 208–11).

[130] E.g. Diom. *GL* 1.330.1; Prisc. 558.2 *RLM*; Schem. Dian. 75.13 *RLM*.

[131] E.g. Arus. *GL* 7.485.22; 26; 487.21.

[132] For the medieval tradition of the *Catilinarians*, see Rouse-Reeve 1983: 62–5; on the influence of the Catilinarian corpus over the centuries, a good survey is Dyck 2008a: 13–6.

[133] Published for the first time by Niebuhr 1820. On the Vatican palimpsest, see Fohlen 1979. The fragment preserving parts of the *pro Rabirio perduellionis reo* is numbered 10 (219). See also Seider 1979: 124–7.

[134] Two fragments of the speech, probably to be integrated after the lacuna at § 19, survive in Quint. *Inst.* 7.1.16 and Serv. A. 1.13. The expression *Cicero De Prasio* in Bede's *De Orthographia* (19.285-6Jones) has tentatively been interpreted as referring to the *pro Rabirio perduellionis reo* (*p* would be an abbreviation for *pro, rasio* a wrong transcription of *rabio*, in turn a contraction for *rabirio*); if this were the case, the sentence *Solis innocens acclamationibus punitus est*, attributed to Cicero by Bede when commenting on the use of the verb *clamo*, should be inserted after chapter 19 of the speech (see Piacente 2014: 97–108).

[135] Niebuhr 1820: 66.   [136] Rouse-Reeve 1983: 91.   [137] Pecere 1982: 112f.

[138] Marek 1983: VI–VII.

To begin with the former, Cicero mentions the invectives against Verres as *Accusationis libri septem* at *Orat.* 103, adopting a progressive numeration for the five speeches included in the second *Actio*.[139] A pentadic system prevailed still in the second century CE, as may be argued from Tacitus (*Dial.* 20.1),[140] Quintilian (*Inst.* 11.2.25), and Gellius (1.7.1; 13.21.16),[141] and then was replaced by a constant oscillation between five- and seven-numeration in the grammatical-rhetorical tradition from the third century onwards.[142] By reason of their length the seven-book body of the *Verrines* hardly entered a volume with other speeches and presumably formed a natural-seeming codex collection. This may have contributed to their propagation as a whole, and there is enough evidence that the oldest written testimonies of the *Verrines*, from which the medieval manuscripts (falling essentially into a French-German family and an Italian one) descend, preserved the seven-book *corpus*.[143]

Moving to the speeches against Antony, Cicero himself called them *Philippics*, intending with this term the creation of a compact corpus of orations named after the Demosthenic model, reproducing then the same political-cultural operation envisaged in the "consular" corpus. As illustrated by Manuwald,[144] the use of the title *Philippici* (*libelli*)/ *Philippicae* (*orationes*) in the Brutus–Cicero epistolary exchange[145] indicates a coherent group, at least in the author's intention. The coexistence of the terms *orationes in Antonium/orationes Antonianae* and *orationes Philippicae* in later periods, as titles of both the whole corpus and individual speeches,[146] denotes the political and literary character of the corpus[147] that survived as a uniform and homogenous group to the medieval manuscripts. The corpus, as we know it, consists of fourteen speeches.[148]

---

[139] Cic. *Orat.* 167; 210.   [140] Mayer 2001: 150–1.
[141] It is not clear whether Sen. *Suas.* 2.19 refers to the entire seven-speech corpus of the *Verrines* or simply to the second *Actio*. On the passage as a critique of the audiences' inattention and negligence in listening to declamations (not as a sign of unfamiliarity with Cicero's text) and the *Verrines* as a paradigmatic instance of a text too long to be plagiarized, see McGill 2005.
[142] Piacente 2014: 75–86.
[143] On the medieval tradition, see Rouse-Reeve 1983: 68–73. For the possible derivation of all the manuscripts of the *Verrines* from the same ancestor, see Clark 1918: 261–5.
[144] Manuwald 2007: 1.47–54; 2008. See also Kelly 2008.
[145] Cic. *ad Brut.* 2.3.4 (2 SB); 2.4.2 (4 SB); Manuwald 2007: 1.51.
[146] Cf. Quint. *Inst.* 3.8.46; Plut. *Cic.* 24.6; 48.6; Lact. *Div. Inst.* 2.3.5; 6.18.28 (*Philippicae*); Gel. 1.16.5; 1.22.17; 6.11.3; 13.1.1; 13.22.6; Quint. *Inst.* 8.4.8; 8.6.70; Macr. 1.5.5 (*Antonianae/orationes in Antonium*).
[147] Manuwald 2007: 1.53–4.
[148] On other *Philippics* that were lost (Arusianus Messius mentions *Philippics* 16 and 17: GL 7.467. 15–7), see Kelly 2008: 22. On a fragment of a lost Philippic, preserved in Sen. *Suas.* 7.5, see Piacente 2014: 23–31.

The oldest and chief manuscript, Vatican, Arch. S. Pietro H. 25 (**V**), written in northern Italy in the ninth century, preserves *Philippics* 1–13.10[149] and is likely to be descended from a *vetustum exemplar*. The other manuscripts apparently derive from mutilated ancestors that might once have contained the whole collection.[150]

A few words are in order, finally, about the speeches delivered by Cicero before Caesar in the years 46–45 BCE, namely the *pro Marcello, pro Ligario* and *pro rege Deiotaro*, commonly called *orationes Caesarianae*. Circulating as independent speeches, they were grouped under the collective heading of *Caesarianae* no earlier than the fourth century CE.[151] Quite interestingly, they appear to have been connected to the *Catilinarians* in the medieval transmission. Granted that the manuscripts belonging to the most reliable family (α) descend from an archetype written in an uncial hand of the late fourth or early fifth century (comparable to the ms. Vatican lat. 5757, the *De republica* palimpsest), it is safe to assume a circulation of the entire corpus, jointed to the *Catilinarians*, at the end of the fourth century.

About other collections or registers of speeches nothing certain can be said. Evidence is too scanty to suppose an *ordo orationum* in Nepos's or Tiro's biographies.[152] Groupings of speeches may be reconstructed from literary texts in the Silver Age, but they appear to be arbitrary arrangements, not defined by textual criteria, and none of them seems to have had any effect on the medieval transmission. The couple *pro Tullio-pro Caecina*, mockingly defined as "unendurable" (*immensa volumina*) by Aper in Tacitus *Dial.* 20.1, pairs off two civic law speeches for their legalistic background and unusual length. Palimpsest leaves of the *pro Caecina* and the *pro Tullio* are preserved in a seventh-century manuscript of Augustine from Bobbio, Turin D.IV.22 (discovered by A. Peyron in 1820),[153] but they do not seem to have been related to each other in sequence. Similarly, in another passage from the Tacitean dialogue (39.5)

---

[149] The manuscript contains in addition Cic. *Pis.* 32–74, *Flac.* 39–54 and *Font.* 11–49; the first work is written in uncials, the other portions in Caroline minuscule. Rouse-Reeve 1983: 73–4; see also Fedeli 1982: V-VI.

[150] Clark 1918: 162–211; Rouse-Reeve 1983: 74–8. On the textual transmission of the *Philippics*, see Magnaldi 2013.

[151] Probus *Cath.* (GL 4.27.18); Serv. *G.* 2.131; *A.* 5.187; 11.438; *Adn. Lucan.* 2.637; 7.260; 313.

[152] On the comparison between Dionysius of Halicarnassus's *Life of Dinarchus* and the biographies of Cicero, which may have included a chronological arrangement of the speeches, see Lo Monaco 1995: 49–50. The name of Tiro has been integrated in a five-space lacuna in the manuscripts of Asconius's commentary, at the point at which the scholiast debates the chronology of the *in Pisonem* (1.6-8C); Kiessling-Schoell 1875: XII–XIII (on Nepos as alternative, see Hildebrant 1894: 15n3; Stangl 1912: *ad loc.*); see also Lo Monaco 1990: 172–3; 1995: 47–8.

[153] Reeve 1992.

Maternus's list of Cicero's speeches, irrespective of chronological consistency,[154] mentions models of republican eloquence fueled by popular participation and social strife.

To sum up so far, it emerges that the *Catilinarians* (separated from the rest of the consular *corpus*), *Verrines* and *Philippics* owed their preservation as a coherent unity throughout the centuries to their textual compactness. The speeches *De lege agraria*, initially disseminated as independent texts, were reassembled in a homogeneous corpus at a later period. Analogously, the creation of a group under the common heading of *Caesarianae* seems to have been a late assemblage of orations sharing Caesar as their addressee. One of the fundamental tenets of classical philology is that the formation of textual bodies – collecting works that had originally been propagated separately – constituted one of the first formative stages in the tradition of the Latin classics.[155] As a defining step towards the current status of the medieval tradition, this form of textual aggregation took place in the fourth and fifth centuries, that is to say, in that age in which the birth and diffusion of the *codex*, "a book-form in which a high number of gatherings could be bound together,"[156] performed as a significant medium of conservation of a large part of classical literature.

The only other case of textual aggregation, which may have taken place in the third and fourth centuries, is the corpus of Cicero's *post reditum* speeches (all delivered in a couple of years, 57/56 BCE), transmitted in its totality in a ninth-century Tours manuscript, Paris. lat. 7794. But before attempting a reconstruction of the history of the *post reditum* corpus, we need to track down traces of textual organization of Cicero's oratory in antiquarian-historical writings and commentaries starting from the Julio-Claudian and Flavian periods. The first-century CE scholar Fenestella, "the source most frequently referred to by Asconius after the *acta*,"[157] commented upon antiquarian, legal and prosopographical aspects of Cicero's speeches,[158] as shown by his remarks on the name of Piso's father-in-law (Asc. 5.8-9C), Cotta's law on the tribunate (Asc. 66.24C)[159] and the condemnation of the Vestal virgins in 113 BCE (Asc. 45.27–46.6C).[160] His attention to chronology, already examined in the miscalculation of the year

---

[154] Maternus mentions the speeches on behalf of Cornelius (delivered in 65), Scaurus (54), Milo (52), Bestia (56) and Vatinius (54); on the passage, see Mayer 2001: 209–11.
[155] Pecere-Reeve 1995; De Nonno 2010: 35–6. [156] De Nonno 2010: 35. [157] Marshall 1985: 53.
[158] On Fenestella's antiquarian and historical production, see Marshall 1980.
[159] Marshall 1980: 350; 1985: 55. On Fenestella as Asconius's source, see Lichtenfeldt 1888: 55–9.
[160] The dates of two of the trials of the Vestals are provided by Fenestella in Macrobius 1.10.5–6: Marshall 1980: 351; 1985: 196.

of delivery of the *pro Roscio Amerino* (Gel.15.28.4), is also reflected in the misdating of Milo's journey to Lanuvium, dated at 17 February instead of 18, as correctly reported by the *Acta* (Asc. 31.13-17C). Though Fenestella's interest in Ciceronian chronology is beyond question, assuming a chronologically organized register of Ciceronian orations is pure speculation. Asconius's criticism of Fenestella, apparently affected by "donnish rivalry,"[161] does not reveal anything about a possible list of speeches. Presumably, Fenestella restricted himself to including generic indications about the chronology of the speeches in his annalistic-style historical account.

## Asconius Pedianus and the *Scholia Bobiensia*

Asconius Pedianus's commentary offers space for a wider discussion. Generally held to have been written under Nero's rule,[162] the text, as we possess it, consists of only five orations commented on, the *in Pisonem, pro Scauro, pro Milone, pro Cornelio* and *in toga candida* in sequence.[163] The medieval manuscripts preserve the speeches in chronological disorder, if we are correct in assuming that the *pro Cornelio* and *in toga candida*, delivered in 65 and 64 respectively, preceded the group including the *in Pisonem, pro Scauro* and *pro Milone*, all delivered between 55 and 52 BCE. Madvig attributed this chronological confusion in the manuscripts to either an accident of transmission – that is, the displacement of the quaternions containing the three-speech group *in Pisonem-pro Scauro-pro Milone* between the two parts of the commentary on *pro Cornelio* – or the incompetence of the copyist, who transcribed the manuscript discovered at St. Gall in the summer of 1416 by Poggio and Bartolomeo da Montepulciano from several copies,[164] adding material as it came to hand.[165]

Scholars argue that Asconius expounded on more than the five speeches currently covered by the commentary.[166] They count no less than sixteen

---

[161] Marshall 1985: 55.
[162] On Asconius's life, senatorial background and literary activity (in addition to his commentary on Cicero's speeches, he wrote a *librum contra obtrectatores Vergilii*, mentioned in Donatus's *Life of Vergil*, a work on Vergil and a *Life of Sallust*), see Marshall 1985: 26–32.
[163] The title of the speech as transmitted in the manuscripts of Asconius is *In senatu in toga candida contra C. Antonium et L. Catilinam competitores*.
[164] Madvig 1828: 32–3; see also Marshall 1985: 1.
[165] On Asconius's textual tradition, see Clark 1907: X–XXII; Reeve 1983. Sozomeno's copy (**S**) surviving in Pistoia, Bibl. Forteguerr. A.37, and Bartolomeo's lost copy (**M**), which generated Florence, Laur. 54.5, were used for the first time by Kiessling-Schoell 1875; Poggio's copy survives in Madrid 8514 (X.81) and was first used by Clark 1907.
[166] Reeve 1983: 24; Marshall 1985: 2.

orations.[167] The number would include the speeches surviving in the *scholia Bobiensia*, apparently indebted to Asconius for some parts, and the invectives against Verres, later commented on by Ps. Asconius.[168] From a series of "straight-out references"[169] it has been postulated that Asconius commented on the *Catilinarians*,[170] the speeches on the agrarian law,[171] *pro Vatinio*[172] and the speech in support of Manilius's proposal.[173] On the ground of cross-references to points Asconius had previously remarked on, one might also suppose that Asconius produced a commentary on the speeches *pro Oppio*,[174] *pro Sestio*,[175] *de domo sua*[176] and *pro Sexto Roscio Amerino*;[177] the latter is confirmed by the previously discussed diatribe over the age of Cicero at the time of the speech's delivery.

While one may plausibly infer that the commentary on the five speeches that has come down to us represents only a selection (not authorial) of a larger commentary on a number of Cicero's orations, the earliest form of the commentary remains a subject of debate.[178] Nothing proves a chronological arrangement of the orations or any order other than the one transmitted. A different, more "positive," story may be narrated about second- and third-century collections of orations. In 1814 A. Mai discovered part of a commentary on Cicero's speeches in the *scriptio inferior* of a Bobbio palimpsest, written in an uncial hand of the later fifth century, preserved in the Ambrosian Library in Milan (E.147 sup, now S.P.9/1–6.11).[179] The manuscript was later reused at the end of the seventh century to put together a Latin translation of the Acts of the Council of Chalcedon. It was still extant in Bobbio in the fifteenth century, as attested by an *Inventarium librorum* of 1461. Mai initially argued for attribution of the text to Asconius Pedianus. In 1828 Madvig demonstrated Asconius's unequivocal influence on the commentary.[180] The discovery of another, consistent section of the same commentary in the Vatican part of Bobbio palimpsest (Vat. Lat. 5750) induced Mai to opt for an undetermined assignment of the corpus of scholia to a *rhetor perantiquus*.[181]

---

[167] Kiessling-Schoell 1875: XIV–XX; Clark 1907: X.   [168] Marshall 1985: 11–19.
[169] Marshall 1985: 2–4.   [170] Asc. 6.3-8C.   [171] Asc. 10.4-6C.   [172] Asc. 18.1-2C.
[173] Asc. 57.1-2C; cf. also 64.17-8C; 65.3-5C; 65.16C.   [174] Asc. 66.19C.
[175] Cf. Asc. 8.12-3C; 11.14-8C.
[176] Asconius's note on *Pis.* 62 (15.13-5C) might refer either to Cic. *Ver.* 2.1.37 or *dom.* 35 (Marshall 1985: 9).
[177] Cf. Asc. 45.22-3C.   [178] Marshall 1985: 21.
[179] On the Bobbio palimpsests, see Lo Monaco 1996: 678–9; 691–3; 2012: 3.
[180] Madvig 1828: 142.   [181] Mai 1828: XI–XII.

*Asconius Pedianus and the* Scholia Bobiensia 79

The Ambrosian (CLA III.28)[182] and Vatican part (CLA I.28)[183] of the Bobbio manuscript, a mosaic of pagan and Christian texts,[184] provide us with extensive remains of a commentary on a number of Cicero's speeches.[185] The commentary, as it has come down to us, includes twelve speeches in the following order: *pro Sulla* (61), *in Clodium et Curionem* (61), *de rege Alexandrino* (65 or 56?),[186] all three transmitted in the Ambrosian part,[187] *pro Flacco* (59), *cum senatui gratias egit* (57), *cum populo gratias egit* (57), *pro Milone* (52), *pro Sestio* (56), *in Vatinium testem* (56),[188] *pro Plancio* (54), *interrogatio de aere alieno Milonis* (53?)[189] and *pro Archia* (62). As the year of speech delivery indicates, the palimpsest presents chronological disorder, arguably due to the confusion and displacement of some four double-leaf gatherings, reassembled in the manuscript in a sequence different from the original one.[190]

It is generally assumed that the *Scholia Bobiensia* are a fourth-century excerpted commentary arising from a larger rhetorical commentary composed in the second century, which in turn might have included further additions from a historical commentary dated at the end of the first century.[191] If the identification of the scholiast with Volcacius, commentator of Cicero's orations mentioned by Jerome (*Adv. Rufin.* 1.16),[192] is plausible, one might establish the approximate date of composition of the

---

[182] In the Ambrosian part the scholia are transmitted by ff. 1–16; 33–52; 117–132; 139–142; 153–154; 159–160; 167–178; 183–194; 315–318; 409–410; 415–416.
[183] In the Vatican part the scholia are contained at ff. 17–28; 31–56; 133–136; 159–164; 169–174; 181–184; 211–226; 229–240; 243–274. For a detailed description of the Vatican part, see Ehrle 1906. For the structure and articulation of the *codex rescriptus*, see Hildebrandt 1907: V–XLIV; Clark 1918: 156–9. In general on the textual history of the scholia, see La Bua 2001: 161 n1.
[184] The palimpsest preserves remains of Fronto's correspondence, the *Explanationes Evangelii S. Iohannis*, fragments of Arian theological writings, a fragment from the *Ascensio Isaiae*, Pliny's *Panegyric* 78.4–80.3, Persius 1.53–104, Juvenal 14.324–15.43 and extracts from Symmachus's speeches.
[185] A partial edition of the scholia, including only the Ambrosian palimpsest, was made by Cramer-Heinrich 1816; Schütz 1823; Beier 1825. The complete text of the preserved commentary was later edited by Orelli-Baiter 1833: 217–376; Orelli-Halm 1845, Hildebrandt 1907, Stangl 1912: 73–179.
[186] On the date of delivery of the *De rege Alexandrino*, see Crawford 1994: 43.
[187] The speech *pro Sulla* occupies ff. 5–6; 33–48; *in Clodium et Curionem* ff. 1–4; 6–16; *de rege Alexandrino* ff. 49–52; Hildebrandt 1907: XXXV–XXXVI.
[188] Four quaternions of the *in Vatinium testem* are in the Ambrosian part, twelve in the Vatican.
[189] On the date and circumstances of the speech, see Crawford 1994: 281–6 (early 52: Lintott 1974: 66).
[190] Hildebrandt 1907: XXIV–XXVI; La Bua 2001: 178–9.
[191] Hildebrandt 1894: 62–3. Stangl 1884a: 430 (for the scholiast as a fourth-century Christian rhetorician with an interest in law and history). For a chronology of the commentary (not excerpted) in the fourth century, see also Schanz 1966–71: 1.448.
[192] Schmidt 1989; Piacente 2014: 49–54 (on Volcacius, cf. also Hier. *Epist.* 70.2). For the identification of the Ciceronian commentator with *Vulcatius Terentianus*, a teacher of eloquence mentioned in the *Life of Gordianus* 25.1, see Buecheler 1908: 194–5; Strzelecki 1961.

commentary in the third and fourth centuries CE, that is, in the period of time that saw the emergence of great commentaries, such as Marius Victorinus's on Cicero's philosophical works or Donatus's on Vergil and Terence.[193] What seems certain is that the *scholia Bobiensia,* in the form of "a set of notes constructed as continuous prose and presented separately from the text itself,"[194] are likely to be only a part of a larger commentary, whose origin might cautiously be traced back to the second and third centuries CE.[195] Whether the copyist of the palimpsest copied out limited sections of the archetype, excerpting the original commentary into the margins of the manuscript, is difficult to say.[196] Yet a process of abbreviation, enlargement and/or contraction, usual in the transmission of scholiastic material,[197] remains a possibility.

That the collection of speeches within the *scholia Bobiensia* represents a selection made from a more substantial corpus of Ciceronian texts seems, furthermore, to be confirmed by a number of places where the scholia include cross-references to discussions not found in the extant text. A note on *Mil.* 16 (118.5-7St) alludes to *Mur.* 75.[198] On a hypothetical series *pro Murena-pro Milone,* Mai suggested an alphabetic order in the Vatican part of the palimpsest.[199] A commentary on the *de domo sua* may also be argued on the basis of a scholion on *Sest.* 48 (131.19-20St). There the scholiast reminds his readers of his previous narration of the episode of Decius's *devotio,* evidently referring to chapter 64 of Cicero's speech on the confiscation of his house.[200] Insufficient evidence is available to assume a commentary on the *in Pisonem* and *De lege agraria.*[201] In consideration of some parallels with the set of marginal notes commonly known as the Gronovian scholiast, one might also suppose a commentary on the *Verrines,* but no clear proof of it exists.

Hildebrandt's idea of a commentary on the whole of Ciceronian oratory is not supported by extant evidence.[202] Yet we may conjecture that the

---

[193] Schmidt 1989: 140–1.
[194] Zetzel 2005: 4 (on specific terminology and the distinction between "commentary" and "scholia").
[195] Schmidt 1989: 140.   [196] Schilling 1892: 28; Hildebrandt 1894: 39f.   [197] Zetzel 2005.
[198] For other references to the *pro Murena* cf. 96.4; 104.7; 166.18St; the scholion on *Planc.* 42 (161.1-5St) might be alluding to *Mur.* 46–7.
[199] Mai 1828: 2.105 (after Niebuhr 1820: 66). The couple *pro Murena-pro Milone* appears in the twelfth-century collection of Ciceronian speeches possessed by the abbey of Cluny, together with the *pro Caelio, pro Cluentio* and *pro Sexto Roscio Amerino.* On Poggio's discovery in 1415 of the ms. Cluniacensis 496, see Clark 1905; Rouse-Reeve 1983: 88 (see also Reeve 1984).
[200] For a likely reference to Cic. *Dom.* 129 (or *Har.* 59) cf. 132.31St; cf. also 133.19-20St for an allusion to *Dom.* 20.
[201] Schol. Bob. 108.27-8St (*Pis.* frg. 10 and 14; 62; cf. Asc. 4C); 109.10–2; 132.15St. (*Agr.* 1.20).
[202] Hildebrandt 1894: 9ff; 33ff.

scholiast expounded on more orations than those preserved in the extant text. A chronological arrangement of the speeches has a sustainable rationale. The group including the orations *pro Flacco, cum senatui gratias egit, cum populo gratias egit, pro Sestio, in Vatinium*, with the insertion of the *de domo sua* before the *pro Sestio*, is made up from speeches delivered in a limited range of years, from 59 to 56 BCE. Except for the *pro Flacco*, we are presented with a small corpus of *post reditum* speeches, all delivered in 57/56 BCE after Cicero's return from exile. Even if we are unable to discern the criteria by which other groups of speeches were assembled,[203] with the exception of the couple *pro Murena-pro Milone* (originally preceding *pro Flacco*), the presence of a compact corpus of post-exile speeches makes a chronological order of orations more than plausible. A note of the scholiast, placed at f. 229 of the Vat. Lat. 5750 after the *explicit* of the *pro Flacco* and the *incipit* of the post-exile thanksgiving speech to the Senate (*Oratio cum senatui gratias egit*),[204] may corroborate this point (108.16-22St):

> Oratio<num ordo> Tulli<anarum> ... <pos>tulabat ut praecedentis commentario eam subiceremus quae inscribitur: Si eum P.Clodius legibus interrogasset, quae oratio videtur post mortem eius inventa. Sed quoniam plurimae consequentur in quibus <eadem> paene omnia dicturus est, eximendam numero arbitratus sum, quando rebus nihil deperdat, quae sine dubio in aliarum tractatione reddentur; nam plurifariam et de consulatu suo et de exilio et contra eundem Clodium locuturus est. Consideremus igitur ...

> "If I had followed the order of the Ciceronian speeches (as I see it), I would have commented upon the speech titled *If P. Clodius had sued him according to law*, appending it to the commentary of the preceding oration. This speech seems to have been discovered after Cicero's death. A good number of speeches, in which the author replicates the same arguments, will follow, however: for that reason, I considered it useful to cut this speech off from the collection. Nothing of Cicero's argumentation shall be missed: there is no doubt that these points will be dealt with in the commentaries of the following speeches, for more than once Cicero will be talking about his consular deeds and his exile, opposing his enemy Clodius. Let us then start with ..."

A model of rhetorical *interrogatio*, as the scholiast himself makes clear in the *argumentum* to the speech *de aere alieno Milonis* (169.20–170.2St),[205]

---

[203] The criteria behind the sequence *pro Plancio-de aere alieno Milonis-pro Archia* are difficult to individuate, though a confusion of the quaternions from the copyist (and a consequent chronological disorder) should be taken into consideration.
[204] For the title of the oration cf. Cic. *Att.* 4.1.5 (73 SB*Att*); *Planc.* 74; schol. Bob. 153.7St; 165.5St.
[205] La Bua 2001: 164–7.

the *Si eum P. Clodius legibus interrogasset* is removed from the *ordo orationum* for being a verbose – and pedagogically irrelevant – repetition of exile topoi. Nothing allows us to suppose a literary evaluation or judgment over the authenticity of the oration behind the commentator's words. I have already addressed the question of the authenticity of the speech, rebuffing contrived attempts to demonstrate its Ciceronian authorship.[206] From a detailed examination of the unusual *inscriptio*, in the form of a hypothetical subjunctive, compared with the traditional title system in Roman oratory, we may infer that the speech was a declamatory exercise about the exile topic.[207] Analogous syntactic structures as declamation incipit are not uncommon.[208] The "Cicero-versus-Clodius" theme, in special reference to the hackneyed diatribe over the illegal condemnation of the Catilinarian conspirators, in addition, was a good topic in the declamation schools, as confirmed by late rhetorical treatises.[209]

As a fictitious *controversia* over the Cicero-Clodius struggle, the *Si eum P. Clodius legibus interrogasset* fills the chronological gap between 59, the date of the *pro Flacco*, and 57 BCE, the year of Cicero's thanksgiving speech to the Senate, his first official oratorical performance after his return from banishment. The collocation of the declamation in the oratorical corpus is conceivably not casual. The *ordo orationum*, which the scholiast was drawing on, evidently included a pre-exile speech focusing on a Cicero-Clodius judicial discussion about the invalidity of the legal measures adopted by Cicero against the conspirators. The tedious replication of defensive arguments by the orator, priding himself on his consular actions and counterattacking Clodius' invectives and threats, compelled the commentator, unconcerned about the speech's authorship, to spare his pupils a boring, useless reading.

Undeniably, the exile motif captured the aspiring declaimers' imagination. It is in fact to the classroom environment that we should trace the origin of another spurious speech, the *Pridie quam in exilium iret,* which opens the collection of *post reditum* speeches in the earliest extant medieval witness, the mentioned Tours manuscript, Paris lat. 7794 (**P**).[210] A sort of

---

[206] La Bua 2001: 167–9.   [207] Crawford 1984: 264–5.
[208] E.g. Sen. *Con.* 1.2; 2.5; 4.7; 7.2; [Quint.] *decl. min.* 294; 332.
[209] Cf. Fortunatianus 84.15 *RLM*. For a similar theme, cf. also [Quint.] *decl. min.* 348: Winterbottom 1984: 550.
[210] Rouse-Reeve 1983: 58–9. In general on the tradition of the *post reditum* speeches, see Peterson 1910; Klotz 1912; 1913; Clark 1918: 266–80; Klotz 1919–23: 1. *praef.* See also Maslowski 1981: V–XXXV; also important is Maslowski-Rouse 1984.

patchwork of Ciceronian themes and sentences,[211] the *Pridie* has been dated to the second century, in view of its linguistic *facies* and its alleged dependence on Plutarch's biography.[212] Yet some lexical peculiarities and the predilection for rhythmic structures validate the interpretation of the *Pridie* as a third- or fourth-century product of rhetorical schools, a *prosopopoeia* on the classic theme of Cicero's exile.[213]

The spurious speeches *Si eum P. Clodius legibus interrogasset* and *Pridie quam in exilium iret* share not only the general subject, that is, the pathetic representation of Cicero accused of illegality in handling the Catilinarian conspiracy and struggling over his liberty before his opponent's attacks, but also their scholastic destination and, most notably, their collocation as introduction to the *corpus* of *post reditum* speeches within a general catalogue of Cicero's oratorical texts. The formation of this *corpus* remains a baffling issue. Of the speeches preserved in the Tours manuscript, namely the *post reditum in senatu, post reditum ad Quirites, de domo sua, pro Sestio, in Vatinium testem, de provincis consularibus, de haruspicum responsis, pro Balbo* and *pro Caelio*, the thanksgiving speeches to the senate and the people must have been thought of as an organic unity, given their similar structure and intonation.[214] A passage from Iulius Victor's *Ars Rhetorica* (402.35 *RLM*) suggests a successive enlargement of the group to the speech "On the answers of the omen-interpreters."[215] However that might be, the presence of a compact group of post-exile orations within the *scholia Bobiensia* would lead us to assume a selection and arrangement of part of the speeches delivered in 57/56 no later than the third or fourth century CE, as suggested by an approximate chronology of the Bobbio commentary. If the tradition of the *post reditum* speeches goes back to an archetype written in capitals with insular influences, moreover, as claimed by Klotz[216] and Clark,[217] it is conceivable to date the formation of the entire corpus to the fourth and fifth centuries, in the same period of time in which other collections of speeches, such as the *Agrarians* and

---

[211] For borrowings and echoes from the *Verrines, Catilinarians, de domo sua* and rhetorical works, see De Marco 1991: 13–25; on the influence of the consular speech *pro Rabirio perduellionis reo* on the fictitious declamation, see Gamberale 1997. A good presentation of the "Ciceronian culture" of the rhetorician, who freely combines passages and commonplaces from different orations, is in Gamberale 1998.
[212] De Marco 1991: 5.   [213] Gamberale 1998: 74.
[214] For a detailed analysis of the two first *post reditum* speeches, see Mack 1937: 18–48; Nicholson 1992: 23ff.
[215] La Bua 2001: 188.   [216] Klotz 1919–23: I.XXXVI–XXXVIII.
[217] Clark 1918: 270; Rouse-Reeve 1983: 60.

*Caesarians,* assumed their definite conformation.[218] From an insular center a copy of the corpus of *post reditum,* circulating as a whole (albeit independent traditions exist for the *post reditum ad senatum* and the *pro Caelio*),[219] must have reached France, perhaps the Carolingian court, in the late eighth or early ninth century, producing then **P**.[220] The corpus was still complete in the middle of the twelfth century, as shown by a florilegium compiled at Orléans (*Florilegium Gallicum*), containing extracts from all the post-exile speeches, with the only exclusion being the *post reditum ad senatum*.

To recap, uncertainty reigns about the number of speeches commented on in the *Scholia Bobiensia,* the original extent of the commentary and the arrangement system of the texts. As we have seen, any assumption about a commentary covering the entire Ciceronian corpus, including the consular speeches, the remaining post-exile orations (*pro Caelio, de provincis consularibus, pro Balbo*) and the speeches delivered in the years following the *pro Archia,*[221] is not supported by the limited evidence available. Yet the *scholia Bobiensia* represent a significant step in the direction of a systematic organization of Cicero's oratorical production on chronological and thematic criteria. Even if we assume an *ordo orationum* limited to specific groups of orations, the plausible chronological arrangement followed by the scholiast, whether preexistent or not to the composition of the commentary, testifies to a scholarly attempt at cataloguing an impressive, confused body of material, presumably for didactic reasons. The history of the medieval transmission of the post-exile orations, furthermore, owes much to the Bobbio *scholia*. Though it is not possible to state whether the scholiast made his own compilation or rather found an already arranged small collection of *post reditum* speeches, his intervention in cutting off the spurious *Si eum P. Clodius legibus interrogasset* from the textual sequence and, most importantly, his focus on the shared content of the speeches delivered in 57/56 BC contributed certainly to the consolidation of the post-exile speeches within a unitary textual body. He paved the way for successive additions resulting in the final, current form of the corpus that came, in its entirety, into our earliest written testimonies.

---

[218] Lo Monaco 1990: 51; 1995: 181.  [219] Rouse-Reeve 1983: 60–1.  [220] Rouse-Reeve 1983: 60.

[221] For a commentary on the speeches delivered before Cicero's consulship in the first forty-five lost quaternions of the palimpsest, see Schmidt 1989: 140–1 (who contemplates the possibility that the scholiast commented on all the post-exile speeches, with the exclusion of *de haruspicum responsis* by reason of his religious beliefs).

## From Publication to the Medieval Manuscripts: Cicero's Speeches in the Schools

Both Asconius's commentary and the *scholia Bobiensia* are visibly embedded in the Roman educational system. They are the product of a regular teaching practice. Following a long-established tradition, Asconius dedicated his work to his sons.[222] A *scriptor historicus*, as defined by Jerome,[223] he supervised his sons' education and provided them with a historical *explanatio* of main passages from Cicero's speeches. His simple notes, usually under the heading *enarratio*,[224] aimed to refine his sons' *historiarum cognitio* and implement their knowledge of Ciceronian oratory.[225] Similarly, the dominant rhetorical tone of the vast majority of the notes included in the Bobbio commentary enables us to postulate an intended readership and audience of budding orators. As we shall see, by expounding upon *status* and *qualitas* of the *quaestio*, in particular in the *argumenta* to any given speech,[226] and scrutinizing Cicero's arguments and aesthetic devices[227] the Bobbio scholiast offers us a specimen lesson at the school of rhetoric. If we turn to the chronological arrangement of groups of speeches, moreover, it evidently sprang from the didactic function of the commentary, intended as a companion work to students engaged in acquiring a comprehensive vision of Cicero's rhetorical technique. The removal of *Si eum P. Clodius legibus interrogasset* from the textual order, as we have observed, is likely to have been encouraged by the limited pedagogical impact of this pre-exile speech.

Asconius and the Bobbio commentary preserve texts not surviving in the medieval tradition. We have already touched upon the loss of a number of orations. Precise reasons for this aspect of Cicero's reception are obviously irrecoverable. As a general principle in the tradition of classical literature, "the nature, modalities and varying outcomes of the transmission process of individual texts (or groups of texts) from ancient Latin literature are the products of several intervening factors, essentially

---

[222] Marshall 1985: 32–33. On the practice of dedicating scholarly works to sons in antiquity, see Kaster 1988: 67.
[223] Jer. *Chron.* under the year of Abraham 2092 (= 76 CE, the seventh year of Vespasian's rule): Marshall 1985: 27–8.
[224] Marshall 1985: 36–7.
[225] Marshall 1985: 37. On the historical perspective dominating Asconius's commentary, intended as a rehabilitation and defense of Cicero as the last orator of the vanished republic, a Roman version of the Greek Demosthenes, see Bishop 2015: 284–94 (who places, however, too much emphasis on the scholiast's obligation to defend Cicero's reputation as a historical figure).
[226] E.g. schol. Bob. 110.10; 112.15–7; 175.14-20St.
[227] E.g. schol. Bob. 90.20; 109.4–5; 120.28; 121.23–4; 167.10St.

unique to their situation."[228] Historical and cultural changes, technical and material factors and "the capricious nature of chance"[229] may have contributed to the disappearance of oratorical texts, regardless of their relevance to Roman educational system. Although we are unable to explain why a number of Cicero's speeches did not escape destruction, it appears that the position that some of the orations had in the curriculum impacted on the current status of the medieval tradition. Thus it is worth attempting to provide readers with a general outline of the role played by the school in the survival of Cicero's orations by drawing on the surviving papyri and palimpsests, examined in parallel with both literary and grammatical-rhetorical sources.

Arguably, all the speeches preserved in the manuscripts of Asconius and the Bobbio scholiast had a good diffusion in the school. To begin with Asconius, the speech *pro Cornelio*, ranked among Cicero's best oratorical performances and exploited as an exemplar of long-winded text in the orality versus writing debate, as we have seen,[230] represents perhaps the most blatant example of how the didactic function attached to a text did not prevent its loss in the successive stages of textual transmission. In spite of an extensive use of the speech as rhetorical model,[231] judicial case law (in relation to the *crimen maiestatis*)[232] and linguistic exemplar,[233] the *pro Cornelio* is known only by indirect external witnesses and none of it survives in the medieval manuscripts. The other lost speech, *In toga candida*, circulated in the schools as an instance of rhetorical *vituperatio*. With the exception of two citations in Quintilian,[234] however, we have no further evidence about the speech. It probably suffered from a comparison with more refined collections of blame *loci*, such as the *in Pisonem* or the *Second Philippic*.

We come now to the Bobbio commentary. The lost speech *de rege Alexandrino* appears to have been appreciated in the school as a valuable set of rhetorical *loci* and figures. It was selected as illustrative of a specific kind of *partitio (communis)*[235] and used to clarify the figure of

---

[228] De Nonno 2010: 32.   [229] De Nonno 2010: 33.   [230] Cf. chapter 1, pp. 39–40.
[231] Quint. *Inst.* 4.3.13; 4.4.8; 5.11.25; 5.13.26; 6.5.10; 8.3.3–4; 9.2.55; 9.4.14; 9.4.122–23; 11.3.164; Grill. *In Cic. Inv.*, 1.5 (35.28Jakobi: *Corn.* II frg4Crawford); 1.20 (89.90: 89.93Jakobi: *Corn.* I frg1Crawford); 1.21 (93.85Jakobi: *Corn.* I frg3 Crawford); Fortunatianus 123.18 *RLM*; Mart. Cap. 170.14Willis; Romanus Aquila 26.31 *RLM*.
[232] Quint. *Inst.* 5.13.18; 7.3.35. See Ferrary 2009.
[233] Prisc. *GL* 2.292.16; 294.2; 361.25; 435.2; 453.24; 527.12; 530.19; Arus. *GL* 7.453.18; 453.20; 455.26; 456.20; 459.9; 465.17; 468.21; 468.23; 468.25; 469.6; 470.9; 470.12; 471.3; 497.11; Prob. *GL* 4.212.8; Ps-Acr. Hor. *Sat.* 1.2.67; schol. Iuv. 7.118; Serv. *A.* 11.708.
[234] Quint. *Inst.* 3.7.2; 9.3.94.   [235] Fortunatianus 115.1 *RLM*.

*compensatio*.²³⁶ The speech *de aere alieno Milonis* owed its place in the scholiast's collection to its evident connection with the Milo-Clodius theme and its interpretation as model of rhetorical *interrogatio*. Yet we have no further references to the speech in late grammarians and rhetoricians. Quite singular, finally, is the case of the *in Clodium et Curionem*. Put into circulation without the orator's permission (Cic. *Att.* 3.12.3; 3.15.3),²³⁷ the speech had a good diffusion in the schools, as attested by citations found in Quintilian (who inserts the oration into the group of Ciceronian invectives, *vituperationes*),²³⁸ Iulius Rufinianus²³⁹ and Nonius Marcellus.²⁴⁰ Material from the speech survived in a palimpsest leaf in the seventh-century manuscript discovered by A. Peyron in the library of Turin (D.IV.22) and subsequently destroyed by fire in 1904.²⁴¹

Our knowledge of the reception of Cicero as *scholasticus auctor* depends, in part at least, on the surviving papyri.²⁴² We possess remains of nine Ciceronian papyri, the largest majority of which preserves material from the *Verrines* and the *Catilinarians*. Dated to the Augustan or Julio-Claudian period, P. Giessen Kuhlmann III.5 (P. Iand. 5.90 inv. 210; CPL 20; CLA 8.1201),²⁴³ a papyrus roll containing *Ver.* 2.2.3–4, is "the oldest witness to any Latin text preserved in medieval manuscripts."²⁴⁴ To the second half of the fourth or the first decades of the fifth century may be dated the parchment fragment of *Ver.* 2.5.39–41, P. Mil. Vogl. inv. 1190 (from Oxyrinchus?).²⁴⁵ In a fifth- to sixth-century half uncial hand are written another three papyri fragments from Oxyrinchus, namely P. Ryl. III.477, which contains §§ 33–37 and 44–46 of the *Divinatio in Q. Caecilium* (CPL 23; CLA 2.226),²⁴⁶ PSI I.20, preserving the first speech of the *Actio Secunda* §§ 60–63 (CPL 27; CLA 3.286)²⁴⁷ and P. Oxy. VIII.1097 + P. Oxy. X.1251 (Brit. Libr. inv. 2057 = P.Lit. Lond. 143) + P. Köln I.49 (inv. 2554 + 3292), which incorporate some chapters

---

[236] Romanus Aquila 26.16 *RLM*; Mart. Cap. 183.2Willis.  [237] Cf. chapter 1, pp. 32–3.
[238] Quint. *Inst.* 3.7.2; cf. also 5.10.92; 8.3.81; 8.6.56; 9.2.26.  [239] Iul. Ruf. 38.8–9; 39.8 *RLM*.
[240] Non. 535L; 700L; 745L; 861L; 863L (frgg21-24Crawford).
[241] Peyron 1824. On the Turin palimpsest, see Clark 1918: 138–46; Rouse-Reeve 1983: 56–7; Reeve 1992; Crawford 1994: 231.
[242] Mertens 1987: 191–5; De Paolis 2000: 43–7 (with further bibliography).
[243] Pack 1965: 2920. See Seider 1975; 1979: 104 n1; 112–13; Buzi 2005: 62; 97 (no. 8): Ammirati 2015: 13.
[244] Rouse-Reeve 1983: 55 n6. For the description of the Giessen fragment, see Seider 1979: 113–4; Ballaira 1993: 83–99.
[245] Gallazzi 1984; Buzi 2005: 62; 98 (no. 10).
[246] Pack 1965: 2919; see Seider 1979: 110–11; Buzi 2005: 98 (no. 11); Ammirati 2015: 19–20; Scappaticcio 2015: 472–5.
[247] Buzi 2005: 62; 100 (no. 16).

from the first and second speeches of the *Actio Secunda* (CPL 24–25; CLA 2.210).[248]

Extracts from the speeches against Catiline are contained in other papyrus scraps. Three fragments from a fourth- or fifth-century papyrus, P. Vindob. inv. G 30885 a+e + P. Ryl I 61 + P. Vindob. inv. L 127 (CPL 21–22; CLA 10.1519; 2.224),[249] are bilingual texts, arranged in parallel columns, one with the Latin original of the first, second and third Catilinarians, one with a Greek translation.[250] We have also remains from another fourth- or fifth-century papyrus, P. Duke inv. 798 (*antea* P. Robin. inv. L 1), bearing traces of nine lines from the First Catilinarian (§§ 13–15),[251] + P.Barc. inv. 128a-149a,[252] preserving the text of *Cat.* 1.6–29 and 30–33, followed by the whole of *Cat.* 2.[253]

Other papyri deserve mention. P.Oxy. 1097 preserves the final chapters of the *de imperio Cn. Pompei* (§§ 60–65; 70–71), in addition to *Ver.* 2.1.1–4;[254] fragments of the *pro Caelio* (§§ 26–35; 35–42 fol. 1; §§ 42–49; 51–55 fol. 2) are transmitted by P. Oxy. 1251.[255] Two Köln papyri contain *de imperio Cn. Pompei* 62–5 (P. Köln 3292) and 68–9 (P. Köln 2554), in addition to *Ver.* 2.1.1–3 (P. Köln 3292) and 2.1.7–9 (P. Köln 2554).[256] Finally, parts of the *pro Plancio* (11.27–8; 19.46–7) are preserved in a fifth-century parchment fragment (in uncial hand) from Hermopolis Magna, P. Berol. 13229 A + B (CPL 26; CLA 8.1043).[257] The fragments of *de imperio Cn. Pompei*, *pro Caelio* and *in Verrem*, collected in P.Oxy 1097 + 1251 (=P. Lit. Lond. 143) and in the Köln papyri (=P.Köln I.49), come from the same manuscript, a fifth-century Oxyrhynchus papyrus written in a small and

---

[248] *Ver.* 2.1.1–4 (P. Oxy. 1097); 2.2.3; 12 (P. Oxy. 1251); 2.1.7–9 (P. Köln 2554); 2.1.1–3 (P. Köln 3292). See Pack 1965: 2918; Hagedorn 1969; Buzi 2005: 98–9 (no. 12).
[249] Pack 1965: 2922–2923; Buzi 2005: 63; 99 (no. 13).
[250] Seider 1979: 128–32. On P. Vindob. inv. G 30885 a+e, see Gerstinger 1937; Axer 1983; 1992; on P. Vindob. inv. L 127, see Harrauer 1982; Maehler 1983. In general see Rochette 1996: 70–9; Capasso 2008: 75. On the Ciceronian bilingual papyri, see Radiciotti 1998: 121–2; Internullo 2011–12; Sánchez-Ostiz 2013; for the digraphism of the Ciceronian papyri, see Radiciotti 2013.
[251] Willis 1963.  [252] Edited by Roca Puig 1977.
[253] The text of the *Catilinarians*, preserved in ff. 1-24a, is followed by a *Psalmus Responsorius* (ff. 24b-28b), a Greek anaphora (ff. 29b-30a), a Greek liturgical text (ff. 30b-32b) and the so-called *Alcestis Barcinonensis* (ff. 33a-36a). See Buzi 2005: 84–7; Ammirati 2015a: 16. For the papyrus fragment of *Cat.* 1.5, see Manfredi 1995.
[254] Hunt 1911: 153–8.
[255] Grenfell-Hunt 1914: 142–61. See Pack 1965: 2918; Seider 1979: 112; 134–5.
[256] Seider 1979: 134–5. See Kramer-Hübner 1976: 1.107.
[257] Pack 1965: 2924; Seider 1979: 109; Buzi 2005: 99 (no. 14). For the fragment of the *pro Plancio*, see Ricci 1910; Olechowska 1984: 7. On the literary texts from Hermopolis, see Minnen-Worp 1993; the papyrus of the *pro Plancio* is numbered 109 (cf. 170).

upright half uncial hand.[258] A close analysis of the readings preserved in the papyrus, in relation with the palimpsests and other written sources, points to a general textual heterogeneousness.[259] The papyrus roll may have contained other Ciceronian speeches.[260] It is conceivable to suppose a small collection of unrelated orations, presumably arranged for didactic purposes and organized by literary genre and author, in line with what we know of the physical organization of ancient booklists.[261]

The remains of papyrus roll containing parts from the *Verrines* and *Catilinarians* are indubitably monuments to the popularity of Cicero's celebrated invectives among readers and students in Latin-speaking regions and Romanized Egypt. It is well known that both the *corpora* soon acquired the status of standard textbooks in the curriculum.[262] Both the *Verrines*, as "a model of prosecution techniques,"[263] and the consular offensives against Catiline, as a powerful example of political invective, served as potentially useful sourcebooks for instructing ancient students of rhetoric in making a right use of argumentative strategy and persuasive aesthetic devices.[264] It has been observed that "à Cicéron les lecteures férus de la literature latine et la jéunesse studieuse d'Egypte demandaient des modéles d'art oratoire."[265] Such a request was evidently fulfilled by the *in Verrem-in*

---

[258] Maslowski 1995: LXXXV–LXXXVI. On the formal features of many of the surviving Ciceronian papyri and palimpsests and the use of the practice of capitulation, meant as a division of the text into sections each beginning with a line that protrudes left, see Butler 2014 (see also Ammirati 2015a).

[259] Grenfell-Hunt 1914: 143.   [260] Seider 1979: 134.   [261] Houston 2009: 243f.

[262] It is interesting to note that, as far as the *Catilinarians* are concerned, the papyri preserve lines from the first and second speeches, less from the third, none from the fourth. This seems to correspond with the status of the rhetorical and grammatical literature, as it emerges from the Index of Authors and Passages quoted in Quintilian's editions, the collection of the *Rhetores Latini Minores* by Halm, and the corpus of the *Grammatici Latini* collected by Keil. In Quintilian we count twenty references to the first speech, two to the second, and one each to the third and fourth; in the late rhetoricians more than thirty citations to the first speech are balanced by only five to the second, three to the third and four to the fourth; in the grammatical literature, finally, we know of seventy quotations from the first speech, thirty-six from the second, sixteen from the third, and fifteen from the fourth. All this leads us to conclude, in Dyck's words, that "the orations were keenly studied in rhetorical schools, albeit ... the first much more than the other three" (Dyck 2008a: 13).

[263] Tempest 2013: 45.

[264] Dyck 2008a: 14 (for the *Catilinarians* as "fodder for school children to the end of the ancient world"). For allusions to the speeches against Catiline in late pagan and Christian writers, see MacCormack 2013: 262; 288; 301; see also Moroni 2009 for the reuse of the *Catilinarians* in fourth- and fifth-century legal texts. On the exordium of Ausonius's *Gratiarum Actio* as modeled after the proem of the *First Catilinarian*, see Green 1991: 239–40; Balbo 2013a. For the reworking of the *incipit* of Cicero's *Fourth Catilinarian* in Ambrosius's *Sermo contra Auxentium* (ep. 75a.1), see Testard 1985; on quotations from the *Catilinarians* in Jerome, see Hagendahl 1958: 287; Adkin 1992; Ferreres 1995; Augustine's references to the orations against Catiline (especially I–III) are examined by Hagendahl 1967: 43–7; 481.

[265] Cavenaile 1958: 22. On the presence of Cicero in the East, see now Licandro 2017: 265–85.

90    Beyond the Author: Cicero's Speeches

*Catilinam* couple, which must have been thought of as having a considerable impact upon the linguistic and rhetorical education of Egyptian students.[266]

Such a didactic approach to Ciceronian oratory is well illustrated by the discovery of bilingual Greek–Latin papyri. A single example may suffice. P. Ryl. III.477 provides Greek and Latin scholia,[267] paraphrases, interlinear glosses and a word-by-word parallel Greek translation of the *Catilinarians* that unfolds the scholastic nature of the material support. These bilingual literary papyri, generally manufactured from the third to the sixth century in Roman Egypt, served the pragmatic function of teaching elementary Latin to middle-class "Latinophone" Greeks in the *pars Orientis* of the empire.[268] Need for a basic knowledge of Latin from members of the Egyptian bureaucracy evidently boosted the production of bilingual texts,[269] especially from the authors most read in the schoolrooms, along with Greek–Latin lexica and bilingual transliterated glossaries, which assisted students in exercises of pronunciation and translation.[270]

Pedagogical reasons may also account for the inclusion of the speech in support of the Manilian law and that on behalf of Caelius in the collection preserved in the Oxyrhynchus papyrus P.Lit. Lond. 143 + P.Köln I.49. To begin with the former, the praise of Pompey's virtues, rated as an excellent example of middle style by Cicero himself,[271] figured as a model of prose panegyric in late pagan literature.[272] Evidence of a rhetorical use of the speech is relatively scanty.[273] Yet Cicero's deliberative speech must have

---

[266] On the *Catilinarians* and the *Verrines* yielding material for students attending the provincial schools in the later Roman empire, see Reynolds 1983: 61; Ward 2015: 311 (who points out that the usage of these speeches "was inferential and illustrative rather than scholarly or extensive"). For echoes from the *Verrines* in late literature, see MacCormack 2013: 263–4 (especially on Ammianus Marcellinus and Cicero; see also Fletcher 1937; 377–81; Blockley 1998); 289; 303; for quotations from the *Verrines* (regarded as *nobilissimae orationes*) in Augustine, see Hagendahl 1967: 50–1; 481.

[267] On the relationship between the scholia and Ps. Asconius, see Cavenaile 1958: 75.

[268] Rochette 1996: 76–9; 2015: 636–7. Brashear 1981: 32 points to "the pedagogical value of transliterated texts in the initial phase of learning a language." On the influence of the Greek translations of Cicero's *Catilinarians* in papyri on the alphabetical bilingual glossaries, see Loewe 1876: 186–94; Ferri 2011b: 159–60; see also Schubert 2012.

[269] Rochette 1996: 62–9. On the diffusion of Latin in the oriental regions of the empire, see in general Rochette 1997; 2013. On the interaction of Greek and Latin linguistic systems and bilingualism in the ancient world, see Adams-Janse-Swain 2002; Adams 2003a.

[270] Brashear 1981: 32–4; Axer 1992: 256. For bilingual glossaria, see Kramer 1983; 2013. In general on the education system in Graeco-Roman Egypt, see Cribiore 1996; 2001 (see also Scappaticcio 2015: 13–31).

[271] Cic. *Orat*. 100–3. Cf. chapter 1, p. 20.

[272] On Cicero's praise of Pompey as a model of "proto-imperial panegyric," see Braund 2012: 106–7.

[273] Surprisingly, Cicero's *pro lege Manilia* appears to have been of limited or no significance to rhetorical theory. The speech is cited by Quintilian on only one occasion (*Inst.* 2.4.40). Only three quotations occur in late rhetoricians: Fortunatianus (114.15 *RLM*) mentions the speech within

been a significant overall model for Pliny's *Panegyricus* and the late antique Gaul *XII Panegyrici Latini*.[274] In combination with the Caesarian speeches and the *Philippics*,[275] Cicero's political tribute to Pompey's grandeur served as an anthology of eulogistic *loci* and sophisticated praise conventions.[276] Furthermore, Cicero's panegyric enjoyed a fair fortune in the Antonine age. As we have seen, Gellius lingers over two alleged syntactic anomalies in the speech, namely the preference for the expression *in potestatem fuisse*, instead of *in potestate fuisse* at § 33 (wrongly tagged as solecism: 1.7.16–7), and the form of the perfect *explicavit* (in place of a weaker and rhythmically feeble *explicuit*) at § 30 (1.7.20), in order to defend Cicero's linguistic oddities against the criticism of *vulgus semidoctum*.[277] Fronto depicts himself as making excerpts from the speech (*Ant.* 4.1: 105.1-3Hout); in *De bello Parthico* (205.2-15Hout) he warmly commends the eulogy of Pompey, who was awarded the title of the Great "not so much by reason of his own merits as of Cicero's praises," for its abundance of meaningful insights into military topics.

The *pro Caelio* too had a substantial diffusion in the ancient school. Frequently referred to in Quintilian's work,[278] the speech furnished rhetoricians and declaimers with an extraordinary collection of *loci* and *figurae*.[279] The portrait of Clodia, the "Medea of the Palatine," provided declaimers with an invaluable model for the character of the "poisoning stepmother" (together with that of Sassia in the *pro Cluentio*).[280] It has also been demonstrated that Apuleius's protean genius manipulated Cicero's figures of Oppianicus and Clodia for the vivid and colorful representation

---

a discussion of the diverse types of "partition" (*partitionis genera*); Iulius Victor (438.25–7 *RLM*) and Emporius (572.17 *RLM*) both refer to the oration as a model of middle style.

[274] Maguiness 1932: 44; Galletier 1949: IX; Nixon-Rodgers 1994: 17; De Trizio 2006: 63; 66.

[275] Levene 1997 (for the influence of Cicero's Caesarian speeches on the panegyrical tradition). See also La Bua 2010b (on the exploitation of the proemial motif of the *insolentia loci* in Cicero's speech in defense of king Deiotarus in Eumenius's panegyric for the restoration of the schools, *Pan. lat.* 9/4).

[276] Manuwald 2011; Hutchinson 2011: 140.

[277] By contrast to what seems to emerge from Gellius's analysis, the use of the speech *de lege Manilia* as a linguistic sourcebook was rather limited in the grammar schools (we know of only seven occurrences).

[278] After the *pro Cluentio*, the *Verrines* and the *pro Milone*, the defense of Caelius stands at the top of Quintilian's list of references to Ciceronian orations (*Inst.* 3.8.54; 4.1.31; 39; 2.27; 5.13.30; 6.3.25; 8.3.22; 4.1; 9.2.15; 39; 47; 60; 99; 4.64; 97; 98; 102; 104; 11.1.28; 1.68; 12.10.61; 11.6).

[279] Romanus Aquila 23–25 *RLM* ; Iul. Ruf. 40.16; 42.10 *RLM*; *Schem. Dian.* 72.19; 73.6 *RLM*; Fortunatianus 124.9; 124.26 *RLM*; Victorin. 250.14 *RLM*; Iul. Sev. 360.27; 369.27 *RLM*; Jul. Vict. 403.27; 426.21; 435.8; 439.36 *RLM*; Mart. Cap. 164.24; 174.9Willis; Isid. 521.1; 558.4; 603.32 *RLM*.

[280] For the characterization of the poisoning stepmother in Roman declamations (cf. Sen. *Con.* 6.6; 9.6.1), as modeled on the figure of Sassia in Cicero's *pro Cluentio*, see La Bua 2006: 201n68. On the figure of the *meretrix* in the *Minor Declamations* and the connections between *Decl. Min.* 297 and Cicero's *pro Caelio*, see Pingoud 2016: 184–88.

of Aemilianus and Pudentilla in his *Apology*.[281] The speech, a standard textbook in the rhetorical school, enjoyed a lasting vogue throughout the centuries.[282] Quoted by Fronto[283] and Gellius,[284] and alluded to in several cases in the corpus of the *XII Panegyrici Latini*,[285] the *pro Caelio* was widely used by late grammarians and scholiasts.[286] By the fourth and fifth centuries it entered the *post reditum* collection, transmitted by the Tours manuscript.[287]

The place of the *pro Plancio* in formal training in rhetoric is more difficult to track down. The speech is mentioned twice in the *Attic Nights* of Gellius, namely at chapter 1.4 in connection with Cicero's use of an *enthymeme*, elucidated by the rhetorician Antonius Iulianus (*Planc.* 68),[288] and at chapter 9.12 for the exemplification of the double meaning, active and passive, of the word *infestus* (*Planc.*1). By contrast to late grammarians,[289] the oration is astonishingly absent from rhetorical handbooks. The motivations behind this silence are difficult to grasp. The fact that the speech was commented on by the Bobbio scholiast makes the question more complicated, in light of the rhetorical nature of the commentary itself. In absence of further evidence, we limit ourselves to stating that the text was evidently deemed as useful to rhetorical training. In addition to the usual definition of the *quaestio* in the *argumentum* (153.13St), the scholiast remarks upon the oratorical features of Cicero's discourse on more than one occasion.[290] The inclusion of the speech in a collection of Ciceronian texts with didactic purposes favors our

---

[281] Harrison 2000: 44–45; May (R.) 2010: 176 n2-3.  [282] Dyck 2013: 26–8.
[283] Cf. *Anton.* 3.1 (97.5-10Hout). On the correspondence between the text of *Cael.* 13, as Fronto had it, and that preserved in the manuscript Pal. lat. 7794, see Hout 1999: 251.
[284] Gel. 17.1.
[285] Plin. *Pan.* 45.4; 85.7; *Pan. lat.* 2 (7).7.4; 12.3; 3 (11).10.3; 4 (10) 3.4; 9 (4) 2.3.
[286] *GL* 1.389.13; 2.489.15; 3.217.13; 437.35; 5.48.16; 6.468.25; 7.118.28; 465.14; 475.3; 487.26; 489.15; 505.5; 508.3; Serv. *A.* 1.203; 2.148; *Buc.* 2.25; Don. Ter. *Eun.* 1072; *H.* 551; *adn. Luc.* 1.602; 2.92; 5.372; Ps.-Acro Hor. *carm.* 3.12.2–3. See also Macr. 3.14.15.
[287] About a late commentary on the *pro Caelio* there is uncertainty. In the set of marginal notes and glosses, commonly ascribed to the Gronovian scholiast **D** (after Stangl), we read two brief comments on the words *versura* (*Cael.* 17) and *sodalitas* (*Cael.* 26). These notes, preserved in the *excerpta* of the ms. Lugd. Octav. 88 (ff. 11r-13r) and published in *CGL* 5.658.33–8 and 659.1, are placed immediately before four glosses on the text of the *Miloniana* in Stangl's edition (323. 28-31St); the commentary on the *pro Caelio* would have followed that on the *pro Milone*, in turn coming after that on the *Pompeiana* (for a further reference to the *pro Caelio* cf. the note on Cic. *Verr.* 1.15 in the Gronovius scholiast **B**, 335.13St; about this passage cf. also Quint. *Inst.* 9.4.98).
[288] Cicero uses this *enthymeme* with slightly different wording at *Red. Pop.* 23 and *Off.* 2.69; cf. also schol. Bob.164.5-24St.
[289] Arus. *GL* 7.479.3; 461.12; 462.21 (the other passages listed in the *Index Scriptorum* by Keil, as taken from the *pro Plancio*, are actually mentioned by the grammarian as deriving from the *pro Sulla*: cf. 7.511.10; 7.511.18); Prisc.*GL* 2.108.18; 335.20; 341.4; 345.2; 3; 527.22.
[290] E.g. 156.32; 158.9; 159.15; 160.6; 163.15; 168.6-9St.

appreciation of the *pro Plancio* as a school text from whose reading students trained in the rhetoric schools could profit.[291]

The papyri can make a good contribution, though only partially, to the study of Cicero as a school author in antiquity. They preserve widely read speeches, presumably included in a canon that was formed very early. Of the greatest significance, moreover, is the fact that we have no papyrus remnant of any speech that did not survive the change from scroll to codex and the transition from antiquity to the Middle Ages. Let us now move on to sketch out other aspects of the reception of Cicero as orator in late antiquity by drawing on the extant parchment manuscripts, which range in age from fifth to seventh century. A palimpsest fragment in rustic capitals, Vatican, Reg. lat. 2077 (CLA 1.115), presumably written in northern Italy, preserves consistent parts of *Verrines* 2.1.[292] A large collection of speeches is included in a fifth-century Bobbio palimpsest in rustic capital hand, Taur.A.II.2 (once D.IV.22; CLA 4.442).[293] The manuscript incorporates five leaves of the *pro Caecina* (§§ 6–9; 13–16; 38–41; 47–50; 62–65), 8 and a half leaf of *pro Tullio* (§§ 1–4; 7–11; 23–36; 37–51; 53–56), four and a half leaves of *pro Scauro* (§§ 2–7; 18–28; 31–36; 46–50), three of *pro Quinctio* (§§ 50–53; 66–70; 92–93), six and a half of *in Pisonem* (§§ 17–23; 33–36; 47–50; 61–63; 64–66; 75–79; 79–82), one of *de lege Manilia* (§§ 40–43), twelve of *pro Cluentio* (§§ 1–7; 18–24; 32–38; 74–78; 92–94; 101–103; 129–131; 145–147), five of *pro Milone* (§§ 29–32; 34–36; 72–75; 86–88; 92–95), and three and a half of *pro Caelio* (§§ 38–42; 54–56; 66–69). The same book transmits also a palimpsest leaf of the *Verrines*, and a consistent number of passages from the *Actio Secunda in Verrem* occur in a fifth-century palimpsest in rustic capitals, Vatican, Reg. lat. 2077 (CLA 1.115). Leaves of the *pro Scauro* (§§ 8–25; 29–45), *pro Tullio* (§§ 4–23), *pro Flacco* (§ 5) and *pro Caelio* (§§ 71–75) are as well preserved in a seventh-century Bobbio manuscript, Milan, Ambros. R. 57 sup. (now S.P. II.66). All these fragments belong to the same book, a fifth-century manuscript in rustic capitals (CLA 3.362–3). Finally, we possess a seventh- or eighth-century Lorsch manuscript, Vatican, Pal. lat. 24 (CLA 1.77), which contains palimpsest fragments from the *pro Rabirio perduellionis* (§§ 32–38), *pro Sexto Roscio Amerino* (§§ 1–5) and *pro*

---

[291] It should also be observed that the political significance of the speech, intended as a further episode of Cicero's post-exile struggle for *dignitas*, might have promoted its knowledge among ancient readers.
[292] Seider 1979: 105; 111.
[293] Seider 1979: 105–6; for a history and reconstruction of the manuscript, see Reeve 1992.

*Fonteio* (§§ 1–6; CLA 1.76); all these scraps come from the same fifth-century manuscript in uncial.[294]

It is not by chance that all the speeches preserved in the oldest extant manuscripts enjoyed a good reputation in the ancient school. We have already remarked on the reception of the *Verrines, de lege Manilia* and *pro Caelio*. As far as the other texts' afterlife is concerned, we try here to briefly delineate their impact on the ancient education system. Following the speech order as transmitted by the manuscript Taur. A.II.2, we begin with the civil law speeches *pro Caecina* and *pro Tullio*, coupled by Tacitus for their unbearable length in *Dialogus* 20.1.[295] Cicero's high regard for the speech in defense of Aulus Caecina as a classic instance of plain style (*Orat.* 102)[296] might have weighed in favor of appreciation of the oration among the rhetoricians. Quintilian amply draws on the *pro Caecina*,[297] whose opening sentence was reputed to be a model period.[298] From the considerable quantity of quotations in late rhetorical treatises, it seems reasonable to suggest a didactic use of the speech as a valuable sourcebook of rhetorical and legal issues.[299] It is quite probable, furthermore, that the debate over the *interpretatio* of the legal category of *dolus malus* in the interdict *de vi armata*, which characterizes Cicero's treatment of the *quaestio*, played a key role in the composition of fictitious *controversiae* questioning the form, wording and application of the law *de vi*.[300]

Clearly connected is the fact that the rhetorical tradition paired up the *pro Caecina* and *pro Tullio* for their shared emphasis on the concept of *voluntas legis* within a more general interpretation of the *scripti et voluntatis status*.[301] In particular, the (apparently limited) diffusion of the *pro Tullio*[302] seems to have been tied to Cicero's manipulation of the *dolus malus* formula: the legalistic discussion of the letter and the spirit of the law was seen as a fascinating example of *dissimulatio* strategy,[303] a demonstration of Cicero's ability to obfuscate the real point of contention and divert the judges' attention from the *quaestio principalis* (in this

---

[294] On the Ciceronian palimpsests, see now Lo Monaco (2012).  [295] Cf. supra p. 75.
[296] Cf. chapter 1, p. 20.
[297] Cf. Quint. *Inst.* 4.2.49 (§ 11); 4.2.132 (§ 23; cf. also Iul. Vict. 427.19 *RLM*); 6.3.56 (§ 27); 5.11.33 (§ 34); 5.10.68 (§ 37); 7.3.17 (§ 42); 5.10.92 and 7.3.29 (§ 43); 7.6.7 (§ 51); 5.10.98 (§ 55); 9.3.22 (§ 82).
[298] Quint. *Inst.* 9.3.80; Romanus Aquila 27.25–30 *RLM*; Mart. Cap. 184.10–4 Willis.
[299] Fortunatianus 107.30; 113.24 *RLM*; Victorin. 193.25 *RLM*; Iul. Vict. 396.33; 35; 400.1; 22; 401.6; 27; 29; 402.23 *RLM*.
[300] On the legal and historical background of *pro Caecina*, see Frier 1983.
[301] Fortunatianus 107.30 *RLM*.
[302] Quintilian mentions the speech twice (*Inst.* 4.3.131 on § 14; 5.13.21 on § 56). See also Iul. Rufin. 40.21 *RLM* (§ 52); Iul. Vict. 397.8 *RLM* (§§ 25 and 34) Mart. Cap. 176.3 Willis (§ 21)
[303] Grill. *In Cic. Inv.* 1.20–21 (93.96 Jakobi); cf. also Victorin. 209.22 *RLM*; Iul. Vict. 419.23–29 *RLM*.

case Tullius's direct involvement in the conflict against Fabius's slaves) to a less relevant topic.[304]

Turning our attention to other speeches transmitted by the Turin palimpsest, the oration on behalf of Scaurus was evidently incorporated in the school canon. Mentioned by Tacitus in *Dial.* 39.9 within a larger group of "popular" speeches, the *pro Scauro*, included in Asconius's commentary, furnished elite male students with a number of rhetorical *sententiae* and *schemata*.[305] In particular, the opening lines served as a model of exordial *prosopopoeia*[306] and an instance of *genus anceps causae*.[307] The *pro Quinctio*, Cicero's earliest delivered speech (81 BCE), attracted fair interest from later rhetoricians,[308] though its scanty use in Quintilian's didactic work argues for a low assessment of the rhetorical and pedagogical potentialities of the text.[309] The invective *in Pisonem*, finally, enjoyed an extraordinary success among grammarians and linguists,[310] in addition to providing students with an extensive repertoire of blame *topoi*.[311]

It is well known that both the *pro Cluentio* and the *pro Milone* met with great success in the schools of rhetoric. To begin with the latter, the reworked speech in defense of Milo was recognized, soon after its dissemination, as Cicero's best oratorical accomplishment. Defined by Quintilian as *pulcherrima* (*Inst.* 4.2.25) and *nobilissima* (*Inst.* 11.3.47), the oration found large employment as a paradigm of rhetorical strategy in the rhetoric schools,[312] not to mention its conspicuous use in the grammarians and scholiasts.[313] The amusing anecdote about the fictitious *in Milonem* by the

---

[304] La Bua 2005.
[305] Iul. Rufin. 47.30 *RLM*; Fortunatianus 123.26 *RLM*. Cf. also Quint. *Inst.* 5.13.28; 40; 6.1.21; 7.2.10 (cf. also Mart. Cap. 164.20 Willis); 9.2.15; 4.122. See also *Adn. Luc.*1.427.
[306] Cf. Quint. *Inst.* 4.1.69 (with further allusion to the presence of the *causa* in the *commentarii*); see also 1.5.8; 11.1.89.
[307] Grill. *In Cic. Inv.* 1.20–21 (94Jakobi).
[308] Romanus Aquila 24.2 *RLM*; Iul. Ruf. 39.28; 41.11; 41.15; 21; 43.22 *RLM*; Fortunatianus 113.24 *RLM*; Victorin. 201.25; 223.4 *RLM*; Iul. Sev. 360.18; 363.20 *RLM*; Mart. Cap. 195.12; 21Willis.
[309] Quintilian cites the speech only twice (*Inst.* 9.3.86; 11.1.89).
[310] Gellius 13.25 quotes the opening chapter of the speech within an erudite discussion about the semantic difference between *praeda* and *manubiae*. The oration must have served as a useful supplement to grammar studies, as may be deduced by the considerable quantity of quotations (thirty-one) registered in the *Index scriptorium* of Keil's edition of the *Grammatici Latini*.
[311] The speech had a marked impact on the panegyrical literature. Pliny the Younger alludes to the invective in *Pan.* 40.3; 56.4; 93.1; likely references to the speech are to be found also in *Pan. Lat.* 9 (4).15.1; 11 (3).1.3; 12 (9).7.1.
[312] On the beginning of the speech as a model of appropriate and rhythmic delivery, cf. Quint. *Inst.* 9.4.74; 11.3.47–51; for judgments on Cicero's tactics in his defense of Milo, cf. Quint. *Inst.* 4.1.20; 31; 3.17; 5.14.20; 6.5.10; 9.4.133; 10.5.20; 11.1.40.
[313] E.g. Diom. *GL* 1.444.8; 467.9; 468.9; 470.23; Char. *GL* I.551.4; Prisc. *GL* 2.105.5; 206.14; 280.8; 307.18; 348.20; 377.5; 393.6; 520.2; 522.24; Arus. *GL* 7.452.24; 26; 454.1; 455.1; 27; 490.15; 494.2; 495.21; 496.4; 500.1; 504.12; 511.7. The speech is cited in the *Adn. Luc.* 1.321 (§ 1); 1.277; 2.252 (§ 10);

declaimer Cestius, reported by Seneca the Elder (*Con.* 3 *praef.* 15–6), implies a good familiarity with Cicero's masterpiece, whose reading was evidently recommended as fundamental to rhetorical training.

In regard to the *pro Cluentio*, we may capture an idea of its marked impact on the curriculum by looking through Quintilian's remarks upon the rhetorical merits of the speech.[314] The most quoted among Cicero's speeches in the *Institutio Oratoria*,[315] the defense of Cluentius, exalted for its excellent articulateness of sentence structure and *ornatus*,[316] attracted Quintilian's interest as a model of rhetorical *iudicium et consilium* (6.5.9), notably as a splendid example of successful judicial strategy aimed at diverting the audience's attention from the *quaestio principalis* towards a pseudo-problem, i.e. the corruption of the trial jury.[317] The literary sensibility of the Silver Age, furthermore, found the speech greatly fascinating. Cicero's emotional style, marked by the use of declamatory *sententiae*,[318] figures of speech and puns, captivated the mind of budding young orators. As Winterbottom remarks, "perhaps Quintilian would have been surprised, had he been miraculously transported to a court addressed by Cicero, to find how Silver the great orator really was."[319]

Contrasting views emerge from a rapid glance at the transmission of other speeches (parts of which are preserved in the Ambrosianus R. 57 sup. and in the Vatican manuscript, Pal. lat. 24). Given the scanty number of references to the speech in late rhetoricians and grammarians, the discourse on behalf of Flaccus apparently had a limited effect on the curriculum;[320] strangely enough, if we reflect upon the fact that Cicero's mockery of the prosecution witnesses commanded attention to the speech as a model of *vis comica*, as may be inferred by

---

1.267 (§ 27); 1.198 (§ 85) and in Pseudo-Acro Hor. C. 1.2.15 (§ 37); chapter 61 is quoted in the scholia of Lactantius Placidus on Statius *Theb.* 2.490.

[314] Mazzoli 1996.
[315] Together with the whole *corpus* of the *Verrines* and *pro Ligario*: Mazzoli 1996: 486.
[316] For the praise of the exordium cf. Quintilian *Inst.* 4.1.35–6; 6.5.9; 8.6.65; 9.4.68; 74; 92; 101.
[317] Mazzoli 1996: 491. On Cicero's strategy in the *pro Cluentio*, see Stroh 1975: 194–227; Classen 1985: 31–121; on Cicero's self-portrait as a professional advocate, see Burnand 2004.
[318] We should keep in mind the celebrated *sententia* of *Cluent.* 199: *uxor generi, noverca filii, filiae paelex*, quoted by Cicero at *Orat.* 107 and recalled by Seneca *Con.* 6.6 and 9.6.1: Winterbottom 1982a: 260.
[319] Winterbottom 1982a: 266.
[320] A general reference to the *pro Flacco*, together with the *pro Fonteio*, is to be found in Iulius Victor *RLM* 423.9. The opening sentences of the speech are cited as an example of *paradoxon* in Isidorus *RLM* 520.23, whereas Grillius in his commentary on Cicero's *De inventione* 1.21 (94.3Jakobi) refers to the exordium of the oration to exemplify *ratio causae ab nostra persona*. As to the grammarians, only three quotations from the speech occur in the *Exempla Elocutionum* of Arusianus Messius (*GL* 7.458.26; 465.10; 493.22).

Macrobius *Sat.* 2.1.13.[321] Additionally, the comments of the Bobbio scholiast upon the rhetorical, linguistic and legal features of the speech[322] make a strong case for the inclusion of the oration in the standard curriculum.

Similarly, the consular speech *pro Rabirio perduellionis reo,* which had a detached transmission, unconnected to that of the other orations included in the consular *corpus* arranged by Cicero in 60 BCE,[323] seems at first glance to have exerted a negligible impact on the education system, if we judge from the remarkable paucity of references to the speech in secondary sources.[324] Yet Cicero's praise of the discourse as a model of magniloquent style (*Orat.*102) must have had an impact on how the school received the speech. The cited *prosopopoeia* on Cicero's exile, the *Pridie quam in exilium iret,* peppered with borrowings from the *pro Rabirio,*[325] is illustrative of a considerable acquaintance with the consular oration on the part of late declaimers. Moreover, if the possible existence of a commentary on the *pro Rabirio* by the third-century scholar Sacer, as suggested in the second book of the *Ars grammatica* of Flavius Sosipater Charisius (273.22B),[326] is taken into consideration, one might conclude that Cicero's defense of Rabirius attracted much interest from antiquarians and literary critics.

The use of the *pro Sexto Roscio Amerino* for didactic instruction is easily proved.[327] We have already pointed out that the oration, deemed a model of Asian exuberant style, as recalled by Cicero himself at *Orator* 107 in reference to his description of the punishment (the *poena cullei*) reserved to

---

[321] The *iocus* in *pro Flacco* is said by Macrobius to have been found in the work of Furius Bibaculus. On Cicero's use of "ironic" devices, such as puns and *aprosdoketa,* in the speech, see Haury 1955: 139–40; Maselli 2000: 22–24 (on this question, cf. chapter 4, pp. 246–7). The only mention of the *pro Flacco* in Quintilian (*Inst.* 11.1.89) alludes to Cicero's tactic of bringing discredit on the credibility of the Greek witnesses (§ 62).

[322] E.g. rhetorical features 94.1–6; 98.30; 101.23; 102.23; 103.23; 105.28; 107.23St; linguistic peculiarities 97.14–6; 104.19; 107.9St; legal questions 97.33–98.2St.

[323] Cf. supra p. 73.

[324] Quintilian cites the speech in four cases: cf. *Inst.* 5.13.20; 7.1.16 (general citations); 11.3.169 (§ 18; also quoted in Iul. Rufin. 46.6; 21 *RLM*); 6.1.49 (§ 24). Gellius (12.3) elaborates on the origin of the term *lictor* (from *ligare*) in *Rab.* 13, relying on the *auctoritas* of Valgius Rufus.

[325] Gamberale 1997; 1998. See also Niebuhr 1820: 68. Cf. supra pp. 82–3.

[326] Suringar 1854: 200; Wessner 1920. Since Charisius's *Ars* incorporates parts of a Latin grammar by C. Iulius Romanus, who was active at around 250–270 CE, it is safe to assume a date for Sacer's work no later than mid- or the second half of the third century. In general on Charisius's and Romanus's chronology, see Kaster 1988: 392–3; 424–5; Schenkeveld 2004: 1–4; 29–30.

[327] For Cicero's oration as a model for parricide trials, see Winterbottom 1982b; Berry-Heath 1997; see also Dugan 2005: 307.

parricides (§ 72),³²⁸ furnished would-be orators and declaimers with a valuable collection of *topoi* related to cases of parricide.³²⁹ The speech must have had an established place in the curriculum. The great number of quotations in rhetorical,³³⁰ grammatical³³¹ and exegetical literature³³² corroborates our understanding of the pedagogical value attached to Cicero's youthful discourse in defense of Roscius, which is also likely to have been expounded on by Asconius.³³³ By contrast, little can be inferred from extant evidence about the scholastic circulation of the speech on behalf of Fonteius (*pro Fonteio*). Quintilian cites the oration in only two cases.³³⁴ Among the late rhetoricians Iulius Victor shows a good knowledge of the text.³³⁵ No citations of the speech occur in the grammarians.

To conclude this section, the speeches preserved in the earliest written testimonies, ranging in date from the first to the fifth or sixth century CE, represent only the smallest part of Cicero's output. Natural accidents of textual transmission prevent us from reading and appreciating speeches that must have been deemed fundamental to the training of upper-class students. As Ward notes, "admirable though this survival pattern may seem, it contains items which modern philology has rejected, and there were many opportunities for textual corruption inherent in the medieval conditions of survival."³³⁶ Yet the evidence put forward so far suggests that a fairly narrow canon of Cicero's speeches was formed early – certainly, before the transition from late antiquity to the Middle Ages. It might also be tempting to affirm that the initial stage of the textual transmission of Cicero's oratory, i.e. the preservation and propagation of the speeches (not

---

[328] It should be added that a late commentator on the speech, the Gronovian scholiast **D**, inserts the speech into the category of the "middle style" (*inter medias haec oratio ponitur*), by reason of Cicero's colored passage about the parricide's punishment (3c2.2St).

[329] Cf. also Val. Max. 4.5; 8.1.a13; 9.11.2.

[330] Quintilian *Inst.* 9.2.53 (general reference); 4.2.3; 19 (§ 60); 126.4 (§ 72); 9.2.41 (§ 98); Fortunat. 110.20; 112.25; 114.11 *RLM*; *Schem. Dian.* 71.14; 73.17; 74.20; 75.17 *RLM*; Iul. Rufin. 43.8; 44.22; 45.10; 47.10 *RLM*; Victorin. 204.6; 210.6; 221.26; 226.13; 15; 229.18; 269.37; 38 *RLM*; Sulp. Vict. 323.15 *RLM*; Iul. Vict. 377.12 *RLM*: Mart. Cap. 152.17; 164.25; 169.20; 172.19; 181.22Willis; Grill. *In Cic. Inv.* 1.20 (87.30Jakobi).

[331] Charisius 267.9 (§ 2); 264.20 (§ 3); 274.19 (§ 4); 147.20 (§ 6); 349.1 (§ 21); 244.25; 295.21 (§ 50); 87.18B (§131); Diom. *GL* 1.389; 393.22; 395.18 (§ 1); 390.17 (§ 2); 402.10 (§ 64); Char. *Excerpta GL* 1.547.26; Prisc. *GL* 2.381.7; 534.24; 3.7.18; 37.9; 72.21; 75.2; 76.28; 366.17; Prob. *GL* 4.212.22; Serg. *GL* 4.431.30; Pomp. *GL* 5.162.24; Phoca *GL* 5.426.24; Eutych. *GL* 5.471.4; Agroec. *GL* 7.119.17; Bede *GL* 7. 228.20; Dosith. *GL* 7.394.24; 404.18; 420.16; 17; Arusian. *GL* 7.451.24; 462.16; 462.23; 468.1; 470.5; 481.6; 485.18; 486.14; 492.10; 493.7; 495.19.

[332] We have a good number of marginal notes on the speech in the Gronovian scholiast **D**: 301. 13–316.6St.

[333] Cf. supra p. 78.  [334] Quint. *Inst.* 6.3.51; 11.1.89.

[335] Iul. Vict. 397.18; 400.12; 423.10 *RLM*. Cf. also Mart. Cap. 187.17-9Willis (*Font.* frg12).

[336] Ward 2015: 310.

infrequently arranged in small groups or collections), was sensibly affected by the role played by the text in liberal education in late antiquity. To put it another way, teaching practice as institutionalized in the ancient school, with its emphasis on texts that could raise standards of education, was crucial to the survival (or loss) of Cicero's speeches. Taken individually, all the speeches served, at different levels, as rhetorical and linguistic models in liberal schools. Given the incredible proportions of the scholastic propagation of Ciceronian oratory, the picture offered by the papyri and our earliest manuscripts is necessarily partial and incomplete – it is worth being reasserted. But if Cicero never died, this was thanks to the schools, which functioned as a sort of "life insurance" against the loss of a great part of Cicero's oratorical masterpieces. Papyri, palimpsests and parchment scraps preserved and propagated a set of exemplars, whose vital function to liberal education had never been questioned throughout the centuries.

CHAPTER 3

# *Between Praise and Blame*
## *Ciceronian Scholarship from the Early Empire to Late Antiquity*

Cicero was "not the name of a person, but of eloquence itself."[1] Quintilian's famous judgment best illustrates the posthumous ancient evaluation of Cicero's cultural legacy. The name of Cicero immediately evoked for later generations rhetorical brilliance and mastery of the Latin language.[2] Everyone, including his opponents, granted Cicero immortal fame as a writer and paid homage to his linguistic and oratorical excellence.[3] Yet Cicero was one of the most controversial figures of the Roman republic. His life, his political history and his death elicited multiple responses from later authors and stimulated reflections on questions of Roman identity.[4] Recently, Gowing has drawn attention to the ambivalent approach to Cicero in the early imperial age.[5] By juxtaposing the positive, eulogistic, portrait of Cicero built up by Quintilian with the equivocal presentation of the orator's life and achievements in Seneca the Younger, Gowing has pointed to the divergent attitude to Cicero in the literary texts subsequent to his death. If Cicero's authority as a prose writer and orator was absolute, as a "player on the historical stage, his impact is seen to be minimal."[6] Held up as a rhetorical model, Cicero was marginalized as a historical figure at the same time.[7] The limited consideration shown the republican orator in the Augustan age is an eloquent testimony to the fact that Cicero "had not earned through his actions a place in the Roman moral and ethical universe that manifested itself in the ever-evolving *exemplum* tradition."[8]

---

[1] Quint. *Inst.* 10.1.112 (*non hominis nomen, sed eloquentiae*). For Quintilian's veneration of Cicero cf. *Inst.* 2.16.7 (Cicero's divine eloquence); 2.5.20 ("love" of Cicero); 9.4.16 (Cicero as *magnus auctor*).
[2] For a good survey of Cicero's oratorical and rhetorical legacy, see Kennedy 2002; see also Clarke 1965. On the reputation of Cicero as a historical and literary figure in the first century, see Winterbottom 1982a; see also Ferguson 1962b; Gambet 1963; Richter 1968.
[3] Sen. *Suas.* 6.24.  [4] Dench 2013.  [5] Gowing 2013.  [6] Gowing 2013: 239.
[7] On Cicero's relegation to a world of aesthetic ideality and the disembedding of the aesthetic from politics, see Dressler 2015: 147.
[8] Gowing 2013: 236.

Let us enlarge upon this point. Remarkably, the name of Cicero is absent from a good part of Augustan literature. This is not to say that Cicero was virtually "proscribed," as incautiously suggested.[9] But it is beyond doubt that the Augustan writers showed little interest in Cicero's biography, an indirect proof that they never endowed Cicero's political and historical achievements with exemplary value.[10] To focus on Vergil, it has been observed that the Augustan poet deliberately omits any mention of Cicero in his survey of Roman history in Book 6 of the *Aeneid* and in the description of the shield of Aeneas in Book 8 (ll. 668–70), where a tortured Catiline and Cato the Younger are paired up to exemplify the opposition between the revolutionary and the defender of law and republican freedom.[11] Whether Vergil was hostile to Cicero, it is hard to say. Rejecting the long-held similarity between the orator and rabble-rouser Drances, depicted as a "typical *popularis* demagogue" in Book 11 of the *Aeneid* (ll. 336–42), and Cicero,[12] it is safer to assume that Vergil was reluctant to promote Cicero as a positive *exemplum* and a model of political integrity.

It was Cicero the orator and writer, as distinct from Cicero the man and politician, that appealed to the Augustan writers. When Vitruvius, in the preface to Book 9 of his treatise *On Architecture* (9. *praef.* 17), singles out Cicero's rhetorical works (together with Lucretius's philosophical work and Varro's *On the Latin language*) as a model for his intellectual project, he implicitly reduces Cicero to a cultural icon, stripped of any political or historical significance.[13] Similarly, in Manilius's *Astronomica* (1.794–5) Cicero is included among the dead heroes in the Milky Way "on account of the wealth of his eloquence" (*censu . . . oris*).[14] It is also important to remember the influence of Cicero's rhetorical and theoretical works on Horace's literary epistles.[15] Furthermore, Cicero's speeches served as

---

[9] Weil 1962: 46. On this point see Gowing 2013: 235.
[10] Interestingly, a resurgence of interest in Cicero's life began at the beginning of the fourteenth century, thanks to Petrarch's investigation. See Cook 2009.
[11] Highet 1972: 141–5; 284–5; Degl'Innocenti Pierini 2003: 4–5. See also Savage 1941.
[12] On the question, see La Penna 1985; Horsfall 2003: 116 (with bibliography). For the "Ciceronian" character of Drances, see Quinn 1968: 241; Canfora 2006: 3–4. On the architecture of Drances's speech, see Estèves 2013.
[13] On Cicero's role in Vitruvius's encyclopedic culture, see Romano 2003. For the image of the well-educated architect as modeled on that of the Ciceronian orator in the *De oratore*, see now Nichols 2017: 8–9.
[14] Volk 2009: 233.
[15] The influence of Cicero's *De officiis* on Horace's *Odes* is examined by Dyck 1996: 40–1. For a recent interpretation of Horace's *Carm.* 3.17 to Lamia as a respectful tribute to Cicero's death, see Marciniak 2011b.

subtexts for Propertius's elegies[16] and Ovid's exile poetry.[17] Beyond doubt, Cicero was referred to or acknowledged as an authority on rhetoric.[18] But none of the Augustan writers regarded Cicero's personal and political life as worthy of eternal memory.

In the Augustan age we find, then, the beginnings of a skeptical treatment of Cicero as a person. Yet traces of hostility to the republican orator and statesman may be detected already in Cicero's lifetime. We start with Catullus 49, a thanksgiving poem addressed to Cicero, generally dated to 56 BCE.[19] The poem is commonly interpreted as an ironic derision of Cicero's political and oratorical pretensions.[20] The formal, solemn apostrophe to Cicero as "the best of all advocates" (*optimus omnium patronus*), in opposition to Catullus's self-definition as the "worst of all poets" (*pessimus poeta*), encourages us to regard the poem as a mock-dedication in which Catullus nicely ridicules the rhetorical achievements of the vaunting orator, at the same time subtly sneering at Cicero's bad reputation as a poet.[21]

It is usual to think of Sallust as unsympathetic to Cicero.[22] We do not intend, of course, to resolve this controversial issue. But it is worth remembering that, if Sallust's admiration for Cicero's eloquence is beyond question, as unambiguously proved by his complimentary remark about the *First Catilinarian*,[23] Cicero is never praised as a model of political virtues in the narration of the Catilinarian conspiracy. It has also been noted that "as a historical source Cicero seems to have held little weight for Sallust."[24] One might add that the intertextual history of the opening words of the *First Catilinarian*, transplanted into Catiline's mouth by

---

[16] For Propertius's adaptation of motifs from Cicero's *pro Caelio* in elegies 4.7 and 4.11, see Duffalo 2003. On the forensic tone of Propertius's elegy 2.32, modeled on the legal context and structure of Cicero's defense of Caelius, see Batinski 2003.

[17] On Ovid's *Tristia* 2 and Cicero's *pro Ligario*, see Ingleheart 2010: 13–5. For Ovid's reformulation of motifs related to Cicero's death in the description of Absyrtus's cruel end in *Trist.* 3.9, see Degl'Innocenti Pierini 2014.

[18] It may be interesting to recall the comparison between Cicero and the mime-writer Publilius in Petronius's *Satyrica* 55.3. In arrogant, bombastic terms the ignorant freedman Trimalchio depicts Cicero as *disertiorem*, "more eloquent," in contrast with Publilius, labeled as *honestior*, "more honest"; the contrast, a rhetorical comparison quite common in literary groups (Schmeling 2011: 224), is obviously a fatuous one but it might reflect a consolidated idea of Cicero as a model of verbal excellence, deprived of moral connotations.

[19] On Cicero's speech in defense of Caelius as the occasion of Catullus's poem, see Quinn 1970: 233–5.

[20] Tatum 1988; Bellandi 2007: 390; Gee 2013: 101–3 (with bibliography).

[21] Gee 2013: 103. On the negative fame surrounding Cicero's poetry cf. Plut. *Cic.* 2.4–5 (with Moles 1988: 149); cf. also Mart. 2.89; schol. Bob. 137.11-3St (on *Sest.* 123); 165.7–9 (on *Planc.* 74).

[22] Syme 1964. For a more appropriate reconsideration of Sallust's alleged "anti-Ciceronian" feelings, see La Penna 1968; Zecchini 1996.

[23] Sal. *Cat.* 31.6. Cf. chapter 1, p. 30 and n101.   [24] Gowing 2013: 234.

Sallust,[25] often interpreted as a mockery of Cicero's consular *persona*,[26] raises further questions about Sallust's re-use of Cicero's self-congratulatory description of the Catilinarian events, since there exists no certain evidence to show whether the phrase *quo usque tandem* was originally Cicero's or Catiline's (readapted by Cicero in an antithetical situation),[27] and, accordingly, no evidence of the source of Sallust's re-contextualization of Catiline's address to his partisans.[28]

Whether and why Sallust had an aversion to Cicero is open to debate. From Sallust's text we may only infer a distance, both ideological and stylistic, between the two writers.[29] Unquestionably, students at the rhetorical schools adopted Sallust's perceived hostility to Cicero as a topic for imaginary speeches, in the guise of conventional invectives. We have two short pieces, an *Invective against Cicero* (*Invectiva in Ciceronem*) ascribed to Sallust and Cicero's purported reply (*Invectiva in Sallustium*), preserved in a good number of manuscripts in conjunction with two anonymous pleas addressed to Caesar and genuine works of Sallust or Cicero.[30] It is generally agreed that the *Invective against Sallust* is a forgery, composed in the rhetorical schools by a writer of poor qualities at a late period. By contrast, the genuineness of the *Invective against Cicero*, considered authentic by Quintilian,[31] has long been debated. I am inclined to believe that, like its natural pendant, the *Invective against Cicero*, whose *terminus ante quem* is commonly fixed at 54 BCE,[32] is a spurious scholastic exercise, in the form of a *prosopopeia*, that originated in the Augustan declamation rooms.[33] Rhetorical practice in the early empire encouraged young students to rework, paraphrase and refashion canonical texts in new ways, usually supplementing them through the creation of fictional situations. Cicero's involvement in the political crisis of the late republic and his dominant role in rhetorical training promoted the production of pseudepigraphic texts to supplement Cicero's biography, in emulation/rivalry with the model.[34] Mock-Ciceronian speeches[35] or invectives in response to Cicero's

---

[25] Sal. *Cat.* 20.9.    [26] Renehan 1976.    [27] Malcom 1979.
[28] For an intertextual re-examination of Sallust's citation of Catiline's words, see Feldherr 2013.
[29] On Sallust's style, modeled on Thucydides's and Cato's prose, see Ramsey 2007a: 10–4.
[30] Novokhatko 2009: 27–110 (on the medieval manuscripts containing the text of the invectives).
[31] Quint. *Inst.* 4.1.68; 9.3.89.
[32] For allusions to the last period of Cicero's political activity in the invective, see Massa 1996.
[33] Syme 1964: 317. On the invective as a rhetorical exercise composed by an opponent to the Augustan regime under the influence of Asinius Pollio's republicanism, see Massa 1996. For a good re-examination of the problem of authorship, see Novokhatko 2009: 111–29.
[34] Peirano 2012.
[35] Sen. *Con.* 3 *praef.* 15 (on Cestius's *Pro Milone*); Quint. *Inst.* 10.5.20 (on Brutus's *Pro Milone*).

orations[36] are well attested in the rhetorical sources. Cicero's texts – and his life – functioned as backdrop for new fictions, which in turn "filled up the blank spaces in the model."[37] Seneca the Elder's *Controversia* 7.2 (on Cicero and Popillius)[38] and the *Suasoriae* 6 and 7 (on Cicero's deliberation whether to beg Antony's pardon)[39] are limpid instances of this creative process of literary refashioning. As Peirano puts it, *Suasoriae* on Ciceronian themes "involve the creation of quasi-fictional scenarios centered on untold episodes and unexplored possibilities in the biography of the orator."[40]

To turn to the *Invective against Cicero,* it might conceivably be interpreted as a fictional exploitation – and reconstruction – of Sallust's supposed antagonism against Cicero. If so, it is to be paralleled with other fictional narratives or speeches, such as the *Fifth Catilinarian,* the *Responsio Catilinae,*[41] the *Declamatio in L. Sergium Catilinam,*[42] all additions to the overused theme of the Catilinarian conspiracy, the *Epistula ad Octavianum,*[43] or the cited *Pridie quam in exilium iret,*[44] in which practitioners reworked traditional Ciceronian motifs to display their knowledge of the "real" Cicero and supplement the model with new "Ciceronian" texts.

In a sense, Ciceronian *pseudepigrapha* shed light on the scholastic reception of Cicero's political legacy.[45] Notably, most of these texts share and manipulate ideas and slogans taken from Cicero's self-promotion campaign, transforming political symbols into instruments of attack and discredit. To concentrate again on the *Invective against Cicero,* the anonymous compiler harshly criticizes the notion of Cicero as *parens patriae,*

---

[36] Asconius Pedianus informs us of two speeches, composed in reply to Cicero's *In toga candida*, one ascribed to Catiline, the other to Gaius Antonius, and touches on the circulation of forged orations falsely attributed to Cicero's competitors (93.24–94.3C *Huic orationi Ciceronis et Catilina et Antonius contumeliose responderunt, quod solum poterant, invecti in novitatem eius. Feruntur quoque orationes nomine illorum editae, non ab ipsis scriptae sed ab Ciceronis obtrectatoribus: quas nescio an satius sit ignorare* ["Catiline and Antonius replied to this speech of Cicero in an insulting manner; they attacked his 'newness', as this was the only instrument of criticism they had. There are in circulation also speeches published in their names, not composed by them but by detractors of Cicero, which I presume it would be better to ignore"]). For Antonius's and Catiline's replies to Cicero cf. also Quint. *Inst.* 9.3.94; App. *BC* 2.2; schol. Bob. 80.13-6St. On Hortensius's defense of Verres, presumably a late rhetorical exercise, cf. Quint. *Inst.* 10.1.23.

[37] Peirano 2012: 10.    [38] Roller 1997.

[39] Sen. *Suas.* 6 *Deliberat Cicero an Antonium deprecetur* ("Cicero deliberates whether to beg Antony's pardon"), 7 *Deliberat Cicero an scripta sua conburat promittente Antonio incolumitatem si fecisset* ("Antony promises to spare Cicero's life if he burns his writings: Cicero deliberates whether to do so").

[40] Peirano 2012: 19.    [41] Edition: De Marco 1991.    [42] Edition and commentary: Shurgacz 2004.

[43] Edition: Lamacchia 1968. For the *epistula* as a second- or third-century declamation composed by an opposer to the Augustan autocratic regime, in the guise of a "Stoic" Cicero, see Tandoi 1992: 297–8 (see also Grattarola 1988).

[44] Cf. chapter 2, pp. 82–3.    [45] Hall 2013: 227–29. See also Peirano 2012: 21–24.

"father of the Fatherland" ([Sal.] *Cic.* 5), by ironically quoting a line from Cicero's poetic commemoration of his consular actions (*O fortunatam natam me consule Romam*! "Fortunate Rome, born in my consulate!").[46] Then, he mocks Cicero's self-portrait as a *dux togatus*, "military commander in civilian dress" ([Sal.] *Cic.* 6), a significant and recurring motif in the celebration of his bloodless victory over the conspirators, by parodying another line from Cicero's poem on his consulship, *concedant arma togae, concedat laurea linguae* ("Let arms yield to the toga, let the laurel yield to the tongue").[47] Again, Cicero is ridiculed for presumptuously tracing his line of ancestry from Scipio Africanus ([Sal.] *Cic.* 1) and branding himself as protected by the immortal gods ([Sal.] *Cic.* 3).

In addition to exploiting the standard topics of blame, such as sexual degeneracy and financial corruption, the author of the invective recycles – and disputes – motifs from Cicero's propaganda campaign in order to present Cicero as an irresponsible and fickle statesman.[48] Significantly, vituperation is sparked off by Cicero's self-portrayal as both a "savior" of the republic and a "new man," ennobled by his own deeds. One point seems clear. The late republic and early empire witnessed a vivid debate on Cicero's Roman self-fashioning and his cultivation of a distinctive political image, a debate connected to nostalgic evocations of Roman past history and its impact on current political conditions. As Dench remarks, "the possibility of characterizing Cicero as a binding-link to the present as much as an epitome of the vanished past encouraged intense engagement with his status as a figure who represented Roman values that were alternatively compromised or continued after Actium."[49] In other words, Cicero's multiple modes of self-construction opened up discussions about Roman identity, not rarely colored by political considerations about the survival and the death of the *res publica,* and what it meant to be Roman in the early imperial period, a "revolutionary" time in which the transition from

---

[46] A satirical reading of this line is in Juvenal (10.122–26).
[47] This is the text given by the author of the invective, in accordance with what we read in Quint. *Inst.* 11.1.24 (presumably a parodic reading). Cicero quotes the verse in a different version (*laurea laudi*) at *Pis.* 74 and *Off.* 1.77. For the revision of the poem *De consulatu* and Cicero's modification of the original term *lingua* into *laus* for political reasons, see Lomanto 1996; a re-examination of the issue and the context of Cicero's line is now in Volk-Zetzel 2015. On the denigration of Cicero as a poet in the invective, see Canfora 1984. Criticism of Cicero as a poet is echoed in a passage of the Bobbio commentary (schol. Bob. 165.7-9St, on Cic. *Planc.* 74: *Nam de consulatu suo scripsit poetico metro: quae mihi videntur opera minus digna talis viri nomine,* "He composed a versified poem on his consulship: this work, however, gives me the impression of being unworthy of the fame of such a great man").
[48] On the content of the invective, see Novokhatko 2009: 18–21.   [49] Dench 2013: 122–23.

## Ethics and Politics: Debating About Cicero

Debating about Cicero's political life implied exploring questions deeply implicated in the history and values of Rome itself. Cicero's rhetoric of "newness," an easy target of criticism, was naturally associated with questions of Roman identity. Similarly, Cicero's alleged inconsistency in public life (*levitas*), a charge that became a regular feature of the scholastic reception of the republican orator ([Sal.] *Cic.* 4–5; Sen. *Con.* 2.4.4),[51] elicited reflections on political and social issues, particularly in terms of morality and conservation of past ethics. Most significantly, the identification of the statesman and orator with the destiny of Rome and, consequently, the symbolic connection between Cicero's epic death, dramatized by the severing of his head and hands, and the injured body of Rome became major themes in later receptions, where evocations of Cicero's struggle with the tyrant Antony, portrayed as a violent oppressor of Rome's citizenry, were inextricably linked to the beginnings of Augustus's principate.[52] From this perspective, it is not casual that the pair *arma-toga*, a clichéd image in Cicero's self-promotion as a *dux togatus*,[53] was parodied in Book 7 of Lucan's epic poem (7.62–66), where Cicero, depicted as a boastful orator, is implicitly accused of fomenting war.[54] In Lucan's gloomy meditation on the causes of civil war it was Cicero, fictitiously placed at the battlefield at Pharsalus, not Pompey, who was invested with responsibility for leading Rome to ruin.[55] As recently remarked, Lucan's fiction "does not put Cicero in an entirely positive light."[56] Cicero's self-representation as a man of peace is overturned by Lucan, who manipulates historical reality in order to present the orator as a belligerent politician, overwhelmed by his desire to defend republican freedom.

---

[50] Dench 2013: 122.
[51] For a positive reassessment of the figure of Cicero charged with *levitas* and a discussion of the nuances of *constantia* as an aristocratic virtue, see Fulkerson 2013.
[52] Dench 2013: 124–5.
[53] Cf. also Cornelius Severus (Sen. *Suas.* 6.26 ... *ille senatus vindex, ille fori, legum iurisque togaeque*).
[54] Narducci 2003b: 82–4.
[55] On Lucan's caricature of Cicero, portrayed as a bellicose "descendant" of the Virgilian Drances, see Fucecchi 2011: 247. See also Galli 2015 (for echoes from Cicero's letters and speeches, especially the *pro Milone* and the *Second Philippic*, in Lucan's epic).
[56] Gowing 2013: 244.

Reflecting on Rome's crisis at the end of the republic and its consequences for changed political conditions was, thus, a key feature of parody of Cicero, or "Cicerokarikatur," to use Zielinski's terms.[57] In this debate over Cicero's engagement in Roman political life, two events of the orator's life attracted most attention: Cicero's consulship and his final struggle with Antony. We have already seen that Cicero's handling of the Catilinarian conspiracy and, in particular, his endless praise of his consular achievements, reaching its highest point in the self-celebratory poem *De consulatu*, found detractors ridiculing – and questioning – Cicero's promotional slogans. Quintilian comments on – and sympathetically justifies – Cicero's need to defend his consular actions, violently criticized by political enemies and *obtrectatores* (*Inst.* 11.1.18–24).[58] The theme of Cicero versus Antony stimulated meditations on vital questions such as freedom of political expression. Students of oratory speculated about Cicero's self-construction as the defender of republican Rome by approaching the *Philippics*, the last documents of "Cicero's free voice," in skeptical terms. These speeches played a crucial role in shaping the image of Cicero as a statesman in the declamation schools, as they "carried the power to preserve and reinforce fundamental republican values at a time of pressure for their abandonment."[59]

Asinius Pollio, a leading political and cultural figure in the late republic and early Augustan age, had an active part in the debate over Cicero's final actions. A strenuous partisan of Caesar and sympathetic to Antonius,[60] he was deemed "the most hostile to Cicero's glory" (*infestissimus famae Ciceronis*: Sen. *Suas.* 6.14). Pollio's oration in defense of the candidate for praetorship in 42, L. Aelius Lamia, a former friend of Cicero, contained a pungent comment on the cowardice of Cicero, fictitiously portrayed as begging Antony's pardon and promising to retract his *Philippics* and recite more favorable speeches. The published version of the *pro Lamia*, a vitriolic attack on Cicero's political choices, was then filled with much more ignoble accusations (*alia sordidiora multo*), so false that Pollio himself never had the effrontery to insert them into his histories (Sen. *Suas.* 6.15).[61]

Pollio's defamatory attacks on Cicero exerted a considerable impact on the propagation of anti-Ciceronian themes in the rhetorical schools.

---

[57] Zielinski 1929.
[58] Cf. Plut. *Cic.* 6.5.24.1–3; Dio 37.38.2; 38.12.7. See Allen 1954; Dugan 2014: 10.
[59] Stevenson-Wilson 2008: 20. On the *Philippics* in the declamation schools, see Wilson (M.) 2008.
[60] On Pollio's political inclinations, see Zecchini 1982. For Pollio's role in contemporary life at Rome and his historiographical method (on the ground of Horace *Carm.* 2.1), see now Morgan L. 2000.
[61] On Pollio and Cicero, see André 1949: 93–8; Gabba 1957; Gambet 1963: 27–34; Massa 2006.

The early third-century Greek historian Cassius Dio's hostility to Cicero owes much to Pollio's polemics and the declamatory manipulation of Cicero's *Philippics*.[62] Not surprisingly, most of the anti-Ciceronian motifs in Fufius Calenus's speech (46.1–28) find analogy in the pseudo-Sallustan invective.[63] As already noted, Cicero's political campaign against Antony for the survival of the *libera res publica* encountered contrasting reactions in the declamation rooms. The *Philippics,* models of the grand style,[64] propagated a double image of Cicero, as both a fierce enemy of the tyrant and an incautious war-monger, fictitiously depicted by Pollio and his followers as a cowardly man mulling over the possibility of destroying his writings in order to save his life.[65] Calenus's defense of Antony collected much of the anti-Ciceronian material previously assembled – and discussed – in the schools, the only suitable place for a re-interpretation of the role of Cicero as a historical figure.

The so-called *reprehensio Ciceronis* involved Cicero's morals as well. Peculiarly, Cicero's exile was a favorite school topic. Students engaged with Cicero's interpretation of his inhuman experience of exile, an event that deprived him of any rational faculty, as explicitly admitted in *Dom.* 97.[66] On the one side, Cicero's undeserved banishment secured him a place in the list of the *boni viri,* unjustly rewarded by their countries.[67] "Un exemple aisément intelligible, essentiellement exemplaire et livresque,"[68] Cicero embodied the characteristics of a political victim whose deeds were not duly appreciated by his fellow citizens. On the other side, Cicero's emphasis on his psychological and moral suffering in exile and, in particular, his refusal of any consolation attracted criticism from later historians and philosophers.[69] It should be remembered that Cassius Dio exploited Cicero's womanish lamentation on his condition of exile as the subject of the dialectical exchange between the orator and a philosopher named Philiscus (38.18–29), a consolation-dialogue in which Philiscus elaborates

---

[62] Gabba 1957; Millar 1961; 1964; Montecalvo 2014. On Dio's knowledge of Cicero, see Rodgers 2008 (who argues that Catulus's speech at 36.31–6 is modeled on Cicero's *pro lege Manilia* and *pro Fonteio*).

[63] Gabba 1957. On the structure of Calenus's speech and its relation with the *Invectiva in Ciceronem*, see Montecalvo 2014: 366–406. For Calenus's depiction of Cicero as a disreputable demagogue, see now Mallan 2016.

[64] For the *granditas verborum* of the *Philippics* cf. Petr. 5.19. See Schmeling 2011: 20.

[65] For this vogue declamatory theme, in addition to Sen. *Suas.* 6 and 7, cf. Quint. *Inst.* 3.8.46 (also Juv. 10.125).

[66] Narducci 1997b.

[67] Sen. *Dial.* 9.16.1; *Ben.* 5.17.2. For Cicero's exile as a privileged historical theme, cf. Sen. *Dial.*4.2.3.

[68] Grimal 1984: 659.   [69] Plut. *Cic.* 32.5.

*Ethics and Politics: Debating About Cicero* 109

on commonplaces from the consolatory tradition to depict a Cicero antithetical to the ideal of Roman senator.[70]

Pollio's assessment of Cicero, as we read it in Seneca the Elder's sixth *Suasoria*, offers further insights into this general, distrustful approach to Cicero as exile. Passing over stylistic quarrels, Pollio pays a reluctant tribute to Cicero's literary qualities and fame and concentrates on Cicero's lack of wisdom in adversity. In Pollio's account Cicero's life was not an *exemplum* of "Stoic" virtues. His political successes resulted from a combination of natural qualities and fortune, supported by divine favor (*munus deum*). But Cicero was unable to predict and resist "storm-clouds of hatred" (*invidiae tempestates*). "Would that he could have shown more temperateness in prosperity, more stoutness in adversity" (*Utinam moderatius secundas res et fortius adversas ferre potuisset!*).[71] The eulogy of Cicero's genius is abruptly reversed by Pollio's fierce, malicious comment on Cicero's absence of *fortitudo*, preliminary to the closing definition of the death of the orator as "pitiable" (*misera*).

In Seneca's view, among the historians Pollio was the only one to narrate Cicero's death grudgingly (*Suas.* 6.24).[72] His description of Cicero's death furnished students with matter for a second *suasoria* on Cicero's deliberation whether to "burn his speeches on Antony's promise of safety," a theme patently false, *inepte ficta* (*Suas.* 6.14).[73] As Seneca reveals, a pro-Cicero stance, entailing an anti-Antony position, dominated the declamatory and historical depiction of Cicero's death.[74] Yet, as

---

[70] Gowing 1998. On Dio's adaptation of the consolatory tradition to the fictitious encounter between Cicero and Philiscus, see Claassen 1996. For some correspondences in the consolation-dialogue between Cicero's exile and Dio's misfortunes, see now Kemezis 2014: 289–90. See also Montecalvo 2014: 231–77.

[71] Text and translation: Winterbottom 1974.

[72] Seneca mentions only two other declaimers adopting an anti-Cicero position, Romanius Hispo (*Con.* 7.2.13) and Varius Geminus (*Suas.* 6.11–2), though the latter declaimed both sides: see Roller 1997: 116 n21. It should be noted that Seneca's *Suasoria* 6 enlists and reproduces extracts about the death of Cicero from Asinius Pollio, Livy, Aufidius Bassus, Cremetius Cordus and Bruttedius Niger, including also the long, poetic description of Cicero's murder in the epic-historical poem of Cornelius Severius (13 *FLP*; 13 *FPL*); see Hollis 2007: 358–67. On Seneca's *suasoriae* and the declamatory use of the theme of Cicero's murder, see Homeyer 1964; Sussman 1978: 72–4; Fairweather 1981: 84–5; 164–5; 316–7; Kaster 1998; Roller 1997; Wright 2001; Degl'Innocenti Pierini 2003; Esposito 2004; Casamento 2004; see also Mazzoli 2006: 52–7; Berti 2007: 106–9; 325–32; Migliario 2007: 121–49; Wilson 2008; Lentano 2014 (with further bibliography). A good commentary on Seneca's sixth *Suasoria* is now in Feddern 2013: 381–482.

[73] Cf. also Quint. *Inst.* 3.8.46. See Wilson 2008: 314.

[74] Roller 1997: 116–17. For the death-of-Cicero theme as a school topic cf. Quint. *Inst.* 3.8.46; Val. Max.1.4.6; 5.3.4; Sen. *Dial.* 9.16.1; Mart. 3.66; 5.69; Tac. *Dial.* 17.3; 24.3; around this topic is also built the cycle of twelve short epigrams in the *Anthologia Latina* known as *Epitaphia M. T. Ciceronis* (603–614Riese = *sap.* 109–120); see Friedrich 2002: 201–27.

correctly noted by Gowing, these pro-Cicero treatments "describe a man whose faults too often cast his virtues into the shadows."[75] To substantiate this claim, Pollio's unfavorable judgment on Cicero's life is reformulated by Livy's celebrated obituary of Cicero (*Suas.* 6.21–22), though less adversarial in tone.[76] Both Pollio and Livy portray Cicero as a man blessed by good fortune. Both comment on Cicero's inability to withstand misfortune, with the exception of his death, a sad and bitter end (*exitus tristis atque acerbus*), the only event faced by Cicero with inspirational courage. Like Pollio, Livy concedes that the pain Cicero suffered from his enemy would not have been different from what Cicero himself would have inflicted on Antony, if victorious. Both Pollio and Livy, finally, judge Cicero by balancing his virtues against his vices. Certainly, Livy mitigates Pollio's malevolent opinion on the orator. His dramatic version of Cicero's death and mutilation largely determined the interpretation of the end of the orator in heroic terms.[77] To Livy, Cicero was "a great and memorable man" (*vir magnus ac memorabilis*): his merits might be fittingly described only by a Cicero as eulogist.[78] Nevertheless, it was Cicero's human voice and eloquence (less his life) that aroused universal – and Livy's – admiration (*Suas.* 6.17).[79]

Livy's emphasis on Cicero's lack of wisdom and imperturbability in enduring misfortune reflects a particular aspect of the debate revolving around the exemplarity of Cicero's life. In his essay *On the Shortness of Life* (*Dial.* 10.5.1) Seneca the Younger portrays Cicero as afflicted by psychological instability, buffeted from side to side, unable to keep calm in prosperity or patient in adversity, constantly cursing his consulate, praised not without reason, but without end (*non sine causa sed sine fine laudatum*).[80] Cicero "has fallen far short of the Stoic ideal of complete and unconditional *libertas*":[81] "half a prisoner," *semiliber,* he impersonates the reversal of Stoic freedom, in contrast to Cato's heroism.[82] Remarkably, Seneca's un-

---

[75] Gowing 2013: 237.   [76] Lamacchia 1975; Pomeroy 1988; Ridley 2013.
[77] Degl'Innocenti Pierini 2003. On Livy's obituary of Cicero, see also Chlup 2004.
[78] Cf. Val. Max. 5.3.4.
[79] As Vasaly 2015 notes, Livy's representation of the ideal politician and orator, especially in the portrayal of T. Quinctius Capitolinus in Book 3, embodies many of the personal qualities envisioned by Cicero for the figure of the *rector rei publicae* (94–5). Nevertheless, Livy subscribes to a different, moralistic idea of the orator, as a virtuous man appealing to the virtuous sentiments of his audience (as shown in Camillus's speech): "the model Livy holds up for his elite readers is at heart Catonian (whether we think of the plain speaking, *severitas,* and moral rigor associated with Cato the Censor or Cato Uticensis) rather than Ciceronian" (132).
[80] On Cicero's psychological need to celebrate his consulate, see Dugan 2014.
[81] Williams (Gareth) 2003: 145.   [82] Degl'Innocenti Pierini 2003: 6–7; 14.

Stoic depiction of Cicero, placed in between Augustus's and Drusus's portraits, assembles motifs largely exploited in the schools. As noted above, Cicero's lack of firmness sparked off contrasting reactions in the rhetorical schools, as may be argued from Sen. *Con.* 2.4.4.[83] Not a few blamed Cicero's morals. Seneca the philosopher was largely responsible for providing – and transmitting – the image of Cicero as an unwise man, whose exemplarity was undermined by weak moral character.[84] Quintilian's rehabilitation of Cicero as both a good man and a good citizen was a vehement response to the prevailing climate of censure surrounding the historical image of the republican orator.[85]

School declamations tended to represent Cicero's death as a heroic act. Yet Cicero was far from being considered a republican martyr. His death was synonymous with the death of eloquence. *Ictaque luctu / conticuit Latiae tristis facundia linguae* ("Struck by grief, the eloquence of the Latin tongue became idle with sadness," Sen. *Suas.* 6.26): Cornelius Severus's poetic lamentation is illustrative of the way declaimers grieved for the doom of eloquence, silenced by the loss of the supreme "artist of the word."[86] Analogously, Velleius Paterculus (2.66–7) treated Cicero's death as the end of eloquence, pointing to its symbolic value rather than its historical and political relevance.[87] What mattered more was Cicero as a cultural icon. As limpidly illustrated by Kaster,[88] the violent murder of the orator favored the identification of the real Cicero (*verus Cicero*) with his writings and his words.[89] Declaimers, historians, philosophers and poets agreed in celebrating Cicero's divine eloquence, sharing the consecration of the republican orator

---

[83] *Nemo sine vitio est: in Catone deerat moderatio, in Cicerone constantia, in Sulla clementia* ("No-one is flawless: Cato lacked moderation, Cicero firmness, Sulla clemency").
[84] For Seneca's moral perspective in letter 51, see Gowing 2013: 240–3.   [85] Quint. *Inst.* 12.1.14–7.
[86] On the expression *Latiae facundia linguae* cf. Ovid. *Pont.* 2.3.75 (also 1.2.67); see Courtney 1993: 325–37; Hollis 2007: 363 (especially for Severus's sentence as an "incorporation of echoes from Cicero's *Brutus*"). A similar formula is in Sextilius Ena's account, *Latiae silentia linguae* (Sen. *Suas.* 6.27): see Hollis 2007: 338–39. *Silentia linguae* is also in Martial's epigram 5.69 (*quid prosunt sacrae pretiosa silentia linguae*, l. 7), a variation (together with 3.66) about the death-of-Cicero theme. For the influence of Seneca's declamation on Martial, see Degl'Innocenti Pierini 2003: 44–7 (on Martial's epigram see Howell 1995: 151–3; Canobbio 2011: 524–30).
[87] Gowing 2013: 237–38 (with further bibliography).   [88] Kaster 1998.
[89] Sen. *Suas.* 7.8: *Quoad humanum genus incolume manserit, quamdiu suus litteris honor, suum eloquentiae pretium erit, quamdiu rei publicae nostrae aut fortuna steterit aut memoria duraverit, admirabile posteris vigebit ingenium tuum, et uno proscriptus saeculo proscribes Antonium omnibus. Crede mihi, vilissima pars tui est quae tibi vel eripi vel donari potest: ille verus est Cicero quem proscribi Antonius non putat nisi a Cicerone posse* ("So long as the human race survives, so long as literature has the honor due to it, eloquence its reward, so long as the fortune of our country holds or its memory is preserved, your genius shall flourish in the admiration of posterity. Proscribed for a generation, you shall proscribe Antony for all generations. Believe me, it is the least valuable part of you that can be taken from you or granted to you. The true Cicero is the one who Antony thinks can only be proscribed by Cicero").

and statesman as an immortal genius.[90] Embellished by declamatory *colores* and fictional figures,[91] the baroque, grandiloquent description of the assassination of the orator laid stress on the survival of Cicero's spiritual legacy through his writings.[92] In a high-flown rhetoric, talented declaimers immortalized Cicero as a language hero.[93]

All the same, none "offered up Cicero's life and career as something worthy of emulation."[94] The reputation of Cicero was affected by his equivocal position in the political life of the late republic. Livy's and Seneca's stance on Cicero's morality and virtues, in particular on his absence of firmness, demonstrate that Cicero never acquired the status of *sapiens*. As has been noted, Cicero was valued "at best as essentially a literary or oratorical figure, at worst as a man whose flawed and perhaps even hypocritical life undermined any claim to ethical authority."[95]

## Morality and Language: Cicero in the Early Empire Debate on Style

There is more at stake in this ambiguous approach to the figure of Cicero in the early empire. Notwithstanding Cicero's recognized superiority in oratory, not a few challenged Cicero's role as a stylistic model in current education.[96] Such a skeptical approach was clearly embedded in stylistic controversies. Depending on literary tastes, the distinctive qualities of Cicero's writings, in particular his observance of linguistic norms, clarity, articulateness of sentence structure and abundance of style, were often treated as stylistic vices.[97] Cicero was fiercely criticized for his wordiness and pomposity by the so-called Atticists.[98] Tacitus, speaking through

---

[90] For the epigram of Tullius Laurea (transmitted by Plin. *Nat.* 31.6–8) and the "miracle" of the *fons*, connected to the consecration of the name of Cicero, see Degl'Innocenti Pierini 2003: 42–4; Morgan L. 2007.
[91] On the "historical record contaminated by a fiction generated by the practice of declamation" and the rhetorical reinvention of the figure of Gaius Popillius Laenas as *Ciceronis interfector*, see Wright 2001, who raises considerable skepticism about the credibility of the anecdote surrounding the involvement of Popillius in Cicero's assassination; see also Roller 1997. On the figuration of Cicero as Popillius's father, see Wilson 2008: 324–33; see also Lentano 2016 (for a political reading of Seneca's declamation and Popillius's act of ingratitude alluding to Octavian's ambiguous treatment of Cicero after Caesar's death).
[92] E.g. Sen. *Suas.* 6.4; 5; 19; 7.2; 7–8; Kaster 1998: 255–56.
[93] Kaster 1998: 256: "Cicero is being spoken of as in language appropriate to a hero – a figure specially marked and set apart (the essence of being *sacer*), enduring and of special worth, a figure looked to as an embodiment of some crucial aspect of right order."
[94] Gowing 2013: 237.   [95] Gowing 2013: 243.
[96] On the ancient literary detractors of Cicero, see Throop 1913.   [97] Powell 2013: 41–2.
[98] Quint. *Inst.* 12.10.12–4 (for the Atticists' depiction of Cicero as "Asianic, repetitive, undisciplined and almost effeminate in his composition"). On the Atticist controversy, see Wisse 1995.

Marcus Aper, informs us that the *obtrectatores Ciceronis*, much more numerous than Vergil's,[99] reproached Cicero for being "bombastic and puffy" (*inflatus et tumens*), "too exuberant" (*supra modum exsultans*), "redundant" (*superfluens*) and "not Attic enough" (*parum Atticus*).[100] Leading figures among Cicero's detractors, Calvus and Brutus labeled the orator as "languid" (*solutus et enervis*) and "effeminate" (*fractus atque elumbis*) respectively.[101] Again, Aper, though admitting to Cicero's stylistic evolution in his last speeches, attached the *vitium antiquitatis* to his early orations, lacking pathos and pointed expressions. Recurring to a well-known simile, he equated Cicero's oratory to an "unfinished building" (*rude aedificium*), whose walls are stable enough but still roughly fashioned.[102]

Pollio's rivalry with Cicero had motivations in stylistic quarrels as well.[103] Seneca the Younger compared Cicero's modulated style with Pollio's abruptness (*ep.* 100.7), an opposition reiterated by Quintilian (*Inst.* 10.1.113; 12.1.22),[104] who celebrated Cicero's elegance in contrast to Pollio's quasi-archaic roughness.[105] Interestingly, stylistic contention between Cicero and Pollio was the subject of the work of Asinius Gallus, Pollio's son (Plin. *Ep.* 7.4.3–6),[106] later opposed by the emperor Claudius (Suet. *Claud.* 41). Gellius reports Gallus's foolish comments on Cicero's style, adding a reference to Largius Licinus's *Ciceromastix* ("The Scourge of Cicero"), another infamous pamphlet on the orator's language (17.1.1).[107] It is a well-known fact, furthermore, that Cicero was later censured as an exponent of the plain, monotonous, classical style, in contrast to the modern, imperial style, incarnated in Seneca's search for abruptness and epigrammatic brilliance.[108] Though the common characterization of Seneca as a "representative of the pointed manner adverse to the periodic style cherished by the famous orator" has been questioned,[109] the perceived discrepancy between Cicero's traditional, pure, language and Seneca's

---

[99] Tac. *Dial.* 12.6.  [100] Tac. *Dial.* 18.4.
[101] Tac. *Dial.* 18.5. On Calvus's Atticism, see Dugan 2001.  [102] Tac. *Dial.* 22.1–3.
[103] Winterbottom 1982a: 241–2.  [104] Austin 1948: 63.
[105] For Quintilian's defense of Cicero's style cf. also *Inst.* 4.5.11 (where the rhetorician reacts against those who criticize the *partitio* of the *pro Cluentio*) and 4.2.59 (in contrast to those who consider a passage from the *pro Milone*, § 28, as "lacking in distinction," Quintilian takes it as an example of Cicero's careful concealment of his art, *ars occulta*). See Bishop 2015: 290.
[106] Danesi Marioni 2001.
[107] For Didymus Calchenterus's six-book criticism of Cicero's philosophy and language cf. Amm. Marc. 22.16.16.
[108] A good analysis of Cicero's linguistic features is provided by Powell 2013; see also Albrecht 2003.
[109] Albrecht 2014: 701–2 (who rejects the long-held view of Seneca as "anti-Cicero," pointing to the correctness and purity of Seneca's language).

concise, Asian style initiated a fierce debate over matters of rhetorical, stylistic and linguistic imitation in the early imperial period.

It has been observed that, by the time of Trajan, interest in Cicero's political life was supplanted by the unanimous recognition of Cicero's superiority as a prose writer, allegorically transformed into an iconic personification of Roman eloquence.[110] This is the period when Quintilian promoted the revival of a neo-Ciceronianism, advocating a pedagogical ideal based on Cicero's universal doctrine and his moral authority. The consecration of Cicero as a standard school author doubtless marked a shift in approach to the republican orator and statesman. Over time Cicero's life lost its attraction as a subject of study or commentary. The orator acquired the symbolic, eternal value of *libera vox rei publicae* and *maximus auctor Romani eloquii*.[111] What mattered more was Cicero's *ingenium*. Yet imitation of Cicero's stylistic qualities remained a controversial issue in literary criticism in the early empire, as demonstrated by the well-rounded discussion of the current state of oratory in Tacitus's *Dialogus de Oratoribus*.[112] Cicero's pivotal role in education – and his importance in the formation of a well-educated élite – was broadly debated. A key point of the dispute was the vitality of ancient models in modern pedagogy.

Let us briefly reassess some basic points of this aspect of Cicero's *Nachleben*. Oratory had significantly changed since Cicero's death. Declamatory exercises on fictitious topics, delivered by schoolboys in the schoolrooms or in private halls, replaced the tumultuous forensic oratory of the late republic. In the guise of imaginary legal cases (*controversiae*) and deliberative speeches to or by Greek and Roman historical and mythical personages (*suasoriae*), the practice of declamation became the core of the school curriculum, superseding the old education system, based on home-upbringing and the *tirocinium fori*.[113] Alongside school declamatory practice,[114] there was also the show declamation,[115] a form of social entertainment akin to public reading or *recitatio*.[116] As stated by Votienus Montanus in the ninth preface of Seneca the Elder's collection, "if

---

[110] For a brief history of the metamorphosis of Cicero from historical figure to paradigm of Roman eloquence, see Moretti 2009.
[111] Luc. 7.62–3.   [112] On the stylistic controversy in the early empire, see Dominik 1997.
[113] On the utility of declamation in rhetorical training, cf. Pliny *Ep.* 2.3.5–6; Quint. *Inst.* 2.10.1–2; 10.5.14.
[114] On declamation in Rome and its role in rhetorical education, see Bonner 1949; Clarke 1953: 85–99; Sussman 1978: 1–17; Bloomer 1997; 1997a; Kaster 2001; Bloomer 2007.
[115] Stramaglia 2016 (for the distinction between "school declamations" and "show declamations").
[116] On the *recitatio* as a social event, see Dupont 1997. For Pliny the Younger's description of aristocratic recitation, see Roller 2011: 215–7.

## Cicero in the Early Empire Debate on Style 115

someone prepares a declamation beforehand, he writes not to win but to please" (*Con.* 9 pr. 1, *Qui declamationem parat, non scribit, ut vincat, sed ut placeat*).[117] An upper-class pastime, largely practiced by leading intellectuals in the early empire, declamation aimed to entertain large educated audiences with elegant and refined style.[118] Both as a rhetorical exercise and as a literary presentation, declamation became a display of virtuosity and cleverness by talented students and professional rhetoricians, a ludic occasion of improvised forensic competition as well as a public exhibition of linguistic abilities.[119]

By the first decades of the imperial age, style too had undergone a radical change. In place of the regularity and symmetry of republican, Ciceronian Latin, literary language adopted a vivid and sophisticated style in "a sort of self-advertising artificiality."[120] Metaphors, allegories, antithesis, personifications and other rhetorical devices were prominent in the new style, a spectacular imitation of public theatrical performances.[121] Imperial writers showed a predilection for a paratactic, unbalanced and epigrammatic, style, more spontaneous and pathetic than classical Latin. "Not only a natural extension of the classical norm and an anxious reaction to the influences of the Augustan classical achievement, but also a response to the oppressive political environment and a reflection of changed social conditions, manners and literary taste,"[122] the post-classical style found its standard-bearer in Seneca the Younger. His brilliance and fondness for pointed expressions symbolized what we might call the "stylistic revolution" in the early empire.[123]

The supremacy of the modern style over republican Latin and the contemporary decline of old training practices, replaced by the unreal, theatrical world of the declamation, were to be the topics of scholarly dispute throughout the first century CE. Notably, a shared feeling of cultural decadence permeated the meditation of intellectuals and writers on the current condition of oratory. The main emphasis was on the notion that the decline of rhetoric was connected to the *luxuria temporum*. Seneca

---

[117] On the presentation declamation, see Hömke 2007.
[118] On the flourishing of declamatory rhetoric, cf. Pliny *Ep.* 2.18; Quint. *Inst.* 1.2.9–15.
[119] For declamation as a form of competitive eloquence, see Roller 2011: 217–9.
[120] Mayer 2005: 62.
[121] On literary images, especially metaphors and similes, in Seneca's prose works, see Armisen-Marchetti 1989; 2015.
[122] Dominik 1997:55.
[123] For the use of rhetorical devices in Seneca's prose, see Wilson 2007; on the declamatory style in Senecan tragedy, see Boyle 1997: 15–31. On Seneca's style in general, see Grimal 1991; Albrecht 2014; Williams (Gareth) 2015.

the Elder is instructive from this perspective, as he lingers over this issue in the first half of the first preface of his declamatory collection.[124] In nostalgic tones, he recalls the golden age of Roman eloquence, embodied by Cicero, and pinpoints the contemporary luxury and laziness of mollycoddled students as the sources of decline.[125] With some variations, Petronius,[126] Seneca the Younger,[127] Quintilian, in his lost work "on the causes of decadent eloquence" (*De causis corruptae eloquentiae*)[128] and pseudo-Longinus, author of the treatise *On Sublimity*,[129] expanded on the idea of decadence as a consequence of moral downfall,[130] implicitly rejecting alternative explanations such as natural growth and decline[131] or the contemporary low estimation of oratorical art.[132]

The moralistic interpretation of the notion of decline was integral to the vivid discussion about the harmful impact of declamation on Roman education. A target of criticism was the triviality and artificiality of declamation topics. The remoteness of modern school training from real life and its extravagance of style were identified as the causes of lower standards of education. Both Seneca the Elder and Quintilian lamented the sterility of declamatory exercises, reasserting the vitality of the concept of the *vir bonus dicendi peritus* at the same time. It is a common assumption that the "social" definition of the orator as a good man is essential to Quintilian's moral pedagogy. Bloomer has recently placed emphasis on moral qualities as vital to rhetorical training. As he puts it, "rhetoric is a moral art because, in Quintilian's thinking, rhetoric needs a community, and in the actual exercises rhetoric imagines community, human relations, and the power of speech to mediate these."[133] Certainly, Quintilian, like Seneca, appreciated the role played by declamation in elite rhetorical preparation. Nevertheless,

---

[124] *Con.* I *praef.* 6–7. See Williams (Gordon) 1978: 7–9; Fairweather 1981: 132ff.
[125] For Seneca's praise of Cicero's republican eloquence cf. also *Con.* I *praef.* 6; 11.
[126] Petr. 1–5. For a good presentation of the discussion between Encolpius and Agamemnon, a teacher of rhetoric, about the collapse of eloquence, see Courtney 2001: 54–62. See also Schmeling 2011: 1–20.
[127] Sen. *Ep.* 114.
[128] For Quintilian's criticism of modern declamatory rhetoric in *De causis*, see Brink 1989: 473–80.
[129] On Longinus's discussion of literary decline in the final chapter of his work (44), see Williams (Gordon) 1978: 17–25.
[130] A general vision of moral decline is formulated by Pliny the Elder (*Nat.* 14.2–6).
[131] This explanation recurs in Velleius Paterculus (1.16–7).
[132] About the theory of loss of prestige of oratorical perfomance cf Seneca the Elder *Con.* I *praef.* 7; see Fairweather 1981: 134–38.
[133] Bloomer 2011: 136. For the intersection between morality and eloquence in Quintilian's educational project, see Winterbottom 1964; for the political implications of the connection between virtue and skill in speaking, see Morgan (T.) 1998a. On the concept of the *vir bonus* as a rhetorically artificial construction, see Dozier 2014.

the unreal atmosphere of the declamation schools, the license (*licentia*) and ignorance (*inscitia*) of the declaimers,[134] the stylistic affectation (*cacozelia*) of declamatory performances[135] and the concurrent decline in morals and taste were perceived as the symptoms of a general social and cultural deterioration, which inevitably led to nostalgia for the past.

It appears, thus, that change in the educational system was synonymous with moral decline. By deploring contemporary school teaching Seneca the Elder and Quintilian showed their concern for the bad effects of declamation's fatuity on the youth's education. Furthermore, the increasing popularity of declamation was seen as a menace to the ideal of practical wisdom, *Romana sapientia,* embodied in the Roman orator.[136] One might say that, more than declamation as a rhetorical exercise in itself, it was declamation's inability to establish the moral foundations of oratorical art that attracted criticism from imperial writers. Apart from the satirical invectives of Petronius and Juvenal,[137] this topic is touched upon in Tacitus's *Dialogus* by Messalla, an optimistic traditionalist, who clearly echoes Quintilian's stance on current and future oratory. Complaining about the scant attention paid to learning and culture in modern schools, Messalla contended that the imitation of reality (*imitatio veritatis*), the practical aim of rhetorical training, requires the breadth of learning that Cicero promoted. In line with Quintilian, Tacitus's Messalla looked at Cicero's universal doctrine as the basis of ideal education. But while Quintilian enthusiastically foresaw a revival of neo-Ciceronianism, without refusing modern teaching methods, Messalla limited himself to drawing an idealized picture of the republican age. In putting past and present into contrast, Messalla distrusted modern rhetorical teaching and resuscitated Cicero's theory of education, as it had been laid out in the *Brutus*.[138] By transferring Quintilian's Ciceronianism back to the Ciceronian age he performed as an anachronistic *laudator temporis acti*, "elevating the principles of a single remarkable individual, Cicero, into a general practice."[139]

Speaking through Messalla, Tacitus apparently joins Seneca and Quintilian in condemning the immorality and vacuity of the modern education system. But Tacitus's Ciceronian-stylized dialogue is far from being a simple reproof of bad pedagogy. Through six paired, competing speeches, placed in three successive sections, the dialogue's characters dispute key issues of the aesthetic controversies of the

---

[134] Quint. *Inst.* 2.10.3. See Brink 1989: 477–8.   [135] Quint. *Inst.* 8.3.56ff.   [136] Leeman 1963: 291.
[137] Juv. 1.1–18; 7.105–214. For Juvenal's criticism of declamation, see Braund 1997.
[138] Leeman 1963: 289.   [139] Mayer 2001: 182.

imperial age.¹⁴⁰ As Goldberg puts it, "Tacitus' work is a dialogue of shifting values and perspectives that pursues no thesis, single or composite, nor does it answer a particular question."¹⁴¹ It patently refuses to convey a uniform message.¹⁴² Through three interconnected perspectives Tacitus discusses the alleged superiority of poetry over oratory and vice versa (Aper-Maternus, *Dial.* 5.3–13.6),¹⁴³ examines the qualities of past and present oratory (Messalla-Aper, *Dial.* 15.1–27.2) and criticizes modern standards of education (Messalla, *Dial.* 28.1–35.5), arguing, with Maternus, for the interdependence of great eloquence and political conditions (*Dial.* 36.1–41.5).¹⁴⁴ He reflects upon contemporary literature, bringing to the focus the social, political and educational reasons lying behind the ostensible decline of oratory.

It has long been assumed that Tacitus endorsed the view of oratory's decline, constructing his dialogue as a pessimistic vision of inexorable literary decadence. However, no speech in the dialogue is refuted.¹⁴⁵ Marcus Aper's claim that oratory must be adapted to the modified cultural situation of the modern age is never condemned by the other speakers. It is hard to say whether Tacitus's feelings are represented in any of the characters of the dialogue. Tacitus likely approved of some of the opinions of Messalla and Maternus, especially criticism against contemporary oratory lacking political substance.¹⁴⁶ But it is equally possible that the historian sympathized with Aper's modernism.¹⁴⁷ As recently argued, to Tacitus style was a dynamic entity, an expression of *Zeitgeist*.¹⁴⁸ Change in aesthetics was an index of new cultural attitudes. Moving away from the stereotypical lament over the death of oratory, Tacitus interpreted changes of style from a historical perspective. Instead of being a simple reassertion of Ciceronian principles, then, Tacitus's *Dialogus* turns out to be an optimistic analysis of contemporary literature, explored in its historical and cultural context. The advent of

---

[140] On the historical and literary background of the dialogue, see Mayer 2001, 1–5; Rutledge 2012; Berg 2014b: 17–51.
[141] Goldberg 1999: 226 (reformulating Brink 1994: 276–77).  [142] Berg 2014a.
[143] For the exchange between Maternus and Aper as a testimony to the emergence of new spaces of literary, social competition, see Roller 2011: 211–15.
[144] On Maternus's arguments and their similarity to Cicero's position on oratory in the *Brutus*, see Goldberg 1999: 235–6.
[145] Williams (Gordon) 1978: 45; Barnes 1986: 236; Luce 1993: 33–5.  [146] Mellor 1993: 18
[147] For a re-appreciation of the role of Aper in the *Dialogus* and an interpretation of Tacitus's work as a meditation on "the dynamics of literary change," a "key work for recovering not just the literary values of the so-called Silver Age, but the forces at work in generating these values," see Goldberg 1999.
[148] Dominik 1997b.

a new oratory/style was a natural reaction to changed social and political conditions.[149]

The notion that oratory and style were evolving represents a cornerstone of literary criticism in the early empire. Though imperial writers generally read the decline of oratory in moral terms, deprecating the damaging effects of declamation on education at the same time, they had a good perception that change in style was a historical and social necessity. As Aper's arguments fully demonstrate, "style changes with altered social conditions and is part of a natural process of aesthetic change in popular taste."[150] To Aper and Tacitus, style is the product of the age. On this concept is also based Seneca the Younger's theory of style in *Ep.* 114.[151] In replying to Lucilius's enquiry about the origin of bad prose style, Seneca starts by associating corruption of prose style with a bad lifestyle, as exemplified by the proverbial "as men's lives, so their speech" (*talis hominibus fuit oratio qualis vita*, 114.2).[152] Then, he singles out three likely sources of bad prose style. First, effeminacy of language may be an expression of a depraved character. Rejecting style that is "broken and drawn out in the fashion of singing" (*infracta et in morem cantici ducta* 114.1), Seneca identifies deterioration of taste and stylistic sophistication with moral decay, as proved by Maecenas's effeminate style (114.3–8).[153] Second, bad prose style may issue from luxury and lavishness. As "style has no fixed laws" (*oratio certam regulam non habet*), tastes inevitably change over the course of time. It is "the usage of the community" (*consuetudo civitatis* 114.13) that determines cultural and literary inclinations. A corrupt manner of speaking and writing may be the natural consequence of altered social and political conditions. Third, imitation of bad models may result in stylistic faults. Intemperate imitation of Sallust's verbal quirks by Arruntius is cited as an instance of how corrupt style originates from excessive admiration of the original author (114.17–9).[154]

---

[149] Dressler 2015: 145 (on Tacitus's paradoxical treatment of Cicero, invoked as an exemplar of past oratory and simultaneously rejected as a canonical author).
[150] Dominik 2007: 332.
[151] On Seneca's ideas of style as expressed in *Ep.* 114, see Laudizi 2004: Takàcs 2005.
[152] On the Greek origin of this proverb, attributed to Socrates, cf. Cic. *Tusc.* 5.47; Quint. *Inst.* 11.1.30. See Möller 2004; Ferriss-Hill 2012.
[153] Cf. also Sen. *Ep.* 19.9. On the application of gender terms to literary style and Seneca's critique of effeminacy in language, see Richlin 1997: 77–8. For Maecenas as the archetype of literary decadence, see Degl'Innocenti Pierini 2013; on the satirical reinterpretation of the so-called "Maecenas-myth" in the Neronian age, see Rosati 2012.
[154] Dominik 1997b: 48–9; Taoka 2011: 128. See also Connolly 2007b. 87.

In Seneca's view style is a reflection of personality and age. He detects stylistic vices in writers before his time. In addition to Maecenas, he gives the historian Sallust as an example of archaism and obscurity, counseling caution in the imitation of his stylistic faults. By contrast, Seneca emphatically describes the qualities of modern style, characterized by "control of language, brevity and the refusal of bombastic images."[155] To Seneca the new, post-classical style constituted an improvement in aesthetic standards. Seneca himself regarded his own style as a fitting response to the contemporary search for elegance and emotional effects, encountering Tacitus's and his contemporaries' approval.[156] Nonetheless, Seneca too was aware that imitation of the wrong models, resulting in an effeminate, inflated language, posed a risk for education. Lining up with Quintilian in recognizing the centrality of imitation to ethics and morality in education, Seneca regarded effeminate prose style as a threat to the formation of well-educated pupils. Paradoxically, as we shall see, Quintilian reprimanded immoderate imitation of Seneca's vices as a menace to youth's education, counseling against excess of stylistic, poetic refinements in oratory;[157] Seneca, in turn, cautioned against unrestrained reproduction of stylistic faults, reassessing the pivotal role of imitation in the cultivation of prose style as well as in the relationship between style and life. Though in different perspectives, Seneca and Quintilian shared concern about the effects of imitation upon ethics and pedagogy.

Amid divergent and shifting approaches to the notion of change and the related concept of moral decline, as suggested by Tacitus's dialogue, literary debate in the early empire was thus marked by an evident bipolarity. On the one side, we see disapproval and severe censure of the futility of declamatory themes, associated with a nostalgic evocation of a socially and politically competitive eloquence. As a result, the perceived decline of oratory was equated to the decline of educational standards, lacking in morality and therefore unable to furnish prospective orators with ethically good exemplars. On the other side, we learn of a general appreciation of declamation as a training instrument. Seneca the Elder and Quintilian, followed up by Pliny the Younger, regarded declamation as a practical, useful manner of rhetorical expression, suited to changed political conditions. Within this context evolution of style was a largely accepted concept. As we have noted above, consciousness of the necessity of change in style was a fundamental component of literary criticism in the early empire. Post-classical style was generally considered a natural manifestation of

---

[155] *Ep.* 59.5.   [156] Tac. *Ann.* 13.3.   [157] Quint. *Inst.* 10.1.28–9.

changed social and cultural situations. Quintilian himself, far from being a "blind traditionalist," praised Seneca the Younger's intellectual style, admitting the historical importance of modern literary language. However, modernists too showed their concern about the damaging impact of effeminacy of language and excess of stylistic affectation upon education. Along with Quintilian, who pondered the perils of immoderately imitating Seneca's stylistic faults, the defenders of the new style meditated upon the relationship between language and morality.

It is time now to return to Cicero and the early imperial debate surrounding his role in modern education. Imitation, supremacy of past tradition and evolution of style were key issues in the literary dispute about the contemporary state of education, a fundamental step towards the construction of a modern, ethical pedagogy. Needless to say, any debate on the effects of imitation of past models on liberal instruction centered upon Cicero, the supreme expression of rhetorical excellence. As illustrated by Tacitus's *Dialogus*, imitation of Cicero as a perennial authority in oratorical ability, or, by contrast, refusal of Cicero as an *antiquus*, a stylistic model no longer valid in the changed political and social climate, was central to the reform of the schooling system, a need largely recognized by intellectuals and writers concerned about the lower moral standards of current education. If we look at Quintilian's lively discussion of imitation, as we read it in Book 10 of the *Institutio*, it is easy to understand how important a good choice of readings was to the rhetorical training of upper-class Roman pupils. Significantly, in chapter 2 Quintilian points to the close study of the model as the prerequisite of good imitation, which implies a conscious, deliberate absorption of the model's virtues followed by an original recreation, in the form of paraphrase, of the chosen text. To Quintilian, the model of rhetorical grandeur was undoubtedly Cicero, who embodied all the stylistic merits of the great orators of the past and surpassed them thanks to his extraordinary ability to manage each case successfully in accordance with the circumstances, in emulation of the best Attic oratory.[158] As recently stressed by Gowing, in his handbook on education Quintilian advanced a new "Ciceronianism," devoid of any political meaning, in order to cultivate the ideal of the "good man skilled at speaking," the *vir bonus dicendi peritus*.[159] He encouraged imitation of the best exemplars in order to preserve the values of the past and make the child a good man.[160] Quintilian reconfigured a new Cicero, a figure of the

---

[158] Quint. *Inst.* 10.1.105–12; 10.2.25; cf. also 12.10.12; 12.1.20.   [159] Gowing 2013: 245.
[160] Bloomer 2011.

rhetorician and orator durable for the future, to whom he "accorded a status that the orator will enjoy in the Middle Ages and the Renaissance, when he becomes the foundation of a good education."[161]

Quintilian's discussion of imitation follows his assessment of Seneca's qualities (*Inst.* 10.1.125–31). Placed at the end of Book 10's reading list for students,[162] Quintilian's judgment of Seneca focuses on the dangerous attractiveness of the philosopher's "corrupt style of speaking" (*corruptum dicendi genus*, 125). To Quintilian, young students' unrestrained imitation of Seneca's verbal license and "exuberance of language"[163] represents a deviation from a morally incorruptible style and produces bad effects upon the cultivation of a good prose style.[164] Though appreciating Seneca's versatility and uncommon talent, Quintilian views Seneca's stylistic legacy as a threat to the foundation of a pedagogical system, firmly rooted in the imitation of the best models of the past. Quintilian was mainly preoccupied with the endurance of Seneca's bad influence and the moral consequences of imitating the philosopher's over-refined style.[165] At the same time, by condemning post-classical style, epitomized in Seneca's elegance, Quintilian initiated a counter-reaction against hostility toward neo-Ciceronianism. Seneca represented a menace to the reinvigoration of a new cult of Cicero's oratorical figure. However influenced by Seneca's use of rhetorical devices Quintilian's writing might have been, by opposing post-classical style Quintilian championed a return to the best oratory of the first century BCE, a re-creation of the past that he regarded as crucial to the moral foundations of modern education. As Dominik puts it, "while Seneca represented the style of a contemporary age that sought expression for its ideas in new and varied forms, Quintilian sought to represent the standard of the best oratory of the past in a modern form."[166]

What mattered to Quintilian was good education and the role played by imitation in the formation of prose style. In this light Quintilian and Seneca shared ideas about intemperate imitation as a cause of bad style and lower moral standards. Yet they embraced two different ideas of Cicero. As we have seen, Seneca promoted a stylistic reform as a response to the modified sensibility of contemporary audiences. Similarly, in the Tacitean *Dialogus* Aper staked out a modernist position and advocated

---

[161] Gowing 2013: 249. See also Connolly 2007a: 262–73.
[162] On the list of Greek and Roman readings in Book 10 of Quintilian's *Institutio*, see Citroni 2005.
[163] Quint. *Inst.* 12.10.73.
[164] For Quintilian's comments on *mollitia* and "effeminate" oratory, see Dozier 2015: 319–25.
[165] For Quintilian's judgment of Seneca, see Gelzer 1970 ; Laureys 1991; Dominik 1997b: 42–9.
[166] Dominik 1997b: 48.

a kind of eloquence that reflected the changed attitudes and circumstances of the early principate. To Seneca and Aper, the new style, more vivid, elegant and sophisticated than the classical, periodic Ciceronian style, suited the popular taste. Thus, Cicero's unadorned style was censured as a product of its age. In Seneca's view, Cicero's well-rounded periods lacked variety; his prose was "too slow" (*gradarius*; Sen. *Ep*. 40.11).[167] Cicero's periodic style – and its imitation – hampered spontaneity of expression, a distinctive quality of post-classical Latin.[168] But there is more. A man speaks as he lives. So, Cicero was not the moral *exemplum* towards which students should strive. Seneca and his followers could not draw a demarcation line between Cicero's work and his life, a life in which Cicero never achieved the supreme ideal of Stoic *libertas*. As underscored on more than one occasion, imitation is not only a literary activity, a subtle intertextual dialogue between the writer and his interlocutor. It also has ethical implications. Imitation of an inadequate model, both formally and ethically, may undermine the moral basis of a good education. In Seneca's view Cicero failed to acquire the status of a moral paradigm. His authority as a rhetorical exemplum "was determined by how he conducted his life."[169] As much as style made Cicero an obsolete model, no longer advisable to young readers, lack of morality made Cicero a "negative" exemplar, whose imitation could engender undesirable effects on the ethical training of Roman pupils.

In contrast, Cicero's speeches were synonymous for Quintilian with the perfection of language. As forcefully affirmed in Book 10 of the *Institutio* (10.1.112), "nothing more beautiful has ever been heard than Cicero's speech."[170] We have already seen that Quintilian's promotion of the historical and cultural relevance of neo-Ciceronianism represented a polemical reply against Cicero's literary detractors, a defense of the pre-eminence of classicist tradition in reaction to the post-classical style and the anti-Ciceronian perspective of the early imperial age. But it is worth restating that in revitalizing Cicero and the ideals embodied in him Quintilian offered up a new Cicero to later generations, contributing to the rehabilitation of Cicero's reputation as a person. Seneca questioned Cicero's moral authority. Quintilian rehabilitated Cicero as a "good man." Being a "good" orator implies being a "good" man. Cicero's political and oratorical career demonstrates that he acted as "the best citizen" and

---

[167] Cf. also *Ep*. 100.7; 114.16.
[168] On the oft-examined relationship between Seneca and Cicero, see Grimal 1984; Setaioli 2003 (with bibliography); Fedeli 2006.
[169] Gowing 2013: 243.    [170] *Illa qua nihil pulchrius auditum est oratio*.

a "perfect orator."[171] In describing Cicero as a wise navigator and sailor (*Inst.* 12 *praef.* 2–4), Quintilian sketched the republican orator as a sort of Platonic philosopher-king, "retrieving him from the dustbin of irrelevance and refashioning him as an imperial *exemplum* par excellence."[172] In the following years Pliny the Younger endorsed Quintilian's project, measuring his epistolographic successes against those of his predecessor.[173] No matter how distant from Cicero's age his own was, Pliny depicted Cicero as "an authority in matters of oratorical choices and as an example of freedom in choosing a poetic lineage."[174] As Riggsby correctly claimed, Pliny's imitation/*aemulatio* of Cicero in oratory, "both in terms of oratorical style and of self-definition as, first and foremost, an orator,"[175] extended beyond literature.[176] He fashioned himself on the model of Cicero as an orator engaged in public life. In other words, he not only reiterated the relevance of Cicero as an oratorical model. He reasserted also the role of Cicero as a political figure, a leading orator involved in politics in the interest of the collectivity.

With Quintilian and his pupil, Pliny, the Cicero debate comes to an end. The opposition between Cicero as a man and Cicero as an orator was no longer of any interest. Cicero's life began fading into the past. What the young students read and emulated was his writings and his impressive ability to arouse passions by his "divine" words. Criticism of Cicero as a man certainly endured throughout the centuries. Evidence of this is provided by a famous passage from Augustine's *Confessions* (3.4.7). There, while assessing the vital role played by Cicero's *Hortensius* in his education, Augustine echoes condemnation of Cicero as a historical figure, implicitly aligning himself with the admirers of Cicero's language (*Ciceronis, cuius linguam fere omnes mirantur, pectus non ita*).[177] But it was Cicero's intellect that dominated the schoolrooms. As MacCormack puts it, "the very stones of Rome spoke of Cicero's linguistic finesse and his personality."[178]

Quintilian's and Pliny's Ciceronianism revitalized and consecrated the figure of Cicero as the greatest orator and advocate of Roman history. But they made another significant contribution to the reception of Cicero in

---

[171] Quint. *Inst.* 12.1.16–9.  [172] Gowing 2013: 249.  [173] Clarke 1965: 83.
[174] Marchesi 2008: 210.  [175] Riggsby 1995a: 130.
[176] On Pliny's imitation/emulation of Cicero, see Schwerdtner 2015, with further bibliography (esp. 67–72, for Cicero as literary "Vorbild").
[177] On Augustine's passage, see Clark (G.) 1995: 143. For a discussion of Augustine's approach to Cicero, see MacCormack 2013: 273–82 (with bibliography).
[178] MacCormack 2013: 251.

the schools. They redefined the public role of the orator, bringing into existence a new Cicero, a Cicero in which mastery of the Latin language and excellence in oratory combined with political activism and engagement in Roman society, something in which the real Cicero was unanimously recognized as an unattainable model.

### *Latinitas* and *Eruditio*: Cicero, Icon of the Latin Language

By Quintilian's time the transformation of Cicero into a cultural icon seems to have been complete. As we have seen, starting from the early Augustan age and the Tiberian period, Cicero's personal and political history ignited a fierce debate over questions of Roman identity and aristocratic ethics, suggesting contrasting interpretations of the history of the late Roman republic and its impact on imperial ideology.[179] Cast as the supreme exemplar of Roman eloquence, Cicero's equivocal figure was revisited and stripped of any political relevance. Reconfigured and transmitted as a Roman cultural and moral authority to posterity, Cicero was reduced to an abstraction, a literary concept, dissociated from political contexts.[180] In this process towards the simplification of Cicero to embodiment of verbal *ingenium* a major role was played by the declamatory manipulation of the death-of-Cicero tradition.[181] With Quintilian, later on, the controversy over Cicero's debatable moral authority petered out. As we have noted, Quintilian held up Cicero as a moral and rhetorical standard, an indisputable model of linguistic excellence bearing testimony to the perfect coincidence between ethics and language. In the end, Cicero entered the scholastic canon as a paradigm of perfect Latin and an icon of eloquence, overshadowing and transcending his perishable image as a human being, unable to counter Antony's violence.[182]

In consequence, the reception of Cicero's speeches in the early empire pivoted on Cicero as a writer and stylist more than as a historical figure.

---

[179] On the "beatification" of Cicero under the Principate and his idealization as "the rhetorical stylist" ("not the statesman who declared himself an enemy of Caesar and Octavian"), see Sinclair 1994: 105 (who correctly points out that "the canonized Cicero served both as a touchstone of unattainable rhetorical talent and as a warning against the political dangers of *libertas*," as demonstrated by the examples of Cassius Severus and Labienus, admirers of Cicero's spirit of *libertas* and banished because of their sharp-tongued criticism against the imperial power).

[180] On Cicero the *person*, as distinct from Cicero the word for eloquence "because he (sc. Cicero) experiences such a 'modern' alienation from himself and then, through his very erasure becomes the template for alienation and enfranchisement through culture," see Dressler 2015: 149ff.

[181] Kaster 1998: 262.

[182] Wilson (M.) 2008: 323: "Declamation asserts, even against the historical evidence, the greater power of the word over the sword. The battle that counts is the battle for the judgment of posterity."

This is not to say that Cicero's political deeds ceased to attract attention from scholars and teachers. As we shall see in the following chapter, ancient exegesis abounds in comments on the historical background of Cicero's oratorical performances and, most importantly, on the interrelation between oratory and power in Cicero's political speeches. But the first- and second-century CE Ciceronian scholarship was patently characterized by attention to stylistic and linguistic features of Cicero's prose. The status of Cicero as *optimus auctor*, fount of incorrupt Latin, stimulated linguistic examinations of the speeches, plundered for select Latin words and sentences. Scholars customarily commented upon Cicero's language, remarking on his fondness for archaisms or *singularia*, drawing attention to alleged deviations from the urban standard and, above all, pinpointing peculiarities in vocabulary and literary register. They expounded on Cicero's ability "to put the right words in the right places, with the right stylistic finish"[183] in order to instruct pupils in the correct use of words (also rare and unusual) deployed in the model.

Before our discussion proceeds further, it is worth refreshing our memory on the relevance of the study of Cicero's language to Roman pedagogy. It is beyond question that the approach to Cicero's orations as linguistic models was a natural response to educational needs. Imitation of Cicero's style, a key point of Quintilian's neo-classicism, as we have seen, satisfied an idealized vision of rhetoric, designed to "give rise to a new kind of orator, *Romanus sapiens* ('a Roman wise man', 12.2.7), who is suited to political leadership because of his moral superiority and unparalleled persuasive ability."[184] Bloomer has nicely demonstrated that Quintilian's pedagogical project, the most reliable testimony to current education theories, sees the child as the subject/agent of a learning process, a gradual movement towards maturity under the guidance of erudite teachers.[185] "Rendering the child moral and making the boy a man".[186] This was the ambitious goal of Quintilian's teacher, in terms of an ethical and cultural development aimed at acquiring propriety of language and intellectual finesse with the support of suitable linguistic models. Within this perspective, a child training in linguistic skills represented the first stage in instruction, commonly termed *eruditio*. By learning to speak properly, *Latine loqui*, the mature child was equipped with the opportunity to play a relevant role in adult society, a public space dominated by an "aristocratic" sense of language.

Naturally, *eruditio* starts with removing what is rude and inappropriate in diction and language. Correctness, the basic stylistic virtue, which

---

[183] Powell 2013: 71.   [184] López 2007: 321.   [185] Bloomer 2011a.   [186] Bloomer 2011a: 111.

formed, together with clarity, appropriateness and ornamentation, the basis of *elocutio*, prose style,[187] was a pedagogical concern. Usually designated by the term *Latinitas*, "Latinness," the Roman equivalent to the Greek *Hellenismós* ("Greekness"),[188] correctness of language relied on the connection of two interchangeable features, "pure speech" (*sermo purus*) and "avoidance of error" (*ab omni vitio remotus*).[189] An expression of the *consensus eruditorum*, the linguistic usage pursued by the educated,[190] *Latinitas* was thought of as the final point of *eruditio*, culminating in the acquisition of pure Latin, nurtured by good examples and practices.[191]

Shaping and fashioning the child's uncultivated mind entailed cleaning up Latin and fixing norms of literary language. In this road to purification (and standardization) of Latin Cicero occupied a special place. His language, a model of regularity, was chosen "as the norm of correct usage."[192] Revered as an expert in linguistic matters by contemporary men of learning,[193] Cicero embodied virtuous language, a perfect synthesis of correctness, lucidity and elegance of diction. As has been observed,

---

[187] Quint. *Inst.* 1.5.1 *Iam cum omnis oratio tris habeat virtutes, ut emendate, ut dilucida, ut ornata sit (quia dicere apte, quod est praecipuum, plerique ornatui subiiciunt), totidem vitia, quae sunt supra dictis contraria, emendate loquendi regulam, quae grammatices prior pars est, examinet* ("Style has three kinds of excellence, correctness, lucidity and elegance – for many include the all-important quality of appropriateness under the heading of elegance. Its faults are likewise threefold, namely the opposites of these excellences. The teacher of literature therefore must study the rules for correctness of speech, these constituting the first part of his art"). Text and translation of Quintilian: Russell 2001.

[188] Morgan (T.) 1998a: 178. A good analysis of the notion of "language correctness" (*Hellenismós*) in the Greek world is now in Pagani 2015.

[189] *Rhet. Her.* 4.12.17 *Latinitas est quae sermonem purum conservat, ab omni vitio remotum. Vitia in sermone quo minus is Latinus sit duo possunt esse: soloecismus et barbarismus* ("It is correct Latinity which keeps the language pure, and free of any fault. The faults in language which can mar its Latinity are two: the solecism and the barbarism"): text and translation: Caplan 2004. Cf. also Varro in Diom. *GL* 1.439.15.

[190] Clackson 2011b: 241. See also Grebe 2001: 161.

[191] Quint. *Inst.* 1.6; 10.1.27–36 (on *sermo Latinus*, based on the combination of *ratio*, "analogy and etymology," *vetustas*, "antiquity of a word," *auctoritas*, "literary authority" and *consuetudo*, "common usage"). On Quintilian's definition of *Latinitas*, see Coleman 2000 (also Maselli 1979: 38–55); for Varro and Quintilian on the "correct speech," see Grebe 2001. On *Latinitas*, "Sprachrichtigkeit," in Servius and the grammatical praxis, see Uhl 1998: 27–40.

[192] Powell 2013: 55. For Cicero's bombastic self-presentation as a model of stylistic fullness in *Off.* 1.2, see Dyck 1996: 60–5.

[193] Particularly instructive is an anecdote reported by Aulus Gellius (10.1.7), concerning the dedication of the temple of Victory placed at the top of the theater of Pompey. Quoting from a letter of Tiro, Cicero's freedman, Gellius informs us that Pompey, puzzling over the correct formulation of the inscription to be incised in the temple (whether *consul tertium* should be written, or *tertio*), a question much disputed by the most learned men of Rome, turned to Cicero to request his advice. Cicero cautiously recommended to use the abbreviation *tert.*, "so that the meaning was shown without writing the whole word, but yet the doubt as to the form of the word was concealed" (*ut verbo non perscripto res quidem demonstraretur, sed dictio tamen ambigua verbi lateret*).

Cicero "happened to live at a time when the Latin language was going through a process of standardization."[194] The educated elite in the late republic cultivated urban and refined language.[195] Cicero cooperated with the members of the Roman aristocracy in polishing up language and defining rules of standard, pure and correct Latin. His attitude, both theoretical and practical, toward linguistic issues, as illustrated in many of his rhetorical works,[196] impacted on determining the notion of *Latinitas*, the idea of correct Latin, "which, as a priority, should embody the usage of the educated urban elite, but which must also take due note of the best practice of the past (thus acknowledging both *vetustas* 'antiquity' and *auctoritas*), albeit with a final outcome subject to minor correction and regularization according to grammatical principle (*ratio*)."[197]

Identifying Cicero's linguistic virtues with the concept of *Latinitas* implies also reassessing the importance of proficiency in Latin language to social and political hierarchies. Since *Latinitas* was the expression of Rome's aristocratic ideals, involving promotion of Roman values through literary activity and the creation of an urban language,[198] facility in language was intrinsic to public reputation. Deeply embedded in the Roman cultural tradition, training in language and consequent appropriation of stylistic "correct modes" interlaced with elite identity and political power. As has been noted, proper pronunciation and grammatical knowledge (along with humor) were natural, aristocratic, types of behavior that revealed a true Roman, a member of the cultivated classes who was expected to promote and transmit notions underlying the very concept of *Romanitas*.[199] As Cicero himself stresses in the *De oratore* (3.37–9; 150–51), good diction (*Latinitas* or *elegantia*) was a prerogative of the educated *civis Romanus*.[200] Learning to *Latine loqui* then played a pivotal role in the run for political leadership. Linguistic competence and command functioned as forms of self-presentation and "the necessary cultural capital needed to be exhibited in order to claim a place in the discourse of the elite."[201]

Within this interaction between language and power, correctness and verbal propriety reinforced and sustained the social order. As has been

---

[194] Powell 2013: 55.
[195] For Caesar's treatise on the principles of correct Latinity (*de ratione Latine loquendi*) cf. Cic. *Brut.* 253. On Caesar's *De analogia*, see now Garcea 2012 (esp. 50–77, for the rhetorical doctrine of *elegantia* and the virtue of *Latinitas*).
[196] Cic. *Brut.* 258; *De orat.* 3.39.    [197] Clackson-Horrocks 2007: 206.
[198] Clackson-Horrocks 2007: 187. See also Krostenko 2001: 123.    [199] Corbeill 2001: 283–4.
[200] Sinclair 1994: 93.
[201] McNelis 2007: 293. On competitive aristocratic eloquence in the late republic and the early empire, see Roller 2011.

noted, Cicero identified ordered style and political order, naturalizing aristocratic beliefs and structures through equation of masculine language with civic virtue.[202] What made the child a "virile man," admitted to the ranks of Rome's elite, was language and its political force, its impact on favoring enhancement of status and social advancement. Thus, mastery of Cicero's urban language marked adolescents out as elite male citizens. "Speaking like Cicero" became assimilated to "speaking like a man." Familiarity with Cicero's *Latinitas* signaled masculinity and secured *auctoritas* in Roman aristocratic society.

It might also be tempting to say that Cicero's *Latinitas* stresses the connection between morals and communication in Roman education system. Knowledge of correct, Ciceronian Latin expanded the linguistic potential of elite male students, who entered the world of political oratory as matured, educated speakers. Fluency in Latin molded the child as a "new Cicero," a good speaker with proper authority and social status. But good acquaintance with Cicero's urban and aristocratic language was also beneficial to the process of maturation. Training in Ciceronian language, a decisive move on the path to maturity and affirmation of the individual, validated the correspondence between the ideal orator, the "modern" *vir bonus dicendi peritus*, and ideal society. As has been said, good Latin was a moral requirement of a good Roman citizen.[203] In a sense, adopting Cicero as a handbook of good Latin was an expression of the desire to preserve Roman identity and propagate ethical values associated with Roman elite culture.

It has often been reiterated that Cicero, model of *Latinitas*, was the quintessence of the perfect pleader. Yet a *perfectus orator* must of necessity be an *optimus civis*.[204] "Men speak as they live".[205] The Greek motto identifies morality with language. Cicero's pure Latin, as a display of both aristocratic ideals and ethics, contributed to shaping the character of the fresh orator and producing a *vir bonus*, a "good man." Speaking like Cicero rendered a young man virtuous, a limpid example of virtuous political community. Turning to Quintilian's pedagogy, we have already pointed to the equation of language with morality, training in language with training in ethics, as the basis of Quintilian's moralized "classicism,"[206] a principled *eruditio*, in which Cicero is elevated to the figure of the ideal orator and man,

---

[202] Cic. *de Orat.*1.34: Connolly 2007b: 92.   [203] Cic. *Brut.* 140; Adams 2003b: 185–6.
[204] Quint. *Inst.* 12.1.16–19.   [205] Sen. *Ep.* 114.1.
[206] Quint. *Inst.* 1.6.44–5 (*Ergo consuetudinem sermonis vocabo consensum eruditorum, sicut vivendi consensum bonorum,* "I will therefore define usage in speech as the agreed practice of educated men, just as where our way of life is concerned I should define it as the agreed practice of all good men").

a perfect embodiment of linguistic and moral virtues. Gowing has well shown that, whereas Seneca expresses reservations about Cicero's moral authority, Quintilian "sets Cicero apart from ordinary mortals," according him a dominant, durable status as both a wise man and a master of language.[207] Quintilian's *Institutio* aspired to producing a ruling educated class, made of manly virtuous speakers, prepared to play a central role in Roman politics and society through the power of the word. Cicero, with his undisputable authority as both a writer and a *vir bonus,* enjoyed a pre-eminent place in the ethically structured universe of Roman education.

## From Quintilian to the Scholiasts: Cicero's Authority on Latin

Let us now home in on the manifold use of Cicero's language in the school. There were various aspects of Cicero's style and language that received scholarly attention in antiquity. Quintilian's chapters on grammar (*Inst.* 1. 4–8) reveal how important Cicero was to the definition of the rules of the *recte loquendi scientia,* "the art of speaking properly," correctly defined as "a systematically proceeding and normative model of language teaching."[208] When dealing with the elementary stages of grammar, concerning spelling and pronunciation, Quintilian supports his comments by drawing on Cicero as a grammatical source. In *Inst.*1.4.11 he calls to mind Cicero's preference for consonantalization of *i* (*aiio, Maiia*).[209] Aspiration of *f* in Greek is explained by reference to Cicero's lost speech *pro Fundanio* (*Inst.* 1.4.14).[210] Quintilian's discussion of grammatical vices, encompassing barbarism, that is, distortion of single words by addition, omission, transposition or substitution of letters, and solecism, a grammatical error produced by the faulty combination of words, also widely relies on Ciceronian examples. At *Inst.* 1.5.8 Quintilian cites the Sardinian word *mastruca,* from Cicero's *pro Scauro,*[211] as an example of barbarism by addition. Barbarism by substitution in prose is legitimized by Cicero's use of *Canopus,* instead of the local name *Canobus,* in the speech *De rege Alexandrino* (*Inst.* 1.5.13).[212] Cicero's authority is further evoked in dismissing the erroneous interpretation of *scripsere* as a case of

---

[207] Gowing 2013: 248. [208] Ax 2011a: 331; see also Ax 2011b: 230–31.
[209] Cf. also Vel. *orth.* V.1 Di Napoli (*GL* 7.54.1–55.10). Cf. *GL* 7.79.1–5 for Velius Longus's praise of Cicero's *elegantia,* exemplified by the deletion of the consonant *n* from words, such as *foresia, Megalesia, hortesia,* in order to produce smoothness of sound, *lenitatis causa.*
[210] According to Quintilian, Cicero mocked the inability of a witness to pronounce the name of Fundanius properly. On Cicero's defense of Fundanius, prosecuted for *ambitus* or *maiestas* in 67 or 66 BC, see Crawford 1994: 57–64.
[211] Frg. h Clark (cf. Isid. *Orig.* 19.23.5).
[212] Frg11Crawford (see Crawford 1994: 56, for a commentary on the fragment).

solecism of number (*Inst.*1.5.44).[213] In addition, in listing Latin and foreign words Quintilian recurs to Cicero's *pro Milone* (§ 28) to introduce the Gallic word *raeda* (*Inst.* 1.5.57). Again, in the section devoted to compound words (*compositae voces*), Quintilian offers Cicero's *subabsurdus* as an example of words with a double prefix (*Inst.* 1.5.65).[214] Finally, in laying down the rules of correct orthography, subjected to frequent change in accordance with *usus*,[215] Quintilian traces back the doubling of *s* to Cicero's times (*Inst.* 1.7.20).[216]

In Quintilian's scientific presentation of grammar Cicero incarnates the demarcation between correct and incorrect Latin. By promoting Cicero as a grammatical *auctor*, Quintilian teams up with his source to exhort his pupils to "avoid anything that did not accord with current educated urban usage, whether unassimilated regionalisms or mistaken analogical formations."[217] Quintilian's treatment of grammatical topics may also be helpful in clarifying the question concerning the use of prose authors in the grammar school. Notoriously, reading and interpretation of prose texts was a significant part of the *rhetor*'s profession. The *enarratio poetarum*, explanation of poetry texts,[218] usually set the grammar school off from both the primary school, the *ludus litterarius*,[219] and the school of the *rhetor*, associated with the study of the prose authors.[220] As is well known, Quintilian recommended Cicero as both pleasant and accessible reading to the beginners at the rhetoric school (*Inst.* 2.5.18–20). Among the *optimi auctores*, listed in the short history of classical literature in Book Ten of Quintilian's *Institutio* (10.1.27–36), Cicero stands out as the undisputed model of Latin prose. Whether Cicero's orations were also read and expounded at the school of the *grammaticus* remains a controversial matter. Ancient evidence does not bear out the perception of Cicero as a standard author in the grammar school.[221] A passage from the second book of

---

[213] Cic. *Orat.* 157.
[214] Cic. *de Orat.* 2.274. Cf. also Quint. *Inst.* 1.5.66 on the word *capsis*, defined by Cicero as a three-noun formation from "*cape si vis*" (Cic. *Orat.* 154).
[215] Quint. *Inst.* 1.7.11.
[216] *Quid quod Ciceronis temporibus paulumque infra, fere quotiens s littera media vocalium longarum vel subiecta longis esset, geminabatur, ut "caussae" "cassus" "divisiones"*? ("Again in Cicero's days and a little later, it was the almost universal practice to write a double *s*, whenever that letter occurred between two long vowels or after a long vowel, as for example in *caussae, cassus, divisiones*").
[217] Powell 2013: 56. On the use of examples in Roman grammarians, see Vainio 2000.
[218] Quint. *Inst.* 1.4.2    [219] Kaster 1983: 334.
[220] On literary instruction in antiquity and the three stages of schooling (primary school or *ludus litterarius*, secondary or grammar school and the school of rhetoric) see Bonner 1977: 34ff; 165ff.; Kaster 1983.
[221] For the list of *auctores* in the grammar school, see Pugliarello 2009; De Paolis 2013b.

Quintilian's handbook (2.1.4)[222] seems to be alluding to the practice of teaching history or prose literature in the school of the *grammaticus*. But *enarratio* of history and oratory was explicitly reserved to the *rhetor*, as underlined by Quintilian himself at 2.5.1. Though it is possible to suppose that the *grammatici* taught some history, at least in the form of basic historical information, arguing that oratory was regularly taught in the grammar schools is much more problematic.[223]

Nevertheless, as has been noted, "the grammarian could not possibly have fulfilled his task of teaching proper grammatical usage without being thoroughly familiar with the texts of the standard prose writers, and he would also frequently refer to them in his classroom commentaries on the poets."[224] According to Quintilian (*Inst.* 1.4.4), the grammarian should not limit himself to reading the poets: "every type of literature must be thoroughly combed" (*excutiendum omne scriptorum genus*) in order to learn "words that acquire authority from their use by a particular author" (*verba, quae frequenter ius ab auctoribus sumunt*). Within this context, Quintilian's frequent use of Cicero as a grammatical source may testify to standard teaching procedures in the grammar school. As MacCormack notes, the boundaries between grammar and rhetoric "were porous" and, as shown by Servius's repeated use of Cicero in his commentary on Vergil, the two disciplines "interpenetrated each other."[225] Conceivably, the grammarian was allowed to explain rules of normative grammar by referring to select passages or sentences of prose authors. Taking a step further, grammarians and schoolteachers set standards of correct Latin usage by looking at Cicero as an authority on Latinity.

To consolidate our perception of Cicero as a source of good Latin, it may be convenient to look through Gellius's sophisticated debates on etymology and meaning of words,[226] which offer us interesting insights into Roman culture in the Antonine age and the role played by Cicero in

---

[222] *Nos suum cuique professioni modum demus: et grammatice, quam in Latinum transferentes litteraturam vocaverunt, fines suos norit, praesertim tantum ab hac appellationis suae paupertate, intra quam primi illi constitere, provecta; nam tenuis a fonte adsumptis †historicorum criticorumque† viribus pleno iam satis alveo fluit* ("Let us assign its proper sphere to each profession. Grammar, which has been translated into Latin as the science of letters, must recognize its own limits, especially as it has encroached so far beyond the boundaries to which its unpretentious name should restrict it and to which its earlier professors actually confined themselves. Springing from a tiny fountain-head, it has gathered strength from the historians and critics and has swollen to the dimensions of a brimming river").
[223] Reinhardt-Winterbottom 2006: 44–46.   [224] Bonner 1977: 218.
[225] MacCormack 2013: 300.
[226] For Gellius's linguistic discussions, see Maselli 1979; Cavazza 1987; Holford-Strevens 2003:48–64; 172–92.

the second-century revitalization of Latin cultural tradition. Preliminarily, it seems necessary to call attention to the ideological and political perspective that dominates Gellius's construction of cultural authority in the *Attic Nights*. As Keulen has shown, Gellius was neither a blind traditionalist fond of linguistic disputes as a form of elite diversion, nor an apolitical anecdotalist. He fashioned himself as a Roman author and actively contributed to the consolidation of Latin cultural tradition by an educational program which stimulated "reflections about cultural identity and literary canons, and about values and competences that mark out a true intellectual aristocracy."[227] Thus, Gellius's interest in language, especially his claim for the superiority of pure Republican Latin, was a relevant part of a cultural and political discourse, which aimed at preserving the collective memory of the past and consolidating Roman authority and identity.[228] By reading, studying and scrutinizing a shared corpus of authoritative texts, the educationalist Gellius legitimated cultural *auctoritas* of past literary precedents and laid the foundations of a scientific language, based on *veritas* and a systematical, methodical approach to ancient texts, recognized as pedagogical authorities and enduring monuments to the traditions of the past.[229]

Gellius's affection for the republican past and his often-ridiculed inquiries into old, pre-classical forms fit into a strategy that combines the notion of authority with the reproduction/replication of Roman cultural values. For Gellius, language was the supreme expression of cultural authority and elite status. Despite recent attempts to undermine the cultural force of the archaizing movement in the Antonine age,[230] Gellius's classicism, his revival of Republican Latin, was intended to convey a moral-educational message, that is, the inculcation of Roman values through the establishment of a written paradigm of *Romanitas* for contemporary society. In this perceived interconnection of good learning and good *mores*,[231] linguistic corruption and contamination with improper training systems, such as normative, modernistic

---

[227] Keulen 2009: 7.    [228] On the *Attic Nights* as *monumenta memoriae*, see Heusch 2011.
[229] For Gellius's critical attitude toward antiquity and his "love" of the past, in terms of an incessant investigation into the mediated transmission of a value system, see Howley 2014.
[230] Swain 2004.
[231] On the union of *doctrina* and *mores* in the literary and cultural program of the *grammaticus*, see Kaster 1988: 60–6 (who points to the opposition between the "centripetal force of learning, tending toward personal distinction and autonomy," and "the centripetal force of *mores*, urging conformity to established values and behavior," a tension resolved in different contexts through a subordination of *doctrina* to *mores*: 65).

grammar,[232] represented a menace to both the moral conduct of the Roman aristocracy and the consolidation of Roman cultural identity.

If "exemplary teaching goes hand in hand with imbibing the pure, uncontaminated language of exemplary authors,"[233] it follows that Cicero represented the pedagogical response to the deterioration of standards of education in the Antonine society. As the incarnation of pure language and *Latinitas*, Cicero established himself as a true cultural authority, radically opposed to the false authority embodied in *litteratores* and professional grammarians. Gellius's concern for purity and correctness of speech reflects his anxiety over wrong education and the moral decline of the youth. As has been demonstrated, behind the "pure milk" of Favorinus, the nourishment of the young, in chapter 12.1 we are invited to recognize the notion of education and learning, metaphorically symbolized by the *fons sanctus*, "the sacred fount" of the uncorrupt language, which preserves the nobility of *corpus* and *animus*, "body" and "soul."[234] It may be tempting to say that behind the *fons sanctissimus* lay the Ciceronian Latin, the recognized example of pure eloquence of the past. Thus, Gellius's *commemoratio* of Cicero's *Latinitas* turns out to be a means of establishing authority and preserving purity of language. Cicero's eloquence nurtures Gellius's ideological and educational program. Through Cicero, Gellius protects linguistic tradition and communicates love for moral and cultural values charismatically associated with the dominant role of the Roman elite.

Counted among those "men of early days who spoke properly and purely" (*veteres qui proprie atque integre locuti sunt*),[235] Cicero is praised for his elegance of diction and fine artistry in a significant number of *loci Gelliani*. Most of them portray Cicero as a "'poet of the word," an artist engaged in revivifying the harmony and musicality of Latin through a proper selection of words and forms. Chapter 1.7 illustrates the controversy over Cicero's archaizing taste in the contemporary society. Gellius legitimates Cicero's predilection for alleged archaic forms, as we have seen.[236] Cicero's preference for the expression *in potestatem fuisse* at *Man.* 33, questioned by the half-educated, and his choice of the perfect *explicavit*, in place of *explicuit*, at *Man.* 30, is defended on rhythmical grounds

---

[232] For Gellius's contempt of school prescriptions and his polemic against the boasted authority of *grammatici*, see Vardi 2001; Holford-Strevens 2003: 172–74; Keulen 2009: 28–32.
[233] Keulen 2009: 34.   [234] Keulen 2009: 32–4.
[235] Gel. 6.11.2. Cicero is ranked among the *veteres* at 1.4.8; 9.12.4; 18.7.8.
[236] On Cicero's archaisms and the related debate over the diffusion of fake Tironian manuscripts in the Antonine age, see chapter 2, pp. 62–66.

## Cicero's Authority on Latin

(1.7.18–20).[237] According to Gellius, both the constructions, producing a rhythmic combination of short and long syllables (ditrochee) more appropriate to the end of cola, would entice readers by being "more agreeable to the ear and better rounded" (*iucundius ad aurem completiusque*). In chapter 2.17.2–3 Gellius touches upon the nature of the prefixes *in* and *con* and approves of Cicero's "musical" interpretation of language, regulated by the "pleasure of the ear" (*voluptas aurium*) and the "principle of euphony" (*ratio suavitatis*).[238] Similarly, at chapter 15.3.1–3 the alteration of the preposition *ab* into *au* in verbs such as *fugio* (*abfugio>aufugio*) and *fero* (*abfero>aufero*) is legitimated by its sound and pronunciation, in line with Cicero's formulation in *Orator* 158.[239]

Admiration for Cicero's linguistic finesse and sensibility permeates Gellius's encyclopedic work. At chapter 13.21, the Antonine scholar agrees with the first-century grammarian M. Valerius Probus, a respected man of learning,[240] in chiding the rigidity and abstractness of school grammar and appreciating musicality of diction. The one who speaks good Latin "follows only the ear, which weighs words according to its own standards" (*solam aurem secuti sunt, suis verba modulis pensitantem* 13.21.23), as demonstrated by Cicero's choice of *fretu* instead of *freto* (*Verr.* 2.5.169), *peccatu* instead of *peccato* (*Verr.* 2.2.191) and *antistitae* instead of *antistites* (*Verr.* 2.4.99), and forcefully affirmed by Cicero himself in *Orator* 168 (13.21.24).[241] In chapter 13.25, the philosopher and polymath Favorinus, a dominant figure in Gellius's collection,[242] while admiring the monumental spaces of Trajan's forum discusses the meaning of the word *manubiae*, joined by significance to its near-synonym *praeda*.[243] The debate centers on the repetition, supposedly idle and inelegant (*inanis et inlepida*), of these two words in a passage of Cicero's first speech on the Agrarian law, a repetition occurring again in the second speech against Rullus (2.59).

---

[237] Holford-Strevens 2003: 187.   [238] Cic. *Orat.* 159.

[239] Gellius seems to opt for a derivation of *au-* from the Greek (Homeric) αὖ: Holford-Strevens 2003: 183.

[240] Probus is referred to in Gellius's work on more than one occasion: cf. 1.15.18; 3.1.5; 4.7.1; 6.7.3; 9.9.12; 15.30.5; 17.9.5. On the literary activity of Probus see *supra* chapter 2, p. 61 n53 (cf. Suet. *Gramm.* 24, with Kaster 1995: 242–69). For the role played by Probus in the *Attic Nights*, see Holford-Strevens 2003: 163–65.

[241] "*Quod qui non sentiunt,*" *inquit idem ipse M. Cicero, cum de numerosa et apta oratione dissereret,* "*quas auris habeant aut quid in hominis simile sit, nescio*" ("'And for those who do not feel this', says Cicero himself, when speaking about appropriate and rhythmical language, 'I know not what ears they have, or what there is in them resembling a man'").

[242] On Favorinus in Gellius, see Holford-Strevens 2003: 98–130. See also Lakmann 1997; Beall 2001; Heusch 2011: 261–70.

[243] On chapter 13.25 and Gellius's strategy of visualizing Roman sites and shaping his reader's perception of Roman identity, see Keulen 2009: 237–41.

To Favorinus, a clever and subtle interpreter of language and an expert in Latin,[244] repetition and accumulation of similar words is not a symptom of linguistic ineptness or feebleness. It is rather a mark of dignity (*dignitas*) and copiousness (*copia*), a sign of both elegance and rhetorical vehemence, as confirmed by Cicero's invectives against Caecilius (*Div.* 19; 11) and Piso (*Pis.* 1). But in the case under discussion, Favorinus says, Cicero has not placed similar words in the same context inconsiderately. Since *manubiae* and *praeda* are differentiated from each other, the former indicating the money collected by the quaestor from the sale of the war booty, the latter the objects which make up the booty, Cicero's conscious juxtaposition of two synonyms displays propriety of language and an uncommon linguistic sensibility (13.25.24–32).[245]

As Holford-Strevens notes, Gellius was not "a beggar but an artist."[246] He was a true lover of words, "little gems" (*gemmulae*),[247] which decorate the architectonic structure of Roman elite language. Within this idealized, aristocratic vision of Latin it is no surprise that Cicero emerges as a master of Latin words.[248] Implicitly contesting Fronto's stylistic authority, Gellius dismisses the label of sophisticated manipulator of *verba pulcherrima,* "the most beautiful words," applied to his cultural model.[249] In chapter 1.15 he scorns vain and empty loquacity and sees the habit of spouting forth a disorderly mass of words "with no exercise of judgment" (*sine ullo iudicii negotio*: 1.15.2) as the epitome of ignorance.[250] In his view, Cicero deserves highest praise for founding his vocabulary on usage (*consuetudo*) and stylistic accuracy[251] and, most importantly, for combining clarity with ornamentation by selecting the *verbum proprium,* the appropriate word

---

[244] Favorinus's interest in Latin is discussed by Beall 2001: 92–5.

[245] Particularly interesting is chapter 17.1, where Gellius defends Cicero from attacks from linguistic detractors (Asinius Gallus and Larcius Licinus) and takes *paeniteat* at *Cael.* 6 in the meaning of "repent," cleverly elaborating on the ambiguity of the verb *paenitere* and rating Cicero's use of the word as "elegant and witty in the highest degree" (*festivissimum adeo et facetissimum* 17.1.10); see Holford-Strevens 2003: 206–7. On Cicero's *urbanitas* and his *calliditas,* "subtlety," cf. also Gel. 12.12.

[246] Holford-Strevens 2003: 49.   [247] Fronto *Ep. M. Caes.* 4.3.6 (58.25Hout).

[248] In chapter 10.21 Gellius comments positively on Cicero's refusal to employ improper words, such as *novissimus* and *novissime*. For Gellius's appreciation of Cicero's language, see also Michel 1992.

[249] Fronto *Ep. M. Caes.* 4.3.3 (57.5-20Hout). Holford-Strevens 2003: 134 (on Fronto's judgment of Cicero, reputed to be "too proud, too lazy, or too diffident to search out the unlooked-for and unexpected word"). For Fronto on Cicero cf. also *Ant.* 3.1.1 (97Hout); 3.8.2 (104.12Hout); *Ver.* 2<1> 14 (124.7Hout); *Amic.* 1.14.2 (180.8-13Hout); *Parth.* 10 (225Hout). See chapter 1, p. 61.

[250] Gel. 1.15.5 (cf. Cic. *De orat.* 1.51; 3.142).

[251] Gel. 12.13.17–29 (on the use of *intra* for *citra* in Cic. *Ver.* 2.3.207; *Fam.* 4.4.4: SB*Fam; Sest.* 58); 13.22.6 (on the word *gallica,* properly used by Cicero at *Phil.* 2.76); 15.5.5–7 (*adfectum,* not *profligatum,* in the sense of "nearly done, finished" in Cic. *Prov.* 19; 29). For Gellius's etymological judgment, see Holford-Strevens 2003: 180–4.

or group of words that allow readers or listeners to discern the speaker's meaning and to appreciate its charming effects on the ear.[252] It follows then that the choice of difficult words, or of words erroneously deemed incorrect, becomes a mark of linguistic acuteness.[253] In the case of similar words, or near-synonyms, which present a subtle gradation of meaning or register, Cicero meticulously pondered their proper significance and application to a specific context.[254] As solemnly affirmed by the teacher of rhetoric Antonius Julianus, while elucidating a Ciceronian syllogism at *Planc.* 68 (in chapter 1.4), what elicits our admiration is the "fine artistry in the way the words are marshalled, something well-rounded that charms the ear by its mere music" (*crispum agmen orationis rotundumque ac modulo ipso numerorum venustum*, 1.4.4). As a visible demonstration of *urbanitas*, when comparing a debt of gratitude with that of money, Cicero artfully substituted *habet* for *debet* in the case of gratitude to preserve "the truth of the proposition" (*sententiae fides* 1.4.5) and retain the "careful balance of the period" (*concinnitatem sententiae*, 1.4.8).[255]

In the *Attic Nights*, Cicero achieves the status of an exemplar of linguistic sensibility and finesse, a model of well-balanced, rhythmical prose. Gellius's educational program of restoration of pure Latinity embraces Cicero as both an icon of correctness and elegance and a Roman cultural authority. Cicero's *verborum proprietas*, his care in selecting the best words, was not admired by everyone, however. Partially dissenting from Gellius, Fronto extolled Cato as the most distinguished among prose writers for his care in searching out unexpected words. In Fronto's view, Cicero was "magnificent above all other orators in embellishing the subject which he wished to set out" (*ante omnes alios oratores ad ea, quae ostentare vellet,*

---

[252] In chapter 10.3.14–5, when comparing passages on the same topic from the speeches of Gaius Gracchus, Cicero and Cato, Gellius contrasts Gracchus's plain narrative with Cicero's pathetic, vigorous description in the fifth Verrine (2.5.161–2) and glorifies Cicero's superiority in the "harmonious arrangement of the words" (*verborum modificatio*).

[253] Gel. 2.6.8 (Cic. *Ver.* 4.122 for the word *vexare*); 4.9.6–7 (Cic. *Att.* 9.5.2: SB*Att*; *Div. Caec.* 3 on the proper meaning of *religiosus*); 7.11.6–13 (Cic. *Sul.* 72; *Agr.* 2.100 for the sense of the verb *deprecor* as "beg off," already in Catullus 92; Cic. *Rep.* 6.2.2; *Caec.* 30; *Ver.* 2.2.192 on *deprecor* as "to avert"); 12.10 (the good old form *aeditumus* in place of *aedituus* is in Cic. *Ver.* 2.4.96). Sometimes Gellius credits Cicero with interpreting some words in a sense that is actually at variance with our evidence; e.g. 1.22 (*superesse* is properly intended as "to overflow, exceed" in Varro and Cic. *Rep.* 3.32; however, *superesse* for "remain to do" in *de Orat.* 3.31); 13.17 (*liberalitas* is regularly interpreted by Varro and Cicero as "education and training in the liberal arts," but *liberalitas* in the Greek sense of "good-feeling towards all men" appears in *Sex. Rosc.* 46, *Q. fr.* 1.1.27: SB); see Holford-Strevens 2003: 177–8.

[254] Gel. 6.11 (Cic. *Phil.* 2.77 on the different use of *levitas* and *nequitia*); 9.12.3–6 (Cic. *Planc.* 1 on the double meaning of *infestus*).

[255] Holford-Strevens 2003: 87–8.

*ornanda magnificum fuisse*).[256] Yet he was "far from disposed to search out words with especial care" (*a quaerendis scupulosius verbis procul fuisse*); he handled all kind of words (literal, figurative, simple, compound, noble and exquisite) but "unexpected and unlooked for terms" (*insperata atque inopinata verba*), hunted out with study and careful exquisition of literary memories,[257] are rarely found in his orations.[258] To put it in other words, Fronto subordinated Cicero to Cato in the search for "special" words. Gellius and Fronto adopted a divergent stance on Cicero's role as a linguistic authority, a literary-scientific debate concentrated primarily upon the notion of *proprietas*, selection of proper words, a core tenet of *Latinitas*.[259]

Creativity in Latin vocabulary, undoubtedly one of the most innovative characteristics of Cicero's style, enchanted ancient scholars.[260] As has been observed, Cicero exploited the unexplored potentialities of Republican Latin by introducing new words (abstract nouns in particular), using non-Latin words and poeticisms, embellishing his style with near-synonyms or terms with a subtle gradation of meaning and adapting nouns and adjectives to the demands of rhythm and a specific literary register.[261] He contributed to the continuous, dynamic, process of lexical coinage. With Cicero "Latin increased the number of its words by reproducing pre-existing patterns and extending its productive groups."[262] Remarkably, Cicero's cultivation (and expansion) of vocabulary, a lynchpin of his idea of *Latinitas*, did not go unnoticed by the modernist Aper, who pointed to Cicero's attentive care for words as one of the distinguishing qualities of the orator's sophisticated style, along with word order and arrangement, metaphors and figures of speech, and the search for pointed expressions

---

[256] Fronto *Ep. M. Caes.* 4.3.3 (57.7-8Hout). The letter well illustrates Fronto's stylistic judgment of Cicero's oratorical prose.

[257] Fronto *Ep. M. Caes.* 4.3.3 (57.8-20Hout).

[258] On the superiority of Cicero's epistles over the orations cf. Fronto *Ad Antoninum Imp. et Invicem Liber III.7* (104.1-3Hout): *Ciceronis epistulas si forte electas totas vel dimidiates habes, inperti aut mone, quas potissimum legendas mihi censeas ad facultatem sermonis fovendam* ("If you have any selected letters of Cicero, either entire or in extracts, lend me them or tell me which you think I ought particularly to read to improve my command of language"); *III. 8* (104.12Hout): *Omnes autem Ciceronis epistulas legendas censeo, mea sententia vel magis quam omnis eius orationes: epistulis Ciceronis nihil est perfectius* ("All Cicero's letters, however, should, I think, be read, in my opinion even more than his speeches. There is nothing more perfect than Cicero's letters").

[259] Seneca the Elder's collection reminds us of some declaimers enchanted with Cicero's affection for archaisms and disused forms: cf. *Con. 4 praef.* 4–11 (on Haterius, who used to recite declamations filled with *antiqua dicta Ciceronis*).

[260] Cf. Cic. *Brut.* 253 on Caesar's praise of Cicero's diction and vocabulary (in his treatise on the principles of correct Latinity).

[261] Powell 2013: 57–9.    [262] Fruyt 2011: 151.

(Tac. *Dial.* 22.2). It is well known that Aper's stylistic appreciation, part of a more general assault on old literature, confines itself to Cicero's last speeches, regarded as the mature results of a process of stylistic refinement. We have already seen that Aper criticized the early Cicero "for being primitive, unsophisticated and utilitarian."[263] He enumerated Cicero's stylistic faults in order to stress the unsuitability of Ciceronian periodic style for the demands of the current age.[264] Yet Aper's words bear testimony to a common way of debating Cicero's style in the schoolrooms and the literate circles of the day. He spotlights and expands on peculiarities of Cicero's style, notably his suavity of language or facetiousness, which attracted considerable attention in antiquity. His emphasis on Cicero's ambition to distance himself from past oratory and to "create" a work of art, a product of stylistic polish, furthermore, is indicative of a consolidated approach to Cicero's orations as masterpieces of Latin language. Indisputably, what aroused interest and admiration from later writers was Cicero's innovative use of Latin language, especially his capacity for enlarging vocabulary and balancing regularity and ornamentation of style. Notwithstanding his reservations concerning outmoded features of republican style, Aper lauded Cicero's stylistic grandeur. His learned judgment demonstrates that, in spite of changes in literary tastes and aesthetics,[265] the distinguishing qualities of Cicero's oratory continued to charm generations of scholars and students throughout the centuries.

Let us now pay attention to the antiquarian-erudite interest in Cicero's archaizing language and his use of obscure or obsolete terms, a style feature of particular fascination for grammarians and school teachers. This scholarly topic is best exemplified by the already mentioned collection of rare words and *singularia* compiled by the second-century scholar Statilius Maximus. A scholarly work categorized as a special glossary, belonging to the genre of erudite glossography typified by Verrius Flaccus's alphabetic lexicon "On the meaning of the words" (*De verborum significatu*), Statilius's list is preserved partially in the chapters *de adverbio* of the early third-century grammarian Iulius Romanus, in turn recollected by the fourth-century grammarian Charisius.[266] Romanus's endorsement of analogy and tradition (*auctoritas*) as defining principles of correct Latinity and,

---

[263] Powell 2013: 70.    [264] Dominik 2007: 331. See also Goldberg 1999.
[265] Clackson 2011b: 255 ("the authorities that are appealed to for justification of a word or construction change from age to age, even from writer to writer").
[266] On Charisius's grammatical compilation and Iulius Romanus's work (titled *Aphormai*), see Schenkeveld 2004 (for the structure of Romanus's chapter on the adverb and its sources: 39–42); see also Uría 2012: 226.

at the same time, his concentration on archaic and classical writers (*veteres*),[267] cited and discussed by reference to glossographical material and other grammatical sources,[268] provide a revealing glimpse into a common erudite attitude towards the Latin language of the republican age, idealized as the supreme fount of linguistic purity.[269]

In examining Statilius's *subscriptio* to Cicero's *De lege agraria* I, we have pointed to the scientific and literary qualities of his revision. Here our focus is on the *singularia* detected by Statilius in Cicero, not the words *semel posita*, corresponding to the Greek *hapax legomena*, but rather rare words or terms and morphological elements of enigmatic signification.[270] As observed by Zetzel, the purpose of Statilius's collection, presumably an alphabetical list of grammatical entries contained in a single work,[271] was "to supply its users with handy justification for the use of rare words and forms, primarily the latter, by giving them a suitable authority, in this case either Cicero or Cato."[272] Though Statilius's list seems to have been spurned as a bargain-basement shortcut to learning by open-minded scholars, like Fronto and Gellius, this kind of grammatical compilation evidently satisfied the second-century archaizing taste and was of practical value for Ciceronian scholars hunting out rare forms and words in the writings of the master of the Latin language.

The passages from Charisius's grammar, in which Statilius is explicitly indicated as a source for Cicero's *singularia*, have accurately been reported and discussed by Zetzel and Merello.[273] Just one point may be made here regarding Statilius's textual criticism. In Charisius's nineteen citations from Statilius's collection, the name of the scholar, usually introduced by *ut*,[274] is associated with the verbal form *notare*, "to annotate, mention."[275]

---

[267] On Romanus and the *veteres*, see Welsh 2010: 260–74 (especially for second-hand quotations from republican authors and Romanus's method of first-hand excerption).

[268] Schenkeveld 2004: 39–53 (on Romanus's critical use of his sources, in contrast to Zetzel's view of the grammarian as a "lazy excerptor," 42).

[269] Schenkeveld 2004: 50–1.

[270] On the category of the *singularia*, see Zetzel 1974: 110–11 (who correctly contrasts *synonyma* and *singularia* to *glossae* on the basis of Fronto *Eloq.* 4.7 (144Hout) and claims for the destination of this type of collections to low-grade scholars, a sort of "poor man's alternative to the years of reading and excepting of a Gellius or Fronto").

[271] On the scope and title of Statilius's work cited by Romanus (*de singularibus apud Ciceronem quoque positis*), see Zetzel 1974: 114 (also Schmidt 1997b: 258).

[272] Zetzel 1974: 114. [273] Zetzel 1974; Merello 1977.

[274] *Ubi Maximus* is used to refer Statilius's comment at Char. 262.21B (*ubi idem Maximus notat*: 280.24B).

[275] The usual expression to introduce Statilius's grammatical note is *ut Maximus (quoque) notat* (275.1B; 276.4B; 277.12B; 278.24B; *ut idem notat* at 282.28; 30B); *notat* is also at 267.16B (in the discussion of the adverb *malitiose*) and 285.22B (on the adverb *taetre*). In three cases only is Statilius's comment introduced by *inquit* (cf. 255.3B; 284.6B; 313.1B). Merello 1977: 113–14.

Interpretation of obsolete or difficult words was a crucial part of the grammarian's duty, a significant step towards a more scientific textual criticism. In this context *notare* functioned as a technical, quasi-formulaic verb that tended to call attention to the meaning or the unusualness of terms no longer readily understood. Zetzel contends that in a least two cases *notare* implies a critical evaluation of Cicero's words. In the fragment numbered as the fifth of the list (Char. 270.28-31B),[276] Statilius *notat*, "criticizes," the use of adverbs in *-im*, such as *ostiatim*[277] and *vicatim*,[278] and encounters the disapproval of Romanus/Charisius, who inserts adverbs ending in *-im* in the category of the "iterative" (*frequentativi*).[279] More enigmatic is the interpretation of the fragment numbered as the first (Char. 252.15-21B). There, Statilius apparently discusses the use of the adverb *saepenumero*, not infrequent in Cicero[280] and attested in Gellius, Fronto and Apuleius.[281] The general sense of Charisius's passage has puzzled modern scholars. It seems useful to reproduce the whole text, as printed by Barwick:

> Et tamen passim "magni te facit" dicimus et "multi", et quia saepenumero contendere a nobis non desinitis, licet Statilius Maximus de singularibus apud Ciceronem quoque positis "saepenumero" notet, ut in ceteris an ratio teneat examen,[282] per easdem vias pedetemptim subire conabimur, quidve sit cum officiis rectae constitutaeque rationis quidve licentius proditum requiramus. Et prius illud praeverbium an adverbium dici debeat disputemus.

> "And yet without difference in meaning we say *He values you highly* (*magni*) and *much* (*multi*). [252.15] Because you never stop to ask us oftentimes (*saepenumero*), you reproach me for this usage, although in his book *On unique words also used by Cicero* Statilius Maximus notes his use of *saepenumero*, for a discussion whether, as in other cases, analogy is preserved here too, we shall try to proceed along the same way gradually, and shall investigate what has been put forward in agreement with the duties of the correct and established theory of analogy and what with greater license. [252.21] And let us first discuss whether this word (*saepenumero*) should be called *preverb* or *adverb*."[283]

---

[276] In the numeration of the fragments I follow Zeztel 1974.  [277] Cic. *Ver.* 2.4.48; 2.4.53.
[278] Cic. *Sest.* 34.
[279] On the adverbs in *-im* and the origin of the forms *ostiatim*, from *ostium* ("from door to door"; cf. Quint. *Inst.* 5.10.122; Apul. *Met.* 2.2), and *vicatim*, from *vicus* ("street by street"; cf. Cic. *dom.* 129; Hor. *Epod.* 5.97; Liv. 10.4.2; Tac. *Hist.* 2.95), see Merello 1977: 126–7.
[280] Cic. *de Orat.* 1.1; *Sen.* 4.  [281] Zetzel 1974: 110.
[282] *Examen* is the reading preserved in the most important medieval witness of Charisius's *Ars grammatica*, the early-eighth-century manuscript written at Bobbio, Naples IV A 8 (**N**). It is accepted by Barwick, Keil and Schenkeveld (2004: 129), who interpret the word as the direct object of *contendere a nobis*, whereas *examinemus* is proposed by Kroll, followed by Zetzel.
[283] English translation: Schenkeveld 2004 (with minor modifications).

At the center of the debate is the exact meaning of *notet* and the definition of its object, not unanimously recognized as the adverb *saepenumero*.[284] More specifically, the second *saepenumero* has inspired metalinguistic interpretations, being in "contrast with its previous common use in order to produce a play on words."[285] That Statilius's analysis focused on the adverb *saepenumero* seems reasonable to me. Less convinced am I that the concessive sentence *licet* ... *notet* suggests a somewhat critical evaluation of the use of the word, in consideration of its relative presence in Cicero's writings.[286] Perhaps, we would better understand *notet* in neutral terms, simply as a notation of an adverbial form, not rare in Cicero's works but surely in need of being signaled to Cicero's students and scholars alike.[287]

Additionally, in the vast majority of Statilius's occurrences in Romanus's chapter *notare* preserves its neutral meaning, a form signaling a lexical singularity or semantic anomaly. This is the case of the comment on the adverb *placate* (Char. 275.1-2B: frg6),[288] *pudenter* (Char. 276.4B: frg. 7),[289] *pariter,* instead of *pariliter* (Char. 277.12B: frg8),[290] *repentino,* rather

---

[284] According to Zetzel 1974: 110, Barwick "mispunctuated the sentence to include at the beginning a preliminary phrase *et tamen 'magni te facit' et dicimus 'multi'* (belonging to the previous period)"; in contrast, Merello (1977: 123–4) assumes that Charisius's main interest was in explaining the sense of the syntactical expressions *magni facere* and *multi facere*. On the question, see now Uría 2012: 228–30, who suggests that "the object of *notet* is neither *saepenumero* nor *magni te facit*, but rather the clause *an ratio teneat*, by way of a simple ἀπὸ κοινοῦ construction" and interprets the whole passage as a discussion of the correctness of rare adverbs, adding that "the concessive sentence *licet* ... *notet* determines both *non desinitis* ... *contendere* and *conabimur* ... *subire*, that is to say 'given that you often insist on asking us (even if Statilius often points out ...) to verify if reason prevails ... we shall try to ... '."

[285] On this metalinguistic, in some way humorous, usage of *saepenumero*, see Zetzel 1974: 110; Schenkeveld 2004: 129; Uría 2012: 227ff.

[286] As *saepenumero* occurs elsewhere in Latin, used by Romanus himself in his sentence *quia saepenumero contendere a nobis non desinitis*, Zetzel (1974: 110) interpreted the reference to Statilius in ironic terms (similarly, Schenkeveld 2004: 129 points to "Romanus' awareness of Statilius' censure of Cicero's use of *saepenumero*, which awareness he ascribes to his audience"); *contra* Merello 1977: 124 and Uría 2012: 228–9.

[287] *Notabile* is also used in connection to rare or disused words in Seneca the Elder's description of Haterius's practice of declamation (*Con.* 4 *praef.* 10). Seneca comments on Haterius's habit of introducing Cicero's archaisms and old words (*antiqua dicta*) into his improvised speech and his expectation that fluency and rapidity of speaking could prevent listeners from recognizing Ciceronian borrowings; but *adeo quicquid insolitum est etiam in turba notabile est* ("How true it is that the unusual stands out even in a crowd").

[288] Cic. *Fam.* 6.1.4 (242 SB*Fam*); *placatius* in Cic. *Fam.* 6.13.3 (227 SB*Fam*). The adverb *placate* is unattested in Fronto, Gellius and Apuleius (who used *placide* instead): see Zetzel 1974: 112.

[289] *Pudenter* occurs in Cic. *Quinct.* 39; *Tul.* 20; *Vat.* 6; *de Orat.* 2.364; cf. also Verg. [*Cat.*] 5.14.

[290] *Pariter* is well attested in Latin (Charisius mentions Verg. *G.* 1.189; *Aen.* 1.174; 11.592; 673). It appears evident, however, that "at least in the second century A.D., *pariter* was less readily understood than *pariliter*" (for *pariter* as archaic cf. Serv. *A.* 11.582 and *DS* on *G.* 1.189): Zeztel 1974: 112.

than *repente* (Char. 280.19-20B: frg10),[291] *stomachose* (282.5-6B: frg13)[292] and *singularie,* instead of *singulariter* (Char. 284.5-6B: frg16).[293] In the presentation of the adverb *rare,* instead of *raro* (Char. 280.24-5B: frg11),[294] Charisius introduces Statilius's comment with the sentence *ubi idem Maximus notat Catonem quoque ita locutum.* Here the sense of *notare* is quite ordinary, being a simple indication that Cato also used the adverb, as confirmed by the immediately subsequent attestation of *rarenter* in *Agr.* 103 (Char. 281.5B: frg12). If it is undeniable that "like the Atticist lexicographers, Statilius not only cited words from his sources, he sometimes criticized their use,"[295] *notare* (with its derivations) belongs to a category of scholarly verbs deployed to identify or pick out rare and unusual forms or words calling for explanation.[296] Zetzel mentions a group of six notes from the already discussed commentary on Cicero's speeches, known as *scholia Bobiensia,* that have in common with Statilius the use of the word *notabile,* regularly employed to signal anomaly or irregularity of rare forms.[297] Obviously, scholarly commentaries offer evidence of the use of other verbs, near-synonyms of *notare,* to signify lexical rarities or archaic forms, such as *considerare*[298] or *animadvertere.*[299] More often, rare words or archaisms are pinned down through specific locutions, usually pointing to the *vetustas* and antiquity of the forms used by Cicero in his speeches.[300]

---

[291] Cic. *Quinct.* 14. *Repentino* is to be found in Apul. *Fl.* 16.24.1; 16.24.23; *Mun.* 16.152.7. Once again, Charisius (not Statilius) pairs the reference to Cicero with a citation of Afranius (cf. Char. 276.4B).

[292] Not attested either in Cicero or in the Antonine literature.

[293] Since *singularie* does not appear in Cicero (*quasi unice Cicero,* comments Statilius), one might presume that the grammarian quoted from a no longer extant work; see Zetzel 1974: 114.

[294] Zetzel (1974: 113) notes that, since *rare* is unattested in Cicero, in contrast to a good number of citations of *raro,* "either the word was found in a now lost work of Cicero, or the source of the word in an extant work has been corrupted to *raro*" (this latter hypothesis is supported by the fact that in the passage from the *Rudens* of Plautus, quoted by Romanus/Charisius, the manuscripts transmit *raro*).

[295] Zetzel 1974: 116.   [296] Schad 2007: 270–71.

[297] *Notabile* is in a scholium on *Flac.* 7, concerned with the uniqueness of the singular form *sordem* (97.13-6St; the scholiast adds the final sentence *hoc igitur de verbis rarioribus adnotemus*) and in another scholium on *Vat.* 41, related to the diminutive *labecula* (152.3-5St). For *notabiliter* cf. 128.31–129.2St (on the form *dixet* in *Sest.* 28, with a further reference to the use of similar forms *apud veteres*) and 131.28-30St (on the singular *aerumna* in *Sest.* 49). The word *scalpellum* (in *Sest.* 135) belongs to *verba notabilia* (141.3St); similarly, the word *fucosa* (in *Planc.* 22) is designated by the scholiast as a rare, archaic form (154.17St). To the six-entry list discussed by Zetzel we can also add schol. Bob. 164.11-2St (on the term *debitio* in *Planc.* 68).

[298] Schol. Bob. 104.18St (on *Flac.* 47).

[299] Schol. Bob. 120.20St (on *Mil.* 29); cf. also schol. Gronov. 346.5-6St (on *Ver.* 2.1.53).

[300] *Vetuste locutus est* (schol. Bob. 120.25St: on *Red. Pop.* 1); *vetus locutio* (Ps. Ascon. 251.4St: on *Ver.* 2.1.125); *vetuste posuit* (Ps. Ascon. 264.13St: on *Ver.* 2.2.33); *antiqua locutio* (schol. Gronov. 290.18St: on *Catil.* 4.13).

Both Statilius's collection of rare forms and scholarly comments on Cicero's syntactical and morphological archaisms tell us much about "the reconciliation of the desire for obscure vocabulary with the unquestioned pre-eminence of Cicero in rhetorical technique."[301] They confirm us in our view that school practices stimulated the need for clarification of linguistic difficulties. The good number of notes on Cicero's linguistic usage in our extant commentaries, a visible product of elite teaching, demonstrates that linguistic oddities or anomalous verbal formations baffled students taking instruction in Latin grammar and rhetoric. Criticism of words was then a significant part of regular teaching. As a school teacher, the scholiast used to expound on the irregularity of nouns, adjectives and adverbs, reminding his students, when necessary, of the rarity of the word attested in the text under scrutiny. To understand this point it may be instructive to return to the Bobbio scholia discussed by Zetzel. In the scholium on *Sest.* 28 (128. 31–129.2St) the commentator stimulates his students' interest in the subjunctive *dixet*, a contracted form of *dixisset* by subtraction of the *media verbi pars*.[302] Curiously, this form is not attested in Cicero, but similar cases, the scholiast says, are fairly common among the *veteres*. Form takes priority over meaning in the remaining scholia. *Sordem*, used in the singular by Cicero at *Flac.* 7 to indicate "meanness of conduct," in contrast to the more common use of the plural *sordes* (97–13-6St),[303] and *aerumna*, "affliction," used to designate the woes of exile at *Sest.* 49 (131.28St),[304] are both signaled as instances of irregularity in number. *Labecula* (from *labes*, "stain") calls attention by being a rare diminutive, similar to *aetatula* and *nubecula* (152.3-5St). *Scalpellum*, "scalpel" (141.3St),[305] and *fucosa*, "sham" (154.17-9St),[306] finally, are counted as rare words.[307]

The Bobbio commentary teems with linguistic notes on words or pairs of words that offer minute variations of meaning.[308] When commenting

---

[301] Zetzel 1974: 118.    [302] *Dixet* is accepted by Maslowski 1986: *praef.* V.
[303] Remarkably, the scholiast comments on the "very frequent usage" (*consuetudo celeberrima*) of the plural *sordes* in reference to "characters particularly inclined to immoderate desire" (*mores ad cupiditatem pecuniae promtiores*). On the singular *sordem* cf. Apul. *Met.* 1.21.
[304] *Aerumna* (singular) is attested in Cic. *Prov.* 17.    [305] *Scalpellum* is also in Cic. *Div.* 2.96.
[306] The word is also found in Cic. *Rab. Post.* 40; *Att.* 1.18.1 (18 SB*Att*).
[307] For the linguistic *curiositas* of the Bobbio commentator cf. 164.11–2 St. (on the word *debitio pecuniae* in *Planc.* 68).
[308] In the note on Cic. *Arch.* 28 (179.9-11St), Stangl (1912: *ad loc.*) reads in the lemma, with Klotz, *hunc ad perficiendum adornavi* (*adoravi* Stangl 1884a: 443); accordingly, the text of the scholium would discuss the difference between *adornare* as *cohortor* and *adorare* as *orare et petere*. In truth, *adoravi* is the reading preserved in the Bobbio palimpsest (*sic* Hildebrandt 1907: *ad loc.*). Two of the best medieval witnesses of Cicero's speech, **G** (Brussels, Bibl. Royale 5352) and **V** (Vatican City, Bibl. Apostolica Vaticana, Pal. lat. 1525), preserve *adortavi*. Moreover, *adorno* in the sense of *hortor* is unattested in Cicero.

on *Flac.* 14 (98.26-7St) the scholiast clarifies the sense of Cicero's colloquial expression *qui domi stare non poterant, largo et liberali viatico commovebat* ("those who were bankrupt he encouraged by a liberal and generous travelling allowance") by pointing to the old use of the verb *stare* as "to hold a good patrimony" (*habere idoneam rem familiarem*).[309] Again, in the scholium on *Flac.* 47 (104.18-9St) *infatuare,* "to make a fool of," is designed as an uncommon verb.[310] Obsolete terms are frequently accounted for by opposition to a word of common use. *Legatio libera,* used by Cicero to indicate the senatorial privilege of free official transport (*Flac.* 86), is contrasted by the commentator with the more recent word *commeatus* (107.8-9St). A passage from the *pro Milone* (29) stimulates the scholiast's reflection on the subtle gradation of meaning between the current word *mulio,* "muleteer," properly employed to designate the class of those who make business by governing vehicles drawn by mules or horses, and its near-synonym, the archaic *redarius,* "coachman" (120.20-6St).[311]

Other scholia deserve mention here. To the scholiast, Cicero's propriety and elegance of language is manifested in the distinction between the word *squalor,* "mourning," and its synonym *maeror,* "sorrow," in *Sest.* 68 (134.17-20St).[312] In *Planc.* 25 the enigmatic meaning of *rogatio,* "request," prompts the commentator to specify the political sense of the word, commonly used by Cicero as a synonym of *petitio,* "process of canvassing for a candidature"(156.14-7St). Particularly interesting is the scholium on *Mil.* 49. The use (more appropriate to poetry) of the past participle of the verb *properare,* "to hurry," instead of an expected abstract *properatio,* offers

---

[309] For a similar use of the verb *stare* the scholiast mentions Cic. *Catil.* 2.21.
[310] Cf. also Cic. *Phil.* 3.22; Sen. *Ep.* 59.13. In the scholium on Cic. *Red. Pop.* 1 (110.24-27St) the scholiast takes notice of the archaic use of the word *convictus.*
[311] The distinction between *mulio* and *redarius* seems to be rectified by what the scholiast says about the designation of Ventidius as *mulio* in Cicero's *Philippics* (120.23-6St): *Quamvis et in Filippicis "mulionem Ventidium" dixerit eapropter, quod de public redemerat iumentorum praebitionem quae esset aput exercitum necessaria* ("Although even in the *Philippics* Cicero baptized Ventidius as *mulio,* in consideration of the fact that he entered into contracts with the government to furnish beasts of burden that were needed by the army"); the words *mulionem Ventidium* are numbered as fragment 5 of the *Philippics* by Fedeli 1982 and Shackleton Bailey 2009. It should be noted that the epithet *mulio* is attributed to Ventidius, on the ground of Cicero's *Philippics,* in a scholium on Juvenal (7.199) and Plin. *Nat.* 7.135. Ventidius, never addressed as *mulio* in the invectives against Antony, is called "muleteer," *mulio,* in Cic. *Fam.* 10.18.3 (395 SBFam), probably the source of the error of both Pliny and the scholiast on Juvenal.
[312] An analogous comment on the difference between *virtus,* ascribed to Milo and intended as *emendatae vitae et honesti animi professio,* and *vis,* prerogative of Clodius, defined as *plerumque corporalis et saepe grassatoribus congruentior,* is made by the scholiast on *Mil.* 30 (121.16-20St). See also 103.18-9St (on *Flac.* 43).

the scholiast the opportunity to think over the distinction of meaning between the verbs *festinare* and *properare* (124.1-9St):

> Verbum hoc properandi non sum nescius aput quosdam indifferenter accipi ac solere unum videri festinare et properare. Visum est igitur mihi propter eos quibus aliquod studium proprie loquendi est auctore ipso M. Catone haec verba distinguere. Quippe aliud esse properare, aliud festinare ipse nos, ut dicebam, Cato docuit in oratione quae inscribitur de virtute sua contra Thermum: eius igitur verba ponamus. Qui sic ait: "Nam aliud est properare aliud festinare; qui unumquodque mature transigit, properat: qui multa simul incipit neque perficit, is festinat."[313]

> "I know well that this verb *properare* is taken by some as a synonym of *festinare*. But it seems appropriate to me to distinguish between these two words in line with those who care about propriety of language drawing on the authority of Marcus Cato. It was he in fact, as I said, who showed us that *properare* is one thing, *festinare* another; he did it in his speech entitled *On his own merits against Thermus* (*de virtute sua contra Thermum*). Let us then reproduce his words: he says as follows: 'Actually *properare*, to hasten, is one thing, *festinare*, to hurry, another: who carries quickly everything through to the end, *properat*, hastens; who starts doing a lot of things simultaneously but cannot bring them to conclusion, *festinat*, hurries.'"

Aligning himself with the men of learning engaged in laying down the rules of correct Latinity, the scholiast relies on Cato's authority to draw a subtle line between two verbs belonging to the same semantic class.[314] The passage from Cato's oration, the *De suis virtutibus contra L. Thermum post censuram*, presumably delivered in 183 BCE,[315] quoted verbatim by Gellius in a chapter of his *Attic Nights* (16.14), is concerned with the *differentia* between the two near-synonyms *properare* and *festinare*.[316] In addition to reporting the fragment from Cato's speech, Gellius comments negatively on the false etymology of *festinare* from *fari* ("to speak"), propounded by Verrius Flaccus, opting for the interpretation of *festinare* as *fessum esse* ("to be exhausted, wearied").[317] Whether Gellius was the source of the Bobbio scholiast's comment is hard to say. Certainly, both the texts

---

[313] *Nam* at the beginning of Cato's sentence is only in the scholium (accepted by Sblendorio Cugusi 1982: 286).
[314] *Properare* and *festinare* are placed side by side in Cicero's *Phil.* 9.6.
[315] On the speech, delivered by Cato to defend his censorship from public allegations of *infelicitas* made by Minucius Thermus, see Astin 1978: 105–6; Sblendorio Gugusi 1982: 277–8 (with bibliography).
[316] On the fragment (44 Iord; 131 *ORF*; 96Sbl.), see Sblendorio Cugusi 1982: 285–6.
[317] Cato's fragment is also cited by Fest. 268.2Lind; Non. 709.18L; Isid. *diff. verb.* 440; ps. Suet. *diff. serm.* 317.19Roth (frg285Reiff.); Serv. *G.* 1.260 (in both Isidorus and Servius there is no indication of the title of Cato's oration). On the verb *festinare* cf. also Serv. *A.* 9.486.

partake in a tribute to Cato the Elder's charisma and linguistic *auctoritas*. More importantly, in the scholium Cato stands out as *idoneus auctor*, a paradigm of linguistic finesse against which educated men should measure themselves. The scholiast elucidates Cicero through Cato, recommended as the embodiment of "noble and dignified language" (*virtutes dignitatesque verborum*).[318] In other words, he acknowledges Cato as a cultural authority, inviting his students to reflect upon linguistic issues under the guidance of a recognized exemplar of correct Latin.[319]

To recapitulate so far, Gellius's annotations on language, in conjunction with Statilius's compilation of *hapax legomena* and the Bobbio commentary, point clearly to the fact that Cicero, along with Cato, was established in a fixed canon of authoritative authors supplying scholars with material for the study of Latin language and literature. He embodied linguistic excellence, the ideal of pure Latin idiom (*Latinitas*), to which Roman elite students aspired. His authority on Latinity oriented both scholarship and the educational system in late antiquity. It seems pertinent, at this point, to consolidate our perception of the influence exerted by the *auctoritas* of Cicero upon Latin language science and textual criticism from imperial times to the Early Middle Ages. Unavoidably, in surveying the place occupied by Cicero in Roman erudite and grammatical tradition we will move backward and forward through grammatical/rhetorical handbooks and scholarly commentaries throughout the centuries. In so doing, we will provide definitive proof of the fact that Cicero as the icon of *Latinitas* in Roman education is a timeless notion. In the eyes of grammarians, scholars and schoolteachers, from the Augustan age to the medieval times, Cicero best illustrated the equivalence of antiquity and correctness/elegance of style. His *auctoritas* consecrated an idealized model of literary Latin and remained inextricably associated with the very concept of education in language and rhetoric from antiquity to the Renaissance.

It has been observed that "mastery of correct language, command of a fairly small number of classical texts, and an ability to turn the knowledge of language and literature to a facility in composition and speech" were the goals of literary instruction, "pursued first in the grammarian's school, then in the rhetorician's."[320] Rules of correct speaking and writing were established on the *auctoritas* of ancient, respectable models, which incarnated

---

[318] Gel.1.23.3: Keulen 2009: 254.
[319] A fragment from Cato's oration on the *Lex Orchia* (53 Iord.; 141 *ORF*; 130Sbl.; the speech is reported as *[Dis]suasio ne lex Orchia derogaretur* in Fest. 220.15; 280.30Lind; on the speech also Macr. *Sat.* 3.17.2) is preserved in the Bobbio scholiast 141.15St (on *Sest.* 138).
[320] Kaster 1988: 11.

the standardized criterion of correctness and provided suitable examples of linguistic appropriateness. The guideline to the selection – and related interpretation – of "good" ancient words or syntagms was the *auctoritas* principle. Conservatism and emphasis on authority were the key words of scholarly works and didactic handbooks on the Roman language, metalinguistic texts, distinct in their typology, formal structure and social-historical background, that formed the rich, wide-ranging tradition of Latin grammar[321] and shared the ideal of correct Latin style, whose acquisition – and consequent fruition – relied on the reading (*lectio*) and explanation (*expositio*) of the classical authors.[322]

This academic attitude toward past Roman literature is well illustrated by Nonius Marcellus's twenty-book dictionary *De compendiosa doctrina*, an "elaborate and chaotic collection of lexicographical, grammatical and antiquarian information,"[323] probably composed in the late fourth or early fifth century.[324] As Nonius Marcellus himself makes it clear, *veterum auctoritas docet* (Non. 231L). The authority of the classical authors is the source of linguistic education.[325] Treading in the footsteps of Verrius Flaccus and Gellius and "displaying an attitude widespread in imperial grammatical discourse, Nonius perceived 'antiquity' and 'authority' as one category, with consequent fusion of the two distinct notions of archaic usage and figurative language of poets and high-register prose writers."[326] His cultural project, aimed at re-evaluating and perpetuating Latin literary heritage, integrated the principle of *auctoritas* into a more articulated discourse on the Roman past.[327] He adopted a conservative approach to the Latin language, whose purity was preserved by the replication of the linguistic standards of republican *Latinitas*.

The notion of *auctoritas* deserves more attention. Ranked among the *idonei auctores*,[328] together with Terence, Vergil and Sallust,[329] Cicero occupied a central place in the specialized institutions of language teaching. He was among the authors most credited with original and elegant words

---

[321] On the multiplicity and variety of grammatical and scholarly work in late antiquity, see De Nonno 2003.
[322] Chahoud 2007: 69 and n3.   [323] White (D. C.) 1980: 112.
[324] For a Severan date (ca. 205–220 CE), see Keyser 1994.
[325] In general, on the concept of *auctoritas veterum* in late antiquity grammarians, see Schmidt 1993.
[326] Chahoud 2007: 72.
[327] Chahoud 2007: 69. On the principle of *auctoritas* in Nonius, see also Barabino 2003.
[328] On the connection between teaching of language and *auctoritas* and the role of the *idonei auctores*, "suitable authors," in Servius's commentary on Vergil, see Kaster 1978. On Servius's interest in the language of the *antiqui* or *veteres*, see also Del Vigo 2013.
[329] In the so-called *quadriga Messi* (cf. Cassiod. *Inst.* 1.15.7).

or expressions. As Barabino has rightly observed, in the ancient grammarians/scholiasts Cicero's *auctoritas* functioned as support to morphological/etymological explanations and, most notably, as a formal, undisputable sign of accreditation of anomalous linguistic forms.[330] As Chahoud puts it, the authority of the model allowed "for the justification of language anomalies at all levels (from morphological irregularities to semantic shifts) on the grounds that an unusual expression (*novum dictum*) meets with the grammarian's approval as long as the usage is found in the *auctores*."[331] The *auctoritas vetustatis*, and Cicero's authority in particular, was mostly summoned to authorize and sanction the use of noteworthy grammatical or lexical forms. The quotations from fourth- and fifth-century grammarians, collected by Barabino,[332] unequivocally testify to the force exerted by Cicero on the formation of a grammar of Latin language. *Tulliana auctoritas sufficit* (Char. 348.26B; Diom. *GL* 1.390.15), "Cicero's authority is enough." To provide some examples, the insertion of the indicative present into a series of subjunctive imperfects is legitimate, according to Charisius and Diomedes, by a passage of the *pro Sextio Roscio Amerino* 21. Analogously, the masculine term *scrupulus* is supported by Cicero's *auctoritas* (cf. *Sext. Rosc.* 6; *Cluent.* 76: ps. Probus *GL* 4.212.21); the use of the ablative, instead of the more common dative, in prepositional phrases expressing place (with the name of towns) appears acceptable on the grounds of Cicero's use in *Phil.* 2.75 (ps. Serg. *GL* 4.511.6; Cledon. *GL* 5.22.13; Pomp. *GL* 5.253.23).[333] Grammar's rigidity allowed a few exceptions; Cicero's *auctoritas* permitted – and justified – linguistic anomalies, especially when competent grammarians felt uneasy in providing a scientific explanation of perceived grammatical irregularities.

As we have seen, correct Latin diction had been associated with the preservation of Roman elite identity and morality since the late republic. Linguistic competence thus maintained and transmitted values and notions inherent in the aristocratic Roman cultural tradition.[334] *Custos Latini sermonis*,[335] the grammarian was the "guardian" of language and tradition, the conservator "of all the discrete pieces of tradition embedded in his texts, from matters of prosody to the persons, events, and beliefs that marked the limits of vice and virtue."[336] Within this context, Cicero's *auctoritas* in language was central to the process of conservation – and protection – of Latin cultural heritage. In ensuring admiration for Cicero's

---

[330] Barabino 1990.  [331] Chahoud 2007: 76.  [332] Barabino 1990: 96–8.
[333] Cf. also Serv. *GL* 4. 419.4 (ps. Serv. *GL* 4. 442.11); Cledon. *GL* 5.65.17; 71.23 (Pomp. *GL* 5.245.3; ps. Augustin. *GL* 5. 516.34); Macrob. *Excerpta Par. GL* 5.600.17. See Barabino 1990: 97–8.
[334] McNelis 2007: 292–3.  [335] Sen. *Ep.* 95.65.  [336] Kaster 1988: 18.

linguistic order and/or legitimating anomalies by appealing to Cicero's *Latinitas* the grammarians preserved and consolidated an aristocratic vision of Roman language. They equated linguistic discipline with ethics and fostered principles of education firmly rooted in an elite vision of the Romans' idealized past.

Resting upon the classic partition of grammar into four parts – glossography/lexicography, exegesis, metrics and technical grammar, as devised by a late commentator of the Alexandrian grammarian Dionysius Thrax[337] – and pursuing a line of enquiry successfully taken by seminal studies on this topic,[338] it may be useful to offer a brief glimpse into Cicero's place in lexicography,[339] a genre encompassing glossaries and word-lists and "combining the didactic necessity to explain literary texts with a scholarly interest in linguistic science."[340] Since Verrius Flaccus's *De verborum significatu* ("On the meaning of words"), a lexicon composed under Augustus's reign, had been lost (it was epitomized by the second- to third-century grammarian Sextus Pompeius Festus, in its turn abridged in the Carolingian work of Paulus Diaconus),[341] we must turn to Nonius Marcellus's encyclopedia. As Lindsay has demonstrated,[342] the North African scholar Nonius arranged his lexicographical material in books or sections of uneven size, "incorporating the characteristics of an *ars grammatica* and of a glossary"[343] and placing himself in the tradition of Roman antiquarianism and glossography that goes back to Varro's idea of *Latinitas*. The guiding principle of Nonius's compilation was the authority of the ancient writers (*auctoritas veterum*). Synonymous with correctness and elegant style, the venerable Roman past incarnated the linguistic ideal of *Latinitas*. Most of his sources were republican authors (with the notable exception of Virgil); as correctly identified by Lindsay, Nonius's collection relied on thirty-three texts of seventeen Latin authors of the third and second centuries BCE and five glossaries in eight volumes (among which are Gellius's *Attic Nights*), for a total of forty-one books.[344] In conformity with the literary canon standardized in the second-century CE revival of early Latin, Nonius pondered lexical, syntactical and morphological questions by reproducing, with

---

[337] *Schol. Dion. Thr. GG* 1.3 (10.8–10 Hilgard).
[338] I refer here to Barwick 1922. A good (though necessarily succinct) survey of the presence of Cicero in the late grammarians is now in De Paolis 2000 (still useful is Karbaum 1885; 1889). For a typology of the citations from classical authors in the grammarians, see in general De Nonno 1990.
[339] In general, see Ferri 2011a (with bibliography). [340] Chahoud 2007: 73.
[341] Glinister-Woods 2007; Lhommé 2011. See also De Nonno 1990: 608–9; Pieroni 2004: 12–5.
[342] Lindsay 1901; White (D. C.) 1980; Chahoud 2007. [343] Chahoud 2007: 74.
[344] Lindsay 1901: 7–10; Chahoud 2007: 72 (and n29). On Nonius's sources and his method of composition, see in particular White (D. C.) 1980. See now Gatti 2011.

mechanical regularity, extracts and words from early and republican Roman epic, tragedy, satire, oratory and philosophy.[345]

Nonius calls upon the *auctoritas* of Cicero quite often.[346] In particular, in the sixth book "on words used metaphorically" (*de impropriis*) Cicero is invoked to legitimate anomalous forms or modifications of gender;[347] similarly, Cicero has a pre-eminent place in Nonius's illustration of etymological issues, especially in Book 1 about correctness of Latin language (*de proprietate sermonum*), and in Book 4 that touches upon questions of polysemy (*de varia significatione sermonum*). On Lindsay's estimations, Nonius used eight books of Cicero's works, inclusive of philosophical dialogues (especially the *Tusculanae Disputationes* and *De officiis*),[348] epistles, rhetorical works (predominantly the *De oratore*)[349] and speeches, with a preference for the *Verrines* and *Philippics*.[350]

---

[345] On the order of Nonius's word entries (he used to place the numbers of the books before each entry), see Lindsay 1901: 3–5; Maggiulli 1980.

[346] Barabino 1990: 92–6.

[347] Cf. Non. 722L (*dotatam*); 722L (*cincinnos ac fucum*); 733L(*opificem*); 738L(*putidum*); 740L(*monumenta*); 743L (*numerum*). Usually, Nonius refers to Cicero with formulas such as *Cicero . . . auctor est, Tullio auctore dicimus . . ., M. Tullius auctor est*. The expression *M. Tullio auctore dicimus* returns in a small fragment, preserved by Nonius 334L, relating to the gender of the word *syngraphas* (feminine), contrasted to the use of the masculine in Plautus's *Asinaria*. As noted by Crawford 1994: 310–11, the fragment "has been too hastily attributed to a speech" of Cicero, titled *pro negotiatoribus Achaeis*; in truth, the words *pro* (*prae* F) *negotiatoribus Achaeis* are part of the quotation from Cicero and nothing suggests the existence of a speech so titled in Cicero's oratorical corpus.

[348] The first book of the *De officiis* (fifty-five quotations) occupies the whole of book twenty of Nonius ("Cicero III"); the second and third books of *De officiis* (forty-three and ninety-five citations, respectively), grouped with the *Hortensius* (seventy-two quotations) and *De senectute* (fifty-eight citations), form the book numbered as twenty-nine ("Cicero V").

[349] We have ninety-one quotations from the three books of the *De oratore* and thirty-two from the treatise *Orator* (both included in book VII).

[350] Both the *Verrines* and the *Philippics* are contained in a single volume of Cicero (styled "M. Tullius"), together with the epistles *ad Caesarem iuniorem* (the volume is numbered "Cicero IV"). The speeches against Verres count two hundred-twenty citations; thirty-two quotations come from the *Philippics* (with an understandable supremacy of citations from the first and second invectives; notably, in discussing the meaning of the verb *tibubare* as *trepidare* Nonius cites a passage from book fourteen, 267L). Quite interestingly, the role played by other speeches of Cicero in Nonius's collection seems to have been minimal. Only five citations come from the *Catilinarians* (one from the first speech, § 6: Non. 529L, four from the second speech, § 1: Non. 652L; § 7: Non. 171L; § 22: Non. 653L; 860L); we have also two quotations from the *pro Plancio* (§ 1 Non. 187L; 68 Non. 299L), two from the *De provinciis consularibus* (§ 19 and 29, cited together in the discussion about the verb *profligare*: Non. 237L), two from the *Sexto Roscio* (§ 18 Non. 285L; 131 Non. 781L), one from the *pro Caelio* 46 (Non. 309L), one from the *pro Cluentio* 94 (Non. 16L), one from the *in Pisonem* (§ 37 Non. 173L) and one again from *De le agraria* (frg. 4, discussed also by Gel. *NA* 13.25.6; cf. Non. 697 L.); *pro Rabirio perduellionis reo* 13 is cited twice, at 73L and 617L). A same passage from *pro Marcello* 2 is quoted in two places: At 357L Nonius discusses the use of the adjective *aemulus* as *sectator, imitator* and cites Cicero's work as *pro Marco Marcello*, whereas at 703L the text of the speech, simply indicated as *in Caesarianis*, is mentioned to

Nonius was not an original thinker. He was rather a "learned amateur,"[351] an "enthusiastic compiler, muddled by reason of his own limitations just as often as he is misled by errors in the texts available to him."[352] His zeal for unusual word formations and etymologies, sanctioned by the *vetustas* and *auctoritas* of the *exemplum*, pervades his entire collection. Nonius's use of a portion of the fragmentary speech *In Clodium et Curionem*, a text already presented as an anomalous case of unauthorized publication in Cicero's oratorical *corpus*,[353] is particularly illuminating. Nonius quotes four fragments from the speech, all belonging to the caustic invective against Clodius, ridiculed for his womanish and ludicrous appearance. In the first fragment, numbered as 21 in Crawford's edition,[354] Nonius comments on the defamatory sense of the adjective *elegans*, not uncommon among the *veteres* (*a veteribus etiam vitio datur*), and cites Cicero's words: "*tu elegans, tu solus urbanus, quem decet mulieris ornatus, quem incessus psaltriae; qui levare vultum mollire vocem potes*" (745L).[355] The rarity of *calautica*, a Greek term for womanish headdress, prompts Nonius to quote another fragment of the speech (in Book 14 *de genere vestimentorum*, "on the variety of clothes"): *M. Tullius in Clodium*: "*tune, cum vincirentur pedes fasceis, cum calauticam capiti accommodares?*" (861L: frg23Crawford).[356] A small part of the same fragment returns at 863 L., in the explanation of the Greek word *strophium*, usually denoting a twisted breast band; another fragment (frg24Crawford), an ironic comment of Cicero on Clodius's fabricated beauty,[357] is cited by Nonius in two places, at 535L, with reference to the temporal notion intrinsic to the adverb *longe*, and at 700L, in the discussion about the difference between *specula*

---

mark out the difference between the terms *aemulatio* and *imitatio*. Finally, Nonius reproduces a small part of a fragment from *pro Cornelio* II, quoted by Cicero himself at *Orator* 232 (277L); a fragment from the speech *pro Gallio* (Nonius discusses the Greek word *logus*, "jest") is cited at 88L; again, in elaborating on the difference between *confiteor* and *profiteor* Nonius quotes the only remaining fragment of the speech *pro Manilio* (700L).

[351] Kaster 1988: 417–18.  [352] Chahoud 2007: 83.  [353] See chapter 1, pp. 32–3.
[354] Crawford 1994: 242; 254–55.
[355] The late rhetorician Iulius Rufinianus reports the fragment (with the words *Tu vero festivus, tu elegans, tu solus urbanus, quem decet muliebris ornatus, et cetera*: 38.8–9 *RLM*) as an instance of ironic language. Cf. also schol. Bob. 89.10-6St (the scholiast defines Cicero's words as a *mixta responsio et facetiis urbanitatis et asperitatis virolentia*, "a response in which polite jokes are combined with bitter harshness," aimed at disclosing Clodius's indecency, *turpitudo*).
[356] The Bobbio scholiast (89.17-20St) reads *Cum calautica capiti accommodaretur* and designates *calautica* as a Κόσμου *genus, quo feminae capita velabant*, a term already used by the republican author of *fabulae togatae*, Afranius, in his *Consobrini* (*cum mitris calauticis*: 37 Ribbeck).
[357] Reported also by the Bobbio scholiast 89.29–90.8St with the lemma *Sed credo, postquam speculum tibi allatum est, longe te a pulchris abesse sensisti*. On this fragment, see Crawford 1994: 256.

and *speculum*.³⁵⁸ Evidently, Nonius's attention was captivated by the concentration (within a single passage) of *loci* and unusual terms about physical appearance and feminine dress. The vilification of Clodius's immoral and effeminate aspect, a standard topic in invective,³⁵⁹ is paired off with some of the most celebrated passages from Cicero's orations for its verbal violence and linguistic exemplarity. Whether Nonius cited from a glossary or inspected Cicero's manuscript personally, it is not easy to ascertain.³⁶⁰ Certainly, the sarcastic presentation of Clodius as a transvestite was of some relevance to Nonius's interpretation and use of Cicero as a linguistic innovator, a manipulator of Latin and foreign terms combined in an elaborate, amusing portrait of an indecorous Roman man.

Latin lexicography deals primarily with the explanation of unusual and rare words, legitimated in their use by the *veteres*. Nonius's second book (*de honestis et nove veterum dictis*) is a glossary of "decorous" and "new" words³⁶¹ found in respectable ancient models, something very similar to Statilius's collection or Verrius's short list of "old words, with examples" (*priscorum verborum cum exemplis libri*).³⁶² Into this group of specialized glossaries we also include Caesellius Vindex's *Stromateis*, also known as *Commentarium lectionum antiquarum*,³⁶³ Velius Longus's *Commentarium de usu antiquae lectionis*³⁶⁴ and Fabius Planciades Fulgentius's *Expositio sermonum antiquorum*.³⁶⁵ Framed according to lexicographical rules is Arusianus Messius's dictionary of exemplary locutions and expressions (*Exempla elocutionum*), a fourth-century alphabetical collection of verbal

---

[358] From a comparison between Nonius and the text preserved in the Turin palimpsest (T), modern scholars have inferred that the North African scholar (or the manuscript he made use of) abbreviated or trivialized Cicero's passage. In fragment n. 21 Nonius transformed Cicero's tricolon *effeminare vultum, attenuare vocem, levare corpus* into a less effective dicolon *levare vultum, mollire vocem* (Puccioni 1960: 121). In a similar way, in fragment n.23, the reading *cum calautica capiti accommodaretur* (instead of Nonius's *cum calauticam capiti accommodares*), transmitted by the Bobbio scholiast 89.17 St. and the Turin palimpsest, is certainly to opt for, as it maintains the "impersonal" sense of the dressing ceremony (usually performed by slaves); Puccioni 1960: 122.

[359] On effeminacy as a "common means of indicating a male opponent's deviance" and "as an aberration of what Roman society deemed as natural behavior," see Corbeill 2002: 209.

[360] On Nonius's collection largely based on a direct consultation (and consequent inventory) of his sources, see White (D. C.) 1980.

[361] On the word *honestas* (*elegantia*) in Nonius, see Chahoud 2007: 76 and n67.

[362] A late Ciceronian glossary is transmitted in a tenth-century Leiden manuscript (Voss. Lat. O. 88; Goetz 1891), part of which is now preserved in the Leiden codex (Voss. Lat. Q. 138), the same manuscript that transmits the *scholia Gronoviana*.

[363] Gel. *praef.* 6f.; 2.16.5; 3.16.11; 6.2.1; 11.15.2; cf. also 18.11 (Prisc. *GL* 2.210.6ff.; 230.11–2; Char. 150.11B). On the lexicographical work of Caesellius Vindex, see Taifacos 1983.

[364] Gel. 18.9.4; see Di Napoli 2011: XXXVI–XXXVII.

[365] Pizzani 1968; Whitbread 1971: 157–75 (with English translation). Strangely enough, Cicero is never mentioned among the sources of the sixty-two cases of hard and rare words discussed by the mythographer.

or nominal constructions, founded on the authority of Vergil, Cicero, Terence and Sallust.[366] Notably, Arusianus's exclusive use of *exempla* taken from the authors of the scholastic *quadriga* and his adoption of a regular system of citation (along with the name of the *auctor* he usually records the title of the work and the number of the book),[367] reflecting a documentary attitude that goes back to the antiquarian/exegetical tradition (already established before Varro), make the *Exempla elocutionum* an erudite handbook, a work *de Latinitate,* to be paralleled with the *De Latinitate* of Flavius Caper or Julius Romanus's Ἀφορμαί.[368] Offering a stimulating meditation on correct Latin consecrated by the *usus* of classical authors, directly consulted and plundered for source material, Arusianus contributed to the preservation and transmission of Roman cultural legacy. In the case of Cicero, the impressive number of citations from the speeches (the rhetorical and philosophical writings are practically absent, with the partial exception of the *De re publica*)[369] ratifies Arusianus's familiarity with Cicero's oratory, a keystone of professional grammar and rhetoric teaching, and demonstrates that the propagation of the ideal of *Latinitas,* validated by Cicero's undisputed authority, was central to Roman education in late antiquity.

Proceeding with our analysis, it may be interesting to consider the relevance of Cicero's *auctoritas* to the formation of late and medieval compilations of synonyms and *differentiae verborum,* the difference between words with similar meaning, a scholarly topic already treated by Nonius (in his fifth book *de differentia similium significationum*).[370] As Brugnoli demonstrated,[371] the didactic urgency to provide lists of

---

[366] On Arusianus's work, dedicated to the consuls Probrinus and Olibrius in 395 CE, see Di Stefano 2011.

[367] For the private nature of Arusianus's dictionary, an unsystematic "domestic" collection of idiomatic expressions, which reveals the scholar's desire to preserve and transmit the linguistic *proprietas* of classical Latin, see Di Stefano 2011: XXXIX–XLV.

[368] Di Stefano 2011: LXVI–LXVII.

[369] In total, Cicero is used as a source by Arusianus in two hundred seventy-three cases. With special regard to the speeches, we count fifty-five quotations from the *Verrines,* thirty-four from the *Philippics* (with the understandable prevalence of citations from the first and second speeches of the corpus), twenty-three from both the *Catilinarians* and the *pro Cluentio,* eighteen from the *in Pisonem,* seventeen from the *pro Cornelio* and fifteen from the speeches addressed to Caesar (nine from the *pro rege Deiotaro,* five from the *pro Ligario,* one from the *pro Marcello*). Arusianus drew also on other orations of Cicero, though with less frequency (*pro Plancio* 7, *pro Scauro* 7, *pro Caelio* 6, *de imperio Cn. Pompeii* 6, *pro Milone* 5, *de domo sua* 5, *pro Sestio* 4, *pro Murena* 4, *pro Flacco* 3, *pro Quinctio* 3, *pro Sulla* 1, *pro Oppio* 1, *cum a ludis contionem avocavit* 1, *cum quaestor Lilybaeo decederet* 1). On Arusianus's oscillation in citing the titles of Cicero's orations, see Di Stefano 2011: LVI-LVII.

[370] Cf. also Fronto's *Liber de differentiis* (*GL* 7.519ff.); on the lists of *differentiae verborum* see Brugnoli 1955: 21–2.

[371] Brugnoli 1955: 7.

synonyms, as a mnemonic device for preserving the literary heritage,[372] encouraged the creation of unorganized collections of *synonyma*, arranged without explanation of the *differentia*, circulating in the schools as reference books. The so-called *Synonima Ciceronis*, a seventh-century pseudo-Ciceronian collection starting with the series *orator auctor defensor*,[373] preceded in some manuscripts by a letter *ad Veterium* (a rude assemblage of Ciceronian expressions),[374] originated evidently from a false attribution to Cicero of lexicographical works.[375] As has been noted, Cicero embodied both theory and practice of the art of synonyms.[376] Attaching the name of Cicero to lexical lists implied recognizing his status of master of the *Ars grammatica*.[377]

As expected, Cicero is scarcely present in the *scriptores de re metrica*, mostly concerned with the study of prosody and metrics.[378] Equally, exegetical works seem to be reluctant to insert long textual citations from the classical *auctores* into a context not primarily concerned with grammar. This happens in the twelve-book *Interpretationes Vergilianae*, attributed to the fourth- to fifth-century rhetorician Tiberius Claudius Donatus.[379] A rhetorical commentary on Vergil's *Aeneid*, the *Interpretationes* reveal a limited use of the authors included in the *quadriga Messi*: Cicero is explicitly cited in two cases only,[380] even if the general shape of the commentary owes much to Cicero's rhetorical theory. In contrast, the early fifth-century commentary on Vergil of Servius, generally held to be based on a lost commentary by Aelius Donatus and transmitted to us in two distinct forms (the longer, commonly known as *Servius Auctus* or *Servius Danielinus*, is probably a seventh- to eighth-century expansion of a shorter form, with addition of material from Donatus's commentary not used by Servius),[381] is known to have made much use of Cicero's oratorical

---

[372] Cf. Fronto *Ant.* 2.19 (144.17Hout): Fronto defines the collections of synonyms and *singularia* as *lucrativa studiorum solacia*, "valuable recreations in the way of study." On the rhetorical use of synonyms cf. Quint. *Inst.* 9.3.45; [Prob.] *GL* 4.120.6.

[373] Brugnoli 1955: 27–37; 1961.  [374] Brugnoli 1955: 29.  [375] On the question see Mordeglia 2016.

[376] Brugnoli 1961: 294.  [377] Brugnoli 1961: 297f.

[378] It may be interesting to observe that knowledge of basic elements of prosody and metrics is deemed preliminary to reading of Cicero in Maximus Victorinus's *Commentarius de ratione metrorum* (*GL* 6.227.25–228.5). In addition, Cicero's *Divinatio* and *Verrines* offer a good repertoire of rhythmical endings in the second book of Marius Plotius Sacerdos's grammatical treatise (*GL* 6.492.25–495.26 = *Cathol. Prob. GL* 4.40.14–43.10). For Cicero as a stylistic model in Manlius Theodorus's *De metris* (*GL* 6.585–601), see Romanini 2007: LXVIII–LXIX.

[379] Squillante Saccone 1985.

[380] Cic. *de Orat.* 3.44–5; *Tusc.* 3.2 (in the note on Verg. *Aen.* 4.367: 1.406.25 Georgii); Cic. *Inv.* 2.2.5 (on Verg. *Aen.* 7.49: 2.13.3–6 Georgii). See Squillante Saccone 1985: 104 and n3.

[381] Kaster 1988: 169–97; Fowler 1997; Murgia 2004. On the so-called *Servius-frage*, see Pellizzari 2003: 15ff.

legacy. Servius's commentary was the "instrument of a teacher."[382] It was primarily devised to make students familiar with the supreme model of Roman poetry and to "teach them to write good Latin."[383] Cicero retained a firm place in Servius's curriculum. As an *idoneus auctor,* he assisted *pueri* taking instruction in language.[384] No surprise thus that Servius drew repeatedly on Cicero's linguistic authority to expound significant Vergilian lines.[385] From Mountford-Schultz's list we know of one hundred sixty-nine quotations of Cicero's works in Servius (sixty-five in the *Servius Auctus*),[386] a good number of which come from the speeches, especially the *Verrines* (26) and the *Catilinarians* (14).[387] The process of acculturation of Roman elite students assumed Cicero as its guide. Instruction in the Latin language, the final purpose of educational manuals and commentaries, required established models. To provide further examples of this linguistic-didactic approach to Cicero, it may suffice to take a quick look at the position occupied by the acclaimed model of Roman prose in Donatus's commentary on Terence's comedies,[388] in the late Horace scholia[389] and in the *Adnotationes super Lucanum*.[390]

A survey of grammatical handbooks in late antiquity lends support to our perception of the role played by Cicero in the curriculum. Though different from each other in typology and nature, the surviving late Latin grammars, ranging in date from the third to the sixth century CE, give evidence of how training in language preserved linguistic and ethical values associated with the aristocratic ideal of *Romanitas*. Thought to be modeled after the Greek grammar of Dionysius Thrax,[391] the Latin *artes* have

---

[382] Kaster 1988: 170.  [383] Cameron 2011: 417. On Servius's language-teaching, see Foster 2017.
[384] Pellizzari 2003: 232. On Servius's use of republican authors, see Lloyd 1961; Jocelyn 1964; Uhl 1998: 221–4 (especially on the notion of *auctoritas*).
[385] Pellizzari 2003: 231–32.  [386] Mountford-Schultz 1930: 39–40.
[387] We also have eleven quotations from the *Philippics*, eight from the *pro Murena*, seven from the group of the speeches addressed to Caesar, four from the *pro Sestio*, three from both the *pro Caelio* and *pro Sex. Roscio Amerino*, two from both the *pro Scauro* and *pro Fundanio* and one from the *in Pisonem, De imperio Cn. Pompeii, pro Quinctio, pro Cornelio, pro Archia, pro Rabirio perduellionis reo* and *de domo sua* respectively. On the relation between Servius and *Servius Auctus* in the use of Cicero's speeches, see Salomies 1997 (who argues that Servius "cannot have been using only Donatus as his source, but must have had other material at his disposal, some of this perhaps coming from his own notes on Cicero" and concludes that "the additions in *Servius Auctus* must have come from a source not identical with Donatus, but from some source able to refer to an unusually large repertory of Ciceronian speeches": 135).
[388] We count twenty-six quotations from Cicero in Donatus (second only to Virgil).
[389] In the scholia of Ps.-Acro, Cicero is quoted in fourteen cases; the scholia of Porphyrio mention the republican orator nine times.
[390] Cicero is quoted fifty-nine times (all from the speeches, with the exception of the scholium on Luc. 3.244, where the commentator makes reference to *Att.* 5.20.3).
[391] Barwick 1922: 89–111; 229–50.

generally been divided into two categories, the "Schulgrammatik-" (or "*ars grammatica*-type"), a typology of systematically structured grammatical texts involved in discussing each part of speech and concretely explaining the properties of nouns and verbs, and the "*regulae*" Artes, "reference works intended for consultation rather than school textbooks designed for systematic study"[392] and filled with a relevant number of examples from classical *auctores*.[393] The first group, including works of variable length like those of Aelius Donatus (*GL* 4.367–402),[394] Marius Victorinus (*GL* 6.3–31), Augustine (*GL* 5.494–96), Asper (*GL* 5.547–54), Consentius (*GL* 5.329–404) and Dositheus (*GL* 7.376–436), tends to make limited use of textual citations, favoring "definitions and explanation at the expense of paradigms and examples."[395] The second category, characterized by a massive presence of paradigms and lists of examples, including (among others) Phocas's *Ars de nomine et verbo* (*GL* 5.410–39),[396] Priscian's compendium *Institutio de nomine, pronomine et verbo* (*GL* 3.443–56)[397] and the *Ps. Aurelii Augustini Regulae* (*GL* 5.496–524),[398] appears more inclined to use the *auctores*, usually quoted by name, in support of the *regula* under discussion.[399] The canon of the prescribed authors covers Latinity in its entirety. Cicero, needless to say, has a privileged space, along with other recognized models of poetry and prose (Vergil, Terence, Sallust, Horace, Plautus, Persius, Juvenal and Lucan).

The antiquarian-erudite tradition *de Latinitate*, exemplified by Flavius Caper's theoretical manual, preserves linguistic *ratio* and order with the

---

[392] Law 1987: 192.
[393] For a distinction between the "Schulgrammatik" and the "*regulae*" grammars in consideration of the different use of the *auctores* as sources of grammatical examples, see Law 1987: 191–94 (see also Luhtala 2010). For the role of the textual citation in the "*regulae*-type" *Artes*, see De Nonno 1990: 630–33.
[394] On Donatus's work, an exemplar of elementary grammar in late antiquity and the early Middle Ages, consisting of the *Ars minor* (an introduction to the parts of the speech) and the three books *Ars maior*, see the fundamental study of Holtz 1981.
[395] Law 1987: 192.   [396] Kaster 1988: 339–41 (§ 121).
[397] A school handbook composed after the eighteen-book *Institutio Grammatica* (upon which it draws heavily): see Kaster 1988; 346–48 (§ 126).
[398] In the *Regulae Augustini* Cicero's speeches are mentioned in five cases (three citations from the *Verrines*, one from the *Catilinarians*, one again from the *Post reditum ad senatum*). For Cicero in Macrobius's treatise *De verborum Graeci et Latini differentiis vel societatibus* (*GL* 5.599–633), see Balbo 1996.
[399] Within this category scholars tend to include the so-called *Ars* of ps. Remmius Palaemon (*GL* 5. 533–47) and the second book of Sacerdos's *Ars grammatica* (*De catholicis nominum atque verborum*: *GL* 6.471–95), an identical version of which has come down to us as the *Catholica* of Probus (*GL* 4. 3–43), correctly designed as "a systematic review of nominal and verbal desinences and a succinct survey of prose rhythm": Kaster 1988: 352–53 (§ 132).

support of the *idonei auctores*.[400] Particularly illuminating are the grammar handbooks produced in the non-Latin environment of the Eastern Empire, which advocate a sort of renaissance of classical Latin.[401] In the three-book *Ars grammatica* of Diomedes (*GL* 1.297–530),[402] the five-book grammar compiled by Flavius Sosipater Charisius (*GL* 1.1–296)[403] and, above all, the monumental *Institutio grammatica* of Priscian (*GL* 2.1–597; 3.1–377) the quotations of *veteres* and *vetustissimi*, stemming from both Caper's lists and collections of *loci* arranged for personal use,[404] serve as practical tools for explaining grammar rules and linguistic deviances. Perhaps most of the citations of Cicero in these handbooks come from previously arranged collections but it is equally possible that the grammarians personally inspected Cicero's works, especially his speeches, as may be inferred from the quotation of forty passages from the oration *de praetura urbana* from the second *actio in Verrem* in Priscian (*GL* 3.255–64).[405] To further specify what kind of text was most used by the grammarians, we have noted on more than one occasion that the selection of Cicero's speeches was inevitably conditioned by school practices. From Keil's *Index* it is easy to gauge how dominant was the role played by the *Verrines*, *Catilinarians* and *Philippics* (together with the *pro Cluentio*) in language training.[406] Presumably most of the citations from these and other orations in medieval glossaries are second-hand citations, coming from Priscian's and Isidorus's handbooks.[407]

The *Tulliana auctoritas* was the conceptual guideline to grammar handbooks and scholarly works on Latin, which looked to Cicero as both a symbol of correct Latin diction and a resource for linguistic research. If we pay attention to the scholia and commentaries on Cicero's orations, they appear intrinsically preoccupied with preservation, consolidation and transmission of the idea of Cicero as "perfect pleader and writer." Not quibbling over Cicero's expertise in Latin, ancient scholarship concentrated on promoting knowledge and appropriation of the best qualities of

---

[400] De Nonno 1990: 638–39 (with further bibliography).
[401] On Latin grammars in the Eastern Empire and the "enseignement du latin pour hellénophones," see Rochette 2015.
[402] Kaster 1988: 270–2 (§ 47).
[403] *GL* 1.1–296. For the numeration of Charisius's pages I follow Barwick's edition. On Charisius in general, see Kaster 1988: 392–94 (§ 200).
[404] Caper's *liber de latinitate* was among Priscian's sources: De Paolis 2000: 58.
[405] De Paolis 2000: 60. Cicero's speeches are among the most used sources of the alphabetical collection of Greek and Latin constructions that forms the last part of Priscian's *Ars* (*GL* 3.278.13–377.18); see Rosellini 2011.
[406] De Paolis 2000: 64.   [407] For Cicero in medieval glossaries, see Cecchini 2000.

the Roman orator. In discussing Gellius's or the Bobbio scholiast's comments we have already pointed out the prominence given to Cicero's innovation in vocabulary and propriety of language, within a revitalization of the ideal of pure and correct Latin diction. By spelling out anomalies of vocabulary, elucidating morphology and syntax and, above all, celebrating Cicero's words and idioms as both intentional archaisms and touches of elegant and sophisticated style, commentators and ancient readers showed an awareness of the extraordinary importance of Cicero's writings to the formation of a classical, correct Latin and directed students' minds towards appreciating the grace and beauty of the master of Roman prose.

Elegance of diction governs the Bobbio scholiast's judgment about Cicero's lexical semantics, as we have seen. Similarly, in Ps. Asconius, a post-Servian commentary on Cicero's *Divinatio in Caecilium* and *in Verrem* 1, act. 2. 1 and 2.2.1–35[408] – a "variorum work" built on earlier scholarship and largely indebted to Servius[409] – the considerable number of linguistic notes, concerned with grammar and etymological issues and the explanation of difficult or obsolete terms, offers insights into the scholiast's admiration for Cicero's accuracy in selecting verbs and nouns suited to context and style register. At the same time, it provides good evidence of the didactic nature of the commentary, a valuable instrument for improving linguistic proficiency. In the majority of cases, these comments appear in the form of concise, quite simplistic observations about near-synonyms with a fine distinction of meaning (presumably, glosses or marginal notes in origin). A few examples should suffice. When treating the difference between *populor* ("to plunder") and *vexo* ("to despoil"), the scholiast makes reference to the action covered by the verb and its cause (*avaritia,* "avarice," for *populor,* whereas *libido et crudelitas,* "excess of desire and cruelty," for *vexo*; cf. 187.15.6St, on *Div.* 2). In a similar way, he explains the subtle demarcation of meaning between other couples or groups of verbs: e.g. *rogare,* "to request," is used for humans, *orare,* "to pray, beseech," for gods (188.6-7St, on *Div.* 3); *accedere causam* means "to undertake a cause," whereas *aspirare causam,* "to hanker after a cause," indicates an aspiration to do something (192.1-2St, on *Div.*

---

[408] It is widely known that the commentary, transmitted together with Asconius Pedianus in the medieval manuscripts and erroneously attributed to the Neronian scholar by A. Mai, was definitely ascribed to a fifth-century grammarian and scholar by Madvig (1828: 84ff.); on Orosius's *Historiae adversus paganos* as a *terminus post quem* for the Verrine commentaries, see Benario 1973: 66–7. The *editio princeps* was published in Venice in 1477, followed by the edition Beraldina (1520), Aldina (1522) and Manutius in 1547: the text, reprinted by Baiter in 1833, is now in the edition of *Ciceronis Orationum Scholiastae* by Stangl (1912: 185–264). On Ps. Asconius's commentary in general, see Stangl 1909.

[409] Zetzel 1981: 171ff. For the relationship between Servius and Ps. Asconius, see Gessner 1888.

20);[410] the association of three verbs, *transigere* ("to settle matters"), *expedire* ("to clear up") and *absolvere* ("to dispose of"), is rhetorically explained by definition of the verbal object (199.3-6St, on *Div.* 45). These examples could be multiplied.[411] This kind of annotation (proper to a school commentary) on grammatical details and the meaning of adverbs, nouns and verbs (usually coupled) was devised to simplify the sense of the word or passage commented upon. Concerned with laying down rules of correct diction, the commentator elucidates Cicero's linguistic peculiarities and novelties by weighing up the meaning of words and implicitly lauding his erudition and refined diction.[412]

The nature of Ps. Asconius's commentary as a "variorum work" accounts for the presence of a significant number of textual annotations, variant readings or variants of collation ("*legitur* variants"), which are commonly considered to have been drawn from manuscript evidence.[413] This point will attract our attention in the following section of this chapter. But since three comments at least, depending on earlier exegetical tradition, are concerned with solecism and grammatical deviances, it seems pertinent to deal briefly with this question here. In the opening words of the *Divinatio* the scholiast interprets *descenderim*, in place of *descendere*, as a solecism of substitution; he suggests the insertion of *et* or *idem* as a possible solution to the grammatical anomaly.[414] These are the scholiast's words (186.19-22St):

---

[410] Cf. Cic. *Div.* 63 (*accedere ad causam/accedere ad periculum*).
[411] E.g. *Div.* 4 (*graviter/acerbe*: 188.12-3St); 8 (*difficultas/paupertas*:189.3St); 19 (*eripuisti/abstulisti*; 191.21-2St); 22 (*ulciscor* as both *punire* and *vindicare*); 26 (*suscipitur/recipitur*; 195.1-2St); 28 (*asportare/deportare*; 195.20-1St); *Ver.* 1.17 (*alacris/alacer/lacer*: 210.22–211.4St); 1.24 (*intellectum/animadversum*; 214.16-21St); 1.55 (*argumentari/dicere*: 222.24-6St); 2.1.33 (*lenones/perductores*: 233.5-7St); 2.1.91 (*syngrapha/chirographa*: 244.29–245.4St); 2.1.132 (*detrimentum/intertrimentum*: 251.26-7St); 2.1.143 (*socius/particeps*: 253.7-8St).
[412] Here I append a list of other linguistic explanations in Ps. Asconius: *Div.* 11 (distinction between the words *patronus, advocatus, procurator* and *cognitor*: 190.4-8St); 12 (*praeiudicium/iudicium*: 190.9-11St); 33 (*mancipes/portorii aut pecuarii*: 196.18-21St); *Ver.* 1.11 (*prodere/oppugnare*: 208.22St); 1.16 (*renuntiatio*: 209.30St); 1.22 (*fiscus/confiscare*: 212.7-12St); 1.36 (*deponitur/accipitur/recipitur*: 218.23St); 2.1.43 (*circumscribere*: 235.7St).
[413] Zetzel 1981: 175–6.
[414] Cicero's passage sounds as follows: *Si quis vestrum, iudices, aut eorum qui adsunt, forte miratur me, qui tot annis in causis iudiciisque publicis ita sim versatus ut defenderim multos, laeserim neminem, subito nunc mutate voluntate ad accusandum descendere* ("It may be, gentlemen, that some of you, or some of the audience, are surprised that I have departed from the line of action which I have pursued for all these years with regard to criminal proceedings; that having defended many accused persons, and attacked nobody, I have now suddenly changed my policy, and entered the arena as a prosecutor"). *Descenderim* is patently a simplification ascribed to the presence of *defenderim* and *laeserim* in the previous verbal units. Klotz 1919-23 (5: *ad loc.*) cautiously suggests that the sequence *defenderit ... laeserit ... descenderit* in Quintilian's paraphrasis of Cicero's sentence (*Inst.* 4.1.49; cf. also Vict. 422.29 *RLM*) might have originated the error.

Si quis vestrum, iudices] Hoc toto capite soloecismi species continetur, nisi addas "et" aut "idem," ut sit: et nunc subito mutata voluntate ad accusandum descenderim: quare multi non descenderim legunt, sed descendere.

"It may be, gentlemen, that some of you] This initial chapter presents a form of solecism, unless one might add '*et*' or '*idem*', so that the sentence sounds as follows: 'and now I have suddenly changed my course of action and entered the arena as a prosecutor'. This is the reason why many commentators read *descendere*, not *descenderim*."

Zeztel correctly observes that Ps. Asconius's addition of *et* or *idem* is "no improvement at all, as it would destroy the asyndeton of the three units."[415] However it might be, the scholiast seems preoccupied with eliminating a possible reason for underappreciating Cicero's stylistic choice. This type of solecism, like hyperbaton, may be justified as a means of rhetorical ornamentation. Yet Ps. Asconius felt obliged to intervene in the dispute in order to prevent students from misunderstanding the syntax of Cicero's passage.

Another case of solecism is detected by Ps. Asconius in *Ver.* 1.25 (214.4-9St). A syntactical anomaly occurs in the use of the infinitive *venisse*, regarded as an example of "illogical locution, like a solecism" (*inconsequens locutio similisque soloecismi*), not so different from that observed at the beginning of the *Divinatio* (*in primo capite Verrinarum*). Ps. Asconius's difficulty with the construction of *venisse* seems unsubstantiated, for the infinitive clearly depends on the previous *audio*: *venissent* is "a trivializing reading invented for supposed grammatical improvement," not based on manuscript evidence.[416]

The third case of solecism spotted by Ps. Asconius, at *Ver.* 1.55 (223.3-6St), seems much more complicated. Cicero's phrase, *nunc id quod facimus, ea ratione facimus ut malitiae illorum consilio nostro occurramus, necessario fieri intellegat*,[417] contains a not easily intelligible repetition of *facimus*.[418] The perceived obscurity of Cicero's expression (*inconsequens locutio et obscura*), which reminds the scholiast of the end of the oration in support of Ligarius,[419] is eliminated by simply suggesting the deletion of

---

[415] Zetzel 1981: 173.   [416] Zetzel 1981: 174.
[417] "For the moment he must see that our line of action, being directed to thwarting, by rational means, the trickery of our adversaries, is the only one possible."
[418] The second *facimus* is given in brackets in modern editions. Peterson 1903: 200–1 suggests <*quia*> *ea ratione* and thinks of a copyist's misinterpretation of the compendium *rē* (*recte*, not *ratione*), propounding thus the reading *nunc id quod facimus et recte facimus ut*).
[419] Stangl (*ad loc.*) tentatively takes Ps. Asconius's words as alluding to *Lig.* 38 (presumably to the chiastic sentence *longiorem orationem causa forsitan postulet, tua certe natura breviorem*). Ricchieri 2017: 100 (who also suggests the insertion of *quoniam* before *id quod facimus*) makes reference to *Lig.* 37 (with emphatic repetition of *facio*).

the redoubled *facimus*. This emendation surely shows a low order of textual ability. Yet it testifies to the concrete, though disputable, effort of Ps. Asconius (and earlier commentators) to confront the complexity and sophistication of Cicero's language and support students in understanding – and solving – real linguistic problems.

In short, the grammarian/scholiast acts as a guide through the learning process. He supervises his students' development toward maturity and *eruditio* by offering Cicero as both a model of pure Latin diction and *idoneus auctor*. Viewed in this way, the teacher's attempts to clarify lexical and/or morphological difficulties are an integral part and parcel of a larger educational program. By elucidating linguistic matters the schoolmaster advocates his own ideal of education, a firm command of classical Latin, achieved through the appropriation and replication of Cicero's abundant and proper vocabulary, his *elegantia*, rhythmical regularity and clear sentence structure. Commenting upon Cicero, thus, was not just a way of making an authoritative classical text more accessible to readers and students. It was, above all, a way to allow each generation to acquire and take advantage of proper Latin usage, a valuable tool for promising orator-politicians. Cicero's *Latinitas* fostered the intellectual and linguistic abilities needed to play a vital role in the quest for prestige and *dignitas* within the elite that dominated Roman society.

In recognizing the pragmatic value of education and promoting Cicero as an authority on Latin, ancient scholars stressed the practical aspects of training in language and reasserted the importance of virile *Latinitas* to intellectual and social advancement. As has been remarked at the beginning of this chapter, mastery of the language was the keyword of Roman liberal education. And mastery of Cicero's language was a determining factor in the pursuit of social esteem and honor status. By systematically reading Cicero's authoritative texts and facilitating the comprehension of the intricacies of Latin grammar, ancient scholars depicted Cicero as the epitome of correct Latin and, most importantly, emphasized *Latinitas* as an honorific value, a sign of elite distinction commonly associated with political and social success.

### *Alii . . . Dicunt, Alii . . . Legunt*: Late Ciceronian Scholarship

The late fourth to fifth century represented a critical period in the history of Latin textual criticism. This was the time that witnessed the emergence of scholarly commentaries, like Servius and Donatus on Vergil and Terence or Marius Victorinus on Cicero the philosopher, in the form of

## Late Ciceronian Scholarship 163

"variorum works" built on earlier scholarship. These variorum commentaries, "separate works of second-order in literature in late antiquity,"[420] assembled earlier materials, discussing (and often refuting) interpretations from earlier scholarly authorities. It is generally believed that Donatus's lost commentary on Vergil "was largely composed of extracts from his predecessors";[421] Servius's commentary, in turn, relied on that of Donatus for the most part. Late surviving Latin scholia are usually thought to represent a survey of previous scholarship, providing us thereby with outstanding evidence of literary and textual criticism from imperial times to early Middle Ages. Both as *editiones variorum,* later abridged and transmitted as marginal excerpts,[422] and organized systems of lemmatized annotations separate from the text commented upon,[423] Latin scholiastic *corpora* systematically assembled and condensed earlier versions, with the addition of a (small) portion of original material.

To turn from the general problem of the Latin scholia to the specific question concerning late commentaries on Cicero, the Bobbio scholiast, Ps. Asconius and other sets of marginal or interlinear notes show that ancient scholarship on Cicero resulted from a progressive, gradual accumulation and conflation of exegetical notes produced on the orations at different times. This is especially evident in those notes that allude (often in polemical tones) to earlier commentaries by means of technical expressions such as *alii . . . legunt/alii . . . dicunt (alii . . . putant).*[424] Within a systematic collation of data, scholars provided their readers/students with a controlled, exhaustive series of different explanations, placed side by side, inviting them thus to familiarize themselves with scholarly debates on the scrutinized text or passage. Equally, comments deprived of any reference to previous scholarship may show traces of earlier material. Through different (not always discernible) stages of transmission, the

---

[420] Zetzel 1975: 337.
[421] Zetzel 1975: 338. On the stages of the transmission of ancient commentaries and Latin scholia, see also Zetzel 2005.
[422] Thus the commentary of Donatus on Terence and the Bembine scholia; see Zeztel 1975; 2005. For the transition of commentaries on literary works into scholia, taking the form of marginalia, see Dickey 2007: 11–12 (with bibliography).
[423] On the absence of a rigid distinction between marginal glosses or annotations and scholiastic commentaries, see now Gioseffi 2014: 177–79 (with further bibliography). For terminology and the difference between scholia and commentaries, see Zetzel 2005: 4–9 (also Montana 2011).
[424] For the expression *alii . . . putant* (and comparable locutions) cf. Ps. Asconius 186.5St; 191.3-4St (*quidam . . . putant*; also 251.1St); 200.1St; 207.18-9St; 211.3St (*sunt qui . . . putant*); 217.10St; 230.33St (*alii sic adnotant . . . alii sic*); 247.23 St. (*alii sic intellegunt*); *alii . . . aiunt* in schol. Gronov. 324.13St. On the use of *aliter* (and similar formulas) in the Vergilian commentaries, see Gioseffi 2014.

scholiographic *corpora* on Cicero originated from a stratified amalgam of sources or earlier scholarly statements. Positioned within a broader historical-cultural context, ancient exegesis of Cicero shows that the speeches were perceived as being a fertile ground for "academic competition" between detractors (*obtrectatores*) and scholars fascinated by Cicero's verbal *ingenium*.

As Wilson observes, "the history of scholia goes back to the time when explanations of literary texts first became necessary, in other words the classical age of Greece, when schoolmasters found that pupils required some explanation of rare words and other difficulties in Homer and the lyric poets, the basic texts of literary education."[425] To apply this statement to the reception of Cicero in antiquity, the exegetical history of the speeches goes back to the end of Roman republic, not long after the death of the republican orator and statesman. Interpretation of Cicero started as soon as the speeches acquired the status of standard schoolbooks. In this light, the material preserved in the commentaries represents our most valuable source for the reconstruction of how critics and scholars read and taught Cicero's oratory, extending from the late republic and early Augustan age to the medieval period. But, as Zetzel clearly puts it, "perhaps the greatest difficulty of scholiastic transmission is the fact that none of these commentaries was an original work, composed by a single critic in the fourth or fifth century. They represent summaries and extracts of a tradition ranging back to the time of the authors who are being explained. We cannot isolate much out of them and ascribe it to an earlier period."[426] Establishing the epoch of composition of the scholia is nearly an impossible task. The ancient scholia were not fixed texts, written by a single commentator. There is no way to ascertain their origin. We may venture to date the Bobbio commentary to the late third or early fourth century CE. Analogously, it is possible to date Ps. Asconius to the early fifth century, in light of its dependence on Servius, as we have seen. Yet there is no doubt that the Bobbio scholiast includes additions from a rhetorical-historical commentary that is presumably to be traced back to the late first or early second century. In the same way, the commentary of Ps. Asconius preserves and discusses material from earlier scholarly texts. Reconstructing any phase of the tradition or determining the chronology and origin of any single annotation is further frustrated by the fact that the scholiasts or earlier critics mentioned or referred to in our commentaries of Cicero have no names and identities. By contrast to Servius and the DS

---

[425] Wilson (N. G.) 2007: 40.   [426] Zeztel 1981: 79.

commentary on Vergil, in which the name of the textual critic is attached to the proposed emendation in a good number of cases, the commentaries and scholia on Cicero (with the only exception being Fenestella in Asconius's commentary)[427] seem to avoid citing or naming earlier scholarly authorities. The identities of earlier commentators are shrouded in mystery. The *commentaria* on Cicero preserve a relevant portion of ancient exegesis, but they tell us very little (or nothing) about the scholars who supplied linguistic or textual annotations on the text expounded upon.

Before enquiring into the relation between the surviving *scholia* on Cicero and earlier exegesis, it is worth calling to mind some figures of textual critics, already encountered in the course of our discussion about first- and second-century scholarship. As we have seen, the activity of these professional scholars, mostly embracing clarification of questions related to style and rhetorical technique or illustration of historical-antiquarian topics, is representative of an "academic" approach to Cicero's text, dissected as a source of information on Roman history and used as both a model of Latin diction and persuasion and an instrument of linguistic research. The first-century historian and antiquarian Fenestella, the author of a twenty-two-book annalistic history of Rome, has already been mentioned as a primary source of Asconius's commentary. Significantly, Fenestella is the privileged target of Asconius's academic polemic. An instructive example of this rivalry (in addition to the cases discussed in the second chapter) is the repeated disagreement of the two scholars about Cicero's alleged defense of Catiline, accused *de repetundis* by the young P. Clodius after his return from Africa,[428] a highly controversial issue suggesting different interpretations of Cicero's ambivalent attitude to political crisis in the years immediately preceding his consulship and the Catilinarian conspiracy.[429]

In a general sense, beneath the competition between Asconius and Fenestella lurks the tendency towards debate, a hallmark of ancient

---

[427] The name of the first-century grammarian and antiquarian Sinnius Capito occurs in the *argumentum* to the speech *de aere alieno Milonis* in the Bobbio commentary. There, the scholiast expands on the term *interrogatio* (included in the *titulum* of the oration) by making a distinction between different types of *interrogationes* (170.1-14St); Sinnius Capito is alluded to as scholarly authority for the third type of inquiry, usually held in a senatorial context (170.8-14 St.).

[428] Asc. 85.13-4C; 86.15-6C. In categorically refusing any involvement of Cicero in the defense of Catiline, Asconius is probably mistaken. He evidently lacked access to Cicero's correspondence with Atticus (in particular he did not take into account Cic. *Att.* 1.2 [11 SB*Att*], a clear statement of Cicero's intention to defend Catiline); see Lewis 2006: 294.

[429] Possibly, Fenestella is the name (lost) to be supplemented in Asconius's discussion of Scipio's permission to the senators to be separated from the rest of the general seating during the Megalensian Games, on the basis of a passage from Cicero's oration *On the answer of the haruspices* (*Har. Resp.* 24); cf. Asc. 70.9-11C.

scholarship. Dispute is obviously integral to interpretation and textual criticism. It largely impacts on the ways a classical text is received by later readers. As has been stated, ancient exegetes "claim for their own work – and indeed for themselves – the right to extract all kinds of meaning from a text and to construct their own line of argument."[430] Each interpreter claims authority. Each interpretation is implicitly legitimated by refuting previous scholarly evaluations. By its very nature, ancient exegesis was a field of debate, an "open space" in which different, contrasting modes of critical discourse intersected with each other and offered practical manifestations of various trends in scholarship and changing cultural and historical perspectives in the approach to ancient texts.

If applied to Cicero, this general statement is of some significance. We have seen that the political and social (not only literary) impact of the speeches colored ancient reception and inspired debates about Cicero as a distinctive figure of Roman republican history. Cicero as a man was naturally debatable and debated. His orations, unanimously recognized as authoritative works, soon earned a reputation as "political documents," expressions of a critical moment of Roman history, attracting thus multiple, different reactions about Cicero's engagement in the political crisis of the late republic. So, the academic divergence between Asconius and Fenestella is not only a good example of scientific debate by means of refusal/approval of contrasting readings. It also tells us more about the political interpretation of the speeches and ancient responses to Cicero in the early imperial period. No doubt, the dispute over the presumed defense of Catiline carried with it political significations, involving reflections on Cicero's exploitation of power and his ambiguous relationships with friends and enemies before and during the Catilinarian crisis. What is more, figuring Cicero as advocating on behalf of Catiline (or mulling over the political convenience lying behind a prospective defense of the soon-to-be conspirator) would have had a considerable impact on later receptions of Cicero as a loyal supporter of the Roman *res publica* and, above all, as a never-to-be-forgotten consul rightly claiming the title of *parens patriae*.

Likely, Asconius's insistence on rejecting any possible involvement of Cicero in the acquittal of Catiline was motivated by political considerations.[431] Modeled on ancient Demosthenes scholarship,[432] Asconius's work reconfigured a "positive" historical Cicero, a Roman

---

[430] Montanari, Matthaios, and Rengakos 2015: 1.XIII.   [431] Asc. 86.16-22C.
[432] On Didymus's historicizing approach to Demosthenes and its influence on Asconius's commentary, see Bishop 2015: 288–90.

Demosthenes, seen (and eulogized) as the republican bulwark against Antony and the rise of imperial tyranny.[433] Yet this was far from being an untroubled operation. In interpreting the speeches, the most representative (and debated) political texts of the Roman republic, Asconius confronted criticism and denigration of his source, a natural (widespread) response to the equivocal involvement of the senator and statesman in the political life of the late republic. Through Cicero students learned Roman history, as we have seen. Most notably, by focusing on Cicero as a historical figure they were stimulated to revisit Roman history and rethink the relation between morality and politics within the vigorous debate over freedom and new forms of dominance. Such was the context in which Asconius stood in defense of Cicero's reputation as a politician, the last champion (like Demosthenes) of republican liberty, a battle no doubt fraught with danger. Whatever the reason behind Fenestella's claim, Asconius had an obligation to react to outrageous criticism about Cicero's political conduct.

Other Ciceronian critics may usefully be remembered in this survey of early empire scholarship. Favorinus and Antonius Julianus, respected men of learning well versed in ancient literature and lauded by Gellius as subtle interpreters of Cicero's stylistic virtues, are prototypical examples of a consolidated scientific attitude towards the text of Cicero.[434] We have seen that interest in Cicero's language, not rarely accompanied by contemptuous criticism,[435] was dominant in second-century scholarship, as may be inferred from grammarians' and *rhetores*' comments on purported archaisms or anomalous constructions in the speeches.[436] A commentary on Cicero may be ascribed to the second-century grammarian Flavius Caper, already mentioned as author of the treatise *De latinitate*, amply used by the later artigraphic and lexicographical tradition, a seminal work in the development of Latin grammatical science and erudite classicism.[437] Evidence of that comes from the prefatory epistle of the fifth-century Agroecius's *Ars de orthographia*, addressed to Eucherius, the bishop of Lyons.[438] After describing his own work as a supplement to Caper's *De orthographia et de proprietate ac differentia sermonum*, the *rhetor* Agroecius pays homage to Caper's learning and exegetical skills paraded at best in his commentary on Cicero (*GL* 7.113.8ff.):

---

[433] Bishop 2015: 290ff. (on Asconius's defense of Cicero).   [434] See supra, pp. 135–6.
[435] On the *obtrectatores Ciceronis* cf. Gel.17.1. For criticism of Cicero's use of false arguments in his dialogue on friendship cf. Gel. 17.5.
[436] Gel. 1.4; 10.3; 13.1; 15.13 20.6; 20.9.   [437] See supra p. 154.   [438] Kaster 1988: 382.

> Libellum Capri De ortographia misisti mihi ... huic ergo Capri libello, qui est De orthographia et de proprietate ac differentia sermonum, quaedam adicienda subieci, non quod vir tantae peritiae aliquid praetermiserit tam multis praesertim litterarum operibus celebratus et in commentando etiam Cicerone praecipuus.

> "You have sent me off Caper's little treatise *On orthography* ... Well, I thought it necessary to add something to this treatise of Caper, entitled *On orthography and propriety and difference between words:* this was not because such a learned man had omitted some points, on the contrary his critical and literary qualities, displayed at most in his commentary of Cicero, are unanimously recognized."[439]

Notwithstanding lack of evidence about the nature and extent of Caper's commentary,[440] it appears that Caper enjoyed considerable fame as a Ciceronian critic.[441] His interest in Cicero's language and rhetorical technique is well attested by second-hand citations in late grammatical handbooks.[442] He was well acquainted with the entirety of Cicero's literary production, as demonstrated by his discussion of a passage from the *Philippics* (13.43).[443] Likely, Caper made an extensive use of Cicero's speeches, epistles and philosophical works in order to complement his discussions *de Latinitate.*[444]

Similarly, the figure of Volcacius as a commentator of Cicero remains obscured in mystery. In the second chapter we pointed to the suggested identification of Volcacius with the author of the Bobbio commentary. In support of this attribution scholars cite a passage from Jerome's *Apology against Rufinus* (1.16). Jerome claims legitimacy here for his exegetical work, undeservedly classed as plagiarism, and details the nature and form of late commentaries. To complement his assertions he also includes a list of illustrious past commentaries, like that of Volcacius on the *orationes Ciceronis,* celebrated along with other significant products of fourth- and fifth-century Latin scholarship (Asper's commentary on Vergil and Sallust, Marius Victorinus, Donatus's exegesis of Terence and Vergil and unspecified commentators on Plautus, Lucretius, Horace, Persius and Lucan).[445] Jerome's text runs as follows:

---

[439] My translation.
[440] Doubts have also been raised about Caper's composition of commentaries on Latin poets and prose-writers comparable, in form and content, to that of Servius and Donatus: see Grafehan 1850: 299; Suringar 1854: 1.191–93. For Caper's *commentarii* cf. also Hier. *Adv. Rufin.* 2.9.
[441] The existence of a commentary on Cicero is postulated by Schmidt 1997a: 236.
[442] For quotations from Cicero's works in Caper, see Karbaum 1889; Hoeltermann 1913: 81–88.
[443] Pomp. *GL* 5.154.11.   [444] Hoeltermann 1913: 87–8.
[445] With the exception of Donatus, Jerome does not mention these commentators elsewhere; see Hagendahl 1958: 175.

Commentarii quid operis habent? Alterius dicta edisserunt, quae obscure scripta sunt, plano sermone manifestant, multorum sententias replicant, et dicunt: Hunc locum quidam sic edisserunt, alii sic interpretantur, illi sensum suum et intelligentiam his testimoniis et hac nituntur ratione firmare, ut prudens lector, cum diversas explanationes legerit et multorum vel probanda vel improbanda didicerit, iudicet quid verius sit, et quasi bonus trapezita, adulterinae monetae pecuniae reprobet. Num diversae interpretationis et contrariorum inter se sensuum tenebitur reus, qui in uno opere quod ediserit, expositiones posuerit plurimorum? Puto quod puer legeris Aspri in Vergilium ac Sallustium commentarios, Vulcatii in orationes Ciceronis, Victorini in dialogos eius, et in Terentii Comoedias praeceptoris mei Donati, aeque in Vergilium, et aliorum in alios, Plautum videlicet, Lucretium, Flaccum, Persium atque Lucanum. Argue interpretes eorum quare non unam explanationem secuti sint, et in eadem re quid vel sibi vel aliis videatur enumerent.

"What is the task of commentaries? They explain the words of another, they elucidate in plain speech what is written in obscure terms, they repeat earlier opinions, and they say: 'There are many who expound on this passage in this way, many others interpret it differently, and by these citations and this method they attempt to confirm their interpretation and opinion', so that the prudent reader, once he has looked through contrasting interpretations and has learned what is worthy accepting or refusing, can make his own judgment on the subject and, like a good money-changer, will reject the false coinage. Now is he to be held responsible for all these different interpretations, and opposing each other, who lays forth in one single work what he has learned concerning the arguments of man? When you were at a very young age, I am sure, you read Asper's commentaries on Vergil and Sallust, the commentary of Volcacius on Cicero's orations, that of Victorinus on Cicero's rhetorical dialogues, and again the commentary of Donatus, teacher of mine, on Terence and Vergil, and other commentaries on other writers, no doubt Plautus, Lucretius, Horace, Persius and Lucan. Attack their interpretations because they have not followed a single explanation, and have instead on each passage enumerated their own views and those of others."[446]

Replying to Rufinus's indictment for plagiarism in his commentary on Ephesians,[447] Jerome elaborates on the typical structure of the commentary as a collation of earlier scholarship. Significantly, he insists on the key role played by the learned and sensible reader, left to question the reliability of the commentary and make thus his own choice between two or more

---

[446] Text and translation: Williams (Megan Hale) 2006: 103.
[447] On Rufinus versus Jerome literary controversy, see Lardet 1993; Gamberale 2013: 153–68.

alternative readings/explanations.[448] Within this dispute, Jerome's catalogue of earlier commentaries is of great value. It represents a condensed survey of classical scholarship. More important to us, in this history of late Latin exegesis a special position is occupied by Volcacius, reputed not inferior to Donatus (Jerome's mentor), Asper and the *rhetor* Victorinus. His commentary on Cicero earned him a reputation as a reliable schoolteacher, rightly associated with other eminent figures of scholars and literary critics.[449]

Jerome's polemical response to Rufinus sheds light on the art of commentary in late antiquity. Basically a compilation of earlier exegetical texts, the typical commentary was intended to explain its source text through paraphrase, discussion of textual problems and elucidation of linguistic complexities, sometimes touching upon historical and cultural matters. At the same time that the scholiast addressed the meaning of the text, he provided students with a survey of different, often contradictory earlier opinions about grammatical or textual issues. This is the key point of Jerome's apologetic argument. He downplays the critical abilities of the commentator, depicted as a simple, passive "medium for instruction," in favor of the dominant position of the reader (charged with estimating the correctness of the various opinions propounded by the commentator). Portraying the commentator (and himself) as a compiler of earlier exegetical texts, Jerome formally justifies his authorial choice and invites his opponent to consider the scientificity of the commentary, a research-based work drawing on a rich legacy of earlier exegesis and aimed at deepening knowledge through a survey of academic disputes. To Jerome, the commentator does not plagiarize previous works. He simply collects earlier material, enabling his readers to form their own opinion about textual issues or linguistic problems, variously explained by earlier professional scholars.

Yet Jerome's self-justifying assertion of "neutrality" cannot be accepted at face value.[450] It turns to be a strategic rhetorical gambit. Obviously, the ancient commentator not only channeled the opinions of earlier authorities. He guided his reader through the intricacies of interpretation and exercised control over the reader's mind and judgment. Refuting or

---

[448] For Jerome's definition of the characters of late commentaries (*consuetudo* or "respect of norms," diversity of the sources, and function of the reader), see Lardet 1993: 81–2.

[449] On other figures of commentators of Cicero we have little or no information. For a commentary on Cicero's *pro Rabirio perduellionis reo* by the third-century scholar and grammarian Sacer, see chapter 2, p. 97.

[450] Lardet 1993: 82.

approving earlier authoritative opinions was the scholiast's task, not the reader's, whose verdict on the text was implicitly (and inevitably) swayed by the commentator's presentation. As a result, when Jerome (and the commentator in general) discusses variant readings or focuses on controversial literary/technical issues, misinterpreted by earlier critics, he implicitly enters into competition with his erudite rivals. He asserts thus his authoritative role as a trustworthy exegete and offers his interpretation as the unique, reliable source of knowledge.

By its very nature the commentary implies a complex, multifaceted relationship between its author and readership, on both theoretical and practical levels, as demonstrated by recent studies on the classical commentary in modern times.[451] So a good commentary was intended to be a "fixed" system of instructions to readers, supplied with explanatory, authoritative (and uncontestable) sentences about discrete questions immanent in the text and thereby inhibited from doing further research. Certainly, the reader responded to spurs to textual investigation. He cooperated with his supervisor and refined his analysis by questioning earlier interpretations. Yet the final verdict was left up to the commentator. His authority guaranteed and certified the reliability of any textual explanation.

Jerome's passage is also relevant to the use of commentaries in support of reading, a practice clearly connected to the training system in the school. On the one hand, Jerome's address to Rufinus *puer* consulting classical commentaries illuminates the dominant role of the *auctores* of the *quadriga Messii,* namely Terence, Sallust, Cicero and Virgil,[452] together with other textual authorities, in the late antique education system.[453] On the other, it gives us every reason to believe that schoolboys solved stylistic or textual problems as they came up during the act of reading by resorting to accompanying commentaries. As has been noted, "later commentaries continued to assume that the reader had a text of the work under comment before him, or perhaps that he had committed it to memory."[454] Presumably, he also used a commentary to enhance his knowledge and acquire a deeper understanding of the text under scrutiny. The commentary, in sum, was intended to function as a didactic instrument, an auxiliary paratext supplying

---

[451] Most 1999; Gibson-Kraus 2002.
[452] Virgil, Sallust and Cicero (along with Plautus, Varro, Livy, Quintilian and Tacitus) are included in the canon of scholastic authors in Sidonius Apollinaris's *Panegyric of Anthemius* (*Carm.* 2.182–92).
[453] On Lucretius's presence in late school curriculum, see Hagendahl 1958: 87–8. For the absence of Statius in Jerome's scholastic list (despite Lactantius Placidus's commentary on the *Thebaid*), see Zetzel 1981: 177.
[454] Williams (Megan Hale) 2006: 105–6.

information necessary for an adequate comprehension of the given primary text.[455] It is easy to assume that by Jerome's times the commentary had entered the school system as both a guide for the reader's perception of the text commented upon and a support for acquiring knowledge of classical Latin.

Turning to the scholia on Cicero, it is reasonable to believe that the Bobbio commentary and Ps. Asconius operated as auxiliary texts in the interpretation of Cicero's oratory, directing the student's mind towards a correct understanding of the sense and content of specific passages. Significantly, they were of practical use in clarifying textual issues. It is known that reconstructing the earliest (authentic) form of the text, by means of *recensio* and careful examination of variant readings, was the main task of the textual critic. But the process of emendation, the first step towards the establishment of a correct text, was also meant to be crucial to the interpretation of classical authors. In this light, it constituted a substantial part of educational training. To employ conceptual categories applied to Alexandrian scholarship, learned scholars showed "a real idea of textual criticism as well as of history of the text."[456] More, as schoolteachers and educationists they realized that textual correctness and appropriateness were of the greatest significance to the reception – and related comprehension – of the text. Textual criticism was firmly rooted in the educational system.

That said, the scholia on Cicero are quite atypical. Both the commentaries and the groups of *scholia* and marginal notes, which surround the text of the orations in many medieval manuscripts, contain a relatively small number of textual annotations (especially by comparison with Vergil).[457] Textual criticism does not seem to have been the main affair of Ciceronian scholiasts. A few examples may suffice to clarify this point. To start with Asconius's commentary, the only textual comment occurs in the scholium on a passage from the first speech on behalf of Cornelius, concerning a much disputed political theme, that is, the secession of the plebs and the establishment of the tribunate (76.13C).[458] The manuscript reading *restituerent*, if accepted, would imply assuming the restoration of formerly

---

[455] For the commentaries as auxiliary texts (and the application of modern theories of communication in understanding the relation between auxiliary texts and condensation of knowledge), see Dubischar 2010.
[456] Montanari 2011: 14.
[457] On variants of collation (or *legitur* variants) as a consistent part of scholarly material in the commentaries on poetry authors (like Servius), see Zetzel 1981: 171ff.
[458] Frg48Crawford (for a commentary on this passage, Crawford 1994: 130–31).

sanctioned sacred laws (*leges sacratae*) and, consequently, an earlier creation of the popular magistracy. Asconius dismisses it as an "error of the copyists" (*menda librariorum*). To him it was implausible that Cicero erred in choosing improper terminology, as he had sure knowledge that "the plebs did not restore religiously sanctioned laws – for it had never had tribunes of the plebs – but then for the first time instituted them" (*plebs sibi leges sacratas non restituit – numquam enim tribunos plebis habuerat – sed tum primum eas constituit*).[459] Asconius's proposal of emending *restituerent* to *constituerent* (probably right) seems to be impelled by historical curiosity. He was visibly preoccupied with the date and origin of the office of tribunate, less with philological accuracy. Textual criticism came along as an incidental accompaniment of an eminently historical commentary. As Zetzel notes, "it does not appear that Asconius was interested in the text of Cicero to any greater extent than to correct in passing an obvious error on a subject of interest to him."[460]

A group of four variants of collation, based on manuscript evidence, in Ps. Asconius has already been examined by Zetzel.[461] Here, I add some marginal notations on these textual scholia. At *Ver.* 2.1.52 (236.16-8St) the Ciceronian manuscripts offer the alternative readings *quaesitorem* (reported by the scholiast in the lemma) and *quaestorem*. In simplistic terms, Ps. Asconius adopts the reading *quaesitor*, "inquisitor" (a banal manuscript error), referring it to Manius Glabrio, the president of the extortion court entrusted with the task of returning illegally confiscated goods to the allies (*cuius cura est ut sociis omnia rapta reddantur*). Similar is the explanation of the reading *quaestor*, the city quaestor charged with redistributing the property of the proscribed.[462] As quite usual, the scholiast does not reject the variant introduced by *legitur* (in this case *quaestor*). He simply limits himself to giving notice of an alternative reading, explained to the reader for the sake of clarity. Incidentally, it may be observed that in the scholium on *Ver.*1.29 (215.24-6St) Ps. Asconius elucidates the meaning of *quaesitor* by quoting a line from the sixth book of Vergil's *Aeneid* (6.432, *Quaesitor Minos urnam movet*). The scholium recalls Servius's comment on the same Vergilian line. It is reasonable to assume, with Stangl,[463] that the figuration of Minos as *quaesitor* (*praetor rerum capitalium*) in the *argumentum* to the *Actio* 2.1 (224.22-5St) is a late

---

[459] Lewis 2006: 283.   [460] Zetzel 1981: 37.   [461] Zetzel 1981: 175–6.
[462] Cf. also schol. Gronov. 345.26-7St (on the difference between *quaestor* and *sector*).
[463] Stangl 1909: 105.

interpolation,[464] inspired by the common designation of the entire second *Actio* as a *liber de criminis repetundarum* (generally concerning Verres's corruption and misconduct in office)[465] and drawing on Ps. Asconius's mentioned explanation.

The second example of variant of collation involves a textual problem. At *Ver.* 2.1.60 the manuscripts read *habeo et ipsius et patris accepi tabulas omnis: accepti* is the reading of Ps. Asconius, who adds that some testimonies have *ab eo . . . accepi* (*legitur et "ab eo" et "accepi"*: 238.20-1St).[466] As has been noted, the combination of *habeo* and *accepi* "generates an undesirable tautology".[467] Furthermore, *accepti* "as a short form of the standard *accepti et expensi*" is not attested elsewhere in Cicero.[468] No doubt, the readings *ab eo* (replacing *habeo*) and *accepi* (in lieu of *accepti*) are simple variants of collation, arising from the attempt to establish a syntactically intelligible text.[469]

Another case of *legitur* variant occurs at *Ver.* 2.1.90 (244.16-7St).[470] The scholiast offers the reading *expectant* in the lemma (preserved in all the manuscripts) and then records the existence of a variant *extimescunt*. The subsequent explanation of the alternative readings as produced by similarity of meaning (both the verbs point to the *metus* surrounding the designation of the consuls-elect) is evidently prompted by didactic needs. Zetzel rightly contends that *extimescunt* "was merely a gloss on *expectant* that had achieved the status of a variant by the time of Ps. Asconius."[471] The scholiast appears to be indifferent to philological accuracy. Restricting himself to reporting variant readings as they are transmitted in the manuscript available to him, he resembles Servius's superficial attitude to textual accuracy and shows no interest in establishing or reconstructing a reliable text.[472]

---

[464] The note on Minos (named *quaesitor*, "inquisitor"), exercising justice in the netherworld (*iudex apud inferos*), is positioned in the middle of a detailed presentation of the legal and rhetorical topics treated in each of the five books, which form the entire second *Actio*.

[465] Ps. Asconius's comment is of some importance to the tradition of Cicero's *Verrines*, as it discusses the "fictionality" of the second *Actio* of Cicero's prosecution of Verres (pointing to the rhetorical strategems that sustain the literary fiction of the trial; on this issue, see chapter 1, pp. 50–1). The scholium also offers indications about numeration and titles of the speeches included in the second *Actio*, each of them dealing with a specific *crimen* (the first *liber* would be devoted to the *anteacta vita*, past misdeeds, the remaining four to the *crimina repetundarum*, divided into *de iure dicendo, de re frumentaria, de signis, de suppliciis*: 224.18-21St).

[466] *Habeo <et> ipsius et patris eius accepti tabulas*] *Id est acceptarum pecuniarum. Legitur et Ab eo et accepi.*

[467] Gildenhard 2011b: 88.   [468] Zetzel 1981: 175.

[469] Peterson (1903: 201–2) omits *habeo* and prints *et istius et patris eius accepi tabulas omnis*.

[470] *Et consulum designatorum nomen expectant*] *Et extimescunt legitur, nam utroque verbo idem significatur.*

[471] Zetzel 1981: 175.   [472] On Servius's textual criticism, see Zetzel 1981: 90ff.

Again, at *Ver.* 2.1.34 (233.8-10St) the scholiast registers the presence of a variant *consule* (rather than *consuli*).[473] This is an obvious case of a "minor variant of collation."[474] The supplement *sed male*, proposed by Stangl to fill a lacuna of six or seven letters at the end of the scholium,[475] appears inconsistent with the scholiast's practice, because of the absence of analogous critical remarks in reporting *legitur* variants within the commentary.[476] If it is true that Ps. Asconius sometimes evaluates earlier opinions in major linguistic and syntactical issues, involving understanding and related appreciation of Cicero's stylistic devices, he never employs philological techniques in textual matters. He acts simply as a collector of variant readings, never expanding on the validity of the recorded variant.

Two further textual scholia deserve attention. In the *Scholia Cluniacensia*, a short group of marginal and interlinear notes on many orations of Cicero,[477] an interesting gloss penetrated the text in the earliest stages of textual transmission. In the scholium on *Cat.* 2.4 (269.21–270.4St), we read in the lemma *quem amare in praetexta calumnia coeperat*. The scholiast initially reports the existence of a variant *praetextata calumnia* (probably a variant based on the exegetical tradition). Then he comments on the locution *praetexta calumnia*, an ironic, scornful expression[478] intended to replace the usual formula, *toga praetexta*, in order to stigmatize Catiline's involvement in a sexual liaison with the lad Tongilius. *Praetexta calumnia* is the reading transmitted by most of the medieval witnesses. It also appears in

---

[473] *Quaestor Cn. Papirio consuli fuisti]* Uno nomine Cn. Papirii Carbonis et tempus criminis significavit et crimen. Legitur tamen et consule, sed male.
[474] Zetzel 1981: 176.   [475] Stangl 1909: 127.
[476] I agree with Zetzel (1981: 176) in considering the note on *Div.* 3 (188.2-3St) as a not "particularly apposite" parallel for the use of *male* in textual scholia (Stangl 1909: 127). This scholium does not record *legitur* variants. It concerns itself with the distinction between *templa* and *delubra* and, as usual in similar notes, Ps. Asconius lists contrasting interpretations from earlier scholars (expressing his rejection of the equivalence of *delubra* with *ligna delibrata* with the final sentence *sed male*).
[477] This set of glosses and marginal notes on Cicero's speeches (specifically, on *Cat.* 1.33; 2.1–2; 4–5; 3.15; 24; 4.1; 4; 9; 10; *Marc.* 9; 13; 17; 20; 31; *Lig.*12; 21; 24; 37; *Deiot.* 1–2; 8; 12; 19; 25–26; 29; *Ver.* 2.2. 1–5; 8) has come down to us in an early ninth-century manuscript written in Caroline minuscule at Tours, later owned by the library of Cluny (London, British Library, Add. 47678, olim Holkhamicus 387: **C**). On the manuscript, see Peterson 1901; Reynolds 1983: 61ff. (**C**, the oldest manuscript that has *Catilinarians, Cesarians* and *Verrines* in order, is commonly thought to be the archetype of the French family of the manuscripts transmitting the *corpus* of the *Catilinarians*). A number of marginal notes on the fourth speech against Catiline and the *Cesarians* orations (perfectly corresponding to those in **C**) are also preserved in a late tenth- or early eleventh-century manuscript written in France (Milan, Biblioteca Ambrosiana, Ambrosianus C 29: **A**). The two groups of scholia were later joined together to form a single scholiastic *corpus* and then published under the heading of *Scholia Cluniacensia et recentiora Ambrosiana* (Stangl 1912: 269–73).
[478] The scholiast designates the abrupt insertion of *calumnia* with the term *paraprosdocia* (*inopinatus exitus*, "unexpected conclusion"); cf. also schol. Gronov. 347.4 St. (107.18St); *Schem. Dian.* RLM 76.23; Eugraph. *Heaut.* 5.1.3.

the fourth- or fifth-century Barcelona papyrus that preserves fragments from the First and Second *Catilinarians*.[479] In the footsteps of Lambinus, modern editors have deleted *calumnia* as a reader's marginal annotation or an explanatory gloss, marked by the sign *k*,[480] pointing to the sense of disapproval implied in Cicero's mockery of the effeminate behavior of Catiline's young partisans and fellows. Likely, by the fourth century the note had crept into the text.[481]

In the *Scholia Gronoviana*, a scholiastic *corpus* including four sets of marginal or interlinear notes by as many commentators,[482] the alternative readings *somnium/somnum* at *Cat.* 3.16 are trivial variants of collations (285.1-4St).[483] In the passage from the *Third Catilinarian* Cicero describes the conspirators' ineptness in contrast to Catiline's exaggerated boldness.[484] Lentulus, the most senior among Catiline's fellow-conspirators, is ironically portrayed as "dull-witted," almost lethargic, oppressed by a continuous state of sleep (*somnum*); the variant *somnium* alludes to Lentulus's ambition of dominating Rome, falsely founded on the Sibylline prophecies.[485] The scholiast offers explanations of both the readings (*somnum* is in the lemma),[486] without commenting upon their validity. It also remains a strong possibility that the commentator simply records earlier interpretations of the alternative readings, as suggested by the expression *utrumque exponitur*.

While textual criticism was peripheral to ancient scholarship on Cicero, language and style attracted considerable interest from scholars and

---

[479] On the papyrus (Fundació Sant Lluc Evangelista, Barcelona: CLA Suppl. 1782), see Roca-Puig 1977.
[480] Cf. Velius Longus *GL* VII, 53, 6 (21.7 Di Napoli): *Et qui "k" expellunt, notam dicunt esse magis quam litteram, qua significamus "kalumniam", "kaput", "kalendas"*; cf. also Scaur. p. 15, 11–14).
[481] Dyck 2008a: 132.
[482] Published for the first time by Jakob Gronovius in 1692. the so-called *scholia Gronoviana*, a numerically consistent series of late glosses or marginal notes on many Ciceronian orations, are preserved in a tenth-century Leiden manuscript (Voss. Lat. Q. 138). After Mommsen (1861; see also Stangl 1884b; 1905–1906), we individuate four different groups of notes ascribed to as many scholiasts. This is the order in which the scholia appear in Stangl's edition (1912: 281–351): scholiast **D** (*Catil.* I, 9; II, 2–29; III *argumentum* + 1–26; IV *argumentum* + 1–21; *pro Ligario argumentum* + 1–24; *pro Marcello* 1–2; 20–34; *pro rege Deiot. argumentum* + 1–10; 31–41; *pro Roscio Am. Argumentum* + 1–21; 34–154; *de imperio Cn. Pomp.* 3–71; *pro Milone argumentum* + 1; 15; 60; 65; 67; *pro Caelio* 17; 26: pp. 281–323St); scholiast **B** (*Divinatio* 3–73 + *actio I in Verrem* 1–45 + *actio II I argumentum* + 1–5: pp. 324–344.7St); scholiast **A** (*Actio II in Verrem* 1. 45–62: pp. 344.9–348.8St); scholiast **C** (*Actio I in Verrem* 16–30: pp. 349–351St).
[483] SOMNUM] *Alii somnium, alii somnum habent. Utrumque exponitur. Si somnum, segnitiem, quia amabat dormire: 'praeter consuetudinem' inquit 'proxima nocte vigilaverat'. Si somnium, vanam spem de fatis Sibullinis, quod dicebat se fore dominum Romae.*
[484] Dyck 2008a: 189.   [485] Cic. *Cat.* 3.9.5–8 (Dyck 2008a: 179ff.).
[486] *Somnium* is the reading of all the Ciceronian manuscripts, with the only exception being a late twelfth-century German manuscript (Munich, Bayerische Staatsbibliothek, Clm 4611), corrected by a second hand.

commentators, as we have seen on numerous occasions. Despite his established reputation as *elegans auctor,* Cicero did not escape censure because of his alleged linguistic faults, syntactical anomalies and logical inconsistencies. As we have seen in the first section of this chapter, early empire literary critics voiced their disapproval (*reprehensio*) over Cicero's excess of stylization, inappropriateness and obscurity of vocabulary or idioms.[487] As a reaction, Gellius and late scholars (including the Bobbio scholiast, Nonius and Ps. Asconius) tended to legitimate anomalies or obsolete forms by recurring to the principle of *vetustas,* automatically associated with the incontestable concept of *auctoritas.* Compelled to dispel any doubts or skepticism about the exemplarity and purity of Cicero's *Latinitas,* scholars and schoolmasters assisted students with notes on linguistic and stylistic issues, with the intent of rehabilitating the undeservedly discredited reputation of Cicero as an authority on Latin.

The scholiographic *corpora* on the speeches offer quite a few examples of this academic confrontation between detractors and defenders of Cicero, a contest over language and stylistic features that began in early imperial literary criticism and continued uninterrupted through the centuries. As we said, such a debate seems to have been a constant feature of ancient exegesis of Cicero, in ways not dissimilar to those typical of other scholarly commentaries (especially Servius and Donatus on Vergil and Terence). In some cases the introduction of earlier explanations appears to be simply intended to offer erudite information, as a required supplement to the interpretation of significant passages. This is peculiar to portions of text involving historical,[488] antiquarian,[489] rhetorical and legal questions.[490]

---

[487] See supra pp. 112ff

[488] Cf. schol. Bob. 130.22-3St (on *Sest.* 43: . . . *ab aliis proditum est*); 142.17St (on *Sest.* 141: . . . *ut quidam putant*): 142.22St (on *Sest.* 141: . . . *alii vero existimaverunt*: Cicero's passage contains a list of Greek heroic *exempla*); 149.5St (on *Vat.* 25: . . . *ut quidam memoriae tradiderunt*). Cf. also 86.29-31St (on *In Clod. et Cur.* frg. 6Crawford: . . . *secundum opiniones aliorum*).

[489] Cf. schol. Bob. 154.26–155.7St on *Planc.* 23 (on the institution of the *Feriae Latinae*); Ps.Asconius 187.25–188.3St on *Div.* 3 (on the difference between *templa* and *delubra*; cf. also schol. Gronov. 324.4-9St); 217.8-15St (on *Ver.* 1.31: again on the origin of the *Ludi Romani*).

[490] Cf. Ps. Asconius 186.4-8St on the origin and meaning of the term *divinatio* (the scholiast records three contrasting definitions of *divinatio*: first, as a speech delivered to determine which of several accusers should conduct the prosecution in the future; second, as an inquiry held by unsworn judges, conjecturing about the prosecutor; last, as a judicial inquiry not contemplating *testes* and proofs, based on presumption about the figure of the accuser: cf. also Gel. 2.4). For other juridical issues and related comments on divergent earlier opinions cf. also Ps. Asconius 190.29–191.4St (*Div.* 14: on the number of the *crimina Syracusanorum*); 220.1-3St (*Ver.* 1.40; on the color of the voting-tablets); 230.32–231.13St (*Ver.* 2.1.26; on the meaning of *comperendinatio,* the adjournment of a trial for two days); 232.32-33St (*Ver.* 2.1.32; on the time allowed to the prosecutor for his speech).

Occasionally, it concerns the meaning and origin of some words[491] or linguistic rules.[492] This tendency to discuss previous scholarly opinions, in censorious, sometimes overly critical, terms, permeated ancient scholarship on the speeches. More than being a sign of scholarly competence, comments on earlier exegetical statements sparked (pseudo-) scientific disputes. Needless to say, the main area of contention remained Cicero's creativity and linguistic talent.

Two cases, occurring again in Ps. Asconius's commentary on the *Divinatio*, deserve consideration. In the note on *Div.* 15 (191.3-4St) the scholiast reminds his readers that many scholars disdain the sentence *ut oculis iudicare possitis* as unsuited to Cicero's *gravitas*:

> Ut oculis iudicare possitis] Hoc quidam leviter a Cicerone dictum et neoterice putant, sed aptum est asseverationi.

> "As your own eyes can tell you] There are many who believe that Cicero pronounced this sentence in a way lacking in seriousness and without force: on the contrary, it well fits the tone of the assertion."

Criticism targets Cicero's inconsistency of style. *Leviter et neoterice* points to the perceived superficiality of the passage of the *Divinatio*.[493] Ps. Asconius shrugs off any question about the appropriateness of the sentence and rehabilitates Cicero's reputation by reasserting the complete congruence between words and the emotional tones of the discourse against Caecilius.

In the second passage Ps. Asconius's response is elicited by criticism of Cicero's search for rhythmical effects. The sentence ending *cuius ego causa laboro* at *Div.* 23 (192.27-30St) has been rejected as unrhythmical by incompetent commentators:

> Cuius ego causa laboro] Inepti sunt homines qui hanc clausulam notant ut malam, cum sit ex spondeo et bacchio de industria durior ad exprimendam sententiam posita more Ciceronis; ut alibi idem: "Non tu eum patria privare, qua caret, sed vita vis."

---

[491] Cf. Ps. Asconius 194.9-13St (*Div.* 24: for the term *quadriplator*, interpreted as *delator criminum publicorum*, "bringer of a criminal accusation," or as *accusator eorum reorum qui convicti quadrupli damnari soleant*, "accuser of those criminals who should be condemned to a quadriplied sanction"); 199.29-200.3St (*Div.* 48: *Alienum* as a *nomen proprium*, stemming from *Allia* – cf. Verg. *Aen.* 7.717, or as near-synonym of *alienum*); 207.18-20St (*Ver.* 1.6: on the contrasted identification of the man charged with collecting evidence against Verres in Achaea); 211.3-4St (*Ver.* 1.17: on the noun *alacer*); 255.7-9St (*Verr.* 2.1.154: on the origin of the term *tensa*, "sacred coach"). Cf. also schol. Gronov. 323.24St (on *Mil.* 65; *popa* either as a person name or as *copo, caupo*, "shopkeeper").
[492] Cf. Priscian. *GL* 3.316 on the use of *kalendarum* in place of *ante kalendas* in Cic. *Cat.* 1.7.
[493] For the adverb *neoterice* in the sense of "modestly, humbly" (not "novel, unfamiliar": cf. Gel.15.14.1; Ps. Asconius 264.23St) cf. Serv. (DS) *A.* 8.731.

"On whose behalf I am working] There are many stupid interpreters who stigmatize this sentence-ending as unrhythmical: but the spondee and bacchius sequence, producing a harsher effect, has deliberately been placed by Cicero at the end of this sentence. This reflects Cicero's stylistic habit, as it occurs elsewhere: 'It is not of the country which he has lost that you desire to despoil him, but of life'."[494]

Ps. Asconius's reply to *inepti* focuses on the aptness of an unmelodious rhythm, produced by the collocation of a spondee and a short-long-short series, to the severity of Cicero's sentence structure, a stylistic pattern not unusual in oratorical prose, as proved by the clausula in the speech on behalf of Ligarius. As in the previous case, Ps. Asconius is preoccupied with reaffirming Cicero's authority on Latin prose. In pointing up clarity of sentence structure and effects of rhythmical endings he depicts Cicero as a model of regular, refined style. Significantly, he insists on Cicero's concern for rhythmical sentences and clausulae harmoniously matching literary register.

Earlier commentators are criticized for professional incompetence, manifested also in misunderstanding of subtleties of meaning and unsound assumptions about Cicero's manipulation of rhetorical devices.[495] On *Div.* 30 (196.1-3St) Ps. Asconius defends Cicero's prosecution strategy against pointless reproaches from earlier commentators.[496] Similarly, in the note on *Div.* 33 (197.1-3St) he laments the incompetence of some exegetes, incapable of appreciating Cicero's silence over Verres's secret robberies as a well-timed rhetorical gesture.[497] The comment on *Ver.* 1.22 is of some

---

[494] Cic. *Lig.* 11 (a cretic-trochee sequence).
[495] In the note on *Ver.* 2.1.66 (240–29–241.7St), a passage concerning a dinner-party organized by Rubrius on behalf of Verres, Ps. Asconius polemicizes against misinterpretation of the expression *Graeco more*, "in Greek fashion" (240.29–241.3St), and then points to the incorrect lengthening of the vowel *o* in the verbal form *poscunt* (unwrongly interpreted as *potant*, "drink"); the sentence *poscunt maioribus (poculis)* would mean *provocant se invicem*, "they challenge each other" to drinking with larger cups (241.4-7St).
[496] *Queritur Sicilia tota]* Inepte quidam mirantur cur haec Tullius in accusando Verre non obiecerit Caecilio, ut multa alia; et non intellegunt haec ad tempus commode adiungi; quae victo Caecilio non sunt necessaria ("It is a general complaint of the Sicilians] There are some who are surprised at seeing Cicero not laying into Caecilius and listing these resentments over Verres, like many other things; they are foolish, since they do not understand that these accusations will be included in the discussion at the right moment. Once Caecilius is defeated, this will be no longer necessary").
[497] *Sunt alia magis occulta furta]* Inepte a quibusdam quaeritur quae sint: nulla sunt enim, sed oratorum est neque laudes [vel] neque crimina ieiune ostendere ("There are other more secret robberies] There are many stupid commentators who ask themselves what these robberies are. They are nothing: it is the orator's goal not to parade either eulogies or crimes scantily").

significance to our understanding of Cicero's adoption of fictional arguments in the *Actio prima* (212.13-9St):

> A quodam senatore ad equitem R.] Hos homines inepte quaerunt: quasi certum sit quod dicitur, et non de industria fingatur a Tullio ad invidiam adversariorum et sui defensionem, qua cogitur novo modo causam agere horis brevioribus quam mos est accusatoribus. Itaque suspicantur senatorem alii Crassum, alii Hortensium; equitem R. alii neminem proferunt, alii Publicium quendam, temporibus illis in dividenda pecunia populo famosissimum.

> "From a particular senator to a particular knight] It is foolish to try to discover the names of these men, as if it were true what the orator says. By design Tullius invents them, in order to both arouse envy from his opponents and sustain his line of defense in a different way; so he is forced to conduct his prosecution in a time inferior to that usually allowed to the accusers. For that reason there are many who suspect that the senator was Crassus, many others Hortensius; many say that the knight does not exist, many others call him Publicius, a man lauded for his ability in distributing money to the people at that time."

The story of money exchanged between unknown members of the senatorial and equestrian order is a fabrication, a strategic artifice aimed at modifying the plan of prosecution. The scholiast rightly plays up the commentators' lack of discernment. The combination of the adverbial locution *de industria* and the verb *fingo* draws attention to Cicero's ability to create and manipulate fictional characters, something which was evidently not so obvious to less astute interpreters.[498]

Similar notes on Cicero's prosecution strategy occur elsewhere in Ps. Asconius. Cicero's recount of his service as quaestor in Sicily in *Div.* 2, irrationally reprehended as out of place in a properly structured prologue (*narrationem in exordio multi admirantur ac<ri cum> reprehensione*), is justified as a "narration adducing arguments to the first partition" of the discourse (*argumentalis narratio ad priorem divisionem*), tailored to support Cicero's self-portrait as the ideal accuser (187.3-5St).[499] In the *argumentum* to the second book of the *Actio secunda* (257.13-5St) the scholiast

---

[498] On earlier commentators' incompetence, cf. also Ps. Asconius 191.23-5St (*Div.* 19: futile censure of Cicero's alleged contradictory statements about sums of money raided by Verres); 251.13-6St (*Ver.* 2.1.128: misinterpretation of Cicero's irony); 264.18-20St (*Ver.* 2.2.34: mispunctuation of the edict *Si quid perperam iudicarit senatus*).

[499] In the Bobbio commentary (in the *argumentum* to the *pro Sestio*: 125.26-7St) the scholiast repudiates disapproval of Cicero's prosecution tactic in the speech as "unconnected to the matter" (*extra causam*).

replies to commentators who, pointlessly (*frustra*), criticize Cicero for not starting his prosecution from the main topic of the speech, that is, the administration of justice (*iurisdictio*) in Sicily. A proper *exordium* – the scholiast says – starts with *magna* and *clariora* ("great and more solemn subjects") and a trained orator treats *crimina* differently. Again, earlier commentators' censure of Cicero's insults to Verres's boy, a blatant sign of stupidity (*stultitia*), fills Ps. Asconius with indignation (*Ver.* 2.1.32: 233.1-4St).[500] Prosecution (*accusatoria ars*) commonly uses defamation and slander in order to prevent pity and compassion from the judges in the peroration (*in epilogis*).[501]

By way of conclusion, we go back to the topic on which this chapter is centered. "Between praise and blame," reverence and censure. The late commentaries on the speeches conjure up a controversial image of Cicero, not very different from what we have presented as peculiar to early imperial literary criticism. From Asconius's historical commentary to the late *marginalia*, Cicero stirred up enthusiasm and condemnation at the same time, as both a prose stylist and a political authority. In a span of six centuries, that is, from the early Augustan age to the Early Middle Ages, scholarship of Cicero was marked by an astonishing, paradoxical combination of positive responses and hostile, sometimes vitriolic attacks on style and speech strategy, implicated in the specific political and rhetorical context of the case. Though in different ways, this "quarrel" over style and content (distant, of course, from the Tacitean quarrel over "ancient" and "modern" in the *Dialogus*)[502] informed the nature and quality of the scholiastic *corpora*.

Debating over aesthetics and rhetoric was intrisic to the reception of Cicero. *Alii ... dicunt, alii ... legunt*. Linguistic and stylistic features of the paramount model of oratorical prose prompted contrasting evaluations. Scholiasts and schoolteachers took up the challenge of confronting criticism of Cicero, something that could unavoidably have negative effects and erode the established reputation of the republican orator as an *idoneus auctor*. Since the appreciation of Cicero as a stylistic model was

---

[500] *Stultissime* ("very foolishly") is the adverbial form used by Ps. Asconius to condemn pointless disapprobation of Cicero from earlier commentators.
[501] For other cases of criticism of earlier exegesis cf. Ps. Asconius 209.21-2St (*Ver.* 1.16); 241.13St (*Ver.* 2.1.70); 247.20–5 St. (*Ver.* 2.1.104); 251.1–2 St. (*Ver.* 2.1.124); schol. Gronov. 282.6-8St (*Cat.* 2.16); 286.27St (*argumentum* to *Cat.* 3); 295.23-32St (*argumentum* to the *pro Marcello*); 296.3-4St (*Marc.* 1); 310.18-9St (*Rosc.* 70); 324.13St (*Div.* 3); 328.13-4St (*Ver.* 1.1); 328.30–329.2St (*Verr.* 1.2); 338.25-7St (*Ver.* 1.32); 342.5-6St (*argumentum* to the first book of the *Actio secunda in Verrem*).
[502] Dressler 2015.

essential to Roman elite students being trained in language and rhetoric, preserving and transmitting Cicero's *auctoritas* was the schoolmaster's chief concern. From this perspective, exegetical tradition made a major contribution to the way generations to come thought about Cicero as the "head and wellspring of Roman eloquence" (*fons atque caput Romanae facundiae*).[503]

---

[503] Fronto *Ep. M. Caes.* 4.3.3 (57.5-6Hout). The expression *M. Tullius summum supremum os Romanae linguae fuit* is found in the margin of the Fronto manuscript (a secondhand addition) in the epistle addressed to the emperor M. Verius (2.1: 124.21Hout). Cf. also *Eloq.* (134.3-5Hout): *contionatur . . . Tullius gloriose . . . iam in iudiciis triumphat Cicero.*

CHAPTER 4

# *Teaching Cicero*

From the Silver Age historical commentary of Asconius Pedianus to the late scholiographic *corpora*, ancient scholarship reveals a great deal about the reception of Cicero as a master of Latin prose and a paradigm of eloquence in the schools of rhetoric. As we have shown in the previous chapter, *Latinitas*, a notion embodied in Cicero's purity and perfection of language, was an ethical and pedagogic concern of Roman education. Grammarians, teachers of rhetoric and learned scholars pursued the holy grail of virtuous and good Latin by looking to Cicero as *idoneus auctor* and inculcating Roman pupils with a set of linguistic and stylistic values strictly associated with the elite ideals of Romanity. They relied on Cicero as a model of pure and correct Latin. By a never-ending search for clarification of linguistic features and aesthetic devices in Cicero's prose ancient rhetorical theorists and educationists aimed to instruct and support the young in acquiring fluency of speech, a skill critical to the art of persuasive speech and an inherent component of the masculine ideal of rhetoric, which was at heart of Roman aristocratic culture and society.[1]

Interpreting Cicero's oratory was not only a didactic, instructional practice connected with linguistic *eruditio* and expected to be undertaken by an elite Roman male. It also constituted a vital part of a cultural and political program, which endeavored to achieve maturation of the boy into a "good man fluent in speaking" (*vir bonus dicendi peritus*). As Quintilian makes it clear, the formation of a well-trained orator was an ethical concept. Formal education (and its related compositional instruction) "aimed to distill, reflect, and reinforce elite attitudes in the next generation of adults," who imitated and reproduced the values of elite culture in their written and spoken compositions.[2] By reading – and learning to understand – Cicero's prose models Roman elite students perpetuated attitudes, values and behaviors that connoted the true, good Roman. They

---

[1] Connolly 2007b (on rhetoric and masculinity).   [2] Gibson 2014: 4.

transformed themselves into high-status citizen-men, members of a society dominated by the moral and political power of the word.

## How to Read a Speech: Quintilian's *Praelectio*

It has been noted that "rhetoric is an art, but it is also a weapon of war."[3] By means of language Roman orators swayed audiences and obfuscated issues, triumphed over their opponents, gained *auctoritas* and enacted their social status. Cicero, the "new man" ascending the political and social hierarchy by words, fascinated teachers and students as the perfect specimen of successful eloquence. Treated as examples of good political oratory, his speeches educated the young to confront prospective, real-life issues in the tumultuous political and oratorical arena. In other words, they served as weapons in the struggle for political leadership and social advancement. Reversing Votienus Montanus's well-known maxim, related to the display declamation, one might say that Cicero's triumphant pleas showed students how "to win, not to please."[4]

The art of advocacy and its potential impact on the formation of a disciplined, virtuous speaker provided the main impulse to the development of an education system founded on Cicero's *auctoritas*, the "Ciceronianism" advocated by Quintilian and governed by an aristocratic ideal of rhetoric, as a social, political and linguistic practice in the hands of men of the dominant order. Under Cicero's authority Roman pupils became competent in the art of politics and public speaking. It was on Cicero's supremacy that schoolmasters relied to supervise the intellectual progress of the boys, from the early stages to maturity and the definitive acquisition of a good man's personality. As MacCormack comments, "given that the primary purpose of education was to prepare the young for public service and for public speaking in the law courts and elsewhere," pagan scholars supplied students with "summaries of the speeches along with notes on historical context and on Cicero's rhetorical method and legal arguments and their desired effects."[5] They clarified content, structural pattern and style features of any single oration in order to instruct budding orators in making an appropriate use of rhetorical devices and stratagems, necessary "tools of war" in oratorical contests. In more or less explicit terms, Roman pupils were encouraged to imitate the model, the only way of becoming accomplished orators.

---

[3] Connolly 2007b: 95.   [4] Sen. *Con.* 9 *praef.* 1. See chapter 3 p. 115.
[5] MacCormack 2013: 261–2.

Before finding out more about the multiple ways in which scholiasts and late rhetoricians illustrated Cicero's rhetorical technique, it may be convenient to look into the classroom procedure for the teaching of rhetoric by re-examining a long, rightly celebrated passage from the second book of Quintilian's educational treatise (*Inst.* 2.5.5–11). "A blueprint for a rhetorical commentary on a speech of Cicero,"[6] this passage is incorporated into a larger presentation of the early stages of rhetorical education, involving treatment of the *progymnasmata* and exercises of thesis and commonplace (2.4.14–40); it follows a summary sketch of the history of declamation, whose origin may be traced to the Latin *rhetores* and the school of Plotius Gallus (2.4.41–2). The "only explicit evidence for the *enarratio* of prose texts by Latin,"[7] to be conducted in parallel with the interpretation of poetry texts from the *grammaticus*,[8] Quintilian's discussion contemplates initial recommendations on the *praelectio*, reading out prose authors in class (2.5.4), whose purpose was to provide the pupil with a first, constructive perception of the written text (perhaps earlier dictated to him), by means of distinction of one word from another and identification of any unfamiliar terms (*minus usitatum*).[9] To Quintilian, an essential part of the teacher's profession was to "point out merits and, where necessary, faults" of the expounded text (*demonstrare virtutes vel, si quando ita incidat, vitia*: 2.5.5). The exposition of the speech, covering first the devising of arguments (*inventio*) and, later, elaboration of style *(elocutio)*, would fruitfully be carried out with the help of a boy appointed as reader (2.5.7–9):[10]

---

[6] Winterbottom 1982a: 247.
[7] Reinhardt-Winterbottom 2006: 120. For the word *enarratio* as "explanation of a text," a basic expository narrative, cf. *Rhet. Her.* 4.55.69 (in addition to Quint. *Inst.* 2.1.5).
[8] Quint. *Inst.* 2.5.1: *Interim, quia prima rhetorices rudimenta tractamus, non omittendum videtur id quoque, ut moneam, quantum sit collaturus ad profectum discentium rhetor, si, quemadmodum a grammaticis exigitur poetarum enarratio, ita ipse quoque historiae atque etiam magis orationum lectione susceptos a se discipulos instruxerit* ... ("In the meantime, as we are discussing the elementary stages of a rhetorical education, I think I should not fail to point out how greatly the rhetorician will contribute to his pupils' progress, if he imitates the teacher of literature whose duty it is to expound the poets, and gives the pupils whom he has undertaken to train, instruction in the reading of history and still more of the orators").
[9] Murphy (J. J.) 1987: XVIII–XXXIV (for a rapid sketch of the teaching methods in Quintilian's pedagogical treatise).
[10] Quint. *Inst.* 2.5.6 (*Nam mihi cum facilius tum etiam multo videtur magis utile, facto silentio unum aliquem, quod ipsum imperari per vices optimum est, constituere lectorem, ut protinus pronuntiationi quoque assuescant* ["It seems to me at once an easier and more profitable method to call for silence and choose someone pupil, and it will be best to select them by turns, to read aloud, in order that they may at the same time learn the correct method of elocution"]). On the mechanics of reading in Quintilian's construction of the ideal orator, see Johnson (W. A.) 2010: 26–31.

Tum, exposita causa in quam scripta legetur oratio (nam sic clarius quae dicentur intellegi poterunt), nihil otiosum pati quodque in inventione quodque in elocutione adnotandum erit: quae in prohoemio conciliandi iudicis ratio, quae narrandi lux brevitas fides, quod aliquando consilium et quam occulta calliditas (8) (namque ea sola in hoc ars est, quae intellegi nisi ab artifice non possit), quanta deinceps in dividendo prudentia, quam subtilis et crebra argumentatio; quibus viribus inspiret, qua iucunditate permulceat, quanta in maledictis asperitas, in iocis urbanitas; ut denique dominetur in adfectibus atque in pectora inrumpat animumque iudicum similem iis quae dici efficiat; (9) tum, in ratione eloquendi, quod verbum proprium ornatum sublime, ubi amplificatio laudanda, quae virtus ei contraria, quid speciose tralatum, quae figura verborum, quae levis et quadrata, virilis tamen compositio. (10) Ne id quidem inutile, etiam corruptas aliquando et vitiosas orationes, quas tamen plerique iudiciorum pravitate mirentur, legi palam, ostendique in his quam multa impropria obscura tumida humilia sordida lasciva effeminata sint; quae non laudantur modo a plerisque, sed, quod est peius, propter hoc ipsum quod sunt prava laudantur.

"The case for which the speech selected for reading was written should then be explained for if this be done they will have a clearer understanding of what is to be read. When the reading is commenced, no important point should be allowed to pass unnoticed either as regards the resourcefulness or the style shown in the treatment of the subject: the teacher must point out how the orator seeks to win the favor of the judge in his exordium, what clearness, brevity and sincerity, and at times what shrewd design and well-concealed artifice is shown in the statement of facts. For the only true art in pleading is that which can only be understood by one who is a master of the art himself. The teacher will proceed further to demonstrate what skill is shown in the division into heads, how subtle and frequent are the truths of argument, what vigor marks the stirring and what charm the soothing passage, how fierce is the invective and how full of wit the jests, and in conclusion how the orator established his sway over the emotions of the audience, forces his way into their very hearts and brings the feelings of the jury into perfect sympathy with all his words. Finally as regards the style, he will emphasize the appropriateness, elegance or sublimity of particular words, will indicate where the amplification of the theme is deserving of praise and where there is virtue in a diminuendo; and will call attention to brilliant metaphors, figures of speech and passages combining smoothness and polish with a general impression of manly vigor. It will even at times be of value to read speeches which are corrupt and faulty in style, but still meet with general admiration thanks to the perversity of modern tastes, and to point out how many expressions in them are inappropriate, obscure, high-flown, groveling, mean, extravagant or effeminate, although they are not merely praised by the majority of critics, but, worse still, praised just because they are bad."

In the scene imagined by Quintilian teachers and students work on the text side by side,[11] scrutinizing each relevant point of the speech (*nihil otiosum pati*).[12] As has been observed, "*lectio* in the early stages requires that the boy stand at the teacher's knee, read aloud, and have the text, at first, interpreted by the master, and, later, inquired into by the master to confirm that the student has sufficient understanding."[13] Much emphasis is placed on the orator's ability to propitiate the judges, made benevolent by a well-articulated proem (*exordium*),[14] and alternate brevity, clarity and straightforwardness with thinly veiled artifices in narrative. Rhetoric is a "practical" art (*ars /téchne*), whose essence stands on the artful use (and re-handling) of technical devices, penetrated only by their *artifex* ("creator") or by a master of rhetoric cognizant of the impact of rhetorical sophistry and cunning, even on those parts of the speech generally intended for a plain illustration of the facts.[15] Then Quintilian (and his ideal teacher) stimulates students' interest in the speech's strategy, demonstrating how the orator's control over his adversaries relies on his command and artificial manipulation of arguments and passions. In Quintilian's view, the student should be informed of the orator's wisdom in dividing the materials (*in dividendo prudentia*) and his capacity for deploying delicate as well as dense arguments (*subtilis et crebra argumentatio*); he should also be guided in appreciating the ways in which the orator inspires passions, utters sharp words about his enemies and dispenses off-the-cuff remarks and witticisms (*ioca*) as a sign of *urbanitas*. In a word, the pupil should be shown how the orator holds sway over the jury's emotions, bursts into the hearts of his listeners (*inrumpat in pectora*) and makes their feelings reflect his words.

Moving to *elocutio*, Quintilian invites his ideal teacher to perform as an interpreter of features of style and language, pointing out the elegance or sublimity of each word and attracting attention to devices of amplification, such as brilliant metaphors and figures of speech, and smoothness of composition, producing effects of masculine oratory (*virilis compositio*: 2.5.8–9).[16] A similar procedure is also recommended in the *enarratio* of bad or faulty speeches (*corruptae et vitiosae orationes*), frequently admired by modern critics (2.5.10–2). Illustrating their vicious elements,

---

[11] On the pupil/teacher relationship and its "human dimension" cf. Quint. *Inst.* 2.3.7; 2.9.1–3 (see Calboli Montefusco 1996: 617–8).
[12] "Leave nothing in peace" (Reinhardt-Winterbottom 2006: 125).    [13] Johnson (W. A.) 2010: 29.
[14] On the function of the *exordium* as preparation of the jurors' or listeners' mind for receiving the orator's words in a sympathetic way, cf. Cic. *Inv.* 1.20; *Rhet. Her.* 1.6–8; Quint. *Inst.* 4.1.5.
[15] Cf. also Quint. *Inst.* 1.11.3.
[16] For the association of authenticity and naturalness of oratorical performance with manliness, see Connolly 2007b.

undeservedly praised, the instructor implicitly arouses admiration for the *recta oratio*, "the correct style," displayed at best in the text under scrutiny.

By the practice of reading, as it is envisaged in Quintilian's didactic project, the student approaches the text of the speech as a model of persuasion. Special attention is paid to the use and manipulation of rhetorical and stylistic artifices as a means of arousing passions and dominating audiences.[17] The good orator is a master of persuasion. He manipulates words, meant to function as stylish embellishments and tools of deceit. What seems to matter is not the case in question or the political or social background behind the performance. A rhetorical reading of a speech is intended to be an exposition of the rhetorical stratagems adopted by the orator to sway the audience. Accordingly, it functions also as an (implicit) invitation to the would-be orators to emulate the model by reproducing similar patterns of argumentation and displaying analogous persuasive abilities. Reading, as a significant part of *exercitatio*,[18] then pushes the boy to compete with the author of the text read, paraphrased and commented upon under the guidance of a skilful teacher.

It goes without saying that Cicero best exemplifies rhetoric as the art of persuasion. After encouraging teachers to test pupils' judgment and critical qualities by posing frequent questions (2.5.13–7), Quintilian pauses to consider the authors suitable for the beginners' reading. The issue is of the utmost importance to Quintilian's elite ideal of education, as it involves the dynamics of reading intimately tied up with the acquisition of speaking and writing skills. Distancing himself from those critics who prescribe unpretentious authors, of inferior merit (only apparently easier to understand), or more florid, elaborate writers (providing nourishment to the still immature minds of the young: 2.5.18), Quintilian opts for the authors he judges best, recommended from the very beginning and never cast aside throughout the instruction process (2.5.19–20):

> Ego optimos quidem et statim et semper, sed tamen eorum candidissimum quemque et maxime expositum velim, ut Livium a pueris magis quam Sallustium (etsi hic historiae maior est auctor, ad quem tamen intellegendum iam profectu opus sit). Cicero, ut mihi quidem videtur, et iucundus incipientibus quoque et apertus est satis, nec prodesse tantum sed etiam amari potest: tum, quem ad modum Livius praecipit, ut quisque erit Ciceroni simillimus.

---

[17] On the exploitation of manipulative techniques and stage-managed effects in oratorical delivery, see Hall 2007.

[18] On *natura, ars* and *exercitatio* as the basis of eloquence and the three kinds of *exercitatio* (writing, reading and speaking), see Calboli Montefusco 1996 (with bibliography).

"I think the best should come both first and always, but among the best the most straightforward and accessible; for example, Livy for boys rather than Sallust – Sallust indeed is the greater historian, but one needs further progress to understand him – Cicero, in my view at least, is both pleasant reading for beginners, and perfectly accessible; he can be not only useful but also a favorite. Next (to follow Livy's advice) should come whoever is most like Cicero."

Cicero teaches the art of "speaking well." From Cicero the young learn so much that they come to venerate and love him. Other authors may be read with benefit, on the condition that they most nearly resemble Cicero.[19] Quintilian's ideal of literary education holds Cicero to be a perennial model of eloquence.[20] Warning against excess of admiration for *antiquitas* and archaic style and equally condemning the pernicious love of modern style's allurements (2.5.21–2),[21] Quintilian points to the best ancient authors as the most suitable models of "vigour and virility" of language (*solida ac virilis ingenii vis*: 2.5.23), once again pushing forward a masculine ideal of rhetoric, nurtured by imitation of good texts. In insisting upon the study of the earlier writers, even at the price of error,[22] and rising up against what he regards as corrupt eloquence Quintilian sets the stage for a new classicism, an ideal (aristocratic) form of rhetorical education relying on the figure of the *vir bonus* and modeled on the system of ethical and literary values incarnated in Cicero's oratory. As correctly stated, Quintilian "models a social order reinforced through language" and, by transposition of Ciceronian public performative ethics into a domestic key, "redefines the enlargement of thought encouraged by Ciceronian rhetoric as the project of becoming a *vir bonus*, 'a good man'."[23]

Quintilian's step-by-step guide through a rhetorical commentary may well serve as a synopsis of a classic, scholastic explanation of a speech of Cicero, presented to students as a model of persuasion, a piece of oratorical writing built around a series of rhetorical and stylistic devices and stratagems, appealing to – and exploiting – the audience's emotions. Cicero furnished the young with multiple examples of oratorical delivery designed

---

[19] Quintilian is following Livy's advice, as it is formulated in a letter (lost) to his son; cf. *Inst.* 10.1.39 (*Fuit igitur brevitas illa tutissima quae est apud Livium in epistula ad filium scripta, legendos Demosthenen atque Ciceronem, tum ita ut quisque esset Demostheni et Ciceroni simillimus*, ["Safest is the brief advice given by Livy in his letter to his son, to read Demosthenes and Cicero, and then others as they are most like Demosthenes and Cicero"]).

[20] Cf. Quint. *Inst.* 10.1.105–22 for the list of the orators recommended as suitable reading at a later stage. López 2007: 316.

[21] Reinhardt-Winterbottom 2006: 138–9.   [22] Quint. *Inst.* 2.5.26.   [23] Connolly 2007a: 255–6.

to achieve success by exploitation of the passions.[24] What was commonly designed in late treatises as the *lectio Tulliana* consisted primarily of a repertoire of rhetorical devices, including not only ornaments of style attractive to the listeners (and so making them more inclined to be persuaded), but also tropes and figures of speech and thought. These were designed as intellectual and emotional implements, adding vivacity and brilliance to words and argumentation and, at the same time, moving the soul of the listener or judge. As expressly stated by the late rhetorician Romanus Aquila, the author of a Ciceronian-based treatise *De figuris sententiarum et elocutionis* ("On the figures of thought and speech": 22–37 *RLM*), by means of figures the orator "exalts small topics and expands on narrow ones" (*et parva extollit et angusta dilatat*: 22.11–2 *RLM*).[25] The pupil (*adulescens*), as an advanced rhetorical practitioner, relying on both his own *ingenium* and the model of Cicero,[26] was thus equipped with an impressive apparatus of rhetorical knowledge to be effectively used in oratorical contests, an apparatus that made it possible to deliver a powerfully persuasive speech.[27]

### Introducing Cicero's Oratory to Beginners

With Quintilian's passage in mind, we are entitled to look into the interpretation of the speeches of Cicero as well-orchestrated performances, carefully planned texts applying manipulative techniques to generate emotions and persuade the audience. As expected, a general introduction and background on the *causa*, covering topography, prosopography and legal-historical issues, served as a natural starting point for a rhetorical commentary (*enarratio*), in line with the principles of teaching as declared by Quintilian (and Varro before him). As illustrated by Asconius's scholarly work, the standard format of the rhetorical *enarratio* usually contemplated an explanatory preface (*argumentum*), consisting

---

[24] For the paradigmatic function of oratorical texts cf. Quint. *Inst.* 8.3.66; 79; 10.1.15 (*Nam omnium quaecumque docemus hinc sunt exempla, potentiora etiam ipsis quae traduntur artibus (cum eo qui discit perductus est ut intellegere ea sine demonstrante et sequi iam suis viribus possit), quia quae doctor praecipit orator ostendit*, ["For in the same sources are to be found examples of everything we teach, examples which are in fact more powerful than those found in the textbooks (at least when the learner has reached the stage of being able to understand without a teacher and follow on his own) because the orator demonstrates what the teacher only prescribed"]).
[25] MacCormack 2013: 262 (see also Elice 2007: 94).
[26] Cf. Romanus Aquila 27.1–9; 37.25 *RLM*. See Elice 2007: 128; 204–5.
[27] On oratory as a dynamic live performance and the arousal of emotions, see again Hall 2007 (also Webb 1997a).

basically of an introduction reporting on the consular dating, circumstances and persons involved in the trial, and a commentary by *lemma* and *scholion*. This was a regular structural pattern, adopted in other scholarly commentaries (the Bobbio commentary and Ps. Asconius included).

Varying in length, these introductory reports or *argumenta* supplied the pupil with invaluable insights into the political circumstances surrounding Cicero's performance. Let us start with Asconius. In the *argumentum* to the *pro Milone*, rightly regarded as Cicero's finest speech,[28] Asconius expands on the scene of the trial and the political turmoil of the year 52 BCE, marked by electoral violence (30-1C). He then offers an exhaustive narrative of the murder of Clodius, adding significant, circumstantial details to Cicero's account of the episode (sometimes at variance with it).[29] In his exposition of the events following Clodius's funeral he supplies data about the emergency measure of the *interregnum* (33.25–34.21C) and scrutinizes the equivocal behaviors of current leading political figures, like Pompey (35.25–36.27C), preparing the ground for illustrating the phases of the trial preceding Cicero's ineffectual delivery (38.14–42.4C).[30] The account of the facts provided by Asconius, designed as an introduction to the subsequent line-by-line commentary, is accurate and historically reliable. It abounds in details, especially if compared with the *argumentum* in the Bobbio commentary, limited to the narration of the battle of Bovillae and Cicero's first, failed, *pro Milone*.[31] The scholiast devises his *argumentum* as a didactic instrument, a source of information to his sons confronting a complex and tricky text, especially in consideration of its political relevance. The only comment he makes is on the line of defense taken by Cicero, grounded on the presentation of Milo's action as self-defense legitimated by the law of nature, something which evidently contrasted with the truth of the matter (41.9-24C).[32]

---

[28] Asc. 42C.  [29] Asc. 31.12–32.17C: see Lewis 2006: 234–6.  [30] Lewis 2006: 239–48.

[31] Schol. Bob. 111.24–112.18St. In the *argumentum* to the *pro Milone*, the Gronovian scholiast **D** (322.19–323.13St) succinctly recounts the chain of events leading up to the murder of Clodius and the *quaestio extra ordinem de morte Clodii* decreed by Pompey, who encircled the trial place with armed troops. Then, he comments on the argumentative strategy, classifying the issue as belonging to the *status relativus* (*hoc est feci, sed meruit, hoc est insidiantem occidi*, "I did it, but he deserved it, that is, I killed a man who threatened") and defines the *genus causae* as *admirabile* (323.11-3St).

[32] In opposition to M. Brutus's line "taken in the speech which he composed for Milo and published as if he had pleaded the case" (*quam formam M. Brutus secutus est in ea oratione quam pro Milone composuit et edidit quasi egisset*), focusing on Clodius's murder as an act *pro re publica*, in the public interest, Cicero structured his whole speech as a counter-plea to the view that Milo set an ambush for Clodius. But, Asconius says, "on that day the battle was unpremeditated by either party" (*nec utrius consilio pugnatum esse eo die*): Clodius and Milo "met by chance" (*verum et forte occurrisse*) and it was well known that "both had often threatened the other with death" (*notum tamen erat utrumque mortem alteri saepe minatum esse*); cf. also schol. Bob. 112.14-8St. See Lewis 2006: 246–7.

Similarly, Asconius's other surviving *argumenta* offer expected information about date and chronology of the speech, sometimes touching on historical and political issues. In the a*rgumentum* to the *In Pisonem* Asconius fleshes out the particular circumstances of the speech, delivered a few days before the magnificent games celebrating the dedication of Pompey's theatre (August 55 BCE),[33] rejecting also the view (held by an unidentified scholar) that Cicero's speech was the last delivered in the following year, during the consulship of L. Domitius and Appius Claudius (1C). The introductory notes on the historical context are restricted to a few words (2.4-10C):

> Argumentum orationis huius breve admodum est. Nam cum revocati essent ex provinciis Piso et Gabinius sententia Ciceronis quam dixerat de provinciis consularibus Lentulo et Philippo consulibus, reversus in civitatem Piso de insectatione Ciceronis in senatu conquestus est et in eum invectus, fiducia maxime Caesaris generi qui tum Gallias obtinebat. Pisoni Cicero respondit hac oratione.

> "To provide an explanatory preface for this speech is no lengthy matter at all. For when Piso and Gabinius were recalled from their provinces in accordance with the views of Cicero which he declared in his speech *On the consular provinces*, in the consulship of Lentulus and Philippus, Piso on his return to the city complained of Cicero's polemics and inveighed against him, especially confident of support from his son-in-law Caesar, who at that time held the Gallic provinces. Cicero replied to Piso in the present oration."

Asconius takes it to be a statement of fact that Cicero's declaration (*sententia*) in his oration on the allocation of the consular provinces (*De provinciis consularibus*, delivered in the summer of 56 BCE) speeded up the recall of Piso and Gabinius from governorships in Macedonia and Syria.[34] Cicero apparently succeeded in making Macedonia a consular province,[35] as demonstrated by the fact that, upon his return, Piso, buoyed up by Caesar's hold on the Gallic provinces, railed at Cicero's polemics (*insectatio*). The *in Pisonem* was the transcription of Cicero's vitriolic response to Piso's verbal assault.

---

[33] Marshall 1985: 81–3. On the question see chapter 1, p. 25 and nn72–3.
[34] Asconius probably overstated the political impact of Cicero's *sententia*; on the question, see Marshall 1985: 84; Lewis 2006: 194; Grillo 2015: 11–2.
[35] In contrast, from *Pis.* 88 we may argue that Gabinius remained as governor of Syria until 54 (Cicero's recommendation was inefficacious): "perhaps Asconius oversimplified the outcome of *Prov.* to magnify Cicero's success" (Grillo 2015: 12).

A brief note on the date of the case is placed at the beginning of the *argumentum* to the *pro Scauro*, delivered in 54 BCE.[36] It precedes a detailed exposition of the political circumstances of the trial, with emphasis laid on the personalities involved in the accusation of Scaurus (18-20C). Again, the political significance of the two-speech *pro Cornelio de maiestate*, a precious piece of evidence about the political circumstances preceding Cicero's consulship, accounts for Asconius's prefatory discussion of the events that occurred during Cornelius's tribunate leading up to the trial (57–62.12C). As has been noted, Asconius's historical reconstruction differs considerably from the version offered by Dio 36.38.4–40.3 but we may surmise that the scholiast checked the order of the events against other historical sources, in addition to Cicero's speech.[37] Finally, the characterization of the political personalities of the time underpins the *argumentum* to the fragmentary speech, titled *In senatu in toga candida contra C. Antonium et L. Catilinam competitores*, delivered in 64 BCE (82–83.12C). Preoccupied with elucidating the occasion for such an oration, Asconius lingers over the enactment of *de ambitu* legislation, vetoed by the tribune of the plebs Q. Mucius Orestinus, which turned out to be the immediate cause of Cicero's invective against the electoral pact (*coitio*) of Catiline and Antonius.[38]

On the grounds of the *argumenta* preserved in other surviving commentaries and sets of Ciceronian scholia, it is possible to obtain a more comprehensive understanding of the ways by which the schoolmaster initiated the young into the perusal of the speech to be commented upon.[39] To turn our attention to the Bobbio commentary, in the explanatory preface to the *In Clodium et Curionem*, delivered in 61 BCE in the senate (as already seen, a written version of it was circulated without Cicero's authorization),[40] the scholiast calls attention to the invective tone of the speech, defined as an "oration no doubt filled with violence and humorous remarks" (*oratio plena sine dubio et asperitatis et facetiarum*),

---

[36] For the source of Asconius's chronology (probably the *Acta*), see Lewis 2006: 216.
[37] Lewis 2006: 262. For a historical introduction to the *pro Cornelio*, see Crawford 1994: 65–70.
[38] Crawford 1994: 159–75.
[39] The *argumentum* could also introduce the structure of the commentary to the young readers. This appears to be the case of the *argumentum* to Ver. 2.1 (*In Verrem de praetura urbana*: 341.11-6St), in which the Gronovian scholiast (**B**) discloses his intention not to treat each point in detail (something which would be *non tantum onerosum ... sed etiam longum*, "not only tiresome but also long"). The purpose of his scholarly *opusculus*, "little work," the scholiast says, is rather to select the most important questions coming up in the course of reading, calling attention to perfection of oratorical style, revealed at its best by digressions and "the greatest examples of each type of figure" (*uberrima exempla per omnium generum figuras*).
[40] See chapter 1, pp. 32–3.

in which the orator "lashes out at the habitual conduct of both the opponents and treats the vices of each of them as bitterly as possible" (*mores utriusque proscindit et de singulorum vitiis quam potest acerbissime loquitur*: 85.5-7St). The scholiast aims to introduce Cicero's speech as a test case of blame rhetoric, alerting his students to the manipulation and distortion of the traditional elements of an epideictic oration. As has been observed, in the speech Cicero applied and reversed the categories commonly used for laudatory speeches, producing a satiric text (*vituperatio*)[41] in which "elements of serious oratory" are combined "with invective and lampoon in a clever and witty fashion."[42] More importantly, if it is true that Ciceronian invective, intended as "public verbal censure of inappropriate behavior,"[43] was endowed with didactic and moralistic implications, providing therefore models "by which future orators could also perceive immorality and thereby expose criminality,"[44] the *In Clodium et Curionem* functioned as a specimen of a moral, socially decent code of conduct, a conspicuous example of how a good orator – and a good citizen accordingly – should blame anti-social, threatening behavior, cultivating and fostering Roman elite values at the same time.[45]

To the scholiast, the invective also served a political purpose at the outset of Clodius's fatal rancor against Cicero (85.8St). In recapping Clodius's desecration of the rites of the Bona Dea,[46] his prosecution for sacrilege (*incestus*) by senate members before a *quaestio extraordinaria*,[47] Cicero's damaging testimony[48] and the unexpected acquittal of the *reus* (presumably, because of bribery),[49] the commentator spells out the reasons behind

---

[41] Quint. *Inst.* 3.7.2 (cf. also *Rhet. Her.* 3.10; Cic. *Inv.* 1.7 for *vituperatio* paired with its antithesis *laus*, "praise").

[42] Crawford 1994: 233 (Nisbet 1961: 194, for a list of specific blame *topoi*). On humor and laughter as a means of destroying the adversary's credibility in Roman delivery practice, see Corbeill 1996; Rabbie 2007 (for the functioning of Roman oratorical invective, see Arena 2007). On Ciceronian invective, see Corbeill 2002 (on Cicero's exploitation of epideictic rhetoric for forensic and political purposes, see Dugan 2001b: 37–43); for themes and practice of Cicero's invective, see in general Booth 2007; Smith-Corvino 2011.

[43] Corbeill 2002: 212.

[44] Corbeill 2002: 214 (who opportunely discusses Cicero's exchange of letters with Marcus Brutus, in which the orator explains the didactic value of invective, as a "lesson for posterity," *in posterum documentum*, teaching readers how they should prosecute their opponents' immoral actions, at the same time abstaining from socially deviant behaviors: cf. Cic. *ad Brut*. 23.10: SB).

[45] On invective as a means of public affirmation of ethical and social norms, Corbeill 1996: 12–3; 24–5; 130–1.

[46] Cf. also schol. Bob. 89.20-8St (see Crawford 1994: 255–6).

[47] The Bobbio scholiast mentions only one of the prosecutors, L. Cornelius Lentulus Crus, and gives further details on the family of the Curiones (Clodius was defended by the elder Curio): 85.17-22St.

[48] Epstein 1986.

[49] Crawford 1994: 227–29. Cf. Cic. *Att*. 1.16.1–11 (for the account of the events leading up to the trial).

Cicero's and Clodius's mutual hostility, a critical moment of Cicero's political history that ultimately led to exile and represented, in some ways, the beginning of the decline of the republican statesman.[50] Though Cicero's involvement in the debate over Clodius's blasphemy (and the reasons for it) remains an unsettled question, it is beyond doubt that this was the point at which Clodius became a *capitalis inimicus*, "a mortal enemy," of Cicero. At the end of the *argumentum*, the scholiast expatiates on the violent *contiones* held by the future tribune against Cicero, who replied, in vehement tones, with a speech addressed to both Clodius and his advocate Curio (86.1-5St).[51]

Among the speeches delivered after the return from exile the *pro Sestio* stands out as the "most didactic." Not only a "tendentious and deceptive speech,"[52] exemplifying at its best Cicero's strategic treatment of rhetorical topics and commonplaces to achieve a practical goal, it also provides readers with a cluster of political slogans and clichés, incorporated into "a lesson for the younger generation to learn,"[53] an excursus about the destiny of the commonwealth and, at the same time, an exhortation to the young to emulate the best citizens, "those who really had the people's interests at heart (oneself and one's allies) against those who claimed to do so out of self-seeking motives."[54] Cicero's defense strategy, its significance and political relevance, forms the essence of the scholiast's prefatory explanation. The bulk of the *argumentum* (125.7–126.5St) is made up of a comparison between Sestius and Milo, both gathering paramilitary forces to confront Clodius's gangs (125.9-15St),[55] supplemented by a rhetorical clarification of the line of defense (*defensio*), hinging upon the

---

[50] Similarly, the Bobbio scholiast focuses on Clodius's hate for Cicero and desire for revenge in the *argumentum* to the fragmentary speech *De aere alieno Milonis*, delivered in the Senate in 53 BCE (169.14-29St). Clodius tried to undermine Milo's credibility as a candidate for the consulship, pointing to the (falsely claimed) extent of his indebtedness (*ad extremum longe minus quam haberet aeris alieni esse professum*), a motivation for not campaigning for the imminent consular elections (*cum igitur obnixe contenderet Clodius non oportere consulatum petere*). As the scholiast makes it evident, Clodius's speech was actually intended to be an aggressive invective against Cicero (*contumeliosa atque aspera*): Cicero replied to Clodius with a speech backing his friend, entitled *interrogatio de aere alieno Milonis* (on the title and the scholiast's explanation, see chapter 2 pp. 81–2). On the speech in general, see Crawford 1994: 265–70.

[51] Following the trial's outcome, Cicero restored a dispirited senate by attacking the jurors, the consul Piso and Clodius: "it is from these remarks that the material for the speech *in P. Clodium et Curionem* was taken, and later published without Cicero's consent" (Crawford 1994: 229).

[52] Kaster 2006: 35.   [53] Cic. *Sest.* 96.   [54] Kaster 2006: 34.

[55] The "digressive" and "ethical" nature of the characterization of Sestius and Milo, opposing their antagonist Clodius, lends weight to Cicero's defense. Similarly, in the trial of Milo, Cicero's client is depicted as a true hero and a tyrannicide, protected by the gods' will. On the emotional tones of Milo's *ethos* in the *pro Milone*, see May 1979.

principle of *compensatio*, "balancing"(125.22St).⁵⁶ Sestius's forming of an armed gang is propounded not as a seditious act or an act of public violence but as an emergency measure in the interests of the state (*pro bona causa et rei p. necessaria*: 125.22St) and, more than that, as a praiseworthy deed leading to the unanimously acclaimed restitution to the *res publica* of a good citizen, entitled to public honors for his merits (*cum bene meritum de salute patriae civem restitui vellet omnium favente consensu*: 125.23-4St). Cicero constructs a plea of self-defense on turning the prosecution's allegations against them and presenting his own "political" version of the facts,⁵⁷ a patently manipulative distortion of illegal actions (justifiably charged under *de vi*).

Cicero's reiterated (sometimes monotonous) recount of the present times, experiencing political violence, attracted reproval for being a strategic deviation (*extra causam*) from the real charge. Significantly, the Bobbio scholiast exonerates Cicero from any blame. He speaks in favor of Cicero's structural plan. Though he admits that Cicero was prone to exaggeration when portraying himself as afflicted or overwhelmed by passions (125.27-9St), his historical narrative, occupying the largest part of the text, is recommended to be treated as a complementary argument, a well-integrated point in the economy of the speech, in harmony with the relevance of the case (*tamen quod hic prolixa quadam turbulentissimi temporis descriptione multum voluminis occupat, non mediocriter videtur ad praesens negotium pertinere*: 125.29-31St). After discrediting unsubstantiated criticism from earlier, unnamed critics, the scholiast insists upon Cicero's need to arouse collective resentment at Clodius's terrorizing actions and stress his miserable condition as exile in order to legitimate Sestius's gathering of armed groups (and relieve him from rumors and the *invidia praesentis criminis*: 125.31–126.3St). He seems to be fully aware of the fact that Cicero's self-portrait as a victim of Clodius's violence aspired to present his recall from exile as a "new foundation" of the republican state.⁵⁸

---

[56] On the *pro Milone* as a "literary" case of *relatio criminis* (Cic. *Inv.* 2.71), in which the defense is carried out within the *qualitas adsumptiva*, by adducing conditions and circumstances of the fact and presenting the benefit (and the common good) occasioned by the deed itself, cf. Quint. *Inst.* 7.4.9; Victor. 191.2 *RLM* (52.24 Riesenweber: *feci, sed profui*); cf. also Fortunatianus 93.3 *RLM*. Lausberg 1998: 76 (§181).

[57] "The charge (against Sestius) was thus a political charge justifying a political defense in what was fundamentally a political trial" (Kaster 2006: 26).

[58] On Cicero's vivid description of his recall, a "drama" in which Roman citizens' actions and stylized gestures made plain the "proposition that Cicero's civic well-being was inseparable from, in fact identical with, the well being of the civil community as a whole," see Kaster 2009 (especially 311).

Yet Cicero's self-praise, a hackneyed theme in the post-exile speeches,[59] met with bitter reproval from anti-Ciceronian scholars.[60] Paying new attention to Cicero's apologetic description of his exile could then result in a repetitive and boring interpretative act, inefficacious in didactic terms. As a master sensitive to the pedagogical effects of his exegesis, the scholiast feels it necessary not to annoy students with discussions of mind-numbing tedium. Accordingly, he promptly eliminates any additional note on this topic, already touched upon in his commentary on other post-return speeches (the reference is to the *Post Reditum ad Senatum*: 126.3-4St).[61] In a direct address to his pupil, he refuses to deal with such a subject once it comes up in the course of reading (126.4-5St).[62]

Cicero's self-heroization and his continual emphasis on the exile as a traumatic experience are salient points of the post-return speeches.[63] Modern scholars have long insisted on the ways Cicero presented himself upon return from exile and tried to rehabilitate his public *persona* by portraying himself as both a victim and a Roman hero and depicting his own decision to depart as an act of *devotio*, "self-sacrifice," in the supreme interest of the republican institutions.[64] In the *argumentum* to the post-return speech of thanksgiving to the People (110.3-12St), the Bobbio scholiast pairs off Cicero's first public speeches upon his return (to the Senate and to the People), viewing the orator's gratitude and obligation to both the members of the Senate and Roman citizens as a self-gratulatory act and a manifesto of Cicero's self-aggrandizement. "Looking to restoring himself to his former glory" (*gloriae suae consulens*: 110.7St). This was Cicero's main concern. He thus felt he had

---

[59] Schol. Bob. 144.20-22St (on *Vat.* 7): *Multis in locis et in plerisque orationibus prae se fert hanc exilii gloriosam patientiam, quam videri volebat non gravate suscepisse, ne populi dissensio propter se commoveretur* ("In a number of places and in many orations Cicero glorifies his own ability to endure exile: he did not want to give the impression that he had grudgingly submitted himself to it, in order to avoid dissensions in the people because of him").

[60] Cicero's excess of arrogance is severely reprimanded by the commentator as not convenient to oratorical performance: schol. Bob. 144.23-145.3St (on *Vat.* 8).

[61] *Multa quidem in orationis cursu praetermittemus quae propter similitudinem causae in commentario proxumae orationis ostendimus* ("In commenting on the oration we will pass over many points, as, because of their similarity, we have already treated them in the commentary on the preceding text").

[62] *Ergo ne expectaveris ut, sicubi inciderit, eadem rursum iteremus* ("So, do not expect that we will return to this subject once again, when it occurs during reading").

[63] Narducci 1997b.

[64] Nicholson 1992; Dyck 2004; Raccanelli 2012: 7–22. Cf. schol. Bob. 130.25-8St (on *Sest.* 45); 168.6-9St (on *Planc.* 86: *Et simul in hoc epichiremate adhibet eundem colorem iam sibi in multis orationibus frequentatum, idcirco se cedere urbe maluisse, ne quid seditiosae dimicationis cum multorum exitio moveretur*, "At the same time, in this piece of dialectical reasoning he introduces an argument that has already been used in many orations, that is, that he has voluntarily made the choice to withdraw from the city in order to not occasion a seditious conflict"); 172.9-12St (on *de aere alieno Milonis* frg. 11).

to offer his recall as a sign of "political harmony," the natural consequence of a general consensus of all the social classes (*omnium ordinum consensu restitutus*: 110.8St). To consolidate the public perception of his return as beneficial to the commonwealth, Cicero recurred to epideictic tones and themes in both speeches. The scholiast detects an "epideictic quality" (*demonstrativa qualitas*) in Cicero's recollection of services (*beneficia*) from his friends and loyal supporters and, at the same time, in the invective against his enemies, in the guise of either instigators of exile or opponents of his recall (110.10-2St).[65] As has been shown, both the thanksgiving speeches, largely based on the practice of the *progymnasmata*, adopted similar methods for praise and blame by means of comparison.[66] In them Cicero made extensive use of a "stock of themes," drawn from epideictic rhetoric, redeployed in subsequent speeches, in combination with "arguments drawn from daily politics or other current concerns."[67]

Cicero's return from exile benefited from a complex network of relations with friends and political *socii*. This point returns in the *argumentum* to the *pro Plancio*, a speech delivered toward the end of summer of 54 BCE on behalf of Cn. Plancius, prosecuted for election bribery under the *Lex Licinia de sodaliciis* of 55 (the prosecution's *subscriptor* was M. Cassius Longinus).[68] Conscious of the uncertainty surrounding the illegal acts of electioneering covered by the law, the Bobbio scholiast seems initially concerned with explaining the legal context of the case and points out that the *lex* imposed a penalty on those candidates who made use of *sodales* or *sodalitates* to distribute money to tribes (152. 21-6St).[69] He comments also on the *iudices editicii*, jurors appointed according to a sortition system contemplated by Crassus's bill: once the jurors were taken from an *album iudicum* (a list of jurors), the prosecutor was allowed to pick out four tribes, from which the defender could subtract only one (152.26-32St).[70]

The commentator then explains the reasons behind Cicero's defense by pointing to the patron–client relationship, enhanced by a "great and sacred

---

[65] Stangl 1910: 103–4.
[66] As Dyck observes (2004: 302), "both speeches consist of (1) a comparison with others who endured a similar fate, (2) invective against enemies and expressions of thanks and/or praise of those who have helped him and of his resolve for the future, and (3) a narrative of the decision to depart and the process of his recall."
[67] Dyck 2004: 302–3.
[68] On the trial Alexander 2002: 128–44 (see also 2009b). On electoral bribery in the Roman republic, see Lintott 1990 (especially 9–10).
[69] Lintott 1990: 9 (on the *lex* presumably embracing public violence, in addition to bribery). See also Craig 1990: 76. On the crime of *ambitus* (and related charges), see also Riggsby 1999: 21–49.
[70] On the *reiectio iudicum* on the grounds of the *Lex Licinia*, cf also schol. Bob. 160.8-12St.

*Introducing Cicero's Oratory to Beginners* 199

intimacy associated with no ordinary services" (*summa et religiosa familiaritas beneficiis non mediocribus copulata*: 153.1-2St). As quaestor in Macedonia in 58, Plancius was the only one who provided sustenance for Cicero as exile with "liberal benevolence and not less loyalty" (*prolixa benignitate et fide non minore*: 153.4-5St). Cicero paid his debt of gratitude to Plancius. He thanked him in public, in both the thanksgiving speeches upon his return (153.7-9St), and, above all, he took on the role as his defender in the prosecution for election bribery, conducted by the young *nobilis* M. Iuventius Lateranensis, a defeated competitor for the curule aedileship of 55 (153.9-13St). Appropriately for a rhetorical commentary, the indication of the *status causae* provides students with the tools needed to grasp the significance of Cicero's defense strategy. The speech is basically founded on a *coniectura* ("conjectured conclusion"),[71] a dispute revolving around whether or not illegal distribution of money was made during the election process (*principaliter quidem coniecturalis defensio est . . .* : 153.13St). As Craig has shown, Cicero, embarrassed by Lateranensis's attacks, counterattacked by offering a positive, heroic portrait of himself.[72] Specifically, as the scholiast says, he focused upon the "probity of customs and actions" (*integritas morum et rerum gestarum*: 153.14-5St) of his client, diverting the jurors' attention from the real issue.[73]

Cicero's laudatory speech in support of the Roman citizenship of the Syrian Greek-speaking poet Licinius Archias, delivered in 62 BCE, the year following the consul's triumph over the Catilinarian conspiracy, is unanimously recognized as an unconventional speech, an epideictic oration in which the legal case is subordinated to cultural arguments, encapsulated in a full-blown praise of poetry and literature, a lengthy *digressio* serving as an instrument of persuasion.[74] As Dugan has nicely observed, Cicero obscured and neutralized legalistic arguments and technicalities by exploiting epideictic *topoi* and identifying himself with his client, a poet naturalized as a Roman in virtue of the excellence of his poetic *genius*.[75] In

---

[71] On the *status coniecturalis* (with its question *an fecerit*), cf. Quint. *Inst.* 3.6.5: Lausberg 1998: 48–9 (§§ 99–103).
[72] Craig 1990. On Cicero's re-establishment of his public image in the *pro Plancio* by means of a double *sermocinatio*, see Grillo 2014.
[73] On the use of ethical arguments in the *Pro Plancio*, see Riggsby 1999: 37–8 (also Craig 1993b: 123–45, for dilemma forms in the speech).
[74] A good analysis of Cicero's literary *digressio* in the *pro Archia*, correctly defined as "an exercise in persuasion," is in Berry 2004b.
[75] Dugan 2001b (on the *pro Archia* as a "splendid example of the performative power of epideictic"). For the use of an "artistic language" in the speech as a means of reinforcing the constructive role of poetry and literature within Roman society, see Nesholm 2009–2010.

blurring the distinction between himself and Archias, Cicero, under attack for his illegal execution of the conspirators, "could justify his own claim to be authentically Roman and, by extension, to have conducted himself as consul in accordance with the *mos maiorum*."[76] What is more, in eulogizing Archias's past services as a poet and encouraging him to compose a poem celebrating his consulate, Cicero charged epideictic style with poetical-political expectations, presenting his speech (and Archias's poem) as a *laudatio funebris*, a form of self-memorialization and textual fixation of his consular *persona*.[77]

Far from disputing the value of Cicero's encomiastic presentation of Archias as a poet, the Bobbio scholiast offers his own rhetorical interpretation of the speech strategy in the explanatory preface (175.3-20St). As usual, he provides information about the legal background of the case: Archias's literary education and his honorary citizenship at Heraclea in Lucania, the provisions of the *Lex Plautia Papiria* of 89 BCE (extending citizenship to "honorary citizens of federate states not resident in those states but nevertheless resident in Italy, provided that they reported to one of the praetors at Rome within sixty days")[78] and the Greek poet's prosecution under the *Lex Papia* of 65 (in absence of tangible proof of the right to claim Roman citizenship: 175.3-14St). Then, he distills Cicero's defense plan as follows (175.14-20St):

> Fit ergo quaestio coniecturalis an adscribtus sit in ordinem Heracliensium et an fecerit omnia quae is facere debuerit qui esset e numero foederatorum. Et deficitur quidem multis probationibus, testimonio tamen Heracliensium et vel maxime, quibus tota occupatur oratio, poeticae facultatis et doctrinae iucundissimae gratia nititur. Est etiam omissa coniectura disceptatio per ipsam qualitatem personae <an> civis Romanus debeat adoptari, etiamsi in praeteritum non sit adscitus.

> "Then, the issue is based upon conjecture, whether or not he was enrolled into the ranks of the citizens of Heraclea and he has done everything needed to be included in the number of the *foederati*, allies. And since he could not provide many proofs, Cicero built upon Heraclean citizens' testimony and, above all, constructed his whole speech of defense as a praise of Archias's poetic skills and very pleasing learning. Once conjecture is not permitted, the issue must of necessity shift to the character of the person, whether or not he could be adopted as a Roman, even if he had not been admitted to citizenship in the past."

---

[76] Dugan 2001b: 45.
[77] Dugan 2001b: 52 (for the *pro Archia* as a hybrid of Greek *epideixis* and the Roman *laudatio funebris*).
[78] Berry 2004b: 293.

The unavailability of evidence to prove Archias's Heraclean citizenship forces the orator to shift from the *status coniecturalis* to the *status qualitatis*,[79] passing over legal and forensic argumentations[80] and focusing instead on the outstanding cultural and moral qualities distinctive to the Greek poet, displayed by his cultivation of poetry and literary doctrine. If the *status coniecturalis*, the dissection of the issue upon conjecture, is not allowed and there is no question of fact, the debate centers by necessity around the *qualitas*, the character of the prosecuted, the only argument at the advocate's disposal to claim outright that Archias could legitimately be regarded as Roman.

In addition to detailing Cicero's defense strategy, the scholiast seems also to offer his students suggestions about the best way of exploiting rhetorical topics in legal actions concerning citizenship issues. In his view, the *pro Archia* turns out to be a sort of ideal *controversia* about citizenship rights, a speech built upon a general or abstract question (*thesis* or *quaestio infinita*), specifically a practical political question (*an adoptandum*).[81] Applied to individuals and definite circumstances, the legal case faced by Cicero relies upon a particular question (*hypothesis* or *quaestio finita*),[82] "whether or not Archias should be granted Roman citizenship" (*an Archias adoptandus sit*). Themes specifically related to questions of citizenship are not contemplated in Cicero's long list of declamation exercises included in a letter to Atticus (9.4.2),[83] nor do the collections of declamations preserved to us from antiquity, the so-called *Major Declamations* and the collection known as the *Minor Declamations*,[84] provide arguments hinging upon fictional citizenship laws. But it appears that the scholiast's presentation of the speech is very reminiscent of declamatory terminology. Beyond offering a magnificent (though manipulative) encomium of the immortal value of poetry and literary *ingenium*,[85] the *pro Archia* provides also an extraordinary test case for the (successful) manipulation of legal controversies about citizenship rights.

As a commentary tailored to students in need of a good grounding in rhetoric, Ps. Asconius abounds in details about the rhetorical *quaestio* (and

---

[79] On the *status qualitatis*, see Lausberg 1998: 62ff. (see also Russell 1983: 55ff.). In general on *stasis*-theory Heath 1994 is useful.
[80] Cf. schol. Bob. 175.23-7St (the scholiast comments on Cicero's choice not to capitalize on forensic arguments).
[81] Lausberg 1998: 497–98 (§§ 1134–1138).   [82] Lausberg 1998: 41 (§§ 73–77).
[83] Gunderson 2003: 106–9 (on the letter and Cicero's declamatory practice).
[84] For themes and argumentations in the *Minor Declamations*, see Winterbottom 1984.
[85] For a stylistic commentary on Cicero's praise of the liberal arts in the *pro Archia*, see Gotoff 1979 (esp. 152ff.).

its *status*) and the *genus causae*, the "degree of defensibility of a party's case gauged either by the content of the *causa* or by the party's level of sympathy among the *iudices*."[86] In the *argumentum* to the *Divinatio in Caecilium* (185.2–186.17St), a long explanatory preface basically centered on Cicero's self-portrait as the ideal accuser (an unprecedented role taken on by the orator in response to the Sicilians' request),[87] the scholiast distinguishes two main lines of argument in Cicero's strategy (*divisio principalis*), "one focused on Cicero himself, the other on the rivalry between the orator and Caecilius" (*una de se ipso, altera de contentione sui et Caecilii*: 186.2-3St). The explanation of the political context of the case (186.9-14St),[88] following a detailed exposition of contrasting interpretations of the term *divinatio* (186.3-8St),[89] precedes the scholiast's note on the treatment of the judicial issue (186.15-7St):

> Genus causae honestum: status: qualitas negotialis comparativa de constituendo accusatore, qui potissimum de duobus aut qui solus accuset; dicit enim Caecilius actore se accusandum esse Verrem aut a se quoque.

> "The class of the case is honorable; about the *status*, this relies on the quality concerned with the content and on a comparison between two potential accusers, to determine who should be preferred as the ideal prosecutor or whether the accused should be prosecuted by only one accuser or two: Caecilius claims in fact that either he must take on the prosecution as a single pleader or Verres pleads guilty."

The audience's sense of justice supports the "honorable" level of defensibility of the case:[90] No discussion exists about the facts, and the

---

[86] Lausberg 1998: 34 (§ 64) on the five levels of defensibility, generally called *genera causarum* (*Rhet. Her.* 1.5; Quint. *Inst.* 4.1.40; Grill. 87.19–88.56Jakobi; Isid. *Orig.* 2.8.1), and classified into *honestum genus* (the audience is entirely favorable to the speaker), *dubium vel anceps* (the case presents a mix of *honestas* and *turpitudo* and the audience is perplexed over the sense of justice of the case itself), *admirabile* (the audience's mind is hostile to the speaker), *humile* (the case is regarded as trivial and inconsequential) and *obscurum* (the technical complexity of the case puts the audience to trouble).

[87] Ps. Asconius notes that Cicero, "at the height of a flourishing career as a defender of his friends at that time" (*illo tempore florentem defensionibus amicorum*), was encouraged to take on the prosecution of Verres for a sense of obligation and debt of gratitude to the Sicilians (*necessitudine copulatum*), a debt contracted when he served as quaestor in Sicily in 75 BCE, under the praetorship of Sex. Peducaeus (185.8-10St). In addition, Cicero gave a speech upon his return to Rome from the province of Sicily in 74 (the title *Cum quaestor Lilybaeo decederet* is reported in the collection of *exempla elocutionum* of Arusianus Messius, who quotes the only surviving fragment of the speech, concerning the use of *detrecto* with the accusative case: *GL* 7.469.1), in which he "promised his generous support to the Sicilians" (*multa his benigne promisisset*: 185.11St). On Cicero's speech and the fragment quoted by Arusianus, see Crawford 1994: 19–22.

[88] For an attentive analysis of the political implications of Verres's case, see Vasaly 2009 (also Brunt 1980).

[89] Cf. chapter 3, p. 177 and n490.    [90] Grill. 87.23Jakobi.

condemnation of Verres's misconduct is unanimous. What is at stake is whether Cicero or his opponent should be picked out as a more effective prosecutor of Verres.[91] The entire case, a "paradigm of highly structured forensic argument" (together with the *Actio Prima*),[92] relies upon a comparison between competing prosecutors, Cicero and Caecilius Niger, Verres's former quaestor in Sicily. In the commentator's opinion, the pupil should thus be instructed in perceiving the *Divinatio* as a rhetorical *synkrisis*, a debate over the qualities of Cicero and Caecilius as would-be good prosecutors,[93] a debate unavoidably resulting in the victory of the speaker able to present himself as the saviour of Sicily, the restorer of moral order, and, above all, the archetypal advocate.[94]

The *Actio Prima* against Gaius Verres has long attracted attention for Cicero's highly performative manipulation of the *testes* ("witnesses"). Cicero deliberately abstained from a long speech, an *oratio perpetua* setting out all of the charges,[95] and treated "each charge as a miniature case, with its own small-scale introductory oration, followed by corroborating witnesses."[96] Cicero himself informs the judges of the unconventional way he is adopting in dealing with the testimony of the witnesses (*Ver.* 1.55). He focuses on the novelty of the *accusatio* ("the method of prosecution"), which presupposes first the treatment of each of the charges and then cross-questioning of supporting witnesses to each particular charge (in limited number). Its purpose is to engage the opponent, Hortensius (the most distinguished orator in Rome at that time), in a direct confrontation with each *testis*. The effect of this strategy, apparently designed to accelerate proceedings, is well described by Ps. Asconius in the *argumentum* to the speech (205.11-15St):

> Hoc commentus est rationis, ut orationem longam praetermitteret neque in criminibus declamatione cumulandis tempus absumeret, sed tantummodo

---

[91] The question was also whether the other potential accuser (not selected as the more suitable prosecutor) should be "assigned as a *subscriptor* (assisting prosecutor)": Craig 1993b: 49. On the *divinatio* process, which contemplated a selection of the most appropriate prosecutor (who was allowed time to investigate the charges abroad, *inquisitio*), see Lintott 2015: 311 (also Lintott 2004: 72).

[92] Enos 1988: 73. On the structure of the *Actio Prima* reproducing the parts outlined by rhetorical theory, see Vasaly 2002: 89–90.

[93] Ps. Asconius (197.20-3St, on *Div.* 37) draws attention to the procedure to be followed in cases involving a comparison process between two would-be plaintiffis: He advises the orator, who hankers to be selected by the jury, to capitalize on any occasion to show off his speaking skills and facility for dealing with the *quaestio* in a practiced manner (*qui praeferri velit, occasionem sibi sumat ostendendi quam perite possit tractare id ipsum de quo agitur*).

[94] On Cicero's self-presentation in the *Divinatio* (and his "highly unusual mode of characterization by comparison"), see Tempest 2011.

[95] Ps. Asconius 222.14-29St (on *Ver.* 1.55).      [96] Vasaly 2009: 111.

citaret testes ad unumquodque crimen expositum et eos Hortensio interrogandos daret: qua arte ita est fatigatus Hortensius, ut nihil contra quod liceret inveniret, ipse etiam Verres desperato patrocinio sua sponte discederet in exilium.

"He so devised this strategy as to eschew a long oration and not to waste time in accumulating and presenting all the crimes; but he limited himself to introduce witnesses to each crime, once he had illustrated it, and to present them to Hortensius for questioning. Hortensius was so tired out by this stratagem that he could not invent anything to contrast it: Verres himself, despairing of any defense, deliberately withdrew into exile."

Ps. Asconius's words accord with what Cicero himself declares about the first part of the trial in the *Actio Secunda*.[97] As Vasaly says, "Hortensius at first complained bitterly of Cicero's refusal to deliver the usual continuous oration, but then he also seems to have remained largely silent, even forgoing the opportunity to examine most of the witnesses."[98] Cicero's adoption of an uncustomary procedure proved to be effective, forcing Hortensius to capitulate and Verres to opt for a voluntary exile.

But there is more at stake in Cicero's prosecution strategy, in Ps. Asconius's view. In addition to their impact on the result of the court case, the miniature orations delivered over the course of the *First Action*, exhibiting a high degree of literacy,[99] confirm Cicero's dexterity in exploiting arguments and proofs in a "political" trial, involving his public image as a defender of the *res publica* and its laws. After commenting on the issue upon which the case turns, a double *status quaestionis, coniecturalis* in relation to the *repetundae* case, *negotialis* in connection with the legal assessment of the question to be made in the future,[100] Ps. Asconius concentrates on the main points (*capita*) by which the oration is articulated (206.6-9St) and points up once again Cicero's cleverness (*astutia*) as essential to victory over his opponents (206.10-4St).[101] Cicero's small-scale oration, built upon a rhetorical device (*artificium dicendi*), appears,

---

[97] Cic. *Ver.* 2.1.20; 24–7; 29.    [98] Vasaly 2009: 112–13.    [99] Ps. Asconius 205.24St.
[100] Ps. Asconius 206.1-5St.: *Status: quantum ad crimina causae repetundarum pertinet, coniectura multiplex inest omnibus libris: quantum ad specialem intentionem libri huius refertur, qualitas negotialis extra scriptum in particula iuris est constituta* ("The issue: if referred to the crimes in the case *de repetundis*, in all the books there is multiple conjecture; if related to the specific scope of this book, we have a *qualitas negotialis* concerning legal matters *extra scriptum*, arising from difficult legal cases in accordance with the specificity of law"). On the *pars negotialis* of the *status qualitatis*, Lausberg 1998: 81–2 (§ 196).
[101] On Cicero's *astutia*, "astuteness," in handling the witnesses (leaving no space to Hortensius's further inquiries) cf. also the scholiast's note on *Ver.* 2.1.24 (230.1St).

to the scholiast's eyes, as an exercise in eloquence and a limpid demonstration of oratorical power (*in hac parte vim oratoris ostendat*: 206.15St).

Upon the artificial nature of the five-book *Actio Secunda in Verrem* modern scholarship has long dwelled, and we have already touched upon this topic in the first chapter of this volume.[102] In the view of many scholars, the singularity of the speech, never delivered and circulated in a written version beforehand, accounts for its non-conformity to the precepts of rhetorical theory and to the standard structure of oratorical texts. Recently, this interpretation has been rejected with reasonable arguments.[103] Treated as a single speech (rather than five separate orations), the *Actio Secunda* abides by the *dispositio* theory and configures itself as "an exercise in persuasion" and "an example of a real speech, whether or not any part of it was actually delivered."[104] Analogously, the debate over the Second Action in antiquity appears to have been centered on the speech's artificiality and its conformity to conventional oratory. Ps. Asconius's *argumentum* to the speech (entitled *Accusatio*: 224.1–225.14St) starts off with a note on the "written" nature of Cicero's accusation (224.2-4St):

> Deinceps haec omnia non dicta, sed scripta sunt contra reum, quod <ita> factum est: Fingit Cicero adesse in iudicio Verrem comperendinatum, respondere citatum et defendi.

> "Everything from this point onward has not been delivered, but written against the accused man, so that the scene appears in the following way: Cicero assumes that Verres is present before the jury, after the adjournment of the trial, that he answers the prosecutor's questions, once summoned, and defends himself."

After commenting on the oratorical virtues displayed by Cicero in his first (unusual) experience as prosecutor (224.3-10St),[105] the scholiast offers a further indication of the "scene" as unreal (224.10-4St):

> Igitur rerum scaena sic ficta est, ut dicit Tullius, non ut acta res est. Adest inquit Verres, respondet, defenditur. Ergo cum prima Actione accusatus sit ac defensus Verres, nunc velut defensus iterum (sic enim mos erat) in altera Actione accusatur ad ultimum rursus oratione perpetua.

---

[102] Chapter 1, pp. 50–1.   [103] Tempest 2007.   [104] Tempest 2007: 22–3.
[105] Interestingly, Cicero's display of oratorical vehemence and doctrine (*vis artis et eloquentiae*) is seen as a sort of "compensation" for taking on the role of accuser (*accusationis officium his libris qui Verrinarum nomine nuncupantur compensare decrevit*), a role deemed to be inglorious to the orator striving for public reputation (*accusare multos indecorum Tullio videbatur*).

"Then the scene is artificially constructed in such a way as Tullius says, not as it has actually happened. Verres is present, he speaks, he answers the questions, he defends himself. So, whereas in the first Action Verres was accused and defended, now, in the second Action he is once again defended (this was the usual procedure at that time) and accused with a continuous speech."

Similar notes on the make-believe setting of the trial occur elsewhere within the commentary. In the same *argumentum*, the scholiast reminds his pupils that the "proems to this book have been composed to simulate reality, as if the accusation had actually taken place against a Verres brave enough to be present and defend himself" (*prohoemia sane huius libri in simulatione constituta sunt quasi verae accusationis in Verrem audentem adesse atque defensum:* 225.8-9St). The very beginning of the speech is defined as a *figmentum Ciceronis* (225.16St).[106] Again, at *Ver.* 2.1.23 Cicero apologizes for his long-winded discourse about the Senate's corruption, justifying it with Verres's and his friends' changed conduct. He admits that "the newborn hope of Verres and his friends, which has suddenly dragged him back to this court-house from the city gate" (*sed spes illorum nova, quae cum Verrem a porta subito ad iudicium retraxisset*), forced him to "enlarge on this topic" (*haec me pluribus verbis ... vobiscum agere coegit*). Preoccupied with supporting his students in discerning the speech's verisimilitude, the schoolmaster interprets the expression *a porta subito retraxisset* as a made-up scene, concluding that such an image has been devised by Cicero to persuade his potential readers to believe the *Second Action* to be a reality-based performance (229.28-30St).[107]

In spite of its fictionality, the *Actio Secunda* must be read as a standard oration, a text structured in line with rhetorical theory. Ps. Asconius devotes a good part of his explanatory preface to illustrating the topic upon which the *confirmatio* (the argumentation) rests; as Cicero himself clarifies, the *confirmatio* is a key part of the speech that "confers trust, authority and foundation on the case by the presentation of argument."[108] After reformulating Cicero's words about the classification of proof deriving from attributes either of persons or of actions (*omnis enim [et] confirmatio ab attributis <personae et ab attributis> negotio sumi solet:* 224.16-

---

[106] Cf. chapter 1, pp. 80–1.
[107] *Hoc comminiscitur Cicero, ut credamus veram fuisse secundam Actionem.* Cf. also Ps. Asconius on *Ver.* 2.1.31 (for the use of the verb *fingo* to indicate Cicero's fabrication of the scene: 232.25St); 2.2.31 (263.5-6St); schol. Gronov. (**B**) 342.14St (on *Ver.* 2.1.1).
[108] Cic. *Inv.* 1.34: *Confirmatio est, per quam argumentando nostrae causae fidem et auctoritatem et firmamentum adiungit oratio.* Lausberg 1998: 160–1 (§ 348).

7St),[109] the scholiast calls attention to Cicero's division of his argument (and books, accordingly) into five categories of accusation related to the quality or species of the crimes (*pro qualitate criminum*). A first, single book (2.1) is occupied by the treatment of Verres's *anteacta vita* (under the common label *De praetura urbana*):[110] Cicero's detailed exposition of Verres's character and crimes is based upon "conjecture" (*ergo hic liber qui de anteacta vita est statum necesse est coniecturalem habeat*: 225.1-2St), and serves as preparatory material to the subsequent accusations.[111] To the disquisition on the *crimen repetundarum* Cicero then dedicates four books: (a) about Verres's judicial mismanagement, commonly referred to as *De iure dicendo* (2.2), (b) about Verres's extortion of taxes from the tithe system, designated *De <re> frumentaria* (2.3), (c) about Verres's robbery of artworks, called *De signis* (2.4), and (d) about Verres as magistrate exercising power to punish, commonly labeled *De suppliciis* (224.18-21St). The titles and content of the speeches forming the *corpus* of the *Second Action* are restated in the *argumentum* to the second book (2.2).[112] Ps. Asconius signals Cicero's transition from the description of Verres's misdeeds in chronological order to the dissection of each crime *per se*[113] and succinctly guides his students through Cicero's digressions about the cases of alleged misconduct. A final, resounding note on the *genus causae* (*admirabile*) of the entire *Verrines* textual body[114] and the main *status* upon which the case hinges (*coniectura*) supports the pupil in recognizing the rhetorical structure of the text.[115]

---

[109] Cic. *Inv.* 1.34.
[110] As the scholiast notes, this book, the first designed for the second hearing, recounts Verres's career before he took on the governorship of Sicily. Cicero follows a chronological order (*ordo temporum*), detailing first Verres's quaestorship, then his actions as legate and pro-quaestor of Dolabella in Cilicia, and finally his misconduct and abuse of judicial powers during the urban praetorship (225.2-4St; cf. also 257.7-8St).
[111] Ps. Asconius 225.6-7St: *anteacta <ad> unum omnia hoc libro comprehensa sunt ad eorum fidem quae post dicuntur* ("all the actions *anteacta vita* are condensed in this single book so that they corroborate what is going to be said in the future"). Cf. also the *argumentum* to *Ver.* 2.2 (257.5St).
[112] Ps. Asconius 257.8-10St: *Ubi ventum est ad causam ipsam et Siciliensia crimina, quattuor libros edidit: unum de iuris dictione, alterum de frumento, tertium de signiis, quartum de suppliciis* ("Once the issue came to be centred on the charge and the crimes committed in Sicily, Cicero published four books, one on the judicial abuse of power, the other on taxation; a third book deals with Verres' theft of artworks, a fourth with his exercise of illegal power in punishment").
[113] Ps. Asconius 257.10-1St: *In qua distributione non ordo temporis, sed facinorum genera et momenta servata sunt* ("In this repartition of the speech he did not follow a chronological order: he instead described all kinds of crime and the time in which they occurred").
[114] On the "shocking degree of defensibility" of the *causa admirabilis* (*turpis*), Lausberg 1998: 36 (§ 64.3).
[115] Just a few words about the *argumentum* to *Ver.* 2.1 (*De praetura urbana*) in the Gronovian scholiast (**B**), 341.3–342.6St. As we have seen, after succinctly listing some of Verres's crimes during his praetorship, the commentator addresses his reader and restates the purpose of his scholarly work, an

Scholars and students of rhetoric – and Roman history – were certainly bemused by Cicero's ambiguous language in the speeches delivered in the period between September 46 and November 45 BCE, commonly known as *Orationes Caesarianae*.[116] Though given on distinct occasions and for distinct purposes, the *pro Marcello, pro Ligario* and *pro rege Deiotaro* share C. Julius Caesar, the *dictator* and *imperator* vested with the supreme judicial authority, as a special spectator. Before Caesar as a single judge, first thanked – and solemnly praised – for his pardon of M. Claudius Marcellus, an anti-Caesarian consul of 51,[117] then implored to be benevolent toward a former Pompeian (Ligarius)[118] and a Galatian tetrarch (Deiotarus),[119] Cicero adopted "the voice of a political critic and advisor,"[120] contemplating a rapport between himself and the new ruler of Roman politics based on mutual respect and cooperation. Forced to deal with an unhoped-for political reality, Cicero, as a "master of the Roman qualities of compromise and pragmatism,"[121] strove for a reconciliation with his former enemy, the only concrete possibility he saw to retrieve his lost authority and a space under modified political conditions.

Yet, as Gotoff has aptly remarked, "a Ciceronian speech can only incidentally mirror his true feelings, and even then identification of the 'real' Cicero amidst the many voices he creates would be an entirely subjective process."[122] This operation is doubtless much more complicated in the case of the *Caesarianae*, orations delivered in equivocal political

---

*opusculum* intended to particularize Cicero's digressions and shed light on his *oratoria virtus*, displayed at its best *in singulis narrandis* ("in the narration of single points"). Then, he reformulates the rhetorical repartition of the proem (*principium*) into four categories, in relation with the "benevolence" of the audience (*a persona iudicum, ex nostra persona, a persona adversariorum, a causa*), labeling the exordial words of Cicero's speech as a *prohoemium a causa adversarii*. Finally, he explains, in quite simplistic terms, the reasons behind the unifying title of the speech as *de praetura urbana* (pointing to Verres's crimes perpetrated during his praetorship as its main subject).

[116] In general on the corpus of the *Caesarianae*, see Gotoff 1993a; 2002.

[117] With the *pro Marcello*, an impromptu thanksgiving speech delivered in the Senate at an extraordinary session in the fall of 46 BCE, Cicero broke his self-imposed silence, *diuturnum silentium* (*Marc.* 1), and launched into a praise of Caesar's magnanimity and clemency. On the narration (in pathetic tones) of Caesar's pardon of Marcellus, cf. Cic. *Fam.* 4.4.3–4 (203 SB*Fam*: a letter to Sulpicius Rufus of September–October 46). See Dugan 2013: 213–14 (also Winterbottom 2002: 29–30).

[118] The *pro Ligario*, a judicial speech in defense of Q. Ligarius (a former Pompeian who fought at Thapsus in 46), was delivered in the Forum in the presence of a *corona* (for the first time since Milo's trial in 52). Ligarius was charged, presumably *de maiestate*, and prosecuted by Q. Aelius Tubero; Caesar presided over the trial as sole judge. On the emotional appeal of Cicero's oratory (Caesar was induced to acquit by the very power of Cicero's words), cf. Plut. *Cic.* 39.7.

[119] The *pro rege Deiotaro*, delivered in November 45, was given in Caesar's private home before the dictator as sole inquisitor; Deiotarus was charged with attempted assassination (of Caesar) by Castor, son of Tarcondarius, and Phidippus, one of Deiotarus's slaves.

[120] Gotoff 2002: 219–20.   [121] Gotoff 2002: 223.   [122] Gotoff 2002: 220.

circumstances and, by their very nature, "open texts," marked by ambiguity and opaqueness of language. Cicero's appeal to Caesar, dictator and judge at the same time, and his praise of clemency appear to be conveying an ambivalent political message, wavering between sincerity and surreptitious censure of the dictatorial regime. Perused and interpreted as an expression of Cicero's genuine desire to cooperate with Caesar in restoring law and order or, in contrast, condemned on ethical and aesthetic grounds[123] or, again, regarded as "ironical" texts, documents of Cicero's covert criticism of the change of direction in Roman politics, the *Caesarianae* transmit a sense of deliberate obscurity, offering us the image of a Cicero simultaneously perplexed over Caesar's real intentions[124] and truly disposed to cooperate with the most powerful man of Rome.

Unlocking the authentic meaning of the *Caesarianae* and extrapolating Cicero's true intentions from such equivocal texts becomes then a complex hermeneutical operation that is implicated in the history of textual reception. As has been noted, the discernment of the message conveyed by the *Caesarianae* had long engaged readers' attention and continues to be a central issue in modern Ciceronian scholarship. In particular the *pro Marcello*, the formal thanksgiving speech to Caesar of mid-September 46, had been the center of a scholarly controversy since late antiquity.[125] On the one hand, it has been seen as a "figured" text, a concealed attack on the dictator, calling even for his assassination.[126] On the other, scholars have read the speech from a historical perspective, contextualizing its apparently equivocal laudatory tone and interpreting it on the grounds of both rhetorical theory and Cicero's controversial role within Roman politics.[127]

As Dugan puts it, "the seeds of the controversy lie in the ancient scholastic tradition in which we find both these strands of thought represented – suspicions of a covert figured criticism vs. contextualization leading to the naturalization of Cicero's praise."[128] The comment on the *incipit* of the *pro Marcello* in the Gronovian scholia (**D**) enables us to

---

[123] Dugan 2013: 213 (especially for condemnation of the *pro Marcello* in Wolf's edition).
[124] "Cicero's relationship with Caesar was one in which ambiguities were constantly being negotiated" (Dugan 2013: 221).
[125] Dugan 2013: 213–4 (and n7, with further bibliography).
[126] Dyer 1990 (for an "ironical" reading of the oration, see also Gagliardi 1997). On the question, Tedeschi 2005: 16–20.
[127] Winterbottom 2002. On the speech as a *suasoria*, see Cipriani 1977; Rochlitz 1993. For the connection between praise and advice in the development of Cicero's ethical argumentation, see Gotoff 2002: 224–35.
[128] Dugan 2013: 214.

penetrate the key points of the debate as it developed in antiquity (295.23–296.2St):

> Plerique statum dederunt in hac oratione venialem, cum in ista oratione nullus status sit: gratiarum actio est. Si necdum dedisset indulgentiam, videretur status venialis. In gratulatione tantum Marcelli qui putant surrexisse Tullium errant. Vidit Caesarem ignoscere: multis enim petenda venia fuerat. Provocat illum ad <ipsum> genus laudis. In extrema parte orationis utitur quasi statu coniecturae, quia dicebat: "Insidias mihi faciunt, ut me occidant," sive me purget ceteros, ne poeniteat ignoscere Caesarem, sive ut Caesarem cautum faceret. Bellis ergo civilibus oratione non fuerat usus, et post bella tamen tacuerat. Haec prima vox fuerat "diuturni silentii."
>
> Plerique putant figuratam esse istam orationem et sic exponent, quasi plus vituperationis habeat quam laudis. Hoc nec temporibus convenit nec Caesari. Nam et tempus tale est, ut vera laude Caesar inducatur ad clementiam, et Caesar orator est qui non possit falli.

> "Most people have considered the point in question in this speech (*status*) as one of pardon (*venia*); but there is not an issue at question: it is instead a thanksgiving speech. If he (sc. Caesar) had had not given his pardon, the *status* would have been *venialis*. Those who think that Tullius rose up to his feet to speak only in felicitation of Marcellus are wrong. He saw that Caesar had forgiven his enemy: mercy had to be secured in fact for a good number of people. He challenged him to the same kind of praise. In the last part of the speech Cicero seems to have resorted to the conjectural issue, for he said: 'They are waiting in ambush to kill me.' These words have been said for two reasons: either he desired to absolve others from allegations (so that Caesar did not come to regret his forgiveness) or he wanted to alert Caesar to be on his guard. Since the civil wars Cicero had not spoken publicly; he also kept silent after the wars. These are the first words he pronounced, 'after a long silence' (*diuturni silentii*).
>
> Most think that this speech is 'figured' and explain it this way, as if the speech has more invective than praise. But this interpretation accords neither with the times nor with Caesar. For in reality both the time was such that it was by true praise that Caesar would be moved to clemency, and Caesar was an orator who could not be deceived."

After concisely summarizing the circumstances leading to the Senate meeting of September 46 and Caesar's act of clemency (295.8-22St),[129] the

---

[129] The scholiast portrays Marcellus as both an orator (he evidently alludes to Cic. *Brut.* 248–51 and chapter 2 of the speech; the definition *Marcellus loquax*, attributed to Lucan, is presumably taken from the scholia on Lucan 6.20: cf. 295.10St) and a leading figure of the anti-Caesarian movement. He lingers over the pathetic, theatrical connotations of the request for clemency to Marcellus, urged

Gronovian scholiast concentrates on the speech's rhetorical form and its intent and political purpose. He points first to earlier misunderstanding of the *status*, erroneously taken to be *venialis*, a *status* that consists in admitting that the deed is bad in itself and justifying it on the grounds of compelling arguments. As explicitly stated in rhetorical handbooks, the *qualitas venialis* (or *concessio*)[130] usually envisages a formal request for pardon or appeal for clemency to the judge (subdivided into *purgatio* and *deprecatio*).[131] But this is a different case. Marcellus has been given pardon before Cicero's words. As a result, the speech cannot be examined in rhetorical terms (the *status* would have been *venialis* only if Caesar had rejected appeals for mercy).

To the scholiast, the *pro Marcello* is not just a *gratiarum actio*, an official expression of thanks for the dictator. In his view, Cicero constructed his performance as a model of rhetorical praise. He challenged his reader/spectator Caesar to enter into dialogue – and competition – with him. In exploiting topoi of praise Cicero tested his own capacities for combining epideictic and politics and offered himself as a trustworthy orator and politician, a man whom the dictator should count on to re-establish a restored, morally reinvigorated republic.[132] It is tempting to say that the ambiguity of Cicero's message, hidden behind a formal, public panegyric of the Caesarian policy of clemency,[133] does rely on this very oscillation

---

by the entire senatorial order, and comments on Caesar's decision, motivated by both violence suffered in the past (*ex superiore iniuria*) and a state of disquiet for the future (*futuro metu*). Exploiting the figure of the *fictio personae*, in the form of the *sermocinatio*, the scholiast then introduces Caesar into the scene and concocts an imaginary dialogue between the dictator and C. Marcellus, dramatizing Caesar's thought process and offering an "open-voiced" exploration of the reasons that led to pardoning the former anti-Caesarian consul (*"Marcelle, hoc contra me fecisti. De superiore iniuria illud fecisti. Deinde audio mihi parari insidias ab his quos servavi. Tamen, quoniam hoc amplissimus ordo postulat, ignosco" – ideo dixit Cicero: tuis vel doloribus vel suspicionibus anteferre; "tamen, quia senatus hoc vult, ignosco"* ["'Marcellus, I know you did it against me. I know about violence in the past: you did it. Now, I have been informed that those whose lives I spared are waiting in ambush to kill me. Nevertheless, since this order, which is the most honorable, demands it, I accord pardon' – this is the reason why Cicero said: 'you placed it above both your resentment and suspicion'; 'however, since this is the Senate's desire, I forgive'"]: 295.17-21St). On the dramatization of the scene of supplication and "stage directions" in the fictitious dialogue between Caesar and Marcellus, see Dugan 2013: 215.

[130] Cic. *Inv.* 1.15; 2.94; Isid. *Orig.* 2.5.6; Victorin. 191.15 *RLM* (53 Riesenweber: see also Riesenweber 2015: 2.92).
[131] Cic. *Inv.* 1.15; Fortunatianus 93.32 *RLM*. See Lausberg 1998: 79 §§ 187–191.
[132] For the conceptual association of stylistic figures with Cicero's discourse of praise and cooperation in the *pro Marcello*, see Krostenko 2005.
[133] On clemency as political virtue and "the sign of a humane temperament," see Konstan 2005 (in particular on the definition of the *clementia Caesaris* in Cic. *Att.* 9.7.6 [174 SB*Att*]; 9.16 [185 SB*Att*] and its reformulation in Seneca's political treatise *De clementia*). For the philosophical connotations of the concept of *clementia Caesaris*, see Griffin 2003. In general, see Picone 2008.

between an apologetic (self-) defense of the past and the expectation for a "moderate" republic, under the guidance of an open-minded dictator and the supervision of a far-sighted politician.[134]

Also politically inspired is the scholiast's interpretation of Cicero's argumentative strategy and his attempt to play down Caesar's fears for his safety (*Marc.* 21–2). In his opinion, Cicero's rhetoric reveals a major shift in his search for political cooperation. As a defender of former anti-Caesarians, "virtuous men" (*boni viri*) who "have fallen not from any evil desires or depravity, but merely from an opinion of their duty," (§ 20)[135] Cicero was compelled to remove Caesar's trepidation by erasing any trace of suspicion over potential lethal conduct by opponents of the regime. This note is reformulated in the lemmatized comment on chapter 21, which marks the beginning of Cicero's political, manipulative treatment of Caesar's complaint (*Nunc venio ad gravissimam querelam:* 296.23-5St). The main purpose of Cicero's argument was to prove the unfoundedness of Caesar's worst fears (*nemo tibi insidias facit,* "no one is waiting to ambush you"). The scholiast discerns political considerations in Cicero's intent to dispel Caesar's anxiety over his life and make him more circumspect (*cautiorem faciendo securum tamen praestat*).[136] His encouragement to prudence and vigilance, a *cautio* shared with the dictator himself and the entire civil body,[137] was peculiar to his role as counselor and political adviser. The scholiast seems also to be conscious that Cicero's actions and words function as polysemous "subtexts," leaving space for different interpretations. More, in "grounding his reading within the facts of the speech act – historical context, persuasive goal, and audience, that is, Caesar himself,"[138] he performs as a correct interpreter of Cicero's *persona*, a *persona* operating under ambiguous and paradoxical conditions but always directing his own action toward the restoration (and conservation) of the *res publica*, though under a non-republican regime.

The scholiast's refusal of an ironical reading of the *pro Marcello* is sustained by careful examination of the speech's specific performative

---

[134] For the speech as oscillating between sincerity and irony, eulogy and condemnation of the new political regime, refusing violence as a means of re-establishing republican order but at the same time calling for a limitation of Caesar's supreme power, see Connolly 2011.

[135] A note of the Cluny scholiast (271.20-6St) explains Cicero's sentence *opinione officii stulta fortasse, certe non inproba* ("a foolish and erroneous opinion of duty perhaps, but certainly not a wicked one") at *Marc.* 20 as a calculated diminution in moral terms of the former Pompeians' choice to fight the future dictator.

[136] "At the same time that he makes him more circumspect he makes him more secure" (296.25St).

[137] The expression in the scholia *ut Caesarem cautum faceret* recalls Cicero's chiastic formulation *tua enim cautio nostra cautio est* (*Marc.* 21).

[138] Dugan 2013: 217.

context. Its chronological framework and recipient do not permit a figurative interpretation of Cicero's eulogistic tone. As Winterbottom notes, "a figured oration fails if its covert meaning is apparent to the person against whom it is directed."[139] And Caesar was such a sophisticated orator that he would have easily detected veiled hostility in Cicero's high-flown rhetoric, if it had been present.[140] Additionally, Cicero's praise of Caesar's clemency in the *pro Marcello* is perfectly consistent with his attitude to the changed political landscape, as illustrated in the letters of the summer of 46.[141] Cicero's literary work at that time brings out into the open a man negotiating political ambiguities, trying to come to terms with dictatorial power, exploring possibilities of cooperating in the new political environment of Caesar's Rome and discussing relationships between free oratory and politics.[142] This does not imply a Cicero entirely sincere in his unstable rapport with the ruling power. From private correspondence and rhetorical-philosophical works of the years 46–45 BCE we witness a Cicero perplexed over Caesar's obscure and suspicious intentions and "tyrannical" conduct. The very fact that the speech, as we have said, has elicited divergent readings since antiquity, tells us much about ambiguity as a natural component of Cicero's relationship with Caesar.[143] Yet the *pro Marcello* presents a Cicero using his authorial voice to exert pressure on Caesar and persuade him to return to constitutional ways. As Winterbottom again puts it, "it was not in his interest, at this juncture, to make a speech that did anything but encourage Caesar to continue treading the present comparatively hopeful path."[144] And the scholiast himself advocates a realistic, historically founded reading of the speech, offering explanations for an "irony-free" interpretation of Cicero's words in his lemmatized commentary[145] and stimulating his readers/students to looking at the text within the circumstances of its performance.[146] While stigmatizing figured reading as a sign of ignorance of both rhetorical theory and historical reality, he "anchors the text in events and actions, and thus

---

[139] Winterbottom 2002: 24.
[140] Dugan 2013: 224. For the *pro Marcello* to be treated as a speech conveying a real political message (not as an *oratio figurata*), see also Craig 2008.
[141] Winterbottom 2002. See also Hall 2009.
[142] On the *Brutus* as a "rich meditation upon the relationship between oratory and politics" and Cicero's investigation of the complex, hermeneutical puzzle involved in the discussion about text (*scriptum*) and intention (*voluntas*) in the *Causa Curiana* of 94 BCE, see Dugan 2013: 219–20.
[143] Dugan 2013: 224.  [144] Winterbottom 2002: 33.
[145] Cf. 296.3-6St (on the scholiast's neutralization of the suspicion that Cicero's mention of "these times," *his temporibus*, at § 1 may be interpreted as a covert accusation against the current times, marked by Caesar's political dominance).
[146] On irony in performance, cf. Quint. *Inst.* 8.6.54.

closes off the slipperiness of signification that may have been present in a more formalistic reading of the text."[147]

Categorized as *deprecatio* by Quintilian,[148] the *pro Ligario* is a highly sophisticated, paradoxical text, closely abiding by traditional rhetorical theory but unusual for its treatment of forensic issues.[149] As Cicero himself makes clear at the outset, the speech refuses argumentative strategies and configures itself as a pure plea for mercy (*omissaque controversia omnis oratio ad misericordiam tuam conferenda est,* § 1). Accordingly, the Gronovian scholiast interprets the issue upon which the speech rests as belonging to the special category of the "pardon" (*venialis*: 292.4-6St):[150]

> Status venialis per casum, per imprudentiam et per necessitatem: omni igitur parte consistit. Narrationem probamus. Genus causae admirabile: quod iste odit reum, quod odiosa persona est Caesari.

> "The status of the speech relies upon pardon, through the categories of chance, thoughtlessness and necessitude: therefore it stands on its own. We admire its narration. The category which the case belongs to is *admirabilis*: for he hates the accused; he is hated by Caesar."

Preceded by a long introductory narration of the historical events involving Q. Ligarius and his participation in conflicts in Africa after Pompey's death (291.4–292.3St),[151] the note on the rhetorical structure of the speech focuses on the absence of issue or controversy. Cicero's claim to refrain from standard judicial arguments (though he treats the legal proceeding in conformity to rhetorical theory and advances arguments in a highly sophisticated form of indirection)[152] prompts the scholiast to resolve problems related to the "genre" of the speech by inserting it into the category of the *status venialis*[153] and cataloging the case, with reference to

---

[147] Dugan 2013: 219.
[148] Quint. *Inst.* 5.13.5; 5.13.31 (on Quintilian's appreciation of the *pro Ligario* as a simple *deprecatio*, see McDermott 1970, skeptical about the sincerity and quality of the speech). For the *pro Ligario* as an instance of *purgatio* cf. Iul. Vict. 381.34–5 *RLM* (*omissis omnibus veniam precamur aut ignoratione aut necessitate aut casu, ut est Marci Tullii pro Ligario sententia*). On the controversy surrounding the meaning and structure of the speech in modern scholarship, see a good survey in Johnson (J. P.) 2004.
[149] Montague 1992.
[150] Cf. also 292.22St (*venialis oratio*); 292.26St (*utitur ad venialem*); 292.32-3St (*venialis per casum et per necessitatem*).
[151] For a brief examination of the events leading up to the trial, see Gotoff 2002: 236–38.
[152] Montague 1992: 562–3.
[153] On the *purgatio* based on three factors, *imprudentia* ("ignorance"), *casus* ("influence of fate") and *necessitas* ("moral or physical compulsion"), cf. *Rhet. Her.* 1.25; 2.23; Cic. *Inv.* 1.15; 2.94; Quint. *Inst.* 7.4.14; Grill. 73Jakobi; Victorin. 191.15 *RLM* (53 Riesenweber); 286.35 *RLM* (187 Riesenweber); Mart. Cap. 159.17Willis; Cassiod. *Inst.* 2.2.5; Isid. *Orig.* 2.5.8; Albin. 532.7 *RLM*.

its legal defensibility, as "paradoxical" (*admirabile*).[154] The effect of incoherency (produced by Cicero's statements, his manipulation of legal-rhetorical arguments and the novelty of the judicial situation) is particularly striking in the opening sentences of the oration. Cicero's words *novum crimen, C. Caesar, et ante hunc diem non auditum* ("a new crime, Caesar, and never heard of before"), a "stereotyped expression of *aporia*,"[155] are explained by the commentator in terms of parody, in line with the common interpretation of this passage in rhetorical handbooks (292.6-8St):[156]

> In ista oratione per hironiam esse principia intellegamus. (§ 1) Novum crimen] Per irrisionem.

> "In this speech the proemial words are to be interpreted ironically. (§1) A new crime] Through parody."

The *exordium* of the *pro Ligario* patently violates the principles that regulate introductory sections of judicial speeches. Gotoff correctly explains it as "a masterpiece of cheerful confidence disguised as unremitting panic, conveyed by obvious exaggeration, self-parody, and sophistic argumentation, suggesting the absurdity and inconsequence of the case before Caesar."[157] Conceding Caesar's ability to appreciate his humorous reversal of Tubero's arguments Cicero admits his confusion in pleading such an anomalous case and breaks with traditional rhetorical techniques. He manipulates the absurdity of the *crimen* to paradoxically shift culpability onto the accusers and flatter his audience, prone to be swayed by the sophisticated, parodic treatment of the charges against Ligarius.[158] Not

---

[154] Cic. *Inv.* 1.20; Quint. *Inst.* 4.1.40; Lausberg 1998: 36 (§ 64.3). The speech in defense of the king Deiotarus too is inserted into the category of the *genus admirabile* by the Gronovian scholiast **D** (298. 29-30St: *Haec causa dicitur in domo Caesaris, non in foro. Adest Cicero. Status coniecturae. Genus causae admirabile; nam offensus est animus Caesaris, sed non satis, quia indulgentiam dederat*, ["This speech was delivered in Caesar's private home, not in the forum. Cicero is present. The issue rests upon conjecture. The category of the speech is *admirabile*; for Caesar feels hurt and offended by the accused, but not so much; he had given him his pardon"]). Cf. also the *argumentum* to the *Sex. Rosc.* (302.4-5St: the scholiast explains the *admirabilitas* of the case as the result of "adversity of time, power of Sulla, and greatness of the crime of parricide").

[155] Montague 1992: 563.

[156] Cf. Quint. *Inst.* 4.1.70 (*divina illa pro Ligario ironia*); Romanus Aquila *RLM* 24.21-4 (also 38.7); Mart. Cap. 182.14Willis (on the figure of *simulatio*). For Quintilian's admiration of Cicero's *pro Ligario* cf. *Inst.* 4.1.39; 4.1.67; 4.2.51; 4.2.108; 4.2.109; 4.2.110; 4.2.131; 5.10.93; 5.11.42; 5.13.20; 5.13.31; 5.14.1.

[157] Gotoff 2002: 241. On salacity in the *pro Ligario* cf. Iul. Vict. *RLM* 438.21-2.

[158] On the level of irony operating in the *exordium* (especially in the comic image of the orator incapable of facing such an unexpected case, visualized in the sentence *itaque quo me vertam nescio*), see Johnson (J. P.) 2004: 384-5.

surprisingly, Cicero's irony has been recognized since antiquity. Ancient commentators engaged their readers and students in admiring Cicero's oratorical wit,[159] a strategy that also proved vital to the deprecatory appeal to Caesar's humanity and clemency in the last part of the oration.[160]

In interpreting Cicero's thanksgiving speech for Caesar's action of pardoning Marcellus as an ambiguity-free text, as we have seen, the Gronovian scholiast "presents himself as fighting a battle against ignorance of rhetorical theory and shoddy reasoning."[161] He depicts himself as a "heroic corrector of error, and one that is advancing a minority opinion against opponents who outnumber him."[162] A similar attitude is displayed in the *argumentum* to the Fourth Catilinarian, a polemical attempt at re-establishing the correctness of a reading based on historical context, *status* theory and performative elements (286.27–287.17St):

> Hoc libro de poena coniuratorum agitur. Et ausi sunt plerique commentatores negotialem dicere. Ubi enim de qualitate poenarum quaeritur, negotialis status est, sed accidens cum ... Melius est ut dicas demonstrationem esse. Status enim negotialis est, ubi intentio et depulsio est. Nihil est tale: quomodo potest esse negotialis? Magis demonstrationis partem esse scilicet orationem debemus dicere.

> "In this speech we face the issue involving punishment prescribed by the law for the conspirators. And most commentators have been so brave as to say that the speech *status* is *negotialis*. When in fact there is a discussion about the type of punishment to be inflicted, then we have the *negotialis status*, but it happens when ... So it would be better to say that the *status* is *demonstrativus*. We have the *status negotialis*, where there is accusation, *intentio*, and defense, *depulsio*. Here nothing similar happens: how it is possible to define it as *negotialis*? We should rather define the oration as a part of the general demonstration of the facts."

As a master of rhetorical doctrine, the scholiast understands Cicero's plea for the execution of the Catilinarian conspirators, delivered in the Senate meeting of 5 December 63 BCE, as based on the categories of the *genus demonstrativum*. The presumptive rhetorical diagnosis of the speech as belonging to the *genus iudiciale*, involving "attack" (*intentio*) and "defense" (*depulsio*),[163] is ridiculed by the commentator, who offers instead his own reconstruction of Cicero's oration on stylistic and political

---

[159] For Cicero's use of wit in the *pro Ligario* (and in the three orations addressed to the dictator Caesar, in general), see Corbeill 1996: 210–11.
[160] On the ironic use of *deprecatio* elements in chapters 32–6 of the speech, see Johnson (J. P.) 2004: 395.
[161] Dugan 2013: 217.   [162] Dugan 2013: 217.   [163] Quint. *Inst.* 3.9.1; 10.1.

grounds and reads the consul's intervention in the senatorial debate as a case study of "performance oratory," showing the powerful influence of Cicero's consular voice.

The scholiast corroborates his hermeneutics by reconsidering in detail the procedure followed by Cicero in putting the question of death penalty before the Senate (286.31–287.17St). As the presiding magistrate, Cicero was not supposed to express his opinion; he could just bring the question to the Senate (*relatio*) and, according to the customary, ancient system (*more maiorum*), call upon the consuls-elect, requesting them to formulate their proposal (*sententia*).[164] Specifically, the consul-elect D. Silanus was first asked for his opinion (*prius interrogatus est*). He proposed the death penalty (*morte multavit coniuratos*), a punishment mitigated by Caesar's proposal of lifelong detention and confiscation of property.[165] Set in parallel with that of Silanus, the view of Caesar was rebuffed by Cato,[166] not by Cicero, whose "ostensibly neutral description"[167] subtly lent credit to Cato's authority and his sense of responsibility to the state.

In line with tradition and *decorum*, Cicero took pains to maintain the appearance of impartiality in relating both proposals. The scholiast calls attention to this move and alerts his students to Cicero's deft manipulation of the senators' fears (287.5-17St). By depicting himself as a neutral magistrate, willing to submit the question to the Senate's advice, Cicero reinforced his status and consular *dignitas*, eliminating any possible suspicion about personal interests in the case. At the same time, as the scholiast himself notes, Cicero endorsed Silanus's proposal and managed to control the senators' opinions.[168] Cape correctly points out that "Cicero desired to argue against Caesar's proposal while avoiding charges that he had decided what to do before he consulted the Senate."[169] In this light, his praise of Caesar is certainly ironic,[170] a faint eulogy and an implicit (and subtle) devaluation of the allegedly moderate, more humane (and falsely "popular") opinion of the praetor-designate, in comparison with that of Silanus,

---

[164] Cape 1995: 260–63.
[165] The scholiast limits his own comment on Caesar's proposal to a simple *Caesar dissuasit* ("Caesar advised against it"): 287.3St.
[166] *Necdum Caesaris sententiam solvit Cicero: nam postea Cato solvit sententiam Caesaris* ("But Cicero has not canceled Caesar's proposal yet; it was afterwards Cato who destroyed the binding force of Caesar's opinion": 287.3-4St).
[167] Dyck 2008a: 218. See also Cape 1995: 264-5.
[168] *Sed laborat orator occidendos esse quantum potest, et suadet aliud agendo quantum potest* ("Yet the orator, as far as he can, spares no effort in putting them to death; he did anything possible to convince the Senate to do that": 287.7-8St).
[169] Cape 1995: 268.
[170] *Laudando vituperat eius sententiam* ("While praising he censures his proposal": 287.8St).

no doubt charged with *crudelitas* but consistent with truly popular examples and the best tradition of the ancestors.

Cicero's intent was clearly to put the Senate under pressure and persuade the senators to vote in support of the proposed death penalty.[171] Yet he oscillated between his own official position, as an impartial presiding magistrate, intent on doing what was correct and appropriate under specific legal circumstances, and his willingness to persuade the jurors to act in respect for the *mos maiorum*, thereby treating Caesar's proposal in a paradoxical way, ironically lauded for its apparent leniency but vituperated for its being in contrast to the liberal-popular ideals. Implicitly arguing against Caesar's view, he tried to maintain the illusion of impartiality.[172]

A similar atmosphere of uncertainty – and fluctuation between legality and severity – seemed to pervade the audience, concerned about legal constraints imposed by the *lex Sempronia* and fearing for the future of the city. The scholiast perfectly captures the feelings of Roman citizens. He makes them voice their conflicting sensations in a rhetorical soliloquy (287.12-4St): *Dicebant enim: "quam necessitatem habet Cicero? Quid est hoc? Si non occiderit, periculosum est civitati: si occiderit, contra leges facit"* ("They considered the situation saying: what necessity induces Cicero to do that? What is this? If he does not put the conspirators to death, there will be a risk for the city; if he does approve of death penalty, he will act against law"). Cicero understands public anxiety and offers himself as the solution, the only magistrate capable of balancing legality with public interest and defending Roman institutions (*debet ergo orator ostendere se securum esse adversus omne periculum*, "the orator must show himself free from any threat or danger"; 287.15-6St). The political significance of Cicero's dexterous negotiation between political positions is well caught by the commentator. He correctly interprets the *Fourth Catilinarian* as a "deft political speech,"[173] a display of oratorical cleverness, irony and astute manipulation of legal-political arguments, in a word, a subtle and

---

[171] As expressly stated by the scholiast, 290.29-30St (on § 18): *Iam hic cohortatio est paene ad occidendos* ("This is all but an encouragement to approve of the death penalty").

[172] Interestingly, the scholiast defines Cicero's move in terms of political dexterity and "oratorical cleverness" (*oratoria astutia*) and comments positively on the orator's ability to cover his real intentions. The sentence rounding off Cicero's dissection of both the proposals (*Decernatur tamen, si placet*, "Still, let this be your decree, if it is your will") in chapter 8 of the speech well illustrates, in the scholiast's opinion, the orator's concern for neutrality in the debate. What mattered was to maintain the appearance of impartiality, a tactic crucial to persuading the audience that the death penalty was (paradoxically) of benefit to the conspirators (288.26-9St).

[173] Cape 1995: 273.

constructive reformulation of the image of Cicero as the ideal prototype of a Roman magistrate.

## Oratory, *Dissimulatio* and Irony: Cicero Teaches the "Art of Illusion"

Let us now turn to the text from which we started in our inspection of the routine practice in the teaching of rhetoric, Quintilian's rhetorical *enarratio* in the second book of the *Institutio*. A key point the master of rhetoric stresses, as we have seen, is the orator's ability to persuade the audience and exercise power over the minds of the judges by mastering and elaborating technical-legal arguments and exploiting rhetorical material in a skillful manner. Quintilian's primary goal is to demonstrate that oratory is the art of *dissimulatio* ("dissimulation").[174] The best way to be successful in winning a case is to influence the jury's verdict by means of rhetorical/dialectic subtleties and manipulative argumentation. This point is underscored in the first chapter of the tenth book by introduction to a list of renowned classical authors expected to be read from potential orators (*Inst.* 10.1.21). Quintilian describes here the orator's strategy of manipulation, perceivable since the beginning of the speech. It is in fact in the proemial part that the speaker usually "prepares his way, dissembles, lays traps" (*saepe enim praeparat dissimulat insidiatur orator*), in other words, starts his tactic of deception that will result in complete control over the souls of baffled judges.

Quintilian's comment on the orator's action leads us to confront the long-debated issue of the immorality of rhetoric, closely linked to the centrality of philosophical knowledge and ethics to oratory.[175] Crucial to the construction of the ideal orator, morality – and the accorded pursuit of what was good – appeared to be a fundamental ingredient of the persona of the advocate.[176] It was imperative that moral standards of advocacy were maintained, as we have already noted in our presentation of Quintilian's Ciceronianism.[177] Cicero certainly recognized the moral force of philosophy for oratory and considered it necessary to practice a "morally correct" eloquence. However, to Cicero's eyes oratory presented practical, more

---

[174] It should be noted that Quintilian rebuts the identification (held by some scholars) of *dissimulatio* with the figure of irony, εἰρωνεία (as a schema), not so much different from irony as a trope (*Inst.* 9.2.44); cf. also 9.1.3 (for irony belonging to figures of thought just as much as to tropes). For this identification cf. Mart. Cap. 182-3Willis; Romanus Aquila 24.21–4 *RLM*.
[175] For this part of my discussion I owe a large debt to Gotoff 1993b.
[176] A good survey of this issue is in Powell-Paterson 2004: 19–29.   [177] See chapter 3, pp. 124–25.

than moral, concerns.[178] As Wisse posits it, in the *De oratore* "the question of the morality of rhetoric is in fact mostly avoided – perhaps precisely because Cicero felt that there was no way to guarantee the integrity of the orator."[179] The primary need of oratory was to master the audience's psychology by application of specific rhetorical devices and stratagems. What mattered to the good orator was to impress the audience and manipulate emotions, a fundamental step towards the final victory.[180]

It follows then that a dogmatic vision of the Roman legal system, founded on an idealized (abstract) notion of justice and moral oratory (the same ideal pursued, as said, by Quintilian), constrasts unavoidably with the reality of Roman advocacy, based on a system of personal relations and obligations, in no way comparable with our modern system of advocacy. As clearly elucidated by Powell and Paterson, personal connections (and political interests) played a role in the advocate's choice to defend a guilty client or prosecute a personal or political enemy.[181] It is known that Cicero sometimes took on difficult cases, based on weak or false evidence. And, as any Roman advocate at that time, he argued "the case on his client's behalf as strongly as possible in the interests of reaching a fair decision."[182] At any cost, regardless of truth, it might be added. So the advocate's duty was to secure the goodwill of the jury/audience by devising and presenting arguments that were expected to be believed as true, because if "it is always the business of a judge in a trial to find out the truth, it is sometimes the business of an advocate to maintain what is plausible, even if it be not strictly true."[183] This manipulation of truth, which is the essence of the art of rhetoric, implied on the advocate's side maximum flexibility, commensurate with the complexity of the concrete case. As Gotoff puts it, "Cicero the advocate is not a single voice or a single personality. Instead he is a variety of *personae* invented and portrayed by Cicero the orator capable of introducing, interpreting, and manipulating the material of the case in an infinite variety of ways; of interacting with his client, his client's accusers, and the judges in an almost infinite variety of tones; of participating in and, therefore, to a large degree creating the ambience in which he operates."[184]

---

[178] Gotoff 1993b: 296.   [179] Wisse 2002b: 393.
[180] On Cicero's ethical rhetorical perspective and the Ciceronian construction of a practical morality, see Remer 2017.
[181] Powell-Paterson 2004: 20–3 (on the defense of Gabinius in 54 BCE as an illuminating case of political "reconciliation": 21 and n81).
[182] Powell-Paterson 2004: 24.
[183] Cic. *Off.* 2.51: *Iudicis est semper in causis verum sequi, patroni est non numquam verisimile, etiamsi minus sit verum, defendere*. Text and translation of Cicero's *De officiis*: Miller 1913.
[184] Gotoff 1993b: 312–3.

In Cicero's "over-arching rhetorical strategy,"[185] aimed at winning the audience's benevolence and stirring emotions,[186] manipulation or even distortion of the truth was the most effective means of persuasion. "Truth was just a ploy."[187] Cicero's courtroom tactic well exploits the basic tension between truth and rhetorical exposition of the case. In close similarity to the dramatist, Cicero, as a *disertus* and *eloquens* orator, fabricated his own reality and achieved credibility "by means of a convincing cast of characters and a seemingly inevitable set of circumstances."[188] Since judicial and political oratory's success resided in the orator's power of persuasion, there are no parameters within which we can measure the sincerity of the words uttered by the speaker. In oratorical and political contests, the jury had to be prevented from distinguishing truth from falsehood. What was believed to be true or not was crucial to victory. Most importantly, telling the truth was not the orator's business. His final goal was to win the case. The good speaker knew that his success depended on the degree and extent of manipulation of truth, a key factor in achieving a positive response from the audience.[189]

Naturally, urbanity of language and irony participate to a large degree in the creation of a successful illusion and "a temporarily plausible reality."[190] Cicero himself makes it clear that urbanity, as a virtue proper to oratory, does not correspond to sincerity.[191] In the second book of the *De oratore* Crassus voices his view in these terms (2.269–70): "irony is also urbane, when things are said otherwise than as you feel" (*urbana etiam dissimulatio est, cum alia dicuntur ac sentias*).[192] An urbane speech "involves dissimulation or a visible (audible) difference between what you mean and what you say."[193] Another eloquent passage, again from the third book of the *De*

---

[185] Wisse 2002b: 387.    [186] Cic. *de Orat.* 2.310.    [187] Gotoff 1993b: 297.
[188] Gotoff 1993b: 290.
[189] Cicero himself makes it plain that, if the circumstances of the case demand it, the advocate may take a position that is opposite to his own. Cf. *Clu.* 139: *Sed errat vehementer, si quis in orationibus nostris, quas in iudiciis habuimus, auctoritates nostras consignatas se habere arbitratur. Omnes enim illae causarum ac temporum sunt, non hominum ipsorum aut patronorum. Nam si causae ipsae pro se loqui possent, nemo adhiberet oratorem* ("But if anyone supposes that, in the speeches which we have delivered in the court, we have expressed our certified opinions, he makes the greatest possible mistake. All those speeches reflect the demands of some particular case or emergency, not the individual personality of the advocate. For if a case could speak for itself no one would employ a pleader"). Text and translation of Cicero's *pro Cluentio*: Hodge 1927.
[190] Gotoff 1993b: 290.
[191] For urbanity and humor in oratory, see also Quint. *Inst.* 6.3.102–12. On the Ciceronian notion of *urbanitas*, still useful is Ramage 1973: 52–76.
[192] Text and translation of Cicero's *De oratore*: Sutton-Rackham 1942.
[193] Miller (P. A.) 2015: 328. See also Vlastos 1991: 28, for the Socratic character of the *eironeía* as feigned ignorance and irony as the "perfect medium for mockery innocent of deceit." Cf. Cic. *de Orat.* 2.270: *Socratem opinor in hac ironia dissimulantiaque longe lepore et humanitate omnibus praestitisse. Genus est perelegans et cum gravitate salsum* ("In this irony and dissimulation Socrates, in my

*oratore* (3.201–8),[194] reproduced in full by Quintilian (*Inst.* 9.1.26–36), illustrates the persuasive effects of stylistic ornaments (figures of thought) on the mind of the hearers. Among the most effective manipulative devices, Crassus (charged with a detailed presentation of figures of language and of thought) lists the deliberate digression, illusion (mockery), exaggeration, overstatement of the truth, figures of hesitation, rhetorical question and self-correction.[195] On the art of dissimulation, "which most easily insinuates itself into people's minds, as it were, and which occurs when you say something different from what you are suggesting" (*quae maxime quasi irrepit in hominum mentes, alia dicentis ac significantis dissimulatio*: 3.203),[196] he recommends it in a conversational speech (rather than in a contentious one).[197]

Oratory, as it emerges from Crassus's and Cicero's words (and Quintilian's later reception), is then the art of manipulation of words, the field of application of artistic, highly stylized and metaphorical language (*artificiosa eloquentia*).[198] It allows in some cases (when necessary) for substitution of falsehood for truth (*dicere falsa pro veris*).[199] The true orator is not a speaker of truth. To use Miller's words, the orator is rather an ironist, who "performs the gap between himself and an ultimately impossible sincerity"[200] and intentionally recurs to figures of thought, verbal artifices and tricks, allegories, and tropes to throw dust into the eyes of his potential hearers and persuade them of the credibility of his assertions. In the sixth book of the *Institutio* Quintilian candidly states that "the peculiar task of the orator arises when the minds of the judges require force to move them, and their thoughts have actually to be led away from the contemplation of the truth" (6.2.5).[201] More importantly, the orator intentionally deceives others, not himself.[202] Another significant passage from Quintilian, inserted into a list of recommendations for current orators, demonstrates that concealment

---

opinion, far excelled all others in charm and humanity. Most elegant is this form and seasoned in seriousness").

[194] Mankin 2011: 290–301.   [195] On this unsystematic catalog, see Fantham 2004: 283–5.
[196] Cic. *Brut.* 292–3; *Orat.* 137; *Ac.* 2.15.
[197] On illusion (*illusio*), a type of allegory in which the meaning is contrary to that suggested by the words, systematized by rhetorical theorists as a performative element and a component essential to the realization of the oration's purpose, cf. Quint. *Inst.* 8.6.54. On irony as a category of allegory, *permutatio*, see *Rhet. Her.* 4.46.
[198] Cic. *Inv.* 1.6; Quint. *Inst.* 2.17.2.   [199] Quint. *Inst.* 2.17.19.   [200] Miller (P. A.) 2015: 334.
[201] *Ubi vero animis iudicum vis adferenda est et ab ipsa veri contemplatione abducenda mens, ibi proprium oratoris opus est.* Cf. also Quint. *Inst.* 12.1.36–9 (for the expediency of false arguments in difficult cases). See Leigh 2004b: 131–4 (for Quintilian's "frank celebration of the delight in emotional effect and of the thrill of subverting any pedantic contemplation of the truth").
[202] Cf. Quint *Inst.* 2.17.20–1 for Cicero's *pro Cluentio* as an example of intentional "oratorical deceit"(*Item orator, cum falso utitur pro vero, scit esse falsum eoque se pro vero uti; non ergo falsam*

of eloquence implicates elegance and virtuosity of the speaker, high literary culture and, above all, an extraordinary capacity for beguiling the judges (*Inst.* 12.9.5):

> Veteribus quidem etiam dissimulare eloquentiam fuit moris, idque M. Antonius praecipit, quo plus dicentibus fidei minusque suspectae advocatorum insidiae forent. Sed illa dissimulari quae tum erat potuit; nondum enim tantum dicendi lumen accesserat ut etiam per obstantia erumperet. Quare artes quidem et consilia lateant et quidquid si deprenditur perit.

"The ancients indeed had the habit of actually concealing eloquence, and Marcus Antonius advises this,[203] as a means of increasing the speaker's credibility and reducing suspicions of advocates' trickery. The eloquence of those days no doubt could be concealed, for there was not as yet that brilliance of oratory that can break through any form of cover. So artifices and stratagems, and anything that cannot survive discovery, should be kept hidden."[204]

Rhetoric of advocacy demands that the advocate's real designs should be masked. True eloquence makes capital out of secrecy.

"Advocacy is a process of persuasion, which takes place over time," as has been observed. Before an unsympathetic audience, the advocate "has first of all to establish his line of communication with the tribunal, and this may require not only that considerable attention should be paid to self-presentation, to flattery of the jury and sometimes to denigration of the opponent's motives, but may also require that the actual points at issue in the case should be initially misrepresented or obscured."[205] This description perfectly fits Cicero's art of disarming his opponent and gaining success, even in the face of hostile conditions, by devising and adapting arguments and commonplaces (*communes loci*)[206] to specific issue contexts and mastering language and style in accordance with the specific needs of

---

*habet ipse opinionem, sed fallit alium. Nec Cicero, cum se tenebras offudisse iudicibus in causa Cluenti gloriatus est, nihil ipse vidit*: ["Similarly an orator, when he substitutes falsehood for the truth, is aware of the falsehood and of the fact that he is substituting it for the truth. He therefore deceives others, but not himself. When Cicero boasted that he had thrown dust in the eyes of the jury in the case of Cluentius, he was far from being blinded himself"]).

[203] Cic. *de Orat.* 2.4.   [204] Cf. also Quint. *Inst.* 2.17.6.   [205] Powell-Paterson 2004: 47.
[206] Cf. Cic. *Inv.* 1.34–43; Quint. *Inst.* 2.1.19; 2.4.22; 27; 5.7.4 (5.1.3 on the general rules for commonplaces to be followed by the orator); 5.13.57; 10.5.12; 11.1.46. For the system of *loci* in Cicero's rhetorical works, see Mortensen 2008. The scholiasts call attention to Cicero's use of commonplaces in a number of cases: e.g. schol. Bob. 78.30St (on Cic. *Sul.* 17: *locus verecundiae*; for the deployment of the *locus communis contra testes* in *Sul.* 79, see Berry 1996a: 292); 164.15St (on Cic. *Planc.* 68: *locus generalis de animi religione*); schol. Gronov. **D** 310.3St (on Cic. *Rosc.* 61; *locus communis de parricidio*). Cf. also schol. Bob. 109.11St, on the *locus communis de superbia*, applied to the description of Capua in Cic. *Agr.* 1.18; 20 and *Red. Sen.* 17.

the case. So it was the cunning and intelligence of the orator, his talent in distorting truth and manipulating the audience, at the center of a typical reading of a speech of Cicero. To students of rhetoric, the speeches of Cicero offered "examples of the techniques for enchanting audiences, discomfiting opponents, changing minds and winning in argument and debate."[207] Cicero appeared to be the living embodiment of oratorical virtuosity. He was destined to arouse admiration throughout the centuries as a clever deviser/manipulator of arguments and a consummate speaker, the model of an advocate expected to mislead the jury and elicit emotions in the audience, by means of linguistic devices, in order to win approval.

Rhetoric as a weapon of deceit may well serve as a conceptual guideline for interpreting and penetrating the goals towards which Cicero directed his verbal efforts in any part of the speech. The notion of advocacy as the art of illusion is intrinsic to Cicero's strategy of persuasion. As mentioned, astuteness (*astutia*) in the devising and arrangement of arguments,[208] not rarely in deviation from the recommended standard order of rhetorical structure, and the strategic use of linguistic devices as a means of enchanting audiences and deceiving the opponent had been recognized as distinctive features of Cicero's art of oratory since antiquity. Quintilian, ancient rhetorical theorists and late commentators foregrounded – and idealized – the importance of Cicero's advocacy as "the art of irony and illusion," a sophisticated and learned act of both self-fashioning and intentional deceit realized by artistic manipulation of pre-planned arguments.[209]

We proceed now with our understanding of ancient interpretations of Cicero's manipulative art of persuasion. Once equipped with a sufficient, preliminary knowledge of the legal, political and rhetorical frameworks by which the *causa* was structured, students were being guided through the speech as an example of artful deception and clever manipulation of the minds of listeners/readers, starting with what was usually styled the *principium* or *exordium*, the introductory portion of an oratorical text. Divided into the normal *exordium* (called *principium*), and the special *exordium* (named *insinuatio*, mostly for the *genus admirabile*),[210] a good, normal

---

[207] Gotoff 1993b: 297.
[208] For the notion of *astutia oratoria* in late scholiasts, cf. supra p 218, n172.
[209] The rhetorical theories of the "arguments by comparison" (*parabole* in Aristotle, *collatio* in Cicero, *similitudo* in Quintilian) point unequivocally to the presence of the concept of "obscurity" and "deception" lying behind the rhetorical and political functions assigned to illustrative fables and hypothetical comparisons. See McCormick 2014.
[210] *Rhet. Her.* 1.4; Cic. *Inv.* 1.20; Quint. *Inst.* 4.1.1; Grill. 86.1–88.26Jakobi; Lausberg 1998: 121–36 (§§ 263–88).

*exordium*, fashioned in line with πρέπον theory,[211] aims to "render the audience well-disposed, attentive and ready to receive instruction" (*iudicem benevolum, docilem, attentum parare*).[212] It is intended to arouse sympathy and benevolence of the judge by means of *perspicuitas* ("clarity of exposition").[213]

Quintilian's ample exploration of prooimial topics in the fourth book of the *Institutio* informs us about the rhetorical use of linguistic and intellectual devices for influencing the audience. In the footsteps of the greatest orators,[214] he lays down the rules for a correct *exordium* and delves into Cicero's oratorical *corpus* to supply students with significant examples of "conciliatory" *exordia*. In listing some of the most useful devices for acquiring good will, Quintilian points to the celebrated opening of the *pro Milone* as a model *exordium* built upon the judges' fear, aroused by the sight of Pompey's soldiers stationed around the court.[215] Interestingly, the *exordium* of the *pro Milone* serves also as a specimen of how the tone should be varied in vocal delivery. When illustrating the art of producing variety (*ars variandi*) and "adapting the voice to suit the nature of the various subjects on which we are speaking and the moods that they demand" (*secundum rationem rerum, de quibus dicimus, animorumque habitus conformanda vox est*: *Inst.* 11.3.45), Quintilian offers the opening of the *oratio nobilissima pro Milone* ("Cicero's magnificent speech in defense of Milo") as an outstanding demonstration of oratorical power built on variation of tone and facial expression *ad singulas paene distinctiones* ("almost at every stop": 11.3.47). Delivered in an atmosphere of intimidation, Cicero's introductory words of his defense of Milo reflect the speaker's sense of anxiety.[216] Notwithstanding the trial's hostile conditions, Cicero displayed boldness and vigor of tone and adapted his *respiratio* ("breath") and voice to the needs of each single moment of his delivery (11.3.47–9).[217]

---

[211] Quint. *Inst.* 4.1.52: Lausberg 1998: 121 (§ 264).
[212] Cic. *Inv.* 1.20; *Rhet. Her.* 1.6; Quint. *Inst.* 4.1.5. On the Roman theory of the *exordium*, see Prill 1986; Loutsch 1994: 21ff. (see also Calboli Montefusco 1988: 8–17).
[213] A re-formulation of the basic, classic theory of the *exordium* is to be found in the *argumentum* to *Ver.* 2.1 in the Gronovian scholiast (**B**): 341.18–342.2St. See also the explanation of the exordial technique in the fifth-century commentary on Cicero's *De inventione* by Grillius (86.1Jakobi).
[214] Quint. *Inst.* 4.1.12.
[215] Quint. *Inst.* 4.1.20; cf. also 4. 1. 31; schol. Bob. 112.5-10St; schol. Gronov (**B**) 323.14-8St. Similarly, the orator may be obliged to bring fear to bear upon the judges, as happens in the invectives against Verres (*Inst.* 4.1.21).
[216] Quint. *Inst.* 11.3.48.
[217] Further references to the *pro Milone* in Quintilian's *Institutio*: 3.6.12 and 93; 4.5.15; 5.14.22; 6.5.10; 7.2.43; 9.2.38; 10.5.20; 11.1.34 and 40; 11.3.115 and 167.

Sometimes external circumstances, relevant to the case, might usefully be capitalized on by the orator in constructing a creditable *exordium*. Such was the case of the proem to the *pro Caelio*, in which the chronological framework of the trial, exceptionally taking place during a public festival, the *Ludi Megalenses* (time usually imposing suspension of business) is "theatrically" and comically exploited by Cicero to mark the contradiction between the professed gravity of the prosecution of Caelius, a distinguished *adulescens* brought to trial under the legal charges of the *lex Plautia de vi*, and the irrelevance of the matters at issue,[218] too insignificant to force the judges to operate in the court in holiday times.[219] Analogously, the unusual *locus* in which Cicero delivered his speech in defense of the king Deiotarus (Caesar's private home), the extraordinary *habitus* of the trial ("appearance of the court") in the *pro Milone* and the public expectation surrounding Verres's trial (*opinio*) might satisfy the orator's preliminary needs for the compassion and benevolence of the judges.[220]

Quintilian provides abundant Ciceronian examples of exordial devices for appealing to the audience's benevolence and attracting attention from the jury.[221] The *pro Cluentio* (among Cicero's speeches the one most cited by the Spanish rhetorician)[222] furnishes the best example of an *exordium* that balances the audience's disposition to listen to a long speech and the structural complexity of the case itself (*Inst.* 4.1.34–6).[223] Taking the prosecution speech as his starting point, Cicero elaborated on the partition of the accusation into two main parts (malevolence, *invidia*, following Oppianicus's contested condemnation, and the question of the charge of poisoning, touched upon "with a certain timidity and diffidence," *timide et diffidenter*), reassuring the judges about his intention not to diverge from the legal treatment of each point. Similar cases, Quintilian adds, motivate a "proposition-*exordium*," a statement of willingness, more than a detailed

---

[218] Cicero's irony in presenting the prosecution of Caelius as a trivial one is stressed by Quintilian at a further point, when he calls attention to the orator's strategical distortion of the adversaries' arguments and words in the exordial lines (successfully used in the *pro Ligario*): cf. *Inst.* 4.1.38–9.

[219] Leigh 2004a: 302 ("Cicero founds his defence on a strategy of trivialization, on the bid to make the jury believe that what is at issue is rather less than his opponents have made out"). On comedy and theatrical features in the speech, see generally Geffcken 1973. On the *exordium* of the *pro Caelio* see Dyck 2013: 58–64 (also Austin 1960: 41–5).

[220] Quint. *Inst.* 4.1.31.

[221] As one might expect, Cicero was criticized for the monotony and tediousness of some exordial portions of his youthful speeches (Tac. *Dial.* 22.3, *lentus in principiis*, "tedious in his introductions").

[222] Mazzoli 1996 (see also La Bua 2006: 185–6).

[223] Cf. also Mar. Vict. 198.10 *RLM*; on the *exordium* of the *pro Cluentio*, see Classen 1965; Patimo 2009: 73–81 (with further bibliography).

expository *exordium*.²²⁴ Cicero refrained from "describing how each thing occurred" (*quomodo quidque sit actum*), simply indicating "the points on which he proposes to speak" (*de quibus dicturus sit*). In so doing, he managed marvelously to achieve maximum attention from the judges, accomplishing the defender's double task to instruct his listeners and render them attentive and ready to look upon the defense's argumentation with favor.²²⁵

In what may be defined as a "scandalous kind of cause" (*turpe genus causae*: *Inst*. 4.1.40), the good speaker should "insinuate himself little by little into the minds of his judges" (*insinuatio surrepat animis*: 4.1.42).²²⁶ Depending on the individual nature of each case, he should concentrate on "those points which are likely to be of profit" (*ad ea quae prosunt refugiamus*: 4.1.44), relying on the character of the client or the peculiar circumstances of the case;²²⁷ again, in those cases calling for insinuation it may be also advantageous to display wit, alleviating the spirits of bored judges, or anticipating the objections raised by the opponents, as Cicero did in the opening lines of the *Divinatio in Caecilium* (4.1.49).²²⁸ At the outset of the speech *pro Rabirio Postumo*, according to Quintilian (*Inst*. 4.1.46), Cicero addressed the jurors hearing the case by depicting himself as a "reliable" and trustworthy advocate, experiencing mental and physical pain for his client's foolhardy, though human (and hence justifiable), conduct. While acknowledging Postumus to be culpable of extortion, he was "engaging in a calculated ploy to forestall objection."²²⁹ He conveyed the impression of acting in defense of a "victim of bad fortune," founding his plea on the appeal to a humane understanding of the errors and imperfections that are intrinsic to man's nature. It might also be added that the speech *pro Rabirio Postumo* provides a good case study of Cicero's duplicity in handling emotional and intellectual arguments to influence his audience. At *Inst*. 3.6.11, Quintilian's treatment of the *simplex causa*, the "simple cause"

---

[224] Quint. *Inst*. 4.1.35.   [225] Quint. *Inst*. 4.1.36–7.
[226] On the *genus obscurum causae* and the *occultatio negotii* in the proem to the speech *pro Tullio*, see La Bua 2005.
[227] In the *gratiarum actio* to the People, upon his return from exile, Cicero builds the *exordium* on a divine transfiguration of his restitution to the civic community, presenting his *misera profectio* as an act of *devotio* and depicting his recall as a "divine and eternal *beneficium*," expression of the protection of the city gods: cf. schol. Bob. 110.15ff. St.
[228] A typical case of *dissimulatio artis* in a special exordium (*insinuatio*) occurs in the *pro Cluentio*, as explicitly stated by Quintilian (*Inst*. 9.2.19), who points to the dubitative expression *quo me vertam nescio* (§ 4) as a deceptive device, aimed at convincing the judges of the presumptive extemporariness of the speech. Cf. also Romanus Aquila 25.11 *RLM*; Mart. Cap. 183 Willis; *Schem. Dian.* 75.4 *RLM*.
[229] Siani-Davies 2001: 110.

(standing on one main *status*, the "basis," which the orator considers the most important point for his defense), makes use of Cicero's oration as an instance of *conflictio causarum*, "conflict of causes." The first portion of the text, in which Cicero "contends that the action cannot lie against a Roman knight" (*in hoc intendit, ut actionem competere in equitem Romanum neget*), appears to be contradicted by the second section, where the orator asserts that "no money ever came into the client's hands" (*nullam ad eum pecuniam pervenisse*). This latter argument is much stronger than the former, Quintilian affirms, since denial of the facts (*non fecit*) proves always to be a more forceful line of defense;[230] similarly in the case of Milo, in which the orator exerts himself to demonstrate "that Clodius lay in wait for Milo and was therefore rightly killed" (*ubi totis viribus insidiator Clodius ideoque iure interfectus ostenditur.* 3.6.12).

Quintilian's insistence on the nature and character of the *exordium* (the *ratio prooemii*) is naturally not devoid of practical, pedagogical implications. As a teacher, his preoccupation was with showing to his pupils how a good *exordium* should be composed (*Inst.* 4.1.52–3):

> Verum quoniam non est satis demonstrare discentibus, quae sint in ratione prooemii, sed dicendum etiam, quomodo perfici facillime possint, hoc adiicio, ut dicturus intueatur, quid, apud quem, pro quo, contra quem, quo tempore, quo loco, quo rerum statu, qua vulgi fama dicendum sit, quid iudicem sentire credibile sit, antequam incipimus, tum quid aut desideremus aut deprecemur. Ipsa illum natura eo ducet, ut sciat, quid primum dicendum sit. 53. At nunc omne, quo coeperunt, prooemium putant et, ut quidque succurrit, utique si aliqua sententia blandiatur, exordium. Multa autem sine dubio sunt et aliis partibus causae communia, nihil tamen in quaque melius dicitur, quam quod aeque bene dici alibi non possit.

> "It is not, however, sufficient to explain the nature of the *exordium* to our pupils. We must also indicate the easiest method of composing an *exordium*. I would therefore add that he who has a speech to make should consider what he has to say; before whom, in whose defense, against whom, at what time and place, under what circumstances he has to speak; what is the popular opinion on the subject, and what the prepossessions of the judge are likely to be; and finally of what we should express our deprecation or desire. Nature herself will give him the knowledge of what he ought to say first. (53). Nowadays, however, speakers think that anything with which they choose to start is a *proem* and that whatever occurs to them, especially if it be a reflection that catches their fancy, is an *exordium*. There are, no doubt, many points that can be introduced into an *exordium* which are common to

---

[230] Cf. also Quint. *Inst.* 4.2.10.

other parts of a speech, but the best test of the appropriateness of a point to any part of a speech is to consider whether it would lose effect by being placed elsewhere."

Quintilian's short, but still detailed register of the points that a budding young orator should consider before launching into composing an *exordium* summarizes the virtues of a good, Ciceronian *exordium*, a both attractive and effective form of improvised proem drawing on the speech of the opponent, producing pleasing effects through simplicity and efficacy of thoughts, style, voice and facial expression (4.1.54–7).

Quintilian's disquisition on the exordial topic also gives due emphasis to style matters. A good *exordium* must not merely instruct the judges, it must also charm and "hypnotize" them by means of a simple and unpremeditated (though elaborate) style, naturally rich in its stylistic and linguistic construction (refusing any unusual word or poetic license). As the *exordium* is, by its very nature, addressed to the judges whose favor the orator aims to win, it may be of some utility to render the prooemial tone more forceful and vehement by recurring to some figures of thought, such as the "apostrophe" (ἀποστροφή, *aversio*).[231] Inspired by his Greek model Demosthenes, Cicero adopted this device in several of his speeches.[232] In the *pro Ligario*, in particular, the expression *Habes igitur, Tubero, quod est accusatori maxime optandum* ("You are, then, in possession, Tubero, of the most desirable advantage that can fall to an accuser": § 2), an unexpected turn and diversion of the orator's words, from the jury to the person of the prosecutor, would have been much less powerful and efficacious if it had been addressed to the judges. Conversely, such a figure (focused upon the audience) would have been deprived of force if the orator had said *Habet igitur Tubero* ("Tubero is then in possession"), limiting himself to simply pointing out a fact (4.1.68).

Again, Quintilian relies on Ciceronian examples to train his pupils in making a proper use of the *apostrophe* and other rhetorical artifices or figures.[233] The famous opening of the First Catilinarian, with its impassioned *Quousque tandem abutere?*, best exemplifies the pathetic effects of the figure of address on the proem of a political speech (4.1.68). A *prosopopoeia* (*fictio personae*) is placed at the beginning of the lost speech

---

[231] Quint. *Inst.* 4.1.64.
[232] Schol. Bob. 126.29-32St (on *Sest.* 10); Ps. Ascon. 230.10-2St (on *Verr.* 2.1.25).
[233] For the use of the *congeminatio* ("doubling") in the proem to the *pro Flacco* (in the pathetic formulation *Si umquam res publica consilium gravitatem sapientiam iudicum imploravit, hoc, hoc, inquam, tempore implorat* in chapter 3 of the speech) cf. schol. Bob. 94.1-2St (also 94.18 on the device of the *addubitatio*, "expression of doubt").

on behalf of Scaurus (charged under bribery); *exempla* are usefully employed in the *pro Rabirio Postumo* and the preserved *pro Scauro* on the charge of extortion, while the "division into heads" (*partitio*) is introduced in the *pro Cluentio* (4.1.69). Other devices, such as metaphors, similes or tropes, usually banned in the *exordia*, may be deployed at times in specific contexts. Illustrative is the case of the *pro Ligario*, a magnificent model of rhetorical irony (4.1.70).[234]

Cicero's *auctoritas* guides Quintilian (and the ideal teacher) through the rhetorical artifices needed to create a correct, persuasive proem. As an undisputed authority on Latin prose, Cicero supplies the rhetorician with material for thematic and linguistic analysis of the *exordium*, offering him the opportunity for a critical discussion of a significant point of the exordial system. What is more, in explaining a good Ciceronian *exordium* Quintilian automatically encourages his students to compose their *exordia* in line with Ciceronian theory and practice.[235] He calls attention, specifically, to the exordial technique as an aspect (though a relevant one) of oratory as the art of insinuation. Winning benevolence or favor from the judges requires that the orator make use, when necessary, of rhetorical stratagems, vital elements in the process of preparation of the jury's mind.

Quintilian also makes it plain that a good *exordium* aims to control the audience and persuade the jury to attend with docile eyes by combining emotional and intellectual appeal and adapting different exordial patterns to the unique conditions of the case. Rhetorical theory (with its standard list of ingredients) "was merely a convenient formula, not a prescriptive rule."[236] There was the possibility of alterations in the standard exordial

---

[234] *Non tamen haec, quia possunt bene aliquando fieri, passim facienda sunt, sed quotiens praeceptum vicerit ratio; quomodo et similitudine, dum brevi, et translatione atque aliis tropis (quae omnia cauti illi ac diligentes prohibent) utemur interim, nisi cui divina illa pro Ligario ironia, de qua paulo ante dixeram, displicet* ("Still such artifices, although they may be employed at times to good effect, are not to be indulged in indiscriminately, but only when there is strong reason for breaking the rule. The same remark applies to *simile*, which must however be brief, *metaphor* and other *tropes*, all of which are forbidden by our cautious and pedantic teachers of rhetoric, but which we shall none the less occasionally employ, unless indeed we are to disapprove of the magnificent example of irony in the *pro Ligario* to which I have already referred a few pages back").

[235] Quintilian ends his long discussion about the *exordium* with some Ciceronian examples of "pseudo-exordia," or portions of the speech that have an introductory function and *exordium*-like force, though they are inserted in other parts, such as the *narratio*, 'statement of facts,' in the *argumentatio* or in the presentation of proofs (*probationes*): 4.1.72–9. Such is the case of the *pro Vareno* (frg. 9; see Crawford 1994: 17) or the passage of the *pro Cluentio* (§ 117), where Cicero announces that he would be attacking the censors; similarly, in the *pro Murena* (§ 7) Cicero offers his apologies (*se excusat*) to Servius (4.1.75; on this sub-prologue in the *pro Murena*, see Leeman 1982: 205n1). Chapter 11 of the *pro Cluentio*, finally, is, to Quintilian, a good example of transition from the *exordium* to the statement of facts (4.1.79).

[236] Powell-Paterson 2004: 46.

theory in accordance with the political, legal and rhetorical specificities of the case. Cicero's authority allowed for some exceptions. His speeches showed students how to break with the rules, when permitted by the *ratio*. Yet Quintilian takes pains to justify and rationalize any deviation from the approved, ordinary rule. It is tempting to say that Cicero's oratory was not only a source of norms and precepts of rhetoric, which the students should apprehend and conform to. It was also a precious handbook of case-study departures from the standard theory, reflecting re-adaptation of general topics to disparate situations in the prosecution case. The teacher's responsibility was to illustrate the sense (and function) of any diversion, authorized by the model and icon of Roman prose, thus inspiring students to follow different patterns of argumentation when needed.

The definition of advocacy as "play of dissimulation and deception" seems much more appropriate when dealing with the *narratio*, "statement of facts," or what modern theorists and writers generally call "narrative."[237] It was in the very narrative, more than in other parts of the speech, that truth might potentially be irrelevant to the advocate.[238] Before fleshing this issue out, however, it seems necessary to spend some preliminary words on the rhetorical theory of the *narratio*. As documented by instructional manuals on rhetoric as well as by extant Roman speeches, in the *narratio* (usually following straight after the *prohoemium*)[239] the orator contrived to achieve credibility for himself and his client by propounding a "simple, short, clear and lucid" exposition of the events, to be proved in the subsequent *argumentatio* or discussion of the legal issues.[240] In the guise of both a biased description of the events before the court and digression (in the judicial speech),[241] the *narratio* had as its primary goal *docere*, "to

---

[237] Levene 2004: 117 (n2).
[238] On the question see the illuminating pages of Powell-Paterson 2004: 25ff.
[239] Quintilian reckons with the often debated issue concerning the correct placement of the narrative at *Inst*. 4.2.24–30. Though admitting alterations of the normal order of the parts of the speech under specific circumstances (as happens for the postponement of the narrative in the "magnificent published defense of Milo," in the *pro Vareno* and in the *pro Caelio*: 4.2.25–7; cf. also Sulpicius Victor 426.9–21 *RLM*; schol. Bob. 112.20–113.8St), Quintilian re-establishes the "practice of the schools," *scholarum consuetudo*, as his guiding principle. Since specified themes, *certa themata*, are posed before the eyes of students practicing declamatory exercises, no changes (or deviations) must be allowed (*nihil est diluendum*) and the narrative always comes after the *exordium* (4.2.28–30).
[240] On the three *virtutes* of the *narratio* (clarity, brevity and plausibility), cf. *Rhet. Her.* 1.14–7; Cic. *Inv.* 1.19; 27–8; *De Or.* 2.83; 2.326–30; *Orat.* 122; *Part. Or.* 31–2; *Top.* 97; Quint. *Inst.* 4.2.31. See Lausberg 1998: 136–60 (§§ 289–347).
[241] It should be noted that Quintilian precedes his theory of narrative with pointed comments about unsubstantiated interpretation of *narratio* as a fixed part of the case (*Inst.* 4.2.4–23). Several instances may be adduced, Quintilian says, to demonstrate that there are "reasons for leaving out the narrative" (*non narrandi causas*: 4.2.9). At the same time, the view of Cornelius Celsus, who

instruct," the audience and attain plausibility (*narratio verisimilis*) by means of brevity and clarity (*narratio brevis et lucida*). Rhetorical theory recommended the use of the three canonical qualities, *virtutes*, of the narrative and their accorded (stylistic) aims throughout the speech (thereby not only associated with the narrative).[242] Nonetheless, theorists saw these qualities as peculiar to the *narratio*. Clarity as a prime virtue of narratives was conventionally expected as matching the standards of rhetorical correctness, demanded to win the audience's favor and support for the speaker's exposition (either true or false) of the facts.[243] As Levene has observed, clarity of narration admits no exceptions.[244] Though handling the matter in deviance from the established rules, the orator was required to produce an account accessible to its presumed hearers, stimulating them to perceive the narrative as a straightforward, morally correct, version of the facts.

Given that plainness and simplicity were commonly associated with masculinity and morality, the persuasive force of a narration rested on merging intelligibility and plausibility with ethics, a combination of theoretical preconceptions and moral code that satisfied the reader's need for an objective, clear and plain exposition of the events.[245] Though potentially admitting deviation from the rule, as said, the primary function of the *narratio* was to preserve – and convey – the sense of correctness and credibility, achieved through plain, moral language.[246] As has been noted, "at Rome in particular, where moral simplicity formed part of the traditional cultural self-image, a positive portrayal of rhetoric is likely to be one that has incorporated such an image within its theory, and ignored or downplayed the alternatives. And given that the theory was presented in such a manner, a person who read speeches for rhetorical training, with

---

held that "there is no narrative when the defendant merely denies the charge" (*non ... esse narrationem cum reus quod obicitur tantum negat*), an opinion basically founded on inspection of cases of bribery and extortion, is refused on the ground that forensic cases may contemplate different types of narrative (even long ones), in accordance with the number of charges (4.2.10–6). Quintilian lists, then, examples of narrative, "not belonging to the cause itself but relevant to it" (*pertinentes ad causam sed non ipsius causae narrationis*: 4.2.17–8). Such is the case with Cic. *Ver.* 2.5.7 (the story of L. Domitius), *Rab. Post.* 28, and *Ver.* 5.26–8 (Verres's journey). Fictitious narratives may sometimes be introduced to arouse emotions (Cic. *Rosc.* 50) or relieve the judges from anxiety by means of humoristic or ornamental, non-functional digressions (*Cluent.* 57; *Ver.* 2.4.106; on the passage from the *pro Cluentio* cf. also *Inst.* 6.1.41; 6.3.39–40).

[242] Quint. *Inst.* 4.2.35. See Levene 2004: 141.    [243] Quint. *Inst.* 4.2.35.
[244] Levene 2004. Cf. Quint. *Inst.* 4.2.32; 64–5.
[245] This point naturally enters into the perennial debate over the "moral" connotations of the art of advocacy (on which see Powell-Paterson 2004: 19–29).
[246] McCormick 2014: 158 (on Quintilian's theory of visibility and palpability in the narrative).

rhetorical theory foremost in his mind, would accordingly be liable to construct his reading in a manner exemplifying the theory."[247]

The teacher's duty was then to tutor his pupils in the *ars* or *vis narrationis* by drawing attention to the orator's search for clarity and plainness within a dexterous, ingenious and sophisticated elaboration (and manipulation) of the narrative's features and language.[248] As expected, from Cicero there derives a stock of relevant models of "good" and "virtuous" narrative,[249] mostly responding to the standardized theory of rhetorical narrative,[250] a number of them contemplating deviations from the ordinary rules.[251] Into this latest category we may incorporate Cicero's description of Sassia's marriage in *Cluent.* 15, a test case for insertion of a "digression" (*excursio*) into a narrative (clear and brief by its very nature), legitimated by indignation and the eruption of violent feelings.[252] The passage, a ferocious condemnation of Sassia's *audacia* and *libido* voiced by a triple, emotional *exclamatio*, must also have served as a significant

---

[247] Levene 2004: 145.
[248] On more than one occasion, Quintilian points out that lucidity and clarity are crucial to the statement of facts (*narratio aperta atque dilucida*), pushing the students to use "words which are appropriate, significant and free from any taint of meanness, but not on the other hand farfetched or unusual" (*verbis propriis et significantibus et non sordidis quidem, not tamen exquisitis et ab usu remotis*) and "adapt delivery to matter, so that the judge will take in what we say with the utmost readiness" (*ipsa etiam pronuntiatione in hoc accomodata, ut iudex quae dicentur quam facillime accipiat*: 4.2.36), while avoiding extravagance (*lascivia*) of statement, language and style at the same time. Clarity and simplicity achieve (and enhance) credibility: "it is just when an orator gives the impression of absolute truth that he is speaking best" (*tum autem optime dicit orator, cum videtur vera dicere*: 4.2.38). Cf. also 4.2.40ff.
[249] It should be useful, however, to remind readers of criticism of Cicero's "art of narrative" in the orations delivered in his youth. Cf. Tac. *Dial.* 22.3; see Mayer 2001: 161.
[250] E.g. Cic. *Caec.* 11 (example of *narratio* omitting circumstances that are irrelevant to the case: Quint. *Inst.* 4.2.49); *Lig.* 4 (recapitulation of facts at the end of the narrative: Quint. *Inst.* 4.2.51; cf. also 4.2.108–9 for the insertion of arguments or a brief defense of the case into the statement of facts, as shown by *Lig.* 2–4); *Ver.* 2.5.118 (Quint. *Inst.* 4.2.106); *Cluent.* 36 (credibility of the statements enhanced by a dialogue; Quint. *Inst.* 4.2.107); *Arch.* 5 (*elegantia* of the narrative: schol. Bob. 176.12-5St). For beginnings and ends of the narrative cf. again Quint. *Inst.* 4.2.129–32.
[251] For the "appeal to the emotions" in the statement of facts as an alleged violation of the standard norms of the *narratio* cf. Quint. *Inst.* 4.2.111–24 (who cites Cic. *Ver.* 2.5.62 and 1.30 as effective means of arousing passions in the audience). The commendation of Sestius's father as a wise man at the beginning of the *pro Sestio* (6) is labeled as a "short narrative" (*narratiuncula*) by the Bobbio scholiast (126.11-6St). It should be added here that the Gronovius scholiast **D**, in his commentary on chapter 5 of the *Rosciana*, considers the expression *Forsitan quaeratis* as the beginning of a "special narrative" (*particularis narratio*), a brief explanation of the case, inserted into the *exordium*, whose aim is to render the judges benevolent and docile (303.8St: for the proem of the *pro Sexto Roscio*, see Dyck 2010: 56–8).
[252] Quint. *Inst.* 4.2.104–5 (cf. also Iul. Vict. 426.30 *RLM*, who labels the passage as *excessus*); Patimo 2009: 197–99 (for a stylistic analysis of Cicero's invective on Sassia's *scelus*). For the special and "theatrical" effects of Sassia's defamation in the *pro Cluentio*, see Hall 2014a: 99ff.

collection of rhetorical figures and verbal plays, producing good sound effects. Alliteration, zeugma, the use of homoeoteleuton within a tricolon and antithesis mark Cicero's sentence out (*perfregit ac prostravit omnia cupiditate et furore: vicit pudorem libido, timorem audacia, rationem amentia*)[253] as a refined example of rhythmical, highly elaborated, and emotionally charged style.[254]

All the same, Cicero himself and Quintilian pointed to the need for false arguments in problematic cases,[255] especially those in which the jury was far from being on the orator's side. As has been stated, "the overwhelming tendency of Latin rhetorical theory is to focus almost exclusively on persuading that jury, and constructing the detail of one's speech with the jury in mind."[256] Under such conditions, a fabricated narrative only apparently contrasted with the profession of reliability and truthfulness, which stands as the theoretical and moral underpinning of the art of advocacy. It was often the case that a prosecution or defense speech needed adaptation of the facts (and manipulation of the truth accordingly) to the circumstances of the trial, especially before evidence of wrongdoing from the accused. To exemplify this point, I select here a passage from the fourth book of Quintilian's work (*Inst.* 4.2.57–9), which explores the *narratio* of the *pro Milone* as an example of Cicero's first-class virtues as narrator. The key point is Cicero's "cunning and astute feint of simplicity" (*callidissima simplicitatis imitatio*) in depicting Milo's serenity and absence of premeditation in the murder of Clodius (*Mil.* 28). Cicero's intention to procure the jury's goodwill and benevolence is favored, in Quintilian's view, by the preliminary presentation of Milo as an unsuspecting victim of Clodius's violence (*praemunitio* or *praestructio*).[257] He achieves credibility (and secures approval from the judges) through a concealed and artful use of narrative devices, which conjure up the innocence and purity of the prosecuted. By means of ordinary, familiar words and "a careful concealment of his art" (*arte occulta*) the great orator, *vir eloquentissimus*, attracts attention to Milo's morality and succeeds in deluding the judges,

---

[253] "She broke down and overthrew everything in her passion and her madness: lust conquered shame, boldness fear, madness reason."
[254] Quint. *Inst.* 9.3.61; 77; 81.  [255] Cic. *Off.* 2.51; Quint. *Inst.* 12.1.36.  [256] Levene 2004: 122.
[257] Cf. also schol. Bob. 119.26St (on *Mil.* 24): *Vigilantissime praeparationibus instructa narratio est* ("The narrative has been forged by means of some preliminary remarks with extreme alertness"); 120.5–6 St. (on *Mil.* 28): *Simul et ad innocentiam Milonis et ad cogitationem sceleratam P. Clodii ferenda praestructio est* ("The narrative is constructed by way of preparation to demonstrate both Milo's innocence and Clodius's criminal thoughts").

primed to receive his reconstruction of the facts with sympathetic eyes.[258]

The narrative of the *pro Milone*, referred to elsewhere in Quintilian's treatise,[259] must have been seen as emblematic of the art of *deceptio*, as may be easily deduced from the comment of the Bobbio scholiast on *Mil.* 29 (120.15-19St):

> Statim complures in hunc faciunt de loco superiore impetum] Pars haec narrationis aliquanto turbatior est; sine dubio in ea multa finguntur. Verum hanc omnem confusissimam permixtionem cursim pratervolat: non enim debent cum mora protrahi quae videri iudicibus possunt aliquod habere figmentum, ne orator, si laciniosus sit, in mendacio deprehendatur.

> "Immediately a number of men attack him from the higher ground] This part of the narrative seems to be somewhat confused. There is no doubt that Cicero counterfeited a lot in it. He passed quickly over this jumbled mixture of events, for arguments that might appear to the judges as containing fictional elements should not be treated lengthily so that the orator might avoid being accused of lying (especially, if he showed himself as blundering in speaking)."

Conscious of pleading a legally difficult case before a hostile audience, Cicero felt it necessary to blur the boundaries between reality and fiction, bewildering and confusing the judges by eliminating or passing over arguments and aspects relevant to the presentation of the violent, fatal confrontation between Clodius's and Milo's armed gangs (or touching upon them rapidly). As clarified by the commentator's use of words related to the semantics of fiction (*finguntur ... figmentum ... mendacium*), the narrative

---

[258] Quint. *Inst.* 4.2.59: *Frigere videntur ista plerisque, sed hoc ipso manifestum est, quomodo iudicem fefellerit, quod vix a lectore deprehenditur. Haec sunt quae credibilem faciant expositionem* ("The majority of readers regard this passage as lacking in distinction, but this very fact merely serves to show how the art which is scarce detected by a reader succeeded in hoodwinking the judge. It is qualities of this kind that make the statement of facts credible"). It is important to note that Quintilian also calls attention to the use of "magnificence of diction" (*magnificentia*, μεγαλοπρέπειαν) as a stylistic expedient in the *narratio* of the *pro Milone* (4.2.61).

[259] *Inst.* 4.2.121 (the sentence *Fecerunt servi Milonis, quod suos quisque servos in tali re facere voluisset*, in *Mil.* 29 is approved of as refreshing the judge's jaded palate; cf. also Sulp. Vict. 427.15 *RLM*); 5.10.50 (the presentation of Clodius, not Milo, as a potential murderer, as he had instruments – and then the will – to act, in the narrative of the *pro Milone* provides a limpid example of "argument of reasoning," based on considering the resources possessed by the parties involved in the case); 7.1.34-7 (the *narratio* enhances its credibility by means of a process of elimination of all possible arguments advanced by the opponent). On the *narratio* of the *pro Milone* as an instance of "clear narrative" (*aperta narratio*) cf. Sulp. Vict. 323.14 *RLM* (on *Mil.* 24); on the appearance of reality and verisimilitude in the narrative, achieved through manipulation of arguments, 323.21-5 *RLM*. Cf. also Iul. Sev. 361.26 *RLM* (on *Mil.* 26).

of the *pro Milone* is just an amalgam of made-up facts and reality, a deceitful (implausible) re-invention of a real conflict, leading the judges to receive the assassination of Clodius as a praiseworthy and moral act of self-defense. Cicero's narrative, a purportedly transparent but manipulative version of real events, implicitly refuses the hallmark of credibility. As Dyck explains, "the awkward gaps in the *narratio* of the *pro Milone* point to a weakness of the cause itself: Cicero simply could not have incorporated the fact of Milo's deliberate order of Clodius' death into a case based on self-defence against *insidiae*."[260]

The vivid account of the battle of Bovillae,[261] a blend of real and false assertions, points to Cicero's sagacity, as stressed by the scholiast in a later comment (120.27–121.8St):

> Partim recurrere ad raedam, ut a tergo adorirentur Milonem]
> Ἐνάργεια coacervatur plena sine dubio falsae adseverationis, quippe vult ita praestruere, ut servi nihil imperante domino fecerint. Et considerato statim miram prudentiam, quod ita narrationem summaverit: Cum dominum crederent interemtum,
> Fecerunt id servi Milonis,]
> Deinde κατ' ἐπένθεσιν
> <Dicam enim aperte non derivandi> criminis causa, sed ut factum est: nec imperante domino nec sciente:]
> ibidemque continuo κλέμμα subiunxit, id est furtum quoddam invidiose commemorationis, quoniam consequens erat ut dicerent: "occiderunt inimicum domini sui." Sed cautius multo existimavit λεληθότως hoc perstringere sic desinendo:
> Fecerunt id quod suos quisque servos ...]

"Some of them ran back towards his chariot in order to attack Milo from behind]
Vividness, [this part] is no doubt filled with false statements, as he (Cicero) aims to prepare the judges so that they think that the servants did it without their master commanding it. And let us consider immediately the orator's remarkable sagacity, as he recapitulated the narrative in such a way: Because they thought that he was slain
The servants of Milo did it]
Then by means of insertion
I am not speaking for the purpose of shifting the guilt onto the shoulders of others, but I am saying what really occurred: they did it, without their master either commanding it, or knowing it]:

---

[260] Dyck 1998: 227.
[261] On the technique of the *evidentia* as a virtue of the *narratio*, adding force and credibility to a truthful exposition of the facts, cf. Quint. *Inst.* 4.2.64–5 (also 8.3.61).

> And there he immediately added (and made use of) an artifice, that is the concealment of an action that may arouse feelings of hate as it was brought to mind, for it would have been a natural consequence that they could say: 'they killed the enemy of their master'. But he used much more circumspection: he thought it useful to furtively and rapidly touch on it by concluding with these words:
> They did what everyone would have wished his servants to do ...]"

In a compressed recapitulation of the key moments of Clodius's murder, Cicero captures the jury's imagination by revitalizing the action of Milo's servants as a noble, "heroic" deed. By means of a continual replication of the dominant role chosen by the servants in the mortal combat, only momentarily interrupted by his voice as narrator (inviting the audience to "appreciate" the truthfulness of his own account), Cicero covers reality up and guides his intended hearers through a false, distorted comprehension of the facts. Cicero's speech in support of Milo teaches, in a word, how to mystify the judges, in a case of patent violation of law and thereby in absence of proofs supporting the professed innocence of the prosecuted. It displays the orator's sagacity and *consilium* in matching his plea to the specific circumstances of the case, by passing by in silence or postponing dangerous arguments or adopting a particular line of defense. Dyck again observes that "Cicero himself was in deadly earnest about the rightness of his cause and was staking his reputation as an advocate and a repayer of *beneficia*."[262] So, Cicero had to ponder individual arguments, sidestepping "a series of pitfalls that could have trapped a lesser advocate"[263] and basing his plea of self-defense on a misleading re-visitation of the fight at Bovillae, a necessary preparation to the subsequent depiction of Milo as a "rescuer of the country."

On this ground, the *pro Milone* instances Cicero's astonishing capacity for manipulating – and distorting – the truth, as reaffirmed by Quintilian in the sixth book (*Inst.* 6.5.10):[264]

> Quid pro Milone? Quod non ante narravit, quam praeiudiciis omnibus reum liberaret? Quod insidiarum invidiam in Clodium vertit, quamquam revera fuerat pugna fortuita? Quod factum et laudavit et tamen voluntate Milonis removit? Quod illi preces non dedit et in earum locum ipse successit?

---

[262] Dyck 1998: 221.   [263] Dyck 1998: 222.
[264] The *pro Milone* pairs up with the *pro Cluentio* as examples of Cicero's rhetorical cleverness (Quint. *Inst.* 6.5.9).

"What again am I to select as an outstanding instance of his sagacity in the *Pro Milone*? The fact that he refrains from proceeding to his statement of facts until he has cleared the ground by disposing of the previous verdicts against the accused? The manner in which he turns the odium of the attempted ambush against Clodius, although as a matter of fact the encounter was a pure chance? The way in which he at one and the same time praised the actual deed and showed that it was forced upon his client? Or the skill with which he avoided making Milo plead for consideration and undertook the role of suppliant himself?"[265]

This point is later expanded on by Quintilian in the first chapter of the seventh book (*Inst.* 7.1.34–7), devoted to the art of arrangement (*dispositio*). The speech on behalf of Milo well displays Cicero's art of directing the audience's mind by "examining all possible arguments and arriving at the best by a process of elimination" (*excutere quidquid dici potest et velut reiectione facta ad optimum pervenire*). The fundamental premise of Quintilian's review of Cicero's "false" narrative is that the defendant could not deny the fact that he killed Clodius. As a result, the plan of defense had to be twofold: on the one hand, to demonstrate that the deed was for the good of the state; on the other hand, to argue that the fight was accidental and unpremeditated. The safest course was to contend that the slaves of Milo killed Clodius "without Milo's orders or knowledge" (*neque iubente neque sciente Milone*). By rounding off his apparently feeble (*timida defensio*) argumentation with the sententious "as every man would have wished his slaves to do under similar circumstances" (*quod suos quisque servos in tali re facere voluisset*), Cicero validated the reasoning behind his line of defense, starting from the vantage point of a favorable response to his tendentious interpretation of the fatal battle. To put it differently, he made the jurors morally complicit in the criminal act by assuring them that they would have felt the same as Milo (and his servants).

The calculated narrative of the *pro Milone*, largely based on distortion of truth, recommends itself as an invincible form of argument.[266] It serves Cicero well throughout the speech, enabling him to win attention from the jury. By falsification of events the orator exerts control over the minds of the hearers, stirring up a general feeling of resentment at

---

[265] Quint. *Inst.* 6.1.27 (for impersonation, *prosopopoeia*, in the *pro Milone*; cf. § 94).
[266] Fotheringham 2007 (on the powerful combination of incompatible arguments in the *pro Milone*, one more rational – the killing of Clodius was an act of self-defense, another more emotional – the killing of Clodius was of great benefit to the *res publica*). See also Riedl 2016.

violence perpetrated by Clodius's gangs.[267] Putting morality over legality (the murder of Clodius was a moral action in the interests of the state), Cicero shows himself unconcerned about the truth, presenting a slanted version of events to make the judges believe what they hear. As already said, the creation of illusion consents to the use of invented or fabricated arguments in the narrative. In Quintilian's words (*Inst.* 11.1.35), the "public man, who is truly wise" (*vir civilis vereque sapiens*) freely employs "every method that may contribute to the end which he seeks to gain by his eloquence, although he will first form a clear conception in his mind as to what aims are honorable and what are not" (*omnia, quae ad efficiendum oratione quod proposuerit valent, libenter adhibebit, cum prius quid honestum sit efficere in animo suo constituerit*).

Before proceeding further, it is worth pausing briefly on some aspects of Cicero's rhetorical strategy as they have been examined by academics in modern times. Relying on interpretation of Cicero's argumentative tactics in ancient readers and theorists, modern scholars have long been exercised about Cicero's strategy of persuasion, his devising and arrangement of arguments and his adoption of different lines of approach (diversified in relation to the specificities of any given case). Cicero's advocacy has emerged as "a mixture of flattery, emotional appeal, and the force of argument,"[268] achieved by means of manipulation of rhetorical schemes and linguistic devices. It has been demonstrated that, among the presentational argument forms, the dilemma (*complexio*),[269] a form of argument in which "irrefutable conclusions can be cast as *ad hominem* argument underscoring the inconsistency of the target's actions in a judicial context,"[270] stands out as a dominant, recurrent device of Cicero's strategy of *argumentatio*, based on Hellenistic rhetorical teaching. As Craig has elucidated, the dilemma, in its different forms accorded with specific issue contexts, recurs in Cicero as a "presentational form of invincible argument,"[271] shaping – and impacting on – the oratorical tactic of persuasion and "interacting with the content of individual arguments to create persuasive effects."[272] Notably, the dilemma as a perceived invincible

---

[267] For Cicero's account of the battle of Bovillae as "the best-attested example of falsehood in a forensic speech," see Lintott 2008: 33–4.
[268] Laws 2004: 408 (who opportunely cites Cic. *Opt. gen.* 1.3).
[269] Cic. *Inv.* 1.45 (*Complexio est in qua, utrum concesseris, reprehenditur, ad hunc modum: "Si improbus est, cur uteris? Si probus, cur accusas?"*, ["A dilemma is a form of argument in which you are refuted, whichever alternative you grant, after this fashion: 'If he is a scoundrel, why are you intimate with him? If he is an honest man, why accuse him?'"]). Text and translation of Cicero's *de Inventione*: Hubbell 1968.
[270] Craig 1993b: 12.    [271] Craig 1993b: 26.    [272] Craig 1993b: 167.

argument form, whose presentational effects are easily accepted by the hearers, emerges as a manipulative device, a mechanism of refutation (and dismissal) of the opponent's flawed assumptions, showed as irrational or inconsistent.[273] The art of obfuscation rests on this very apparent clarity. Powell correctly points out the fact that "too great a complexity in the style might sound a warning that there is some argumentative trickery going on: hence simplicity of presentation may pay dividends."[274]

As to what is commonly called the "dilemma style,"[275] Quintilian's discussion is particularly revealing as it offers a good number of cases of arguments by elimination (*argumentorum genus ex remotione*), which intensify the force of Cicero's captious argumentation.[276] Once an argument is eliminated or proved as false, only "that which remains is true" (*modo id, quod relinquitur, verum*).[277] The examples provided from the *pro Caecina* (§ 37) and the *pro Caelio* (§ 64) show Cicero's "knack of using an apparent dilemma form in order to increase the air of invincibility that surrounds his arguments."[278] A significant impact on the defense strategy is made, moreover, by what may be defined as a common dilemma structure, intended as a special kind of "division" (*divisio*), in the form of two alternative conditions offered to the opponent, both of which will result in an unfavorable outcome (*utraque facit accusatori contraria*).[279] In this context, an interesting annotation on Cicero's manipulative effects of the dilemma technique is rendered by the Bobbio scholiast, who defines the argument form of *Sul.* 10 as an "extremely clever dilemma with the force of dialectics" (*acutissimum* δίλημμα *prope ad vim dialecticorum*: 77.6St).[280] The scholiast rounds off his comment by pointing to the character of testimony, functioning as self-defense, assumed by the device,[281] used to neutralize "any ambivalence

---

[273] In addition to Craig 1993b, see also Powell-Paterson 2004: 48–9.  [274] Powell 2013: 65.
[275] Powell 2013: 66.  [276] Quint. *Inst.* 5.10.65–70.  [277] Quint. *Inst.* 5.10.66.
[278] Powell 2013: 65.  [279] Quintilian (*Inst.* 5.10.69) cites from the lost *pro Oppio* and *pro Vareno*.
[280] On Cicero's passage, see Berry 1996: 148ff. (for the dilemma form see Craig 1993b: 92–3).
[281] Schol. Bob. 77.12-3St: *Et hic iam se animis iudicum latenter insinuat, ut praesens defensio in testimonii vicem cedat* ("And here already he covertly insinuates himself into the minds of the jurors, so that the present defense may serve in place of testimony": English translation: Craig 1993b). Another case of "dilemma," explicitly cited as *complexio*, is detected by Ps. Asconius at *Div.* 45 (198.27-9St). Here the sentence *factum esse necne* ("whether a thing has or has not happened") gives a clue to the classic definition of dilemma (*si probabilis est, vincitur, si necessaria, solvi non potest*, "if this is probable, the opponent is defeated, if necessary, he cannot defend himself"); on this passage, Craig 1993b: 60. It may also be added here that Ps. Asconius appears to have interpreted the conditional clause *Atque utinam neges* (at *Ver.* 2.1.61) as introducing a dilemma structure. He explains the sentence in such terms (239.20-2St: *Cum enim confiteris, etsi improbe, videris tamen aliquid dicere, cum dicis: Emi, non rapui. Si autem negaveris, et convinceris et huiusmodi defensione nudaberis*, ["If you admit the fact, you will appear to say something, though insolently, when you say: 'I bought it,

the jury may feel about the range of motives that the orator may have for defending a man as wealthy and well connected as Sulla."[282]

Other forms of persuasion and argumentative structures, not only based on logical or dialectical reasoning, have been investigated with success.[283] Recent research has explored specific aspects of ethical argumentation.[284] As ethos played a crucial role in the rhetoric of advocacy, proving itself as an effective source of persuasion, Ciceronian oratory has been read as an artistic application (and manipulation) of ethical characterizations grappling with the rhetorical, political and judicial circumstances provided by each case. The analysis conducted by May on fifteen speeches (starting from the pre-consular speeches through the consular and *post reditum* speeches to the Third and Twelfth Philippics) has revealed how vital to success verbal persuasion relying on ethos and character was. It is quite superfluous here to remind readers of the impact exercised on the jury's emotions by speeches in character, such as the frequently used *prosopopoeia* and *sermocinatio*, whose comical effects (in the trial of Caelius, for example) have been recognized since antiquity.[285] Character descriptions, personifications and ethical narratives, in addition, conjure up a picture of Cicero as an artist of words, a speaker at ease with handling ethical arguments.[286] As May notes, "in the hands of a master orator with the skill and personality of Cicero, the effective presentation of character becomes not only a powerful persuasive weapon but also a vehicle for artistic expression in the speech."[287]

We turn now to scrutinize the ways by which ancient teachers and scholars approached Cicero's proficiency in manipulating ethical proofs

---

I didn't despoil it.' But if you deny it, you will be proved guilty and deprived of such a defense argument"]).

[282] Craig 1993b: 93.
[283] Neumeister 1964; Classen 1982; Leeman 1982 (especially on Cicero's *pro Murena*). See also Vasaly 1993 (on the use of trial places as means of persuasion); Dyck 2001 (for clothing as "a component of Cicero's rhetorical toolkit"). For Cicero's strategy of appropriation and reversal of the opponent's argument, see Riggsby 1995b.
[284] May 1988. See also May 1981; Craig 1981 (on the portrayal of the *accusator* as *amicus* and its relevance as ethical argumentation). On the recourse to emotional appeals in the rational process of deliberation, see Arena 2013 (who focuses on Cicero's emotional eloquence and grand style as essential to the rational appreciation of the arguments from the captivated audience).
[285] For the Ciceronian use of the *prosopopoeia* in the defense of Caelius cf. Quint. *Inst.* 1.83; 6.1.25; 4.1.69; 11.1.41 (as presentation or invention of a character); 9.2.29–37 (as a figure); 2.1.2; 3.8.49; 52 (as exercise); 3.8.49–54 (in general about tone and purpose of the *prosopopoeia*); 4.1.28; 4.2.103; 6.1.25–7 (on its use in other parts of speech). See May 1988: 112ff; Duffalo 2001; Piras 2017. For the use of theatrical devices as instruments of persuasion in Ciceronian oratory, see Hall 2014a (also Axer 1989).
[286] May 1988: 167, rightly refers to Quintilian's well-known judgment on Cicero's felicity and spontaneity of style (*Inst.* 10.1.111–12).
[287] May 1988: 166.

or deploying artistic devices with persuasion effects. We have already observed that ancient readers recognized Cicero's clarity and neatness of style as a forceful, effective instrument of persuasion and a means of obfuscating truth, both in the exordial part of the speech and in the narrative. Since a complete survey of all the citations from Ciceronian orations in rhetorical handbooks and scholarly commentaries is not possible here, I will pick out a few significant passages that bear relevance to our discussion of Cicero *scholasticus*. The Murena case of 63 BCE, a trial for bribery in electioneering involving Cicero's standing and conduct as consul, offers a convenient starting point for further discussion of Cicero's manipulative oratory. As has been demonstrated, the case required a dexterous treatment and exploitation of arguments and characters.[288] To the prosecution's attempts to undermine his *auctoritas* Cicero had to respond with care and moderation, by eschewing *ad personam* attacks and defusing the opponent's argument with ironic wit.[289] It was essential to the elected consul – and to the consolidation of his role as supreme magistrate and defender of the *res publica* – to refute charges of arrogance and remind the jury of the *beneficia* accorded to the state by his consular actions. This tactic did not escape Quintilian's notice. He lauded Cicero for his *ratio moderationis* in addressing the characters of Cato and Servius Sulpicius (*Inst.* 11.1.69–71). In depicting Sulpicius's virtues with a courteous and deferential language (*decenter*) and behaving towards Cato delicately and with "a light touch" (*molli articulo*), Cicero handled an embarrassing situation with grace, playing down the prosecution's claims in inoffensive tones and camouflaging criticism through the pretense of affection.[290] He made the most of his opponents' character by "disparaging" the virtuous Sulpicius and the Stoic Cato "without giving offence" (*detrahere aliquid salva gratia*: 11.1.71).[291] The efficacy of this line of defense resided in the refutation of the charges with moderate and diplomatic language:[292] Quintilian adds that the more effective the defense, the more it offered

---

[288] For the historical and legal context of Murena's trial, see Fantham 2013: 5–22.
[289] Paterson 2004: 89–91.
[290] On Cicero's concern for the audience and his conciliatory language towards conservative politicians, see Fantham 2013: 29–30.
[291] Leeman 1982: 210 (for the comical effects of the description of Sulpicius, see Bürge 1974). On Cicero's gentle attack of Cato, "an exercise in smiling condescension," see Craig 1986: 233. For Cicero's adoption of *topoi* traditionally used for invective in the attempt to weaken Cato's *ethos*, see van der Wal 2007.
[292] For a succinct examination of Cicero's Isocratean language in the *pro Murena*, see Fantham 2013: 24–30.

the impression of necessity and external pressure behind the defender's response.[293]

Irony is peculiar to Cicero's persuasion tactic in his pleading for Murena, as has been noted.[294] The well-known mock comparison between jurisprudence and military glory in *Mur.* 22–4,[295] appreciated by Quintilian as an example of rhetorical *thesis*[296] and cited under the category of the figure of *comparatio* with the force of proof,[297] serves Cicero as an effective means of denigration and diminution of the prosecutor's *persona* in authority.[298] Other features of Cicero's persuasive manipulation in the *pro Murena* were looked upon with favor by Quintilian. In addition to the *partitio*, admired as a model of "lucidity and conciseness" (*Inst.* 4.5.12), Quintilian singled out the speech for its brilliant combination of an invocation to the immortal gods with an appeal to the ancestral values of serenity and peace in the proem (9.4.107), a theme of prayer and religious dignity, re-elaborated in the final sections of the text and in the *deprecatio* (§§ 88–90). It may be added that, according to Quintilian, Cicero's strategy appeared to be dominated by the concept of *utilitas* (6.1.35). Conscious of confronting "men of the greatest distinction" (*clarissimi viri*), before a not-entirely-convinced audience, the orator felt obliged to go through a middle way, persuading the judges that "nothing was more necessary in view of the critical position of affairs than that Murena should assume the consulship on the thirty-first of December,"[299] a tactic obviously recognized as no more fruitful in times of imperial domination.[300]

---

[293] Quint. *Inst.* 11.1.72. For Cicero's elegance of language in defending the actions of disreputable persons, as manifested by the case of Gabinius and Vatinius and, most notably, by the defense of Scamander in the speech on behalf of Cluentius (§ 17), cf. Quint. *Inst.* 11.1.73–4.

[294] Leeman 1982: 210 points to the humorous attack on Murena's credibility as a *iurisconsultus* as a means of persuasion and calls attention to Cicero's carefulness in presenting rational argument, especially given the delicacy of the case from the legal point of view.

[295] Cicero offers the comparison in terms of a *studiorum atque artium contentio* (§ 22).

[296] Quint. *Inst.* 2.4.24.

[297] Quint. *Inst.* 9.2.100. At 9.3.32 Quintilian discusses the passage *Vigilas tu ... castra capiantur* (Cic. *Mur.* 22) as a case of *primorum verborum alterna repetitio in contrapositis vel comparativis* ("alternating pattern of repetition of first words in antitheses and comparisons"). For this passage as source of inspiration of the antithetical comparison of soldier and lover in Ovid's *Amores* 1.9 see Fantham 2013: 115 (on Ovid's elegy and the comparison of the lover's life with that of a soldier, see McKeown 1989: 257–60).

[298] For Cicero's tact towards his prosecutors and his ironic presentation of Servius Sulpicius's profession and Cato's Stoic character, see also Fantham 2004: 202.

[299] *Persuasitque nihil esse ad praesentem rerum statum utilius quam pridie Kalendas Ianuarias ingredi consulatum.*

[300] For other citations from the *pro Murena* in Quintilian cf. *Inst.* 5.11.23 (§ 4); 4.1.75 (§ 7); 4.5.12 (§ 11); 9.2.26 (§ 14); 5.11.11 (§ 17); 5.13.27 (§ 21); 8.3.22 (§ 25); 7.1.51 (§ 26); 8.3.79 and 9.3.36 (§ 29); 8.6.49 (§ 35); 8.3.80 (§36); 8.6.30 (§ 60); 7.3.16 (§ 73); 9.3.82 (§ 76); 6.1.35 (§ 79); 9.2.18 (§ 80); 5.10.99 (§ 83).

Ridicule and mockery of Cato's Stoic philosophy in the *pro Murena* prompts us to dwell over Cicero's *argutia* and witticism in emotional and logical argumentation, one of the most distinctive features of the orator's technique of manipulation. Humor and verbal jokes (*ioca*), "among the most effective weapons in an advocate's armory,"[301] have been associated with the attractiveness of Cicero's art of eloquence since antiquity.[302] A collection of *facetiae*, ascribed to Cicero, is said to have been compiled by the freedman Tiro, as Quintilian reports.[303] Cicero himself attached great importance to humor as a means of persuasion, a forceful instrument for demolishing the opponent's statements.[304] Amid occasional criticism,[305] Cicero's witticism attracted considerable interest among his contemporaries and later commentators, turning even into a topic for imitation in the schools.[306] Inspired by Cicero, Quintilian covered the topics of jokes in oratory in a long chapter of his *Institutio* (6.3).[307] A systematic treatment of terminology of wit, Quintilian's discussion provides us with a useful catalogue of categories of the laughable, based on content or on words and illustrated by examples drawn from Ciceronian speeches in the majority of cases.[308] As expressly remarked at the outset of the chapter, Cicero possessed a "remarkable turn of wit," *mira urbanitas*, precisely that urbanity founded on humor and wit as much as on virtuosity of language (6.3.3).[309] He

---

[301] Powell-Paterson 2004: 51.
[302] Corbeill 1996: 6–7. On verbal jests in Cicero's speeches, still useful is Holst 1925.
[303] Quint. *Inst.* 6.3.5; Plut. *Cic.* 25–7 (on Quintilian's chapter on wit, Rabbie 2007: 215–7). For a collection of *dicta* made by Caesar, cf. Cic. *Fam.* 9.6.14 (181 SB*Fam*); Suet. *Jul.* 56.7. On Cato's collection of *apophthegmata*, cf. Cic. *Off.* 1.104; *de Orat.* 2.271; Plut. *Cat. Ma.* 2.4 (Astin 1978: 188).
[304] Cic. *de Orat.* 2.216 (*Suavis autem est et vehementer saepe utilis iocus et facetiae*). For Cicero's excursus on the use of humor and jokes in oratory in *De oratore* 2.216–90, see Fantham 2004: 186–208; Rabbie 2007: 208–12 (a theory of jokes also in Cic. *Or.* 87–90 and *De Off.* 1.103–4). In general, on Cicero's humor and his discussion of the role of wit in Roman oratory, see Corbeill 1996: 20–30 (also Gotoff 1993b: 298–99).
[305] Sen. *Con.* 7.3.9; Quint. *Inst.* 6.3.2–5; 12.10.12; Tac. *Dial.* 23.1 (also Plut. *Cic.* 5.6; 27.1; 50.5). In respect of the above-discussed mockery of Cato's severity in the *pro Murena*, it should be interesting to note that Cicero laid himself open to criticism for his treatment of serious matters with ironical joviality and pleasantry, as expressly stated by Plutarch in *Comp. Dem. et Cic.* 1.5 and *Cat. Mi.* 21.5 (who records Cato's celebrated reply to Cicero's jokes: "What a funny man we have, my friends, for consul").
[306] Corbeill 1996: 7.    [307] Kühnert 1962.
[308] For example, Quintilian lists some jests drawn from names for their relevance to Cicero's prosecution against Verres (*Inst.* 6.3.55–6); again, Cicero provides a good number of jests depending on metaphors and allegories (6.3.84–92).
[309] For Quintilian's definition of the concept of *urbanitas* as a "language with a smack of the city in its words, accent, and idiom, further suggesting a certain tincture of learning derived from associating with well-educated men" (*sermonem praeferentem in verbis et sono et usu proprium quondam gustum urbis et sumptam ex conversatione doctorum tacitam eruditionem*), in opposition to the concept of "rusticity" (*rusticitas*), cf. *Inst.* 6.3.17. On the critique of Domitius Marsus's interpretation as expressed in his treatise *De urbanitate*, cf. *Inst.* 6.3.102–112.

"produced more good jests than any other in his daily speeches as much as in his disputes in court and in his examination of witnesses" (6.3.4).[310] Cicero was a master of witticism.[311] He made a major contribution to the affirmation of irony as a standard mechanism of rhetorical invective.[312] But humor in Cicero was also endowed with political and ethical significance, as we have already seen. Laughter functioned as a form of political and moral humiliation. Aggressive humor impacted on the system of beliefs shared by the members of Roman elite society. Corbeill has persuasively argued that "humor helped shape the ethical standards current during the politically convulsive period of the late Republic."[313] Not only recreation and amusement to the judges or a persuasive rhetorical device, humor also represented a political joke with strong implications in ethics and social reality. In Corbeill's words, "within each instance of abuse reside values and preconceptions that are essential to the way a Roman of the late Republic defined himself in relation to his community."[314]

In the persuasion strategy, wit and humor work as powerful instruments of deceit. Quintilian clarifies this point at *Inst.* 6.3.6:

> Ridiculum dictum plerumque falsum est (hoc semper humile), saepe ex industria depravatum, praeterea numquam honorificum

> "Sayings designed to raise a laugh are generally untrue – and falsehood always involves a certain meanness – and are often deliberately distorted, and, further, never complimentary."

Whatever the essence and nature of humor may be, laughter implies deformation of reality. Since humor cannot be removed from derision,[315] it turns out to be an effective means of deceiving the opponent and making him small. Cicero's cleverness, his ability to invent and adapt jests to the nature and circumstances of the case, displays itself in the use of ridicule as an instrument of persuasion, one of the most effectual devices to secure the goodwill of the audience.

---

[310] *Nam et in sermone cotidiano multa et in altercationibus et interrogandis testibus plura quam quisquam dixit facete.*
[311] On Cicero's natural inclination to humor cf. also Plut. *Cic.* 5; 7 (for the recurrent use of jokes in the speeches against Verres); 9 and 26 (on Cicero's sarcastic portrait of Vatinius); 27 (again on Cicero's indiscriminate attacks for the sake of raising laughs).
[312] Rabbie 2007: 217.   [313] Corbeill 1996: 5.   [314] Corbeill 1996: 5.
[315] Quint. *Inst.* 6.3.8 (from Cic. *de Orat.* 2.236).

The speech in defense of Lucius Flaccus is dominated by sparkling wit and elegant, humorous tones, as explicitly noted by Macrobius.[316] We have already touched upon Cicero's *vis comica* in the *pro Flacco* in the second chapter of this volume.[317] Here we note that the Bobbio commentator frequently pointed out Cicero's elegance and urbanity of language, appearing in the refined, ironic use of ambivalent verbal forms, such as *amplecteretur* at § 43,[318] and in the insertion of proverbs, such as *cornici oculum (configere)* at § 46,[319] a facetious expression already used at *Mur.* 25.[320] *Festivitas*, "wit," is a recurrent concept in the explanation of many passages of the speech. In his comment on § 41 the scholiast appends this note to Cicero's sentence *homini enim Frygi, qui arborem numquam vidisset, fiscinam ficorum obiecisti*[321] (102.20-1St):

> Summa cum festivitate discussit inridens veneni criminationem, quod hic videretur unus de numero accusatorum Flacci repentina morte defunctus.

> "With extreme humor he [Cicero *sc.*] mocked his opponents and dispelled the charge of poisoning. Among the accusers of Flaccus he [the Phrygian] was the only one who appeared to have passed away in a sudden death."

An analogous comment on Cicero's strategy of ironic argumentation is made later (102.23-4St):

> Notemus igitur quasdam criminationes non pugnaci argumentatione, sed etiam festiva urbanitate dissolvi.

---

[316] Macr. *Sat.* 2.1.13 (*Atque ego, ni longum esset, referrem in quibus causis, cum nocentissimos reos tueretur, victoriam iocis adeptus sit, ut ecce pro L. Flacco, quem repetundarum reum ioci opportunitate de manifestissimis criminibus exemit*, ["And if it wouldn't take too long, I'd tell you about the cases in which he was defending clients who were dead guilty but nonetheless got them off with his jokes: take the case of Lucius Flaccus, for example, whom Cicero got off with a timely joke when he was on trial for extortion and his crimes were as plain as black and white"]: English translation: Kaster 2011).

[317] Cf. p. 96 and n321.

[318] Schol. Bob. 103.18-9St (the scholiast calls attention to the ambiguity of the verb *amplector*, used both in reference to an erotic act – in the sense of "to lift lovingly in the arms" – and to the immoderate desire of possession of material things – in this latter sense as "to cling to, to refuse to give up," an evident ironic allusion to Lysanias's conviction for peculation).

[319] Schol. Bob. 104.8-13St: the proverbial locution *cornici oculum configit* ("he picked out a crow's eye") is explained by the commentator in reference to the act of deception and, specifically, to Hermippus, the dupe of the unscrupulous Heraclides.

[320] Cf. also Jer. *Adv. Ruf.* 2.27. On other idiomatic expressions (with satiric intent) cf. Cic. *Flac.* 26 (*intentis oculis*); 72 (*pedibus compensari pecuniam*: this maxim is attributed to Cato the Elder by Cicero).

[321] "You threw a basket of figs at the Phrygian fellow who had never seen a fig-tree" (text and English translation: MacDonald 1976). On the name pun *frugi/Phrygi* and similar wordplays in Cicero's speeches, see Corbeill 1996: 95n (with Ahl 1985).

"Let us thus note that a few charges have not been dismissed through a fierce line of reasoning: he made use rather of a humorous urbanity."[322]

and again in the same note (102.27-30St):

> Leve putavit orator diligentissimus hanc suspicionem veneficii sola urbanitate discutere: conclusit etiam breviter argumentatione validissima nullum Flacco emolumentum fuisse in eius interitu qui iam testimonium dixerat et vim criminationis ediderat.

"The orator, very scrupulous as he was, thought it was ineffectual to dispel this poisoning speculation by means of irony only. He also produced the strongest argument by concluding that Flaccus took no advantage from the death of a man who had already submitted his testimony and disclosed the violence of the crime."

In the same vein, the adverb *festivissime* introduces the commentator's clarification of Cicero's punchline *consortes mendicitatis*, "partners of beggary,"[323] humorously tagging Sextilius's brothers at § 35 (101.2St).[324] Cicero's inclination to witticism is also recognized by the scholiast in the verbal pun *Mithridatico crimine* at § 41, an exemplary case of elegant and sophisticated play on the word *crimen*, immediately reminding hearers of the war waged by King Mithridates (103.1-3St),[325] as well as in the ironic description of Laelius's pang of jealousy at Decianus's oratorical incapacity (106.15-7St).[326]

Cleverness and sense of humor are standard features of invective style, as already said. Allegory, involving irony and art of illusion,[327] extends through Cicero's attack on Clodius and Curio, a speech often mentioned

---

[322] A very similar comment occurs in the scholion on *Clod.* fr26 Crawford (90.20St: *Notemus verborum medietates elegantissime ab oratore suspendi*, ["Let us point to the orator's extremely refined play on leaving unsettled the basic meaning of the words"]). The scholiast also calls attention to Cicero's ability to retort to Clodius's arguments against him (*has sententias . . . in vituperationem convertit*: 90.26-7St).

[323] Petrone 1971: 38.

[324] *Festivissime* occurs also in a note on a fragment of the invective *In Clodium et Curionem* (frg24Crawford): 89.31St.

[325] Here the scholiast talks of *elegantia* and *oratorius stomachus*, the latter term being translated as "taste proper to good oratory" (on the use of the term *stomachus* as "feeling, taste" cf. Cic. *Fam.* 7.1.2 [24 SB*Fam*]). On this concept and "well digested" jests in oratory cf. Quint. *Inst.* 6.3.93 (*Iucundissima sunt autem ex his omnibus lenia et, ut sic dixerim, boni stomachi*, ["But the most agreeable of all jests are those which are good humoured and easily digested"]); cf. also 6.3.112 (and 2.3.3): Corbeill 1996: 209–10. On the notion of *stomachus* as conveying a sense of emotional "indignation" at political events (especially in Cicero's epistolary collection), see Hoffer 2007.

[326] In his note on the term *strangulatus*, "strangled," employed by the accuser Decimus Laelius to remind the judges of the execution of the conspirators, the commentator points out Cicero's shrewdness, *calliditas* (95.5-8St: on Cic. *Flac.* frg1).

[327] Quint. *Inst.* 8.6.54.

for being a prototype of invective rhetoric. Referring to Cicero's sarcastic presentation of Clodius as a man of integrity and probity, Quintilian draws attention in his discussion to some cases of allegory (*Inst.* 8.6.56). The fragment (frg29Crawford),[328] noticeable for its triple, asyndetic structure *integritas tua te purgavit, mihi crede, pudor eripuit, vita anteacta servavit*,[329] is explicitly regarded as a fine example of mock-praise, in which the speaker "says the opposite of what he desires to be understood" (*in risu quodam contraria dicuntur iis quae intelligi volunt*).[330] Analogously, in *Inst.* 9.2.96 Quintilian quotes another fragment from the speech (fr13Crawford), part of which is also in the Bobbio commentary (87.20St), for Cicero's parodic allusion to Clodius's illicit (and sacrilegious) participation in the rites of the Bona Dea.[331]

To add flesh to this point, witticism is spotted by the Bobbio scholiast in Cicero's ridicule of Clodius's effeminate dress, a topic largely present in invective contexts,[332] elaborated through sophisticated puns and abusive vocabulary.[333] Cicero's ironic self-definition as a "country bumpkin," *rusticus*, dressed (along with other senators) in dull-colored tunics, suited to the established standards of the virtue and severity of a Roman citizen, is interpreted by the commentator as a "response mixing urbanity and sense of humour with severity and verbal violence" (*mixta responsio et facetiis urbanitatis et asperitatis virolentia*: 89.10St on *Clod.* fr21Crawford).[334] Again, a note on Cicero's sarcasm (*festivitas*) in depicting Clodius's physical appearance and ugliness (as revealed by the mirror), blatantly discrepant with the nobility of his ancestors, is placed at the beginning of a history-like excursus on the *gens* Claudia and the first Pulcher, P. Claudius, son of Appius Claudius Caecus (89.29–90.8St: on *Clod.* fr24Crawford).[335]

Not only sarcastic mottoes, aphorisms and jokes depending on words were employed. The orator relieved anxiety and moved the judges to laughter through *fabellae* (or *fabulae*), short narratives ridiculing and

---

[328] Crawford 1994: 260.
[329] "Believe me, your well-known integrity has cleared you of all blame, your modesty has saved you, your past life has been your salvation."
[330] For other fragments of the *in Clodium et Curionem* in Quintilian cf. *Inst.* 8.3.81 (example of simile) and 5.10.92 (on the way a comparison is made starting *ex faciliore*, "from something easier"). See Crawford 1994: 247–8.
[331] Crawford 1994: 250–1.  [332] Crawford 1994: 254 (for Cic. *de har. resp.* 44).
[333] Crawford 1994: 254, talks of "heavy-handed, but amusing nonetheless" mockery. For Nonius's linguistic appreciation of this section of the speech, see chapter 3, pp. 140–1.
[334] For Cicero's harshness and severity of language in the invective cf. schol. Bob. 86.15St (on *Clod.* fr2 Crawford); 86.24St (on *Clod.* fr5 Crawford); 87.12St (on *Clod.* fr11 Crawford). See also the already discussed *argumentum* to the speech (85.5-7St: supra pp. 193–4).
[335] Crawford 1994: 256–7.

heaping scorn on the opponents. A representative example of this is provided by the celebrated episode of the Cepasii brothers in Cic. *Cluent.* 57–8.[336] Quintilian expressly describes the digression about the Cepasii brothers (*circa fratres Caepasios*) as a charming and entertaining piece, full of elegance and wit (*Inst.* 4.2.19). Adduced as a model of *genus facetiarum* (or rather *cavillatio*) by later rhetoricians,[337] the story was familiar to students of rhetoric, who were encouraged to read it as a humorous hiatus in the treatment of the case, a narrative device guiding hearers into a state of momentary relaxation. In his articulated discussion of arguments or narrative producing laughter, *risus*, Quintilian mentions the story of Cepasius and Fabricius in the *pro Cluentio* as a case study for proving that the narration of *salsa*, producing laughing effects, pertains to the domain of oratory (*Inst.* 6.3.39–40). The most striking feature of this form of oratorical entertainment is given by the combination of elegance and charm (*elegans et venusta expositio*) with a sense of humor, as patently demonstrated by Cicero's account of Fabricius's voluntary flight from the court (6.3.40–1), a well-known episode (*nam est notus locus*) enriched with additional details of a light, humorous tone.

That irony and humor were forceful "instruments of war" in the hands of would-be orators is also demonstrated by a series of didactic notes on Cicero's laughter in late commentaries, part of which have already been registered. "Jokes usually presuppose (even rest on) a significant amount of shared knowledge between the speaker and his audience," as has aptly been said.[338] Wit was easily discerned, understood and appreciated by its contemporary hearers and readers. But this assertion inevitably loses its force if applied to late readers (and students), often in need of explanation of *facetiae* and plays on humor, arousing laughter in the audience and winning benevolence toward the facetious orator. The practical utility of irony as a rhetorical device and tool of persuasion evidently created the conditions for instruction in the art of humor. Students had to be taught how to scorn opponents or elicit passions through sarcasm and urban language. Not surprisingly, ancient commentaries are abundant in comments illustrating the grandeur and simplicity of Cicero's art of irony, implicitly promoting humor as a necessary component of the discipline of rhetoric.

A significant passage from the *Pro Plancio* (§ 85) is interpreted by the Bobbio scholiast as a specimen of Cicero's art of witticism (167.8-18St):

---

[336] Patimo 2009: 455–6.　[337] Jul. Vict. 428.17ff. *RLM* (also Iul. Ruf. 39.16 *RLM*).
[338] Rabbie 2007: 207.

Admonefecisti etiam, quod in Creta fuisses, dictum aliquod in petitionem tuam dici potuisse] Scolastica levitate, quasi nimio adfectantem huiusmodi iocos,[339] M. Tullium videbatur denotasse Laterensis, quod multa, quae facetius dici possent cum aliqua figurandi suptilitate, non praetermitteret. Itaque hoc eum dicto perstrinxerat: habuisse materiam de vocabulo Cretae insulae aliquid in se ioculariter dicendi nec tamen id excogitasse. Constabat enim Laterensem fuisse in Creta provincia, et solebant omnes candidati alba creta oblinire cervicem, ut populo notabiliores essent. Ergo ... dixit eum iocari potuisse, si ad hoc adiecisset ingenium, ut id inveniret quod poterat occurrere. Sed acute rapuit ex eodem proposito validam responsionem, ut magis eum cupidum lacessendi ostenderet qui sibi ea ultro suggereret quae potuisse dici fateretur nec tamen dicta sint.

"You reminded me also, since you had been in Crete that something might have been said against your offering yourself as a candidate] With rustic simplicity[340] Laterensis appeared to have censured Tullius Cicero for his excessive fondness for verbal jokes of such a tone: he in fact did not let slip any occasion to talk about a lot of arguments with irony and fineness of metaphorical language. So he tried to offend him with this saying, since the island of Crete had furnished him with the opportunity of making fun about himself, though it was not he who devised such a term. It was in fact well known that Laterensis had been in the province of Crete and, as customary, all the candidates smeared their head with whitish clay, so that they could be much more visible to the people. For that reason ... [Cicero] said that he might have played on that: if he had exercised his *ingenium* to that scope, he would then have come across with what could be useful to him. But Cicero cleverly made profit of this point and replied with vigor: he did it in order to show that his opponent was much more eager for verbal assault and, though he confessed that he might have said things that were supplied to him spontaneously, he did not do that."

Relying on the usual ethical representation of the *accusator* as *amicus*,[341] in the *pro Plancio* Cicero ironically portrays his opponent (and prosecutor of Plancius), Laterensis, as an accomplished man, a noble character whose authority is neutralized by his moral qualities.[342] Cicero's irony resides in the reversal of the traditional virtues of a good Roman citizen. In this

---

[339] This passage is visibly corrupted in the palimpsest (that reads *nimica spectante huiusmodi locus*). On the proposed corrections, see Stangl in the apparatus (here I limit myself to recording Hildebrant's reading *quasi mimica spectantem*: 1907 ad l.).

[340] The term *scholasticus* as *rusticus* is never attested in rhetorical treatises, as far as I know. Quite interestingly, in Quintilian (*Inst.* 7.1.58) *rusticus* is a correction by Regius, in place of *scolastica* transmitted by all the manuscripts.

[341] Craig 1981. May 1988: 118 points to Cicero's persona in the speech as that "of a concerned friend and also a friendly mentor."

[342] May 1988: 120–1. On Cicero's irony in the speech, see also Haury 1955: 154–6.

specific passage, Cicero sneers at his adversary's bad *ingenium*. He ridicules Laterenensis's doltishness, his incapacity to gain advantage of jests or verbal jokes offered to him by casual situations.[343] This helps Cicero to create a straightforward opposition between himself and his opponent's lack of linguistic intelligence. Both Cicero and Laterensis are "covetous of smart sayings" (*cupidus dicti*).[344] Yet, whereas Laterensis seems to possess limited oratorical virtues, the orator opportunely balances pro and contra of irony and humor and is able to make an appropriate use of witticism. He thus may well claim victory on his slow-witted opponent. Such a contrast is well explained by the commentator, who sketches Laterensis as a *rusticus*, a definition that is crucial to Cicero's ethical argumentation, filled with touches of refined irony.

Cicero's self-declaration as being a lover of jokes and humorous sayings in a former passage of the same speech is of some relevance to our understanding of Cicero's conception of humor. In chapter 35, in reply to false allegations of injurious language against Plancius, Cicero complains about the insane habit of ascribing to him sayings of other men, patently unworthy of his urbanity.[345] The strategy of identification of patron and client, a standard ethical argument, shifts here to the comparison of the orator's urban, refined language with that of the prosecuted. Plancius is worthy of admiration for restraint and consistency of language (§§ 33–4). He has certainly reproved Crassus's and Antonius's designs with witty remarks, but too many sayings, uttered by others, have unreasonably been attributed to him. Cicero, his defender, has suffered from a similar situation. He admits to his predilection for tongue-in-cheek humor and jesting tones.[346] But he rehabilitates his persona of urban speaker by

---

[343] For a similar comment on Laterensis's tendency for captious verbal attacks on Cicero cf. schol. Bob. 166.16-25St (on *Planc.* 83).
[344] Cic. *Planc.* 85.
[345] *Quamquam, iudices, – agnosco enim ex me – permulta in Plancium quae ab eo numquam dicta sunt conferuntur. Ego quid dico aliquid aliquando non studio adductus, sed aut contentione dicendi aut lacessitus, et quia, ut fit in multis, exit aliquando aliquid si non perfacetum, at tamen fortasse non rusticum, quod quisque dixit, me id dixisse dicunt* ("Although, o judges, for thus much I know of my own knowledge, many things are attributed to Plancius which were never said by him. In my own case, because sometimes I say something, not from any deliberate intention, but either in the heat of speaking, or because I have been provoked, and because it is natural that, among the many things which I say in this manner, something comes out at times if not excessively witty, still perhaps not altogether stupid, the consequence is that, whatever anyone else says people say that I have said"). Text and translation of the *pro Plancio*: Watts 1979.
[346] Interestingly, Cicero's self-image as a passionate deviser of jokes, even amid political troubles, emerges in a passage from the *Second Philippic* (2.39). Here Cicero rebuts Antony's allegations of immoderate witticism during his residence in Pompey's camp at Pharsalus, pointing rather to the cathartic relief produced by humor on the spirits of fatigued soldiers. See Corbeill 1996: 185–6.

claiming that each word is pondered with special care, chosen in accordance with urbanity and refinement of language. He implicitly reacts to criticism of rustic language and excess of witticism, a good topic of anti-Ciceronianism, later echoed by Plutarch.[347] Whatever is worthy of a well-educated and learned man enters into the realm of Cicero's urban Latin. The scholiast comments on Cicero's tactic in these terms (159.16-22St):

> Ad quod optinendum contra insimulationes inimicorum subnectit exemplum Cicero ipse de se: quem non ignoramus multum facetiis et urbanioribus dictis indulsisse, id quod locis pluribus in Verrinis orationibus potuimus adgnoscere. Hoc ergo ait: quoniam soleo quaedam non ingrata festivitate secundum sales urbanitatis dicere, idcirco plerique huiusmodi omne quod dicitur, etiam si ab alio dictum sit, in me conferunt. Quare nihil mirum est si quaedam falso etiam de Planci libertate iactentur.

> "In order to obtain it and reject his opponents' allegations Cicero provided himself as example. We know well that Cicero was very fond for jokes and urbane sayings, something which we can easily observe and verify in the orations against Verres.[348] For that reason he said: since I am used to insert humorous words in my discourse, in line with the concept of urbane irony, there are many who ascribe to me anything that is said with humor, even if this has been said by others. So it is not surprising that some words have falsely been hurled about Plancius's freedom."

In providing the jury with a self-portrait as a *cultor Latinitatis* Cicero deflates his opponent and reinforces his credibility as *patronus*, a subtle and learned connoisseur of Latin and thereby a facetious orator. The commentator grasps the sense of Cicero's argumentation and reminds his readers of irony as a pervasive feature of Cicero's style.[349] Yet he implicitly recommends to them a measured use of witticism. Cicero himself "warns against using witticisms injudiciously" in the second book of *De oratore* (2.244–6) and points to "propriety, morality and taste" as essential to an appropriate, effective use of humor.[350] The power of jokes may be hampered by their abuse, coming into conflict with the notion of *Latinitas* and encountering disapproval from educated men.

Mockery and derision based on name puns is a standard category of invective.[351] An interesting explanation of a name pun occurs in a note of the Bobbio scholiast on *Sest.* 135 (140.11-7St):

---

[347] See supra p. 244, and n.305.   [348] Cf. Plut. *Cic.* 7.
[349] Cf. also schol. Bob. -9St (on *Planc.* 33).   [350] Wisse 2013: 182–3.   [351] Corbeill 1996: 57–98.

Unus leo, ducenti bestiarii] Cum Vatinius invidiam sibi magnam conflasset de apparatu gladiatorum, simulaverat se bestiarios potius habere quam gladiatores, et unum gladiatorem confitebatur cui nomen Leoni fuit. Hanc igitur stultitiam M. Tullius inridens unum leonem dicit, ducentos bestiarios, id est venatores: sine dubio volens intellegi omnem hanc manum gladiatoriam seditionis causa comparatam. Hoc etiam dictum de Leone Tullius Tiro, libertus eiusdem, inter Iocos Ciceronis adnumerat.

"One lion, two hundred beast fighters] Vatinius inspired feelings of hate when he put forward the argument of the equipment of the gladiators. He pretended he had beast fighters rather than gladiators, and confessed to have just one gladiator, named Lion. Tullius made fun of this evident foolishness and said that he had one lion and two hundred beast fighters, that is, hunters. Out of doubt he wanted the audience to understand that Vatinius had assembled this entire group of gladiators to provoke sedition. This saying about the Lion has been enlisted among the 'Jests of Cicero' by the freedman Tullius Tiro."

In chapters 132–5 of the speech (preceding the final peroration) Cicero launches a biting attack on Vatinius, who testified against Sestius and lashed out at him through Vettius the informer, "devising every form of criminal snare" (*omnis insidias sceleratissime machinatus*: § 133).[352] Here Cicero alludes to Vatinius's violation of the *lex Tullia de ambitu* of 63 BCE, "forbidding anyone from giving gladiatorial shows within two years of standing, or intending to stand, for office."[353] Cicero's *jeu d'esprit* is in scoffing Vatinius's self-defense based on two pleas. In the first plea, Cicero says, Vatinius pretended that no violation of law had occurred since he had given shows for beast fighters, not gladiators; in the second, he alleged that he had "put on not gladiators, plural, but a single gladiator" (*dicet se non gladiatores, sed unum gladiatorem dare*, 135), founding his entire aedileship on his act of liberality. The pun is evidently intended for a political effect. Cicero's jest (preserved in Tiro's collection) is on the name "Lion," the name of the single gladiator summoned by Vatinius,[354] but, as the scholiast notes, Cicero offers a slightly different interpretation of the term *bestiarii*,

---

[352] English translation of the *pro Sestio* : Kaster 2006.
[353] *Quae* (sc. *lex*) *vetat gladiatores biennio quo quis petierit aut petiturus sit dare*.
[354] Another interesting case of etymological game, exploited to ridicule the opponent's name, occurs at *Sest.* 72. There, Cicero comments on the political resonance of the nickname Gracchus applied to the tribune Numerius Quintius Rufus and compares him to a *nitedula*, a "red field mouse," pointing to the humorous use of the cognomen *Rufus* as "a label for a red-haired non-Roman" (Corbeill 1996: 86). The sense of Cicero's mockery is well recognized by the Bobbio scholiast 134.28-9St (*Quod esset non tantum statura depressus, verum etiam colore rubidus, nitedulam nominavit*, "He called him *nitedula* because he was not only short in stature, but red in color": English translation: Corbeill 1996).

"hunters," putting on display the subversive intents behind assembling a number of "fake gladiators." As has been observed, "Vatinius' gladiators are not costly specimens selected and trained for their roles but the inmates of 'workhouses' (*ergastula*) where slaves good only for brute labor were kept."[355] According to the scholiast, we might add, Cicero equated the concept of "gladiatorial show" with that of "conspiracy," an equivalence already exploited in the consular speeches and in the post-return invectives against Clodius.

Mockery of the adversary's physical appearance was also a relevant part of Cicero's persuasion strategy. Corbeill rightly points to mockery of physical deformities as a phenomenon peculiar to invective and underpins the sense of "social deviance" implied in negativity of physical exterior.[356] As fully revealed by the invective *Against Vatinius*, "identifying publicly an opponent's physical deficiencies provided a powerful rhetorical means for excluding that opponent from society."[357] Particularly, Vatinius suffered from *struma*, "scrofula," a tuberculous infection of the lymphatic glands resulting in swellings in the neck and face. This infection, a good opportunity for sarcasm,[358] turns out to be a motif of political meditation on the diseased conditions of the body of the state in the final lines of Cicero's invective in the *pro Sestio* (135). Ironically labeled as *pulcherrimus* in the *familia gladiatoria*, the troupe of slaves and gladiators recruited to seditious plans (134), Vatinius is metaphorically immortalized as the *struma civitatis*, a "plague on the civil community," whose removal could eventually lead to healing of the infected *res publica*.[359] Cicero's joke on Vatinius's tumor is filled with political relevance. In urging the men of the highest distinction, the "best sort" (*optimates*) to cure the commonwealth by cutting out the scrofula of the state,[360] Cicero makes his opponent the symbolic origin of the plague of sedition, the epicenter of the subversion of republican institutions. The exterior congenital malformation of Vatinius mirrors

---

[355] Kaster 2006: 376.
[356] Corbeill 2002: 207 (also Corbeill 1996: 14–56). On the combination of physiognomics, natural philosophy and political competition in Ciceronian attacks on the physicality of his opponent, see Corbeill 2004: 111–39.
[357] Corbeill 2002: 208.
[358] Cf. Cic. *Att.* 2.9.2 (29 SB*Att*); *Vat.* 4; 10; 39; Plut. *Cic.* 9.3; 26.2; Corbeill 1996: 46–56; Bonsangue 2013: 62–72 (especially on the passages from the *In Vatinium*).
[359] On the use of medical imagery in political contexts, see Bonsangue 2013: 60–2; La Bua 2014b.
[360] Cic. *Sest.* 135 (*Ii medentur rei publicae qui exsecant pestem aliquam tamquam strumam civitatis*, "The people who cure the commonwealth are those who cut out a plague on the civil community as though it were scrofula").

the interior "evil" spreading disease across the city.[361] The scholiast is eloquent in this respect (141.9-12St):

> definiens aliter, quid sit mederi rei p., incommoda scilicet ei et pericula detrahere. Sed quod ait strumam civitatis, πλαγίως intellegere debemus: pertinet enim ad ipsum Vatinium, qui traditur fuisse strumosa facie et maculoso corpore.

> "he defines it differently, intending 'to cure the commonwealth' in the sense of 'to relieve the state from any danger and political trouble'. As to the expression 'the scrofula of the city', we should intend it as an indirect reference to Vatinius himself, who was said to suffer from swellings on the face and disfiguring marks on the skin."

He correctly interprets the political sense of the medical metaphor and invites his students to penetrate the allegorical – and humorous – tone of the Ciceronian definition,[362] transforming his opponent's infection into a powerful symbol of the illness looming over the body of the state.

To recap, humor had devastating effects on the *persona* of the opponent.[363] By humor a good orator could potentially annihilate the credibility and morality of his adversary.[364] Witticism was then a powerful weapon in the talented speaker's armory, a great asset to delivery and the oratorical persuasive strategy.[365] Yet a proper, urbane sense of humor represented a requirement of good oratory. As we have seen, an incautious recourse to jokes could attach a stigma of incompetence to the figure of the orator. As Wisse notes, "jokes could also backfire, and making the right criticism before the right audience must also have been difficult."[366] It follows that Quintilian and later commentators focused not only on the force of persuasion implied in jokes and criticism of the opponent's deviant behavior. They also held a pedagogical view of witticism, directing their

---

[361] Corbeill 1996: 51–2.
[362] The adverb πλαγίως is also found in a note of the Bobbio scholiast on the use of tragic poets in Cicero's speech in defense of Sestius (137.4-6St, on *Sest.* 122).
[363] For other comments on Cicero's irony cf. schol. Bob. 148.14St (on *Vat.* 23); Ps. Asconius 190.15St (on *Div.*13); 197.4St (on *Div.* 33); 199.22St (on *Div.* 47); 219.9St (on *Ver.* 1.38); 238.17St (on *Ver.* 2.1.60; a similar note is in schol. Gronov. **A**, 347.21St); 247.18St (on *Ver.* 2.1.104); 253.5St (on *Ver.* 2.1.243); schol. Gronov. **D**, 309.3St (on *Rosc.* 52); 313.27St (on *Rosc.* 120). Cicero's comic comment on Verres's use of the famous verse *Fato Metelli Romae fiunt consules*, attributed to the poet Naevius, at *Ver.* 1.29 is remarked on by Ps. Asconius with the adverb *subtiliter* (215.23St).
[364] Interestingly, in the *argumentum* to the *Pro Sex. Roscio Amerino*, the Gronovian scholiast **D** notes that Cicero discredits Erucius's credibility as a prosecutor by means of "very sophisticated jokes," *urbanissimis salibus* (301.29St).
[365] On Cicero's use of arguments from immorality to characterize his opponent as a man unfit for political influence, worthy of exclusion from Roman society, see in general Hammar 2013.
[366] Wisse 2013: 178.

student's minds towards a moderate and appropriate use of irony and provocative jokes, in line with the rules imposed by urbanity of language.

Illustration of irony, in its pragmatic application within the process of persuasion, was thus a relevant part of rhetorical exegesis in antiquity. It served the practical purpose of demonstrating Cicero's facility for subverting his opponents' arguments by means of ridicule and jeers. In a more general context, by pointing to humor as a powerful mode of persuasion the schoolmaster recommended that his students approach the orations of Cicero as concrete models of successful eloquence, a concentration of argumentative and non-argumentative, emotional means, to be analyzed in their presentation, purpose and momentary impact on the persuasion strategy. Through irony Cicero established himself as the master of illusion, the ideal orator capable of devising arguments, inventing anecdotes, manipulating unexpected courtroom situations, reacting to – and discrediting – the opponent's assertions with *ex tempore* responses and fascinating audiences with a manipulative and ironic language (in a clever combination of high-literary and colloquial style). In their function as "general guides on actual performed oratory,"[367] extant late commentaries on the speeches guided Roman elite students through Cicero's persuasive strategy and his art of humor. Their final intent was to provide practitioners in rhetoric with a set of principles to adopt in speaking, in particular that (felicitous) use of irony deemed indispensable to persuade – and amuse – the public and win the cause.

To resume our analysis of ancient readings of the speeches, Cicero's flexibility in adapting multiple means of persuasion to the specificity of the case and, above all, his humor were the criteria by which teachers and students judged the persuasive force and success of his oratorical performance.[368] Quintilian and late commentators dilated on Cicero's capacity for devising and deploying persuasive arguments on more than one occasion. They amply discussed Cicero's manipulative strategy, implicitly preparing – and encouraging – the students to meet the needs of any given case by diversifying patterns of argumentation and style registers in response to the opponent's statements and then developing different persuasion strategies, potentially designed to achieve victory. Some further examples of this scientific-didactic approach may usefully be provided here. We start with the *argumentatio* of the *Second Catilinarian* (§§ 17–27), a moral vignette of

---

[367] Arena 2013: 195.
[368] Cic. *Brut.* 208 (on Cicero's adaptation of different means of persuasion to each point raised by his opponent).

Catiline's followers divided into six groups, the first four of which "wrestle in different ways with debt."[369] This section of Cicero's consular discourse is interpreted by the Gronovian scholiast (**D**) as a special, artful form of *divisio*, a (satirical) picture of the immoral conspirators, afflicted by vices and alienated by Roman society (282.16-24St). To each individual group – and to each individual vice accordingly – is offered a "cure" (cf. *sanare* § 17). The sharp-sighted consul proposes a medical treatment for each vice, leaving out only the last two groups, assembling criminals and immoral youths (§§ 22–3), categories of individuals for whom no remedy is available.[370] In plain words the ancient commentator illustrates the basic layout of the *argumentatio* (282.16-7St).[371] More than than, he captures the sense of Cicero's strategy, connecting the partition of Catiline's army (*exercitum Catilinae*) into types of vice (*per genera vitiorum*) – and the related picture of the conspirators as immoral citizens – with the necessity of silencing those who complained that Catiline had been forced to leave the city by the consul, something which could sound like an implicit allegation of a secret accord between the magistrate and Catiline's depraved followers (282.23-4St).[372]

The youthful speech in defense of Sextus Roscius of Ameria, "a staple of the rhetorical schools"[373] in spite of criticism of its not-yet-mature style,[374] was a case based on weak arguments (by analogy to the *pro Milone* and the *Fourth Catilinarian*). As Dyck notes, "Cicero's lengthy speech in defense of his client is mostly the product of his imagination, deployed to derive maximum advantage from scanty materials."[375] The Gronovian scholiast (**D**) is actively engaged in clarifying Cicero's line of defense, basically founded on the *constitutio coniecturalis*, i.e. denial of the crime (306.1-20St). At the outset of the *refutatio* (§ 37) the scholiast reads the initial sentence *occidisse patrem* [*Sex. Roscius arguitur*] as a form of rhetorical exaggeration, which "foregrounds the shocking charge"[376] and makes the crime (parricide) more implausibile, because of its gravity.[377] This figure of speech has its place in both prosecution and defense speeches (306.2-5St):

---

[369] Dyck 2008a: 148.  [370] On this passage Dyck 2008a: 148–57; La Bua 2014b: 43–44.
[371] *Dicit genera vitiorum et statim infert remedium* ("He lists the different types of vice and suddenly applies a remedy to each of them"). Cf. also schol. Gronov. **D** 282.11–3 (*vitia sociorum Catilinae per genera enumerat*, ["He divides the vices of Catiline's supporters into categories"]).
[372] On the moral *synkrisis*, comparison of virtues and vices, at chapter 25 of the speech cf. Isid. 518.5–17 *RLM*.
[373] Dyck 2010a: 19. Cf. Cic. *Off.* 2.51. On the presence of the speech in the schools of grammar and rhetoric in antiquity, cf. chapter 2, p. 97.
[374] Cf. chapter 2, pp. 97–8. For the exuberant use of wordplay and abundance of diction in the speech, see Dyck 2010a: 13.
[375] Dyck 2010a: 17.  [376] Dyck 2010a: 109.
[377] Cf. Quint. *Inst.* 9.2.53 (cf. also Victorin. 71.2; 95.2 Riesenweber).

> Extollit magnitudinem criminis, ut fides derogetur: quanto enim quaeque magna sunt, tanto in credendo difficilia. Hoc in defensionibus recte facimus ante probationem, in accusationibus autem probato crimine debemus augere. Item dixit principia, dixit narrationem, excessus, nunc summam dicit: summa autem dicitur criminis collectio.

> "He exaggerates the gravity of the crime to reduce its credibility: the more things become bigger, the more they become incredible. We correctly do that in the defense speeches, before giving proofs: in the prosecution speeches, instead, we have to increase the seriousness of the crime, after demonstrating that it has been committed. Not otherwise, he pronounced the proem, a narrative, and a digression: now he recapitulates the whole issue: the whole is generally intended as a recapitulation of the crime."

From a didactic point of view, the comment of the scholiast on Cicero's tactic sounds like an implicit recommendation to adopt a similar strategy in defense cases that are based on the denial of crime. In alignment with standard rhetorical theory,[378] Cicero constructed his plea of defense based on the fact that accusing Roscius of such a serious crime was a blatantly implausible claim. His client's character and previous life could hardly have fomented an action, such as parricide, whose exceptionality and monstrosity would have required a deviant human behavior. This provides a rationale for the three-part arrangement of the speech, i.e. proem, narrative and digression, in which Cicero gradually dismisses the opponents' arguments, before recapitulating the points at issue (*criminis collectio*) and launching himself into a detailed refutation of the prosecutor's charges.

Deploying arguments *ex persona* (306.6-7St), Cicero replied to Erucius's allegations by depicting his client as a young man of pure character, not indulging in violence or luxury. As lucidly demonstrated by Riggsby, Cicero's defense of Roscius serves as a prime example of the technique of "appropriation and reversal" of the opponent's argument, which is at heart of Cicero's art of manipulation.[379] Interestingly, this mechanism is elucidated by the scholiast (306.8-15St):

> Patrem occidit]Congessit schemata oratoria: nam per quaesitum argumentatur, responsionem facit. Quotienscumque coniectura est, summa ponitur, incipiens a genere criminationis, naturae conveniens: "causa lucri, causa inimicitiarum patrem occidit" naturae conveniens. Erucius volens aptam sceleri designare personam, descripsit feram quandam fuisse naturam Roscii, dicens: "miramini si <indomita cupiditate fuit> iste homo, qui in

---

[378] Cf. *Rhet. Her.* 2.5 (*probabile ex vita*).   [379] Riggsby 1995b: 245–6 (and Dyck 2010a: 111).

agro et solitudinibus cum nullo vixerit?" Cicero arripuit luxuriae partes, expugnavit obiectionem Eruci: "si enim solus in silvis fuit, luxuriosus esse non potuit".

"He killed his father] He assembled oratorical modes: the argumentation is based in fact on questions and replies. Each time the issue lies on conjecture, there is a recapitulation of facts which starts from the type of crime and its consistency with nature and character: 'he killed his father out of avarice, out of personal enmities'. Erucius aimed to demonstrate that the prosecuted was naturally prone to misdeeds and then described Roscius as a rude character: he said: 'Why are you bewildered at the fact that a man who lived alone in deserted lands had immoderate desires?' Cicero jumped at the luxury argument and counteracted Erucius's accusation: he replied: 'If he was alone in the forests, he could not be a licentious man'."

The commentator well discerns the effectiveness of Cicero's procedure in discrediting Erucius's reputation and refuting charges of misconduct or luxurious lifestyle on the part of his client. He usefully describes Cicero's strategy in terms of "to jump at the opponent's argument" (*arripere ... partes*) and "to counteract the opponent's argument" (*expugnare obiectionem*),[380] a tactic aimed at stripping the prosecutor of any authorial voice.[381] Particularly revealing is the charge of *luxuria*. Erucius's point that Roscius was *ferus* and *agrestis*, used to live alone in the country and then developed unrestrained desires "is turned to account by Cicero as proof that he did not indulge in luxurious living."[382] Notably, Cicero's positive re-interpretation, or rather re-adaptation, of Roscius's rural lifestyle (*agrestis vita*) dominates the first part of the *argumentatio* (§§ 37–51), basically founded on the contrast between the rustic virtues of parsimony and diligence and the city vices, connected with immoderate behavior.[383] As Dyck notes, Cicero's portrait of Roscius turns out to be a "paean in praise of Rome's origins and the qualities that made the city great: Roscius, represented as a hard-working rustic, is thus allowed to bask in those reflected glories."[384]

Another example, taken from the *pro Sulla*, is crucial to clarifying the ways by which ancient theorists approached Cicero's tactic of persuasion.

---

[380] A similar expression, *obicere quaestionem*, "to throw the issue back in the opponent's face," occurs in Ps. Asconius 238.7-8St (on *Ver.* 2.1.58).

[381] Another instance of Cicero's tactic of forcing his opponent to silence is spotted by Ps. Asconius in the First Verrine (Hortensius is unable to continue with his discourse after Cicero's formal inquiry of the witnesses: 230.1-3St, on *Ver.* 1.24).

[382] Dyck 2010a: 111.

[383] The Gronovian scholiast discusses at length Cicero's strategic manipulation of the argument *de rusticitate*: cf. 308.5-9St (on *Rosc.* 49); 308.16-22St (on *Rosc.* 50); 310.29-30St (on *Rosc.* 75).

[384] Dyck 2003: 237. See also Vasaly 1985 (for the picture of Roscius as a naïve and virtuous *rusticus*).

The trial of P. Cornelius Sulla, charged under the *lex Plautia de vi*,[385] was probably held sometime between May and October 62 BCE.[386] It represented a significant moment in Cicero's political career, as it was on this very occasion that the former consul, the hero of the Catilinarian conspiracy, felt himself constrained to defend – and rehabilitate – his political position in the face of the charge of having attempted to establish *regnum* at Rome and, more than that, of having illegally executed Roman citizens (without regular trial). The initial sections of the speech (esp. §§ 2–10) concentrate on Cicero's rejoinder to the accusations of inconsistency and tyrannical behavior, formally presented by the chief prosecutor at the trial, the young L. Manlius Torquatus, who had complained vehemently about the former consul's decision to accept the defense of Sulla, accused of having conspired with Catiline.[387] Torquatus's allegation emerges as a serious assault on Cicero's consular *auctoritas*, understandably founded on popular anger and resentment (a consequence of Cicero's controversial handling of the Catilinarian conspiracy) and stirred up by his political enemies, among whom stood out the tribunes Q. Caecilius Metellus Nepos and L. Calpurnius Bestia, who had prevented the outgoing consul from delivering the customary retiring valedictory.[388] So it follows that Cicero conceived his plea on behalf of Sulla as a self-defense speech, a public (self-gratulatory) reconstruction of his role as consul and restorer of the political order. Cicero devoted a third of his speech (an ample digression, including chapters 2–35, with the exclusion of the *partitio* at chapters 11–14) to justifying his acceptance of the case and defending his political position. As Berry puts it, Sulla's trial enabled the *homo novus* Cicero "to display his *lenitas* and shake off the image of a *rex peregrinus*, substituting the more congenial picture of himself as the merciful savior of the Roman state."[389]

Cicero neutralized Torquatus's charges by depicting himself as a man of integrity, a trustworthy politician committed to the common cause. This strategy revealed its usefulness in particular in Cicero's rebuttal of Torquatus's charge of "tyrannical capriciousness" in handling the case of the guilty P. Autronius Paetus. By refusing his support to Autronius, Cicero displayed in fact a comportment strikingly contrasting with the humane and kind treatment reserved to the innocent

---

[385] Schol. Bob. 84.21-22St. See Alexander 2002: 189–205 (for the charges against Sulla).
[386] Berry 1996a: 14.
[387] Sulla was also accused of complicity in the first conspiracy of 66 (Cic. *Sul.* 11; cf. also schol. Bob. 77.19-26St): on the question see Berry 1996a: 151ff.
[388] On the sources see Berry 1996a: 206 (on Cic. *Sul.* 34.2).     [389] Berry 1996a: 28.

Sulla.³⁹⁰ The Bobbio scholiast expands on Cicero's ethical argumentation, stressing first the persuasive force of the dilemma device at § 10 (77.6-13St)³⁹¹ and pointing to the orator's disingenuous, cynical self-presentation as a man not sufficiently informed of the political events of 66 (77.19-26St).³⁹² Then he emphatically comments on Cicero's "rhetorical acuteness" (*oratoria suptilitate*), calling attention to the opposition of "the brash and evil Autronius with the decorous and decent Sulla"³⁹³ as the central point of the orator's self-defense. Cicero's insistence on Sulla's innocence and his own compassionate nature is read as a powerful response to Torquatus's attack, an extremely profitable form of argumentation (79.9-16St):

> Veniebat enim ad me et saepe veniebat Autronius] Salubriter institit huic parti: multis et inpensis precibus auxilium defensionis commemoratis amicitiae veteris officiis Autronium postulasse multosque alios ad hoc impetrandum pro se deprecatores adhibuisse nec tamen extorsisse ut patronus ei et defensor adsisteret: ne hoc dicere adversarius posset: "Idcirco Autronium non defendisti, quod non satis egerit ut a te defenderetur." Sed si hoc impensissime deprecatus est nec impetravit, videri iam potest idcirco ad defendendum Syllam venire, quod de eius innocentia certus sit.

> "For to me Autronius would come, and would come often] He dwelled on this point to good effect: he said that Autronius had often and repeatedly implored him to act in his support by reminding him of their consolidated friendship and calling in many other intercessors to obtain his service: however, he could not be persuaded to assist him as both a patronus and a defender, so that the prosecutor [Torquatus] could not sustain his argument and say: 'You have not supported Autronius, because he had not done enough to convince you to accept his defense.' But the point was: if he [Autronius] prayed without any stint and he could not obtain it, it would become apparent that he decided to defend Sulla, because he was absolutely certain about his innocence."

The tale of Autronius's passionate and persistent pleading (at § 18) provides a showcase for Cicero's integrity and kindly nature. In portraying Autronius as a *supplex* Cicero deliberately misrepresents his role in the political events of 66 and 63, implicitly dramatizing the gravity of the crime (Autronius's proven involvement in the conspiracy) and offering thereby his own negative reaction to the conspirator's appeal for aid in justification of his choice to act in behalf of Sulla. From the refusal to defend Autronius

---

³⁹⁰ Craig 2014: 213.  ³⁹¹ Craig 1993b: 92–3.  ³⁹² Cf. also schol. Bob. 78.7-8St.
³⁹³ Craig 2014: 214.

the jury was entitled to infer Sulla's innocence. As the scholiast understands, "the fact that not even the most persistent appeals could induce Cicero to defend a guilty conspirator is intended to suggest that Cicero's defense of Sulla implies the latter's innocence."[394] Cicero resisted Autronius's appeals because of his proven misconduct. A feeling of anger, *indignatio*, pervades Cicero's rejection of Autronius. As Craig has recently observed, in the *pro Sulla* "Cicero portrays his own emotional trajectory in an internal decision-making process driven by the competing feelings of pity and outrage."[395]

Cicero's elaborate self-depiction as a compassionate and mild man makes an ideal starting point for the reply to Torquatus's more forceful (and potentially damaging) *regnum* accusation, a charge of autocratic power directly involving Cicero's actions as consul. Here too the scholiast's comments help us to shed light on Cicero's self-fashioning as a moderate, law-abiding consul, subservient to senatorial authority. Torquatus's allegation of exercising "regal" and absolute power is countered by Cicero by recalling his consulship as an example of "moderation, probity and virtue" (*consulatum suum talia edidisse moderationis et continentiae et virtutis exempla*: 79.21-2St) and, above all, by depicting the execution of the conspirators as a crackdown on *regnum*, a self-defense act in reaction to the tyrannical ambitions of Catiline and his followers (*regnum adfectantibus*: 79.22St). In a standard *reductio ad absurdum* Cicero quickly eliminates any suspicion of autocratic power in his handling of the conspiracy and turns the *regnum* accusation back in the face of his opponent, connecting the term *regnum* to the conspiracy act. As the scholiast notes, with such action Cicero "freed his authority from enmity and discredit and made the sense of what he was going to say to achieve Sulla's acquittal more obscure" (*et invidia liberat auctoritatem suam et impenetrabilius facit quod ad Syllae victoriam locuturus est*: 79.23-4St).

Cicero's strategy of removal of *invidia*, through the usual *retorsio argumenti* (turning the argument round),[396] is perceived by the scholiast as essential to the orator's self-praise. As we have seen, the *regnum* argument, a nodal point in Torquatus's accusation, is turned to prove that the prosecutor himself was guilty of what he had alleged. More significantly, the *peregrinitas* argument, a leitmotif of political invective in the late republic and a stock feature of anti-Ciceronian invectives,[397] is counterattacked by Cicero by adducing illustrious examples of both "foreign kings" (Tarquinius and Numa) and eminent political figures of *municipalis* origin

---

[394] Berry 1996a: 168.   [395] Craig 2014: 216.   [396] Cic. *Inv.* 1.90; Quint. *Inst.* 5.13.29.
[397] Schol. Bob. 80.12-7St; Berry 1996a: 182.

(Cato the Elder, Ti. Coruncanius, M. Curius Dentatus and C. Marius) and ingeniously designating Torquatus himself as a "foreigner."[398] Cicero's tactic of "appropriation and reversal," filled with indignation,[399] clears the way for the final, emphatic self-portrayal as a magistrate devoted to the supreme interests of the state. As the scholiast comments, Cicero boasts about his great services to the *res publica* (*gloriose in hunc locum decurrit orator, laudibus suis plurimisque meritis erga rem p. tribuens*: 81.15-6St) and his refusal of a honest retirement after completing a long political career.[400] In "teleological" tones the orator connects his action as a far-sighted and prudent consul with the gods' will (*divino quodam mentis instinctu*: 81.28-9St),[401] a stratagem (often used in the speeches) correctly interpreted by the commentator as preparatory to demonstration of Sulla's innocence (81.30-82.3St). Concerned to play his consulship up, Cicero makes the most of Torquatus's allegations and depicts himself as a "divine" consul, a common topic in the consular and post-return speeches. The terms of Cicero's self-praise are well absorbed by the schoolteacher, who displays competence and good critical judgment. Taking a step further, one might venture to say that the scholiast proposes Cicero's sophisticated and brilliant combination of rhetorical/ethical arguments and self-fashioning as an effective means of persuasion in cases of political relevance.

Before closing this long section, I want to draw attention to a note of the Gronovian scholiast (**D**) on the initial words of the speech on behalf of the king Deiotarus. The note runs as follows (299.1-7St):

> Tum in hac causa ita me <m.> perturbant] Amamus periclitantibus subvenire. Hac arte dixit quemadmodum in Corneliana et in Cluentiana. Et dedit exemplum Virgilius. Sinon <nisi> miserabilem personam sumpsisset: et non haberet quemadmodum Troianis extorqueret misericordiam, quippe hostis. Ut eius fallax audiretur oratio, finxit turbari: turbatus inquit inermis constitit. Sic et modo Cicero, quia apud Caesarem de hoste Caesaris loquitur, finxit se moveri, ut eius audiatur oratio.

> "Then in this case I am so perturbed by many things] We usually long to support those who are in danger. By means of this device Cicero pleaded in

---

[398] Cic. *Sul.* 25 (the Bobbio scholiast uses the verb *humilitare* [*humiliare*], "humiliate," to design Cicero's demolition of Torquatus's reputation: 81.5St).
[399] Schol. Bob. 80.21-4St. For further comments on the "appropriation and reversal" tactic cf. also schol. Bob. 90.26-7St (on *Clod.* frg26); 140.4St (on *Sest.* 133).
[400] In the scholiast's opinion, Cicero would have imitated a passage from an oration of C. Gracchus (1.190*ORF*): 81.18-24St.
[401] On this recurrent theme in Cicero's orations (especially on divine favor as a self-promotion instrument), see Gildenhard 2011a: 255–98.

such a manner as he had spoken in the speeches in behalf of Cornelius and Cluentius. Vergil gave an example of this. If Sinon had not taken on a pitiable figure, he would not have had any possibility to induce the Trojans to clemency, as he was an enemy. He pretended to be perturbed so that they would listen to his false and deceitful speech; he said: 'I am anxious' and he stood unarmed. Similarly Cicero, for he spoke before Caesar on behalf of an enemy of Caesar, pretended to be perturbed, so that his speech could be paid attention to."

Perhaps the "most baffling of Cicero's speeches,"[402] the *pro rege Deiotaro*, from its very outset, presents an anxious lawyer pleading a case before a single trial judge who, by "chance," has also been the target of an alleged killing plot. The anomalous situation occasions the pleader's anxiety. Cicero is very eloquent in this respect in the opening lines of the speech. He manipulates the disadvantages of the trial to elicit compassion from the judge and deploys an emotional tactic to make Caesar benevolent. As Gotoff observes, "the *exordium* that began with Cicero in panic ends with him supremely confident because of the virtues of his judge."[403] The ancient commentator takes notice of Cicero's strategy, comparable with an analogous tactic used in the (lost) two speeches in behalf of Cornelius[404] and in the *pro Cluentio*. The allusion is clearly to the technique of the *insinuatio*, which Cicero draws on in the opening lines of the *pro Cornelio*[405] and in the proemial section of the *pro Cluentio*,[406] a cunning ploy designed to win the jury's sympathy by way of demonstration of the difficulties faced by the lawyer in handling the case. Interestingly, the scholiast exemplifies Cicero's manipulation of the jurymen through the archetypal figure of Vergilian liar Sinon, the mendacious Greek orator "well-trained in trickery and Pelasgian craft" (*dolis instructus et arte Pelasga*),[407] and indirectly hints at the opening words of Sinon's speech in the second book of Vergil's *Aeneid* (2.77–80).[408] The passage resembles Grillius's comment on Cicero's *De inventione* 1.20 (in particular the mentioned note on the *insinuatio*), in which the scholar quotes a Vergilian line (*Aen.* 2.79: *neque me Argolica de gente negabo*), taken from Sinon's speech (without specifying the name of the speaker), after reporting the *exordium* of Cicero's *pro Cornelio* as an instance of

---

[402] Gotoff 2002: 251.   [403] Gotoff 2002: 258.
[404] This passage is not included among the *testimonia* of the speech in Crawford 1994.
[405] Grill. 89.88-91Jakobi. On the *exordium* of the *pro Cornelio*, see Crawford 1994: 98–100.
[406] On the emotional effects of the *insinuatio* strategy in the opening sections of the *pro Cluentio*, see Patimo 2009: 73–81.
[407] Verg. *Aen.* 2.152.
[408] An useful commentary on Sinon's speech is in Horsfall 2008: *ad loc.* (see also Highet 1972: 247–8).

*insinuatio per circuitionem* (89.88-92Jakobi).[409] A consolidated *synkrisis* in rhetorical handbooks, Cicero and Sinon share the art of illusion, the faculty for manipulating and swaying the minds of potential hearers. And like Sinon, whose lying appearance and mendacious speech led ultimately to Troy's ruin, Cicero as an orator establishes himself as a potential liar, a trained manipulator prepared to arouse passions and destroy his opponent's credibility by means of tricky language. In addition to being a common exordial device, the fiction of anxiety bears witness to oratory, *ars dicendi*, as a potential tool of deceit in the hands of talented and astute speakers.[410]

Cicero's final purpose was to win his case. He deployed and applied different patterns of argumentation to each specific case in order to enhance his point of view and gain approval. But, if we focus upon the intended readership of Cicero's oratory and the didactic context in which the speeches were supposed to be read and interpreted, it is clear that the reader/student might have trouble in understanding the historical and political framework of the case and, above all, in appreciating the rhetorical and linguistic features of every single speech only on the basis of the information contained within the text.[411] Levene has correctly noted that "the reader has problems of his own in interpreting the speech, and so will approach it through preconceptions derived from a rhetorical theory that is itself only partly connected to the pragmatics of rhetoric."[412] So ancient teachers guided their students through the complexities of each speech by elucidating historical and political references, focusing upon perceived rhetorical effects, illustrating deviations from ordinary rules and, above all, pointing to Cicero's impressive ability in manipulating arguments and rhetorical material. Each passage of the speech was read as an instance of Cicero's facility for devising and commanding arguments and exploiting linguistic and emotional devices in an urbane manner. Yet there was more. Cicero was a master of oratory as the art of illusion. Like the Vergilian Sinon, Cicero misled his audience. In Gorgian terms, he was a "leader of souls" (*psychagogos*), a sort of magician enchanting his listeners through psychological and aesthetic strategies.[413] As we have seen, throwing dust

---

[409] Sinon's rhetorical tactics is commented upon by Serv. Dan. *Aen.* 2.69 (the scholiast places particular emphasis upon Sinon's strategy for arousing pity and making the listeners docile and benevolent).
[410] Cicero's feeling of uneasiness, manifested by the opening words of chapter 4 (*perturbat me etiam illud*), is described as a rhetorical stratagem (*ars dicendi*) by the scholiast: cf. 299.19St.
[411] Levene 2004: 140 (who opportunely takes into account Quintilian's didactic prescriptions at *Inst.* 10.1.20–3 and 2.5.7).
[412] Levene 2004: 146.   [413] López Eire 2007: 341.

into the eyes of the judges and concealing the truth was the art in which Cicero was without equal, the only way he had sometimes to accomplish his goal, especially in weak cases or before patently hostile audiences.[414] In offering the speeches as instructive examples of practical advocacy and focusing upon Cicero's crafty and artful use of rhetorical devices the schoolmasters grasped the sense of the art of advocacy. Most significantly, they exposed the persuasion effects of Cicero's strategy and made their students sensible to the potentialities of manipulative oratory, encouraging them to tread on Cicero's footsteps in order to manage each case successfully and achieve victory. Under the guide of teacher trainers Roman elite students looked through Cicero's speeches in the hope of making personal success in real-life oratory.

## *Eleganter Dixit Cicero*

In the Second Book of his *Institutio* Quintilian expatiates on the long-debated issue of the content and end of rhetoric (2.17). Confronting earlier criticism of rhetoric as a "purposeless art" he spells out the primary goal of the profession of speaking (2.17.22–3):

> Aiunt etiam omnes artes habere finem aliquem propositum, ad quem tendant: hunc modo nullum esse in rhetorice, modo non praestari eum, qui promittatur. Mentiuntur: nos enim esse finem iam ostendimus, et quis esset diximus. (23) Et praestabit hunc semper orator, semper enim bene dicet. Firmum autem hoc, quod opponitur, adversus eos fortasse sit, qui persuadere finem putaverunt. Noster orator arsque a nobis finita non sunt posita in eventu. Tendit quidem ad victoriam qui dicit: sed cum bene dixit, etiamsi non vincat, id quod arte continetur effecit.

> "My opponents also assert that every art has some definite goal towards which it directs its efforts, but that rhetoric as a rule has no such goal, while at other times it professes to have an aim, but fails to provide what it promises. They lie: I have already shown that rhetoric has a definite purpose and have explained what it is. (23) And, what is more, the orator will always make good his professions in this respect, for he will always speak well. On the other hand this criticism may perhaps hold good as against those who think persuasion the end of oratory. But our orator and his art, as we define

---

[414] On the reasons inducing a good man (*vir bonus*) to conceal the truth from the judge (*auferre aliquando iudici veritatem*), cf. Quint. *Inst.* 12.1.36–45 (who exploits the basic tension between morality and oratory and legitimates manipulation of truth as a necessity dictated by the circumstances of the case, not infringing moral laws and the orator's integrity of purpose, *honesta voluntas*: cf. *Inst.* 12.1.45).

it, are independent of results. The speaker aims at victory, it is true, but if he speaks well, he has lived up to the ideals of his art, even if he is defeated."

Rhetoric satisfies its ideal if the orator succeeds in the virtues of diction (*elocutio*). Termed "artistic eloquence" (*artificiosa eloquentia*) by Cicero,[415] rhetoric is intended to function as a display of linguistic abilities. Its main aim consists of good, virtuous language. Quintilian clarifies this concept in a later passage (2.17.25–6):

> Ita oratori bene dixisse finis est. Nam est ars ea, ut post paulum clarius ostendemus, in actu posita non in effectu. (26) Ita falsum erit illud quoque, quod dicitur, artes scire quando sint finem consecutae, rhetoricen nescire. Nam se quisque bene dicere intelligit.

"So too the orator's purpose is fulfilled if he has spoken well. For the art of rhetoric, as I shall show later, is realized in action, not in the result obtained. (26) From this it follows that there is no truth in yet another argument which contends that arts know when they have attained their end, whereas rhetoric does not. For every speaker is aware of when he is speaking well."

Quintilian's view of rhetoric as the "art of speaking well,"[416] an ethical concept embedded in the elite ideal of Romanity, as we have seen, is intrinsic to his pedagogical project. In defining ornateness and appropriateness of language as virtues of the "really eloquent speaker,"[417] Quintilian holds *elocutio*, style, to be the central part of rhetorical training, since without its power "all the preliminary accomplishments of oratory are as useless as a sword that is kept permanently concealed within its sheath."[418] A disciplined style, produced by a dynamic fusion of verbal ornaments and propriety of language (*urbanitas*), is the fruit of reading and imitation, followed by exercise in composition. It results from a long cultivation of authoritative texts, the only source of knowledge of good Latin. Once supplied with adequate linguistic resources (carefully acquired beforehand), the budding orator is expected to deliver a powerful speech, in a perfect combination of persuasive arguments and suitable style producing admiration and pleasure in the audience.[419]

---

[415] Cf. Quint. *Inst.* 2.17.2 (from Cic. *Inv.* 1.6); Victorin. 172.32 *RLM*. See supra p. 222 and nn197–98.
[416] Cf. also Quint. *Inst.* 8 pr. 6 (*rhetoricen bene dicendi scientiam et utilem et artem et virtutem esse*).
[417] Quint. *Inst.* 8 praef. 13 (on Cic. *de Orat.* 1.94).
[418] *Sine quo supervacua sunt priora et similia gladio condito atque intra vaginam suam haerenti* (Quint. *Inst.* 8 *praef.* 15). For Crassus's discussion of the theory of *elocutio* in the third book of *De oratore*, see Fantham 2004: 237–66.
[419] Quint. *Inst.* 8 *praef.* 28–33.

Excellence and elegance of style would not only render the speech more effective. Beautiful style could also testify to the good character of the speaker, who presents himself as a trustworthy man by means of reasonable arguments and elegant diction. What distinguishes the good orator from the bad one is his capacity for deploying elegant stylistic devices, which are entirely congruent with the content of the speech.[420] Through language the good speaker portrays himself as having a good "moral" character. As has been shown, criticism of technical and oratorical faults is often "intricately linked with general Roman views of what was and was not becoming, fitting, and generally morally acceptable."[421] In terms of oratorical effectiveness, speaking well and showing good judgment, propriety of language and technical competence could give the speech the kind of credibility that is crucial to persuasion.[422]

Naturally, Quintilian's encouragement to strive for good Latin has to do with the long-shared idea of oratory as a "dynamic live performance,"[423] whose persuasive effect was secured not only by force of arguments but also by correct diction and a proper use of voice (*pronuntiatio*) and gesture (*actio*). Preoccupied with corruption and degeneration of style in his own times,[424] Quintilian emphasized the importance of *Latinitas* as a means of exerting influence on the hearers' minds. At the same time, he turned the spotlight on the importance of delivery as a form of political and social promotion. Like Cicero, he endorsed the orator as a master of the skills of public speaking. Voice, nonverbal language, emotional gestures and image management: all played a part in augmenting the persuasive power of a speech. As Hall notes, "the Roman orator laid himself open to criticism and ridicule every time he spoke in public. Plebeian and patrician alike were quick to mock perceived flaws in a speaker's performance."[425] On this ground, a well-staged, effective oratorical performance was fundamentally inseparable from the acquisition of power and authority within Roman aristocratic society. Oratory was a performing art rather than a literary

---

[420] On the "bad" orator, see the exhaustive discussion of Wisse 2013.    [421] Wisse 2013: 172.
[422] Quint. *Inst.* 8.3.5: *Sed ne causae quidem parum confert idem hic orationis ornatus. Nam, qui libenter audiunt, et magis attendant et facilius credunt, plerumque ipsa delectatione capiuntur, nonnumquam admiratione auferuntur* ("But rhetorical ornament contributes not a little to the furtherance of our case as well. For when our audience find it a pleasure to listen, their attention and their readiness to believe what they hear are both alike increased, while they are generally filled with delight, and sometimes even transported by admiration").
[423] Hall 2007: 218.
[424] Quint. *Inst.* 8 pr. 18–28 (on oversophistication and deteriorioation of style); see Connolly 2007b: 93–4 (for a discussion of Quintilian's condemnation of ornament's emasculation of speech). On the theatricalization of rhetoric and effeminacy of performance, see Enders 1997.
[425] Hall 2014b: 43.

genre.[426] Clearness, elegance and appropriateness of style (*decorum*)[427] certainly fired the enthusiasm of the audience and paved thereby the way towards oratorical success. An excellent delivery, resulting from a correct use of voice tone and gesture[428] and the adoption of a "masculine" posture,[429] offered the ambitious Roman elite orator the occasion to create his own public space and acquire high social visibility into the bargain.[430] As Quintilian makes it clear when dealing with the extraordinary success of Cicero's *pro Cornelio*, "sublimity, splendor, brilliance and weight of eloquence" (*sublimitas, magnificentia, nitor et auctoritas*) won general, public approbation.[431] Transported by admiration, the listeners blessed the orator with *dignitas* and authority.

Attention has recently been paid to the doctrine of the "rhetoricity of language," the power of *logos*, that is, the deployment of emotional and stylistic strategies to attract and lead the souls of the hearers.[432] In a philosophical approach to language (an approach favored by Gorgias, the various sophists, and Aristotle), "rhetoricity"opposes the notion of truth as the main aim of rhetorical discourse and admits to the use of pathetic and stylistic devices to move and delight the listeners' or judges' minds. As clearly stated, "rhetoricity is the quality or capacity that persuades listeners through a logical but not necessarily strict or true argument, and especially with psychological and aesthetic strategies based on language in action and derived from language itself."[433] In this context, rhetorical language is not very dissimilar from the language of poetry.[434] Both the orator and the poet aim to inspire emotions in their potential hearers/readers. What counts in language is its capacity for impressing the audience and living up to general expectation of aesthetic delight by means of an elegant style. In the case of oratory, obviously, "rhetoricity" implies persuading the judge-hearer by appeals to emotion and attractive linguistic stratagems.

Applied to Roman oratory and Cicero's style in particular, the concept of "rhetoricity of language," as it has been described, makes sense of many

---

[426] Hall 2007: 234.
[427] Arena 2013: 198 (for the importance of *decorum* as "the self-regulating means which permits the perfect orator to choose the most appropriate style, according to the subject matter and the character of both speaker and audience"). On the concept of *decorum* cf. Cic. *Orat.* 69; 97 (for the literary and stylistic notion of *decorum* as a conjunction of ethics and aesthetics, see Guérin 2009).
[428] On the theory of gesture in antiquity, see Aldrete 1999.
[429] For "masculinity" in oratorical performance, see Gleason 1995; Richlin 1997; Gunderson 2000.
[430] On Roman preoccupations with the morality of the elite, see Edwards 1993 (esp. 12–28).
[431] Quint. *Inst.* 8.3.3–4.    [432] López Eire 2007.    [433] López Eire 2007: 343.
[434] Cic. *de Orat.* 1.70. On the interaction between rhetoric and poetry, see in general Webb 1997.

emotional and stylistic strategies exploited by the orator to influence the opinions of the judges. Cicero's use of psychological and aesthetic strategies in his speeches reflects his belief in language as a powerful means of persuading the judges. Through the variety of ornaments, such as figures, repetitions, metaphors and intensifying linguistic devices, he shaped his personal style, a style founded on the requirements of effectiveness and appropriateness of language. Conscious of the persuasive effects of rhetorical strategies based on language, Cicero aimed to impress his hearers by means of pathetic and sophisticated stylistic devices, offering his own eloquence as an instance of oratorical success relying on rational arguments and charming language. In Cicero's opinion, victory could only be secured by means of the rhetorical tools proper to the grand style, i.e. "the appeal to emotions, the recourse to *ornatus*, the implementation of rhythm in prose, the deployment of the *loci communes*, as well as the theatrical devices of the *actio*."[435]

If correctness (*Latinitas*) and lucidity (*perspicuitas*) were thought of as virtues of good Latin, pursued by any trained orator, it was on the quality of distinction or ornament (*cultus, ornatus*)[436] that the attractiveness and the persuasive force of a speech most relied. Quintilian explicitly affirms that the speaker who possesses the virtue of ornament "fights not merely with effective, but with flashing weapons" (*Inst.* 8.3.2).[437] Since the attention of the audience is increased by aesthetic pleasure, one who admires beauty of language is generally inclined to believe what he hears (*Inst.* 8.3.5).[438] Ornament then fulfills a psychological and aesthetic function. More importantly, as already said, it fulfills a persuasive function, resulting in the most effective weapon of oratorical competition. To put it differently, eloquence that appeals to the emotions of the audience by linguistic devices would induce belief and play a decisive role in the final act of deliberation. As has correctly been said, "leading to a rational appreciation of the arguments, ornament strengthens deliberation, rather than interfering with it."[439]

Yet the aesthetic devices associated with the virtue of *ornatus* must naturally be adapted to the specific content of each case, "appropriate," so to speak, to the occasion or the right moment. It follows that the fourth virtue of style,[440] "appropriateness" (*aptum, decorum*), inextricably

---

[435] Arena 2013: 198.   [436] Cic. *de Orat.* 1.144 (Quint. *Inst.* 8.3.1).
[437] *Nec fortibus modo, sed etiam fulgentibus armis proeliatur.*
[438] *Nam qui libenter audiunt et magis attendunt et facilius credunt, plerumque ipsa delectatione capiuntur, nonnumquam admiratione auferuntur.*
[439] Arena 2013: 205.
[440] Cic. *de Orat.* 1.144; 3.37; 3.210; *Orat.* 21; 79; *Rhet. Her.* 4.17–8; Quint. *Inst.* 1.5.1; 8.1.1; 11.1.1 (on the basis of the fourfold division of the virtues of diction in Theophrastus's lost treatise *On diction*). Kirchner 2007: 182.

## Eleganter Dixit Cicero

connected to the "rhetoricity of language,"[441] becomes the main concern of the good speaker, who has to make the style of his speech suit the genre, audience, speaker and occasion (*causa, auditor, persona, tempus*)[442] and adapt ornamentation to the type of diction (plain, middle and grand style) required by the specific circumstances of the speech. As Quintilian says, "words that are both good Latin and significant and graceful" (*verba et Latina et significantia et nitida*) and embellishments of style (by means of elaborate figures and rhythms) remain ineffectual unless they are in harmony with the matters at issue and the purposes of the speech.[443] Only language suited to the case enables the orator to construct and deliver a persuasive speech based on emotional arguments and stylistic strategies. Appropriate style produces credibility and makes the orator a "good," moral character, as already said. If read in didactic terms, appropriateness becomes a tenet of rhetorical education. Engaged in the formation of the ideal orator, Quintilian places great emphasis on the orator's employment of appropriate and elegant language as a mark of good oratory (*Inst.* 11.1.6).[444]

Ancient theorists and commentators devoted much of their scholarly efforts to illustrating the features of Cicero's elegant style. The explanation of Cicero's stylistic strategies was integral to the reception of the speeches in the schools of rhetoric. The icon of the Latin language, as we have shown in the previous chapter, Cicero was also reputed to be a master of *elegantia*, "refined style," involving clarity and lucidity of language, rhythmical prose[445] and presentation of arguments in dignified words.[446] Ancient commentators pointed often to *elegantia* as a distinctive feature of Cicero's style.[447] Cicero personified the power of artistic eloquence, associating persuasion with a

---

[441] López Eire 2007: 347.   [442] Cic. *de Orat.* 3.210.   [443] Quint. *Inst.* 11.1.2.
[444] *Quare notum sit nobis ante omnia, quid conciliando, docendo, movendo iudici conveniat, quid quaque parte orationis petamus* ("For this reason, it is of the first importance that we should know what style is most suitable for conciliating, instructing or moving the judge, and what effects we should aim at in different parts of our speech").
[445] On rhythm in prose composition cf. Quint. *Inst.* 9.4.121–46. In general, see Hutchinson 1995; Powell 2013: 59–62.
[446] Stucchi 2013 (for the use of *elegantia* in Cicero's works); see also Krostenko 2001: 116–17 (on *elegantia* as propriety of language). Cicero is associated with the *elegantissimi veteres* in Gel. 18.7.8–9.
[447] Here it may be convenient to list some passages from the scholia that contain specific comments on the elegance of Cicero's diction: schol. Bob. 90.20St (on *Clod.* frg26: *elegantissime*); 103.2St (on *Flac.* 41: *eleganter et oratorio stomacho*); 103.18St (on *Flac.* 43: *eleganti verbo usus est amplecteretur*); 104.3St (on *Flac.* 46: *eleganter*); 124.24St. (on *Mil.* 103: *elegantissime*); 127.7St (on *Sest.* 12: *et eleganter*); 134.18St (on *Sest.* 68: *distinxit haec verba eleganti proprietate*); 163.13St (on *Planc.* 64: *consideremus quam eleganter . . .*); 169.6St (on *Planc.* 102: *ita eleganter*); 176.13St (on *Arch.* 5: *sed eleganter . . . in hac parte narrationis ostendit*); schol. Gronov. (**D**) 306.21St (on *Rosc.* 41: *eleganter*); schol. Gronov. (**B**) 334.33 (*eleganter*).

vigorous rhetorical language, founded on a variety of stylistic ornaments and appropriateness of style. It follows that his speeches served as examples of the proper application of linguistic forms and devices to rhetorical argumentation, in line with the requirements of correctness, clarity, distinction and appropriateness, as presented by Roman rhetorical handbooks.[448]

According to Theophrastus,[449] magnificence and efficaciousness of ornament could be achieved through word choice, figures and sentence structure. Adopting this established threefold classification, we can start to look at the ways by which ancient theorists and scholiasts approached Cicero's use of emotional and linguistic tools. Our presentation will of necessity be selective, since a detailed analysis of the different linguistic phenomena occurring in Cicero's oratorical prose (and their related interpretation) would entail a monograph of its own, a work already done in good part by eminent Ciceronian scholars and language specialists.[450] In regard to word choice (*dilectus verborum*), a large part of our discussion has already been dedicated to the selection of appropriate words as a long-appreciated virtue of Cicero's language.[451] Analogously, due attention has been paid to Cicero's vocabulary, encompassing neologisms, archaisms and abstract nouns, as a sign of cultivated style.[452] In addition to what has been said about appraisal of Cicero's propriety of language in antiquity, here we may briefly add that ancient scholars frequently called attention to the correct and appropriate use of words in the speeches. Just to give some examples, the Bobbio scholiast eulogizes Cicero for the use of a potent and eloquent verb, such as *iacto*, at *Mil.* 7 (112.26St).[453] Similarly, according to Ps. Asconius, Cicero accurately selected words to shape the hearers' minds, such as *occido* at *Ver.* 2.1.90, a verb serving the orator's intent to make the audience skeptical about the opponent's arguments (*suspiciosum verbum*: 244.25St).

Among the tools for embellishing a speech, the trope, defined by Quintilian as "a change of a word or phrase from its proper meaning into another for the sake of effect" (*Inst.* 8.6.1),[454] produces a major impact

---

[448] For the *elocutionis virtutes et vitia*, see Lausberg 1998: 216–471 (§§ 458–1077).
[449] Dion. Hal. *De Isocr.* 3.1.   [450] Albrecht 2003; Powell 2013.   [451] See chapter 3, pp. 138–62.
[452] For Crassus's discussion of individual words (divided into words used singly and words used in combination) in the doctrine of *ornatus* in Cic. *de Orat.* 3.148–86 (cf. also *Or.* 80–1; *Part.* 16–8), see Mankin 2011: 234–80. On Cicero's propriety in the use of words, cf. Quint. *Inst.* 8.2.
[453] The expression *iactata sunt* conveys a threefold signification (*non decreta, non statuta, non iudicata*) according to the scholiast, who points to the effectiveness of the word used by Cicero (*verbo usus est efficaciter*).
[454] *Tropus est verbi vel sermonis a propria significatione in aliam cum virtute mutatio.* Cf. also Quint. *Inst.* 9.1.5 (tropes include metaphor, metonymy, antonomasia, metalepsis, synecdoché, catachresis, allegory, and hyperbole, concerning either words or things).

on the disposition and structure of thoughts and sentences. The trope commonly known as metaphor (*translatio*),[455] the "commonest and by far the most beautiful of tropes,"[456] adds ornament to the speech in a number of ways and, if correctly and properly applied, secures persuasive effects. Cicero was thought of as a master of metaphors and suggestive allegories (extended metaphors),[457] as testified by Quintilian's numerous references to metaphors in the speeches.[458] We also have a number of notes on Cicero's imaginative use of metaphors in the commentaries. For example, the word *ministrator*, "attendant," in *Flac*. 53 (referred to Maeandrius) is interpreted as a metaphorical transposition of the figure of the gladiatorial assistant into that of the legal attorney by the Bobbio scholiast (105.17-9St).[459] Metaphors are detected at *Red. Sen*. 18 (109.23St)[460] and *Sest*. 71 (134.23-4St).[461] The celebrated metaphor of the shipwreck of the republic at *Sest*. 15 attracts interest from the scholiast, who points to the appropriateness of the verbs *colligere* ("to repair") and *reficere* ("to restore") and explicitly invites his students to respect the norms of propriety and choice of words when creating allegories (*aptissimis verbis et congruentibus*: 127.19-20St). Again, figurative language derives from the terminology of war,[462] medicine,[463] law[464] and nature's elements,[465] as regularly observed by the scholiasts. Teachers and students looked at Cicero's speeches as a valuable source of rhetorical metaphors. One might also observe that Cicero's mastery of metaphorical language reminded practitioners of rhetoric of the rules of correct Latin. Cicero himself showed that a "gross metaphor" (*deformis translatio*) or excess in the use of metaphor betrayed a lack of

---

[455] Lausberg 1998: 250–6 (§§ 558–564). On the use of metaphor and devices related to metaphor, cf. Cic. *de Orat*. 3.155–70 (and Mankin 2011: 241–70).

[456] Quint. *Inst*. 8.6.4.   [457] Quint. *Inst*. 9.2.46 (a continued metaphor develops into allegory).

[458] Quint. *Inst*. 8.6.4–18 (Quintilian draws largely on Cicero and Vergil to offer instances of effective metaphors). For Cicero's use of metaphors in humorous contexts, cf. Quint. *Inst*. 6.3.69.

[459] According to the commentator, the term *ministrator* designates a gladiator assistant (properly a man charged with providing gladiators with weapons). For the word *ministratrix* cf. Cic. *de Orat*. 1.76; 2.305.

[460] The commentator points to the metaphorical use of the verb *occido* in the expression *Nondum palam factum erat occidisse rem publicam* ("It was not yet openly known that the republic had fallen").

[461] Cicero's description of Piso and Gabinius as *duo vulturii paludati*, "two vultures wearing the cloak," is deemed a "fitting metaphor" (*congruentissima* metaphora), because of the rapaciousness and violence of the tribunes.

[462] Schol. Clun. 269.11St (on Cic. *Cat*. 2.1: *motus est*); Ps. Asconius 333.19St (on Cic. *Ver*. 1.11: *oppugnavit ac prodidit*).

[463] Schol. Clun. 269.19St (on Cic. *Cat*. 2.2: *evomuerit*).

[464] Schol. Clun. 271.10St (on Cic. *Marc*. 9: *curriculum* as *forense officium*).

[465] Schol. Gronov. (**D**) 317.3-4St (on Cic. *Man*. 7: *emergere*, *translatio a sole*); schol. Gronov. (**B**) 342.17St (on Cic. *Ver*. 2.1.1: *emanarat*: marine metaphor).

oratorical skills.[466] In advancing Cicero as a model of a "temperate and felicitous use of metaphor" (*modicus atque opportunus usus: Inst.* 8.6.14), Quintilian cautioned the young against an inappropriate and irrational use of metaphors that could generate obscurity of language.[467] In other words, Cicero's proper use of allegorical language served Quintilian's didactical purposes. Imitation of Cicero's metaphors – and adhesion to the rules of correctness and propriety in consequence – was presented as crucial to the formation of the ideal orator.

Other tropes in the speeches fascinated ancient readers. Synecdoche,[468] metonymy,[469] emphasis,[470] litotes,[471] periphrasis,[472] hyperbaton[473] and antonomasia[474] occur often in Cicero's orations. Quintilian abounds in detail about these stylistic devices based on word choice and substitution, with specific reference to Cicero (along with Vergil) as a prime example of the correct use of these poetical tools of ornamentation. In particular, hyperbole, "a metaphor with vertical gradations and evocative, poetical effect,"[475] stands out as one of the finest and most vivid linguistic stratagems of amplification (or exaggeration) and, as such, is strongly recommended as an effective means of persuasion. If used with moderation, hyperbole amplifies the magnitude of the facts and ridicules the opponent, distorting the truth by augmentation or attenuation of actual events.[476] This is the case of Cicero's description of Antony's vomiting and drunkenness at *Phil.* 2.63, offered by Quintilian as a limpid example of hyperbole by exaggeration (*Inst.* 8.6.68). The passage evidently formed the core of any study of the "rhetoric of amplification." As the model of "augmentation" of style by introduction of "a continuous and unbroken series in which each word is stronger than the last" (*Inst.* 8.4.8–9)[477] and the form of amplification based on both comparison (*Inst.* 8.4.10)[478] and "reasoning,"

---

[466] Cic. *de Orat.* 3.164 (and Quint. *Inst.* 8.6.15–6).   [467] Quint. *Inst.* 8.6.14–18.
[468] Quint. *Inst.* 8.6.19; 28. Lausberg 1998: 260–62 (§§ 572–577).
[469] Quint. *Inst.* 8.6.23. Lausberg 1998: 256–60 (§§ 565–571).
[470] Quint. *Inst.* 8.2.11; 8.3.83; 86. Lausberg 1998: 262–63 (§ 578).
[471] Lausberg 1998: 268–9 (§§ 586–588).   [472] Lausberg 1998: 269–71 (§§ 589–598).
[473] Quint. *Inst.* 8.6.62–4: on the use of hyperbaton (in addition to parenthesis) as a source of obscurity in the sentence *At quemadmodum, iudices, venerint* at Cic. *Ver.* 2.2.11 cf. Ps. Asconius 259.21-2St. A good analysis of the linguistic phenomenon of hyperbaton in Cicero's prose is now in Powell 2010b.
[474] Quint. *Inst.* 8.6.29–30. Lausberg 1998: 264–66 (§§ 580–581).
[475] Lausberg 1998: 263–4 (§ 579).   [476] Quint. *Inst.* 8.6.74–6.
[477] Quintilian specifically applies his definition of augmentation (*augendi genus*) to Cicero's sentence *In coetu vero populi Romani, negotium publicum gerens, magister equitum* ("Before an assembly of the Roman people, while performing a public duty, while master of the cavalry-men").
[478] In Cicero's phrase *Si hoc tibi inter cenam et in illis immanibus poculis tuis accidisset, quis non turpe duceret? In coetu vero populi Romani* ("If this had befallen you at the dinner-table in the midst of your amazing potations, who would not have thought it unseemly? But it occurred at an assembly

*ratiocinatio* (*Inst.* 8.4.16),[479] Antony's vomit illustrated the qualities of Cicero's descriptive style, founded on the elegant treatment of different types of amplification in order to produce pleasure and admiration, and, above all, to fill the audience with disgust and horror.

As a "graded enhancement of the basic given facts by artistic means, in the interest of the party,"[480] *amplificatio* is a psychological and emotional device, determined by the sequence of words in composition. If achieved by augmentation (*incrementum*, or *modus per incrementa*, law of growing members)[481] or the accumulation of words and sentences identical in meaning (*congeries*), the *species amplificandi* lends grandeur and magnificence even to elements that are comparatively insignificant[482] and excites emotions at the same time. In addition to being a form of ornament, amplification thus constitutes itself as a powerful tool of persuasion, "an exacerbation of emotions generated in the audience,"[483] to be effectively employed in oratorical performances. A number of comments in the scholia draw on Ciceronian examples of *amplificatio* to instruct students in the political and rhetorical manipulation of this linguistic and aesthetic implement.[484] Cicero's use of the vocabulary of crime in the potent expression *Quae malum est ista audacia atque amentia* at *Ver.* 2.1.54 represents, according to the Gronovian scholiast **A**, an exemplary case of accumulation for the sake of indignation. This piling up (*congregatio*) of words or *loci* appears to be especially suitable to prosecutorial contexts, in which the orator sees the judge's anger and resentment at the opponent as beneficial to his strategy of persuasion (346.17-21St).[485] Amplification acts

---

of the Roman people"), Quintilian finds an example of amplification depending on comparison (the *incrementum* goes from the less to the greater).

[479] Cicero's reproachful expression *Tu istis faucibus, istis lateribus, ista gladiatoria totius corporis firmitate* ("You with such a throat, such flanks, such burly strength in every limb of your prize-fighter's body") is interpreted as a form of amplification produced by reasoning, as it leads the readers to infer the sense of the sentence by moving from one point to another (from throat and flanks it is possible to estimate the quantity of wine that Antony drank at Hippias's wedding and was unable to digest despite his bodily strength). The passage is cited also as an example of word arrangement and increasing structural constituents, from the minor to the major (Quint. *Inst.* 9.4.23). See also Rowe 1997: 153.

[480] Lausberg 1998: 118 (§ 259).

[481] Quint. *Inst.* 8.4 (on amplification by "augmentation, comparison, reasoning, and accumulation"). To illustrate amplification by augmentation Quintilian cites a passage from Cicero's *Fifth Verrine* (2.5.170).

[482] Quint. *Inst.* 8.4.3 (*incrementum est potentissimum, cum magna videntur etiam quae inferiora sunt*).

[483] Leigh 2004b: 125.

[484] E.g. Ps. Asconius 223.9St (on Cic. *Ver.* 1.56); schol. Gronov. (**B**) 324.25St (on Cic. *Div.* 4); 333.7 (on Cic. *Ver.* 1.11); 333.25St (on Cic. *Ver.* 1.12); 343.7St (on Cic. *Ver.* 2.1.2); schol. Gronov. (**A**) 345.5St (on Cic. *Ver.* 2.1.47).

[485] Quintilian offers Cic. *Lig.* 9 and *Ver.* 2.5.118 as instances of amplification by accumulation (*Inst.* 8.4.27; for the passage from the *pro Ligario* cf. also Iul. Sev. 369.7 *RLM*). On the use of amplification

also as a means of self-fashioning in Cicero's sentence *Quod ausus esset pro cive, pro bene merito cive, pro amico, pro re publica deprecari* (*Sest.* 29).[486] The Bobbio commentator points to the gradual accumulation of words and clauses in a stunning crescendo, which ends in the emphatic identification of Cicero with the destiny of the state (129.5-7St). In regard to the technique of amplification we quote here an eloquent passage from the Gronovian scholiast **A** (344.11-21St):

> Velim tamen et in hac brevitate perspicias non abesse Ciceronis studium τῆς αὐξήσεως. Id tamen egit, ut, quamvis proponeret, tamen acerbitatem mali facinoris extolleret. Ignem parum erat dixisse: subiecit ex lignis viridibus, quod est intolerabilius; addidit etiam umidis, quo spiritus magis magisque auferri solet. Superposuit in loco angusto, ubi densior fumus animam haurientes urgeret. Post haec deinde intulit hominem ingenuum, domi nobilem, P.R. socium amicum, fumo excruciatum semivivum reliquit. Totum si gradatim consideres, αὐξητικὸν est. Et nihilominus visus est tantum proposuisse, non et exaggerasse, cum robustius non potuerit augere. Ita si rem spectes, magna copia est; si verba numeres, summa brevitas.

"Nevertheless, I would like you to consider that this passage, though concise, shows Cicero's fondness for amplification. He did it with intention to exaggerate the cruelty of the punishment, while bringing the facts to the general attention. Fire was not enough: he added of green wood, which is more unbearable; he also added moist, so that life is gradually taken away. At the end of the sentence he placed in a confined spot: there a denser, swirling smoke would oppress those who are dying. After that he added a free-born man, a man of high rank in his own town, one of the allies and friends of Rome, was put through the agonies of suffocation and left there more dead than alive. If you examine the passage step by step, it is clearly based on a process of accretion. Nonetheless, he appeared to have only narrated events, not exaggerated them, since he could not amplify his account in a more powerful way. So, if you inspect the whole story, there is great abundance of details; if you count the words: there is extreme brevity and conciseness."

A sort of school lesson in rhetorical amplification, the scholiast comments on Cicero's sophisticated version of the penalty inflicted on the magistrate of Sicyon by the governor Verres (*Ver.* 2.1.45), in the form of a restricted sequence of words or small clauses arranged by a graded augmentation. Cicero's artistic virtuosity creates a short story, which captures the admiration of the audience and, by a calculated addition of significant

---

to move listeners to pity cf. also Cic. *Mil.* 102 (*Quid respondebo liberis meis? Quid tibi, Quinte frater?*): schol. Bob. 124.15-9St.

[486] "Because he (*sc.* L. Lamia) had dared to make an entreaty on behalf of a citizen, on behalf of a citizen who had given good service, on behalf of a friend, on behalf of the commonwealth."

words, causes a sense of consternation among the hearers, terrified by the inhuman punishment. If examined in a didactic context, the scholiast's words imply that brevity is an effective means of achieving clarity and perspicuity.[487] Yet brevity may be attained without rejecting emotional and aesthetic devices. As a tool for embellishing an oration and inflaming passions, amplification renders a narrative (however terrifying it might be) more attractive and agreeable.

Amplification is naturally peculiar to the language of *indignatio* (or *exaggeratio*), a dominant feature of invective literature. As Craig puts it, *indignatio* "is in its broader and non-technical sense a key element of the hostile emotional response that the prosecution tries to excite in the jury."[488] Ancient commentaries teem with notes on Cicero's technique of *indignatio*, especially his use of vehement, harsh words conveying a sense of anger and revulsion.[489] As observed by Webb, the emotional effect of *indignatio*, together with that of pity (*miseratio* or *misericordia*), may also result from vivid descriptions (*enargeia, ekphrasis*) of pitiful or indignant scenes that make the listeners feel as they were present and thereby personally involved in the case.[490] Emblematic of this is Cicero's evocation of the former splendor of Henna in Sicily in the *Fourth Verrine* (*Ver.* 2.4.107). Captivated by the sense of beauty and grace produced by Cicero's description, the hearer is moved to indignation by Verres's sacrilegious theft of cult statues.[491] As a means of arousing emotions in invective, *indignatio* turns out to be a self-defense instrument.[492] On this point is centered the Bobbio scholiast's concise examination of Cicero's outburst of *indignatio* against Torquatus in the *pro Sulla* 40–45 (83.31–84.2St). Accused of having falsified the accounts of the interrogation of Volturcius and the Allobroges, Cicero replied with indignant tones.[493] The scholiast justifies Cicero's violent rejoinder by noting the monstrosity of the charge, concluding that similar counterattacks, by turning around the deeds of illustrious citizens, could be easily transformed into self-celebration.[494] By his

---

[487] For the persuasive force of *brachylogia* (*brevitas*), a succinct condensation of ideas (assigned to *argumentatio*), cf. schol. Gronov. **A** 345.1-2St (on Cic. *Ver.* 2.1.46: *ipsa velocitas magnam habet virtutem probandi*).
[488] Craig 2010: 75.
[489] Schol. Bob. 91.32St (on *de rege Alexandrino* frg1); 104.27St (on *Flac.* 51); 106.20St (on *Flac.* 83); 109.3-4St (on *Red. Sen.* 16); 128.1St (on *Sest.* 18); 163.34-5St (on *Planc.* 67); 168.12St (on *Planc.* 87); 170.22St (on *De aere alieno Milonis* frg2); 173.12St (on *De aere alieno Milonis* frg19); schol. Gronov. **B** 339.15St (on *Ver.* 1.40).
[490] Webb 1997: 120–21 (who draws on *Rhet. Her.* 4.39 and Cic. *Inv.* 1.104).
[491] Webb 1997: 124–5.   [492] Craig 2010: 75.   [493] On this passage, see Berry 1996a: 216–24.
[494] *Hae sunt defensiones quae in personis inlustribus quendam spiritum laudis imitantur* (84.1-2St).

indignant rebuttal Cicero shares memory of his consulship with his audience and constructs his image as a reliable consul, whose evocation in the mind of the listener was expected to produce an emotional effect similar to that manifested by the orator in reaction to the false allegations of his opponent.

It is now time to call attention to one of the most significant parts of the theory of ornament, that of *figurae*, commonly divided into figures of speech (*figurae elocutionis*) and figures of thought (*figurae sententiae*), regarded by Quintilian as "innovative forms of expression produced by some artistic means."[495] As stated in a passage from the third book of *De oratore* mentioned above (3.201), reported *verbatim* by Quintilian (*Inst.* 9.1.26–36), in the composition of a "continuous speech" (*in perpetua oratione*) the good speaker must "lend brilliance to its style by frequent embellishments, that is to say, figures of thought and of speech" (*quasi luminibus distinguenda et frequentanda omnis oratio sententiarum atque verborum*).[496] Cicero would regard figures of speech, concerning the arrangement of words in a sentence, and figures of thought, "patterns which provide an orator with various ways to address his audience and to arrange his thoughts,"[497] as both a sign of sophistication and an effective means of persuasion. He drew on figures in various ways and for different purposes, taking care not to "exceed the bounds of ordinary language, and not to let the self-conscious employment of such devices create an impression of insincerity." Cicero's fondness for figures of speech and of thought is displayed at best in the speeches, an invaluable source of figurative material for practitioners of rhetoric, as testified by late Latin rhetorical handbooks written for educational purposes.[498] Quintilian himself strongly recommended that his students follow Cicero as a guide to the formation and arrangement of figured statements (*Inst.* 9.2.1).

Among the figures that lend vitality and persuasive force to Cicero's oratory, those of interrogation (or rhetorical questions) occupy a special place. Cicero's

---

[495] *Ergo figura sit arte aliqua novata forma dicendi* (Quint. *Inst.* 9.1.14).

[496] On Crassus's confusing and obscure list of figures in the *De oratore* and Quintilian's critique at *Inst.* 9.3.90–7, see Mankin 2011: 292–93.

[497] Kirchner 2007: 189. For the classification of figures of words and figures of thought in ancient rhetoric, see also Rowe 1997.

[498] In addition to Quintilian (*Inst.* 9.2–3), we mention here the early first-century treatise of Rutilius Lupus (*Schemata Lexeos*: 3–21 *RLM*), the Ciceronian-based *De figuris sententiarum et elocutionis liber* written by Romanus Aquila (third century CE: 22–37 *RLM*), and the third- or fourth-century compilation by Iulius Rufinianus (37–47 *RLM*). To these works we can add the late anonymous collection of figures, titled *Schemata dianoeas (quae ad rhetores pertinent)*, edited by Halm 1863 (71–77 *RLM*).

Eleganter Dixit Cicero 279

famous opening of the *First Catilinarian* (*Inst.* 9.2.7),[499] a sequence of three short, impatient rhetorical questions,[500] has long attracted attention for its aggressive tones, which strengthen the orator's apostrophe and pepper the opponent with provocative language.[501] Questions add strength and cogency to the argument (*acrior et vehementior fit probatio*: Quint. *Inst.* 9.2.6), as demonstrated by relevant passages from the *pro Ligario*[502] and the *pro Cluentio*.[503] Similarly, figures of anticipation (*prolepsis*),[504] usually divided into *praemunitio* ("preparatory defense"), *confessio* ("confession"), *praedictio* ("prediction"), *emendatio* ("self-correction"), and *praeparatio* ("preparation"),[505] as well as figures of hesitation (*dubitatio*)[506] and of communication (*communicatio*),[507] function, in Quintilian's view, as "powerful weapons of persuasion," as may easily be evinced by Cicero's speeches.[508]

As might be expected, the scholiasts provide us with interesting comments on Cicero's use of rhetorical figures and linguistic artifices and their related effects.[509] "Preterition" (*praeteritio*), a word figure of omission

---

[499] Cf. also Quint. *Inst.* 4.1.68.
[500] *Quo usque tandem abutere, Catilina, patientia nostra? Quam diu etiam furor iste tuus nos eludet? Quem ad finem sese effrenata iactabit audacia?* ("How long, Catiline, will you take advantage of our forebearance? How much longer yet will that madness of yours make playthings of us? When will your unbridled effrontery stop vaunting itself?"). See Dyck 2008a: 63–5.
[501] Late rhetoricians mention this passage on several occasions: cf. Iul. Rufinian. 44.9 *RLM*; Schem. Dian. 72.21 *RLM*; Iul. Vict. 439.23 *RLM* (as a colon divided into short sentences); Rufin. 581.12 *RLM*.
[502] Quint. *Inst.* 9.2.7 (from *Lig.* 9); 9.2.14 (from *Lig.* 7).
[503] Quint. *Inst.* 9.2.8 (from *Cluent.* 103); 9.2.15 (a case of "imaginary interrogation," from *Cluent.* 39). The third-person question at Cic. *Ver.* 2.1.109 (*rata esse patietur?*) is classed as a rhetorical reply (ὑπόκρισις), filled with indignation, by Ps. Asconius 248.17-8St. For figures of address, such as *apostrophe*, cf. schol. Bob. 119.11St (on *Mil.* 22); 124.12St (on *Mil.* 101); 126.29St (on *Sest.* 10); Ps. Asconius 230.10St (on *Ver.* 2.1.25). In general on apostrophe, see Lauberg 1998: 338–39, §§ 762–765.
[504] On the persuasive force of the figure of "anticipation" cf. Quint. *Inst.* 4.1.49 (also 9.3.99).
[505] Quint. *Inst.* 9.2.16-8.    [506] Quint. *Inst.* 9.2.19.    [507] Quint. *Inst.* 9.2.20-5.
[508] The *Divinatio in Q. Caecilium* provides readers with an instance of *praemunitio*, whereas the *pro Rabirio Postumo* serves as an example of *confessio* (Quint. *Inst.* 9.2.17). Cicero's simulated hesitation at *Cluent.* 4 (*quo me vertam nescio*, "I do not know where to turn") works as a stratagem aimed at convincing the judges of the orator's sincerity (Quint. *Inst.* 9.2.19; also 9.4.75): on the figure of *addubitatio* in *Flac.* 4 (*quem enim appellem, quem obtester, quem implorem?*), cf. schol. Bob. 94.17St. The artifice of "anticipation" is detected by Ps. Asconius at Cic. *Ver.* 2.1.117 (in the expression *Ipse in Siciliensi edicto*: 250.13St).
[509] Here it may be convenient to append a list of figures of speech and of thought, as they are presented in the scholiasts: schol. Bob. 93.21St (on Cic. *de rege Alex.* frg9: *gradatio*); 129.17 (on Cic. *Sest.* 31: a form of *correctio*); 136.17St (on Cic. *Sest.* 119: *protherapeusis*, "a *correctio* before the shocking utterance as a prophylactic preparation of the audience": Lauberg 1998: 348; the term *protherapeusis* occurs also in Don. *Ter. Ad.* 481); 164.9St (on Cic. *Planc.* 68: *compensatio*); Ps. Asconius 214.28St (on Cic. *Ver.* 1.26: *dilogia*, figure of *ambiguitas*); 215.8St (on Cic. *Ver.* 1.27: *epitherapeusis*); 222.13St (on Cic. *Ver.* 1.54: *figura zeuma*); 235.9St (on Cic. *Ver.* 2.1.44: ἀνακεφαλαίωσις, recapitulation); schol. Gronov. D 302.7St (on Cic. *Rosc.* 1: *pleonasmos*); 302.17St (on *Rosc.* 2: *antiptosis*, i.e. *soloecismus per casus*, change of case); 304.7St (on Cic. *Rosc.* 9: *prosapodosis*, a form of addition: cf.

(*figura per detractionem*),⁵¹⁰ is a common device of Cicero's prose. The Bobbio scholiast's comment on Cic. *Flac.* 79 (*Mitto quod aliena, mitto quod possessa per vim*) draws attention to the frequent use of this figure in the orations, a rhetorical device easily discernible by any perceptive reader (106.2-3St). Anaphora (*repetitio*), a figure of addition by which the orator replicates the same word or group of words in successive sentences or clauses, is peculiar to Cicero's strategy of argumentation as well.⁵¹¹ As Quintilian observes, it produces pleasure in the audience while impressing a point in the minds of the hearers through a particularly insistent effect.⁵¹² Ps. Asconius invites his students to reflect upon the persuasive force of anaphora in his note on *Ver.* 2.1.7 (226.9-13St):

> Agunt eum praecipitem]Proprium Ciceronis et in orationibus et in dialogis et in epistolis eandem saepe sententiam dicere et uti eloquentiae diversis modis, iisdem sententiis tamen ab aliqua occasione repetitis. Nam et hic repetitio furoris, in qua videtur insaniae Verris causa velle monstrari. Est enim hic locus de suppliciis irrogatis, ubi ostendit cives R. Verrem <pro> praedonibus occidisse.
>
> "He is being swept into madness] It is typical of Cicero's style to repeat the same sentence, in the speeches as well as in the dialogues and epistles, in various ways and for different occasions. Here there is a repetition of the notion of 'fury', by which he aims to show Verres's madness. This is in fact the point of the speech concerning the infliction of punishments, in which the orator demonstrates that Verres has executed Roman citizens as if they were brigands."

Here, the scholiast dwells on Cicero's reiterated attack on Verres's madness as a means of arousing public anger at the governor's illegal and impious behavior. He also draws attention to repetition as a pervasive feature of Cicero's style, not limited to the orations. Repetition of the same word or sentence (though with some variations) occurs as a forceful instrument of persuasion.⁵¹³ Ps. Asconius elaborates again on this point

---

Quint. *Inst.* 9.3.93–6); schol. Gronov. **B** 338.14St (on Cic. *Ver.* 1.30: πεῦσις, *pusma* or *quaesitum*: Lausberg 1998: 342 § 772, under *subiectio*, mock-dialogue).
⁵¹⁰ Lausberg 1998: 393–94 (§§ 882–886).
⁵¹¹ Powell 2013: 69. Cf. Cic. *de Orat.* 3.206 (Quint. *Inst.* 9.1.33).
⁵¹² Quint. *Inst.* 9.2.4 (also 9.3.29, for the similarity between *geminatio* and *repetitio*; 9.3.47).
⁵¹³ A special variant of *geminatio* (*anadiplosis, reduplicatio*), based essentially on the repetition of the last member of a synctatic or metrical word group, occurs in Cic. *Cat.* 1.2 *Hic tamen vivit, vivit? Etiam in senatum venit* (Quint. *Inst.* 9.3.44; Cassiod. 499.22 *RLM*; Isid. 517.23 *RLM*). See Lausberg 1998: 348 (§ 785), who interprets Cicero's passage as "a repetition within a *correctio*, precisely a *res*-variant of *correctio*."

at *Div.* 65 (203.19-20St)⁵¹⁴ and *Ver.* 1.17 (210.18-21St). In the latter case, the repetition of *nullus* (*nulla nota, nullus color, nullae sordes*)⁵¹⁵ produces emphatic effects and enables Cicero to turn the opponent's arguments into a powerful tool of self-defense.⁵¹⁶

Cicero enlivened his orations with a series of pathetic and intensifying linguistic devices, intended to stir up emotions and strengthen the case. Any reader of Cicero is familiar with the grandiloquent exclamation, preceded by the interjection *o*, occurring in the first line of chapter 2 of the *First Catilinarian* (*O tempora, o mores*).⁵¹⁷ "Typical of the *elocutio* of the emotive grand style,"⁵¹⁸ exclamations tend to be scattered throughout Cicero's heart-breaking *conquestio* (*miseratio*), the final "appeal to pity."⁵¹⁹ Ideally suited to heightening emotion, exclamations are "simulated and artfully designed figures" (as Quintilian says), working on the judges' sense of compassion.⁵²⁰ The beginning of the *conquestio* in the speech on behalf of Sulla (*O miserum, infelicem illum diem*: § 91) gives voice to the orator's (calculated) lament about the imminent catastrophe threatening his client.⁵²¹

The term *sententia*, maxim or aphorism (the Greek γνώμη), is generally applied to a self-evidently true statement involving human life. It may also be employed to designate a pointed expression or sentence, usually introduced at the end of periods, *in clausulis*. As elements of ornamentation, according to the author of the *Rhetorica ad Herennium* (4.24–6) and Quintilian (*Inst.* 8.5), *sententiae* provide a good complement to Cicero's refined and magniloquent style. A good example is offered by the commendable axiom *Nihil est tam populare quam bonitas* ("Nothing is as popular as goodness of heart"), introduced at the close of *Lig.* 37 (Quint.

---

⁵¹⁴ *Vide firmamenta argumentorum quotiens in oratione sine metu fastidii repeti solent* ("You should consider how many times the basic points of the argumentation are being replicated in the speech, without any fear of producing tedium").

⁵¹⁵ Cf. also Cic. *Cael.* 1.

⁵¹⁶ *Etsi haec Cicero, quia sibi contra Hortensium prosunt, saepissime repetit, tamen in qua causa et a quo et quomodo haec facta sint meminimus in Divinatione narrasse* ("Cicero most often repeats these things, which he can take advantage of against Hortensius: however, we remind you that we already shown in which case and from whom and in which way this has been done in our commentary on the *Divinatio*"): cf. 218.18-20St.

⁵¹⁷ Dyck 2008a: 66.

⁵¹⁸ Winterbottom 2004: 223 n38. On the *exclamatio* device, see Lausberg 1998: 358 (§ 809).

⁵¹⁹ Cic. *Inv.* 1.106.   ⁵²⁰ Quint. *Inst.* 9.2.26.

⁵²¹ The Bobbio scholiast regards Cicero's exclamation as an "oratorical lamentation" (*oratorie deplorat*): 84.16St. The exclamation at *Div.* 7 (*Quid est pro deum hominumque fidem*) is interpreted by the Gronovius scholiast (**B**) as an effective tool of persuasion (*ad probationem commoditatis pertinet*: 325.26-7St). Cf. also 130.25-8St (on the oratorical force of the exclamation *Te, te, patria, testor et vos, penates patriique*, at *Sest.* 45).

*Inst.* 8.5.3).[522] The post-exile speeches, in particular, reveal Cicero's predilection for sententious style. This is hardly surprising, since the post-return orations are "specimens of epideictic oratory, showpieces," admitting a "good deal of grandeur and elaborate ornamentation."[523] It is thus probably not by chance that the surviving part (a small one) of the Bobbio commentary dedicated to the post-return thanksgiving speech to the Roman people (110.1–111.20St) is primarily concerned with the explication of Cicero's *sententiae*. The phrase *Non tantae voluptati erant suscepti, quantae nunc sunt restituti* (*Red. Pop.* 2)[524] is defined as a *concepte posita sententia* (110.29St). Cicero's emphatic description (in the form of a simile) of his return as a recovery from illness occupies a good part of the initial sections of the speech. Starting from the sentence *Sed tamquam bona valetudo iucundior est iis qui e gravi morbo recreati sunt* (*Red. Pop.* 4),[525] the scholiast dilates on this creative re-use of a metaphor derived from human life. He explains Cicero's sentence with a similar maxim (*quippe sensus incommodorum commendabilia facit illa quae prospera sunt*: 111.1-2St)[526] and substantiates his explanation with a line from Vergil's *Aeneid* (1.203)[527] and two extracts, from Plato's *Republic* (9.583 C.D) and Isocrates's *To Demonicos* (35) respectively (111.2-8St).[528] Again, the saying *A parentibus, id quod necesse erat, parvus sum procreatus, a vobis natus sum consularis* (*Red. Pop.* 5)[529] is explained as a *popularis magis quam pressa et gravis sententia*, a saying appealing to popular taste (111.11-2St).

Pointed expressions or epigrams were mostly associated with poetry rather than with prose and reflected a tendency toward the modernist, declamatory style, the "Senecan" epigrammatic style that was to become a hotly contested topic of debate in the early empire. Illustrative of this is the fact that the proverbial sentence *Difficile est*

---

[522] The speech on behalf of Ligarius supplies Quintilian with a variety of *sententiae* (cf. *Inst.* 8.5.7, on *Lig.* 38; *Inst.* 8.5.10, on *Lig.* 10, as *enthymeme*; *Inst.* 8.5.13, on *Lig.* 2, as *conclusio*).

[523] Nicholson 1992: 121.

[524] "Yet my original acceptance of the responsibilities they brought to me was attended with less joy than their present restoration to me" (English translation: Watts 1979).

[525] "But as good good health is sweeter to those who have recovered from grievous sickness."

[526] "It is in fact experience and perception of disadvantages that makes commendable what is felicitous in itself."

[527] *Forsan et haec olim meminisse iuvabit* ("Perhaps even this distress will some day be a joy to recall").

[528] It should be noted that this is the only case in the Bobbio commentary in which the explanation of a passage from Cicero is supported by quotations from the text of Vergil and Greek authors. Plato's dialogue *Phaedon* is mentioned, together with the first book of the *Tusculan Disputations*, in the comment on Cicero's presentation of different theories about the destiny of souls after death in the *pro Sestio* 47 (130.32St).

[529] "As a babe, it was to my parents, in the course of nature, that I owed my being; but now it is to you that I owe my veritable birth as a consular."

*tacere, cum doleas*,⁵³⁰ at *Sul.* 31, is presented as a "rare feature of style in Cicero's orations" (*genus in Tullianis orationibus rarum*) by the Bobbio scholiast (82.13-4St). *Sententiae* such as this, "clever thoughts in the form of a brief comment" (in Quintilian's terms),⁵³¹ were evidently perceived as a symptom of Asiatic rhetoric. Arguably, Quintilian's position on this aspect of Cicero's prose was not very dissimilar. Conscious of the fact that Cicero could be reproached for his fondness for Asiatic style, he steered a middle course. He reminded his readers that delight (*delectatio*) of the audience was, together with the interests (*utilitas*) of the case, at the heart of Cicero's oratorical practice (*Inst.* 12.10.45). Embellishments, such as those commonly called *sententiae*, were designed to produce pleasure and emotion in the hearers, provided that they had substance (*rem contineant*) and were not over-abundant (*copia non redundent*). By their very brevity epigrams and *sententiae* could render the argumentation much more effective and contribute to the final victory (*Inst.* 12.10.47–8).⁵³²

This type of ornamentation, rejected by the ancients and the early Greeks, appealed to Cicero's aesthetic taste. He recurred to the use of *sententiae*, axioms, and pointed expressions to render his thought more agreeable and effective. In Cicero's view, *sententiae* worked as means of embellishment and persuasion. *Apud Ciceronem enim invenio* ("I do find it in Cicero"), says Quintilian in simplistic terms (*Inst.* 12.10.48). And a more circumstantial account is given by Aper in the Tacitean *Dialogus* (22.2), who remarks on Cicero's proclivity for epigrammatic expressions in the late speeches.⁵³³ Cicero's love of *sententiae* linked him with his successors and the Asiatic style of the Silver Age. Yet Cicero saw pointed sentences and epigrams as an ingredient of his *ornatus*, to be deployed with an eye to appropriateness and consistency of style. As with any other aesthetic device, he cautioned against excess and overabundance of style. So, I suspect that Quintilian's endorsement of a moderate, beneficial use of *sententiae* serves as an implicit recommendation for treading in Cicero's footsteps (a usual procedure in Quintilian's pedagogy). As Winterbottom remarks, "the Silver Age, again, merely expands on something that Cicero

---

⁵³⁰ "It is hard to stay silent, when you are afflicted." See Berry 1996a: 200.

⁵³¹ Quint. *Inst.* 4.2.121 (he cites *Mil.* 29 and *Cluent.* 14 as examples of pointed sentences).

⁵³² *Feriunt animum et uno ictu frequenter impellunt et ipsa brevitate magis haerent et delectatione persuadent* ("They strike the mind and often produce a decisive effect by one single blow, while their very brevity makes them cling to memory, and the pleasure which they produce has the force of persuasion": *Inst.* 12.10.48).

⁵³³ Winterbottom (1982a: 260) opportunely notes that the cited *sententia* in chapter 31 of the *pro Sulla*, a consular speech, demonstrates that Cicero did not restrain himself from using this form of *ornatus* in orations, which belonged to a mature (not late) phase of his oratorical activity.

had used with restraint: he learned it, perhaps, from his Asiatic preceptors, but brought to it a moderation they did not practise."[534] One might add that Quintilian, too, advocated moderation in epigrammatic style, in line with Cicero's theory and practical application.

It goes without saying that prose rhythm was one of the most intriguing and fascinating aspects of Cicero's style, an aspect regarded as essential to *elegantia* and ornamentation by Cicero himself.[535] As declared by Crassus in the third book of *De oratore* (3.175), the good speaker "desires the word-order to resemble verse in having a rhythmical cadence, and to fit in neatly and be rounded off" (*eam coniunctionem, sicuti versum, numerose cadere et quadrare et perfici volumus*): a "polished speech" (*polita oratio*) must have a rhythmical shape (*numerosa oratio*),[536] and a continuous flow of words in prose "is much neater and more pleasing if it is divided up by joints and limbs than it is carried right on without a break."[537] But rhythm is not only an element of decoration. As has been noted, "by pointing to the pauses within a passage of prose, it acts as a guide to the structure of sentences, and thereby to the general movement of thought."[538] Rhythm and pronunciation, along with a skillful arrangement of words, impact on the hearer's perception and discernment.[539] In his long chapter about the doctrine of *compositio*, which presupposes a three-part division into word order and arrangement (*ordo*), contiguity of the sentence elements (*iunctura*) and rhythm or a calculated succession of long and short syllables (*numerus*),[540] Quintilian endows good composition with a persuasive power (*Inst.* 9.4.9): What is pronounced "with energy, grace and elegance" (*vehementer, dulciter, speciose*)[541] arouses emotions, appeals to the audience's cultivated taste and conveys a much more effective message. To Quintilian and late rhetoricians interested in word order and sentence rhythm, the basic elements of composition provided a clue for a stylistic analysis.[542] Nonetheless, they were aware that a periodic style and a sequence of rhythmical cola might well serve the orator's purpose, becoming fundamental ingredients of the strategy of persuasion.

With regard to the laws of *numerus*, Quintilian followed Cicero in supplying students with the conventions of artistic prose rhythm. Since

---

[534] Winterbottom 1982a: 261.   [535] Cic. *de Orat.* 3.177–186.   [536] Cic. *de Orat.* 3.184.
[537] *Continuatio verborum haec soluta multo est aptior atque iucundior si est articulis membrisque distincta quam si continuata ac producta* (Cic. *de Orat.* 3.186). See Mankin 2011: 279.
[538] Berry 1996a: 50–1.   [539] Cic. *de Orat.* 3.196.
[540] *In omni porro compositione tria sunt genera necessaria: ordo, iunctura, numerus* ("Further, in all composition, there are three necessary elements: order, linkage, and rhythm"): Quint. *Inst.* 9.4.22.
[541] Quint. *Inst.* 9.4.13.   [542] Habinek 1985: 21–41.

oratorical prose was governed by a set of prosodic and metrical rules (*ratio pedum*) which considerably differed from that of poetry (*Inst.* 9.4.60),[543] he recommended a proper, "natural" use of rhythmical (and poetic) patterns and meters, especially in the final clauses of the period, *clausulae*, the point of the phrase that elicits most attention from the audience.[544] Cicero's conformation to generic prescriptions of prose rhythm, as inherited from Hellenistic Greek oratory, was not a factor of restriction or limitation of rhetorical skills, however. Quintilian (and later critics) noticed Cicero's propensity for favorite or pet rhythms. The celebrated *esse videatur* clausula or Cicero's considerable use of cretic-spondee or cretic-trochee sequences (with their resolved forms) show undoubtedly that the individuality of the trained orator might determine the rhythmical profile of the speech. Here there is no place for a larger discussion of prose rhythm as a hallmark of Cicero's style. Since Zielinski's seminal study,[545] "the first large-scale scientific exposition of Latin prose rhythm,"[546] Cicero's rhythmical prose had been at the center of scholarly interest,[547] with invaluable results not only for a deeper appreciation of Cicero's style but also for textual criticism and questions of genuineness and authenticity.[548] What matters here is to restate the value of prose rhythm as an aesthetic and emotional device and its pedagogical function. Students of rhetoric had to be acquainted with rhythmical shapes that, if opportunely employed, might well serve the speaker's interest. More than any other prose text, Cicero's speeches provided would-be orators with many instructive examples of periodic structure and elegant rhythms at colon and sentence endings.

So much then for Cicero's style in rhetorical handbooks and ancient commentaries. Cicero dominated the study of rhetoric not only as a master of *ornatus*, however. He was also unanimously recognized as an authority on the practice of oratorical delivery. As we have seen, Cicero's style won the admiration of ancient exegetes throughout the centuries. But aesthetic and linguistic devices would have lost their effect if they had not been accompanied by a proper delivery. "Delivery is the dominant factor in oratory" (*Actio in dicendo una dominatur*). This quasi-formulaic sentence, by which Crassus starts off his discussion of performance in the third book of the *De oratore* (3.213),[549] illustrates the central role of oratorical delivery in securing persuasion, a delivery rooted in both natural talent and a proper use of vocal phrasing, gesture, facial expression, bodily comportment and

---

[543] Cf. also Quint. *Inst.* 10.1.28.   [544] Quint. *Inst.* 9.4.62.   [545] Zielinski 1904.
[546] Berry 1996b: 47.   [547] Habinek 1985; Nisbet 1990.   [548] Berry 1996b.
[549] Mankin 2011: 305 (on Theophrastus as the likely source of Crassus's treatment of performance).

stage-managed theatrical effects.[550] As asserted by Quintilian, "a mediocre speech supported by all the power of delivery will be more impressive than the best speech unaccompanied by such power" (*Inst.* 11.3.5).[551] Delivery, as a form of communication, impacted on the orator's success.[552] It was on the speaker's force of communicating the fire of his passion to the hearers that the Romans judged the orator's achievement.[553]

Cicero was very sensitive to the fact that the audience's reaction to delivery, in terms of aesthetic appreciation, was the best gauge of a speech's effectiveness.[554] Public approbation was cited as a primary factor in deciding whether an orator had succeeded in pleasing his listeners and stirring emotions.[555] An eloquent passage from Cicero's *Divinatio* (§ 39) stresses the primary role played by an attentive and passionate audience in the orator's success.[556] Again Cicero reminds his readers that conveying meaning without words, by voice tones and a sophisticated system of hand and body gestures (*sermo corporis*),[557] is "at least as influential in swaying an audience as the words of the oration" (*Orat.* 55–6).[558] Aldrete notes that "when a Roman spoke before an audience, he was simultaneously communicating in two languages, one verbal and one nonverbal, and the messages the two conveyed could be identical, complementary, or different."[559]

As a live performance embracing vocal delivery and bodily gesture, *actio* is, of course, "the domain where the overlap between acting and oratory is most pronounced and where the dangers that an orator's body may engage

---

[550] For modern discussions of *actio* and oratorical delivery, see Fantham 1982; May 2002b: 66–8; Hall 2007; Cavarzere 2011; see also Porter 2009. On the comparison between orators and actors as performers and the application of theatrical techniques to the sphere of oratory, see Fantham 2002.

[551] *Equidem vel mediocrem orationem commendatam viribus actionis adfirmarim plus habituram esse momenti quam optimam eadem illa destitutam.* Cf. Cic. *de Orat.* 3.213; *Or.* 56.

[552] On the aesthetics of delivery, see Corbeill 1996: 16–30; Corbeill 2004: 111–16; Wisse 2013; Hall 2014 (also Hall 2007). See Bell 2013: 175, on successful oratory as depending upon physicality and visibility.

[553] Quint. *Inst.* 11.3.3.   [554] Bell 2013: 176.

[555] Cic. *Brut.* 185. See Steel 2017a: 88 (on the perils of forensic oratory and the orators' need "to earn their audience, and keep on earning it, by offering speech which was important enough and interesting enough to hold its attention, and in many cases its presence").

[556] *Dicenda, demonstranda, explicanda sunt omnia: causa non solum exponenda, sed etiam graviter copioseque agenda est. Perficiendum est, si quid agere aut perficere vis, ut homines te non solum audiant, verum etiam libenter studioseque audiant* ("You have to mention everything, establish every fact, expound everything in full. You have not merely to state your case; you have to develop it with impressive wealth of detail. If you wish to achieve any sort of success, you must not only make people listen to you; you must make them listen with pleasure, with eagerness"). See Tempest 2013: 41.

[557] Cic. *Orat.* 55 (*Est enim actio quasi corporis quaedam eloquentia, cum constet e voce atque motu*, "For delivery is a sort of language of the body, since it consists of movements or gesture as well as of voice or speech").

[558] Cic. *Orat.* 56.   [559] Aldrete 1999: 6.

in an indecorous theatricality are most present."[560] The reciprocal entanglement of acting and oratory, an association complicated by deep-rooted prejudices about effeminate attributes of actors,[561] appears to have been a major concern for theorists engaged in the intellectual construction of the ideal orator. Cicero's treatment of theatrical style in *De oratore*[562] and Quintilian's discussion of stage effects and tricks, taught by the actor-trainer and practiced by students of rhetoric,[563] confirm that theatricality was crucial to good oratory.[564] Persuasion demanded an emotive delivery, leading to oratorical success by means of a moderate, self-regulating use of stage devices. Yet the threat of feminization posed by the fictionality, extravagance and comedic mannerisms of the *actor* induced Cicero and Quintilian to offer specific instructions for the avoidance of all effeminate forms of delivery[565] that originated from an indecorous use of stage techniques.[566] Anxiety about the perils of stage oratory was thus brought under control by consciousness of the oratorical benefits produced by an emotional and theatrical delivery. On the other hand, while acknowledging the utility of certain aspects of the actor's technique to a successful performance,[567] Cicero and Quintilian both distinguished the figure of orator from that of professional actor, who adopted a bodily posture that often contravened the rules of senatorial *dignitas*. As Quintilian puts it, the task of a teacher is "not to form a comic actor, but an orator" (*Inst.* 11.3.181).[568] Unlike stage performance, oratory "consists in serious pleading, not in mimicry" (*oratio actione enim constat, non imitatione*: *Inst.* 11.3.182), a pointed expression reminiscent of Cicero's definition of the stage actor as an "imitator of reality," opposing the more noble activity of the orator as "creator and agent of truth itself."[569] While endorsing Cicero's comments on the mutual implication of oratory and theatrical performance,[570] Quintilian recommended exercise of moderation in deploying stage-managed devices at the same time. Good oratory required control of theatrical and emotional delivery. Any excess of theatricality or unrestrained desire to

---

[560] Dugan 2005: 137–8.
[561] On the Roman elite's disapproval of acting, see Edwards 1993: 98–107.
[562] Cic. *de Orat.* 3.213–227 (also 1.251). On this passage, see Mankin 2011: 304–22.
[563] Quint. *Inst.* 11.1; 3.
[564] In general, see Graf 1991; Fantham 2002; Dugan 2005: 133–47. See also Hall 2007: 230; Harries B. 2007: 131–2.
[565] On Roman anxiety about the subversion of gender role and behavior, see Edwards 1993: 87–90.
[566] Fantham 2002: 372–4. See also Fantham 1982: 259 ("Like Cicero, he [Quintilian *sc.*] deprecated the flamboyance of stage gesture, with its twin excess of mimicry and unmanly gracefulness"). On the connections/affinities between stage and oratory, see Nocchi 2013: 7–25.
[567] Quint. *Inst.* 11.3.19.    [568] *Non enim comoedum esse, sed oratorem volo*.
[569] Cic. *de Orat.* 3.214.    [570] Cic. *Orat.* 122; *Brut.* 141.

attain the elegance of the stage performer might undermine the moral and social authority of the good and virtuous man (Quint. *Inst.* 11.3.184).[571]

The distinction of orator from actor could also be taken as a means of self-fashioning. In drawing a parallel between the stage actor and the orator and, at the same time, providing a set of rules for the ideal delivery, characterized by "dignity and grace" (*graviter et venuste*)[572] and accompanied by a proper use of voice and gesture, Cicero (and Quintilian in turn) implicitly promoted the figure of the ideal orator-actor, adopting an emotional and masculine manner of delivery and self-presentation. It has been observed that the theoretical (moral) separation of the sphere of oratory from that of stage performance, by short-circuiting "the sort of anxieties about the impropriety of theatricality that are a constant theme throughout the Roman rhetorical tradition,"[573] allowed Cicero to legitimize the orator's claim on *actio* and his use of theatrical stratagems to persuasive effects. Yet Cicero's legitimization of the actor-orator, ethically separated from the stage performer, might also be interpreted as a form of self-promotion, a means of fashioning himself as a "good orator" and a "good actor." Cicero extolled Servius Galba's theatrical defense as an instance of successful manipulation of emotional devices and stage tactics (*de Orat.* 1.226–7).[574] To some extent, his appreciation and approval of theatrical oratory implied, on the readers' side, recognition of the persuasive force of oratorical delivery, founded on a masterful, restrained employment of comic and tragic devices and a masculine emotive style.[575]

Quintilian remains our most useful resource to reconstruct the basic elements of oratorical delivery (*Inst.* 11.3).[576] Since we have little evidence about Cicero's own practices of oratorical delivery and the ways in which Roman orators "turned their words into effective live performance,"[577] Quintilian's chapter on delivery is our chief source of insights into the importance and complexity of performance in late republic and early

---

[571] *Sed iam recepta est actio paulo agitatior et exigitur et quibusdam partibus convenit, ita tamen temperanda, ne, dum actoris captamus elegantiam, perdamus viri boni et gravis auctoritatem.*
[572] *Rhet. Her.* 4.69; Cic. *de Orat.* 1.142. See Krostenko 2001: 99–100.    [573] Dugan 2005: 138.
[574] Cf. also Cic. *Brut.* 82.
[575] It may be interesting to note that Ps. Asconius points to Cicero's manipulative deployment of expressions derived from the stage in *Ver.* 2.2.18 (260.26-8St).
[576] Quintilian's long chapter 11.3 is divided into a preface (1–13), discussion of the voice (14–65), facial expression, including eyes and neck (65–87), and gesture proper (88–149). The following paragraphs (150–77) deal with delivery in a courtroom speech; the chapter is closed by a few sections concerned with the similarities between the orator and the art of a stage-actor (178–85). See Fantham 1982; Fantham 2002: 370ff; Hall 2004.
[577] Hall 2004: 143. Tempest 2013: 41–2 (on Cicero's paucity of self-referential comments on the practice of vocal delivery and gesticulation in his rhetorical works).

empire Roman society. Yet it is useful to observe, before proceeding further, that Quintilian, like other authors of rhetorical treatises, seems not to have considered the possibility that the speeches, as he and his students read them, might not be identical to the delivered texts. As Webb puts it, Quintilian – and the common reader of a speech – approached the text as if he were "a member of a live audience" (favored by the practice of reading aloud).[578] The basic equivalence of the act of reading and that of "listening to a live performance," an immediate communication between speaker and listener, was fundamental to the reception of written texts in antiquity. The relationship between rhetorical theory and rhetorical practice and, relatedly, the still-debated issue of how closely a written, delivered speech reproduced the words actually delivered at the trial had little or no relevance to ancient discussions of norms of oratorical performance. As Tempest says, "the imaginability of a text's performance was thus arguably more important to the student of oratory than its actual delivery."[579] What counted was the impact of delivery and performative language on the listener/reader, an impact that continued to be preserved even if the text had been rewritten or reworked to some extent.[580] Quintilian's reaction to a passage from Cicero's *Fifth Verrine* (*Ver.* 2.5. 86)[581] testifies to the continuity of aesthetic and emotional effects on readers distanced in time and space, experiencing feelings and sensations as if they were attending a live performance. Cicero's power of language enabled readers to conjure up a picture of the trial long after the original act of delivery.[582]

Dissociating himself from the taxonomical approach to the topic of performance, typical of the Hellenistic rhetorical tradition and favored by the author of the *Rhetorica ad Herennium*,[583] Quintilian offers an emotional reading of the art of delivery. His basic tenet is the congruence between performance and emotion. In his detailed examination of vocal delivery (*Inst.* 11.3.14–65),[584] he launches into a forceful condemnation of faults and mannerisms of delivery and provides examples of vocal art and

---

[578] Webb 1997: 113.  [579] Tempest 2013: 43.
[580] On the reader as the true addressee of the written performance and the notion of "fictive orality," see Fuhrmann 1990. For the question, see Tempest 2013: 42–44 (see also Nisbet 1992 for the dialogue between the orator and his readers in Cic. *Ver.* 2.2.92–5).
[581] Quint. *Inst.* 8.3.64–6 (similar to the reaction to Cicero's description of a luxurious banquet in the lost speech *pro Gallio*: 8.3.66). See Webb 1997: 114.
[582] On the use of vivid descriptions (prefaced by verbal cues) to promote an emotional response in the audience (even in never delivered speeches like Cicero's *Actio Secunda in Verrem*), see Innocenti 1994.
[583] *Rhet. Her.* 3.19–28.
[584] On vocal delivery in antiquity, see Schulz 2016 (esp. 142–50); see also Hall 2007: 220–24.

variations of tone as a means of arousing emotion. In this association of specific voice nuances with arousal of emotions, Quintilian is clearly indebted to Cicero's presentation of vocal delivery in *De oratore* (3.217–9).[585] For both Cicero and Quintilian, vocal delivery was a product of an emotional state (*motus animorum*). The voice is the "index of the mind" (*mentis index*). The primary function of the good speaker was to employ definite tones to convey different emotions and feelings (*Inst.* 11.3.61–5).

As a teacher solicitous about the intellectual progress of his pupils, Quintilian shows an interest in the emotional power of voice as a means of expressing feelings and passions, shared by a captivated audience. Illustrative texts are, of course, chosen from Ciceronian oratory. The opening sentences of the *pro Milone* display the orator's ability to modulate vocal pitch and sound and adapt them to each single colon or structural member.[586] Gradations of tone are opportunely employed by Cicero to excite interest and kindle the feelings of the judges.[587] Vehement tones alternate with lower (though charming) tones in the *pro Ligario* (*Inst.* 11.3.166); a sweet-sounding utterance characterizes Cicero's words in a passage from the *Second Philippic* (2.63);[588] again, a "tone not far removed from chanting, and dying away to a cadence"[589] typifies Cicero's praise of the power of poetry in *Arch.* 19 (*Inst.* 11.3.167). Drawing on Cicero as well as his own experience as an advocate,[590] Quintilian teaches correct voicing and the cultivation of a vocal delivery entirely in keeping with the specific moments of the speech. What makes the speaker's achievement all the more impressive is harmonizing of speech and voice, achieved by evenness (*aequalitas*) and variety of tone (*varietas*).[591] By his voice the good orator captures the souls and minds of the hearers. In the hands of a trained and talented speaker such as Cicero, vocal delivery emerges as a manipulative tool for exploiting emotions and enhancing the persuasive power of the speech.

An extensive vocabulary of gestures for oratorical use (more ample than Cicero's)[592] is also provided by Quintilian's discussion of the mechanisms of nonverbal body language, including a detailed presentation of even the smallest gestures involving the hands (*Inst.* 11.3.65–149).[593] As it happens in

---

[585] Cf. also Cic. *Or.* 56–9.   [586] Quint. *Inst.* 11.3.47–51 (see supra p. 187). Gunderson 2000: 44.
[587] Cic. *Orat.* 56–7 (for variation of voice tones).   [588] Quint. *Inst.* 11.3.167.
[589] *Iam cantici quiddam habent sensimque resupina sunt.*
[590] Fantham 1982 (on the practice of citation from Cicero in Quintilian's treatment of performance).
[591] Quint. *Inst.* 11.3.43–6 (also Cic. *de Orat.* 3.225; *Or.* 59).   [592] Fantham 1982: 252–3.
[593] For gesture in rhetorical theory, see Aldrete 1999; Corbeill 2004; Hall 2004; Hall 2007: 224–27. In particular on gesticulation as a part of delivery and the conventionality of rhetorical and theatrical gestures, see Graf 1991. See also Maier-Eichhorn 1989 (for Quintilian's treatment of hand gestures).

his theoretical examination of the voice, Quintilian follows Cicero in associating gesture and bodily movement with emotions. Gesticulation reveals internal passion, as explicitly stated by Cicero at *Brut.* 278.[594] As has been noted, hand and body gesture added "an emotional gloss to the verbal content of a speech."[595] Quintilian's systematic study of bodily movement thus offered the budding orator a catalogue of gestures and theatrical techniques to be exploited in order to stimulate emotions and convey the desired feeling. As has been noted, "Quintilian's treatment is admirable for its interest in the finer details of hand gestures, the precision of its descriptions, and the methodical way in which he addresses each aspect that contributes to the orator's performance as a whole."[596] No stranger to the communication system of Roman society, Quintilian showed that the universal language of the hands was of the utmost importance to oratorical success and social promotion.

By virtue of this connection between delivery and emotion,[597] it is hardly surprising that Quintilian and later commentators elaborated on Cicero's exploitation of emotional strategies and stage-managed effects to reinforce argumentation and arouse pity for the defendant. Cicero's prosecution and defense speeches showcase the orator's control of emotional techniques that amplify all the arguments from character (*ex persona*) and intensify the persuasive power of the speech. Emotive devices were instrumental in the orator's self-fashioning as an impassioned pleader. As has been said, we owe to Quintilian the first explicit treatment of emotional manipulation integrated in *actio* (*Inst.* 6.1).[598] In reply to writers of no small authority (*clari auctores*) who reject arousal of passions on moral grounds (*Inst.* 5.1.1), Quintilian recognizes control over an emotional and passionate audience, genuinely moved by the feelings stirred by the speaker, as the essence of eloquence and forensic oratory (*Inst.* 6.2.4).[599] The morality of rhetoric is understandably the main point of contention here.[600] We have already touched upon this issue and shown that the pragmatic orator was permitted to deceive the audience and distort the truth, if the case required it.[601] What was right or wrong

---

[594] Quint. *Inst.* 11.3.128; 155–56.   [595] Aldrete 1999: 17.   [596] Hall 2007: 227.
[597] On this topic, see Webb 1997. An excellent discussion of Roman concepts of emotion is provided by Kaster 2005.
[598] On the exploitation of emotions as part of a rhetorical system, cf. Arist. *Rh.* 1.2.4–7; Cic. *de Orat.* 2.188–214: see Hall 2007: 232 (for Cicero's passage, see Wisse 1989: 257–81). For Aristotle's examination of emotional response in rhetoric, see Fortenbaugh 1975; Konstan 2007 (for manipulation of emotions in Greek rhetoric).
[599] *Atqui hoc est quod dominetur in iudiciis, haec eloquentia regnat.*   [600] Leigh 2004b.
[601] See supra pp. 219–24.

was not an abstraction or a moral notion detached from the trial at hand. What might look bad in abstract might be justified by the case, and on this assumption the orator's manipulation of the emotions could have been regarded as ethically acceptable and, above all, not opposed to the virtues of loyalty and dignity proper to the *vir bonus*. Cicero and Quintilian both felt obliged to defend the moral propriety of oratory and its emotional force, but both admitted the necessity of arousing passions as a means of persuasion, even if it involved mystification or distortion of reality.[602] Quintilian frankly states that "even a wise man is at times allowed to tell a lie and the orator must of necessity excite the passions, if that be the only way by which he can lead the judge to do justice" (*Inst.* 2.17.27).[603]

In their discussion of emotional performance Cicero and Quintilian stress that an effective appeal to emotions is strongly favored, and sometimes generated, by the representation of the orator himself as a victim of misfortune. In the second book of *De Oratore* (2.189), Cicero makes Antony say that "it is impossible for the hearer to grieve, to hate, to envy, to become frightened by anything, to be driven to tears and pity, unless the selfsame emotions the orator wants to apply to the juror seem to be imprinted and branded onto the orator himself."[604] Simply put, in order to arouse compassion and *pathos* in his listeners the good orator has to be moved by the same emotions.[605] This claim is resumed by Quintilian, who reveals that the secret of emotional arousal resides in the extent to which the orator can be said to take on the feelings he aims to generate in his audience (*Inst.* 6.2.25–6).[606] Significantly, Quintilian attributes his knowledge of this emotional relationship between the speaker and his audience to personal experience and nature. It is on real experience of pain and suffering that Quintilian may claim that "the speaker generating pity for his client must imagine that the sufferings which he laments are

---

[602] Hall 2007: 233–4.
[603] *Nam et mendacium dicere etiam sapienti aliquando concessum est, et adfectus, si aliter ad aequitatem perduci iudex non poterit, necessario movebit orator.*
[604] *Nec fieri potest, ut doleat is, qui audit, ut oderit, ut invideat, ut pertimescat aliquid, ut ad fletum misericordiamque deducatur, nisi omnes illi motus, quos orator adhibere volet iudici, in ipso oratore impressi esse atque inusti videbuntur.* On the orator's sincere display of emotions, see Wisse 1989: 257–69.
[605] Wisse 1989: 257–8.
[606] *Summa enim, quantum ego quidem sentio, circa movendos adfectus in hoc posita est, ut moveamur ipsi* ("The prime essential for stirring the emotions of others is, in my opinion, first to feel those emotions oneself": Quint. *Inst.* 6.2.26). On Quintilian's discussion of the role of emotional effects in the peroration in *Inst.* 6.2, see Leigh 2004b.

indeed his own and must speak as he would were that indeed the case" (*Inst.* 6.2.34–6).[607]

In the spectacular manifestation of pain complemented by tears, actors and orators perform the role of the afflicted. They engage emotions that are expected to be believed to be true. This theatrical scenario involves the direct, emotional participation of the putative audience. Moods of despair and anxiety, triggered by the actor-orator lamenting his own misfortune, guide the audience's reaction and final judgment. Quintilian admits that one of most powerful means of obtaining victory consists in "stirring the emotions of the judges, and moulding and transforming them to the attitude which we desire" (*Inst.* 6.2.1). This applies especially to the *peroratio*, where the appeal to pity and emotions occupies the most prominent place and the effectiveness of a planned *miseratio* can be measured against the judges' emotional participation in the defendant's fate.[608] As Quintilian says, "in the epilogue we have to consider what the feelings of the judge will be when he retires to consider his verdict, for we shall have no further opportunity to say anything and cannot any longer reserve arguments to be produced later" (*Inst.* 6.1.10).[609] In Winterbottom's words, "the judges are, at this finale stage of the speech, more than ever before at the forefront of the orator's mind."[610]

Emotional appeals in the peroration, involving a carefully managed use of tone voice, gestures, facial expressions and tears, as an external manifestation of internal turmoil, are quite common in Cicero's orations. Winterbottom provides us with a close examination of a series of final supplications.[611] This set of case-studies can be usefully compared with Quintilian's precepts about choreography aimed at moving the court to pity and tears (*Inst.* 6.1.30–4).[612] There Quintilian concentrates on the custom of "bringing accused persons into court wearing squalid and unkempt attire, and of introducing their children and parents," an emotional device exploited by Cicero toward the end of the *pro Flacco* (106) and the *pro Cluentio* (192). Similarly, lying prostrate and embracing the knees of the judges was a not-unknown practice, a form of physical supplication that Cicero profitably used in the *Pro Quinctio* (96–7). A passage from

---

[607] Leigh 2004b: 138. Quintilian himself admits that he has achieved a standing reputation for his talent for mimicking (*Inst.* 6.2.36). On Quintilian's discussion of the art of emotional appeal (and the rules to be followed to arouse an emotional response in the judge), see Katula 2003.
[608] In general, see Winterbottom 2004.
[609] *In epilogo vero est, qualem animum iudex in consilium ferat, et iam nihil amplius dicturi sumus nec restat quo reservemus.*
[610] Winterbottom 2004: 230.   [611] Winterbottom 2004 (also Hall 2007: 227–9).
[612] Winterbottom 2004: 220–3.

Asconius's commentary on the *pro Scauro* (28C) informs us that those who were pleading on behalf of the defendant embraced the judges' knees in a suppliant-like manner. In addition, the young Faustus Cornelius "gave a testimonial in humble vein and with tears" and "moved his hearers no less than Scaurus himself had done" (*Is in laudatione multa humiliter et cum lacrimis locutus non minus audientes permovit quam Scaurus ipse permoverat*).[613] As Winterbottom notes, "we cannot be sure that such scenes were enacted, or even physically possible, in the conditions of a court in the Ciceronian period."[614] However, the simple fact that Cicero offers examples of these theatrical devices prompts us to argue that, at least in some cases, the orator was permitted to adopt a histrionic style in the attempt to exploit the emotions.

Crying as a means of arousing pity and winning the jury's goodwill[615] is notoriously a dominant feature of the peroration in Cicero's defense of Milo (§§ 92–5).[616] Conflating the roles of actor and orator, Cicero is a suppliant, who creates compassion by assimilating his own misfortune to that of the defendant.[617] As has been said, "what moves Cicero is that Milo is threatened by the fate Cicero himself had suffered before and from which Milo had saved him."[618] In the guise of an emotional, distressed Milo, Cicero "substitutes his own for Milo's missing tears,"[619] rounding off his final request for mercy with a spectacularly pitiful scene[620] and exploiting his memory of exile to move the judges to compassion. Tears spring from a strategy of personification. In recalling the inhuman experience of banishment Cicero links his exile to that of his savior, conscious though he is that nothing could prevent Milo from being condemned and sent to exile.[621] Deeply moved by Cicero's and Milo's wretched destiny, the listeners associate themselves with the tragic heroes. They are induced by Cicero's lamentation to relate Milo's misfortune to themselves and so fear a painful

---

[613] Lewis 2006: 229.   [614] Winterbottom 2004: 222.
[615] Hagen 2016: 201–2. Cf. also Heckenkamp 2010.
[616] On the rhetorical strategy in the peroration of the *pro Milone* and the use of the figure of *prosopopoeia/sermocinatio* as a self-praise instrument, see Tzounakas 2009. See also Casamento 2004b (for Cicero's manipulative use of crying in the *pro Milone*).
[617] Quint. *Inst.* 6.1.24–5 (citing *Mil.* 102).   [618] Heckenkamp 2010: 180.
[619] Heckenkamp 2010: 179 (from Casamento 2004b: 55–8).
[620] Overpowered by the strain of grief and fatigue, at the end of his impassioned plea Cicero confesses to being unable to utter any words for tears anymore (*neque enim prae lacrimis iam loqui possum*: Cic. *Mil.* 102). Cf. Quint. *Inst.* 11.3.173.
[621] Cic. *Mil.* 102: *Revocare tu me in patriam, Milo potuisti per hos, ego te in patria retinere non potero?* ("You, Milo, were able with the help of these gentlemen to call me back to my country: and shall I, in spite of their aid, be unable to retain you in that country?").

experience similar to that of the prosecuted.[622] From the orator to the prosecuted and the jury, crying is an expression of internal distress that connects the speaker's destiny to that of the defendant and, ultimately, of the audience, moved to pity and tears by past memories and future fears. Interestingly, in the case of the tearful peroration in the speech of Milo, Cicero's theatrical performance and his appeal to pity served later as the model for the pathetic ending of a speech. Illustrative of that is the tragicomic caricature of Cicero-Milo in Lucius's spectacular defense at the *Risus* festival in Apuleius's novel (Apul. *Met.* 3.3.1–11).[623]

In a not dissimilar way, Cicero's strategy in the speech on behalf of Plancius relies largely on the weapons of emotional manipulation.[624] The emotive power of *vicinitas* has been seen as crucial to Cicero's ethical presentation of Plancius as a very popular figure in Southern Latium, seemingly beloved by the people of Atina and surrounding municipalities.[625] Cicero dwells on the pathetic image of Plancius's supporters, a *multitudo* of Roman knights, tribunes of the treasury and ordinary municipal people thronging the court as suppliants (*Planc.* 21),[626] in order to touch the judges and move them to pity and compassion by a demonstration of loyalty and collective suffering. The Bobbio scholiast gives due consideration to the sight of the people's shabbiness and mourning (*squalor et luctus*) as a means of arousing pity and establishing an emotional connection between the client, his friends and partisans, and the judges (154.13-6St). *Vicinitas*, as a moral and civic quality keeping alive the ancient spirit of kindliness, is not a counterfeit emotion, Cicero adds (*Planc.* 22). The scene of collective mourning for Plancius's misfortune (not unlike the public expression of grief for Cicero's exile) thus generates a true emotional response from the audience that reads the defendant's painful life-experience as its own, in a transfer of emotions from the individual to the community.[627] Cicero exploits the political and social notion of *vicinitas* as part of his emotional delivery, endowing a concept embedded in the world of civic patronage and local obligations with a persuasive power and creating a network of moral and social ties – between Plancius, the people from Atina and southern Latium, the advocate and the jury – based on emotional involvement and a shared feeling of compassion.

---

[622] For this worked-out emotional strategy cf. Cic. *de Orat.* 2.211.  [623] La Bua 2013b.
[624] See supra pp. 198–9 (on the legal and political context of the speech).
[625] Lomas 2004: 112–13.
[626] *Quam quidem nunc multitudinem videtis, iudices, in squalore et luctu supplicem vobis.*
[627] Riggsby 1999: 45–7 (on the "economy of *gratia* and *beneficium*" in the trial and Plancius's social position).

Cicero's strategy of "embarrassment" in the Plancius case has already attracted our interest.[628] Here it is useful to recall a significant point of the prosecutor Laterensis's attack on Cicero's credibility. In reference to the case of C. Cispius, defended by Cicero in 56 BCE without success, the prosecutor had raised doubts about the advocate's behavior and tactics (*Planc.* 75–77). In particular, he had reprimanded the orator for his ostentatious and insincere display of compassion, manifested in "a poor little tear" (*lacrimula*; cf. *Planc.* 76)[629] and presented thereby to the jury as characteristic of a man untrue to his friends, exploiting emotional devices to deceive the audience and win approval. Cicero's response is brilliant. Appropriating and turning to his advantage Laterensis's reproach, Cicero invites his opponent to spot his talented use of tears, engaging him in a dispute over the abundance of crying as a symptom of pity and true solicitude for the client's misfortune.[630] At the heart of Cicero's apologetic reply is sincerity, effective as an emotional device, basic to obligations of friendship and feelings of *gratia*. By tears the orator assumes the posture of a true, loyal friend and supporter. Cicero makes his point clearly by validating his crying as a means of reinforcing social and personal ties and offering the picture of a trustworthy orator.[631] In this connection it is also significant that the Bobbio scholiast calls attention to Laterensis's ridicule and mockery of Cicero's "too pathetic and tear-jerking" perorations (*epilogi ... nimium flebiles et miserationis pleni*)[632] and synthesizes

---

[628] See supra p. 249–50.
[629] *Et mihi lacrimulam Cispiani iudicii obiectas. Sic enim dixisti: "Vidi ego tuam lacrimulam." Vide, quam me verbi tui poeniteat. Non modo lacrimulam, sed multas lacrimas, et fletum cum singultu videre potuisti* ("You reproach me with the 'one poor tear' I shed at the trial of Cispius. 'I marked your one poor tear', say you. Mark now how short of the truth your expression seems to me to fall; you could have seen on that occasion not merely 'one poor tear', but floods of them, sighs and weeping commingled").
[630] Alexander 2002: 143–4 (in particular on Laterensis's reproach of Cicero's tendency to characterize every prosecution as a personal attack on his credibility as an advocate).
[631] Cic. *Planc.* 76: *An ego, qui meorum lacrimis me absente commotus simultates, quas mecum habebat, deposuisset meaeque salutis non modo non oppugnator (ut inimici mei putarant) sed etiam defensor fuisset, huius in periculo non dolorem meum significarem?* ("Would you have me exhibit no symptoms of grief when danger threatened one who had been so affected by the tears of my dear ones, when I myself was far away, that he had waived his old differences with me, and, so far from standing forth, as my enemies had anticipated, as the assailant of my well-being, had actually become its champion?").
[632] On the use of tears in the peroration of the *pro Plancio* cf. also schol. Bob. 166.22St (on *Planc.* 83); 169.1-2St (on *Planc.* 101: *lacrimosis lemmatibus iam perorat, adfectus animi sui cum varia miseratione proluens, ut tantum auxilii reus habeat, quantum suo dolori patronus adiecerit*, "He makes his final appeal by adding tearful sentences and displays his own emotions by a flood of tears and expressions of grief, so that the defendant could get a support comparable to the degree of suffering and pain demonstrated by his advocate"). For tearful sentences in the peroration of the *pro Flacco* cf. schol. Bob. 108.11St (on *Flac.* 106).

Cicero's statements about the emotional and persuasive power of tears as expressed in the *Orator* (165.20-2St).[633] The scholiast goes on to elucidate Cicero's ethical and emotional strategy as dictated by friendship and mutual obligations (165.2-6St). But what seems to be the strongest point of the scholiast's argument is that any emotional device, in order to be effective, must be applied properly and reflect true feelings on the speaker's part. In a larger sense, this claim reiterates Quintilian's pedagogical concern about a weak and inappropriate use of crying that might result in collective laughter and even be detrimental to the orator's authority (*Inst.* 6.1.44).[634]

As Winterbottom notes, "the orator has to ensure that he speaks words he can best act, as well as that he accompanies his words with effective *actio*."[635] Cicero spoke brilliantly, performed as a consummate stage-actor and joined doctrine with creativity to produce a powerful and persuasive delivery, with an eye upon the standards of a masculine, aristocratic performance. His speeches demonstrated that training in rhetorical theory was ineffective unless accompanied by the skills of a gifted performer. Bell well points out that Cicero claimed that "eloquence was not a product of rhetorical theory but rather theory developed from eloquence."[636] Cicero's specimens of oratorical performance offered students of rhetoric the opportunity to come into contact with the transformation of theory into action and the power of eloquence. By his artful and modulated use of voice, his posture and gestures, his stage-managed delivery and, above all, his manipulative deployment of aesthetic and emotional devices the young were instructed in adapting style and oratorical gestures to the needs of a specific performance. In other words, if Cicero's speeches "were indeed theory in action,"[637] it was from the practical actions performed by the speaker that would-be orators apprehended the basic principles of successful delivery.

At the end of his circumstantial presentation of matters that are crucial to *actio* and appropriate delivery (*apta pronuntiatio*),[638] Quintilian recapitulates the characteristics of a good delivery, depending upon the orator's

---

[633] Cic. *Orat.* 130 (cf. also *Brut.* 190; Quint. *Inst.* 11.1.85).
[634] *Illud praecipue monendum, ne quis nisi summis ingenii viribus ad movendas lacrimas aggredi audeat; nam ut est longe vehementissimus hic, cum invaluit, adfectus, ita, si nihil efficit, tepet; quem melius infirmus actor tacitis iudicum cogitationibus reliquisset* ("It is especially important to warn against venturing to arouse tears, unless one has a really powerful talent: this emotion, when successfully aroused, is by far the most effective of all, but if the attempt fails it is a lukewarm business, and a weak performer, *infirmus actor*, would do better to leave it all to the silent thoughts of the judges").
[635] Winterbottom 2004: 223.   [636] Bell 2013: 174.   [637] Bell 2013: 177.
[638] Cf. Quint. *Inst.* 11.3.61 (for appropriateness of delivery).

ability to secure a conciliatory, persuasive or emotional effect and win the goodwill of the audience by charming stylistic stratagems (*Inst.* 11.3.154).[639] He then offers recommendations and prescriptions about the method the good orator should follow to give a persuasive delivery, responding with creative variety to the requirements of each portion of the speech (*Inst.* 11.3.155–83). As expected, Cicero is the inspiration for Quintilian's theory of delivery. His precepts, as expressed in the *Orator* (§ 122) and the *Brutus* (§ 141), form the basic conceptual framework for any discussion of oratorical performance (*Inst.* 11.3.184). But Cicero left to posterity not just a set of instructions about correct delivery. He also left a series of splendid examples of emotional delivery, as the product of a perfect fusion of elegant style and theatrical devices. And this appeared all the more impressive in times of degeneracy and decline, like those experienced by Quintilian, concerned about the possible negative impacts of an effeminate and extravagant performance (*Inst.* 11.3.184).[640] It is on Cicero, and only on Cicero, that the would-be orator should rely to form his successful delivery. Doctrine, nature[641] and, ultimately, Cicero, the incarnation of artistic eloquence: The pupil of Quintilian perceived Cicero as the transcendant expression of oratorical supremacy founded on rhetorical rules and personal skills and depending upon a visible emotional delivery.

## Manipulating the Past

Modern scholarship has long dwelled on the relationship between history and rhetoric in Cicero's writings.[642] In an eminently literary approach, Fox has reconsidered Cicero's undogmatic vision of Rome's history in his philosophical (especially the *De republica*) and rhetorical treatises and presented an orator-statesman constantly engaged in a dialectic process of reconstruction and reinterpretation of the teleology of Roman power.[643] Scholarly attention has also been paid to Cicero's theory of historiography

---

[639] *Tris autem praestare debet pronuntiatio: conciliet, persuadeat, moveat, quibus natura cohaeret, ut etiam delectet* ("There are three qualities which delivery should possess. It should be conciliatory, persuasive and moving, and the possession of these three qualities involves charm as a further requisite").

[640] Cf. supra pp. 286–8.

[641] Quint. *Inst.* 11.3.180: *Quare norit se quisque, nec tantum ex communibis praeceptis, sed etiam ex natura sua capiat consilium formandae actionis* ("Consequently, every man must get to know his own peculiarities and must consult not merely the general rules of technique, but his own nature as well with a view to forming his delivery").

[642] For rhetoric and historiography in Roman culture and literature, a good survey is in Laird 2009. See also Nicolai 1992; Cape 1997; Damon 2007 (with further bibliography).

[643] Fox 2007.

in the second book of the *De oratore*,[644] his ideal of literary history[645] and the role of *inventio* in the construction of a true or truth-like narrative. The passage from the *De legibus* (1.5), supporting the claim that historiography is "predominantly a task for orators" (*opus . . . unum oratorium maxime*), has prompted learned discussions about the use of rhetorical technique in historical narratives and the connection between truth (as the domain of historiography) and probability in oratorical discourse.[646] From a different, more pragmatic, perspective, other scholars have reminded modern readers of the impact of Rome's history on Cicero's strategy of persuasion, reconfiguring – and recording for posterity – an image of an orator and politician who exploited and manipulated Rome's past events in order to control the audience's emotions[647] and stimulate reflection on issues of Roman morality and cultural identity.[648]

In this section our interest is not in Cicero's theory of literary history or his sophisticated, often ambiguous interpretation of the Roman past. Our focus is rather on the role played by Cicero's speeches as sources of historical knowledge in the ancient educational system.[649] The main emphasis will be on the endless fascination provided by Cicero's evocation and reconstruction of the past by means of historical and personal *exempla*. Defined as a "statement which strengthens or weakens a case by reference to the authority or situation of an individual or an event" (Cic. *Inv.* 1.49),[650] the *exemplum* (*parádeigma*)[651] is a form of inartificial proof, a *probatio* drawn from history or mythology, intended to persuade and enchant the audience.[652] Cicero himself makes it clear that "the mention

---

[644] Cic. *de Orat.* 2.36; 51–64: in general on Cicero's views on historical writing in the dialogue, see Fantham 2004: 152–8. On Cicero as a historian, see also Fleck 1993; Woodman 2011.

[645] Cic. *Fam.* 5.12 (epistle to Lucceius: 22SB*Fam*). On the letter to Lucceius, see Fantham 2004: 157–60; Fox 2007: 256–64 (with bibliography). On Cicero's construction of a literary history (based on stylistic perfection), see Feldherr 2003. See also Brunt 2011 (for ornamentation in historical writings and Cicero's ideal of elegant narrative history).

[646] Laird 2009: 199–203.

[647] Blom 2010: 67–72; Hanchey 2014 (on Cicero's overall use of historical references as a means of creating a fictional Roman past and establishing an intersubjective and empathetic relationship with his audience, prompted to cooperate with the orator in reshaping the republic's present). For Cicero's manipulation of history in connection with the physical setting of oratory, see Vasaly 1993.

[648] Dench 2013. Also important is Gowing 2005.

[649] On the exploitation of Roman history in Roman oratory, see Steel 2006: 57 (who draws attention to the role of the audience as "a privileged and exclusive group" entering into a historical dialogue with the speaker). For the extent of historical knowledge among Roman citizens, see Morstein-Marx 2004: 68–118.

[650] *Exemplum est quod rem auctoritate aut casu alicuius hominis aut negotii confirmat aut infirmat.*

[651] For the Greek term *parádeigma*, applied to historical parallels, cf. Quint. *Inst.* 5.11.1.

[652] Cf. Cic. *Ver.* 2.3.209 (for the combination of persuasion effects and aesthetics in the use of an *exemplum*, see Blom 2010: 73–7). See also Hanchey 2014: 67.

of antiquity and the citation of examples give a speech authority and credibility as well as affording the highest pleasure to the audience" (*Orat.* 120).[653] This point is reiterated in the prologue of the *De oratore* (1.18): "Moreover, one must know the whole past with its storehouse of examples and precedents, nor should one fail to master statutes and the civil law."[654] In keeping with Cicero's theory of the *exemplum*, Quintilian insists on the rhetorical effectiveness and practicality of exemplary actions (or individuals) that are relevant to the trial at hand and contribute to the persuasive technique.[655] To Quintilian, "what is properly called *exemplum*" consists of a commemoration of an "event which either took place or is treated as having taken place, in order to make your point convincing" (*Inst.* 5.11.6).[656] Since any proof aims to establish credibility, the speaker introduces the historical or fictitious example by an inductive method,[657] evaluating its appropriateness to the case according to different degrees of similarity (*Inst.* 5.11.6–16). For each *exemplum* chosen via induction and similarity Cicero offers the most appropriate specimens (*Inst.* 5.11.11).[658] The *exemplum totum simile*, in which equal importance is given to the deed under examination in the *causa* and the proposed example, is illustrated by a passage from *Mur.* 17;[659] the *exemplum ex maiore ad minus ductum* from *Mil.* 7; the *exemplum ex minore ad maius ductum* from *Mil.* 72;[660] and, finally, the *exemplum dissimile* from *Cluent.* 88–96.[661]

Persuasion is the target of forensic and political oratory. It follows that an *exemplum* served the argumentative tactic. It was instrumental in lending force, credibility and aesthetic value to the speaker's arguments. In appealing to the *auctoritas maiorum* or choosing and presenting family *exempla* or stock historical figures that carried specific connotations familiar to a Roman audience, Cicero strengthened his case, delighted his audience and forced the judges – and the Roman people consequently – to impose a moral judgment on a past action and deliver a verdict based on

---

[653] *Commemoratio autem antiqitatis exemplorumque prolatio summa cum delectatione et auctoritatem orationi affert et fidem.*
[654] *Tenenda praeterea est omnis antiquitas exemplorumque vis, neque legum ac iuris civilis scientia neglegenda est.*
[655] Quint. *Inst.* 3.8.66 (for *exempla* in the *suasoriae*); 10.1.34 (on the knowledge of historical facts and precedents as an indispensable instrument of persuasion); 12.4.1 (on the abundance of examples, both old and new, available to the orator); 12.11.17.
[656] *Quod proprie vocamus exemplum, id est rei gestae aut ut gestae utilis ad persuadendum id quod intenderis commemoratio.*
[657] Quint. *Inst.* 5.11.3 (on the *inductio* cf. Cic. *Inv.* 1.51).
[658] *Singula igitur horum generum ex Cicerone (nam unde potius?) exempla ponamus* ("Let us set out some individual examples of these kinds from Cicero; where could we find better?").
[659] Quint. *Inst.* 5.11.11.    [660] Quint. *Inst.* 5.11.12.    [661] Quint. *Inst.* 5.11.13.

the exemplary value of legal precedents[662] and historical *exempla*.[663] But exemplarity had also a didactic-moral value. The ethical power of the propounded *exemplum* stimulated imitation. Roman citizens attending the trial (and later readers) were spurred on to emulate the deeds of the ancestors or the individuals presented as models of political and moral virtue.[664]

This ethical and pedagogical deployment of the past, which Roller has termed "an exemplary view of the past" and which "assumes ethical and social continuity, or at least homology, over space and time,"[665] illuminates Cicero's historical discourse as a way of preserving and transmitting memories of actions and fashioning himself as a model of behavior to be followed and imitated by others.[666] To Cicero, history (and the use of historical and personal *exempla* accordingly) exceeded the immediate aims of persuasion or aesthetic pleasure. Antonius's splendid definition of history as the "witness of the ages, the illuminator of reality, the life force of memory, the teacher of our lives and the messenger of times gone by" in the second book of the *De oratore* (2.36)[667] suggests that at the heart of exemplary discourse was memorialization and imitation of past actions. In offering an *exemplum* the orator preserved and reinvigorated memory of exemplary deeds. By engaging his audience in evaluating the ethical force of a historical *exemplum* Cicero played upon Roman respect for the *mos maiorum*, instilling – and perpetuating – traditional social and moral values shared by the Roman collectivity.[668] Most significantly, he proposed an exemplary deed or individual for imitation.[669] A rightly celebrated passage from the second book of the *De officiis* (2.46) illustrates how imitation of *exempla* of past generations was thought of as having a great impact on the learning process.[670] Imitation, crucial to rhetorical training (together with

---

[662] Quint. *Inst.* 5.2.1 (for *praeiudicia*, decisions in previous courts on similar cases, termed *exempla*). Cf. also Ps. Asconius 190.9-11St (*praeiudicium dicitur res quae cum statuta fuerit, affert iudicaturis exemplum quod sequitur*, ["*praeiudicium* is usually called a verdict reached in previous cases that provides the judges with an example to follow"]).
[663] McCormick 2014 (on the ancient discussion of exemplarity).
[664] For the moral-didactic function of the *exemplum*, see Blom 2010: 67.
[665] Roller 2009: 216. See also Roller 2004 (for exemplary discourse in Roman culture, which involves action, audience, values and memory).
[666] On Cicero's promotion of the self, see Blom 2010: 287–324.
[667] *Historia vero testis temporum, lux veritatis, vita memoriae, magistra vitae, nuntia vetustatis.*
[668] On the audience for history in Rome, see Marincola 2009: 12–3.
[669] For the use of the historical exempla in judicial speeches, see David 1980.
[670] *Facillime autem et in optimam partem cognoscuntur adulescentes, qui se ad claros et sapientes viros bene consulentes rei publicae contulerunt; quibuscum si frequentes sunt, opinionem afferunt populo eorum fore se similes, quos sibi ipsi delegerint ad imitandum* ("Young men win recognition most easily and most favorably, if they attach themselves to men who are at once wise and renowned as well as

art, natural ability and practice), was at the core of any informed choice between paradigmatic models of morality and virtue.[671] By a calculated selection of historical and personal *exempla* the speaker acted as a teacher and adviser to the Roman people and the younger generations of orators and politicians.

Conscious of the powerful ideological effects embedded in exemplarity, Cicero set himself up as a model for imitation. He advertised himself as a follower of specific moral and political models of behavior and promoted himself, at the same time, as an *exemplum* worthy of imitation. By replicating ancient role models and expressing pride in his own political achievements he created an image of himself as a credible statesman and an exemplary advocate. As Blom puts it, "Cicero's use of personal *exempla* was geared to promote his own agenda and public persona."[672] Any Ciceronian scholar is well acquainted with Cicero's project of figuring himself as a trustworthy political adviser and an exemplary citizen. His speeches, as well as his other genres of writing, abound with references to his own exemplarity, displaying the orator's constant preoccupation with reputation and self-advertising policy.[673] Principled and loyal advocate, *homo novus*, exemplary consul, citizen and consular suffering unjust banishment, strenuous defender of the *res publica*, political adviser, ideal statesman and orator: by reminding his readership of all his political and cultural achievements, Cicero portrayed himself as both a true politician acting in the interests of the state and the ultimate exemplum of Roman orator and intellectual.[674] To quote Roller, Cicero "acted with a view toward being observed, evaluated, monumentalized, and imitated."[675]

Of course, Cicero's anxiety over his own exemplarity advises us to be extremely cautious about the orator's sincerity and the true reasons behind the employment of historical and personal exempla. As has been said, "a

---

patriotic counsellors in public affairs. And if they associate constantly with such men, they inspire in the public the expectation that they will be like them, seeing that they have themselves selected them for imitation"). See Dyck 1996: 429; Blom 2010: 315.

[671] On Cicero's discussion of imitation of rhetorical models in the second book of the *De oratore* (2.87–97), see Fantham 1978a. On imitation as a "law of nature" cf. Quint. *Inst.* 10.2.2 (*Atque omnis vitae ratio sic constat ut quae probamus in aliis facere ipsi velimus*, "And it is a universal rule of life that we should wish to copy what we approve of others"); cf. also 1C.1.3; for imitation of other persons' character (*ethopoia, mimesis*) 9.2.58 (1.3.1 for the didactic power of imitation).

[672] Blom 2010: 293.

[673] For an interpretation of Cicero's strategy of self-fashioning as a response to the nature of advocacy in Rome, see Paterson 2004. In general, on Cicero's self-promotion as an *exemplum*, see Blom 2010: 287–324.

[674] Lintott 2008: 129–211 (for historical topics and Cicero's self-perception in the speeches).

[675] Roller 2004: 7.

historical *exemplum* is never a neutral or objective entity, but will always be a subjective (re)interpretation of the past made to fit the user's aims. A historical exemplum is not a static but rather a fluid element which can be interpreted and reinterpreted in both words and action."[676] The same concept can be applied to Cicero's manipulative use of personal *exempla* and, in a broader context, to the speeches as records of events. As Lintott notes, "Cicero knew the laws of history, that one should neither venture to say anything false nor fail to venture to say anything true."[677] If in his theoretical writings Cicero propounded "an idealized historical narrative of early Rome, articulated by figures who are themselves somewhat idealized,"[678] in the speeches the republican advocate offered his own (mainly apologetic) interpretation of Roman history, within a calculated representation (and occasional misrepresentation) of historical events for the sake of self-promotion.[679] A speech is, by its nature, a historical event. It takes place at a definite time under specific circumstances, recounts (and distorts) facts, delineates political personalities and provides hearers and readers with a variously constructed historical vision depending on the needs of each particular case. Cicero as an advocate could not be an impartial narrator.[680] The desire for glory, combined with the aim of persuasion, prompted him to manipulate – and intermingle – truth and fiction, as the narrative of the battle of Bovillae in the *pro Milone* has demonstrated.[681] From Roman memories and his own political life Cicero built up his strategy of persuasion and self-promotion, offering himself as an exemplary model of successful *homo novus* and ideal orator.

Before enquiring into the reception of Cicero's discourse of exemplarity in the ancient schools, a few words are in order about history in the Roman education system. From Cicero's mastery of exemplary history in judicial and political contexts and its intended pedagogical impact we are allowed to assume that instruction on the past was fundamental to human education and the construction of the ideal orator. That history did not have a secondary place in the formation of the orator is beyond dispute. We have already mentioned Cicero's and Quintilian's assertions of the importance of historical knowledge for the orator. Marincola calls attention to Quintilian's survey of Latin historians in the tenth book of the *Institutio* (10.1.101–4) as an indication of the fact that reading history was of the

---

[676] Blom 2010: 62.   [677] Lintott 2008: 3.   [678] Fox 2007: 111.   [679] Lintott 2008.
[680] Steel 2013c: 68 ("An orator seeks the best possibile presentation of his case, and not balance, fairness, or accuracy – unless such qualities will assist him in securing his aim in speaking, whatever that may be").
[681] Cf. supra pp. 220–5.

greatest significance in rhetorical training.[682] Yet it might seem necessary to be reminded that study of the past did not enter into the practice of teaching as an autonomous discipline.[683] As Gibson puts it, "history as a formal discipline or academic field of study did not exist in antiquity, and nobody was formally trained to take up a profession called 'historian'."[684] What ancient students gained was a general historical knowledge, acquired from the examination of personages and events of the past that came up in the course of reading. To quote Gibson again, "ancient students learned literature, and they learned how to manipulate historical exempla in creating spoken and written discouse, but they did not learn history."[685] So paradigms from ancient history complemented the study of prose and poetry texts. They served as ancillary didactic instruments. They had an instrumental function, supporting the would-be orators in developing the skills of cultural competence.[686] In turn, as we have seen, historical events and exempla participated in the overall construction of a morally good speaker. They reinforced and perpetuated ethical norms, which formed part of the spiritual patrimony of the dominant elite.

It might be observed in passing that an analogous situation could be assumed for legal education. As has been shown, there is no evidence of a formal, standardized, instruction in law in the late republic.[687] Before the emergence of specialized schools of law in the early decades of the empire, the "Sabinian" or Cassian school and "Proculian" school, legal training was not practiced and law was usually taught in the context of the so-called *tirocinium fori*. It was only after the establishment of the imperial power that we witness a formalized legal instruction and the composition of legal textbooks with instructional purposes, like the mid-second-century *Institutions* of civil law of Gaius.[688] About the procedures of teaching in these law schools we have little evidence, and one might just claim that the discussion of law issues had a consistent part in mock-trial exercises or fictitious school controversies. Recently, a significant number of scholarly contributions on the connection between law and Roman declamations has emphasized the role played by the Hermagorean *status* theory (or the system of the *status legales*) in the application of standard legal criteria to

---

[682] Marincola 2009: 14. [683] On the question, see Nicolai 2007 (also Nicolai 1992: 32–83).
[684] Gibson 2004: 106. [685] Gibson 2004: 107.
[686] That history was an ancillary science is made clear by Asconius's historical commentary, which, as has been said, was intended to serve as a companion and a training aid to his sons. On the nature and purpose of Asconius's scholarly work, see Bishop 2015: 292–4.
[687] Riggsby 2010: 57–66. See also Riggsby 2015 (and Lintott 2004). [688] Riggsby 2015: 447.

declamatory exercises.[689] And, in turn, as much as the well-to-do young men attending the school of the *rhetor* exploited legal contexts and principles to construct persuasive speeches, the jurists or the young members of the Roman upper classes receiving instruction in law at the imperial legal schools used rhetorical devices or argumentative theory to strengthen their cases and argue their legal opinions.[690]

Even if law, like history, was not an autonomous field of study in the rhetorical schools, it is beyond doubt that the would-be orator was required to have a good knowledge of civil law.[691] Crassus's promotion of legal education in the first book of the *De oratore* (1.166–203) is an eloquent testimony to the importance of legal science in rhetorical advocacy.[692] Ignorance of civil law and the customs and religious practices of the republic might undermine the advocate's reliability.[693] And Cicero's impassioned eulogy of the *ius civile* and the jurists in the *pro Caecina* (§§ 65–78), "the earliest clear enunciation of the theory of autonomous law,"[694] appears to be rooted in the practical conception of legal knowledge as providing a self-consistent set of norms and instruments to be applied to individual cases. The orator used law to present a persuasive case. In order to do that, he had to be fairly competent in the legal system and the rules governing juridical argumentation. Cicero was not a jurist and he never wrote a work on jurisprudence.[695] Yet he showed a deep knowledge of civil and criminal law in his theoretical writings and, above all, in his speeches, where uncontested rules of law served persuasion in the competitive arena of forensic discussion.[696] The speeches were later received as valuable sources of knowledge of the late republican legal system. Asconius and late scholiasts, as expected, wrote abundant notes on laws, rogations and legal issues.[697] But it should be noted that, just as Cicero manipulated

---

[689] Amato-Citti-Huelsenbeck 2015.
[690] Leesen 2010: 317 (for the use of the topical tradition, as developed in Cicero's *Topica* and Quintilian, in the school controversies treated by Gaius).
[691] Cic. *de Orat.* 1.159.   [692] Fantham 2004: 102–30.   [693] Quint. *Inst.* 12.3.1–3.
[694] Frier 1985: 188.
[695] On Cicero's planned systematic treatment of civil law in the treatise *de iure civili in artem redigendo* cf. Cic. *Leg.* 1.12–3; 17. See Fantham 2004: 112.
[696] For the "agonistic" view of legal cases in Cicero's speeches, see Frier 1985: 115–38. On Cicero's handling of law in the forensic speeches, see Harries 2004, 2006 and 2013.
[697] For a list of laws in Asconius, see Lewis 2006: 333–35. Legal explanations in the Bobbio scholiast occur at 78.35St (*leges Cornelia et Calpurnia*); 84.21St (*lex Plautia de vi* et the procedure of the *reiectio iudicum*); 97.32St (*lex iudiciaria*); 148.10St (*lex Aelia et Fufia*); 149.13St; 150.17St (on the *lex Vatinia*); 152.21St; 160.2St (*lex Licinia*). For Ps. Asconius, cf. 189.10St (*leges iudiciariae*); 193.7St (*divinatio* process); 210.1St (*reiectio iudicum*); 230.20–231.13St (*comperendinatio*, a compulsory two-part trial); 248.3St (*lex Voconia*); 249.15St (*lis vindiciarum*). A note on the procedure of the *sortitio iudicum* occurs in the Gronovius scholiast B 335.21St.

historical narratives in his orations and offered misleading accounts of events in order to deceive his audience, he displayed a great talent for manipulating legal argumentations and law to win approval. Harries correctly advises us that Cicero's forensic speeches "were not dispassionate elucidations of legal points, and concentrated only on issues germane to his argument (or effective distractions from its weakness). As an account of the law, the speeches were tendentious, selective and designed to entertain as well as, in a limited sense, to inform."[698]

Turning to the persuasive and instructional effects conveyed by historical and personal *exempla* in the speeches, we should attend to the scholiasts' comments upon Cicero's strategic use of exemplary history. Let us briefly concentrate on the *exemplum* as a means of persuasion. In his commentary on the *pro Archia*, the Bobbio scholiast reminds his readers of Cicero's plan to legitimate Archias's claim to citizenship on moral and cultural grounds.[699] As demonstrated by Berry, Cicero had to persuade the jury, unsympathetic to a Greek poet, that his client deserved to be a Roman citizen because of his intellectual merits.[700] Cicero's lengthy and elaborate lecture in praise of literature represents, in this light, a necessary transition from legal arguments to the portrayal of Archias as a poet combining *natura* with *doctrina*, whose talent was of practical utility to Roman politics and society. A gifted poet – and Archias as such – could immortalize in verse the military glory of the Roman people and, as Cicero affirms at the end of his literary *digressio* (§§ 28–30), "without praise men would have no incentive to perform great deeds."[701] Exemplarity plays a central role in this glorification of poetry as a creative art that confers glory and immortality on the country. To prove Archias's superiority as an intellectual Cicero mentions a number of eminent public figures of previous generations who were on close terms with the poet or enjoyed the study of literature. At § 6 the orator shows that his client was held in high esteem by Rome's leading families. The scholiast briefly comments on each one of Archias's patrons (176.16–177.14St), and then he appends a note on the purpose of Cicero's catalogue of *exempla* (177.14-7St):

> Densitas igitur haec exemplorum quae ad personas nobilis transfertur multum praesenti negotio patrocinatur; ut Archias tot amicis et tam inlustribus nixus perquam facile <ad> honorem civitatis potuerit pervenire.

---

[698] Harries 2007: 28.
[699] E.g. 176.3-7St (on Archias's astonishing promptness of versification as a significant part of Cicero's argument).
[700] Berry 2004b.   [701] Berry 2004b: 310.

"This abundance of exempla referring to illustrious men is of much value to the present case: the purpose is to show that Archias, who had enjoyed the favor of so many and such noble friends, could be easily granted the honor of citizenship."

As Berry again notes, "the effect on the jury of this roll-call of aristocratic names must have been considerable."[702] Sensitive to the ideological power of *exempla*, Cicero worked on the evocation of past patronage to fashion Archias as an intellectual firmly rooted in Roman tradition and culture. The subsequent set of great Romans who devoted themselves to the study of literature for practical reasons contributes to this persuasive strategy. Cicero cites "Scipio and Laelius as examples of men who attained to preeminence because of a mental culture joined to a superior endowment of nature" (§§ 15–6).[703] Then he mentions a number of military commanders who treated poets as familiar friends (§§ 19–27), first and foremost Pompey, who was close to his diarist, Theophanes of Mytilene (§ 24). The scholiast appears to understand Cicero's exemplary discourse when commenting on the *exemplum* of Sulla (§ 25), who would have granted Roman citizenship to Archias in return for his literary favors had the Greek poet not already possessed it (178.22-5St).[704] By means of *exempla* the orator lends force to his argument. In the case of Archias, exemplarity provides good grounds for accepting literature as a laudatory representation of military and political power into the Roman cultural system.

Didactic notes on the persuasive effects of exemplarity occur elsewhere in the Bobbio commentary. The remembrance (*commemoratio*) of the deeds of Manius Aquilius, consul in 101 BCE, accused of extortion and released because of his victorious campaign against runaway slaves in Sicily, begins a series of examples of leading citizens cited by Cicero for their support of the common safety in the *pro Flacco* (§ 98).[705] The scholiast puts the accent on the practical function of this *enumeratio exemplorum* (108.3-6St). By evaluating the ethical and political value of illustrious precedents the audience will form its own judgment on the trial at hand and return a verdict of acquittal in consideration of Flaccus's great services to the *res publica*. The discourse of exemplarity appears to be a dominating feature in the defense of Milo, a difficult case forcing Cicero to capitalize on past models in order to legitimate Milo's murder of Clodius as beneficial to the

---

[702] Berry 2004b: 300.   [703] Taylor (J. H.) 1952: 68.
[704] To the scholiast the *exemplum* of Sulla strengthens Cicero's argument (*ab exemplo adiudicando . . . haec argumentatio impletur*).
[705] Aquilius is repeatedly mentioned in the *Verrines* (cf. *Div.* 69; *Ver.* 2.3.125; 2.5.3; 5; 7; 14): cf. Ps. Asconius 204.1St (on *Div.* 69).

state. The ancient commentator dilates on Cicero's strategy of exemplarity in the speech at several points. The *exemplum* provided by the soldier of Marius, who repelled violence by violence (*Mil.* 9), is considered pertinent to the plea that T. Annius Milo killed his political rival Clodius in self-defense (114.20-1St). Cicero's proposition that self-defense against violence is mandatory when required by the interests of the state (*Mil.* 13–4), a claim crucial to the orator's campaign of vilification of Clodius, is supported by commemoration of exemplary past "political murders," as noted by the scholiast (116.21-2St).[706] Again, at *Mil.* 16 the scholiast comments on Cicero's recourse to "many and valid exempla" (*multis et fortibus exemplis immoratur*) to persuade the judges that no special process should be proposed for inquiry into Clodius's death (117.32-3St).

A fascinating fusion of history and myth permeates Cicero's exemplary discourse at *Mil.* 7–8. The *exempla* of Marcus Horatius, sentenced to death for having killed his sister but freed by an assembly of the Roman people (§ 7), and other leading political figures of the past who were tried for murder and acquitted for having acted lawfully, serve Cicero's intention to demonstrate that no act of killing deserves punishment if it has been carried out in the interest of the republic (§ 8).[707] The Bobbio commentator stresses the illustrative and normative purposes behind Cicero's use of exemplarity (114.1-2St),[708] then elucidates the way by which the orator inserts a mythical *exemplum* into a series of "true" *exempla* from the Roman past (114.4-10St):

> Eum qui patris ulciscendi causa matrem necavisset] Μυθῶδες hoc exemplum videri poterat, de Oreste scilicet, a quo acultera mater occisa est; noluit id in primo constituere nec in postremo, sed in medio, ut utrimque firmitatem de exemplis verioribus mutuetur; cui tamen et ipsi, quamvis aliquantum levi et fabuloso, consideremus quanto ingenio firmitatem pariat orator, ita inferens: "atque hoc, iudices, non sine causa etiam fictis fabulis." Levitatem habent summam fictiones fabularum, sed quid adiecit? "Doctissimi homines memoriae prodiderunt"; ut scriptorum peritia det exemplo quamvis minus idoneo firmitatem.
>
> "One who killed his mother to avenge his father] This exemplum, regarding Orestes, who killed his adulterous mother, could be interpreted as

---

[706] *Et hoc munit exemplis pluribus eorum quos ex usu rei p. constabat occisos* ("And this argument is strengthened by a number of examples of those who had been killed in the interests of the state").

[707] In discussing these historical *exempla* from *Mil.* 8 Quintilian draws attention to previous knowledge of the exemplary deed, its usefulness to the case (*utilitas causae*), and style (*decor*) as factors impacting on the speaker's presentation of the *exemplum* (*Inst.* 5.11.15–6).

[708] *Necessario igitur hanc enumerationem facit, qua plenius doceat nonnumquam caedes iure optimo fieri posse* ("Then he provided this list of examples out of necessity, so that he could demonstrate with stronger arguments that sometimes homicide can be justified on legal grounds").

pertaining to the domain of fable. Cicero decided to place this *exemplum* neither at the beginning nor at the close but in the middle, so that it could receive strength from more credible *exempla* on both sides. Let us appreciate the orator's talent in lending force to his argument by means of an *exemplum*, however unsubstantial and fictional it might be. He added such a supplementary comment: 'And so too, gentlemen, it is not without reason that even in their fictions . . . '. The fictional examples from the legendary past possess the greatest unreliability: what did he attach? 'Accomplished poets narrated it'. In doing so, he loaned credibility to an *exemplum*, though less appropriate to the context, by drawing on the authority of ancient writers."

Cicero's thesis that a homicide can be ethically and lawfully approved of rests upon a fabulous *exemplum* (the acquittal of Orestes), drawn from Greek tragedy, whose evocative power is reinforced by exemplary past actions firmly rooted in collective memory.[709] Quintilian cites in full Cicero's *exemplum* and emphasizes the speaker's ability to present examples drawn from poetic fables (of less probative force by their very nature) as credible (*Inst.* 5.11.17–8).[710] The scholiast appears to take this a step further. He tries to clarify (though in banal terms) Cicero's manipulative technique of adapting a fictional *exemplum* to a set of significant *res gestae* that are directly relevant to the point at issue, that is, the justification of killing in self-defense against violence.[711] As a master of the art of illusion, Cicero handles and exploits the availability of exemplary deeds, both mythical and historical, in line with the oratorical goal of persuasion.[712]

The explanatory, rather than illustrative, force of the scholiast's comment reminds us of the importance of the *exemplum* as a rhetorical tool. Introduced from outside the *causa* by induction and similarity, an *exemplum* establishes actions to be imitated or avoided and allows the orator to convey a plausible message founded on the normative power of exemplarity. Yet persuasiveness must be achieved by the *exemplum*'s congruency with the context. This seems to have been a matter of concern for ancient schoolteachers, if we judge from the note on the passage from the *pro*

---

[709] For a recent examination of the comparison between Orestes and Milo (and the manipulation of Greek tragedy in Cicero's speech), see Brook 2016.
[710] Cf. also *Rhet. Her.* 1.13.
[711] On Cicero's argumentation and the structural patterns of this section of the speech (*Mil.* 7–11), see Fotheringham 2013: 135–54.
[712] Another instance of Cicero's exploitation of historical *exempla* as part of a rhetorical strategy is offered by *Planc.* 33, where Plancius senior's frankness is justified on illustrious past precedents (Q. Mucius Scaevola, consul in 95 BCE, and P. Cornelius Scipio Nasica, consul in 111): cf. schol. Bob. 158. 9-22St.

*Milone* discussed above and the comment of the Gronovian scholiast **D** on the Medea *exemplum* at *Manil.* 22. The note reads as follows (318.27-31St):

> Primum ex suo regno] Incongruum videtur exemplum, quod imperatori feminam comparavit, sed omni parte quadrare monstratur; primum ex loco, quod Mithridates Ponticus fuit, quae patria Medeae est; ex facto, quod, ut illa parricidium fecit, sic et iste auctore Sallustio et fratrem et sororem occidit; ad postremum comparans exitum.

> "In the first place from his kingdom] This example may seem inconsistent with the argument because of a comparison between a king and a woman. Yet it appears to fit the context in each part. First of all, the place: Mithridates came from Pontus, which happened to be the country of Medea; second, the action: as Medea committed parricide, Mithridates killed his brother and sister, as we understand from Sallust;[713] finally, the similar fate."

The scholion provides a framework in which to interpret the didactic approach to the use of the *exemplum* in oratorical contexts. Cicero introduces the parallel Mithridates-Medea to exemplify the similarity of the two kings' running away.[714] As Medea in her flight "scattered the limbs of her brother along the track" to hamper his father's pursuit, so Mithridates "left behind him the whole of his vast store of gold and silver and all his treasures" and "slipped through the hands of the soldiers" engaged in collecting all these goods.[715] Given the apparent disharmony and inconsistency reflected in a poetic *exemplum* that puts in parallel two figures contrasting each other (a historical king and a fabulous woman), the ancient commentator concentrates on showing how the *exemplum* is congruent with the context of the speech and therefore legitimate. His reasoning is quite banal and simplistic. Failing to capture the real significance of Cicero's exemplary discourse, he centers his explanation on parricide as the act shared by both the kings (319.7-9St)[716] and supplies his students with a

---

[713] *SHR* 1.91 (*Hist.* 2 frg76).

[714] *Primum ex suo regno sic Mithridates profugit, ut ex eodem Ponto Medea illa quondam profugisse dicitur* ("In the first place the flight of Mithridates from his kingdom reminds us of the way in which Medea in the legend fled long ago from the same Pontus"). English translation: Hodge 1927.

[715] *Medea ... quam praedicant in fuga fratris sui membra in iis locis, qua se parens persequeretur, dissipavisse, ut eorum collectio dispersa maerorque patris celeritatem persequendi retardaret. Sic Mithridates fugiens maximam vim auri atque argenti pulcherrimarumque rerum omnium ... in Ponto omnem reliquit. Haec dum nostri colligunt omnia diligentius, rex ipse e manibus effugit.*

[716] *Bene Mithridatem Medeae comparavit. Nam et ipse parricida est: fertur enim fratrem suum occidisse et matrem bello superiore contra Sullam* ("He drew a correct comparison between Mithridates and Medea. He was in fact a parricide: it is known that he killed his brother and mother during the earlier war against Sulla").

"pseudo-historical" note on Medea's deeds and flight (319.1-6St). Yet for our purpose the scholiast's note seems all the more significant as it points to a didactic interest in questioning the appropriateness of an *exemplum* as a tool of persuasion. Students of rhetoric were not engaged only in grasping the sense of historical or mythical exempla supporting the advocate's argumentation. They were also stimulated to reflect on the suitability and logical correctness of the proposed *exemplum*, being thereby invited to imitate the model in appropriately choosing *exempla* to be inserted into the texture of their speeches.

The persuasiveness and effectiveness of an *exemplum* depended on its evaluation by the audience, whether judges or spectators at the trial, who deliberated on its appropriateness and "place[d] it in a suitable ethical category."[717] A "good" reception of an *exemplum* demanded also a considerable degree of acculturation on the part of the audience. A meaningful *exemplum*, producing an emotional engagement in the audience, could be an effective tool of persuasion and convey crucial social and ethical values only if it was propounded before an audience whose members were sufficiently familiar with the Roman past and able thereby to give it value and purpose. And if an *exemplum* drawn from fables might be "more attractive to rude and uneducated minds" (*fabellae ... ducere animos solent praecipue rusticorum et imperitorum*), as affirmed by Quintilian (*Inst.* 5.11.10), a historical *exemplum*, commemorating an ideology embedded in the cultural and ethical patrimony of the Roman people, presupposed and implied a literate, well-educated readership, able to appreciate the persuasive effects of the monumentalized deed.

Cicero's expression of concern about the judges' response to his producing "old-fashioned and out of date" *exempla* of Roman integrity and virtue in *Ver.* 2.1.56 testifies to the significant role played by the audience in transforming a historical *exemplum* into an effective rhetorical device and, most importantly, into an exemplary action laden with social and ethical value.[718] The Gronovian scholiast **A** (346.26-8St) finds it necessary to explain that "*exempla* drawn from the past are less effective if propounded to uneducated judges, as they are likely to be believed to have been made up

---

[717] Roller 2004: 5.
[718] In *Ver.* 2.1.55 Cicero produces a list of Roman commanders involved in Rome's imperial expansion (the catalogue starts with the figure of Marcus Claudius Marcellus, the conqueror of Syracuse in 212 BCE, and recalls, in chronological order, the military deeds of Lucius Scipio, T. Quinctius Flamininus, Lucius Paulus, and Lucius Mummius, who sacked Corynth in 146) and establishes a contrast between the parsimony of the ancestors and Verres's greed for riches and art treasures.

by the orator."[719] Antiquity was often equated with the authority in Roman culture of exemplarity. Yet this notion defies simplification. The controversy over the historical and ethical significance of past precedents was intrinsic to Roman historiography. Cicero showed himself to be aware that the rhetorical and ethical force of an *exemplum* required historical competence, a prerequisite to detecting the meaning and purpose of exemplary figures in the specific context of any given case.

Even if it is true that their fictional character could render mythical *exempla* less credible, *exempla* from the Roman stage conveyed a message freighted with moral significance. The father/son relationship is at the heart of Cicero's early defense of Roscius of Ameria. Cicero relies on the extravagant world of Roman comedy to counterattack Erucius's allegations of murder against the young Roscius. In reply to the prosecutor's scoffing at *ineptiae*, "silly stuff," *exempla* drawn from Caecilius's comedy (*Rosc.* 46) and therefore inappropriately transferred to a case of parricide, Cicero vindicates the legitimacy of exemplarity based on comic *mores* and arguments as a reliable reproduction and imitation of daily life (§ 47). The note of the Gronovian scholiast **D** is a distilled version of Cicero's self-defense (307.13-7St):

> Quid ad istas nugas abis? Inquit] Coepit dicere adversarius: "Quamdiu me" inquit "ad fabulas vocas?" Dicit Tullius: "Ego quidem habeo multorum exempla quae proferam, vel amicorum, sed forsitan isti se nominari nolunt. Quamquam quos magis debemus ad exempla proferre quam comicos? Qui ideo a poetis inducuntur, ut illorum actibus vitae nostrae videamus imaginem."

> "Why go off into such irrelevancies? He said] The prosecutor started his reply saying: 'How long will you address me with fictional examples?' Tullius answers: 'I would certainly have many examples to bring forward, or even examples of friends, who probably would not like their names to be given. Yet what kind of example is more suitable than that drawn from the comic stage? These examples are in fact introduced by the poets to give us a picture of our daily life as reflected in the actions and characters of the persons represented on the stage.'"

Current scholarship on the *pro Sexto Roscio Amerino* has successfully focused on Cicero's manipulation of theatrical *exempla* to defeat Erucius's rigid moralism.[720] As has been noted, "by citing the behavior of characters

---

[719] *Aput ineruditos iudices exempla de vetustate prolata minus efficaciae habent, quoniam videri possunt ab oratore confingi.* It should be noted that the scholiast supports his reasoning by quoting a passage from the speech *Against Aristogeiton 2* attributed to Pseudo-Demosthenes (26.7): 346.28-30St.

[720] Harries (B.) 2007: 135–6.

known from Roman comedy, Cicero includes subsidiary arguments explaining Erucius' apparent failure to understand the underlying psychological mechanisms and establishing the suitability of such material as proof in court."[721] Relying on the common belief that comedy truly represents life, Cicero turns Erucius's argument on its head and invites his audience to ponder the complexity and instability of familiar relationships. Whether Cicero's verbal altercation with his opponent has to do with the dispute around the use of characters or stratagems derived from the stage in the oratorical arena is here not of interest. What is at the core of Cicero's strategy is his use of a comic *exemplum* as a powerful tool of invective. A historical or mythical *exemplum* reinforces the orator's argumentation and memorializes an exemplary figure or deed. A "stage *exemplum*" was expected to serve an extra function. It discredited the opponent and strengthened the *ad hominem* attack, asserting, at the same time, the exemplarity and monumentality of a stage character that assumed "historical" proportions in the hands of a gifted orator.[722]

Of course, commemorating and transmitting a memorable figure or action produced particular ways of knowing the past and enabled viewers or readers to enlarge their historical consciousness.[723] The scholiasts' comments on Cicero's discourse of exemplarity reveal that learning history involved understanding the significance of the propounded *exemplum*. Asconius's basically historical approach to Cicero's oratorical texts points to Roman students' need for support when confronting Roman republican events or institutions.[724] His explanatory notes on the historical background of the speeches or the political actors behind or within the trial demonstrate that knowledge of Roman republican history was far away from being absorbed and interiorized in the early decades of the Roman empire. In this need for historical competence the *exemplum* emerged as a powerful instrument of knowledge. It perpetuated an exemplary deed or

---

[721] Dyck 2010a: 115.
[722] Another interesting instance of Cicero's exploitation of a stage character as *exemplum* is detected by the Bobbio scholiast at *Sest.* 126 (138.1.12St). Here Cicero's quotation of a verse from Pacuvius's tragedy *Iliona*, '*Mater, te appello*' (197 Ribbeck), establishes a comparison between Polydorus's *umbra*, who laments his fate and supplicates his mother in black clothes, and Appius Claudius the praetor, Clodius's brother, entering the public arena furtively, like a "ghost," driven by his bad conscience.
[723] Roller 2009: 217.
[724] Marshall 1985: 32–6 (for Roman young readers generally unfamiliar with republican institutions and history). See also Bishop 2015: 293 (who opportunely recalls Asconius's note on the inability of his sons to understand the meaning of the expression *dividere sententiam*, "to divide up a proposal," cited at *Mil.* 14: cf. Asc. 43C).

image, deepened historical erudition and enabled the young to acquire an intimacy with the monuments of the past.

Crammed with discursive and repetitive notes on exemplary actors or deeds, the ancient commentaries guided students through the different phases of Roman history by synthesizing the political and military achievements of leading past figures. They used Cicero's historical references to improve their historical competence and preserve memory of the past. To exemplify this point, it is sufficient to note that these historical scholia provided students and ancient readers with information about key figures of Roman past history, such as Marius and Sulla,[725] Crassus[726] and Scipio Aemilianus.[727] Through such notes students participated in the story of eminent personages of the Roman past, like Appius Claudius Pulcher,[728] Livius Drusus[729] and Lentulus Spinther;[730] a long note on *Scaur.* 34 (preserved in the small set of marginal notes known as *Scholia Ambrosiana*) calls to students' minds the origins of the Roman senate and the social struggles between patricians and plebeians in the early republic (274.23–275.23St). Cicero's speeches focused on the remote and more recent past to elicit reflections on the cultural and ethical value of Roman exemplary history. By means of *exempla* he recreated (and manipulated) the Roman past, forging the sense of continuity between past and present. One might say that the ancient commentators and schoolteachers relied on Cicero's reinvigoration of the Roman past to reinforce their young pupils' historical consciousness.

As Roller states, "exemplary actors and deeds could be adduced as cognitive or ethical models to provide guidance and standards to later Romans as they contemplated actions of their own, or evaluated the actions of others."[731] Inspiring imitation was a prime function of an *exemplum*, which was placed before the audience as a model of ethical behavior to be appreciated and reproduced.[732] Beyond its persuasive purpose, any given *exemplum* transmitted memory of the past and constituted a "normative

---

[725] Cf. schol. Bob. 932.35–93.3St (on *de rege Alex.* frg6); 109.28-32St (on *Red. Sen.* 38); 156.20-4St (on *Planc.* 26); schol. Gronov. D 286.1-18St (on *Catil.* 3.24: here we read a long account of the conflict between Marius and Sylla).
[726] Schol. Bob. 92.5-16St (on *de rege Alex.* frg2: Crassus's *opulentia* is here described by reference to Cic. *Off.* 3.75).
[727] Schol. Bob. 118.6-17St (on *Mil.* 16: the scholiast quotes a passage from Laelius' *laudatio funebris*, mentioned by Cicero at *de Orat.* 2.341 and *Mur.* 75).
[728] Schol. Bob. 90.1-8St (on *Clod. et Cur.* frg24).
[729] Drusus's death is briefly recounted by the scholiast in a note on *Mil.* 16 (117.32–118.3St).
[730] Schol. Bob. 122.22-7St (on *Mil.* 39: here the scholiast cites a passage from Cic. *Fam.* 1.7.8).
[731] Roller 2009: 214.  [732] Lowrie 2007: 92.

*Manipulating the Past* 315

deed, potentially capable of transmitting values or spurring imitation."[733] Imitation was at the heart of Cicero's policy of self-exemplarity. On several occasions we have seen that Cicero displayed himself and his actions as *exempla* worthy of imitation, encountering criticism from his detractors (both ancient and modern), who not rarely reprimanded his excessive vanity and love of self.[734] The debate over Cicero in the early empire involved invective against his lack of restraint in praising himself as the ideal consul and the *homo novus* achieving a reputation based on great deeds and the power of his eloquence.[735] The Bobbio scholiast remarks on the hostility to Cicero as *homo novus* as a mark of republican anti-Ciceronianism and draws attention to Cicero's rhetoric of *novitas* founded on past *exempla* of *novi homines* claiming political office in virtue of their personal qualities (80.13-24St).[736] In particular, Cicero's self-advertisement came to a climax in the experience of exile, described as an *exemplum rei publicae conservandae* ("the model for acting to preserve the commonwealth")[737] and an act of *devotio*, "self-sacrifice," in the supreme interests of the *res publica*.[738] In Cicero's self-promotion as an unjustly exiled consular and a loyal "lover" of the Roman people, exemplary figures of exiled and recalled in the past supported his metaphorical figuration of exile as a praiseworthy *exemplum* of political cleverness and devotion on behalf of the state. Cicero's strategy of exemplarity in depicting his exile and triumphant recall must have been a good topic in the schools, as evinced by the number of scholiastic comments relating to the use and exploitation of *exempla* of Greek and Roman exiles, whose misfortune provided a point of comparison with the consular's fate.[739] The Bobbio scholiast's note on the cluster of exemplary exiles (*Sest.* 142), who acted to protect their fellow citizens and thereby achieved lasting fame, sheds further light on Cicero's tactic (143.20-4St):

> Omnibus itaque peregrinis exemplis subicit Romanorum documenta breviter et congeste, quasi eminentiorem gloriae commemorationem: ad quos imitandos provocari debeant ingenia iuventutis. Nec tamen recedit usquam a P. Sesti defensione, quoniam et ipsum pro re p. videri studet ad restituendum dignitati suae Tullium laborasse.

---

[733] Roller 2009: 216.   [734] Lowrie 2007: 92.   [735] See Chapter 3, pp. 150–8.
[736] Blom 2010: 153–94 (especially 158–65 on Cicero's list of exemplary *novi* in *Ver.* 2.5.180–2 and *Mur.* 17).
[737] Cic. *Sest.* 49.
[738] For Cicero's exile as modeled after the Roman ritual of the *devotio ducis*, see Dyck 2004.
[739] E.g. schol. Bob. 99.3St (on *Flac.* 16); 131.8-17St (on *Sest.* 48; *exemplum* of Erectheus); 131. 19-24St (on *Sest.* 48; *exemplum* of the Decii).

> "In addition to all these foreign *exempla* he [Cicero] put forward and assembled Roman precedents to stimulate memory of a more outstanding glory. The aim of this list was to encourage the young to imitation. However, he never moved away from the defense of Sestius: he strove to demonstrate that Sestius had devoted a lot of effort to restore him to his former dignity in the interests of the state."

After lingering over the precedents of Themistocles, Miltiades, Aristides and Hannibal, all victims of the people's wrath (*iracundia*) and irresponsibility (*levitas*),[740] the commentator stresses the function of the *exempla* as a spur to imitation, adding a necessary note on the coherence and consistency of Cicero's strategy of defense in the *pro Sestio*. By a close correlation between himself and past statesmen's achievements on behalf of the republic, Cicero built up a strong and credible public image and promoted himself as an outstanding example of politician and champion of republican *libertas*.

Later generations recognized Cicero's repeated attempts to position himself as an *exemplum*, as we have seen, and "Cicero's wish to guide the young men appears to be a common trait of his career, at least from the consulship onwards."[741] The peroration of the *pro Sestio* (§ 136) preserves a passionate exhortation to young people to follow in the footsteps of their ancestors:[742]

> Sed ut extremum habeat aliquid oratio mea, et ut ego ante dicendi finem faciam quam vos me tam attente audiendi, concludam illud de optimatibus eorumque principibus ac rei publicae defensoribus, vosque, adulescentes, et qui nobiles estis, ad maiorum vestrorum imitationem excitabo, et qui ingenio ac virtute nobilitatem potestis consequi, ad eam rationem in qua multi homines novi et honore et gloria floruerunt cohortabor.
>
> "But to bring my speech to a close, and to make certain that I finish speaking before you finish listening so attentively, I shall conclude my remarks on the Best Sort of men and on those who lead them and defend the commonwealth, and I shall stir those of you young men who are notables to imitate your ancestors and urge those who are capable of achieving notability through your manly talent to follow the course that has brought success adorned by public office and glory to many new men."

Cicero's political speech is a "lesson to the younger generation." Everything Cicero did, in politics as well as in his forensic activity, had

---

[740] On this passage of the *pro Sestio* (§§ 141–2), see Kaster 2006: 384–7. See also Blom 2010: 213–6 (for the Greek *exempla* of exiles).
[741] Blom 2010: 312.   [742] Kaster 2006: 379.

the young as its privileged recipient. Instruction, according to the customs of the ancestors, was a paternal duty.[743] Cicero exercised his authority as "Father of the Fatherland" (*pater patriae*) to teach the younger generations how to become accomplished orators and good politicians. This was the lesson Cicero imparted to his "pupils": to imitate the past exemplary actions and imitate himself as a model of excellent statesman and orator.[744] Cicero did not realize in full his ambitious project. As a political figure he was thought unworthy of imitation, as we have showed on more than one occasion. But his reputation as an orator has survived unaltered throughout the centuries. And the young, even in our times, look upon Cicero as the supreme incarnation of the "art of word."

---

[743] Cf. Cic. *Ver.* 2.3.159–61.
[744] On the "personal quality" of the finale of the *pro Sestio* and Cicero's self-promotion as an outstanding model of civic excellence to imitate, see Gildenhard 2011a: 381–2.

# *Conclusion*

Quam ob rem disces tu quidem a principe huius aetatis philosophorum, et disces, quam diu voles; tam diu autem velle debebis, quoad te, quantum proficias, non paenitebit; sed tamen nostra legens non multum a Peripateticis dissidentia, quoniam utrique Socratici et Platonici volumus esse, de rebus ipsis utere tuo iudicio (nihil enim impedio), orationem autem Latinam efficies profecto legendis nostris pleniorem. Nec vero hoc arroganter dictum existimari velim. Nam philosophandi scientiam concedens multis, quod est oratoris proprium, apte, distincte, ornate dicere, quoniam in eo studio aetatem consumpsi, si id mihi assumo, videor id meo iure quodam modo vindicare (Cic. *Off.* 1.2).

"You will, therefore, learn from the foremost of present-day philosophers, and you will go on learning as long as you wish; and your wish ought to continue as long as you are not dissatisfied with the progress you are making. For all that, if you will read my philosophical books, you will be helped; my philosophy is not very different from that of the Peripatetics (for both they and I claim to be followers of Socrates and Plato). As to the conclusions you may reach, I leave that to your own judgment (for I would put no hindrance in your way), but by reading my philosophical writings you will be sure to render your mastery of the Latin language more complete. But I would by no means have you think that this is said boastfully. For there are many to whom I yield precedence in knowledge of philosophy; but if I lay claim to the orator's peculiar ability to speak with propriety, clearness, elegance, I think my claim is in a measure justified, for I have spent my life in that profession."[1]

Cicero promoted himself as a master of eloquence. He secured his posthumous fame by drawing on his extraordinary ability in speaking and writing and creating a self-referential literature, entrusted with the propagation of an idealized image of *vir bonus* relying on his personal qualities to carve out a role of prestige in Roman elite society. In the proem to the *De*

---

[1] English translation: Miller 1913.

*Officiis* Cicero encourages his son Marcus to develop his linguistic potentialities by reading his corpus of oratorical and philosophical works.[2] He recommends his work as an exemplary combination of those oratorical virtues which form the grounding for a thorough education in rhetoric and philosophy. To Cicero's eyes young Marcus incarnates the ideal reader, "someone on the verge of a career in public life."[3] As future speaker and leader, he needs to be presented with a textual body that serves as an authoritative source on Latinity and a prime example of rhetorical excellence.

As Steel correctly notes, "Cicero wished to enhance his own achievements in the written record he left behind by emphasizing the decisive role he played in political life by virtue of his skill as a speaker, and at the same time demonstrate that his skill was unique or, at the very least, rare."[4] Cicero dedicated his entire life to creating a distinctive political image. Passionately devoted to the moral and political principles on which Rome's elite dominance was founded, he fashioned himself as "savior of the country" and restorer of the *res publica*. He managed to disseminate promotional material to consolidate his image as a true patriot concerned for the welfare of the state and disposed to self-sacrifice to maintain the republican *libertas*. Through an unprecedented mass of oratorical pieces Cicero also conveyed his views on politics and society and stimulated later reflections on Roman identity and issues of cultural authority.[5] He offered himself then as an *exemplum* of moral virtues, the embodiment of the traditional values that laid the basis for Roman aristocratic power. It has often been restated that oratory was essential to political leadership. And oratory, in its written form, fostered and promoted political values crucial to the preservation of the Roman elite's supremacy. When inviting his peers and educated readers to peruse his speeches as models of reasoned political strategy, Cicero managed to ensure eternal memory of his achievements. He invited budding orators and politicians to rely on his personal history in order to enhance public reputation and acquire a high social and political position in the elite community. As Hall remarks, the perennial association of the labels "savior of the republic," "father of the fatherland" and *dux togatus* with the figure of Cicero testifies to the success of his self-promotion policy, secured by "the place that his writings assumed in the literary canon of later generations."[6]

Cicero worked hard to become the epitome and ultimate personification of rhetorical and political excellence. Yet his dream came true only

---

[2] On the preface to Cicero's work, see Dyck 1996: 60–5.   [3] Schofield 2013: 85–6.
[4] Steel 2013b: 162.   [5] Dench 2013.   [6] Hall 2013: 228–9.

partially. This volume has frequently called attention to the tension between opposed representations of Cicero from the late republic to at least the first decades of the second century CE. If, on the one hand, Cicero was severely reprimanded for his political conduct and his behavior, especially in the aftermath of the Catilinarian conspiracy and during the tragic experience of exile, while encountering criticism from men of letters and philosophers alike, on the other, not a trace of reproval brought discredit upon him as a writer and leading public speaker. Marginalized as a political figure and held up as a model of oratorical perfection: Gowing well illustrates this aspect of Cicero's reception, as we have seen, opportunely pointing to the pervasive presence of Cicero within the culture of the imperial period.[7] We have devoted a good part of our study to demonstrating that Cicero's fame was sensibly affected by contradictory attitudes towards his political and personal achievements. Blamed for political inconsistency and incapacity to endure misfortunes, and acclaimed as a hero of language at the same time, Cicero never achieved the status of positive *exemplum*, notwithstanding Quintilian's efforts to rehabilitate his illustrious predecessor as a high-principled man.

Readers and students exploited this oscillation between praise and blame in the rhetorical schools, the ideal place for questioning, reevaluating and renegotiating the role of Cicero in Roman politics and culture. The school played an active part in annihilating Cicero as a historical figure and turning him into an icon of eloquence, the embodiment of the power of word. The recount of Cicero's death in heroic terms and, in particular, the equation of his violent end with the loss of "free speech" was the response of talented students and declaimers to repeated attempts to discredit Cicero's posthumous reputation. In confronting the question of Cicero's character, Quintilian reformulated the classic, moral equivalence between "good man" and "good orator," as we have observed.[8] But in composing fictitious exercises about a confrontation between Cicero and Mark Antony the declaimers made a major contribution to putting an end to the debate over Cicero as a person. They implicitly rejected criticism against Cicero as an individual, reasserting his symbolic value as pure intellect and *ingenium*. Cicero began to live only as an abstraction. He was redefined as the incarnation of the absolute power of word. Biography of Cicero was of no interest for would-be orators craving for public reputation. As MacCormack puts it, "it was once Cicero's personal characteristics, his wit and gift for repartee, his passionate devotion to the *res*

---

[7] Gowing 2013: 233.   [8] Gowing 2013: 244–6.

*publica*, his periodic fragilities and propensity for vain glory, whether real or amplified by critics and admirers, were beginning to fade into the past, that his intellectual presence became more distinct."[9]

In renegotiating Cicero as a historical and literary figure, Roman readers and students reconfigured – and transmitted to us – a "new" Cicero, a Cicero treated as an academic abstraction, whose figure was rapidly dissociated from politics and the turbulent history of the late republic. Approached uniquely as the prime example of perfect Latin prose, Cicero "became a character larger – and more important – than his life."[10] Refashioned as a symbol, Cicero was elevated to the status of hero of eloquence. It is tempting to say that in the declamation schools we witness the creation of what one might call the "Cicero myth." Identified as the voice of Latinity, Cicero survived the accidents of time by virtue of his reduction to pure *ingenium*.

Naturally, imitation was a critical component of Cicero's reception. In the schools "the young studied and sought to emulate his polish and charm, his marvellous confidence as a speaker, his ability to lead his listeners to the desired result and, in a word, his 'divine eloquence'."[11] In reading and interpreting him, reproducing his linguistic and rhetorical strategems, replicating his wit, and, above all, emulating his modes of acting and speaking, Roman students mythologized Cicero as the *vox* of Romanity. And in critically thinking and debating about Cicero, they not only deprived him of any political relevance. They also started a process of idealization that ended in the identification of Cicero with the art of speaking.

Cicero's name immediately denoted "eloquence," as we have seen on a number of occasions. The schools of grammarians and rhetors were largely responsible for promoting Cicero's prodigious talent as a speaker and prose writer. In the school environment Cicero as orator was scrutinized, rethought, examined and presented as a model worthy of emulation. Schoolteachers engaged in an incessant critical revisitation of Cicero's massive oratorical output by compiling textual selections and assembling groups of orations by thematic, chronological or stylistic criteria, dissecting variant readings, commenting upon significant passages and guiding students through the intricacies of the world of rhetoric. What Cicero and which text of Cicero we read and, in particular, how we read Cicero. These are the key questions we posed in the Introduction. The response to each of these questions is unequivocal. We read the Cicero that Roman students in

---

[9] MacCormack 2013: 253.   [10] Gowing 2013: 250.   [11] MacCormack 2013: 251.

antiquity used to read. Most importantly, how we read and understand Cicero's oratory depends largely on the incessant interpretative explanation of the speeches conducted by schoolteachers and students at the schools of grammar and rhetoric from the late republic onwards. This is the most important legacy we have inherited from the school. Our Cicero is the same Cicero Roman boys studied and looked at as example of the art of speaking. What remains of Cicero, which text of Cicero has come down to us and, in particular, the modes of approaching, reading, criticizing, even questioning Cicero are all the result of a process of analytic evaluation and interpretation of Cicero's oratory that started in the last years of the Roman republic and took place in the classrooms, that is, in the space ideally suited to a pedagogical re-appropriation of Cicero as the paradigm of Roman eloquence.

## Publication, Text and *Emendatio*

Cicero's speeches conveyed his ideology. They contained and transmitted Cicero's views on rhetoric, politics and Roman society. Most importantly, to his oratorical performances, reworked and polished up for publication, Cicero committed his authorial self-portrait, at the same time engaging his listeners/readers in a process of imitation/emulation of his oratorical and political achievements. The initial chapter of this book examined Cicero's presentation of writing as a supreme form of memorialization. It drew particular attention to Cicero's desire to perpetuate his image as leading orator and statesman through a body of written texts. Cicero's reformulation of the doctrine of the three styles in the *Orator* and, more than that, his Demosthenic assemblage of some of the consular speeches reflect his ambition to exercise control over his own work by means of canonical texts, intended as a medium for instructing contemporary and later readers in the art of both politics and public speaking. In transferring his acclaimed live performances to writing, Cicero created his own textual *corpus*, redefined the parameters of oratory as a literary genre and established himself as a first-class intellectual, a leading figure in Roman elite society. In a word, by writing he memorialized his own persona. And by writing he conveyed his message, that is, the ideal fusion of "good writing" and "good politics" as essential to the formation of the *vir bonus dicendi peritus*.

Focusing on the articulated relationship between Cicero's political and oratorical career and his writings, we have also re-addressed the long-debated issue of publication, taking Stroh's arguments as our starting point and considering Cicero's dialogue with the Roman youth as a foundational element of his self-fashioning project. Close evaluation of many passages from private epistolary collections has revealed that Cicero's policy of publication (as well as of non-publication) was essential to his ambition of becoming the ideal literate and politician. Publication was the main instrument of self-memorialization. In instructing the young in the art of speaking and prolonging his political actions far beyond time by publication, Cicero fulfilled his dream of textual longevity and handed his exemplary record of oratorical and political achievements down to posterity.

Collective, editorial revision was crucial to the production and dissemination of an authoritative text. Notably, a collectively revised text was intended to enhance the public reputation of its author. In submitting his speeches to revision by a literate community, Cicero committed his own persona to public scrutiny. A good part of our analysis has been devoted to Cicero's policy of self-*emendatio* and editorial revision as integral to the construction of the oratorical and political self. The letters, in particular, provide an interesting case study of Cicero's practice of self-correction. By textual cooperation with literate friends, Cicero promoted his own ideal of "aristocratic" *emendatio*, strictly embedded in the elite ideal of collective text exchange, and longed to establish his position as a leading intellectual in Roman society. Cicero's ambition to memorialize his public figure is also reflected in his decision to publish speeches that he had never delivered. Such is the case of the *Second Actio in Verrem* and the *Second Philippic*. More significantly, in rewriting and producing a new *pro Milone*, one of his finest pieces of advocacy, Cicero tried to cancel the memory of his inglorious past. As has been said, Cicero managed to propagate a corpus of authoritative texts that could consolidate his oratorical and political self. The first, failed *pro Milone* marked the lowest point of his career. Cicero's strategy of self-promotion dictated a drastic editorial revision, the elimination of a "wrong" text potentially damaging to its author's reputation.

Cicero's intent to transform himself into an icon of eloquence is also of some relevance to the long-disputed question of the relationship between delivered and published speeches. Revisiting and partially rejecting Humbert's arguments, modern scholarship is inclined to take the written speeches, as they have come down to us, as a fairly close reproduction of what Cicero actually said during the trial. Though stylistic adjustments and refinements could be admitted, especially in transferring an oral text to writing, Cicero's published oration appears to be a sort of transcript of the delivered text, a polished-up version of forms, rhythms and patterns used during the live performance. Without diverging from this line of enquiry, this study has adopted a different approach to the issue. Concentrating on the early empire debate over orality and writing, we have pointed to the equation of the "oration on paper" (*oratio*) with the "spoken text" (*actio*), a guiding principle of the Ciceronian ideology of good rhetoric. As restated by Quintilian and Pliny the Younger, the complete congruence between "speaking well" and "writing well" was crucial to ideal oratory and forensic success. A well-written speech was a charter of elite community, as we have said. It met the elite's demands and enhanced public reputation. Cicero created a text harmoniously blending *actio*, performative elements and acts, and *oratio*, replication of visual and oral features in writing. No doubt, Cicero reworked his performances in order to achieve credibility as a writer. Yet what mattered more to him was producing a style model – an exemplar of perfection of language – that could reproduce the vibrant atmosphere and modes of delivery and thereby instruct students and readers in the art of "speaking and writing well."

## Oratory and School Canon

To memorialize his public persona Cicero relied on the cooperation of contemporary readers and literate friends. Atticus, Nepos and Tiro participated in the textual process of editorial revision and dissemination of Cicero's speeches. In particular, the name of Tiro has stimulated our interest in the production and circulation of Ciceronian editions in the early empire, a question that is at the outset of any scholarly discussion about the reception of Cicero in antiquity. Re-examining a renowned passage from Fronto's letter to Marcus Aurelius, a self-eulogizing piece of writing celebrating the names of well-known copyists of the past, we have surveyed ancient available evidence of surviving copies of Ciceronian texts bearing a form of "Tironian" subscription or authentication. Concern over textual correctness spurred Gellius's search for old manuscripts and handwritten copies preserving good variant readings. Yet antiquity may not be synonymous with reliability. Questioning the perceived trustworthiness of the Tironian manuscripts, Zetzel has cast doubts upon the authenticity of some of the archaic forms found in the Gellian copies, propounding a systematic counterfeiting of copies of famous books in response to the second-century archaistic literary taste. The issue has been approached under a double, interconnected perspective. On the one side, in the footsteps of Timpanaro's scholarly arguments, a meticulous analysis of Cicero's style in his early oratorical production has validated Gellius's assessments about the archaic or disused forms attested in the Tironian manuscripts.

On the other, we have queried whether the name of Tiro attached to a manuscript implied the genuineness (and antiquity) of the *emendatio*. Regardless of its authenticity, a "Tironian" revision acted as a sort of textual authentication, a guarantee of quality, later affixed to an old manuscript to ensure its reliability and thereby its circulation among men of letters and readers fascinated by early republican literature and style.

One point seems quite clear. The dissemination of Ciceronian manuscripts in the early empire is strictly connected to the status of school *auctor* achieved by Cicero. The increasing demand for high-value emended manuscripts testifies to the widespread diffusion and knowledge of Cicero and, in particular, to the need for a "correct" Cicero. Textual accuracy was naturally essential to instruction in language. It was a pedagogical notion, evidently embedded in a larger cultural project aimed at revitalizing purity of Latin against current linguistic degeneration, as revealed by Gellius's encyclopaedic classicism. Within this cultural context, the second-century grammarian and scholar Statilius Maximus's *subscriptio* certifying the *emendatio* of the *De lege agraria* I (numbered as the twenty-fourth speech in an allegedly private collection of Cicero's orations), carried out with the support of the six earliest manuscripts of the text, is a significant example of accurate revision. In addition to being an eloquent witness to the established practice of copying out and emending classical texts by checking copies' reliability against their exemplar, Statilius offers good evidence of a consolidated linguistic interest in Cicero's oratory, resulting in a careful examination of variant readings and archaic forms.

Statilius's subscription is also of the greatest significance to early empire scholarly interest in assembling Cicero's speeches according to chronology or stylistic exemplarity, a philological activity dictated by pedagogical needs. Starting from Statilius's collection for personal use, we have focused on forms of textual aggregation and arrangement from the late republic onwards and revisited the history of Cicero's most important oratorical *corpora* (*Catilinarians, Verrines, Philippics* and *Caesarianae*), whose survival as coherent groups had a significant impact on medieval tradition. Obviously, the process of collecting and cataloguing Cicero's impressive oratorical material contributed to the permanence of his work in the school canon. The selection and related arrangement of the speeches in a coherently articulated collection was a specific didactic requirement. Not that explaining "separated," occasional texts was beyond the scholarly competence of Cicero's literate readers. But the disposition of individual speeches into a distinct collection functioned as a didactic tool for the conveyance of Cicero's oratorical message. By its textual compactness a *corpus* of orations facilitated and supported student learning. In constructing an organic textual collection, later readers and schoolteachers thus created a canonical Cicero. They responded to Cicero's dream of textual longevity by inscribing him into an established literary canon and providing posterity with a Ciceronian oratorical "encyclopedia."

In this light, Asconius's commentary on five speeches (presumably only a small part of a larger commentary) and the *scholia Bobiensia*, a fourth-century excerpted commentary on a consistent group of Ciceronian orations, display the didactic impulse to systematize disparate material into organic and thematically coherent textual units. In particular, in the Bobbio commentary the conceivable presence of a compact *corpus* of post-exile orations, preceded by a spurious declamatory exercise (the *Si eum P. Clodius legibus interrogasset*), has enabled us to appreciate the role played by later scholars and schoolmasters in the process of textual aggregation and formation of textual bodies. In assembling speeches interrelated to each other by virtue of their joint subject, as with the specific case of the *post reditum* speeches all covering Cicero's self-presentation after his triumphal return after exile and his personal fight against Clodius, and in sometimes cutting off texts deemed irrelevant to training and teaching, schoolteachers significantly contributed to the establishment of Cicero's reputation as a key canonical orator. It has often been repeated that the creation of textual collections, a fourth- to fifth-century phenomenon, represented a formative stage in classical tradition. Applied to the reception of Cicero, this notion makes sense of the formation of a canon of orations as a decisive step towards the consolidation of Cicero as school *auctor*.

From the *scholia* and late commentaries we can also obtain precious indications about the place many speeches had in the school curriculum. It comes as no surprise that many of the orations commented upon by the scholiasts had an established position in the literary canon. At the same time, it is conceivable that the formation of compact textual bodies might have affected the current status of the medieval tradition. A thorough examination of Cicero's speeches in papyri scraps and palimpsests, in conjunction with literary evidence and grammatical and rhetorical tradition, has permitted us to reconsider the vital role that teaching practices in late antique schools played in the survival of an extensive portion of Cicero's oratory. Taking stock of our results, we owe our knowledge of Cicero's oratory to the school and to the pedagogical function with which some speeches were invested by sensitive schoolmasters, mindful of the impact of Ciceronian literature on the formation of highly cultured men.

## Politics, Oratory and Morality

"Cicero's reception inextricably involves the influence of his enemies no less than his friends."[12] Altman's statement may well be placed at the beginning of the long story of criticism and adulation that had long permeated Cicero's afterlife. Starting from Catullus's ironic praise in poem 49 and the so-called Augustan silence, we have investigated the early empire's multivalent reaction to Cicero's legacy as orator and statesman. Roman intellectuals recognized and revived the excellence of Cicero's prose, admiring his elegant and refined style and making him an untouched ideal of perfect oratory. At the same time, they offered contrasting interpretations of Cicero's political behavior, his morality and ethical conduct not matching traditional Roman *mores*. As expected, the school was the ideal place for such a debate. The pseudo-Sallustian invectives, presumably scholastic exercises by untalented declaimers, and a good number of the mock-Ciceronian speeches and *pseudepigrapha* originated in the classrooms, which saw a protracted, fierce controversy over Cicero's disputed involvement in the political crisis of the late republic and his impact on Roman current history. If, on the one side, Seneca's *Suasoriae* 6 and 7, as we have seen, reflect the tendency towards a positive revisitation of the historical Cicero, rehabilitated as a hero of republican *libertas* against the tyrant Antony, on the other, Asinius Pollio's invective, a prolonged attack on Cicero's politics that will have considerable effects on subsequent anti-Ciceronian propaganda, attests to the prevailing climate of political censure that pervaded the reception of Cicero among literate readers and students, engaged with a constant, sometimes contradictory, renegotiation of the role played by the republican orator and statesman in Roman politics and society.

Cicero's political deeds opened up a heated discussion about the survival of republican values in the early Roman empire. Yet it was the exemplarity of his life that attracted the most interest from philosophers and historians. In readdressing Livy's obituary in Seneca's Sixth *Suasoria*, in relation with Pollio's and Seneca the Younger's skeptical portraits of Cicero, we have pointed to the general reluctance to identify Cicero with the ideal *sapiens*, an established form of *reprehensio* that stemmed from Cicero's professed physical and mental inability to endure misfortune. His heroic death served only as a partial posthumous rehabilitation, as we have said. Cicero's life never assured him a place of honor among exemplary

---

[12] Altman 2015: 10.

characters. Obviously, the early empire's debate over Cicero centered on stylistic and linguistic matters as well. In spite of unanimous recognition of Cicero's authority as a prose writer, his style, firmly anchored in the notion of *Latinitas*, encouraged reflections on the survival of republican Latin in the early imperial period and its relevance to modern education. Not only Cicero's perceived pomposity, a distinguishing feature of his early orations, encountered criticism from later intellectuals. It was the role Cicero could play in a renovated educational system that most elicited interest from first-century writers, concerned with the maintenance of elevated, moral standards of education within modified cultural and political conditions.

Closely connected to the long-debated issue of the decline of oratory and the related gradual replacement of traditional training practices by modern, unreal forms of educational entertainment, the question of the supremacy of old, republican "Ciceronian" style over modern, epigrammatic "Senecan" style and the place occupied by imitation of the past in the formation of educated Romans informed literary criticism over the course of the first and second centuries CE. In taking a fresh look at ancient discussions about the decadence of eloquence, with particular emphasis on Tacitus's *Dialogus*, we have drawn attention to the notion of "change" in style as a natural reaction to altered cultural and social conditions. Notwithstanding nostalgic evocations of the past, change in aesthetics was seen as a historical necessity. Roman intellectuals tended to harmonize a modernistic vision of literature and culture with morality in rhetorical education. Within this context, Seneca the Younger and Quintilian confronted the problem of degeneration of style from a pedagogical perspective, both of them showing deep concern about the consequences of bad, effeminate language to ethics and morality in education. They agreed in identifying good style with morality, a central tenet of their educational project. In a sense, the axiomatic expression *talis hominibus oratio fuit qualis vita* (Sen. *ep.* 114.2) functioned as a promotional slogan to good education. But Seneca and Quintilian did not accord Cicero the same place in their educational program. To Seneca, Cicero was far from being a moral *exemplum*. Imitation of Cicero had ethical more than stylistic implications. As Gowing puts it, "it was left to Quintilian to reconcile the facts of Cicero's life with his authorial and oratorical legacy."[13] He advocated a neo-Ciceronianism that spurred revitalization of Cicero as a model of oratorical prose, an *exemplum* of pure Latin whose imitation was reputed to be crucial to the formation of the *vir bonus dicendi peritus*.

[13] Gowing 2013: 244.

Moreover, he promoted a new Cicero, as both "good man" and "good orator," thereby creating a splendid fusion between ethics, politics and oratory that contributed significantly to the propagation of Cicero's message throughout the centuries.

## Education and *Latinitas*

Good style was a pedagogical concern, as we have seen. Quintilian's educational plan encouraged imitation of Cicero's style and language as essential to the intellectual and moral development of the child, supported by exemplary linguistic models in his process towards maturity. Within the established connection between *eruditio* and correctness of language, or *Latinitas* – pure Latin, acquired by imitation of good prose examples – we have observed Cicero's impact on the cultivation of a refined, aristocratic language and the consequent creation of a model of regular Latin. Cicero was soon established as a paradigm of *Latinitas*. His correctness and elegance of style were integral to the process of maturation and social affirmation of the child trained in the acquisition of linguistic values associated with aristocratic culture and power. By imitating and replicating Cicero's language, Roman students promoted a moralized classicism, a return to the universal *exempla* of linguistic and moral virtues. *Latinitas*, a notion integrated into a consolidated system of aristocratic values, assisted Roman pupils in transforming themselves into virtuous speakers, destined to hold a respectable position in Roman elite society.

Cicero personified the art of speaking properly, *recte loquendi scientia*. This metaphorical association has guided us through the history of the reception of Cicero as a linguistic authority from the early empire onwards. Following a rapid presentation of Quintilian's treatment of Cicero as a source of good Latin, special attention has been paid to Gellius's educational project of revitalization of Latin cultural tradition, a renovated form of classicism aimed at consolidating paradigms of *Romanitas* against current linguistic and moral corruption. Cicero played a relevant part in the revival of ancient educational models in the Antonine age. His care for proper words, *proprietas verborum*, his creativity in vocabulary and *urbanitas* made him a model of linguistic finesse. Gellius's predilection for Cicero as a cultural authority and *exemplum* of elegant diction and stylistic accuracy thus contributed to the identification of Cicero with incorrupt Latin. From Gellius onwards the label "icon of the Latin language" was definitely associated with the figure of Cicero.

It is well known that Gellius's discussion of rare and obsolete words reflects second-century scholarly interest in archaizing language. Statilius Maximus's collection of *singularia*, in conjunction with linguistic scholia (especially from the Bobbio commentary), provides us with a good illustration of how Cicero's linguistic anomalies and structural complexities stimulated curiosity from scholars and schoolteachers, concerned with elucidating style and grammar features in response to specific educational needs. As an *idoneus auctor*, Cicero furnished students with very impressive material for the acquisition of the rules of correct Latin. His *auctoritas* profoundly impacted on the development of the science of the Latin language. It was up to grammarians, scholars and schoolmasters to direct students towards appreciating the role played by Cicero in the formation of a linguistic system based on the *auctoritas* principle and imitation of exemplary texts. Reading Cicero, commenting upon his style and exploiting his nominal, adjectival or verbal forms to illustrate the precepts of good Latin soon became established scholastic and academic practices. Nonius Marcellus's collection of lexicographical and antiquarian material, a limpid instance of a conservative approach to Roman cultural tradition; Latin glossaries and erudite handbooks; Servius's commentary and late grammars are all significant monuments to the importance of Cicero to the antiquarian-erudite tradition *de Latinitate* and the preservation of linguistic and ethical values strictly associated with the elite ideal of *Romanitas*. As *custos Latini sermonis*, "guardian of language," the grammarian protected Latin cultural heritage. Cicero's *auctoritas* was crucial to this cultural-educational process of conservation and replication of the past. His works not only supplied schoolmasters and students with linguistic material, used mostly in support or justification of morphological and syntactical anomalies. Cicero's authority on Latinity also served scholars' cultural strategy to place the past at the very heart of Roman elite education.

Cicero's role in the preservation of Roman past language is well illustrated by the number of scholia and linguistic notes that occur in our extant commentaries. By providing students with explanations of morphology, syntax, word formations and compounds and offering clarification of grammatical deviances the schoolmasters fostered knowledge of the Latin language and corroborated the universal identification of Cicero with the perfect pleader and writer. Simultaneously, they set a pattern for learning and advocated an idea of education relying on the acquisition and replication of Cicero's *Latinitas*. This is the easiest conclusion of our analysis of textual and linguistic scholia in the Bobbio commentary and Ps. Asconius's commentary on the *Verrines*: Cicero's expertise in Latin was crucial to the formation and intellectual maturation of the youth. By inviting their students to read and interpret Cicero, schoolteachers in antiquity endorsed the elite ideal of conservation of the Roman past and its linguistic heritage.

## Textual Criticism, Ancient Scholarship and the Art of Commentary

As "variorum works" or *editiones variorum*, the extant *corpora* of scholia on Cicero's speeches represent the ultimate end of a long exegetical process that started in Cicero's immediate afterlife. Whether as coherent arrangements of notes and text or in the form of marginal and scattered annotations, the scholiastic corpora collect and discuss earlier material and constitute therefore the result of a stratifying editorial and exegetical tradition. More importantly, they reflect the status of school *auctor* achieved by Cicero from the early empire onwards. In addition to supplying us with adequate information about ancient Ciceronian scholarship, scholia and late commentaries convey a reliable image of Cicero as model of Roman prose, a school text recommended as beneficial to rhetorical and linguistic training. They enable us to perceive how and to what extent Cicero impacted on the curriculum.

We have often drawn attention to the debate in antiquity over the reputation of Cicero as literary model and the equivocal relationship between Cicero as a man and Cicero as a prose writer. Cicero's dominant position in language and rhetorical training as well as his role in Roman political life had ignited debate among literate men and scholars since the late republic. The surviving scholia and commentaries give us the chance to reconstruct some aspects of what may be called an "anti-Ciceronian tradition," a widespread tendency toward criticism involving, among other things, textual and style issues. They tell us much about detractors of Cicero, even if earlier scholarly authorities remain generally unnamed. Through scholiography we can build up a picture of the fascinating story of the *scholasticus* Cicero, a story marked by admiration and censure, enthusiastic eulogy and condemnation, an ambivalent attitude that unequivocally originated in the impact exercised by Cicero's powerful figure on Roman culture and education.

This is the perspective that has guided us in surveying renowned figures of Ciceronian critics and scholars from the late republic onwards, putting special emphasis on the eminently linguistic, historical and erudite interest in Cicero's oratorical prose. The academic dispute between Asconius and Fenestella over Cicero's presumed defense of Catiline serves as a reference point for evaluating current criticism of Cicero's controversial involvement in the political crisis of the late republic. The debate over Cicero revolved also around language and style issues, as may be argued by an outline of second- and third-century scholarship. Within this context, we have focused on the role of the commentary as a primary source on ancient scholarship. Jerome's discussion of the function and purpose of a standard commentary, inserted into an apologetic reply to Rufinus's denunciation of plagiarism in his commentary on Paul's epistle to the Ephesians, is particularly illuminating. After celebrating a number of past commentators (among whom is Volcacius, commentator of Cicero), Jerome sketches out a theory of classical commentary, a second-order literature work contemplating a fixed system of instruction to readers and assembling earlier scholarship. As an auxiliary paratext, a commentary enhanced understanding and supplied students/readers with required details about content, style and language. It also served as a collection of earlier scholarly comments, a sort of handy guide for pupils longing for a critical comprehension of the text and its exegetical history.

*Alii dicunt . . ., alii legunt . . .* This set expression, a recurrent formula in the scholia and scholarly commentaries, may well illustrate the creation of a multistratified exegesis of Cicero's text over time. It alludes to the multiple ways in which commentators interpreted Cicero's text, relating and discussing earlier comments and offering their own interpretation as a didactic tool and support for a more solid understanding of the inspected text. In this light, Jerome's explanation of the nature of the commentary helps us to clarify the function of Ciceronian commentaries. As paratexts, the Bobbio commentary and Ps. Asconius are exemplary of a consolidated academic and didactic attitude toward Cicero as a master of Roman language. They operated as didactic instruments, fostering learning and assisting students in their knowledge of Cicero's reception in earlier times.

It seems that textual criticism was not the main concern of Ciceronian scholars. In conducting a general survey of linguistic and textual notes in the commentaries, we have remarked scanty interest in issues concerning textual correctness, though a few scholia discussing *legitur* variants or variants of collation offer some indication of alternative readings (often glosses or banal manuscript errors) creeping into the text at different times. More numerous are annotations on matters of style and language that testify to the scholars' efforts to celebrate Cicero's refined Latin. Ps. Asconius's commentary is particularly instructive, as it displays a clear tendency to refute unsubstantiated criticism of Cicero as an example of good Latin. It confirms that the preservation of Cicero's linguistic *auctoritas* was an essential component of Roman elite education.

## Illusion, Irony and Practical Oratory

Cicero's *Latinitas* and mastery of Roman prose were of practical utility in the transformation of a boy into a *vir bonus dicendi peritus*, a true, good citizen-man destined to become a respectable member of Roman elite society. Male students relied on Cicero – and imitation/emulation of his oratory – to improve confidence about their speaking and writing ability. Of course, training in language and rhetoric contemplated standard didactic methods. Quintilian's discussion of the *praelectio* of prose texts in the classroom, in the second book of his *Institutio* (2.5), imparts seminal information on the usual procedure in the teaching of rhetoric and also provides crucial clues to the interpretation of oratory as the art of persuasion and illusion. To Quintilian the true orator was a trained manipulator of arguments and passions, a virtuoso speaker holding sway over the jury's emotions by means of an elegant and sophisticated use of rhetorical and linguistic devices. Words were tools of deceit. Cicero typified oratory as an artificial exploitation of verbal stratagems. He taught the art of persuasion and incarnated the figure of the vigorous and virile speaker exercising control over his audience by manipulative language.

Quintilian's *praelectio* and his elaboration of the theory of oratory draw unequivocally on Cicero, presented as model of Roman prose and example of successful persuasive eloquence. Taking Quintilian's passage as our reference text, we have looked at the typical *enarratio* of a speech of Cicero starting from what was commonly intended to be the explanatory preface, called *argumentum* in the scholarly commentaries, a didactic introduction to the historical and rhetorical background of the text that usually preceded the sequence *lemma-scholion*. From the *argumenta* in Asconius and the Bobbio commentary we have derived vital information about the ways in which schoolmasters illustrated Cicero's prosecution or defense strategy within specific political circumstances. Similarly, Ps. Asconius's mainly rhetorical introduction to the invectives against Verres and the comments of the Gronovian scholiast on the nature and purpose of the speeches addressed to Caesar (in particular, the *pro Marcello*) disclose fascinating aspects of Cicero's argumentative tactic, illuminating as well his self-promotion strategy, not rarely dictating deviations from the standard rhetorical doctrine. Cicero emerges as a master of persuasion and dissimulation, a powerful manipulator of the minds of the judges/listeners, relying on his extraordinary abilities to sway the audience and achieve final victory. Cicero's treatment of exordial topics in many of his speeches and, more than that, his manipulation and creation of fabricated narratives (illuminating the case of the *narratio* of the *pro Milone*) support the established identification of Cicero with a sophist-like speaker, a skilful constructor and deviser of ethical arguments or proofs and a talented exploiter of artistic and linguistic devices with persuasion effects.

The image of the orator as a master of "dissimulation" is crucial to any discourse on the morality of oratory and the impact of a principled and ethical eloquence on the Roman political system. By revisiting Cicero's rhetoric of advocacy, based on manipulation and distortion of the truth, and contextualizing his strategy of persuasion in the reality of the Roman legal system we have put emphasis on the figure of the orator as an astute advocate, intent on misleading the jury and arousing passions in the audience by means of a persuasive, tricky language. Cicero's advocacy is a self-evident example of what oratory was meant to be in the late republic, that is, a deceitful misrepresentation of reality through a manipulative use of linguistic and rhetorical stratagems. Rhetoric was a weapon of deceit, as we have said on a number of occasions. The parallel drawn by the Gronovian scholiast between Cicero, displaying anxiety and resorting to the technique of *insinuatio* to elicit Caesar's compassion in the proem to his speech on behalf of the king Deiotarus, and the mendacious Greek-orator Sinon, the prototypical figure of Vergilian liar, makes it clear that Cicero had an established reputation as a well-trained manipulator of passions and a master of the art of illusion. His oratory set out a practical test case for how would-be orators could succeed by manipulating reality and exploiting crafty and cunning language.

Of course, irony was a central component of Cicero's strategy of manipulation. Special attention has accordingly been paid to Cicero's use of mockery and ridicule in the speeches, with an eye to the didactic function of witticism in rhetorical training. Quintilian's critical presentation of Cicero's *urbanitas*, along with a number of scholarly comments on the political and rhetorical exploitation of humor (especially in the Bobbio commentary), has shown that Cicero's tactic of appropriation and reversal of opponents' argumentation by means of ridicule and irony was intended to be crucial to oratorical success, achieved through a strategy of demolition of the adversary's credibility. Ancient commentators pointed to Cicero's sophisticated application of sarcastic mottoes or jokes and fabrication of arguments and narratives producing laughter. Exemplary of this treatment of Cicero's irony are the comments on the Murena case, the speeches in defense of Flaccus and Plancius and, notably, the political invectives against Clodius and Vatinius. The strict connection between humor and politics and the related definition of irony as a form of political and social humiliation, a point duly elaborated by Corbeill, appears to have been central to the interpretation of Cicero's strategy of persuasion in antiquity. As demonstrated by a close analysis of a number of scholia, schoolmasters called frequent attention to Cicero's ingenious use of ridicule as a constructive tool of persuasion, promoting humor as one of the most essential components of oratory and, at the same time, reminding students of the perils incurred by an immoderate exploitation of jokes and humorous sayings.

Teaching Cicero meant developing students' appreciation of his manipulative use of ethical argumentations, his finesse of language and style and his exploitation of past and personal *exempla* as a means of persuasion. The scholia best illustrate how Cicero's use of ethical and emotional arguments or his adoption of presentational argument forms, such as the dilemma, were reputed to be crucial to the development of a powerful strategy of persuasion, based on obfuscation of the jurors' minds and neutralization of the opponent's argumentative force. Additionally, as we have seen, Cicero's speeches offered instructive examples of diversified patterns of argumentation and style registers in accordance with the specific needs of the case. This has prompted us to observe the ways in which Quintilian and late commentators expatiated on Cicero's construction of his tactic of persuasion in connection with his self-fashioning strategy. The Gronovian scholiast's interpretation of the *argumentatio* of the *Second Catilinarian* and his examination of the defense plan adopted in Cicero's speech on behalf of Roscius of Ameria, as well as the Bobbio scholiast's analysis of Cicero's self-portrait as *homo novus* in the *pro Sulla*, provide elucidatory comments on Cicero's capacity to integrate his self-praise into an elaborate combination of ethical and emotional arguments, designed to arouse sympathy from the audience.

Elegance of style and diction marked the true orator. This study has often reminded readers of the importance of good Latin to the intellectual maturation of the young. Cicero's *Latinitas* was a significant part of training in language, as we have seen. Placing at the beginning of our investigation Quintilian's comments on *elocutio* and the impact of propriety of language and excellence of style on the formation of an ethical orator, we have touched upon the so-called doctrine of the "rhetoricity of language" and the interpretation of language as a psychagogic tool of persuasion. Viewed from this perspective, Cicero's style, and his use of psychological, emotional and aesthetic strategies, reflects his belief in language as a powerful means of enchanting the audience and achieving final victory. *Eleganter dixit Cicero*: An entire section of the fourth chapter was dedicated to examining this aspect of Cicero's fortune, that is, his capacity to fascinate generations of scholars and students by a pathetic and charming style. *Ornatus*, ornament, a virtue best displayed in the speeches, appealed to later readers for its potential psychological and persuasive function. Always with an eye to "appropriateness" (*decorum*) and correct adaptation of diction to the specific content of the case, ancient theorists celebrated Cicero as the personification of artistic and elegant eloquence by elucidating tropes, metaphors, allegories, devices of amplification, figures of speech and thought and illustrating the relevance of epigrammatic style (*sententiae*) and prose rhythm (*numerus*) to the strategy of persuasion.

Good delivery was the key to oratorical success. As public approbation was crucial to political and social promotion, an effective, theatrical delivery could enhance the orator's status in Roman elite society. Quintilian and late commentators hinged on Cicero to discuss emotional delivery, involving bodily gesture, voice and stage-managed devices. In particular, Quintilian's treatment of delivery (*Inst.* 11.3) illustrates the emotional power of voice and the mechanisms of nonverbal, body language, by adducing a series of examples taken from Ciceronian oratory. Replicating Cicero's comments on proper delivery and elaborating on his carefully stage-managed application of tone of voice, gestures, facial expressions and tears as pathetic tools of persuasion, Quintilian concentrates on the effectiveness of an emotional, theatrical *actio*, warning at the same time against effeminate and extravagant performances that could be detrimental to the orator's reputation as a "good man." The issue of theatricality and the association between oratory and acting, a long-debated question emanating from ancient reflections about the didactic relevance of stage oratory and the threat posed to moral education by comedic mannerisms, is settled by Quintilian (and late scholars) by inviting students to a moderate deployment of stage-managed devices. As expected, it was Cicero who personified the "best orator" and the "best actor." Students were encouraged to act as trained orators and actors by emulating Cicero and his outstanding ability to produce an emotional delivery, a persuasive and masculine performance depending on the perfect fusion of charming style and stage effects.

Exemplarity played a relevant role in the strategy of persuasion. The evocation of exemplary deeds from the past participated in the construction of a credible, powerful *actio*. Beyond stimulating historical interest, memory of the past strengthened the case and functioned as a proof, a form of irrefutable argument lending force to the orator's prosecution and/or defense tactic. Yet the *exemplum* had not only probatory value. In propounding exemplars of political and moral virtue, the good speaker spurred imitation/emulation. He invested the *exemplum* with a didactic and ethical function, contributing to the preservation of the past and instilling respect of Roman tradition and *mos maiorum* in the cultivated minds of the young members of the Roman elite. Cicero did something more. He promoted his public persona by advertising himself as a moral and political *exemplum*. By means of personal *exempla* Cicero monumentalized his history, as a man and an advocate, and set himself up as a model worthy to be imitated by contemporaries and generations to come. In a word, he satisfied his desire for immortal glory by portraying himself as a shining example of political and moral virtues. Within a more general reconsideration of the place occupied by history (and law) in the curriculum, we have concentrated on Cicero's strategic manipulation of past history and his normative discourse of exemplarity as it was received by later readers and scholars. Cicero's use of exemplarity in many of his political orations was of the greatest significance to rhetorical training. In the commentaries we observe how the schoolmasters pointed to the need for historical knowledge and, more importantly, to the deployment of past and personal *exempla* congruent with the case as crucial to the art of persuasion. Cicero's texts best illustrated the persuasive and moral force of history. They instructed the young in exploiting the past and increasing their authority and credibility as speakers.

Cicero was at the center of the Roman educational system. Ancient educational theorists and schoolteachers grounded the intellectual formation of the young in imitation/emulation of Cicero, propounded as the icon of Roman eloquence, the embodiment of *Latinitas* and the master of oratory as the art of persuasion. More significantly, at the center of Cicero's reading and interpretation in antiquity lay the debate over the role of imitation of classical authors in education. In some sense, Cicero transformed the Roman educational system. As the master of Roman prose and authority on Latinity, he elicited reflections about issues of cultural identity, the connection between oratory and politics and the relevance of good Latin to the enhancement of public status. Cicero's oratory was essential to the construction of an elite ideal of education, based on the transmission and replication of ethical, linguistic and oratorical values associated with upper-class culture. My hope is that this volume has demonstrated that any young member of the ruling elite longing for a respectable position in Roman society had to become a "new" Cicero.

# Bibliography

Abbamonte, G., Miletti, L., Spina, L. (2009) (eds.) *Discorsi alla prova*, Naples: Universita degli Studi di Napoli Federico II.
Abbenes, J. G. J., Slings, S. R., Sluiter, I. (1995) (eds.) *Greek Literary Theory after Aristotle*, Amsterdam: VU University Press.
Achard, G. (2000) "L'influence des jeunes lecteurs sur la redaction des discours cicéroniens," in Achard and Ledentu (2000): 75–88.
Achard, G., Ledentu, M. (2000) (eds.) *Orateur, auditeurs, lecteurs: à propos de l'éloquence romaine à la fin de la République et au début du Principat*, Paris: De Boccard.
Adams, J. N. (2003a) *Bilingualism and the Latin Language*, Cambridge.
  (2003b) "*Romanitas* and the Latin Language," *CQ* 53.1: 184–205.
Adams, J. N., Janse, M., Swain, S. (2002) (eds.) *Bilingualism in Ancient Society: Language Contact and the Written Word*, Oxford.
Adkin, N. (1992) "Hieronymus *Ciceronianus*: the *Catilinarians* in Jerome," *Latomus* 51:408–20.
  (1997) "Cicero *Pro Marcello* 12 and Jerome," *Philologus* 141.1:137–40.
Ahl, F. (1985) *Metaformations. Soundplay and Wordplay in Ovid and Other Classical Poets*, Ithaca: Cornell University Press.
Albrecht, M. von (2003) *Cicero's Style. A Synopsis*, Leiden, Boston: Brill.
  (2014) "Seneca's Language and Style," in Damschen and Heil (2014): 699–744.
Aldrete, G. (1999) *Gestures and Acclamations in Ancient Rome*, Baltimore: Johns Hopkins University Press.
Alexander, J. J. G., Gibson, M. T. (1976) (eds.) *Medieval Learning and Literature: Essays Presented to Richard William Hunt*, Oxford.
Alexander, M. C. (1976) "Hortensius' Speech in Defense of Verres," *Phoenix* 30: 46–53.
  (2002) *The Case for the Prosecution in the Ciceronian Era*, Ann Arbor: University of Michigan Press.
  (2007) "Oratory, Rhetoric, and Politics in the Republic," in Dominik and Hall (2007): 98–108.
  (2009a) "The *Commentariolum Petitionis* as an Attack on Election Campaigns," *Athenaeum* 97: 31–57; 369–95.
  (2009b) "Locating the Trial of Plancius between Rules and Persuasion," in Santalucia (2009):339–55.
Allen, W. Jr. (1954) "Cicero's Conceit," *TAPhA* 85:121–44.

Altman, W. H. F. (2015) (ed.) *Brill's Companion to the Reception of Cicero*, Leiden: Brill.
Amato, E., Citti, F., Huelsenbeck, B. (2015) (eds.) *Law and Ethics in Greek and Roman Declamation*, Berlin, Boston: De Gruyter.
Ammirati, S. (2015a) "Leggere Cicerone in Egitto: osservazioni paleografiche (e filologiche)," in De Paolis (2015): 11–29.
   (2015b) *Sul libro latino antico. Ricerche bibliologiche e paleografiche*, Pisa, Rome: Fabrizio Serra Editore.
Ancona R. (2007) (ed.) *A Concise Guide to Teaching Latin Literature*, Norman: Oklahoma University Press.
André, J. (1949) *La vie et l'oeuvre d'Asinius Pollion*, Paris: C. Klincksieck.
Andrisano, A. M. (2007) (ed.) *Biblioteche del mondo antico. Dalla tradizione orale alla cultura de ll'impero*, Rome: Carocci.
Arena, V. (2007) "Roman Oratorical Invective," in Dominik and Hall (2007): 149–160.
   (2013) "The Orator and his Audience: the Rhetorical Perspective in the Art of Deliberation," in Steel and Blom (2013): 195–209.
Armisen-Marchetti, M. (1989) *Sapientiae facies. Étude sur les images de Sénèque*, Paris.
   (2015) "Seneca's Images and Metaphors," in Bartsch and Schiesaro (2015): 150–60.
Ash, R., Mossman, J., Titchener, F. B. (2015) (eds.) *Fame and Infamy. Essays for Christopher Pelling on Characterization in Greek and Roman Biography and Historiography*, Oxford.
Ash, T. (ed.) (2012) *Tacitus*, Oxford.
Asso, P. (2011) (ed.) *Brill's Companion to Lucan*, Leiden, Boston: Brill.
Astarita, M. L. (1993) *La cultura nelle Noctes Atticae*, Catania: Centro di studi sull'antico cristianesimo, Università di Catania.
   (1997) *Frontone oratore*, Catania: Centro di studi sull'antico cristianesimo, Università di Catania.
Astin, A. E. (1978) *Cato the Censor*, Oxford.
Austin, R. G. (1948) *Quintilianis Institutio Oratoria Liber XII*, Oxford.
   (1960) *M. Tulli Ciceronis Pro M. Caelio Oratio*, 3rd ed., Oxford.
   (1964) *P. Vergili Maronis Aeneidos Liber Secundus*, Oxford.
   (1977) *P. Vergili Maronis Aeneidos Liber Sextus*, Oxford.
Auvray-Assayas, C., Delattre, D. (2001) (eds.) *Cicéron et Philodème: la polémique en philosophie*, Paris: Rue d'Ulm.
Ax, W. (2011a) "Quintilian's Grammar (Inst. 1.4–8) and Its Importance for the History of Roman Grammar," in Matthaios, Montanari, and Rengakos (2011):331–46.
   (2011b) *Quintilians Grammatik (Inst. orat. 1, 4–8): Text, Übersetzung und Kommentar*, Berlin, Boston: De Gruyter.
Axer, J. (1983) "Reedition of the Viennese Fragments of Cicero, In Catilinam I (P. Vindob. G. 30885 a+e)," in Harrauer (1983):468–82.

(1989) "Tribunal-Stage-Arena: Modelling of the Communication Situation in M. Tullius Cicero's Judicial Speeches," *Rhetorica* 7: 299–311.

(1992) "Un'edizione bilingue di *In Catilinam* I di Cicerone della fine del IV secolo. Problemi paleografici," in Capasso (1992):253–64.

Bagnal, R. S., Browne, G. M., Hanson, A. E., Koenen, L. (1981) (eds.) *Proceedings of the Sixteenth International Congress of Papyrology*, Chico, CA: Scholars Press.

Baiter, J. G. (1863) "Über Handschriften des Cicero. I: Der alte Ambrosianus C 29," *Philologus* 20:335–50.

Balbo, A. (1996) "La presenza di Cicerone nel trattato *De verborum Graeci et Latini differentiis vel societatibus*," in *De tuo tibi. Omaggio degli allievi a I. Lana*, Bologna, Pàtron:439–50.

(2013a) "Sulla presenza ciceroniana nella *Gratiarum Actio* di Ausonio," *Aevum* 87.1:157–67.

(2013b) "Marcus Junius Brutus the Orator: Between Philosophy and Rhetoric," in Steel and Blom (2013):315–28.

Ballaira, G. (1993) *Esempi di scrittura latina dell'età romana. Vol. I: Dal III-II secolo a.C. al I secolo d.C.*, Turin: Edizioni dell' Orso.

Balot, R. K. (2009) (ed.) *A Companion to Ancient Greek and Roman Political Thought*, Malden: Wiley.

Barabino, G. (1990) "L'*auctoritas* di Cicerone nei grammatici tardo-antichi," in *Tradizione dell'antico nelle letterature e nelle arti d'Occidente. Studi in memoria di M. Bellincioni Scarpat*, Rome, Bulzoni: 90–103.

(2003) "Il tema dell'*auctoritas* in Nonio Marcello," in Bertini (2003): 81–108.

Barber, K. A. (2004) *Rhetoric in Cicero's Pro Balbo*, New York, London: Routledge.

Barchiesi, A., Scheidel, W. (2010) (eds.) *The Oxford Handbook of Roman Studies*, Oxford.

Barlow, J. (1994) "Cicero's Sacrilege in 63 B.C." in Deroux (1994):180–9.

Barnes, T. D. (1986) "The Significance of Tacitus' *Dialogus de Oratoribus*," *HSCP* 90:225–44.

Bartsch, S., Schiesaro, A. (2015) (eds.) *The Cambridge Companion to Seneca*, Cambridge.

Barwick, K. (1922) *Remmius Palaemon und die römische Ars grammatica*, Leipzig: Dieterich'sche Verlagsbuchhandlung.

Bastianini, G., Lapini, W., Tulli, M. (eds.) (2012) *Harmonia*, Florence: Firenze University Press.

Batinski, E. E. (2003) "*In Cynthiam/Pro Cynthia*: Propertius 2.32," *Latomus* 62.3: 616–26.

Batstone, W. W. (1994) "Cicero's Construction of Consular *Ethos* in the First Catilinarian," *TAPhA* 124:211–66.

Beall, S. M. (2001) "*Homo fandi dulcissimus*: the Role of Favorinus in the *Attic Nights* of Aulus Gellius," *AJPh* 122.1: 87–106.

Beard, M. (2002) "Ciceronian Correspondences: Making a Book out of Letters," in Wiseman (2002),103–44.

Beier, C. (ed.) (1825) *M. Tulli Ciceronis In P. Clodium et Curionem Orationis Fragmenta*, Leipzig: Teubner.
Bell, A. (2013) "Cicero, Tradition and Performance," in Steel (2013a):171–80.
Bellandi, F. (2007) *Lepos e pathos. Studi su Catullo*, Bologna: Pàtron.
Benario, H. W. (1973) "Asconiana," *Historia* 22.1: 64–71.
Benz, L. (ed.) (2001) *ScriptOralia Romana: Die römische Literatur zwischen Mündlichkeit und Schriftlichkeit*, Tübingen: G. Narr.
Berg, C. S. van den (2014a) "Intratext, Declamation and Dramatic Argument in Tacitus' *Dialogus de Oratoribus*," *CQ* 64.1: 398–415.
(2014b) *The World of Tacitus' Dialogus de Oratoribus*, Cambridge.
Berry, D. H. (1993) "Pompey's Legal Knowledge – or Lack of It. Cic. *Mil.* 70 and the Date of *pro Milone*," *Historia* 42, 4:502–4.
(1996a) *Cicero Pro P. Sulla Oratio*, Cambridge.
(1996b) "The Value of Prose Rhythm in Questions of Authenticity: the Case of the *De Optimo Genere Oratorum* Attributed to Cicero," *PLLS* 9: 47–74.
(2004a) "The Publication of Cicero's *Pro Roscio Amerino*," *Mnemosyne* 57.1: 80–7.
(2004b) "Literature and Persuasion in Cicero's Pro Archia," in Powell and Paterson (2004): 291–311.
(2016) "Neglected and Unnoticed Additions in the Text of Three Cicero Speeches *(In Verrem II.5, pro Murena, pro Milone)*," in Hunter and Oakley (2016): 10–21.
Berry, D. H., Erskine, A. (eds.) (2010) *Form and Function of Roman Oratory*, Cambridge.
Berry, D. H., Heath, M. (1997) "Oratory and Declamation," in Porter (1997): 393–420.
Berti, E. (2007) *Scholasticorum Studia. Seneca il Vecchio e la cultura retorica e letteraria della prima età imperiale*, Pisa: Giardini.
Bertini, F. (2003) *Prolegomena Noniana 2*, Genua: Università di Genova.
Bianchetti, S. (2001) (ed.) *Poikilma. Studi in onore di M.R. Cataudella*, La Spezia: Agorà.
Bishop, C. (2015) "Roman Plato or Roman Demosthenes? The Bifurcation of Cicero in Ancient Scholarship," in Altman (2015): 283–306.
(2015–16) "How to Make a Roman Demosthenes: Self-Fashioning in Cicero's *Brutus* and *Orator*," *CJ* 111.2:167–92
Blänsdorf, J. (1995) *Fragmenta Poetarum Latinorum*, Stuttgart, Leipzig: De Gruyter.
(2001) "Cicero auf dem Forum und im Senat: Zur Mündlichkeit der Reden Ciceros," in Benz (2001):205–28.
Blockley, R. (1998) "Ammianus and Cicero: The Epilogue of the History as a Literary Statement," *Phoenix* 52.3–4: 305–14.
Blösel, W., Hölkeskamp, K. J. (2011) (eds.) *Von der militia equestris zur milita urbana: Prominenzrollen und Karrierefelder im antiken Rom*, Stuttgart: Franz Steiner Verlag.

Van der Blom, H. (2010) *Cicero's Role Models. The Political Strategy of a Newcomer*, Oxford.
Bloomer, W. M. (1997a) "A Preface to the History of Declamation: Whose Speech? Whose History?," in Habinek and Schiesaro (1997): 199–215.
  (1997b) "Schooling in Persona: Imagination and Subordination in Roman Education," *ClAnt* 16: 57–78.
  (2007) "Roman Declamation: The Elder Seneca and Quintilian," in Dominik and Hall (2007): 297–306.
  (2011a) "Quintilian on the Child as a Learning Subject," *CW* 105.1:109–37.
  (2011b) *The School of Rome: Latin Studies and the Origins of Liberal Education*, Berkeley, Los Angeles, London: University of California Press.
  (2013) "The Ancient Child in School," in Grubbs and Parkin (2013): 444–461.
  (2015) (ed.) *A Companion to Ancient Education*, Malden, MA: Wiley-Blackwell.
Bonner, S. F. (1949) *Roman Declamation in the Late Republic and Early Empire*, Liverpool: University Press of Liverpool .
  (1977) *Education in Ancient Rome: From the Elder Cato to the Younger Pliny*, London: Routledge.
Bonsangue, V. (2013) "L'irosa eloquenza delle *strumae*," *Rhetorica* 31.1: 58–72.
Booth, J. (2007) (ed.) *Cicero on the Attack. Invective and Subversion in the Orations and Beyond*, Swansea: Classical Press of Wales.
Borgo, A. (2014) "Tra storia e retorica: il contrasto tra Cicerone-Antonio nella settima suasoria di Seneca il Vecchio," in Grisola and Matino (2014): 9–24.
Boulanger, A. (1940) "La publication du *Pro Murena*," *REA* 42:382–7.
Boyle, A. J. (1997) *Tragic Seneca. An Essay in the Theatrical Tradition*, London, New York: Routledge.
Brashear, W. (1981) "A Greek-Latin Vocabulary," in Bagnall, Browne, Hanson, and Koenen (1981): 31–41.
Braund, S. M. (1997) "Declamation and Contestation in Satire," in Dominik (1997):120–35.
  (2012) "Praise and Protreptic in Early Imperial Panegyric: Cicero, Seneca, Pliny," in Rees (2012): 85–108.
Braund, S. M., Gill, Chr. (1997) (eds.) *The Passions in Roman Thought and Literature*, Cambridge.
Bremmer, J., Roodenburg, H. (1991) (eds.) *A Cultural History of Gesture: From Antiquity to the Present Day*, Cambridge.
Bright, D. F., Ramage, E. S. (eds.) *Classical Texts and Their Traditions*, Chicago: Scholars Press.
Brink, C. O. (1989) "Quintilian's *De causis corruptae eloquentiae* and Tacitus' *Dialogus de Oratoribus*," *CQ* 39: 472–503.
  (1994) "Can Tacitus' *Dialogus* be dated? Evidence and Historical Conclusions," *HSPh* 96:251–80.
Brook, A. (2016) "Cicero's Use of Aeschylus' *Oresteia* in the *Pro Milone*," *Ramus* 45.1: 45–73.
Brugnoli, G. (1955) *Studi sulle Differentiae Verborum*, Rome: Signorelli.

(1961) *"I Synonyma Ciceronis,"* in *Atti I Congresso Internazionale di Studi Ciceroniani*, Rome, I:283–99.
Brunt, P. A. (1980) "Patronage and Politics in the *Verrines*," *Chiron* 10:273–89.
(2011) "Cicero and Historiography," in Marincola (2011):207–40.
Buckley, M. (2002) "Atticus, Man of Letters, Revisited," in Sidwell (2002): 15–33.
Buecheler, F. (1908) "Prosopographica," *RhM* 63:190–96.
Bücher, F., Uwe, W. (2006) "Mit Manuskript in den Senat? Zu Cic. *Planc.* 74," *RhM* 149:237–40.
Bürge, A. (1974) *Die Juristenkomik in Ciceros Rede Pro Murena*, Zürich: Juris.
Burckhardt, L. (1990) "The Political Elite of the Roman Republic: Comments on Recent Discussion of the Concepts *Nobilitas* and *Homo Novus*," *Historia* 39, 1: 77–99.
Burnand, Chr. (2004) "The Advocate as a Professional: the Role of the Patronus in Cicero's *Pro Cluentio*," in Powell and Paterson (2004): 277–289.
Butler, S. (2002) *The Hand of Cicero*, London, New York: Routledge.
(2014) "Cicero's Capita," in Jansen (2014): 73–111.
Buzi, P. (2005) *Manoscritti latini nell'Egitto tardo-antico*, Imola: Editrice La Mandragora.
Cairns, D. L., Fulkerson, L. (2015) (eds.) *Emotions between Greece & Rome*, BICS Supplement 125, London.
Cairns, F., Fantham, E. (2003) (eds.) *Caesar against Liberty?: Perspectives on His Autocracy*, Cambridge.
Calboli, G. (1978) *Oratio Pro Rhodiensibus. Catone, l'Oriente greco e gli imprenditori romani*, Bologna: Pàtron.
(2001) (ed.) *Papers on Grammar VI*, Bologna: Pàtron.
Calboli Montefusco, L. (1979) *Consulti Fortunatiani Ars Rhetorica*, Bologna: Pàtron.
(1988) *Exordium Narratio Epilogus. Studi sulla teoria retorica greca e romana delle parti del discorso*, Bologna: Pàtron.
(1996) "Quintilian and the Function of the Oratorical *Exercitatio*," *Latomus* 55.3:615–25.
(2006) (ed.) *Papers on Rhetoric VII*, Rome: Herder.
(2007) (ed.) *Papers on Rhetoric VIII, Declamation*, Rome: Herder.
(2008) (ed.) *Papers on Rhetoric IX*, Rome: Herder.
(2010) (ed.) *Papers on Rhetoric X*, Rome: Herder.
Cameron, A. (2011) *The Last Pagans of Rome*, Oxford.
Canfora, L. (1974) *Conservazione e perdita dei classici*, Padua: Stilo Editrice.
(1984) "Altri riferimenti ai poemi ciceroniani nell'*Invectiva in Ciceronem*," *Ciceroniana* 5:101–9.
(2006) "Immagine tardoantica di Cicerone," in Narducci (2006): 3–16.
Canobbio, A. (2011) *M. Valerii Martialis Epigrammaton Liber Quintus*, Naples : Loffredo.
Capasso, M. (1992) (ed.) *Papiri letterari greci e latini*, Galatina: Congedo Editore.
(1998) (ed.) *Ricerche di papirologia letteraria e documentaria*, Galatina : Congedo Editore.

(2008) "I papiri e le letterature greca e latina ser," *A & R* 2, 2: 58–79.
Cape, R. W., Jr. (1995) "The Rhetoric of Politics in Cicero's Fourth Catilinarian," *AJPh* 116.2:255–77.
  (1997) "Persuasive History: Roman Rhetoric and Historiography," in Dominik (1997a):212–28.
  (2002) "Cicero's Consular Speeches," in May (2002a):113–58.
Caplan, H. (2004) *[Cicero] Rhetorica ad Herennium*, reprinted (originally published 1954). Cambridge.
Carcopino, J. (1947) *Les secrets de la correspondance de Cicéron*, 2 vols., Paris : L'Artisan du Livre.
Carilli, M. G. (1984) "L'orazione *pro Ligario* in Quintiliano," *SRICC*, 6: 15–33.
Casamento, A. (2004a) "Clienti, patroni, parricidi e declamatori. Popillio e Cicerone (Sen. *Contr.* 7, 2)," *P&P* 59:361–77.
  (2004b) "Parlare e lagrimar vedrai insieme. Le lacrime dell'oratore," in Petrone (2004): 41–62.
  (2010) "La Pro Milone dopo la Pro Milone," in Calboli Montefusco (2010): 39–58.
Casamento, A., van Mal Maeder, D., Pasetti, L. (2016) (eds.) *Le declamazioni minori dello Pseudo-Quintiliano. Discorsi immaginari tra letteratura e diritto*, Berlin, Boston: De Gruyter.
Castagna, L., Lefévre, E. (2003) (eds.) *Plinius der Jüngere und seine Zeit*, Munich, Leipzig: De Gruyter.
Castagna, L., Riboldi, C. (2008) (eds.) *Amicitiae templa serena. Studi in onore di G. Aricò*, 2 vols., Milan: Vita e Pensiero.
Cavallo, G., Fedeli, P., Giardina, A. (1990) (eds.) *Lo Spazio Letterario di Roma Antica*, 1–5, Rome: Salerno Editrice.
Cavarzere, A. (1994) "Nota alla *In Pisonem* di Cicerone," *MD* 33: 157–176.
  (2011) *Gli arcani dell'oratore. Alcuni appunti sull'actio dei Romani*, Rome: Editrice Antenore.
Cavazza, F. (1987) "Gellio grammatico e i suoi rapporti con *l'ars grammatica romana*," in Taylor (1987): 85–105.
  (1995) "Gli aggettivi in –ĭ-tĭmus e il rapporto fra *aedituus* e *aeditumus*," *Latomus* 54: 577–91; 784–92.
Cavenaile, R. (1958) *Corpus Papyrorum Latinarum*, Wiesbaden.
Cecchini, E. (2000) "Citazioni ciceroniane in lessici e glossari medievali," *Ciceroniana* 11: 69–78.
Celentano, M. S. (2006) "Dalla scrittura all'eloquenza: le regole e i modelli nel decimo libro *dell'Institutio Oratoria*," in Calboli Montefusco (2006): 31–47.
  (2010) "L'oratore impara a scrivere. Principi di scrittura professionale *nell'Institutio Oratoria* di Quintiliano," in Galand, Hallyn, Lévy, and Verbaal (2010): 47–66.
Cerutti, S. M. (1994) "Further Discussion on the Delivery and Publication of Cicero's Second Philippic," *CB* 70:23–8.

(1996) *Cicero's Accretive Style. Rhetorical Strategies in the Exordia of the Judicial Speeches*, Lanham, MD: University Press of America.
Chahoud, A. (2007) "Antiquity and Authority in Nonius Marcellus," in Scourfield (2007): 69–96.
Champlin, E. (1980) *Fronto and Antonine Rome*, Cambridge, MA, London: Harvard University Press.
Chlup, J. T. (2004) *"Vir magnus et memorabilis fuit:* Livy on the Death of Cicero," in Egan and Joyal (2004): 21–32.
Cichorius, C. (1964) *Untersuchungen zu Lucilius*, Zurich, Berlin: Weidmannsche Buchhandlung.
Cipriani, G. (1977) "La *Pro Marcello* e il suo significato come orazione politica," *A & R* 22:113–25.
Citroni, M. (2005) "Finalità e struttura della rassegna degli scrittori greci e latini in Quintiliano," in Gasti and Mazzoli (2005): 15–38.
Citroni Marchetti, S. (2000) *Amicizia e potere nelle lettere di Cicerone e nelle elegie ovidiane dall'esilio*, Florence: Università degli Studi di Firenze.
(2009) "Words and Silence: Atticus and the Dedicatee of *De Amicitia*," *CW* 103.1: 93–99.
Claassen, J. M. (1996) "Dio's Cicero and the Consolatory Tradition," *PLLS* 9: 29–45.
Clackson, J. (2011a) *A Companion to the Latin Language*, Malden: Wiley-Blackwell.
(2011b) "Classical Latin," in Clackson (2011a):236–56.
Clackson, J., Horrocks, G. (2007) *The Blackwell History of the Latin Language*, Malden: Wiley-Blackwell.
Clark, A. C. (1895) *M. Tulli Ciceronis Pro T. Annio Milone ad Iudices Oratio*, Oxford.
(1902) "Peterson's *Cluniacensis* Ms. of Cicero," *CR* 16:322–27.
(1905) *The Vetus Cluniacensis of Poggio Being a Contribution to the Textual Criticism of Cicero Pro Sex.Roscio, Pro Cluentio, Pro Murena, Pro Caelio and Pro Milone*, Anecdota Oxoniensia, Oxford.
(1907) *Q. Asconii Pediani Orationum Ciceronis Quinque Enarratio*, Oxford.
(1909) *Inventa Italorum*. Anecdota Oxoniensia, Oxford.
(1918) *The Descent of Manuscripts*, Oxford.
Clark, G. (1995) *Augustine Confessions Books I–IV*, Cambridge.
Clark, M., Ruebel, J. (1985) "Philosophy and Rhetoric in Cicero's *Pro Milone*," *RhM* 128: 57–72.
Clarke, M. L. (1953) *Rhetoric at Rome. A Historical Survey*, London: Routledge.
(1965) *"Non Hominis Nomen, Sed Eloquentiae,"* in Dorey (1965): 81–107.
(1971) *Higher Education in the Ancient World*, London: Routledge.
Classen, C. J. (1965) "Cicero *Pro Cluentio* 1–11 im Licht der rhetorischen Theorie und Praxis," *RhM* 108:104–42.
(1982) "Ciceros Kunst der Überredung," in Ludwig (1982): 149–192.
(1985) *Recht-Rhetorik-Politik. Untersuchungen zu Ciceros rhetorischer Strategie*, Darmstadt: Wissenschaftliche Buchgesellschaft.

Cole, N. P. (2013) "Nineteenth-Century Ciceros," in Steel (2013a):337–49.
Coleman, R. (2000) "Quintilian 1.6 and the Definition of *Latinitas*," in Moussy 2000:917–30.
Connolly, J. (2007a) *The State of Speech. Rhetoric and Political Thought in Ancient Rome*, Princeton: Princeton University Press.
  (2007b) "Virile Tongues: Rhetoric and Masculinity," in Dominik and Hall (2007): 83–97.
  (2009) "The Politics of Rhetorical Education," in Gunderson (2009):126–41.
  (2011) "Fantastical Realism in Cicero's Postwar Panegyric," in D'Urso (2011): 161–78.
Cook, B. L. (2009) "Tully's Late Medieval Life: the Roots of the Renaissance in Cicero's Biography" *C & M* 60:347–70.
Corbeill, A. (1996) *Controlling Laughter: Political Humor in the Late Roman Republic*, Princeton: Princeton University Press.
  (2001) "Education in the Roman Republic: Creating Traditions," in Too (2001):261–88.
  (2002) "Ciceronian Invective," in May (2002a): 197–217.
  (2004) *Nature embodied. Gesture in Ancient Rome*, Princeton: Princeton University Press.
  (2007) "Rhetorical Education and Social Reproduction in the Republic and Early Empire," in Dominik and Hall (2007): 69–82.
Courtney, E. (1993) *The Fragmentary Latin Poets*, Oxford.
  (2001) *A Companion to Petronius*, Oxford.
Cox, Ward (2006) (eds.) *The Rhetoric of Cicero in its Medieval and Early Renaissance Commentary Tradition*, Leiden, Boston: Brill.
Craig, C. P. (1981) "The *Accusator* as *Amicus*: an Original Roman Tactic of Ethical Argumentation," *TAPhA* III: 31–7.
  (1986) "Cato's Stoicism and the Understanding of Cicero's Speech for Murena," *TAPhA* 116:229–39.
  (1990) "Cicero's Strategy of Embarrassment in the Speech for Plancius," *AJPh* III.I: 75–81.
  (1993a) "Three Simple Questions for Teaching Cicero's 'First Catilinarian'," *CJ* 88.3: 255–267.
  (1993b) *Form as Argument in Cicero's Speeches*, Atlanta: Scholars Press.
  (2002) "A Survey of Selected Recent Work on Cicero's Rhetorica and Speeches," in May (2002a): 503–531.
  (2004) "Audience, Expectations, Invective, and Proof," in Powell and Paterson (2004): 187–213.
  (2008) "Treating *oratio figurata* in Cicero's Speeches: the Case of *pro Marcello*," in Calboli Montefusco (2008): 91–106.
  (2010) "Means and Ends of *indignatio* in Cicero's *Pro Roscio Amerino*," in Berry and Erskine (2010): 75–91.
  (2014) "Rhetorical Expectations and Self-Fashioning in Cicero's Speech *Pro Sulla*, §§ 18–19," *Rhetorica* 32.3:211–21.

Craik, E. M. (1990) (ed.) *"Owls to Athens": Essays on Classical Subjects Presented to Sir Kenneth Dover*, Oxford.
Cramer, A. G., Heinrich, C. F. (1816) *M. Tullii Ciceronis Orationum Pro Scauro, Pro Tullio, Pro Flacco partes ineditae cum scholiis ad orationem pro Scauro item ineditis*, Kiel: Apud. A. Hesse.
Crawford, J. W. (1984) *M. Tullius Cicero. The Lost and Unpublished Orations*, Göttingen: Vandenhoeck & Ruprecht.
  (1994) *M. Tullius Cicero. The Fragmentary Speeches*, Atlanta: Scholars Press.
Cribiore, R. (1996) *Writing, Teachers, and Students in Graeco-Roman Egypt*, Atlanta: Scholars Press..
  (2001) *Gymnastics of the Mind: Greek Education in Hellenistic and Roman Egypt*, Oxford.
Cugusi, P. (2003a) "Qualche riflessione sulle idee retoriche di Plinio il Giovane: *Epistulae* 1, 20 e 9, 26," in Castagna and Lefévre (2003): 95.
  (2003b) "Lucio Anneo Cornuto esegeta di Virgilio," in Gualandri and Mazzoli (2003):211–44.
Czapla, B., Lehmann, T., Liell, S. (1997) (eds.) *Vir bonus dicendi peritus. Festschrift f. Alfons Weische zum 65. Geburtstag*, Wiesbaden: Reichert.
D'Alessandro, P. (1997) (ed.) *MOYSA. Scritti in onore di Giuseppe Morelli*, Bologna: Pàtron.
Damon, C. (2007) "Rhetoric and Historiography," in Dominik and Hall (2007): 439–50.
Damschen, G., Heil, A. (2014) (eds.) *Brill's Companion to Seneca Philosopher and Dramatist*, Leiden, Boston: Brill.
Danesi Marioni, G. (2001) "All'ombra di un grande padre: Asinio Gallo in Seneca retore e in Tacito," in Bianchetti (2001):323–31.
Darab, A. (1995) "Cicero bei Plinius dem Älterem," *ACD* 31: 33–41.
David, J.-M. (1980) "*Maiorum exempla sequi*: l'*exemplum* historique dans les discours judiciaires de Cicéron," *MEFRM* 92.1: 67–87.
Degl'Innocenti Pierini, R. (2003) "Cicerone nella prima età imperiale. Luci e ombre su un martire della Repubblica," in Narducci (2003): 3–54.
  (2013) "Seneca, Mecenate e il ritratto in movimento," in Gasti (2013): 45–66.
  (2014) "Cicerone a Tomi? Rileggendo Ov. *Trist.* 3.9," *Prometheus* 40:215–23.
Della Casa, A. (1977) *Arusianus Messius. Exempla Elocutionum*, Milan: Marzorati.
Del Vigo, M. L. (1990) "*L'emendatio* del filologo, del critico, dell'autore: tre modi di correggere il testo? (I)," *MD* 24: 71–110.
  (1995) "Ambiguità *dell'emendatio*: edizioni, riedizioni, edizioni postume," in Pecere and Reeve (1995): 7–38.
  (2013) "Servio e i *veteres*," in Stok (2013): 83–100.
De Marco, M. (1991) *M. Tulli Ciceronis opera omnia quae exstant. Orationes spuriae, I: Oratio pridie quam in exilium iret; Quinta Catilinaria; Responsio Catilinae*, Milan: Mondadori.
Dench, E. (2013) "Cicero and Roman Identity," in Steel (2013a):122–37.
De Nonno, M. (1990) "Le citazioni dei grammatici," in Cavallo, Fedeli, and Giardina (1990): 3. 597–646.

(2003) "Grammatici, eruditi, scoliasti: testi, contesti, tradizioni," in Gasti (2003): 13–28.
  (2010) "Transmission and Textual Criticism," in Barchiesi and Scheidel (2010): 31–48.
De Paolis, P. (2000) "Cicerone nei grammatici tardoantichi e altomedievali," *Ciceroniana* 11: 37–67.
  (2012) (ed.) *Manoscritti e lettori di Cicerone tra Medioevo e Umanesimo*, Cassino: Università Cassino.
  (2013a) (ed.) *Le Filippiche di Cicerone tra storia e modello letterario*, Cassino: Università Cassino.
  (2013b) "Le letture alla scuola del grammatico," *Paideia* 68:465–87.
  (2015) (ed.) *Dai papiri al XX secolo. L'eternità di Cicerone*, Cassino: Università Cassino.
  (2016) (ed.) *Cicerone nella cultura antica*, Cassino: Università Cassino.
  (2017) (ed.) *Cicerone oratore*, Cassino: Università Cassino.
Deroux, C. (1994) (ed.) *Studies in Latin Literature and Roman History VII*, Brussels: Latomus.
De Trizio, M. S. (2006) "Echi ciceroniani nel panegirico di Mamertino per l'imperatore Massimiano (289 d.C.)," *InvLuc* 28: 61–74.
Dickey, E. (2007) *Ancient Greek Scholarship: a Guide to Finding, Reading, and Understanding Scholia, Commentaries, Lexica, and Grammatical Treatises, from Their Beginnings to the Byzantine Period*, Oxford.
Dickey, E., Chahoud, A. (2010) (eds.) *Colloquial and Literary Latin*, Cambridge.
Diggle, J., Hall J. B., Jocelyn, H. D. (1989) (eds.) *Studies in Latin Literature and its Tradition in Honour of C. O. Brink*, Cambridge.
Di Napoli, M. (2011) *Velii Longi De orthographia*, Hildesheim: Weidmann.
Dinter, M. T., Guérin, C., Martinho, M. (2016) (eds.) *Reading Roman Declamation. The Declamations Ascribed to Quintilian*, Berlin, Boston: De Gruyter.
Di Stefano, A. (2011) *Arusiani Messi Exempla Elocutionum*, Hildesheim: Weidmann.
Dominik, W. J. (1997a) (ed.) *Roman Eloquence: Rhetoric in Society and Literature*, London: Routledge.
  (1997b) "The Style is the Man: Seneca, Tacitus, and Quintilian's Canon," in Dominik (1997a): 42–56.
  (2007) "Tacitus and Pliny on Oratory," in Dominik and Hall (2007):323–38.
Dominik, W. J., Garthwaite, J., Roche, P. A. (2009) (eds.) *Writing Politics in Ancient Rome*, Leiden, Boston: Brill.
Dominik, W. J., Hall, J. (2007) (eds.) *A Companion to Roman Rhetoric*, Malden: Wiley-Blackwell.
Dorandi, T. (2007) *Nell'officina dei classici. Come lavoravano gli autori antichi*, Rome: Carocci.
Dorey, T. A. (ed.) (1965) *Cicero*, London: Basic Books.
Dortmund, A. (2001) *Römisches Buchwesen um die Zeitenwende. War T. Pomponius Atticus (110–32 v.Chr.) Verleger?*, Wiesbaden: Harassowitz.
Douglas, A. E. (1957) "A Ciceronian Contribution to Rhetorical Theory," *Eranos* 55: 18–26.

(1966) *M. Tulli Ciceronis Brutus*, Oxford.
(1973) "The Intellectual Background of Cicero's *Rhetorica*: A Study in Method," *ANRW* 1.3: 95–138.
Dozier, C. (2014) "Quintilian's *ratio discendi* (*Institutio* 12.8) and the Rhetorical Dimension of the *Institutio Oratoria*," *Arethusa* 47.1: 71–88.
(2015) "Innovative Invective: Strength and Weakness in Horace's *Epodes* and Quintilian's *Institutio Oratoria*," *AJPh* 136.2:313–52.
Dressler, A. (2015) "Cicero's Quarrels. Reception and Modernity from Horace to Tacitus," in Altman (2015):144–71.
Dubischar, M. (2010) "Survival of the Most Condensed? Auxiliary Texts, Communications Theory, and Condensation of Knowledge," in Horster and Reitz (2010): 39–67.
Duffalo, B. (2001) "'Appius' Indignation: Gossip, Tradition, and Performance in Republican Rome," *TAPhA* 131: 119–42
(2003) "Propertian Elegy as Restored Behavior: Evoking Cynthia and Cornelia," *Helios* 30.2:163–79.
Dugan, J. (2001a) "Preventing Ciceronianism: C. Licinius Calvus Regimens for Sexual and Oratorical Self-Mastery," *CPh* 96:400–28.
(2001b) "How to Make (and Break) a Cicero: 'Epideixis', Textuality, and Self-Fashioning in the *Pro Archia* and *In Pisonem*," *CA* 20.1: 35–77.
(2005) *Making a New Man: Ciceronian Self-Fashioning in the Rhetorical Works*, Oxford.
(2013) "Cicero and the Politics of Ambiguity: Interpreting the *Pro Marcello*," in Steel and Blom (2013):211–25.
(2014) "*Non sine causa sed sine fine*: Cicero's Compulsion to Repeat his Consulate," *CJ* 110.1: 9–22.
Dupont, F. (1997) "*Recitatio* and the Reorganization of the Space of Public Discourse," in Habinek and Schiesaro (1997): 44–59
D'Urso, G. (2011) (ed.) *Dicere laudes: elogio, comunicazione, creazione del consenso*, Pisa: ETS Edizioni.
Dyck, A. R. (1996) *A Commentary on Cicero, De Officiis*, Ann Arbor: University of Michigan Press.
(1998) "Narrative Obfuscation, Philosophical Topoi, and Tragic Patterning in Cicero's *Pro Milone*," *HSPh* 98:219–41.
(2001) "Dressing to Kill: Attire as a Proof and Means of Characterization in Cicero's Speeches," *Arethusa* 34.1:119–30.
(2002) "The Other *Pro Milone* Reconsidered," *Philologus* 146:182–85.
(2003) "Evidence and Rhetoric in Cicero's *Pro Roscio Amerino*: the Case against Sex. Roscius," *CQ* 53.1:235–46.
(2004) "Cicero's *Devotio*: the Roles of *Dux* and Scape-Goat in His Post-Reditum Speeches," *HSPh* 102: 299–314.
(2008a) *Cicero Catilinarians*, Cambridge.
(2008b) "Rivals into Partners: Hortensius and Cicero," *Historia* 57.2:142–73.
(2010a) *Cicero Pro Sexto Roscio*, Cambridge.

(2010b) "Cicero's Abridgment of His Speeches for Publication," in Horster and Reitz (2010):369–74.
(2013) *Cicero Pro Marco Caelio*, Cambridge.
Dyer, R. R. (1990) "Rhetoric and Intention in Cicero's *pro Marcello*," *JRS* 80: 17–30.
Easterling, P., Hall, E. (2002) (eds.) *Greek and Roman Actors: Aspects of an Ancient Profession*, Cambridge.
Edwards, C. (1993) *The Politics of Immorality in Ancient Rome*, Cambridge.
Egan, R. B., Joyal, M. (2004) (eds.) *Daimonopylai: Essays in Classics and the Classical Tradition Presented to Edmund G. Berry*, Winnipeg: University of Manitoba Centre for Hellenic Civilization.
Ehrle, F. (1906) *Codices e Vaticanis selecti, voll. 3*, Milan: Biblioteca Ambrosiana.
Eigler, U., Gotter, U., Luraghi, N., Walter, U. (2003) (eds.) *Formen romischer Geschichtsschreibung von den Anfängen bis Livius*, Darmstadt: Wissenschaftliche Buchgesellschaft.
Elice, M. (2007) *Romani Aquilae De Figuris*, Hildesheim: Olms.
Enders, J. (1997) "Delivering Delivery: Theatricality and the Emasculation of Eloquence," *Rhetorica* 15.3:253–78.
Enos, R. L. (1988) *The Literate Mode of Cicero's Legal Rhetoric*, Carbondale: Southern Illinois University Press.
Epstein, D. F. (1986) "Cicero's Testimony at the Bona Dea Trial," *CPh* 81:229–35.
Erskine, A. (2013) (ed.) *A Companion to Ancient History*, Malden: Wiley-Blackwell.
Esposito, P. (2004) "La morte di Cicerone da Livio a Fruttero & Lucentini," in Narducci (2004): 82–104.
Esposito, P., Walde, Ch. (2015) (eds.) *Letture e lettori di Lucano*, Pisa: Edizioni ETS.
Estèves, A. (2013) "*Seditione potens:* le discours de Drancès, de l'altercation personnelle comme stratégie de subversion politique (*Énéide* XI 336–375)," *Exercices de rhétorique* 183.2
Evans, T. V. (2012) "Latin in Egypt," in Riggs (2012):516–25.
Fairweather, J. (1981) *Seneca the Elder*, Cambridge.
Fantham, E. (1975) "The Trials of Gabinius in 54 B.C.," *Historia* 24: 425–443.
  (1978a) "Imitation and Evolution: the Discussion of Rhetorical Imitation in Cicero *de Oratore* 2.87–97 and Some Related Problems in Ciceronian Theory," *CPh* 73.1: 1–16.
  (1978b) "Imitation and Decline: Rhetorical Theory and Practice in the First Century after Christ," *CPh* 73.2:102–16.
  (1982) "Quintilian on Performance. Traditional and Personal Elements in *Institutio* 11.3," *Phoenix* 36:243–63.
  (1996) *Roman Literary Culture: from Cicero to Apuleius*, Baltimore: Johns Hopkins University Press.
  (2002) "Orator and/et Actor," in Easterling and Hall (2002):362–76.
  (2003) (ed.) *Caesar against Liberty. Perspectives on His Autocracy*, Cambridge.
  (2004) *The Roman World of Cicero's De Oratore*, Oxford.
  (2013) *Cicero Pro L. Murena Oratio*, Oxford.
Feddern, S. (2013) *Die Suasorien des älteren Seneca. Einleitung, Text und Kommentar*, Berlin, Boston: De Gruyter.

Fedeli, P. (1982) *M. Tulli Ciceronis In M. Antonium Orationes Philippicae XIV*, Leipzig: Teubner.
  (2006) "Cicerone e Seneca," *Ciceroniana* 12, Rome:217–37.
Feldherr, A. (2003) "Cicero and the Invention of Literary History," in Eigler, Gotter, Luraghi, and Walter (2003): 196–212.
  (2009) (ed.) *The Cambridge Companion to the Roman Historians*, Cambridge.
  (2013) "Free Spirits: Sallust and the Citation of Catiline," *AJPh* 134.1: 49–66.
Ferguson, J. (1962a) (ed.) *Studies in Cicero*, Rome: Centro di Studi Ciceroniani.
  (1962b) "Some Ancient Judgments of Cicero," in Ferguson (1962a): 11–33.
Ferrary, J.-L. (2009) "Lois et procès *maiestatis* dans la Rome républicaine," in Santalucia (2009):223–49.
Ferreres, L. (1995) "Deux reminiscences des *Catilinaires* dans saint Jérome et Saint Augustine," *Faventia* 17:119–20.
Ferri, R. (2011a) (ed.) *The Latin of Roman Lexicography*, Pisa, Rome: Fabrizio Serra Editore.
  (2011b) "*Hermeneumata Celtis*. The Making of a Late-Antique Bilingual Glossary," in Ferri (2011a):141–69.
Ferriss-Hill, J. L. (2012) "'*Talis oratio qualis vita*': Literary Judgments as Personal Critiques," in Sluiter and Rosen (2012):365–91.
Fleck, M. (1993) *Cicero als Historiker*, Stuttgart: De Gruyter.
Fletcher, G. B. A. (1937) "Stylistic Borrowings and Parallels in Ammianus Marcellinus," *RPh* 63:377–95.
Fohlen, J. (1979) "Recherches sur le manuscript palimpseste Vatican, Pal. Lat. 24," *S & C* 3: 195–222.
Fortenbaugh, W. W. (1975) *Aristotle on Emotion*, London: Duckworth..
Foster, F. (2017) "Teaching Language through Virgil in Late Antiquity," *CQ* 67.1: 270–83.
Fotheringham, L. S. (2007) "Having Your Cake and Eating It: How Cicero Combines Arguments," in Powell (2007): 69–90.
  (2013a) *Persuasive Language in Cicero's Pro Milone: A Close Reading and Commentary*, BICS Supplement 121, London.
  (2013b) "Twentieth/Twenty-First-Century Cicero(s)," in Steel (2013a):350–73.
  (2015) "Plutarch and Dio on Cicero at the Trial of Milo," in Ash, Mossman, and Titchener (2015): 193–207.
Fowler, D. (1997) "The Virgil Commentary of Servius," in Martindale (1997): 73–8.
Fox, M. (2007) *Cicero's Philosophy of History*, Oxford.
  (2013) "Cicero during the Enlightenment," in Steel (2013a):318–36.
Frazel, T. D. (2004) "The Composition and Circulation of Cicero's *In Verrem*," *CQ* 54.1:128–42.
Friedrich, A. (2002), *Das Symposium der XII Sapientes. Kommentar und Verfasserfrage*, Berlin, New York: De Gruyter.
Frier, B. W. (1983) "Urban Praetors and Rural Violence: The Legal Background of Cicero's *Pro Caecina*" *TAPhA* 113: 221–241.

(1985) *The Rise of the Roman Jurists: Studies in Cicero's Pro Caecina*, Princeton: Princeton University Press.
Fröhlich, U. (2011) "*Nulla salus bello*: Vergil's Drances," in Heil, Korn, and Sauer (2011): 15–20.
Fruyt, M. (2011) "Latin Vocabulary," in Clackson 2011a:144–56.
Fucecchi, M. (2011) "Partisans in Civil War," in Asso (2011):237–56.
Fuhrmann, M. (1990) "Mündlichkeit und fictive Mündlichkeit in den von Cicero veröffentlichten Reden," in Vogt-Spira (1990): 53–62.
Fulkerson, L. (2013) "Cicero's Palinode: Inconsistency in the Late Republic," *G & R* 60.2:246–61.
Gabba, E. (1957) "Note sulla polemica anticiceroniana di Asinio Pollione," *RSI* 69: 317–41.
Gagliardi, P. (1997) *Il dissenso e l'ironia. Per una rilettura delle orazioni 'cesariane' di Cicerone*, Naples: M. D'Auria.
Galand, P., Hallyn, F., Lévy, C., Verbaal, W. (2010) (eds.) *Quintilien Ancien et Moderne*, Turnhout: Brepols Publishers.
Galewicz, C. (2006) (ed.) *Texts of Power. The Power of the Text. Readings in Textual Authority across History and Cultures*, Kraków: Nydawn.
Gallazzi, C. (1984) "P. Mil. Vogl. Inv. 1190: Frammento di Cicero, in *C. Verrem Act. Sec. Lib. V*," *ZPE* 54:21–6.
Galletier, E. (1949) *Panégyriques Latins*, I, Paris: Les Belles Lettres.
Galli, D. (2015) "Lucano lettore di Cicerone," in Esposito and Walde (2015): 73–84.
Gamberale, L. (1969) *La traduzione in Gellio*, Rome: Edizioni dell'Ateneo.
  (1977) "*Autografi Virgiliani e movimento arcaizzante*," in *Atti del Convegno Virgiliano sul Bimillenario delle Georgiche*, Naples:359–67.
  (1989) "Gli *Annali* di Ennio alla scuola del *grammaticus*," *RFIC* 117: 49–56.
  (1997) "Dal falso al vero Cicerone. Note critiche all'orazione Pridie quam in exilium iret e alla Pro Rabirio perduellionis reo, 31," in D'Alessandro (1997): 331–43.
  (1998) "Dalla retorica al centone nell'*Oratio Pridie quam in exilium iret*. Aspetti della fortuna di Cicerone tra III e IV secolo," in AA.VV., *Cultura latina pagana tra terzo e quinto secolo dopo Cristo*, Florence: 53–75.
  (2013) *San Gerolamo intellettuale e filologo*, Rome: Edizioni di Storia e Letteratura.
Gamberini, F. (1983) *Stylistic Theory and Practice in the Younger Pliny*, Hildesheim, Zürich, New York: Olms.
Gambet, D. G. (1963) *Cicero's Reputation from 43 B.C. to A.D. 79*, Dissertation University of Pennsylvania: Philadelphia.
  (1970) "Cicero in the Works of Seneca Philosophus," *TAPhA* 101:171–83.
Ganz, D. (1990) "On the History of Tironian Notes," in Ganz, P. (1990): 35–51.
Ganz, P. (1990) *Tironische Noten*, Wiesbaden: Harrassowitz.
Garcea, A. (2012) *Caesar's De Analogia*, Oxford.
Gasti, F. (2003) (ed.) *Grammatica e grammatici latini: teoria ed esegesi*, Atti I Giornata Ghisleriana, Pavia: Ibis.

(2013) (ed.) *Seneca e la letteratura greca e latina, Atti IX Giornata Ghisleriana*, Pavia: Ibis.
(2016) "Aspetti della presenza di Cicerone nella tarda antichità latina," in De Paolis (2016): 27–54.
Gasti, F., Mazzoli, G. (2005) (eds.) *Modelli letterari e ideologia nell'età flavia*, Pavia: Ibis.
Gatti, P. (2011) "Nonio Marcello e la *Compendiosa Doctrina*," in Ferri (2011a): 49–62.
(2017) "Cicerone nella Controriforma. Girolamo Ragazzoni umanista e vescovo," *Acme* 2:113–30.
Gee, E. (2013) "Cicero's Poetry," in Steel (2013a): 88–106.
Geffcken, K. (1973) *Comedy in the pro Caelio*, Leiden: Bolchazy-Carducci Publishers.
Geiger, J. (1985a) *Cornelius Nepos and Ancient Political Biography*, Stuttgart: Steiner.
(1985b) "Cicero and Nepos," *Latomus* 44:261–70.
Gelzer, Th. (1970) "Quintilians Urteil über Seneca. Eine rhetorische Analyse," *MH* 27:212–23.
Gerstinger, H. (1937) "Ein neuer lateinischer Papyrus aus der Sammlung Papyrus Erzherzog Rainer," *WS* 55: 95–106.
Gessner, A. (1888) *Servius und Pseudo-Asconius*, Zurich: F. Schulthess.
Giardina, A. (1986) (ed.) *Società romana e impero tardoantico*, 4 vols., Rome: Laterza.
Gibson, C. A. (2004) "Learning Greek History in the Ancient Classroom: the Evidence of the Treatises on Progymnasmata," *CPh* 99.2:103–29.
(2014) "Better Living through Prose Composition? Moral and Compositional Pedagogy in Ancient Greek and Roman Progymnasmata," *Rhetorica* 32.1: 1–30.
Gibson, R., Steel, C. (2010) "The Indistinct Literary Careers of Cicero and Pliny the Younger," in Hardie and Moore (2010):118–37.
Gibson, R. K., Kraus, Christina Shuttleworth (2002) (eds.) *The Classical Commentary. Histories, Practices, Theory*, Leiden, Boston: Brill.
Gildenhard, I. (2007) *Paideia Romana. Cicero's Tusculan Disputations*, Cambridge.
(2011a) *Creative Eloquence. The Construction of Reality in Cicero's Speeches*, Oxford.
(2011b) *Cicero, Against Verres, 2. 1.53–86*, Cambridge.
Giomini, R. (1975) *M. Tullius Cicero De Divinatione De Fato Timaeus*, Leipzig: Teubner.
Gioseffi, M. (2014) "A Very Long Engagement. Some Remarks on the Relationship between *Marginalia* and Commentaries in the Virgilian Tradition," in Montana and Porro (2014):176–91.
Gleason, M. (1995) *Making Men: Sophists and Self-Presentation in Ancient Rome*, Princeton: Princeton University Press.
Glinister, F., Woods, C. (2007) (eds.) *Verrius, Festus, & Paul. Lexicography, Scholarship, & Society*, London: Institute of Classical Studies.

Goetz, G. (1891) "Zu den Gronovscholiasten des Cicero," *Jahrb. Klass. Philol.* 143: 429–32.
Goldberg, S. M. (1999) "Appreciating Aper: the Defence of Modernity in Tacitus' *Dialogus de Oratoribus*," *CQ* 49.1:224–37 (= Ash 2012: 155–79).
Gotoff, H. C. (1979) *Cicero's Elegant Style. An Analysis of the Pro Archia*, Urbana, Chicago, London: University of Illinois Press.
  (1993a) *Cicero's Caesarian Speeches. A Stylistic Commentary*, Chapel Hill, London: The University of North Carolina Press.
  (1993b) "Oratory: the Art of Illusion," *HSPh* 95: 289–313.
  (2002) "Cicero's Caesarian Orations," in May (2002a):219–71.
Gotzes, P. (1914) *De Ciceronis Tribus Generibus Dicendi in Orationibus pro A. Caecina, de imperio Cn. Pompei, pro C. Rabirio perduellionis reo adibiti*, Rostock.
Gowing, A. M. (1998) "Greek Advice for a Roman Senator: Cassius Dio and the Dialogue between Philiscus and Cicero (38.18–29)," *PLLS* 10:373–90
  (2000) "Memory and Silence in Cicero's *Brutus*," *Eranos* 98: 39–64.
  (2005) *Empire and Memory: the Representation of the Roman Republic in Imperial Culture*, Cambridge.
  (2013) "Tully's Boat: Responses to Cicero in the Imperial Period," in Steel (2013a):233–50.
Gozzoli, S. (1990) "La *In Pisonem* di Cicerone: un esempio di polemica politica," *Athenaeum* 78: 451–463.
Gräfenhan, A. (1850) *Geschichte der Klassischen Philologie im Altertum*, Bonn: H.B. Koenig.
Graf, F. (1991) "Gestures and Conventions: the Gestures of Roman Actors and Orators," in Bremmer and Roodenburg (1991): 36–58.
Grafton, A. (2004) "Conflict and Harmony in the *Collegium Gellianum*," in Holford, Strevens, and Vardi (2004):318–42.
Grandsen, K. W. (1991) *Virgil Aeneid Book XI*, Cambridge.
Grattarola, P. (1988) *Un libello antiaugusteo. La lettera dello pseudo Cicerone a Ottaviano*, Genoa: Tilgher.
Grebe, S. (2001) "Views of Correct Speech in Varro and Quintilian," in Calboli (2001):135–64.
Green, R. P. H. (1991) *The Works of Ausonius*, Oxford.
Greenwood, L. H. G. (1978) *Cicero VII. The Verrine Orations*, vols. 2, Cambridge.
Greetham, D. C. (1995) (ed.) *Scholarly Editing. A Guide to Research*, New York: Modern Language Association of America.
Grenfell, B. P., Hunt, A. S. (1914) *The Oxyrhynchus Papyri*, X, London: Egypt Exploration Fund.
Griffin, M. (2001) "Piso, Cicero and their Audience," in Auvray-Assayas, and Delattre (2001): 85–99.
  (2003) "*Clementia* and Caesar: from Politics to Philosophy," in Cairns and Fantham (2003):157–83.
Grillo, L. (2014) "A Double *Sermocinatio* and a Resolved Dilemma in Cicero's *Pro Plancio*," *CQ* 64.1:214–25.

(2015) *Cicero's De provinciis consularibus oratio*, Oxford.
Grimal, P. (1984) "Sénèque juge de Cicéron," *MEFRA* 96.2:655–70.
  (1991) (ed.) *Sénèque et la prose latine, Entretiens 36*, Vandoeuvres-Genève: Fondation Hardt.
Grisolia, R., Matino, G. (2014) (eds.) *Arte della parola e parole della scienza. Tecniche della comunicazione letteraria nel mondo antico*, Naples: M. D'Auria.
Grubbs, J. E., Parkin, T. (2013) (eds.) *The Oxford Handbook of Childhood and Education in the Classical World*, Oxford.
Gualandri, I., Mazzoli, G. (2003) (eds.) *Gli Annei. Una famiglia nella storia e nella cultura di Roma imperiale*, Como: New Press.
Guérin, Ch. (2006) "Cicero as User and Critic of Traditional Rhetorical Patterns: Structural Authority from *de Inventione* to *de Oratore*," in Galewicz (2006): 61–86.
  (2009) "Philosophical *Decorum* and the Literarization of Rhetoric in Cicero's *Orator*," in Woerther (2009):119–39.
Gunderson, E. (2000) *Staging Masculinity: The Rhetoric of Performance in the Roman World*, Ann Arbor: University of Michigan Press.
  (2003) *Declamation, Paternity, and Roman Identity. Authority and the Rhetorical Self*, Cambridge.
  (2009) (ed.) *The Cambridge Companion to Ancient Rhetoric*, Cambridge.
Gurd, S. (2007) "Cicero and Editorial Revision," *ClAnt* 26.1: 49–80.
  (2010) "Verres and the Scene of Rewriting," *Phoenix* 64.1–2:80–101.
  (2012) *Work in Progress: Literary Revision as Social Performance in Ancient Rome*, New York: Oxford.
Gwynn, A. (1926) *Roman Education from Cicero to Quintilian*, Oxford.
Haarhoff, T. (1920) *Schools of Gaul. A Study of Pagan and Christian Education in the Last Century of the Western Empire*, Oxford.
Habinek, T. (1985) *The Colometry of Latin Prose*, Berkeley, Los Angeles, London: University of California Press.
  (1998) *The Politics of Roman Literature. Writing, Identity, and Empire in Ancient Rome*, Princeton: Princeton University Press.
  (2009) "Situating Literacy at Rome," in Johnson and Parker (2009): 114–140.
Habinek, T., Schiesaro, A. (1997) (eds.) *The Roman Cultural Revolution*, Cambridge.
Hägg T. (2012), *The Art of Biography in Antiquity*, Cambridge.
Hagedorn, D. (1969) "Neue Bruchstüche aus dem Cicerokodex Pack$^2$ 2918 (*De imp. Cn. Pomp.* 62–65.68–69; *Verr.* II 1, 1–3.7–9)," *ZPE* 4: 73–80.
Hagen, J. (2016) "Emotions in Roman Historiography: the Rhetorical Use of Tears as a Means of Persuasion," in Sanders and Johncock (2016): 199–212.
Hagendahl, H. (1958) *Latin Fathers and the Classics: a Study on the Apologists, Jerome, and Other Christian Writers*, Stockholm: Almqwist & Wiksell.
  (1967) *Augustine and the Latin Classics*, Göteborg: Almqwist & Wiksell.
Haines, C. R. (1920) *Fronto Correspondence, 2 vols.*, Cambridge, MA, London: Harvard University Press.

Hall, J. (2002) "The *Philippics*," in May (2002a): 273–304.
  (2004) "Cicero and Quintilian on the Oratorical Use of Hand Gestures," *CQ* 54:143–60.
  (2007) "Oratorical Delivery and the Emotions: Theory and Practice," in Dominik and Hall (2007):218–34.
  (2009) "Serving the Times: Cicero and Caesar the Dictator," in Dominik, Garthwaite, and Roche (2009): 89–110.
  (2013) "Saviour of the Republic and Father of the Fatherland: Cicero and Political Crisis," in Steel (2013a):215–29.
  (2014a) *Cicero's Use of Judicial Theater*, Ann Arbor: University of Michigan Press.
  (2014b) " Cicero's *Brutus* and the Criticism of Oratorical Performance," *CJ* 110.1: 43–59.
Hammar, I. (2013) *Making Enemies. The Logic of Immorality in Ciceronian Oratory*, Lund: Lund University.
Hanchey, D. (2014) "Days of Future Passed: Fiction Forming Fact in Cicero's Dialogues," *CJ* 110.1: 61–75.
Hardie, P., Moore, H. (2010) (eds.) *Classical Literary Careers and their Reception*, Cambridge.
Harrauer, H. (1982) "Ein neues bilingues Cicero-Fragment auf Papyrus (P. Vindob. L 127)," *WS* 95:212–19.
  (1983) (ed.) *Papyrus Erzherzog Rainer (P. Rainer Cent.)*, Vienna: Brüder Hollinek.
Harries, B. (2007) "Acting the Part: Techniques of the Comic Stage in Cicero's Early Speeches," in Booth (2007):129–47.
Harries, J. (2004) "Cicero and the Law," in Powell and Paterson (2004):147–63.
  (2006) *Cicero and the Jurists: From Citizens' Law to the Lawful State*, London: Bristol Classical Press.
  (2007) *Law and Crime in the Roman World*, Cambridge.
  (2013) "The Law in Cicero's Writings," in Steel (2013a):*107–21*.
Harris, W. V. (1989) *Ancient Literacy*, Cambridge, MA, London: Harvard University Press.
Harrison, S. J. (2000) *Apuleius. A Latin Sophist*, Oxford.
  (2005) (ed.) *A Companion to Latin Literature*, Malden: Wiley-Blackwell.
Haury, A. (1955) *L'ironie et l'humour chez Cicéron*, Leiden: Brill.
Haverling, G. V. M. (2015) (ed.) *Latin Linguistics in the Early 21st Century*, Uppsala: Uppsala Universitet.
Heath, M. (1994) "The Substructure of *Stasis*-Theory from Hermagoras to Hermogenes," *CQ* 44:114–29.
  (2007) "Teaching Rhetorical Argument Today," in Powell (2007):105–22.
Heckenkamp, M. (2010) "Cicero's Tears," in Calboli Montefusco (2010):173–82.
Heil, A., Korn, M., Sauer, J. (2011) (eds.) *Noctes Sinenses. Festschrift f. F.-H. Mutschler*, Heidelberg: Universitätsverlag Winter.
Helm, C. (1979) *Zur Redaktion der Ciceronischer Konsulatsreden*, Göttingen: Georg-August-Universität zu Göttingen.

Henderson, C., Jr. (1964) (ed.) *Classical, Mediaeval and Renaissance Studies in Honor of B.L. Ullman*, 2 vols., Rome: Edizioni di Storia e Letteratura.
Herzog, R., Schmidt, P. L. (1989) (eds.) *Handbuch der lateinischen Literatur der Antike, V*, Munich: C. H. Beck.
   (1997) (eds.) *Handbuch der lateinischen Literatur der Antike, IV*, Munich: C. H. Beck.
Heusch, C. (2011) *Die Macht der Memoria. Die Noctes Atticae des Aulus Gellius im Licht der Erinnerungskuktur des 2. Jahrhunderts n. Chr.*, Berlin, New York: De Gruyter.
Heyworth, S. J. (2007) (ed.) *Classical Constructions: Papers in Memory of Don Fowler, Classicist and Epicurean*, Oxford.
Higbie, C. (2017) *Collectors, Scholars, and Forgers in the Ancient World*, Oxford.
Highet, G. (1972) *The Speeches in Vergil's Aeneid*, Princeton: Princeton University Press.
Hildebrandt, J. P. (1894) *De Scholiis Ciceronis Bobiensibus Dissertatio Inauguralis*, Berlin: Mayer & Mueller.
   (1907) *Scholia in Ciceronis Orationes Bobiensia*, Leipzig: De Gruyter.
Hodge, H., Grose, (1927) *Cicero Orations. Pro lege Manilia, pro Caecina, pro Cluentio, pro Rabirio perduellionis reo*, Cambridge, MA, London: Harvard University Press.
Hoeltermann, A. (1913) *De Flavio Capro grammatico*, Dissertatio Universitatis Bonnensis: Bonn.
Hömke, N. (2007) "Not to Win, but to Please: Declamation beyond Education," in Calboli Montefusco (2007):103–27.
Hoffer, S. E. (2007) "Cicero's 'Stomach': Political Indignation and the Use of Repeated Allusive Expressions in Cicero's Correspondence," in Morello and Morrison (2007): 87–106.
Hofmann, J. B., Szantyr, A. (1963) *Lateinische Syntax und Stilistik*, Munich: C. H. Beck.
Holford-Strevens, L. (1988) *Aulus Gellius*, Oxford.
   (2003) *Aulus Gellius. An Antonine Scholar and his Achievements*, Oxford.
Holford-Strevens, L., Vardi, A. (2004) (eds.) *The Worlds of Aulus Gellius*, Oxford.
Hollis, S. A. (2007) *Fragments of Roman Poetry c. 60 BC–AD 20*, Oxford.
Holst, H. (1925) *Die Wortspiele in Ciceros Reden*, Oslo: Some & Co.
Holtz, L. (1981) *Donat et la tradition de l'enseignement grammatical. Étude sur l'Ars Donati et sa diffusion (IV$^e$–IX$^e$ siècle) et édition critique*, Paris: CNRS.
Homeyer, H. (1964) *Die antiken Berichte über den Tod Ciceros und ihre Quellen*, Baden-Baden: Grimm.
Horsfall, N. (1989) *Cornelius Nepos. A Selection, Including the Lives of Cato and Atticus*, Oxford.
   (2003) *Virgil Aeneid 11. A Commentary*, Leiden: Brill.
Horster, M., Reitz, Chr. (2010) (eds.) *Condensing Texts-Condensed Texts*, Stuttgart: Franz Steiner Verlag.
Houston, G. W. (2002) "The Slave and Freedman Personnel of Public Libraries in Ancient Rome," *TAPhA* 132:139–76.

(2009) "Papyrological Evidence for Book Collections and Libraries in the Roman Empire," in Johnson and Parker (2009):233–67.
Hout, M. P. J. van den (1999) *A Commentary on the Letters of M. Cornelius Fronto*, Leiden, Boston, Cologne: Brill.
Howell, P. (1995) *Martial. Epigrams V*, Warminster: Aris & Phillips.
Howley, J. A. (2014) "Valuing the Mediators of Antiquity in the *Noctes Atticae*," in Ker and Pieper (2014):465–84.
Hubbard, Th. (2008) "Getting the Last Word: Publication of Political Oratory as an Instrument of Historical Revisionism," in Mackay (2008): 185–202.
Hubbell, H. M. (1939) *Cicero. Orator*, Cambridge, MA, London: Harvard University Press.
　(1949) *Cicero. De inventione De optimo genere oratorum Topica*, Cambridge, MA, London: Harvard University Press.
Humbert, J. (1925) *Les plaidoyers écrits et les plaidoyers réelles de Cicéron*, Paris: Olms.
Hunt, A. S. (1911) *The Oxyrhynchus Papyri*, VIII, London: Egypt Exploration Fund.
Hunter, R., Oakley, S. P. (2016) (eds.) *Latin Literature and its Transmission*, Cambridge.
Hutchinson, G. O. (1995) "Rhythm, Style, and Meaning in Cicero's Prose," *CQ* 45.2:485–99.
　(1998) *Cicero's Correspondence. A Literary Study*, Oxford.
　(2011) "Politics and the Sublime in the *Panegyricus*," in Roche (2011):125–41.
Ingleheart, J. (2010) *A Commentary on Ovid, Tristia, Book 2*, Oxford.
Innocenti, B. (1994) "Towards a Theory of Vivid Description as Practised in Cicero's *Verrine* Orations," *Rhetorica* 12.4:355–81.
Internullo D. (2011–12) "Cicerone latino-greco. Corpus dei papiri bilingui delle *Catilinarie* di Cicerone," *PapLup* 20–21:25–150.
　(2016) "P.Vindob. L17 identificato: Cicerone *In Catilinam* I, 14–15 + 27," *ZPE* 199: 36–40.
Inwood, B. (2005) *Reading Seneca. Stoic Philosophy at Rome*, Oxford.
Jahn, O. (1851) "Über die Subscriptionen in den Handschriften römischer Classiker," *Berichten der sächs. Ges. der Wissenschaft zu Leipzig, Phil.-Hist. Klasse* 3:327–72.
Jakobi, R. (2005) *Grillius. Überlieferung und Kommentar*, Berlin, New York: De Gruyter.
Janeras, S. (1987) (ed.) *Miscellània Papirològica Ramon Roca-Puig*, Barcelona: Fundacio Salvador Vives Casajuana.
Jansen, L. (2014) (ed.) *The Roman Paratext. Frame, Texts, Readers*, Cambridge.
Jocelyn, H. D. (1964) "Ancient Scholarship and Virgil's Use of Republican Latin Poetry," I *CQ* 14:280–95.
　(1984) "The Annotations of M. Valerius Probus," *CQ* 34.2:464–72.
　(1985a) "The Annotations of M. Valerius Probus, II," *CQ* 35.1:149–61.
　(1985b) "The Annotations of M. Valerius Probus, III: Some Virgilian Scholia," *CQ* 35.2:466–74.

Johnson, J. P. (2004) "The Dilemma of Cicero's Speech for Ligarius," in Powell and Paterson (2004):371–99.
Johnson, W. A. (2010), *Readers and Reading Culture in the High Roman Empire: a Study of Elite Communities*, Oxford.
Johnson, W. A., Parker, H. N. (2009) (eds.) *Ancient Literacies. The Culture of Reading in Greece and Rome*, Oxford.
Johnston, D. (2015) (ed.) *The Cambridge Companion to Roman Law*, Cambridge.
Karbaum, H. (1885) *De auctoritate ac fide grammaticorum Latinorum in constituendo lectione Ciceronis orationum in Verrem,* in Dissertatio Philologicae Halenses VI.1: Halis Saxonum, 71–110.
　(1889) *De origine exemplorum, quae ex Ciceronis scriptis a Charisio, Diomede, Arusiano Messio, Prisciano Caesariensi, aliis grammaticis Latinis allata sunt,* Wernigerode: B. Angerstein.
Kasten, H. (1972) *M. Tullius Cicero Oratio Pro L. Murena*, Leipzig: Teubner.
Kaster, R. A. (1978) "Servius and *Idonei Auctores,*" *AJPh* 99.2: 181–209.
　(1980) "Macrobius and Servius: *Verecundia* and the Grammarian's Function," *HSPh* 84:219–62.
　(1983) "Notes on 'Primary' and 'Secondary' Schools in Late Antiquity," *TAPhA* 113:323–46.
　(1988) *Guardians of Language: the Grammarian and Society in Late Antiquity*, Berkeley, Los Angeles, London: University of California Press.
　(1995) *C. Suetonius Tranquillus De Grammaticis et Rhetoribus*, Oxford.
　(1998) "Becoming Cicero," in Knox and Foss (1998):248–63.
　(2001) "Controlling Reason: Declamation in Rhetorical Education at Rome," in Too (2001):317–37.
　(2005) *Emotion, Restraint, and Community in Ancient Rome*, Oxford.
　(2006) *Marcus Tullius Cicero. Speech on Behalf of Publius Sestius*, Oxford.
　(2009) "Some Passionate Performances in Late Republican Rome," in Balot (2009):308–20.
　(2011) *Macrobius Saturnalia*, 3 vols., Cambridge, MA, London: Harvard University Press.
Kasulke, C. T. (2005) *Fronto, Marc Aurel und kein Konflikt zwischen Rhetorik und Philosophie im 2. Jh.n.Chr.*, Munich, Leipzig: De Gruyter.
Katula, R. A. (2003) "Emotion in the Courtroom. Quintilian's Judge – Then and Now," in Tellegen and Couperus (2003):145–56.
Kelly, D. (2008) "Publishing the *Philippics*, 44–43 BC," in Stevenson and Wilson (2008): 22–38.
Kemezis, A. M. (2014) *Greek Narratives of the Roman Empire under the Severians. Cassius Dio, Philostratus and Herodian*, Cambridge.
Kendeffy, G. (2015) "Lactantius as Christian Cicero, Cicero as Shadow-like Instructor," in Altman (2015): 56–92.
Kennedy, G. A. (1972) *The Art of Rhetoric in the Roman World, 300 BC–AD 300*, Princeton: Princeton University Press.
　(2002) "Cicero's Oratorical and Rhetorical Legacy," in May (2002a): 481–502.

Kenney, E. J. (1982) "Books and Readers in the Roman World," in Kenney and Clausen (1982): 3–32.
Kenney, E. J., Clausen, W. V. (1982) (eds.) *The Cambridge History of Classical Literature. 2. Latin Literature*, Cambridge.
Kenty, J. (2017) "Cicero's Representation of an Oral Community in *De Oratore*," in Slater (2017):351–76.
Ker, J., Pieper, Chr. (2014) (eds.) *Valuing the Past in the Greco-Roman World*, Leiden, Boston: Brill.
Keulen, W. (2009) *Gellius the Satirist. Roman Cultural Authority in Attic Nights*, Leiden, Boston: Brill.
Keyser, P. T. (1994) "Late Authors in Nonius Marcellus and Other Evidence of his Date," *HSPh* 96:369–89.
Kiessling, A., Schoell, R. (1875) *Q. Asconii Pediani orationum Ciceronis quinque enarratio*, Berlin: Wiedmann.
Kinsey, T. E. (1975) "Cicero's Speech for Roscius of America," *SO* 50.1: 91–104.
Kirby, J. T. (1990) *The Rhetoric of Cicero's Pro Cluentio*, Amsterdam: Brill.
Kirchner, R. (2007) "*Elocutio:* Latin Prose Style," in Dominik and Hall (2007):181–94.
Klotz, A. (1912) "Zur Kritik einiger ciceronischen Reden," *RhM* 67:358–90.
  (1913) "Zur Kritik einiger ciceronischen Reden," *RhM* 68: 477–514.
  (1919–23) *M. Tulli Ciceronis Scripta quae manserunt omnia*, 7 vols., Leipzig: Teubner.
Knox, P., Foss, C. (1998) (eds.) *Style and Tradition: Studies in Honor of W. Clausen*, Stuttgart, Leipzig: Teubner.
Konstan, D. (2005) "Clemency as a Virtue," *CPh* 100:337–46.
  (2007) "Rhetoric and Emotion," in Worthington (2010):411–25.
Koster, S. (1980) *Die Invektive in der griechischen und römischen Literatur*, Meisenheim am Glan: A. Hain.
Kramer, B., Hübner, R. (1976) *Kölner Papyri*, Bd. 1, Opladen Westdeutscher Verlag R. Habelt.
Kramer, J. (1983) (ed.) *Glossaria bilingua in papyris et membranis reperta*, Bonn.
  (2013) "Les glossaires bilingues sur papyrus," in Marganne and Rochette (2013): 43–56.
Kremmydas, Chr., Powell, J., Rubinstein, L. (2013) (eds.) *Profession and Performance. Aspects of Oratory in the Greco-Roman World*, BICS Supplement 123, London.
Krostenko, B. A. (2001) *Cicero, Catullus, and the Language of Social Performance*, Chicago, London: University of Chicago Press.
  (2005) "Style and Ideology in the *pro Marcello*," in Welch and Hillard (2005): 279–312.
Kubiak, D. P. (1989) "Piso's Madness (Cic. *in Pis.* 21 and 47)," *AJPh* 110.2:237–45.
Kühnert, F. (1962) "Quintilians Erörterung über den Witz (*Inst. Or.* 6.3)," *Philologus* 106: 29–59;305–14.
Kumaniecki, K. (1970) "Les discours égarés de Cicéron pro Cornelio," *Med. Kon. Vlaam. Acad. Belg.* 32: 3–36.

La Bua, G. (2001) "Sulla pseudo-ciceroniana *Si eum P. Clodius legibus interrogasset* e sull'ordine delle orazioni negli *Scholia Bobiensia*," RFIC 129.2:161–91.
  (2005) "*Obscuritas* e *dissimulatio* nella *pro Tullio* di Cicerone," *Rhetorica* 23.3: 261–80.
  (2006) "Diritto e retorica: Cicerone *iure peritus* in Seneca retore e Quintiliano" *Ciceroniana* 12, Rome: 181–203.
  (2010a) "*Aiebat se in animo scribere* (Sen. *Contr.* 1 praef. 18): Writing in Roman Declamations," in Calboli Montefusco (2010):183–99.
  (2010b) "Patronage and Education in Third-Century Gaul: Eumenius' Panegyric for the Restoration of the Schools," *JLA* 3.2:300–15.
  (2013a) "*Quo usque tandem cantherium patiemur istum?* (Apul. *Met.* 3.27): Lucius, Catiline and the 'Immorality' of the Human Ass'," *CQ* 63.2:854–59.
  (2013b) "Mastering Oratory: the Mock-Trial in Apuleius *Metamorphoses* 3.3.1–7.1," *AJPh* 134.4: 675–701.
  (2014a) "Cicero's *Pro Milone* and the Demosthenic Style: *De optimo genere oratorum* 10," *G & R* 61.1: 29–37.
  (2014b) "*Medicina consularis*: Cicerone e la cura dello stato," in De Paolis (2014): 29–51.
Lacey, W. K. (1986) *Cicero: Second Philippic Oration*, Warminster: Liverpool University Press.
Laird, W. (2009) "The Rhetoric of Roman Historiography," in Feldherr (2009): 197–213.
Lakmann, M. L. (1997) "Favorinus von Arelate: Aulus Gellius über seinen Lehrer," in Czapla, Lehmann, and Liell (1997):233–43.
Lamacchia, R. (1968) *[M. Tulli Ciceronis] Epistula ad Octavianum*, Florence: Le Monnier.
  (1975) "Il giudizio di Tito Livio su Cicerone," *SU* 49:421–35.
Lamberton, R., Keaney, J. J. (1992) (eds.) *Homer's Ancient Readers: the Hermeneutics of Greek Epic's Earliest Exegetes*, Princeton: Princeton University Press.
Lange, C. H., Madsen, J. M. (2016) (eds.) *Cassius Dio. Greek Intellectual and Roman Politician*, Leiden, Boston: Brill.
La Penna, A. (1968) *Sallustio e la rivoluzione romana*, Milan: Mondadori Bruno.
  (1985) "Drance (*Drances*)," *EV* II, Rome:138–40.
Lardet, P. (1993) *L'Apologie de Jérôme contre Rufin. Un commentaire*, Leiden, New York, Cologne: Brill.
Larsen, J. (2008) "Cicero, Antony and the Senatus Consultum Ultimum in the Second Philippic," in Stevenson and Wilson (2008):168–80.
Laudizi, G. (2004) "Seneca (*ep.* 114) e la corruzione dello stile," *BStudLat* 34: 39–56.
Laurand, L. (1936–1938) *Études sur le style des discours de Cicéron*, 3 vols., 4th ed., Paris: Les Belles Lettres.
Laureys, M. (1991) "Quintilian's Judgment of Seneca and the Scope and Purpose of *Inst.* 10.1," *A & A* 37:100–25.
Lausberg, H. (1998) *Handbook of Literary Rhetoric. A Foundation for Literary Study*, Leiden, Boston, Cologne: Brill.

Law, V. (1987) "Late Latin Grammars in the Early Middle Ages: a Typological History," in Taylor (1987): 191–204.
Laws, J. (2004) "Epilogue: Cicero and the Modern Advocate," in Powell and Paterson (2004):401–16.
Leach, E. W. (1990) "The Politics of Self-Presentation: Pliny's Letters and Roman Portrait Sculpture," *ClAnt* 9: 14–39.
Ledentu, M. (2000) "L'orateur, la parole et le texte," in Achard and Ledentu (2000): 57–73.
  (2007) (ed.) *Parole, media, pouvoir dans l'Occident romain*, Paris: De Boccard.
Leeman, A. D. (1963) *Orationis Ratio. The Stylistic Theories and Practice of the Roman Orators, Historians, and Philosophers*, 2 vols., Amsterdam: A. M. Hakkert.
  (1982) "The Technique of Persuasion in Cicero's Pro Murena" in Ludwig (1982): 193–236.
Leesen, T. G. (2010) *Gaius Meets Cicero: Law and Rhetoric in the School Controversies*, Leiden: Brill.
Leigh, M. (2004a) "The *Pro Caelio* and comedy," *CPh* 99.4:300–35.
  (2004b) "Quintilian on the Emotions: *Institutio Oratoria* 6 preface and 1–2," *JRS* 94:122–40.
Lennon, J. (2010) "Pollution and Ritual Impurity in Cicero's *De domo sua*," *CQ* 60.2:427–45.
Lentano, M. (2014) "La città dei figli. Pensieri di un declamatore ai funerali di Cicerone," in Pepe and Moretti (2014):223–44.
  (2016) "Parlare di Cicerone sotto il governo del suo assassino. Una lettura della controversia VII, 2 di Seneca e la politica augustea della memoria," in Poignault and Schneider (2016):375–91.
Levene, D. S. (1997) "God and Man in the Classical Latin Panegyric," *PCPhS* 43: 66–103.
  (2004) "Reading Cicero's Narratives," in Powell and Paterson (2004):117–46.
Lewis, R. G. (2006) *Asconius Commentaries on Speeches of Cicero*, revised edition, Oxford.
Lhommé, M.-K. (2011) "De l'encyclopédie au glossaire: Festus et son adaptation par Paul Diacre," in Ferri (2011a): 29–47.
Licandro, O. (2017) *Cicerone alla corte di Giustiniano. "Dialogo sulla scienza politica"* (Vat. gr. 1298), Rome: L'ERMA di Bretschneider.
Lichtenfeldt, C. (1888) *De Q. Asconii Pediani fontibus ac fide*, Diss. Breslau: Vratislaviae, apud G. Koebner.
Lindsay, W. M. (1901) *Nonius Marcellus' Dictionary of Republican Latin*, Oxford.
Lintott, A. (1974) "Cicero and Milo," *JRS* 64: 62–78.
  (1990) "Electoral Bribery in the Roman Republic," *JRS* 80: 1–16.
  (2004) "Legal Procedure in Cicero's Time," in Powell and Paterson (2004): 61–78.
  (2008) *Cicero as Evidence. A Historian's Commentary*, Oxford.
  (2015) "Crime and Punishment," in Johnston (2015):301–31.
Liou-Gille, B. (1994) "La perduellio: Le process d'Horace et de Rabirius," *Latomus* 58: 3–58.

Lloyd, R. B. (1961) "Republican Authors in Servius and *Scholia Danielis*," *HSPh* 65: 291–341.
Loewe, G. (1876) *Prodromus corporis glossariorum Latinorum*, Leipzig: Teubner.
Lomanto, V. (1996) "*Cedant arma togae,*" in *De tuo tibi. Omaggio degli allievi a I. Lana*, Bologna: Pàtron, 115–41.
Lomas, K. (2004) "A Volscian Mafia? Cicero and his Italian Clients in the Forensic Speeches," in Powell and Paterson (2004): 97–116.
Lo Monaco, F. (1990) "Lineamenti per una storia delle raccolte antiche di orazioni ciceroniane," *Aevum(ant)* 3:169–85.
  (1995) "Paralipomeni alle collezioni antiche di orazioni ciceroniane," in Pecere and Reeve (1995): 39–61.
  (1996) "*In codicibus... qui Bobienses inscribuntur*: scoperte e studio di palinsesti bobbiesi in Ambrosiana dalla fine del Settecento ad Angelo Mai (1819)," *Aevum* 96.3: 657–719.
  (2012), "Cicerone palinsesto," in De Paolis (2012): 1–20.
López, J. F. (2007) "Quintilian as Rhetorician and Teacher," in Dominik and Hall (2007):307–22.
López Eire, A. (2007) "Rhetoric and Language," in Worthington (2007):336–49.
Loutsch, C. (1994) *L'exorde dans les discours de Cicéron*, Brussels: Latomus.
  (2007) "Remarques sur la publication du *Pro Caelio* de Cicéron," in Ledentu (2007): 53–74.
Lowrie, M. (2007) "Making an Exemplum of Yourself: Cicero and Augustus," in Heyworth (2007): 91–112.
Luce, T. J. (1993) "Reading and Response in the *Dialogus*," in Luce and Woodman (1993): 11–38.
Luce, T. J., Woodman, A. J. (1993) (eds.) *Tacitus and the Tacitean Tradition*, Princeton: Princeton University Press.
Ludwig, W. (1982) (ed.) *Éloquence et rhétorique chez Cicéron, Entretiens sur l'antiquité classique 28*, Vandoeuvres- Genève: Fondation Hardt.
Luhtala, A. (2010) "Latin Schulgrammatik and the Emergence of Grammatical Commentaries," in Horster and Reiz (2010):209–43.
MacCormack, S. (2013) "Cicero in Late Antiquity," in Steel (2013a): 251–305.
MacDonald, C. (1976) *Cicero Orations. In Catilinam 1–4. Pro Murena. Pro Sulla. Pro Flacco*, Cambridge, MA, London: Harvard University Press.
Mack, D. (1937) *Senatsreden und Volksreden bei Cicero*, Würzburg: K. Triltsch.
Mackay, E. A. (2008) (ed.) *Orality, Literacy, Memory in the Ancient Greek and Roman World*, Leiden, Boston: Brill.
Madvig, J. N. (1828) *De Q. Asconii Pediani et aliorum veterum interpretum in Ciceronis orationes commentariis disputatio critica*, Copenhagen.
Maehler, H. (1983) "Bemerkungen zu dem neuen Cicero-Fragment in Wien," *ZPE* 52:57–9.
Maggiulli, G. (1980) "Il numero dei libri nelle citazioni di Nonio," *Studi Noniani* 6:117–22.
Magnaldi, G. (2002) "Lezioni genuine e glosse nelle *Filippiche* di Cicerone," *Lexis* 20: 61–78.

(2004) *Parole d'autore, parola di copista. Usi correttivi ed esercizi di scuola nei codici di Cic. Phil. 1.1 13.10*, Alessandria: Edizioni dell'Orso.

(2013) "Cicerone a scuola di grammatica: la tradizione manoscritta delle Filippiche," in De Paolis (2013a): 27–44.

Maguiness, W. S. (1932) "Some Methods of the Latin Panegyrists," *Hermathena* 47: 42–61.

Mai, A. (1828) *Classicorum auctorum e vaticanis codicibus editorum*, 2 vols, Rome.

Maier-Eichhorn, U. (1989) *Die Gestikulation in Quintilians Rhetorik*, Frankfurt am Main: Peter Lang.

Malcom, D. A. (1979) "*Quo usque tandem* . . . ?," *CQ* 29.1:219–20.

Mallan, Chr. (2016) "*Parrhêsia* in Cassius Dio," in Lange and Madsen (2016): 258–75.

Maltby, R. (1991) *Lexicon of Ancient Latin Etymologies*, Leeds: Francis Cairns.

Manfredi, M. (1995) "*Lessico a Cic. In Cat. I 5,*" in *Dai Papiri della Società Italiana*, Florence: 5–9.

Mankin, D. (2011) *Cicero De Oratore Book III*, Cambridge.

Manuwald, G. (2007) *Cicero Philippics 3–9, 2 vols*, Berlin, New York: De Gruyter.

(2008) "Cicero Versus Antonius: On the Structure and Construction of the *Philippics* Collection," in Stevenson and Wilson (2008): 39–61.

(2011) "Ciceronian Praise as a Step towards Pliny's *Panegyricus*," in Roche (2011): 85–103.

(2016) (ed.) *The Afterlife of Cicero*, BICS Supplement 135, London: Institute of Classical Studies.

Marache, R. (1952) *La critique littéraire de langue latine et le development du gout archaisant au II siècle de notre ère*, Rennes: Plihon.

(1957) *Mots nouveaux et mots archaïques chez Fronton et Aulu-Gelle*, Paris: Presses Universitaires de France.

Marchesi, I. (2008) *The Art of Pliny's Letters. A Poetics of Allusion in the Private Correspondence*, Cambridge.

Marciniak, K. (2008) "Cicero und Caesar. Ein Dialog der Dichter," *Philologus* 152.2:212–22.

(2011a) (ed.) *Birthday Beasts' Book: Where Human Roads Cross Animal Trails . . .*, Warsaw: Institute for Interdisciplinary Studies "Artes Liberales".

(2011b) "Cicero's Crow in a Brave New World," in Marciniak (2011a): 193–206.

Marek, V. (1983) *M. Tullius Cicero Orationes De Lege Agraria Oratio Pro C. Rabirio Perduellionis Reo*, Leipzig: Teubner.

Marganne, M. H., Rochette, B. (2013) (eds.) *Bilinguisme et digraphisme dans le monde gréco-romain*, Liège: Presses Universitaires de Liège.

Marincola, J. (2007) (ed.) *A Companion to Greek and Roman Historiography*, 2 vols., Malden, Oxford: Wiley-Blackwell.

(2009) "Ancient Audiences and Expectations," in Feldherr (2009): 11–23.

(2011) (ed.) *Greek and Roman Historiography*, Oxford.

Marinone, N. (1946) *Elio Donato, Macrobio e Servio commentatori di Virgilio*, Vercelli: Presso l'Autore.

Marrou, H. I. (1965) *Histoire de l'éducation dans l'antiquité*, 6th ed., Paris: Seuil.

Marsh, D. (2013) "Cicero in the Renaissance," in Steel (2013a):306–16.
Marshall, B. A. (1975) "The Date of Delivery of Cicero's *In Pisonem*," *CQ* 25: 88–93
  (1980) "Asconius and Fenestella," *RhM* 123:349–54.
  (1985) *A Historical Commentary on Asconius*, Columbia: University of Missouri Press.
  (1987) "Excepta Oratio, the Other *Pro Milone* and the Question of Shorthand," *Latomus* 46:730–36.
Marshall, P. K. (1977) *The Manuscript Tradition of Cornelius Nepos*, London: Institute of Classical Studies.
Martin, D. E. (1984) "The Statilius-Subscription and the Editions of Late Antiquity," in Bright and Ramage (1984):147–54.
Martin, G. (2011) "*Meorum periculorum rationes utilitas rei publicae vincat*. Zur Historizität der vierten Catilinaria," *Philologus* 155.2:307–25.
Martindale, Ch. (1997) (ed.) *The Cambridge Companion to Virgil*, Cambridge.
Maselli, G. (1979) *Lingua e scuola in Gellio grammatico*, Lecce: Milella.
  (2000) *Cicerone. In difesa di Lucio Flacco*, Venice: Marsilio.
Maslowski, T. (1981) *M. Tullius Cicero Orationes Cum senatui gratias egit Cum populo gratias egit De domo sua De haruspicum responsis*, Leipzig: Teubner.
  (1986) *M. Tullius Cicero Oratio Pro P. Sestio*, Leipzig: Teubner.
  (1995) *M. Tullius Cicero Orationes in P. Vatinium testem pro M. Caelio*, Stuttgart, Leipzig: Teubner.
  (2007) *M. Tullius Cicero Oratio De Provinciis Consularibus Oratio pro L. Cornelio Balbo*, Berlin: De Gruyter.
Maslowski, T., Rouse, R. H. (1984) "The Manuscript Tradition of Cicero's Post-Exile Orations I: The Medieval History," *Philologus* 128: 60–104.
Massa, G. (2006) "Sallustio contro Cicerone? I falsi d'autore e la polemica anticiceroniana di Asinio Pollione," *Athenaeum* 94:415–66.
Matthaios, S., Montanari, F., Rengakos, A. (2011) (eds.), *Ancient Scholarship and Grammar. Archetypes, Concepts and Contexts*, Berlin, New York: De Gruyter.
Mazzarino, A. (1955) *Grammaticae Romanae Fragmenta Aetatis Caesareae*, I, Turin: Loescher.
Mazzoli, G. (1996) "Quintiliano e la *pro Cluentio*," *RIL* 130.2:483–94.
  (2006) "La guerra civile nelle declamazioni di Seneca il Retore," *Ciceroniana* 12, Rome: 45–57.
May, J. M. (1979) "The *ethica digressio* and Cicero's *pro Milone*: a Progression of Intensity from *logos* to *ethos* to *pathos*," *CJ* 74.3:240–46.
  (1981) "The Rhetoric of Advocacy and Patron-Client Identification: Variation on a Theme," *AJPh* 102:308–15
  (1988) *Trials of Character: the Eloquence of Ciceronian Ethos*, Chapel Hill, New York, London: The University of North Carolina Press.
  (2001) "Cicero's *Pro Milone*: an Ideal Speech of an Ideal Orator," in Wooten (2001):123–34.
  (2002a) (ed.) *Brill's Companion to Cicero: Oratory and Rhetoric*, Leiden: Brill.
  (2002b) "Ciceronian Oratory in Context," in May (2002a): 49–70.
  (2007a) "Cicero as Rhetorician," in Dominik and Hall (2007):250–63.

(2007b) "Ciceronian Scholarship in the Latin Classroom," in Ancona (2007): 71–89.
May, R. (2010) "The Function of Verse Quotations in Apulius' Speeches: Making the Case with Plato," in Berry and Erskine (2010): 175–192.
Mayer, R. (2001) *Tacitus Dialogus de Oratoribus*, Cambridge.
(2003) "Plinius and the *Gloria Dicendi*," in Morello and Gibson (2003):227–34.
(2005) "The Early Empire: AD 14–68," in Harrison (2005): 58–68.
McCormick, S. (2014) "Argument by Comparison: an Ancient Typology," *Rhetorica* 32.2:148–64.
McDermott, W. C. (1970) "In Ligarianam," *TAPhA* 101:317–47.
(1972a) "Cicero's Publication of his Consular Orations," *Philologus* 116:277–84.
(1972b) "M. Cicero and M. Tiro," *Historia* 21:259–86.
McDonnell, M. (1996) "Writing, Copying, and Autograph Manuscripts in Ancient Rome," *CQ* 46.2:469–91.
McGill, S. (2005) "Seneca the Elder on Plagiarizing Cicero's Verrines," *Rhetorica* 23.4:337–46.
(2010) "Plagiarism as Imitation? The Case of Abronius Silo in Seneca's the Elder's *Suasoriae* 2.19-20," *Arethusa* 43.1:113–31.
(2012) *Plagiarism in Antiquity*, Cambridge.
McKeown, J. C. (1989) *Ovid: Amores. Text, Prolegomena and Commentary*, Leeds: Francis Cairns.
McNelis, C. (2007) "Grammarians and Rhetoricians," in Dominik and Hall (2007):285–96.
Melchior, A. (2008) "Twinned Fortunes and the Publication of Cicero's *Pro Milone*," *CPh* 103.3:282–97.
Mellor, R. (1993) *Tacitus*, New York, London: Routledge.
Merello, M. (1977) "Statilio Massimo," *Studi e Ricerche dell'Istituto di Latino Facoltà di Lettere Università di Genova* 1:113–36.
Mertens, P. (1987) "Les papyrus littéraires latins d'auteurs classiques durant les deux dernières décennies," in Janeras (1987): 189–204.
Michel, A. (1992) "*Aulu-Gelle et Cicéron*," in AA.VV. *Au miroir de la culture antique*, Mélanges offerts au prèsident Renè Marache, Rennes Presses Universitaires de Rennes:355–60.
Migliario, E. (2007) *Retorica e Storia. Una lettura delle Suasoriae di Seneca Padre*, Bari: Edipuglia.
Millar, F. (1961) "Some Speeches in Cassius Dio," *MH* 18: 11–22.
(1964) *A Study of Cassius Dio*, Oxford.
(1988) "Cornelius Nepos, Atticus and the Roman Revolution," *G & R* 35: 40–55.
Miller, J., Prosser, M. H., Benson, T. W. (1973) (eds.) *Readings in Medieval Rhetoric*, Bloomington: University of Indiana Press.
Miller, J. F., Damon, C., Myers, K. S. (2002) (eds.) *Vertis in usum. Studies in Honor of E. Courtney*, Munich: De Gruyter.
Miller, P. A. (2015) "Placing the Self in the Field of Truth: Irony and Self-Fashioning in Ancient and Postmodern Rhetorical Theory," *Arethusa* 48.3:313–37.

Miller, W. (1913) *Cicero De Officiis*, London, New York: Heinemann.
Mindt, N. (2014) "Cicero und Seneca d. J. in den Epigrammen Martials," *Gymnasium* 121: 69–89.
Minnen, van P., Worp, K. A. (1993) "The Greek and Latin Literary Texts from Hermopolis," *GRBS* 34.2:151–86.
Moatti, C. (2015) *The Birth of Critical Thinking in Republican Rome*, New York: Cambridge.
Möller, M. (2004) *Talis oratio-qualis vita. Zu Theorie und Praxis mimetischer Verfahren in der griechisch-römischen Literaturkritik*, Heidelberg: Universitätsverlag Winter.
Moles, J. L. (1988) *Plutarch. The Life of Cicero*, Warminster: Liverpool University Press.
Mommsen, Th. (1861) "Handschriftliches," *RhM* 16:135–47.
Montague, H. W. (1992) "Advocacy and Politics: the Paradox of Cicero's *pro Ligario*," *AJPh* 113.4:559–74.
Montana, F. (2011) "The Making of Greek Scholiastic *Corpora*," in Montanari and Pagani (2011):105–61.
Montana, F., Porro, A. (2014) (eds.) *The Birth of Scholiography. From Types to Texts*, Trends in Classics 6.1, Berlin, New York: De Gruyter.
Montanari, F. (1993) (ed.) *La philologie grecque à l'époque Hellénistique et Romaine, Entretiens 40*, Vandoeuvres-Genève: Fondation Hardt.
  (2011) "Correcting a Copy, Editing a Text. Alexandrian Ekdosis and Papyri," in Montanari and Pagani (2011): 1–15.
Montanari, F., Matthaios, S., Rengakos, A. (2015) (eds.) *Brill's Companion to Ancient Greek Scholarship*, 2 vols., Leiden, Boston: Brill.
Montanari, F., Pagani, L. (2011) (eds.) *From Scholars to Scholia. Chapters in the History of Ancient Greek Scholarship*, Berlin, New York: De Gruyter.
Montecalvo, M. S. (2014) *Cicerone in Cassio Dione. Elementi biografici e fortuna dell'opera*, Lecce: Pensa Multimedia.
Mordeglia, C. (2016) "I *Synonyma Ciceronis*. Storia di una falsa attribuzione e aggiornamenti critici," in De Paolis (2016): 55–77.
Moreau, P. (1980) "Cicéron, Clodius et la publication du *pro Murena*," *REL* 58: 220–37.
Morello, R., Gibson, R. (2003) (eds.) "Re-Imagining Pliny the Younger," *Arethusa* 36.2: 110–262.
Morello, R., Morrison, A. D. (2007) (eds.) *Ancient Letters. Classical and Late Antique Epistolography*, Oxford.
Moretti, G. (2009) "Cicerone allegorico: la metamorfosi del personaggio storico in paradigma dell'eloquenza romana," in Pernot (2009):153–65.
Moretti, G., Torre, C., Zanetto, G. (2009) (eds.) *Debita dona. Studi in onore di I. Gualandri*, Naples: M. D'Auria.
Morgan, L. (2000) "The Autopsy of C. Asinius Pollio," *JRS* 90: 51–69.
  (2007) "*Natura narratur*: Tullius Laurea's Elegy for Cicero (Pliny, *Nat.* 31.8)," in Heyworth (2007):113–40.
Morgan, T. (1998a) *Literate Education in the Hellenistic and Roman Worlds*, Cambridge.

(1998b) "A Good Man Skilled in Politics: Quintilian's Political Theory," in Too and Livingstone (1998):245–62.
Moroni, B. (2009) "Lettori di Cicerone nella cancelleria imperiale tra IV e V secolo," in Moretti, Torre, and Zanetto (2009):349–71
Morstein-Marx, R. (2004) *Mass Oratory and Political Power in the Late Roman Republic*, Cambridge.
Mortensen, D. E. (2008) "The *Loci* of Cicero," *Rhetorica* 26.1: 31–56.
Most, G. (1999) (ed.) *Commentaries-Kommentare*, Göttingen: Vandenhoeck & Ruprecht.
Mountford, J. F. (1925) *Quotations from Classical Authors in Medieval Latin Glossaries*, New York, London: Cornell University Press.
Mountford, J. F., Schultz, J. T. (1930) *Index rerum et nominum in scholiis Servii et Aelii Donati tractatorum*, Ithaca: Cornell University Press.
Moussy, C. (2000) (ed.) *De lingua Latina novae quaestiones*, Louvain: Peeters.
Müller, C. (2015) (ed.) *Conflict/Dialogue? Augustine's Engagement with Cultures in "De civitate Dei,"* Würzburg: Augustinus bei echter.
Murgia, Ch. (1985) "Pliny's Letters and the *Dialogus*," *HSPh* 89: 171–206.
(2003) "The Dating of Servius Revisited," *CPh* 98: 45–69.
(2004) "The Truth about Virgil's Commentators," in Rees (2004): 189–200.
Murphy, J. J. (1987) *Quintilian on the Teaching of Speaking and Writing, Translations from Books One, Two, and Ten of the Institutio Oratoria*, Carbondale: Southern Illinois University Press.
(1990a) (ed.) *A Short History of Writing Instruction from Ancient Greece to Twentieth-Century America*, Davis: Routledge.
(1990b) "Roman Writing Instruction as Described by Quintilian," in Murphy (1990a): 19–76.
Murphy, T. (1998) "Cicero's First Readers: Epistolary Evidence for the Dissemination of His Works," *CQ* 48.2: 492–505.
Narducci, E. (1997a) *Cicerone e l'eloquenza romana*, Bari, Rome: Laterza.
(1997b) "Perceptions of Exile in Cicero: the Philosophical Interpretation of a Real Experience," *AJPh* 118: 55–73.
(1998) *Marco Tullio Cicerone. La casa*, Milan: Biblioteca Universale Rizzoli.
(2002a) "*Brutus*: the History of Roman Eloquence," in May (2002a): 401–425.
(2002b) "*Orator* and the Definition of the Ideal Orator," in May (2002a): 427–443.
(2003a) (ed.) *Aspetti della fortuna di Cicerone nella cultura latina*, Florence: Le Monnier.
(2003b) "Cicerone nella *Pharsalia* di Lucano," in Narducci (2003a): 78–91.
(2004) (ed.) *Cicerone tra antichi e moderni*, Florence: Le Monnier.
(2006) (ed.) *Cicerone nella tradizione europea. Dalla tarda antichità al Settecento*, Florence: Le Monnier.
Nesholm, E. J. (2009–2010) "Language and Artistry in Cicero's *Pro Archia*," *CW* 103:477–90.
Neumeister, Chr. (1964) *Grundsätze der forensischen Rhetorik gezeigt an Gerichtsreden Ciceros*, Munich: Hueber.

Nicolai, R. (1992) *La storiografia nell'educazione antica*, Pisa: Giardini.
  (2007) "The Place of History in the Ancient World," in Marincola (2007): 13–26.
Nichols, M. F. (2017) *Author and Audience in Vitruvius' De Architectura*, Cambridge.
Nicholson, J. (1992) *Cicero's Return from Exile. The Orations Post Reditum*, New York: P. Lang.
  (1994) "The Delivery and Confidentiality of Cicero's Letters," *CJ* 90: 33–63.
Niebuhr, B. G. (1820) *M. Tulli Ciceronis Orationum pro M. Fonteio et pro C. Rabirio fragmenta*, Rome.
Nisbet, R. G. M. (1961) *M. Tulli Ciceronis In L. Calpurnium Pisonem oratio*, Oxford.
  (1965) "The Speeches," in Dorey (1965): 47–64.
  (1990) "Cola and Clausulae in Cicero's Speeches," in Craik (1990):349–59.
  (1992) "The Orator and the Reader: Manipulation and Response in Cicero's Fifth Verrine," in Woodman and Powell (1992): 1–18.
Nixon, C. V. E., Rodgers, B. S. (1994) *In Praise of Later Roman Emperors. The Panegyrici Latini*, Berkeley, Los Angeles, Oxford: University of California Press.
Nocchi, F. R. (2013) *Tecniche teatrali e formazione dell'oratore in Quintiliano*, Berlin, Boston: De Gruyter.
Nótári, T. (2008) *Law, Religion and Rhetoric in Cicero's Pro Murena*, Passau: Schenk Verlag.
Novokhatko, A. A. (2009) *The Invectives of Sallust and Cicero*, Berlin, New York: De Gruyter.
Nünlist R. (2009), *The Ancient Critic at Work. Terms and Concepts of Literary Criticism in Greek Scholia*, Cambridge.
O'Donnell, J. J. (2015) "Augustine – Cicero 'Redivivus'," in Müller (2015):103–14.
Olechowska, E. (1984) *Pro Plancio et Pro Rabirio Postumo. La transmission des textes*, Wroclaw: Polskiej Akademii Nauk.
Orelli, J. C., Baiter, J. G. (1833) *M.Tulli Ciceronis opera quae supersunt omnia ac deperditorum fragmenta*, V.2, Zurich: Io. Mueller.
Orelli, J. C., Baiter, J. G., Halm, C. (1845) *M.Tulli Ciceronis opera quae supersunt omnia ac deperditorum fragmenta*, Zurich: Io. Mueller.
Ott, F.-T. (2013) *Die Zweite Philippica als Flugschrift in der späten Republik*, Berlin, Boston: De Gruyter.
Pack, R. A. (1965) *The Greek and Latin Literary Texts from Graeco-Roman Egypt*, Ann Arbor: University of Michigan Press.
Págan, V. E. (2012) (ed.) *A Companion to Tacitus*, Malden: Wiley-Blackwell.
Pagani, L. (2015) "Language Correctness (Hellenismos) and Its Criteria," in Montanari, Matthaios, and Rengakos (2015): I. 798–849.
Papaioannou, S., Serafim, A., Da Vela, B. (2017) (eds.) *The Theatre of Justice. Aspects of Performance in Greco-Roman Oratory and Rhetoric*, Leiden: Brill.
Parker, H. N. (2009) "Books and Reading Latin Poetry," in Johnson and Parker (2009): 186–229.

Pasquali, G. (1952) *Storia della tradizione e critica del testo*, Florence: Le Monnier.
Paterson, J. (2004) "Self-Reference in Cicero's Forensic Speeches," in Powell and Paterson (2004): 79–95.
Patimo, V. M. (2009) *La Pro Cluentio di Cicerone. Introduzione e commento dei §§ 1–81*, Nordhausen: Verlag T. Bautz.
Pecere, O. (1982) "La *subscriptio* di Statilio Massimo e la tradizione delle *Agrarie* di Cicerone," *IMU* 25: 73–123.
  (1986) "La tradizione dei testi latini tra IV e V secolo attraverso i libri sottoscritti," in Giardina (1986), 4: 19–81; 210–46.
  (2010) "Il manoscritto dell'autore latino: un sondaggio," in Perrin (2010): 79–90.
Pecere, O., Reeve, M. D. (1995) (eds.) *Formative Stages of Classical Traditions: Latin Texts from Antiquity to the Renaissance*, Spoleto: Centro Italiano di Studi sull'Alto Medioevo.
Peirano, I. (2012) *The Rhetoric of the Roman Fake. Latin Pseudepigrapha in Context*, Cambridge.
Pellizzari, A. (2003) *Servio. Storia, cultura e istituzioni nell'opera di un grammatico tardoantico*, Florence: L. S. Olschki.
Pepe, C., Moretti, G. (2014) (eds.) *Le parole dopo la morte. Forme e funzioni della retorica funeraria nella tradizione greca e romana*, Trento: Università degli Studi di Trento.
Perlwitz, O. (1992) *Titus Pomponius Atticus. Untersuchungen zur Person eines Einflussreichen Ritters in der Ausgehenden Römischen Republik*, Stuttgart: Franz Steiner Verlag.
Pernot, L. (2009) (ed.) *New Chapters in the History of Rhetoric*, Leiden, Boston: Brill.
Perrin, Y. (2010) (ed.) *Neronia VIII. Bibliothèques, livres et culture écrite dans l'empire romain de César à Hadrien*, Brussels: Latomus.
Perry, E. E. (2000) "Notes on *Diligentia* as a Term of Roman Art Criticism," *CPh* 95.4:445–58.
Peterson, W. (1901) *Collations from the Codex Cluniacensis s. Holkhamicus, a Ninth-Century Manuscript of Cicero, Anecdota Oxoniensia*, Oxford.
  (1903) "Emendations of Cicero's *Verrines*," *CR* 17: 198–202.
  (1910) "Cicero's Post Reditum and Other Speeches," *CQ* 4:161–71.
Petersson, T. (1920) *Cicero. A Biography*, Berkeley: University of California Press.
Petrone, G. (1971) *La battuta a sorpresa negli oratori latini*, Palermo: Palumbo.
  (2004) (ed.) *Le passioni della retorica*, Palermo: Palumbo.
Peyron, A. (1824) *M. Tulli Ciceronis orationum pro Scauro, pro Tullio et in Clodium fragmenta inedita*, Stuttgart: Libraria Joannis Georgii Cottae.
Pfeiffer, R. (1968) *History of Classical Scholarship. From the Beginnings to the End of the Hellenistic Age*, Oxford.
Phillips, J. J. (1986) "Atticus and the Publication of Cicero's Works," *CW* 79.4: 227–37.

Piacente, L. (2014) *Cicerone a riflettori spenti. Episodi della tradizione testuale di orazioni ed epistole*, Bari: Edipuglia.
Picone, G. (2008) (ed.) *Clementia Caesaris. Modelli etici, parenesi, e retorica dell'esilio*, Palermo: Palumbo.
Pieroni, P. (2004) *Marcus Verrius Flaccus De significatu verborum in den Auszügen von Sextus Pompeius Festus und Paulus Diaconus: Einleitung und Teilkommentar (154, 19–186, 29 Lindsay)*, Frankfurt am Main: Peter Lang.
Pingoud, J. (2016) "Le théâtre dans les *Petites Déclamations*," in Casamento, Mal, Maeder, and Pasetti (2016):157–89.
Piras, G. (2017) "La prosopopea di Appio Claudio Cicero (Cic. *Cael*. 33–34): tradizione letteraria, memoria familiare e polemica politica," in De Paolis (2017): 63–100.
Pizzani, U. (1968) *Fulgenzio. Definizione di parole antiche*, Rome: Edizioni dell'Ateneo Roma.
Plasberg, O. (1926) *Cicero in seinem Werken und Briefen*, Leipzig: Wissenschaftlische Buchgesellschaft.
Poel (van der), M. (2009) "The Use of *Exempla* in Roman Declamation," *Rhetorica* 27.3:332–53.
Poignault, R., Schneider, C. (2016) (eds.) *Fabrique de la declamation antique (controverses et suasoires)*, Lyon: Maison de l'Orient et de la Méditerranée.
Pomeroy, A. J. (1988) "Livy's Death Notices," *G & R* 25:172–83.
  (1991) *The Appropriate Comment. Death Notices in the Ancient Historians*, Frankfurt am Main, Bern, New York: P. Lang.
Porter, J. J. (1992) "Hermeneutic Lines and Circles: Aristarchus and Crates on the Exegesis of Homer," in Lamberton and Keaney (1992): 67–114.
  (1999) (ed.) *Constructions of the Classical Body*, Ann Arbor: University of Michigan Press.
  (2009) "Rhetoric, Aesthetics, and the Voice," in Gunderson (2009): 92–108.
Porter, S. E. (1997) (ed.) *Handbook of Classical Rhetoric in the Hellenistic Period 330 B.C. –A.D. 400*, Leiden, Boston, Cologne: Brill.
Powell, J. G. F. (2007) (ed.) *Logos. Rational Argument in Classical Rhetoric*, BICS Supplement 76, London: Institute of Classical Studies.
  (2010a) "Court Procedure and Rhetorical Strategy in Cicero," in Berry and Erskine (2010): 21–36.
  (2010b) "Hyperbaton and Register in Cicero," in Dickey and Chahoud (2010): 163–85.
  (2013) "Cicero's Style," in Steel (2013a): 41–72.
Powell, J. G. F., Paterson, J. (2004) (eds.) *Cicero the Advocate*, Oxford.
Prill, P. (1986) "Cicero in Theory and Practice: the Securing of Good Will in the *Exordia* of Five Forensic Speeches," *Rhetorica* 4.2: 93–109.
Prost, F. (2017) *Quintus Cicéron Petit manuel de la campagne électorale. Marcus Cicéron Lettres à son frère Quintus I, 1 et 2*, Paris: Les Belles Lettres.
Puccioni, G. (1960) "Prolegomeni ad una nuova edizione dei frammenti delle orazioni perdute di Cicerone," *Ciceroniana* 2: 97–124.

Pugliarello, M. R. (2009) "A lezione dal *grammaticus*: la lettura degli *auctores*," *Maia* 61: 592–610.
Querzoli, S. (2009) "Giuristi ed esperti di diritto nelle Notti Attiche di Gellio," in Andrisano (2009):146–62.
Quinn, K. (1968) *Virgil's Aeneid*, London: Routledge & K. Paul.
  (1970) *Catullus. The Poems*, London: Routledge & K. Paul.
Rabbie, E. (2007) "Wit and Humor in Roman Rhetoric," in Dominik and Hall (2007):207–17.
Raccanelli, R. (2012) *Cicerone, Post Reditum in Senatu e Ad Quirites. Come disegnare una mappa di relazioni*, Bologna: Pàtron.
Rackham, H. (1938–43) *Pliny Natural History*, 10 vols., Cambridge, MA, London: Harvard University Press.
Radice, B. (1969) *Pliny Letters and Panegyricus, 2 vols.*, Cambridge, MA, London: Harvard University Press.
Radiciotti, P. (1998) "Manoscritti digrafici grecolatini e latinogreci nell'antichità," in Capasso (1998):107–46.
  (2013) "Digrafismo nei papiri latini," in Marganne and Rochette (2013): 57–69.
Radke, G. (ed.) (1968) *Cicero: Ein Mensch seiner Zeit*, Berlin: De Gruyter.
Raina, G. (2008) "*Contendere potius quam sequi (Inst. Or.* 10, 2, 9). Dinamiche del rapporto con i grandi del passato in Quintiliano," in Castagna and Riboldi (2008): 1387–1409.
Ramage, E. S. (1973) *Urbanitas. Ancient Sophistication and Refinement*, Norman: University of Oklahoma Press.
Ramsey, J. T. (2003) *Cicero Philippics I–II*, Cambridge.
  (2007a) *Sallust's Bellum Catilinae*, 2nd ed., Oxford.
  (2007b) "Roman Senatorial Oratory," in Dominik and Hall (2007):122–35.
  (2014) "The Recovery of More Ennius from a Misinformed Ciceronian Scholiast," *CQ* 64.1:160–5.
Rees, R. (2004) (ed.) *Romane Memento. Virgil in the Fourth Century*, London: Bristol Classical Press.
  (2007) "Panegyric," in Dominik and Hall (2007): 136–148.
  (2012) (ed.) *Latin Panegyric*, Oxford.
Reeve, M. D. (1983) "Asconius," in Reynolds (1983):24–5.
  (1984) "Before and after Poggio: Some manuscripts of Cicero's Speeches," *RFIC* 112.3: 266–284.
  (1992) "The Turin Palimpsest of Cicero," *Aevum* 66: 87–94.
Reinhardt, T., Winterbottom, M. (2006) *Quintilian Institutio Oratoria Book 2*, Oxford.
Remer, G. (2017) *Ethics and the Orator: the Ciceronian Tradition of Political Morality*, Chicago: University of Chicago Press.
Renard, M., Schilling, R. (1964) (eds.) *Hommages à Jean Bayet*, Brussels: Latomus.
Renda, C. (2007) *La Pro Sestio fra oratoria e politica*, Soveria Mannelli: Rubbettino.
  (2009) "I riceventi della *pro Sestio:* tre livelli di struttura, lettura, ricezione del testo ciceroniano," in Abbamonte, Miletti, and Spina (2009): 375–389.

Renehan, R. (1976) "A Traditional Pattern of Imitation in Sallust and His Sources," *CPh* 71: 97–105.
Reynolds, L. D. (1983) *Texts and Transmission. A Survey of the Latin Classics*, Oxford.
Reynolds, L. D., Wilson, N. G. (1974) *Scribes and Scholars. A Guide to the Transmission of Greek and Latin Literature*, 2nd ed., Oxford.
Ricchieri, T. (2017) "Emendazioni alle *Verrine* di Cicerone alla luce del commento dello Ps.-Asconio (*Div. Caec.-Verr. 1*)," *RFIC* 145: 75–105.
Ricci, S. (1910) "Un fragment en onciale du 'Pro Plancio' de Cicéron," in *Mèlanges offerts à M. Emile Chatelain*, Paris:442–47.
Richlin, A. (1997) "Gender and Rhetoric: Producing Manhood in the Schools," in Dominik (1997): 74–90.
  (1999) "Cicero's Head," in Porter (1999): 190–211.
Richter, W. (1968) "Das Cicerobild der römischen Kaiserzeit," in Radke (1968): 161–97.
Ridley, R. T. (2013) "Death and the Historian: Livy's *Benignitas*," *Latomus* 72.3: 689–710.
Riedl, P. (2016) "Das Spiel mit der Wirklichkeit. Der Irrealis in Ciceros *Pro Milone*," *RhM* 159.3–4:369–91.
Riesenweber, T. (2015) *C. Marius Victorinus Commenta in Ciceronis Rhetorica. Bd. 1: Prolegomena; Bd. 2: Kritischer Kommentar und Indices*, Berlin, Boston: De Gruyter.
Riggsby, A. M. (1995a) "Self-Fashioning in the Public Eye: Pliny on Cicero and Oratory," *AJPh* 116:123–35.
  (1995b) "Appropriation and Reversal as a Basis for Oratorical Proof," *CPh* 90: 245–56.
  (1998) "Self and Community in the Younger Pliny," *Arethusa* 31: 75–97.
  (1999) *Crime and Community in Ciceronian Rome*, Austin: University of Texas Press.
  (2002) "The *Post Reditum* Speeches," in May (2002a):159–95.
  (2010) *Roman Law and the Legal World of the Romans*, Cambridge.
  (2015) "Roman Legal Education," in Bloomer (2015):444–51.
Roca-Puig, R. (1977) (ed.) *Cicerò. Catilinàries (I et II in Cat.): Papyri Barcinonenses*, Barcelona: Grafos.
Roche, A. (2011) (ed.) *Pliny's Praise the Panegyricus in the Roman World*, Cambridge.
Rochette, B. (1996) "Papyrologica bilinguia Graeco-Latina," *Aegyptus* 76: 57–79.
  (1997) *Le latin dans le monde grec. Recherches sur la diffusion de la langue et des lettres latines dans les provinces hellénophones de l'Empire romain*, Brussels: Peeters.
  (2013) "Papyrologie latine et bilinguisme gréco-latin: des perspectives nouvelles," in Marganne and Rochette (2013): 11–20.
  (2015) "L'enseignement du Latin à Costantinople: une mise au point," in Haverling (2015):626–39.

Rochlitz, S. (1993) *Das Bild Caesars in Ciceros "Orationes Caesarianae." Untersuchungen zur "clementia" und "sapientia Caesaris,"* Frankfurt am Main: P. Lang.
Rodgers, B. S. (2008) "Catulus' Speech in Cassius Dio 36.31-36," *GRBS* 48: 295–318.
Rolfe, J. C. (1927) *The Attic Nights of Aulus Gellius*, Cambridge, MA, London: Harvard University Press.
Rolfe, J. C., Ramsey, J. T. (2013) *Sallust I: the War with Catiline; the War with Jugurtha*, edited and revised, first published 1921, Cambridge, MA, London: Harvard University Press.
Roller, M. B. (1997) "Color-Blindness: Cicero's Death, Declamation, and the Production of History," *CPh* 92.2:109–30.
  (2004) "Exemplarity in Roman Culture: the Case of Horatius Cocles and Cloelia," *CPh* 99.1: 1–56.
  (2009) "The Exemplary Past in Roman Historiography and Culture," in Feldherr (2009):214–30.
  (2011) "To Whom Am I Speaking? The Changing Venues of Competitive Eloquence in the Early Empire," in Blösel and Hölkeskamp (2011): 197–221.
Romanini, F. (2007) *Malli Theodori De Metris*, Hildesheim: Olms.
Romano, E. (2003) "Il ruolo di Cicerone nella formazione di una cultura tecnica," in Narducci (2003a): 92–111.
Ronconi, A. (1981) *Da Omero a Dante: scritti di varia filologia*, Urbino: Argalìa.
Ronconi, F. (1998) *"De optimo genere oratorum*: storia di un abbozzo," *ARF* 1: 43–68.
Rosati, G. (2012) "Mecenate senza poeti, poeti senza Mecenate: la distruzione di un mito augusteo," in Bastianini, Lapini, and Tulli (2012):405–24
Rosellini, M. (2011) "Le citazioni latine nel lessico sintattico del libro XVIII di Prisciano (GL, III, 278, 13–377, 18)," *MD* 67:183–99.
Rosillo López, C. (2013), "The Common (Mediocris) Orator of the Late Republic: the Scribonii Curiones," in Steel and Blom (2013):287–98.
  (2017) (ed.) *Political Communication in the Roman World*, Leiden: Brill.
Rouse, R. H., Reeve, M. D. (1983) "Cicero. Speeches," in Reynolds (1983): 54–98.
Rouse, R. H., Rouse, M. A. (1976) "The *Florilegium Angelicum*: its Origin, Content, and Influence," in Alexander and Gibson (1976): 66–114.
Rowe, G. O. (1997) "Style," in Porter (1997):121–57.
Russell, D. A. (1983) *Greek Declamation*, Cambridge.
  (2001) *Quintilian. The Orator's Education*, 5 vols., Cambridge, MA, London: Harvard University Press.
Rutella, F. (1977) "Chi fu Flavio Capro," *Studi e Ricerche Istituto Latino Genova*, 1: 143–59.
Rutledge, S. H. (2012) "Tacitus' *Dialogus de Oratoribus*: A Socio-Cultural History," in Págan (2012): 62–83.
Sabbadini, R. (1971) *Storia e critica di testi latini*, Padua: Antenore.

Salomies, O. (1997) "Quotations from Cicero's Speeches in the Commentaires of Donatus and Servius," in Vaahtera and Vainio (1997):126–35.
Sánchez-Ostiz, A. (2013) "Cicero Graecus: Notes on Ciceronian Papyri from Egypt," *ZPE* 187:144–53.
Sanders, E., Johncock, M. (2016) (eds.) *Emotion and Persuasion in Classical Antiquity*, Stuttgart: Franz Steiner Verlag.
Santalucia, B. (2009) (ed.) *La repressione criminale nella Roma repubblicana fra norma e persuasione*, Pavia: IUSS Press.
Santini, P. (2006) *L'auctoritas linguistica di Cicerone nelle "Notti Attiche" di Aulo Gellio*, Naples: Loffredo.
Savage, J. J. (1941) "Catilina in Vergil and Cicero," *CJ* 36.1:225–6.
Sblendorio Cugusi, M. T. (1982) *M. Porci Catonis Orationum Reliquiae*, Turin: Paravia.
Scappaticcio, M. C. (2015) *Artes Grammaticae in frammenti. I testi grammaticali latini e bilingui greco-latini su papiro*, Berlin, Boston: De Gruyter.
Schad, S. (2007) *A Lexicon of Latin Grammatical Terminology*, Pisa, Rome: F. Serra.
Schanz, M. (1966–71) *Geschichte der römischen Literatur bis zum Gesetzgebungswerk des Kaisers Justinian*, 4th ed. revised by C. Hosius and G. Krüger, 4 vols, Munich: Beck.
Schenkeveld, D. M. (1993) "Scholarship and Grammar," in Montanari (1993): 263–301.
  (2004) *A Rhetorical Grammar. C. Iulius Romanus, Introduction to the Liber De Adverbio as Incorporated in Charisius' Ars Grammatica II.13*, Leiden, Boston: Brill.
Schilling, B. (1892) *De Scholiis Bobiensibus*, Leipzig: Teubner.
Schmeling, G. (2011) *A Commentary on the Satyrica of Petronius*, Oxford.
Schmidt, P. L. (1989) "Volcacius? Commentarii in Orationes Ciceronis (Scholia Bobiensia)," in Herzog and Schmidt (1989):140–42 (§ 526.1).
  (1993) "De honestis et nove veterum dictis: die Autorität der veteres von Nonius Marcellus bis zu Matheus Vindocinensis," in Vosskamp (1993):366–88.
  (1997a) "Flavius Caper," in Herzog and Schmidt (1997):232–56 (§ 438).
  (1997b) "Statilius Maximus," in Herzog and Schmidt (1997):256–8 (§ 445.3).
Schmiedeberg, P. (1905) *De Asconii codicibus et de Ciceronis scholiis Sangallensibus*, Vratislaviae: Grass.
Schmitzer, U. (2000) *Velleius Paterculus und das Interesse an der Geschichte im Zeitalter des Tiberius*, Heidelberg: Universitätsverlag Winter.
Schofield, M. (2013) "Writing Philosophy," in Steel (2013a): 73–87.
Schubert, P. (2012) "L'apport des papyrus grecs et latins d'Égypte romaine," in Schubert (2012a):243–71.
  (2012a) (ed.) *Les Grecs hèritiers des Romains*, Entretiens 59, Vandoeuvres-Genève: Fondation Hardt.
Schulz, V. (2016) "Rhetoric and Medicine – The Voice of the Orator in Two Ancient Discourses," *Rhetorica* 34.2:141–62.

Schurgacz, K. (2004) *Die Declamatio in L. Sergium Catilinam*, Trier: Wissenschaftlicher Verlag.
Schütz, Ch. G. (1823) *M.Tullii Ciceronis Opera quae supersunt omnia ac deperditorum fragmenta, 16.3*, Leipzig: Gerhard Fleischer.
Schwerdtner, K. (2015) *Plinius und seine Klassiker. Studien zur literarischen Zitation in den Pliniusbriefen*, Berlin, Boston: De Gruyter.
Sciarrino, E. (2004) "Putting Cato the Censor's *Origines* in Its Place," *ClAnt* 23.2: 323–57.
 (2007) "Roman Oratory before Cicero: the Elder Cato and Gaius Gracchus," in Dominik and Hall (2007): 54–66.
 (2011) *Cato the Censor and the Beginnings of Latin Prose: From Poetic Translation to Elite Transcription*, Columbus: The Ohio State University Press.
Scourfield, D. (2007) (ed.) *Texts and Culture in Late Antiquity. Inheritance, Authority, and Change*, Wales: Classical Press of Wales.
Seider, R. (1975) *Zur Paläographie des Giessener Ciceropapyrus*, Giessen: Universitätsbibliothek Giessen.
 (1979) "Beiträge zur Geschichte und Paläographie der antiken Cicerohandschriften," *B&W* 13:101–49.
Setaioli, A. (1976) "On the Date of Publication of Cicero's Letters to Atticus," *SO* 51:105–20.
 (2003) "Seneca e Cicerone," in Narducci (2003a): 55–77.
Settle, J. N. (1962) *The Publication of Cicero's Orations*, Chapel Hill: University of North Carolina Press.
 (1963) "The Trial of Milo and the other Pro Milone," *TAPhA* 94:268–80.
Shackleton Bailey, D. R. (1965–1970) (ed. and comm.) *Cicero's Letters to Atticus*, 7 vols., Cambridge.
 (1986) "*Nobiles* and *Novi* Reconsidered," *AJPh* 107: 255–260.
 (1991) *Cicero Back from Exile: Six Speeches upon his Return*, Atlanta: Scholars Press.
 (2009) (ed.) *Cicero Orations Philippics*, revised by J. T. Ramsey and G. Manuwald, 2 vols., Cambridge, MA, London: Harvard University Press.
Sherwin-White, A. N. (1966) *The Letters of Pliny. A Historical and Social Commentary*, Oxford.
Shipley, F. W. (1924) *Velleius Paterculus. Compendium of Roman History*, Cambridge, MA, London: Harvard University Press.
Siani-Davies M. (2001) *Cicero's Speech Pro Rabirio Postumo*, Oxford.
Sidwell, K. (2002) (ed.) *Pleiades Setting. Essays for Pat Cronin on his 65th Birthday*, Cork: Department of Ancient Classics, University College Cork.
Sinclair, P. (1994) "Political Declensions in Latin Grammar and Oratory 55 BCE–CE 39," *Ramus* 23.1–2:92–109.
Slater, N. W. (2017) (ed.) *Voice and Voices in Antiquity*, Leiden: Brill.
Sluiter, I., Rosen, R. M. (2012) (eds.) *Aesthetic Value in Classical Antiquity*, Leiden, Boston: Brill.
Small, J. P. (2007) "Memory and the Roman Orator," in Dominik and Hall (2007): 195–206.

Smith, Chr.-Covino, R. (2011) (eds.) *Praise and Blame in Roman Republican Rhetoric*, Swansea: Classical Press of Wales.
Sommer, R. (1926) "T. Pomponius Atticus und die Verbreitung von Ciceros Werken," *Hermes* 61: 389–422.
Springer, C. P. E. (2017) *Cicero in Heaven: the Roman Rhetor and Luther's Reformation*, Leiden, Boston: Brill.
Squillante Saccone, M. (1985) *Le Interpretationes Vergilianae di Tiberio Claudio Donato*, Naples: Società Editrice Napoletana.
Stangl, Th. (1884a) "Zur Textkritik der Scholiasten ciceronischer Reden," *RhM* 39: 231–238; 428–445;566–80.
  (1884b) *Der sogennante Gronovscholiast zu elf ciceronischen Reden*, Leipzig: Kessinger Publishing.
  (1905–1906) "Zur Textkritik des Gronovoschen Ciceroscholiasten," *Wochenschr. Klass. Philol.* 1905:443–5; 1906:360–66; 382–391; 471–77.
  (1909) *Pseudoasconiana. Textgestaltung und Sprache der anonymen Scholien zu Cicero vier ersten Verrinen*, Paderborn: F. Schöningh.
  (1910) "Bobiensia. Neue Beiträge zu den Bobiensier Cicero-Scholien 1.," *RhM* 65: 88–120.
Starr, R. J. (1987) "The Circulation of Literary Texts in the Roman World," *CQ* 37:213–23.
Steel, C. E. W. (2001), *Cicero, Rhetoric and Empire*, Oxford.
  (2003) "Cicero's *Brutus*: the End of Oratory and the Beginning of History?," *BICS* 46: 195–211.
  (2005) *Reading Cicero. Genre and Performance in Late Republican Rome*, London: Bristol Classical Press.
  (2006) *Roman Oratory*, Cambridge.
  (2012) "Cicero's Autobiography: Narratives of Success in the Pre-Consular Orations," *Cahiers Glotz* 23:251–66.
  (2013a) (ed.) *The Cambridge Companion to Cicero*, Cambridge.
  (2013b) "Cicero, Oratory and Public Life," in Steel (2013a):160–70.
  (2013c) "Oratory," in Erskine (2013): 67–76.
  (2017a) "Speech without Limits: Defining Informality in Republican Oratory," in Papaioannou, Serafim, and Da Vela (2017): 75–88.
  (2017b) "Defining Public Speech in the Roman Republic: Occasion, Audience and Purpose," in Rosillo and López (2017): 17–33.
Steel, C. E. W., Blom, H. van der (2013) (eds.) *Community and Communication. Oratory and Politics in Republican Rome*, Oxford.
Stella, C., Valvo, A. (1996) (eds.) *Studi in onore di A. Garzetti*, Brescia: Ateneo di Brescia.
Stem, R. (2012), *The Political Biographies of Cornelius Nepos*, Ann Arbor: University of Michigan Press.
Stevenson, A. J. (2004) "Gellius and the Roman Antiquarian Tradition," in Holford-Strevens and Vardi (2004):118–55.
Stevenson, T., Wilson, M. (2008) (eds.) *Cicero's Philippics: History, Rhetoric, and Ideology*, Auckland, N.Z.: Polygraphia.

Stone, A. M. (1980) "*Pro Milone:* Cicero's Second Thoughts," *Antichthon* 14: 88–111.
Stok, F. (2013) (ed.) *Totus scientia plenus. Percorsi dell'esegesi virgiliana antica*, Pisa: ETS.
Stramaglia, A. (2016) "The Hidden Teacher. Metarhetoric in Ps.-Quintilian's *Major Declamations*," in Dinter, Guérin, and Martinho (2016): 25–48.
Strezlecki, W. (1961) "Volcacius," in *RE*, IX.A.1 (Stuttgart): 758.
Stroh, W. (1975) *Taxis und Taktik. Die advokatische Dispositionkunst in Ciceros Gerichtreden*, Stuttgart: Teubner.
  (1983) "Ciceros demosthenische Redezyklen," *MH* 40: 35–50.
  (2004) "De *Domo Sua*: Legal Problem and Structure," in Powell and Paterson (2004):313–70.
Stroup, S. C. (2003) "*Adulta Virgo*: the Personification of Textual Eloquence in Cicero's *Brutus*," *MD* 50: 115–140.
  (2010) *Catullus, Cicero, and a Society of Patrons*, Cambridge.
Stucchi, S. (2013) "Notazioni sul concetto di *elegantia* in Cicerone," *Latomus* 72.3: 642–59.
Suringar, W. H. D. (1834) *Historia critica scholiastarum Latinorum*, Leiden: S. J. Luchtmans.
Sussman, L. (1978) *The Elder Seneca*, Leiden: Brill.
Sutton, E. W., Rackham, H. (1942) *Cicero. On the Orator Books 1–2*, Cambridge, MA, London: Harvard University Press.
Swain, S. (2004) "Bilingualism and Biculturalism in Antonine Rome. Apuleius, Fronto, and Gellius," in Holford, Strevens, and Vardi (2004): 3–40.
Syme, R. (1964) *Sallust*, Berkeley: University of California Press.
Taifacos, I. G. (1983) "The Lexicographical Work of Caesellius Vindex and its Arrangement," *Hermes* 111–4: 501–5.
Takàcs, L. (2005) "Metamorphosis and Disruption. Comments on Seneca's 114th *Epistula Moralis*," *AAH* 45: 399–411.
Tamburi, F. (2013) *Il ruolo del giurista nelle testimonianze della letteratura romana. I. Cicerone*, Naples: Edizioni Scientifiche Italiane.
Tandoi, V. (1992) "Medicina e politica (da Platone a Cic. De rep. IV 1 e all'-*Epistola ad Octavianum*)," in Id., *Scritti di filologia*, Pisa, I:287–98
Taoka, Y. (2011) "Quintilian, Seneca, *Imitatio*: Re-Reading *Institutio Oratoria* 10. 1.125-131," *Arethusa* 44:123–37.
Tarrant, R. J. (1995) "Classical Latin Literature," in Greetham (1995): 95–148.
  (2012) *Virgil Aeneid Book XII*, Cambridge.
Tatum, W. J. (1988) "Catullus' Criticism of Cicero in Poem 49," *TAPhA* 118: 179–84.
  (1999) *The Patrician Tribune: Publius Clodius Pulcher*, Chapel Hill: University of North Carolina Press.
Taylor, D. J. (1987) (ed.) *The History of Linguistics in the Classical Period*, Amsterdam, Philadelphia: John Benjamins Publishing.
Taylor, J. H. (1952) "Political Motives in Cicero's Defense of Archias," *AJPh* 73.1: 62–70.

Taylor, L. R. (1964) "Cornelius Nepos and the Publication of Cicero's Letters to Atticus," in Renard and Schilling (1964):678–81.
Taylor-Briggs, R. (2006) "Reading Between the Lines: the Textual History and Manuscript Transmission of Cicero's Rhetorical Works," in Cox and Ward (2006): 77–108.
Tedeschi, A. (2005) *Lezione di buon governo per un dittatore. Cicerone, Pro Marcello: saggio di commento*, Bari: Edipuglia.
Tellegen-Couperus, O. (2003) (ed.) *Quintilian and the Law. The Art of Persuasion in Law and Politics*, Leuven: Leuven University Press.
Tempest, K. L. (2007) "Cicero and the Art of *Dispositio:* the Structure of the *Verrines*," *LICS* 6.02.
  (2011) "Combating the Odium of Self-Praise: the *Divinatio* in Q. Caecilium," in Smith and Covino (2011):145–63.
  (2013) "Staging a Prosecution: Aspects of Performance in Cicero's *Verrines*," in Kremmydas, Powell, and Rubinstein (2013): 41–71.
Testard, M. (1985) "Observations sur la rhétorique d'une harangue au peuple dans le *Sermo contra Auxentium* de Saint Ambroise," *REL* 63: 123–209.
Thilo, G. (1881) *Servi Grammatici qui feruntur in Vergilii Carmina Commentarii*, Lipsiae (repr. Hildesheim 1961): Teubner.
Thomas, R. (1988) *Virgil Georgics, 2 vols.*, Cambridge, New York, Sydney: Cambridge University Press.
Throop, G. R. (1913) "Ancient Literary Detractors of Cicero," *WUS* 1.2: 19–41.
Timpanaro, S. (1986) *Per la storia della filologia virgiliana antica*, Rome: Salerno.
  (2001) *Virgilianisti antichi e tradizione indiretta*, Florence: Olschki.
Titchener, F. (2003) "Cornelius Nepos and the Biographical Tradition," *G & R* 50.1: 85–99.
Too, Y. L. (2001) (ed.) *Education in Greek and Roman Antiquity*, Leiden: Brill.
Too, Y. L., Livingstone, N. (1998) (eds.) *Pedagogy and Power. Rhetorics of Classical Learning*, Cambridge.
Tyrrell, B. W. M. (1978) *A Legal and Historical Commentary to Cicero's Oratio Pro C. Rabirio Perduellionis Reo*, Amsterdam: Hakkert.
Tyrrell, R. Y., Purser, L. C. (1901–33) *The Correspondence of M. Tullius Cicero, 7 vols*, Dublin: Hodges, Foster, & Figgis.
Tzounakas, S. (2009) "The Peroration of Cicero's *Pro Milone*," *CW* 102:129–41.
Uhl, A. (1998) *Servius als Sprachlehrer: zur Sprachrichtigkeit in der exegetischen Praxis des spätantiken Grammatikerunterrichts*, Göttingen: Vandenhoeck & Ruprecht.
Urìa, J. (2012), "Iulius Romanus and Statilius Maximus (Char. *Gramm.* 252, 14–31): A Reappraisal," *MD* 69.2:225–38.
Vaahtera, J., Vainio, R. (1997) (eds.) *Utriusque linguae peritus. Studia in honorem Toivo Viljamaa*, Turku: Turun Yliopisto.
Vainio, R. (2000) "Use and Function of Grammatical Examples in Roman Grammarians," *Mnemosyne* 53.1: 30–48.

Van der Wal, R. L. (2007) "What a Funny Consul We Have! Cicero's Dealings with Cato Uticensis and Prominent Friends in Opposition," in Booth (2007): 183–205.
Vardi, G. (2001) "Gellius against the Professors," *ZPE* 137: 41–54.
Vasaly, A. (1985) "The Masks of Rhetoric: Cicero's *Pro Roscio Amerino*," *Rhetorica* 3.1: 1–20.
  (1993) *Representations. Images of the World in Ciceronian Oratory*, Berkeley, Los Angeles, Oxford: University of California Press.
  (2002) "Cicero's Early Speeches," in May (2002a): 71–111.
  (2009) "Cicero, Domestic Politics, and the First Action of the *Verrines*," *CA* 28.1:101–37.
  (2015) *Livy's Political Philosophy. Power and Personality in Early Rome*, Cambridge.
Vessey, D. W. T. C. (1994) "Aulus Gellius and the Cult of the Past," *ANRW* II.34.2:1863–917.
Vickers, B. (1982) (ed.) *Rhetoric Revalued*, Binghamton, New York: Center for Medieval & Early Renaissance Studies.
Vitale, M. T. (1977) "Cesellio Vindice," *Studi e Ricerche Istituto Latino Genova*, 1: 221–58.
Vlastos, G. (1991) *Socrates, Ironist and Moral Philosopher*, Ithaca: Cornell University Press.
Vössing, K. (2008) "Mit Manuskript in den Senat!: zu Cic. *Planc.* 74," *RhM* 151, 1: 143–50.
Vogt-Spira, G. (1990) *Strukturen der Mündlichkeit in der römischen Literatur*, Tübingen: Gunter Narr Verlag.
Volk, K. (2009) *Manilius and his Intellectual Background*, Oxford.
Volk, K., Zetzel, J. E. G. (2015) "Laurel, Tongue and Glory (Cicero *De Consulatu Suo* Fr. 6 Soubiran)," *CQ* 65.1:204–23.
Vosskamp, W. (1993) (ed.) *Klassik im Vergleich: Normativität und Historizität europäischer Klassiken*, Stuttgart: Metzler.
Vretska K. (1976) *C. Sallustius Crispus De Catilinae Coniuratione*, 2 vols., Heidelberg: Carl Winter Universitatsverlag.
Walters, B. (2017) "The Circulation and Delivery of Cicero's *Post Reditum ad Populum*," *TAPhA* 147: 79–99.
Ward, J. O. (2015) "What the Middle Ages Missed of Cicero, and Why?," in Altman (2015):307–26.
Watts, N. H. (1979) *Cicero Pro Archia Post Reditum ad Quirites Post Reditum in Senatu De Domo Sua De Haruspicum Responsis Pro Plancio*, Cambridge, MA, London: Harvard University Press.
Webb, R. (1997a) "Imagination and the Arousal of the Emotions in Greco-Roman Rhetoric," in Braund and Gill (1997):112–27.
  (1997b) "Poetry and Rhetoric," in Porter (1997):339–69.
Weil, B. (1962) *2000 Jahre Cicero*, Zurich: W. Classen.
Weische, A. (1972) *Ciceros Nachahmung der attischen Redner*, Heidelberg: Carl Winter Universitatsverlag.

(1989) "Plinius d. J. und Cicero. Untersuchungen zur römischen Epistolographie in Republik und Kaiserzeit," *ANRW II* 33/1 (1989):375–86.
Welch, K., Hillard, T. W. (2005) (eds.) *Roman Crossings: Theory and Practice in the Roman Republic*, Swansea: The Classical Press of Wales.
Welsh, J. T. (2010) "The Grammarian C. Iulius Romanus and the *Fabula Togata*," *HSCP* 105:255–85.
Wessner, P. (1920) "Sacer (2)," *RE* 2.2, (Stuttgart):1628–29.
Whitbread, L. G. (1971) *Fulgentius the Mythographer*, Columbus: The Ohio State University Press.
White, D. C. (1980) "The Method of Composition and Sources of Nonius Marcellus," *Studi Noniani* 8: 111–211.
White, P. (2009) "Bookshops in the Literary Culture of Rome," in Johnson and Parker (2009):268–87.
  (2010) *Cicero in Letters. Epistolary Relations of the Late Republic*, Oxford.
Williams, Gareth D. (2003) *Seneca De Otio De Brevitate Vitae*, Cambridge.
  (2015) "Style and Form in Seneca's Writings," in Bartsch and Schiesaro (2015): 135–49.
Williams, Gordon (1978) *Change and Decline. Roman Literature in the Early Empire*, Berkeley, Los Angeles, London: University of California Press.
Williams, Megan Hale (2006) *The Monk and the Book. Jerome and the Making of Christian Scholarship*, Chicago, London: University of Chicago Press.
Willis, W. H. (1963) "A Papyrus Fragment of Cicero," *TAPhA* 94: 321–328.
Wilson, M. (2007) "Rhetoric and the Younger Seneca," in Dominik and Hall (2007):425–38.
  (2008) "Your Writings or Your Life: Cicero's *Philippics* and Declamation," in Stevenson and Wilson 2008:305–34.
Wilson, N. G. (2007) "Scholiasts and Commentators," *GRBS* 47: 39–70.
Winterbottom, M. (1964) "Quintilian and the *Vir Bonus*," *JRS* 54:90–7.
  (1974) *Seneca the Elder. Declamations, 2 vols.*, Cambridge, MA, London: Harvard University Press.
  (1982a) "Cicero and the Silver Age," in Ludwig (1982):236–74.
  (1982b) "Schoolroom and Courtroom," in Vickers (1982): 59–70.
  (1984) *The Minor Declamations Ascribed to Quintilian*, Berlin, New York: De Gruyter.
  (1989) "Cicero and the Middle Style," in Diggle, Hall, and Jocelyn (1989): 125–31.
  (2002) "Believing the *pro Marcello*," in Miller, Damon, and Myers (2002): 24–38.
  (2004) "Perorations," in Powell and Paterson (2004):215–30.
Winterbottom, M., Reinhardt, T. (2006) *Quintilian Institutio Oratoria Book 2*, Oxford.
Wiseman, T. P. (1971) *New Men in the Roman Senate, 139 B.C.–A.D. 14*, Oxford.
  (2002) (ed.) *Classics in Progress. Essays on Ancient Greece and Rome*, Oxford.
Wisse, J. (1989) *Ethos and Pathos from Aristotle to Cicero*, Amsterdam: Hakkert.

(1995) "Greek, Romans, and the Rise of Atticism," in Abbenes, Slings, and Sluiter (1995): 65–82.
(2002a) "The Intellectual Background of Cicero's Rhetorical Works," in May (2002a):331–74.
(2002b) "*De Oratore*: Rhetoric, Philosophy, and the Making of the Ideal Orator," in May (2002a): 375–400
(2007) "The Riddle of the *pro Milone*; the Rhetoric of Rational Argument," in Powell (2007): 35–68.
(2013) "The Bad Orator: Between Clumsy Delivery and Political Danger," in Steel and Blom (2013):163–94.
Woerther, F. (2009) (ed.) *Literary and Philosophical Rhetoric in the Greek, Roman, Syriac, and Arabic Worlds*, Hildesheim: Olms.
Wolverton, R. E. (1964) "The Encomium of Cicero in Pliny the Elder," in Henderson (1964): 1. 159–64.
Woodman, A. J. (1983) *Velleius Paterculus: The Caesarian and Augustan Narrative (2.41–93)*, Cambridge.
(2011) "Cicero and the Writing of History," in Marincola (2011):241–90.
Woodman, A. J., Powell, J. G. F. (1992) (eds.) *Author & Audience in Latin Literature*, Cambridge.
Wooten, C. W. (1983) *Cicero's Philippics and their Demosthenic Model*, Chapel Hill, London: University of North Carolina Press.
(2001) (ed.) *The Orator in Action and Theory in Greece and Rome*, Leiden, Boston, Cologne: Brill.
Worthington, I. (2007) (ed.) *A Companion to Greek Rhetoric*, Malden, Oxford: Wiley-Blackwell.
Wright, A. (2001) "The Death of Cicero. Forming a Tradition: The Contamination of History," *Historia* 50.4:436–52.
Yakobson, A. (2010) "Traditional Political Culture and the People's Role in the Roman Republic," *Historia* 59.3: 282–302.
Yon, A. (1964) *Cicéron. L'Orateur. Du meilleur genre d'orateurs*, Paris: Les Belles Lettres.
Zecchini, G. (1982) "Asinio Pollione: dall'attività politica alla riflessione storiografica," *ANRW II* 30.2:1265–96.
(1996) "Cicerone in Sallustio," in Stella and Valvo (1996):527–38.
Zehnacker, H. (2009) *Pline le Jeune Lettres Livres I–III*, Paris.
Zetzel, J. E. G. (1973) "*Emendavi ad Tironem*: Some Notes on Scholarship in the Second Century A.D.," *HSPh* 77:225–43.
(1974) "Statilius Maximus and Ciceronian Studies in the Antonine Age," *BICS* 21:107–23.
(1975) "On the History of Latin Scholia," *HSPh* 79:335–54.
(1980) "The Subscriptions in the Manuscripts of Livy and Fronto and the Meaning of *Emendatio*," *CPh* 75.1: 38–59.
(1981) *Latin Textual Criticism in Antiquity*, New York: Arno.
(2005) *Marginal Scholarship and Textual Deviance. The Commentum Cornuti and the Early Scholia on Persius*, BICS Supplement 84, London: Institute of Classical Studies.

(2009) *Marcus Tullius Cicero. Ten Speeches*, Indianapolis, Cambridge: Hackett.
Zielinski, Th. (1904) *Das Clauselgesetz in Ciceros Reden*, Leipzig: Dieterich.
  (1929) *Cicero im Wandel der Jahrhunderte*, 4th ed., Leipzig: Teubner.
Ziolkowski, J. M., Putnam, M. (2008) (eds.) *The Virgilian Tradition. The First Fifteen Hundred Years*, New Haven, London: Yale University Press.

# *General Index*

*Amplificatio*
  in Cicero's speeches, 275–8
Ancient scholarship, 162–84
  on Cicero, 9–10, 126, 163–82
*Argumenta*
  in the commentaries, 191–219
Arusianus Messius, 153–4
Asconius Pedianus
  *argumenta* in, 191–3
  as *scriptor historicus*, 85, 304, 313
  commentary of, 77–8
  on Cicero, 166–8
  textual criticism in, 172–3
Asinius Pollio
  on Cicero, 107–13
Atticism, 112
Atticus (Titus Pomponius Atticus)
  and the propagation of Cicero's works, 56
  and the revision of Cicero's speeches, 44–50
Augustine
  on Cicero, 124

Cassius Dio
  on Cicero, 108
Cato the Elder, 17, 146–7
Catullus
  and Cicero, 102
Cicero
  *Actio Prima in Verrem*, 203–5
  *Actio Secunda in Verrem*, 50–1, 205–7
  and the creation of his textual persona, 30
  and the doctrine of the three styles of speaking, 19–21
  and the relationship between spoken and written versions of extant speeches, 35–42
  and the Roman youth, 24, 31
  and the use of archaisms in his early orations, 62–3
  as a cultural icon, 3, 100, 111–12, 125
  as a poet, 102, 105
  as a style model, 112–25, 147
  as *optimus auctor*, 126, 148
  as the Latin Demosthenes, 20
  *Caesarianae*
    transmission of, 75, 208–16
  *Catilinarians*
    *Second Catilinarian*, 256–7
  consular speeches, 27, 72
    transmission of, 72–3
  *contra contionem Q. Metelli*, 43
  creativity of in Latin vocabulary, 138–59
  *de aere alieno Milonis*, 87
  *De domo sua*, 26
  *de lege Agraria*
    transmission of, 73
  *de lege Manilia*
    its fortune, 90–1
  *de rege Alexandrino*, 86
  death of in the rhetorical schools, 109–12
  *Divinatio in Caecilium*, 202–3
  early empire debate on Cicero's self-fashioning, 105–12
  exile of as a schooltopic, 82, 108–12
  *exordia*, 225–31
  his *corpus* of oratorical works, 18
  his oratory as art of illusion, 224–66
  his practice of self-correction, 42–54
  his speeches as rhetorical models, 21, 86–99, 188–90
  *homo novus*, 23, 315–16
  *In Clodium et Curionem*, 32, 87, 193–5
  *In Pisonem*, 24, 95, 192
  in Roman education, 5, 120–2, 129–30, 147, passim
  in the Silver Age, 96
  *In toga candida*, 86, 193
  *In Vatinium*, 254–5
  master of *elegantia*, 271–83
  narrative in the speeches, 233–9
  on early Roman orators, 18–22
  on history, 301
  on writing, 17–22

384

personal exempla in the speeches, 302–17
Philippics
    reception of in the rhetorical schools, 107
    *Second Philippic*, 47–50
    transmission of, 74–5
*post reditum* speeches
    transmission of, 81–4
*pro Archia*, 199–201, 306–7
*pro Caecina*, 94
*pro Caelio* 91–2, 226
    its fortune in the rhetorical schools, 91–2
*pro Cluentio*, 96, 226, 233, 249
*pro Cornelio*, 59, 86, 193, 264
*pro Flacco*, 96, 246, 307–8
*pro Fonteio*, 98
*pro Ligario*, 208, 214, 224, 230
*pro Marcello*, 208–13
*pro Milone*, 51–4, 95, 191, 225, 234–9, 294–5, 307–8
    narratio, 234–9
*pro Murena*, 242–3
*pro Plancio*, 198–9, 249–51
    as rhetorical model, 92
    emotional strategy in, 295–7
*pro Quinctio*, 95
*pro Rabirio perduellionis reo*, 97
*pro Rabirio Postumo*, 227–8
*pro rege Deiotaro*, 214, 264
*pro Scauro*, 95, 193, 230
*pro Sestio*, 195–7, 252, 315–17
*pro Sexto Roscio Amerino*, 97, 257–9, 312
*pro Sulla*, 259–63
*pro Tullio*, 94
[Ps. Cic.] *Pridie quam in exilium iret*, 82–3
[Ps. Cic.] *Si eum P. Clodius legibus interrogasset*, 82–3
    reception of, 4, passim
    reception of the speeches in the school, 9, 86–99
    revision of his speeches, 33–54
*Verrines*
    transmission of, 74
Ciceronian critics, 167
Clodius (Pulcher), 145, 152, 238, 247–8
*Commentarii*, 34, 60
*Commentariolum Petitionis*, 23
Commentary
    commentaries on Cicero's speeches, 163–82
    form and use, 171
    in late antiquity, 170–2
Cornelius Nepos
    and Cicero, 56–9
Cornelius Severus, 111

Declamation, 114–9
    artificiality of, 116
    show declamation, 114

*Decorum*, 269
    ideal of, 20, 269–71
Delivery
    and emotion, 291
    in ancient oratory, 285
    Quintilian on, 288–98
    theatrical style, 287
Demosthenes
    as model of Cicero, 28
*Differentiae verborum*, 154
Dilemma, 239
    in Cicero's speeches, 239–41

Education
    and publication of the speeches, 31–33, passim
    early imperial debate about, 4, 110–30
    rhetorical education, 5, passim
*Elocutio*, 127–30, 267
*Emendatio*
    and publication, 34–47
*Exemplum*, 299–317
    and persuasion, 300
*Exordium*, 224–31

Fenestella, 58, 76
    and Asconius Pedianus, 165–8
*Figurae*
    in Cicero's speeches, 278–81
Flavius Caper, 167
Forgery
    Ciceronian *pseudepigrapha*, 104–6
    mock-Ciceronian speeches, 103
    of Ciceronian manuscripts, 63–6
Fronto
    and Cicero, 60–1, 137–8

Gellius (Aulus)
    and Cicero as model of *Latinitas*, 134–8
    and Cicero's manuscripts, 62–6
    cultural program of, 133–4
    on language, 132–4
Grammar
    Cicero as grammatical source, 130–2, 147–62
    grammatical handbooks, 156
    prose authors in the grammar school, 131–2

History
    and rhetoric, 298–317
    in the Roman education system, 303
Horace, 101
Humor
    and invective, 245–56
    Cicero as master of, 245
    in Cicero's speeches, 244–56

Imitation, 7, 126, 301–2, 314–17
  and education, 120–22
  of Cicero, 114–21
*Insinuatio*, 264
*Invectiva in Ciceronem*, 103
  manipulation of Ciceronian slogans, 104
*Invectiva in Sallustium*, 103

Jerome
  on commentary, 168–72

Language
  rhetoricity of, 269–71
*Latinitas*, 6, 127, 183, 268
  Cicero as model of, 127, 137–8, 147–62, 301
Law
  in oratory, 305
  in the Roman education system, 304
*Lectio Tulliana*, 190
Lexicography, 150, 153
Livy
  his obituary of Cicero, 110
Lucan
  and Cicero, 106

Manilius
  on Cicero, 101
Manuscripts
  Ciceronian palimpsests, 93–9
Metaphor
  use of in Cicero, 273–4

*Narratio*
  theory of, 231–9
Nonius Marcellus, 148, 150
  on Cicero, 151–3

*Obtrectatores Ciceronis*, 107, 113
Oratory
  art of *dissimulatio*, 219
  decline of, 15–21
  orality and writing in ancient oratory, 38
*Ornatus*, 270
Ovid, 102

Papyri
  Ciceronian papyri, 87–92
*Peroratio*, 293–8
Pliny the Elder
  and Cicero, 71–2
Pliny the Younger
  and imitation of Cicero, 124
  on orality and writing, 39–41
Propertius, 102
Prose rhythm
  in Cicero, 284–5
Ps. Asconius
  *argumenta* in, 201–7
  commentary of, 159, 164
  linguistic notes in, 159–62
  textual scholia in, 173–82
  variant readings in, 160
Publication
  and textual revision, 33–47
  in ancient Rome, 55
  of Cicero's *Actio Secunda in Verrem*, 50, 174
  of Cicero's *pro Milone*, 51
  of Cicero's *Second Philippic*, 47–50
  of Cicero's speeches, 22–33

Quintilian
  and Cicero, 7, passim
  and Ciceronianism, 117, 121, 124–5, 129, 184
  ideal of literary education in, 120–3, 126, 189, 268–9
  on Cicero's eloquence, 100
  on Cicero's life, 111, 123
  on Cicero's speeches, 123
  on Cicero's style, 266–78
  on grammar, 130–2
  on imitation, 121–5
  on orality and writing, 39–41
  on rhetoric, 266–71
  on Seneca the Younger, 120
  on the *exordium*, 225–30
  on the teaching of rhetoric, 185–90, 201
  on wit, 244–8
  pedagogical project of, 2, 116–18, 126, 129–30, 183–4

Revision
  of Cicero's *pro Ligario*, 45–7
Roman oratory
  and political power, 16

Sallust
  and Cicero, 102
Scholia, 7, 158–65
  comments on Cicero's style, 177–81, 272
  comments on Cicero's use of exempla, 306–17
  debate over Cicero in the scholia, 177
  notes on Cicero's humor, 246–51
  notes on Cicero's strategy of manipulation, 246–51, 256–66
  origin of Latin scholia, 164
*Scholia Bobiensia*, 8, 78–84
  *argumenta* in, 193–201

chronological arrangement of the speeches
    in, 81
  cross-references in, 80
  date and origin of, 79, 164
  linguistic scholia in, 144–50
*Scholia Ciceronis*, 7, passim
*Scholia Cluniacensia*, 175
*Scholia Gronoviana*, 176
  *argumentum* to Cicero's *in Catilinam* IV, 216–19
  *argumentum* to Cicero's *pro Ligario*, 214–16
  *Argumentum* to Cicero's *pro Marcello*, 209–13
School
  the survival of Cicero's orations in, 86–99
Seneca the Elder
  on Cicero's death, 108–12
  on declamation, 114–15
  on decline of oratory, 116
Seneca the Younger
  on Cicero, 110–13, 122–3
  theory of style in, 119–20
*Sententiae*
  in Cicero's speeches, 281–4
Servius, 155
Speech
  collections of Cicero's speeches in antiquity, 71–7
  preparation and publication of, 34
Statilius Maximus
  and his *subscriptio* in the manuscript of Cicero's *de lege Agraria*, 66–70
  *singularia*, 139–44

*Subscriptio*, 66–9
*Synonima Ciceronis*, 155

Tacitus
  *Dialogus de oratoribus*, 117–19
  on style, 118–19, 138–9
Textual criticism, 162–82
Textual transmission, 8, 85–6
Tiberius Claudius Donatus, 155
Tiro
  and Cicero, 59–66
Tropes
  in Cicero's speeches, 272

*Urbanitas*
  and *dissimulatio*, 221

Variant readings
  in Ciceronian manuscripts, 62
Velleius Paterculus, 1
  on Cicero's death, 111
Vergil
  and Cicero, 101
*Vir bonus dicendi peritus*, 116, 121, 183, 189
  ideal of, 41, 183
Vitruvius
  on Cicero, 101
Volcacius, 79, 168

Writing
  and Latin literature, 16
  and memory, 18

# *Index Locorum*

Agroecius
  *GL* 7.113.8ff., 167
Ammianus Marcellinus
  22.16.16, 113
Apuleius
  *Met.* 3.3.1–11, 295
Asconius Pedianus
  2.4-10 C, 192
  18-20 C, 193
  28 C, 294
  30-1 C, 191
  33.25–34.21 C, 191
  35.25–36.27 C, 191
  38.14–42.4 C, 191
  41.24–42.4 C, 51
  41.9-24 C, 191
  57–62.12 C, 193
  76.13 C, 172
  82–83.12 C, 193
  85.13-4 C, 165
  86.15-6 C, 165
  87.9-12 C, 35
  93.24–94.3 C, 104
Augustine
  *Conf.*
    3.4.7, 124

Catullus
  49, 102
Charisius
  164.7B, 64
  252.15-21B, 141
  270.28-31B, 141
  275.1-2B, 142
  276.4B, 142
  277.12B, 142
  280.19-20B, 143
  280.24-5B, 143
  281.5B, 143
  282.5-6B, 143
  284.5-6B, 143

  348.26B, 149
Cicero
  *Agr.*
    2.3–4, 23
  *Arch*
    15–27, 307
    28–30, 306
  *Att.*
    1.13, 42–3
    1.16.8–10, 32
    13.12.2, 46
    13.19.2, 45
    13.44.3, 46
    15.13.1, 48
    15.13a, 48
    16.11, 49
    16.5.5, 57
    2.1.3, 28
    3.12.2, 32
    4.2.2, 26–7
  *Balb.*
    18–9, 23
  *Brut.*
    91–3, 18
    122–3, 19
    278, 291
  *Caec.*
    65–78, 305
  *Catil.*
    1.2, 280
    2.17–27, 256
  *Cluent.*
    15, 233
    57–8, 249
    139, 221
    192, 293
    199, 96
  *de Orat.*
    1.18, 300
    1.150, 39
    1.166–203, 305

388

## Index Locorum

1.226–7, 288
2.36, 301
2.189, 292
2.244–6, 252
2.269–70, 221
3.37–9, 128
3.150–51, 128
3.175, 284
3.201, 278
3.201–8, 222
3.213, 285
*Div. Caec.*
39, 286
*Fam.*
5.12, 299
*Flac.*
41, 246
43, 246
46, 246
53, 273
79, 280
98, 307
106, 293
*Inv.*
1.34, 206
1.45, 239
1.49, 299
*Leg.*
1.5, 299
*Lig.*
37, 281
*Manil.*
22, 310
*Marc.*
21–2, 212
*Mil.*
7, 272
7–8, 308
9, 308
13–4, 308
16, 308
28, 234
92–5, 294
102, 294
*Mur.*
15–7, 23
22–4, 243
*Off.*
1.2, 318
2.46, 301
2.51, 220
*Orat.*
55–6, 286
100–112, 19

120, 300
200, 39
*Phil.*
2.39, 251
2.63, 274
*Planc.*
21, 295
22, 295
33–4, 251
35, 251
74, 35
75–77, 296
85, 249
*Q. fr.*
3.1, 24–6
*Quinct.*
96–7, 293
*Red. Pop.*
2, 282
4, 282
5, 282
*Red. Sen.*
18, 273
*Rosc.*
46–7, 312
*S. Rosc.*
1–5, 23
*Sest.*
15, 273
29, 276
71, 273
72, 253
96–143, 38
126, 313
132–5, 253
135, 252
136, 316
142, 315
*Sul*
2–10, 260
10, 240
18, 261
31, 283
40–45, 277
91, 281
*Ver.*
1.55, 203
2.1.23, 206
2.1.54, 275
2.1.56, 311
2.1.7, 280
2.1.45, 276
2.1.90, 272
2.4.107, 277

*Dio Cassius*
  38.18–29, 108
  40.48–55, 52
  46.1–28, 108

*Diomedes*
  GL 1.368.28, 70
  GL 1.390.15, 149

*Fronto*
  Ad Antoninum Imp. et Invicem
    III. 8 (104.12Hout), 138
    III. 7 (104.1-3Hout), 138
  Amic.
    2.2 (187.10Hout), 61
  Ant.
    4.1 (105.1-3Hout), 91
  Aur.
    1.7 (13.17–16.3Hout), 60
  Ep. M. Caes.
    4.3.3 (57.7-8Hout), 138
  Parth.
    205.2-15Hout, 91

*Gellius*
  NA
    1.4, 137
    1.7.1, 62, 74, 134
    1.15, 136
    2.17.2–3, 135
    9.12, 92
    9.14.6–7, 62, 134
    10.1.7, 127
    12.1, 134
    12.10.6, 62
    13.21, 135
    13.21.16, 62, 74
    13.25, 135
    15.3.1–3, 135
    15.28.1–2, 57
    15.28.4–5, 58
    17.1, 136
    17.1.1, 113

*Grillius*
  89.88-92Jakobi, 265

*Iulius Severianus*
  358.23–4 RLM, 24

*Jerome*
  Contra Iohannem
    12, 59
  Contra Rufinum
    1.16, 79, 168

*Lucan*
  BC
    7.62–66, 106

*Macrobius*
  Sat.
    2.1.13, 246

*Manilius*
  Astr.
    1.794–5, 101

*Nonius Marcellus*
  231 L, 148
  535 L, 152
  700 L, 152
  745 L, 152
  861 L, 152
  863 L, 152

*Petronius*
  Sat.
    55.3, 102

*Pliny the Elder*
  Nat.
    7.116–7, 71–3

*Pliny the Younger*
  Ep.
    1.20, 38, 39–41
    7.4.3–6, 113

*Plutarch*
  Cic.
    35, 52

*Priscian*
  GL 3.255–64, 158

*Ps. Asconius*
  185.2–186.17St, 202
  186.19-22St, 160
  186.4-8St, 177, 202
  187.15.6St, 159
  187.3-5St, 180
  188.2-3St, 175
  188.6-7St, 159
  191.3-4St, 178
  192.1-2St, 159
  192.27-30St, 178
  196.1-3St, 179
  197.1-3St, 179
  197.20-3St, 203
  198.27-9St, 240
  199.3-6St, 160
  203.19-20St, 281
  205.11-15St, 203
  206.10-4St, 204

206.15St, 205
206.1-5St, 204
206.6-9St, 204
210.18-21St, 281
212.13-9St, 180
214.4-9St, 161
215.24-6St, 173
223.3-6St, 161
224.10-4St, 205
224.1–225.14St, 205
224.16-7St, 207
224.18-21St, 207
224.22-5St, 173
225.1-2St, 207
225.16-8St, 50
225.16St, 206
225.6-7St, 207
225.8-9St, 206
226.9-13St, 280
229.28-30St, 206
233.1-4St, 181
233.8-10St, 175
236.16-8St, 173
238.20-1St, 174
239.20-2St, 240
240–29–241.4-7St, 179
244.16-7St, 174
244.25St, 272
257.10-1St, 207
257.8-10St, 207
257.13-5St, 180–1

Quintilian
Inst.
   1.4.11, 130
   1.4.14, 130
   1.4.4, 132
   1.4–8, 130
   1.5.1, 127
   1.5.13, 130
   1.5.44, 131
   1.5.57, 131
   1.5.65, 131
   1.5.8, 130
   1.6.44–5, 129
   1.7.20, 131
   2.1.4, 132
   2.17.20–1, 222
   2.17.22–3, 266
   2.17.25–6, 267
   2.17.27, 292
   2.5.1, 185
   2.5.13–7, 188
   2.5.18–20, 131
   2.5.19–20, 188

   2.5.21–2, 189
   2.5.23, 189
   2.5.5–11, 185
   2.5.6, 185
   3.6.11, 227
   3.6.12, 228
   4.1.34–6, 226
   4.1.38–9, 226
   4.1.40, 227
   4.1.42, 227
   4.1.44, 227
   4.1.46, 227
   4.1.49, 227
   4.1.52–3, 228
   4.1.54–7, 229
   4.1.68, 229
   4.1.69, 230
   4.1.70, 45, 230
   4.1.72–9, 230
   4.2.121, 235
   4.2.19, 249
   4.2.24–30, 231
   4.2.25, 95
   4.2.36, 233
   4.2.38, 233
   4.2.4–23, 231
   4.2.57–9, 234
   4.2.59, 113
   4.2.111–24, 233
   4.5.11, 113
   4.5.12, 243
   5.1.1, 291
   5.10.50, 235
   5.11.10, 311
   5.11.17–8, 309
   5.11.6, 300
   5.11.6–16, 300
   6.1.10, 293
   6.1.30–4, 293
   6.1.35, 243
   6.1.44, 297
   6.2.1, 293
   6.2.4, 291
   6.2.25–6, 292
   6.2.34–6, 293
   6.2.5, 222
   6.3, 244
   6.3.6, 245
   6.3.17, 244
   6.3.39–40, 249
   6.5.10, 237
   6.5.9, 96
   7.1.34–7, 235
   8.3.2, 270
   8.3.3–4, 269

*Quintilian* (cont.)
  8.3.5, 270
  8.6.1, 272
  8.6.14, 274
  8.6.56, 248
  9.2.1, 278
  9.2.19, 227
  9.2.6, 279
  9.2.7, 279
  9.2.96, 248
  9.3.32, 243
  9.4.107, 243
  9.4.60, 285
  9.4.9, 284
  10.1.39, 189
  10.1.101–4, 303
  10.1.112, 100, 123
  10.1.113, 113
  10.1.125–31, 122
  10.1.21, 219
  10.1.27–36, 131
  10.7.30–1, 60
  10.7.30–2, 34
  11.1.18–24, 107
  11.1.6, 271
  11.1.35, 239
  11.1.69–71, 242
  11.3, 288
  11.3.14–65, 289
  11.3.154, 298
  11.3.155–83, 298
  11.3.166, 290
  11.3.167, 290
  11.3.180, 298
  11.3.181, 287
  11.3.182, 287
  11.3.184, 288, 298
  11.3.45, 225
  11.3.47, 95
  11.3.47–9, 225
  11.3.5, 286
  11.3.65–149, 290
  12 *praef.* 2–4, 124
  12.1.22, 113
  12.1.36–45, 266
  12.10.45, 283
  12.10.47–8, 283
  12.10.49–56, 39
  12.2.7, 126
  12.9.5, 223

*Rhetorica ad Herennium*
  4.12.17, 127
*Romanus Aquila*
  22.11–2 *RLM*, 190

*Sallustius*
  *Cat.*
    31.6, 30, 102
  [*Sal.*]
    *Cic.*
      1, 105
      3, 105
      5, 105
      6, 105
*Scholia Ambrosiana*
  274.23–275.23St, 314
*Scholia Bobiensia*
  77.12-3St, 240
  77.19-26St, 261
  77.6-13St, 261
  77.6St, 240
  79.21-2St, 262
  79.23-4St, 262
  79.9-16St, 261
  80.13-24St, 315
  81.15-6St, 263
  81.28-9St, 263
  81.30–82.3St, 263
  82.13-4St, 283
  83.31–84.2St, 277
  85.5-7St, 194
  85.8St, 194
  86.1-5St, 195
  89.10-6St, 152
  89.10St, 248
  89.17-20St, 152
  89.29–90.8St, 248
  90.20St, 247
  97–13-6St, 144
  98.26-7St, 145
  101.2St, 247
  102.20-1St, 246
  102.23-4St, 246
  102.27-30St, 247
  103.1-3St, 247
  103.18-9St, 246
  104.18-9St, 145
  104.8-13St, 246
  105.17-9St, 273
  106.15-7St, 247
  106.2-3St, 280
  107.8-9St, 145
  108.16-22St, 81–2
  108.3-6St, 307
  109.23St, 273
  110.1–111.20St, 282
  110.29St, 282

110.3-12St, 197
111.11-2St, 282
111.1-2St, 282
111.24–112.18St, 191
111.2-8St, 282
112.26St, 272
112.7-13St, 51
114.1-2St, 308
114.20-1St, 308
114.4-10St, 308
116.21-2St, 308
117.32-3St, 308
119.26St, 234
120.15-19St, 235
120.20-6St, 145
120.23-6St, 145
120.27–121.8St, 236
120.5–6 St, 234
121.16-20St, 145
124.1-9St, 146
125.7–126.5St, 195
126.3-4St, 197
126.4-5St, 197
127.19-20St, 273
128.31–129.2St, 144
129.5-7St, 276
131.28St, 144
134.17-20St, 145
134.23-4St, 273
134.28-9St, 253
138.1.12St, 313
140.11-7St, 252
141.3St, 144
141.9-12St, 255
143.20-4St, 315
144.20-22St, 197
144.23–145.3St, 197
152. 21-6St, 198
152.26-32St, 198
152.3-5St, 144
153.1-2St, 199
153.13St, 199
153.14-5St, 199
153.4-5St, 199
154.13-6St, 295
154.17-9St, 144
156.14-7St, 145
159.16-22St, 252
165.20-2St, 297
165.22-6St, 297
165.7-9St, 105
167.8-18St, 249
169.1-2St, 296
169.14-29St, 195
175.3-20St, 200

176.16–177.14St, 306
177.14-7St, 306
178.22-5St, 307
179.9-11St, 144
*Scholia Cluniacensia*
   269.21–270.4St, 175
   271.20-6St, 212
*Scholia Gronoviana*
   282.16-24St, 257
   285.1-4St, 176
   286.27–287.17St, 216–17
   291.4–292.3St, 214
   292.4-6St, 214
   292.6-8St, 215
   295.23–296.2St, 210
   295.8-22St, 210
   296.23-5St, 212
   296.3-6St, 213
   298. 29-30St, 215
   299.1-7St, 263
   303.8St, 233
   306.1-20St, 257
   307.13-7St, 312
   318.27-31St, 310
   319.1-9St, 310
   322.19–323.13St, 191
   341.11-6St, 193
   341.3–342.6St, 207
   344.11-21St, 276
   346.17-21St, 275
   346.26-8St, 311
Seneca the Elder
  Con.
    2.4.4, 106, 111
    3 *praef.* 15–6, 96
    4 *praef.* 10, 142
    4 *praef.* 4–11, 138
    9 *praef.* 1, 115
  Suas.
    6.14, 109
    6.15, 107
    6.17, 110
    6.21–2, 110
    6.24, 109
    6.26, 111
    7.8, 111
Seneca the Younger
  Dial.
    10.5.1, 110
  ep.
    40.11, 123
    100.7, 113
    114, 119
Suetonius
  Claud.

Suetonius (cont.)
    41, 113
Sulpicius Victor
    323.14 *RLM*, 235
    323.21–5 *RLM*, 235

Tacitus
    *Dial.*
        12.6, 113
        15.1–27.2, 118
        18.4, 113
        20.1, 74, 75
        22.1–3, 113
        22.2, a619.1, 283
        28.1–35.5, 118
        36.1–41.5, 118
        39.5, 75
        39.9, 95

Velleius Paterculus
    2.66.4–5, 1
    2.66–7, 111
Vergil
    *Aen.*
        8.668–70, 101
        11.336–42, 101
Vitruvius
    *De arch.*
        9 *praef.* 17, 101